THE

WORLD
OF THE NEW

TESTAMENT

THE
WORLD
OF THE NEW
TESTAMENT

CULTURAL, SOCIAL,
AND HISTORICAL CONTEXTS

JOEL B. GREEN
LEE MARTIN MCDONALD

EDITORS

B
Baker Academic
a division of Baker Publishing Group
Grand Rapids, Michigan

© 2013 by Baker Publishing Group

Published by Baker Academic
a division of Baker Publishing Group
P.O. Box 6287, Grand Rapids, MI 49516-6287
www.bakeracademic.com

Paperback edition published 2017
ISBN 978-0-8010-9861-1

Printed in the United States of America

The Library of Congress has cataloged the hardcover edition as follows:
    The world of the New Testament : cultural, social, and historical contexts / edited by
Joel B. Green and Lee Martin McDonald.
      pages cm
    Summary: "A team of distinguished specialists introduces the Jewish, Hellenistic, and Roman backgrounds necessary for understanding the New Testament and the early church"— Publisher's summary.
    Includes bibliographical references and index.
    ISBN 978-0-8010-3962-1 (cloth)
    1. Jews—History—586 B.C.–70 A.D. 2. Jews—Palestine—Social life and customs—To 70 A.D. 3. Judaism—History—Post-exilic period, 586 B.C.–210 A.D. 4. Civilization, Greco-Roman—Social aspects. 5. Bible. N.T.—History of biblical events. 6. Bible. N.T.—Criticism, interpretation, etc. 7. Church history—Primitive and early church, ca. 30–600. 8. Palestine—History—To 70 A.D. 9. Greece—History—146 B.C.–323 A.D. 10. Rome—History—Empire, 30 B.C.–476 A.D. I. Green, Joel B., 1956– editor of compilation. II. McDonald, Lee Martin, 1942– editor of compilation.
    DS122.W67 2013
    225.95—dc23   2013003341

17 18 19 20 21 22 23   7 6 5 4 3 2 1

Contents

Illustrations

Maps

Diagrams

Contributors

S. Scott Bartchy (PhD, Harvard University), University of California, Los Angeles

Michael F. Bird (PhD, University of Queensland), Ridley Melbourne Mission and Ministry College

James H. Charlesworth (PhD, Duke University), Princeton Theological Seminary

Bruce Chilton (PhD, University of Cambridge), Bard College

Lynn H. Cohick (PhD, University of Pennsylvania), Wheaton College (IL)

David A. deSilva (PhD, Emory University), Ashland Theological Seminary

David J. Downs (PhD, Princeton Theological Seminary), Fuller Theological Seminary

James D. G. Dunn (PhD, University of Cambridge), University of Durham

C. D. Elledge (PhD, Princeton Theological Seminary), Gustavus Adolphus College

Everett Ferguson (PhD, Harvard University), Abilene Christian University

John T. Fitzgerald (PhD, Yale University), University of Notre Dame and North-West University (South Africa)

Gene L. Green (PhD, University of Aberdeen), Wheaton College (IL)

Joel B. Green (PhD, University of Aberdeen), Fuller Theological Seminary

Daniel M. Gurtner (PhD, University of St. Andrews), Bethel Seminary

Thomas R. Hatina (PhD, University of Bristol), Trinity Western University

Larry R. Helyer (PhD, Fuller Theological Seminary), Taylor University

Moyer V. Hubbard (DPhil, University of Oxford), Talbot School of Theology, Biola University

DAVID INSTONE-BREWER (PhD, University of Cambridge), Tyndale House

MICHELLE LEE-BARNEWALL (PhD, University of Notre Dame), Biola University

KENNETH D. LITWAK (PhD, University of Bristol), Azusa Pacific University

NATHAN MACDONALD (PhD, University of Durham), University of Cambridge

LEE MARTIN MCDONALD (PhD, University of Edinburgh), Acadia Divinity College

MICHAEL S. MOORE (PhD, Drew University), Arizona State University and Fuller Theological Seminary

LIDIJA NOVAKOVIC (PhD, Princeton Theological Seminary), Baylor University

NICHOLAS PERRIN (PhD, Marquette University), Wheaton College (IL)

THOMAS E. PHILLIPS (PhD, Southern Methodist University), Arapahoe Community College

E. RANDOLPH RICHARDS (PhD, Southwestern Baptist Theological Seminary), Palm Beach Atlantic University

TORREY SELAND (DArt, University of Trondheim), School of Mission and Theology, Norway

PAUL TREBILCO (PhD, University of Durham), University of Otago

MARK WILSON (PhD, University of South Africa), School of Divinity, Regent University

JOHN D. WINELAND (PhD, Miami University), Kentucky Christian University

BEN WITHERINGTON III (PhD, University of Durham), Asbury Theological Seminary

ARCHIE T. WRIGHT (PhD, University of Durham), School of Divinity, Regent University

KENT L. YINGER (PhD, Sheffield University), George Fox University

Abbreviations

General

AD	*anno Domini*, year of the Lord	i.e.	*id est*, that is
ANE	ancient Near East(ern)	KJV	King James Version
b.	ben	km	kilometer(s)
BC	before Christ	LXX	Septuagint
BCE	before the Common Era	m	meter(s)
ca.	*circa*, approximately	MT	Masoretic Text
CE	Common Era	NIV	New International Version
CEB	Common English Bible	NJPS	*Tanakh: The New Jewish Publication Society Translation*
cf.	*confer*, compare		
chap(s).	chapter(s)	NKJV	New King James Version
d.	died	NRSV	New Revised Standard Version
DSS	Dead Sea Scrolls	NT	New Testament
ed(s).	edited by, editors, *or* edition	OT	Old Testament
e.g.	*exempli gratia*, for example	par.	and parallel(s)
esp.	especially	pl.	plural
ESV	English Standard Version	R.	Rabbi
ET	English Translation	rev.	revised
et al.	*et alii*, and others	RSV	Revised Standard Version
etc.	*et cetera*, and the rest	sg.	singular
fl.	flourished	trans.	translator, translated by
frg(s).	fragment(s)	v(v).	verse(s)
HB	Hebrew Bible	vol(s).	volume(s)

Contemporary Literature

A1CS	The Book of Acts in Its First Century Setting	ABRL	Anchor Bible Reference Library
		AGJU	Arbeiten zur Geschichte des antiken Judentums und des Urchristentums
AB	Anchor Bible		
ABD	*Anchor Bible Dictionary*. Edited by David Noel Freeman. 6 vols. New York: Doubleday, 1992.		
		AJEC	Ancient Judaism and Early Christianity

ANF   *Ante-Nicene Fathers*. Edited by
           Alexander Roberts and James
           Donaldson. 10 vols. 1885–87.
           Repr., Grand Rapids: Eerd-
           mans, 1978.

ANRW   *Aufstieg und Niedergang der
           römischen Welt: Geschichte
           und Kultur Roms im Spiegel
           der neueren Forschung*. Edited
           by H. Temporini and W. Haase.
           Berlin: de Gruyter, 1972–.

BA   *Biblical Archaeologist*

BBR   *Bulletin of Biblical Research*

BCH   *Bulletin de correspondence
           hellénique*

BibSem   Biblical Seminar

BIS   Biblical Interpretation Series

BR   *Biblical Research*

BRev   *Bible Review*

BThS   Biblisch-Theologische Studien

BZAW   Beihefte zur Zeitschrift für die
           alttestamentliche Wissenschaft

BZNW   Beihefte zur Zeitschrift
           für die neutestamentliche
           Wissenschaft

CBQ   *Catholic Biblical Quarterly*

CBR   *Currents in Biblical Research*

CIG   *Corpus inscriptionum
           graecarum*

CIJ   *Corpus inscriptionum
           judaicarum*

CIL   *Corpus inscriptionum
           latinarum*

CIS   *Corpus inscriptionum
           semiticarum*

CJ   *Classical Journal*

ConBNT   Coniectanea biblica: New Tes-
           tament Series

CPJ   *Corpus papyrorum judaico-
           rum*. Edited by V. Tcherikover.
           3 vols. Cambridge, MA:
           Harvard University Press for
           Magnes Press, 1957–64.

CRINT   Compendia rerum iudaicarum
           ad Novum Testamentum

DJD   Discoveries in the Judaean
           Desert

DLNTD   *Dictionary of the Later New
           Testament and Its Develop-
           ments*. Edited by Ralph P.
           Martin and Peter H. Davids.
           Downers Grove, IL: InterVar-
           sity, 1997.

DNTB   *Dictionary of New Testa-
           ment Background*. Edited by
           Craig A. Evans and Stanley E.
           Porter. Downers Grove, IL: In-
           terVarsity, 2000.

DSE   *Dictionary of Scripture and
           Ethics*. Edited by Joel B.
           Green. Grand Rapids: Baker
           Academic, 2011.

EDEJ   *Eerdmans Dictionary of Early
           Judaism*. Edited by John J.
           Collins and Daniel C. Harlow.
           Grand Rapids: Eerdmans,
           2010.

EDSS   *Encyclopedia of the Dead Sea
           Scrolls*. Edited by Lawrence H.
           Schiffman and James C.
           VanderKam. 2 vols. Oxford:
           Oxford University Press, 2000.

EEC   *Encyclopedia of Early Chris-
           tianity*. Edited by Everett Fer-
           guson, Michael P. McHugh,
           and Frederick W. Norris. 2nd
           ed. 2 vols. New York: Garland,
           1999.

ExpTim   *Expository Times*

GBS   Guides to Biblical Scholarship

GNS   Good News Studies

GRBS   *Greek, Roman, and Byzantine
           Studies*

HBD   *Harper's Bible Dictionary*. Ed-
           ited by Paul Achtemeier. New
           York: Harper & Row, 1985.

HeyJ   *Heythrop Journal*

HSM   Harvard Semitic Monographs

HTR   *Harvard Theological Review*

HTS   Harvard Theological Studies

HUT   Hermeneutische Untersuchun-
           gen zur Theologie

ICC   International Critical
           Commentary

IDBSup	*Interpreter's Dictionary of the Bible: Supplementary Volume.* Edited by Keith Crim. Nashville: Abingdon, 1976.	JTS	*Journal of Theological Studies*
		LCL	Loeb Classical Library
		LDSS	Library of the Dead Sea Scrolls
ILLRP	*Inscriptiones latinae liberae rei publicae.* By Attilio Degrassi. 2 vols. Florence: La Nuova Italia, 1957–63.	LEC	Library of Early Christianity
		LNTS	Library of New Testament Studies
		LSAM	*Lois sacrées de l'Asie Mineure.* Edited by F. Sokolowski. Paris: de Boccard, 1955.
ILS	*Inscriptiones latinae selectae.* Edited by Hermann Dessau. 3 vols. Berlin: Weidmann, 1892–1916.		
		LSTS	Library of Second Temple Studies
ISBE	*The International Standard Bible Encyclopedia.* Edited by Geoffrey W. Bromiley. Rev. ed. 4 vols. Grand Rapids: Eerdmans, 1979–88.	MNTS	McMaster New Testament Studies
		NA²⁷	*Nestle-Aland: Novum Testamentum Graece.* Edited by Barbara Aland and Kurt Aland et al. 27th rev. ed. Stuttgart: Deutsche Bibelgesellschaft, 1993.
JAAR	*Journal of the American Academy of Religion*		
JBL	*Journal of Biblical Literature*		
JBQ	*Jewish Bible Quarterly*	NEAEHL	*New Encyclopedia of Archaeological Excavations in the Holy Land.* Edited by Ephraim Stern et al. 5 vols. New York: Simon & Schuster, 1993–.
JNES	*Journal of Near Eastern Studies*		
JQR	*Jewish Quarterly Review*		
JR	*Journal of Religion*		
JRitSt	*Journal of Ritual Studies*		
JRS	*Journal of Roman Studies*	*NIDB*	*New Interpreter's Dictionary of the Bible.* Edited by Katharine Doob Sakenfeld. 5 vols. Nashville: Abingdon, 2009.
JSJ	*Journal for the Study of Judaism in the Persian, Hellenistic, and Roman Periods*		
JSJSup	Journal for the Study of Judaism in the Persian, Hellenistic, and Roman Periods: Supplement Series	NIGTC	New International Greek Testament Commentary
		NovT	*Novum Testamentum*
		NovTSup	Supplements to Novum Testamentum
JSNT	*Journal for the Study of the New Testament*	*NPNF¹*	*The Nicene and Post-Nicene Fathers,* series 1. Edited by Philip Schaff. 14 vols. 1887–1900. Repr., Grand Rapids: Eerdmans, 1956.
JSNTSup	Journal for the Study of the New Testament: Supplement Series		
JSOT	*Journal for the Study of the Old Testament*	*NPNF²*	*The Nicene and Post-Nicene Fathers,* series 2. Edited by Philip Schaff and Henry Wace. 14 vols. 1890–1900. Repr., Grand Rapids: Eerdmans, 1952.
JSOTSup	Journal for the Study of the Old Testament: Supplement Series		
JSPSup	Journal for the Study of the Pseudepigrapha: Supplement Series		
		NTL	New Testament Library
JSPub	Judea and Samaria Publications	NTOA	Novum Testamentum et Orbis Antiquus

NTS	*New Testament Studies*	*SIG*	*Sylloge inscriptionum grae-*
NTTS	New Testament Tools and		*carum.* Edited by W. Ditten-
	Studies		berger. 3rd ed. 4 vols. Leipzig:
OCM	Oxford Classical Monographs		Hirzel, 1915–24.
OGIS	*Orientis graeci inscriptiones*	SJLA	Studies in Judaism in Late
	selectae. Edited by W. Ditten-		Antiquity
	berger. 2 vols. Leipzig: Hirzel,	SNTSMS	Society for New Testament
	1903–5.		Studies Monograph Series
OTP	*Old Testament Pseudepig-*	StPB	Studia post-biblica
	rapha. Edited by James H.	*StudOr*	*Studia orientalia*
	Charlesworth. 2 vols. Garden	SUNT	Studien zur Umwelt des Neuen
	City, NY: Doubleday, 1983–85.		Testaments
PAST	Pauline Studies	*SVF*	*Stoicorum veterum fragmenta.*
PNTC	Pillar New Testament		Edited by H. von Arnim. 4 vols.
	Commentary		Leipzig: Teubner, 1903–24.
PTSDSSP	Princeton Theological Sem-	TENTS	Texts and Editions for New
	inary Dead Sea Scrolls Project		Testament Study
RB	*Revue biblique*	*TLNT*	*Theological Lexicon of the*
RVV	Religionsgeschichtliche Versu-		*New Testament.* By Celsus
	che und Vorarbeiten		Spicq. 3 vols. Peabody, MA:
SA	Series of Antiquity		Hendrickson, 1994.
SAC	Studies in Antiquity and	TSAJ	Texte und Studien zum antiken
	Christianity		Judentum
SBEC	Studies in the Bible and Early	*TynBul*	*Tyndale Bulletin*
	Christianity	UCOP	University of Cambridge Ori-
SBLABS	Society of Biblical Literature		ental Publications
	Archaeology and Biblical	*VC*	*Vigiliae christianae*
	Studies	VCSup	Supplements to Vigiliae
SBLBMI	Society of Biblical Literature		christianae
	The Bible and Its Modern	*VEcc*	*Verbum et ecclesia*
	Interpreters	*VT*	*Vetus Testamentum*
SBLDS	Society of Biblical Literature	VTSup	Supplements to Vetus
	Dissertation Series		Testamentum
SBLSBS	Society of Biblical Literature	WBC	Word Biblical Commentary
	Sources for Biblical Study	WF	Wege der Forschung
SBLSCS	Society of Biblical Literature	WMANT	Wissenschaftliche Monogra-
	Septuagint and Cognate Stud-		phien zum Alten und Neuen
	ies Series		Testament
SDSSRL	Studies in the Dead Sea Scrolls	*WTJ*	*Westminster Theological*
	and Related Literature		*Journal*
SEJC	Studies in Early Judaism and	WUNT	Wissenschaftliche Unter-
	Christianity		suchungen zum Neuen
SI	*Scripture and Interpretation*		Testament

Hebrew Bible/Old Testament

Gen.	Genesis	Exod.	Exodus

Lev.	Leviticus	Isa.	Isaiah
Num.	Numbers	Jer.	Jeremiah
Deut.	Deuteronomy	Lam.	Lamentations
Josh.	Joshua	Ezek.	Ezekiel
Judg.	Judges	Dan.	Daniel
Ruth	Ruth	Hosea	Hosea
1–2 Sam.	1–2 Samuel	Joel	Joel
1–2 Kings	1–2 Kings	Amos	Amos
1–2 Chron.	1–2 Chronicles	Obad.	Obadiah
Ezra	Ezra	Jon.	Jonah
Neh.	Nehemiah	Mic.	Micah
Esther	Esther	Nah.	Nahum
Job	Job	Hab.	Habakkuk
Ps(s).	Psalm(s)	Zeph.	Zephaniah
Prov.	Proverbs	Hag.	Haggai
Eccles.	Ecclesiastes	Zech.	Zechariah
Song	Song of Songs	Mal.	Malachi

Old Testament Apocrypha/Deuterocanonical Books

Add. Esth.	Additions to Esther	Pr. Azar.	Prayer of Azariah
Bar.	Baruch	Pr. Man.	Prayer of Manasseh
Bel	Bel and the Dragon	Sir.	Sirach (Ecclesiasticus, or Ben
1–2 Esd.	1–2 Esdras		Sira)
Jdt.	Judith	Sus.	Susanna
Let. Jer.	Letter of Jeremiah	Tob.	Tobit
1–4 Macc.	1–4 Maccabees	Wis.	Wisdom of Solomon

New Testament

Matt.	Matthew	1–2 Thess.	1–2 Thessalonians
Mark	Mark	1–2 Tim.	1–2 Timothy
Luke	Luke	Titus	Titus
John	John	Philem.	Philemon
Acts	Acts	Heb.	Hebrews
Rom.	Romans	James	James
1–2 Cor.	1–2 Corinthians	1–2 Pet.	1–2 Peter
Gal.	Galatians	1–3 John	1–3 John
Eph.	Ephesians	Jude	Jude
Phil.	Philippians	Rev.	Revelation
Col.	Colossians		

Old Testament Pseudepigrapha

Apoc. Zeph.	Apocalypse of Zephaniah	Jos. Asen.	Joseph and Aseneth
2 Bar.	2 Baruch (Syriac	Jub.	Jubilees
	Apocalypse)	L.A.B.	Liber antiquitatum bibli-
1 En.	1 Enoch		carum (Pseudo-Philo)

Let. Aris.	Letter of Aristeas	Sib. Or.	Sibylline Oracles
Mart. Isa.	Martyrdom of Isaiah	T. Mos.	Testament of Moses
Pss. Sol.	Psalms of Solomon		

New Testament Apocrypha/Pseudepigrapha

Acts Paul Thec.	Acts of Paul and Thecla	Gos. Pet.	Gospel of Peter
Gos. Jud.	Gospel of Judas	Gos. Thom.	Gospel of Thomas

Apostolic Fathers

Barn.	Epistle of Barnabas	Ign. Eph.	Ignatius, To the Ephesians
1–2 Clem.	1–2 Clement	Ign. Magn.	Ignatius, To the Magnesians
Did.	Didache	Mart. Pol.	Martyrdom of Polycarp
Diogn.	Epistle to Diognetus	Pol. Phil	Polycarp, To the Philippians
Herm. Mand.	Shepherd of Hermas, Mandate		

Other Early Christian Writers

Augustine

Civ.	De civitate Dei (The City of God)
Conf.	Confessions
Doctr. chr.	De doctrina christiana (On Christian Doctrine)

Clement of Alexandria

Strom.	Stromata (Miscellanies)

Epiphanius

Pan.	Panarion (Refutation of All Heresies)

Eusebius

Eccl. Hist.	Ecclesiastical History

Hippolytus

Haer.	Refutatio omnium haeresium (Refutation of All Heresies)

Irenaeus

Adv. haer.	Adversus haereses (Against Heresies)

Jerome

Comm. Isa.	Commentary on Isaiah
Epist.	Epistulae (Letters)

Justin Martyr

Dial.	Dialogue with Trypho

Origen

Cels.	Contra Celsum (Against Celsus)
Comm. Cant.	Commentary on Canticles (Song of Songs)
Comm. Matt.	Commentary on Matthew
Ep. Afr.	Epistle to Julius Africanus
Hom. Lev.	Homily on Leviticus
Princ.	On First Principles

Tertullian

Apparel	On the Apparel of Women
Idolatry	On Idolatry
Pat.	On Patience
Prescript.	On Prescription against Heretics

Targum

Tg. Ps.-J.	Pseudo-Jonathan

Papyri

P.Egerton	Egerton Papyri	P.Par.	Paris Papyri
P.Lond. Inv.	London Papyri	P.Vindob.	Papyrus Vindobonensis
P.Mich.	Michigan Papyri	P.Zen.	Zenon Papyri
P.Oxy.	Oxyrhynchus Papyri		

Dead Sea Scrolls and Related Texts

CD	Cairo Genizah copy of the *Damascus Document*	4QFlor	*Florilegium*, from Qumran Cave 4
1QGenAp	*Genesis Apocryphon*, from Qumran Cave 1	4QMMT	*Halakic Letter*, from Qumran Cave 4
1QH^a	*Thanksgiving Hymns*, copy a, from Qumran Cave 1	4QNum^b	Numbers, copy b, from Qumran Cave 4
1QM	*War Scroll*, from Qumran Cave 1	4QpaleoExod^m	Paleo-Hebrew Exodus, copy m, from Qumran Cave 4
1QpHab	*Pesher on Habakkuk*, from Qumran Cave 1	4QpNah	*Pesher on Nahum*, from Qumran Cave 4
1QS	*Rule of the Community*, or *Manual of Discipline*, from Qumran Cave 1	4QpPs^a	*Pesher on the Psalms*, copy a, from Qumran Cave 4
1QSa	*Rule of the Congregation*, from Qumran Cave 1	4QTest	*Testimonia*, from Qumran Cave 4
4QDeut^h	Deuteronomy, copy h, from Qumran Cave 4	11QT^a	*Temple Scroll*, copy a, from Qumran Cave 11

Rabbinic Literature

'Abod. Zar.	'Abodah Zarah	Nid.	Niddah
'Abot R. Nat.	'Abot de Rabbi Nathan	Pesaḥ.	Pesaḥim
b.	Babylonian Talmud	Qidd.	Qiddušin
B. Bat.	Baba Batra	Rab.	Rabbah (+ biblical book)
Ber.	Berakot	Roš Haš.	Roš Haššanah
'Ed.	'Eduyyot	Šabb.	Šabbat
'Erub.	'Erubin	Sanh.	Sanhedrin
Giṭ.	Giṭṭin	Šeqal.	Šeqalim
Ḥag.	Ḥagigah	t.	Tosefta
Ketub.	Ketubbot	Ta'an.	Ta'anit
Kipp.	(see Yoma)	Ter.	Terumot
m.	Mishnah	y.	Jerusalem (Palestinian)
Ma'aś. Š.	Ma'aśer Šeni		Talmud
Meg.	Megillah	Yad.	Yadayim
Menaḥ.	Menaḥot	Yoma	Yoma (= Kippurim)
Miqw.	Miqwa'ot	Zebaḥ.	Zebaḥim
Naz.	Nazir		

Other Ancient Authors and Writings

Aelius Aristides
Her.   Heracles

Aeschines
Ctes.   In Ctesiphonem (Against
              Ctesiphon)

Alciphron
Ep.   Epistulae (Letters)

Apollodorus
Lib.   The Library

Appian
Syr.   Syrian Wars

Apuleius
Apol.   Apology
Metam.   Metamorphoses (The Golden
              Ass)

Aristotle
Ath. pol.   Athēnaiōn politeia (Constitu-
              tion of Athens)
Eth. nic.   Ethica nicomachea (Nicoma-
              chean Ethics)
Metaph.   Metaphysics
Pol.   Politics
Virt. vit. De virtutibus et vitiis (On Vir-
              tues and Vices)

Cicero
Agr.   De lege agraria (On the Agrar-
              ian Law)
Att.   Epistulae ad Atticum (Letters
              to Atticus)
Br.   Epistulae ad Brutum (Letters
              to Brutus)
Cat.   Cato maior de senectute (Cato
              the Elder on Old Age)
Fam.   Epistulae ad Familiares (Let-
              ters to His Friends)
Flac.   Pro Flacco (In Defense of
              Flaccus)

Font.   Pro Fonteio (In Defense of
              Fonteius)
Pis.   In Pisonem (Against Piso)
Prov. cons. De provinciis consularibus
              (On the Consular Provinces)
Q. Fr.   Epistulae ad Quintum fra-
              trem (Letters to His Brother
              Quintus)
Sest.   Pro Sestio (In Defense of
              Sestius)
Tusc.   Tusculanae disputationes
              (Tusculan Disputations)
Verr.   In Verrem (The Verrine
              Orations)

Dio Cassius
Hist.   Roman History

Dio Chrysostom
Or.   Oration(s)

Diodorus Siculus
Lib. Hist. The Library of History

Diogenes Laertius
Lives   Lives of Eminent Philosophers

Dionysius (of Halicarnassus)
Ant. rom.   Antiquitates romanae (Roman
              Antiquities)

Epictetus
Diatr.   Diatribai (Discourses)

Gaius
Inst.   Institutes

Herodotus
Hist.   History

Horace
Sat.   Satires

Iamblichus
Vit. pyth. De vita pythagorica (On the
              Pythagorean Life)

Josephus

Ag. Ap.	Against Apion
Ant.	Jewish Antiquities
J.W.	Jewish War
Life	The Life

Julian

Or.	Orations

Juvenal

Sat.	Satires

Livy

Hist.	Roman History

Lucian

Icar.	Icaromenippus

Ovid

Fast.	Fasti (The Festivals)

Pausanias

Descr.	Description of Greece

Petronius

Sat.	Satyricon

Philo

Abr.	De Abrahamo (On the Life of Abraham)
Cher.	De cherubim (On the Cherubim)
Conf.	De confusione linguarum (On the Confusion of Tongues)
Congr.	De congressu eruditionis gratia (On the Preliminary Studies)
Contempl.	De vita contemplativa (On the Contemplative Life)
Flacc.	In Flaccum (Against Flaccus)
Hypoth.	Hypothetica
Leg.	Legum allegoriae (Allegorical Interpretation)
Legat.	Legatio ad Gaium (On the Embassy to Gaius)
Migr.	De migratione Abrahami (On the Migration of Abraham)
Mos.	De vita Mosis (On the Life of Moses)
Praem.	De praemiis et poenis (On Rewards and Punishments)
Prob.	Quod omnis probus liber sit (That Every Good Person Is Free)
Somn.	De somniis (On Dreams)
Spec.	De specialibus legibus (On the Special Laws)
Virt.	De virtutibus (On the Virtues)

Philostratus

Vit. Apol.	Vita Apollonii (Life of Apollonius of Tyana)

Plato

Apol.	Apology
Leg.	Leges (Laws)
Parm.	Parmenides
Phedr.	Phedrus
Prot.	Protagoras
Rep.	The Republic

Pliny the Elder

Nat. Hist.	Natural History

Pliny the Younger

Ep.	Epistulae (Letters)

Plutarch

Alex.	Alexander
Ant.	Antony
Arist.	Aristides
Caes.	Julius Caesar
Conj. praec.	Conjugalia praecepta (Advice to the Bride and Groom)
Flam.	Titus Flamininus
Mor.	Moralia (Morals)
Stoic. rep.	De Stoicorum repugnantiis (On Stoic Self-Contradictions)
Sull.	Sulla

Polybius

Hist.	Histories

Pseudo-Diogenes

Ep.   Epistulae (Letters)

Ptolemy

Geogr.   Geography

Quintilian

Inst.   Institutio oratoria (The Ora-
             tor's Education)

Seneca

Dial.   Dialogues
Epist. mor. Epistulae morales (Moral
             Letters)

Sextus Empiricus

Pyr.   Outlines of Pyrrhonism

Soranus

Gyn.   Gynecology

Stobaeus

Flor.   Florilegium (Anthology)

Strabo

Geogr.   Geography

Suetonius

Aug.   Augustus
Cal.   Caligula
Claud.   Claudius
Vesp.   Vespasian

Tacitus

Ann.   Annals
Hist.   Histories

Valerius Maximus

Fact. dict. mem. Factorum et dictorum
                  memorabilium (Memo-
                  rable Deeds and Sayings)

Virgil

Aen.   Aeneid

Xenophon

Cyr.   Cyropaedia (The Education of
             Cyrus)
Mem.   Memorabilia

Anonymous Ancient Works

Dig.   Digesta (Digests)

1

Introduction

JOEL B. GREEN AND LEE MARTIN MCDONALD

One of the characteristics of the Jewish and Christian Scriptures is that they are eminently translatable. A quick survey of the available English translations of the Bible is enough to demonstrate this truism, but translation into English is only a relatively recent example of the phenomenon. The "Bible" (what Christians today call the "Old Testament") for most of the earliest Christians and the writers of the New Testament (NT) books was a translation from Hebrew into Greek. Synagogues were the sites of ongoing translation of the Hebrew Scriptures into Aramaic, the vernacular of the day in Palestine. The NT documents, written in "common Greek," were quickly translated into various Coptic dialects and into Latin. And on the story goes, with the result that today the Bible or portions of the Bible are available in more than two thousand of the world's languages.

Although we celebrate the accessibility of the Scriptures in the language of the people, we cannot overlook the basic fact that it is far easier to translate words on a page than it is to capture the deeper sense of those words. Linguists have long been aware that most of what is communicated is not actually expressed in words but is assumed among those involved in the communicative act. The history Paul shared with the Corinthians, the cultural assumptions Luke shared with his audience, those experiences of imperial Rome shared between the author and addressees of the book of Revelation—such shared histories, assumptions, and experiences shape how these authors' words and phrases might be heard. They thicken the significance of the words of parables or letters or homilies. Precisely because these pools of assumptions could simply be taken for granted by Paul, Luke, and John, they therefore do not sit on top of the pages of our New Testament. This is true whether we are reading the NT in English, in Greek, or in some other language. We need more than the words on the page. We need to be oriented to the background assumed by people in the NT era. We need context.

Students taking university or seminary biblical courses will often hear their professors say that the key to understanding the Bible is its context. They quickly learn the mantra of formal biblical studies: "Context, context, context! Without a context, texts easily become little more than pretexts." Although we need more than cultural, social, and historical context in order to attend well to the NT message, we certainly do not need less. Greater awareness of the context within which the NT books were written helps us better to hear its words and to interpret them with greater precision.

This volume provides the reader with a more informed understanding of the context within which the events described in the NT would have taken place and within which the NT books themselves were written. Describing the world in which we live today would be a complex business. It is no less so for the first-century world of the NT. This is not because the first-century Mediterranean world was so much more complicated than our own, but because the day-to-day world of

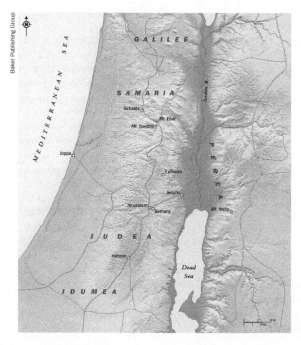

1.1. Israel at the time of Jesus.

Roman antiquity is so much less familiar to us. Too easily we mistake its thought forms for our own or imagine that people everywhere and at all times are like us. Holding Bibles written in our languages, we easily assume that our assumptions are shared by its writers, its first-century audiences. We forget that reading the pages of the NT is for everyone in the twenty-first century a cross-cultural experience. To attend to the NT, we need a better grasp of the first-century world of Peter and Paul, Priscilla and Phoebe, as well as of the years, movements, struggles, and literatures that gave the NT era its shape.

The articles of this book are gathered into five major sections, each of which will foster greater understanding of the NT world as well as open fresh opportunities for further research. These articles provide orientation to the issues they discuss and thus serve as important first steps for gaining essential information on the background of the NT. Annotated bibliographies at the close of each chapter direct readers to some of the best resources available on each topic and will enable them to continue their research in greater depth.

For example, students today quickly learn that it is important to know the Jewish context of early Christianity. After all, Jesus was a Jew, and his earliest followers were Jews. Most of the writers of the NT documents were Jewish. They were reared in Jewish cultures, which influenced how they thought, taught, and responded within their various circumstances. Until recently, it was common to speak of a "normative Judaism" in the first century, and thus to make pronouncements about "the Jews" of the NT era—what "they" believed, "their" hopes, "their" practices, and so on. This was the key for unlocking the mission and message of Jesus, Paul, and other NT figures, whose beliefs, hopes, and practices were often understood as counterpoints to the beliefs, hopes, and practices of "the Jews." We now know that this approach was working with little more than a caricature, a cartoon picture of the Jewish people in the Second Temple period.[1] Plainly stated, there was no singular expression of Judaism in the time of Jesus—no more than we can speak generically of "Christian beliefs in the US at the turn of the twenty-first century." (Which Christians? Rich or poor? Old or young? Mainline or emerging? Socially progressive or conservative? Whose definition?) Although Jews shared some common characteristics, such as the practice of circumcision and Sabbath observance, they could differ, sometimes widely, on other issues, such as messianic expectation, perspectives on life after death, which religious writings were acknowledged as sacred Scripture, and precisely how to keep Torah. By filling in our understanding of the Jewish people during the NT era, we find a more complex picture than was often assumed in earlier days, and we find more continuity than we might have anticipated between these various expressions of Judaism and the beliefs and practices of the early Jesus movement. Indeed, in one of the essays that follows, we read that some twenty expressions of Judaism can be traced in the time of Jesus.

1. See the glossary for definitions of "Second Temple period" and a number of other words and phrases used in NT study.

Similarly, numerous and varied Jewish books and resources informed elements of early Christianity. These include the books that compose the Old Testament (OT), but also many of the so-called apocryphal and pseudepigraphic writings that were written before, during, and after the time of Jesus. Those who want to know more about the social and religious context of the NT and early Christianity should also familiarize themselves with the many books of Philo from Alexandria, Egypt (who was roughly a contemporary of Jesus), and the historical writings of Josephus, from the last quarter of the first century. It is also important to have a sense of the writings preserved by one of the Jewish sects that thrived before AD 70, namely, the Essenes—some of whom would have been contemporaries with Jesus—who produced many of the Dead Sea Scrolls (DSS) and preserved numerous other Jewish religious texts they welcomed into their community. Since this collection of writings was written and copied just prior to the time of Jesus, their importance for understanding the world and literature of the NT is obvious.

What of those Jews who survived the war with Rome and the destruction of Jerusalem and its sacred temple (AD 66–74), and who found ways to continue to express their faith in God and faithfulness to Torah? These Jews produced a wealth of literature that often, though not always, reflects traditions that both precede and are contemporary with the time of Jesus and the earliest Christians. Some of their writings reflect Jewish thinking one or more generations removed from the time of Jesus, but some of it is useful for understanding Jewish practices before and during the time of Jesus. The literature these pious Jews produced or collected and preserved from the second to the sixth centuries AD is known as the rabbinic tradition.

Following the destruction of the Jerusalem temple and the concomitant cessation of temple worship, some rabbis asked Rome for permission to gather at Jamnia (or Yavneh) to determine how a faith that was bound to the sacrificial system practiced in Jerusalem might continue after the temple's destruction. Over several centuries these rabbis collected and produced a large body of important literature that includes the Mishnah, the Tosefta, and the two Talmuds (or Talmudim). This literature must be read with discernment since it does not always reflect perspectives contemporary with NT times; nonetheless, it provides a wealth of material useful in interpreting various NT texts.

One of the more important advances in our study of the NT was the discovery that not only were a number of Jewish perspectives present in the land of Israel in the time of Jesus, but also Judaism itself did not exist in isolation from the dominant culture of its day. In fact, the various ways of being Jewish to which we have already called attention are a corollary of Greek and then Roman cultural influences. How is faithfulness to the God of Israel to be measured and lived in a world of Greek and Roman overlords and in the wake of pressing influences from Greek and then Greco-Roman education, religion, architecture, economics, and politics? Following the conquests of Alexander the Great in the late fourth century

BC, the Jewish people came under the control of the Greek (or Hellenistic) culture that influenced many of their learned leaders. And this influence continued right up to the time of Jesus and his followers.

And what of Jews living outside the land of Israel, that is, living in the Diaspora? Since the rabbinic tradition and its literature were produced only in Hebrew and Aramaic, Jews to the west, north, and south of Israel who spoke Greek and Latin were largely unaffected by that tradition until much later, in the eighth or ninth centuries AD. Jews living in the larger Mediterranean world read their Scriptures in the Greek translation of the Jewish Scriptures regularly called the Septuagint (LXX). This Greek translation of the books of the Hebrew Bible (HB), with certain other books composed in Greek, would constitute the Scriptures of the early churches. What was it like to navigate Jewish beliefs and faithful practices in a predominately gentile setting? What happened among Jews who could not assume that their neighbors shared their commitments to the one God of Israel or their commitments to Sabbath and purity?

Another example: after the Romans became the foremost power over the land of Israel in 63 BC, Hellenistic culture remained dominant; when traveling throughout the Mediterranean world, one could easily communicate effectively in the Greek language and encounter pervasive evidence of the influence of Hellenistic culture. Some NT writers show considerable familiarity with classical writers; moreover, some of the people and many of the events they mention are also found among the writings of Greek and Roman historians and poets. Some NT texts are set in sharper relief when read alongside the literature that originated in the worlds of Greece and Rome—their epics, histories, philosophies, religious beliefs and practices, and so on. Indeed, even on the relatively mundane level of dating events mentioned in the NT—such as the birth of Jesus and beginning of his ministry, aspects of Paul's itinerant mission, and a number of other incidents mentioned in the Gospels and Acts—we would have little with which to work if we were unable to draw on Greco-Roman writings.

According to John's Gospel, "the Word became flesh and made his home among us" (1:14 CEB). That is, even if the gospel it presents has a timeless appeal, the Christ to whom the NT bears witness was born on real soil found in a particular time and place. Paul, Aquila, and Priscilla had dirty hands from their work with leather (Acts 18:3). The Corinthians knew the smell of meat sacrificed to idols, and those Christ-followers to whom 1 Peter is addressed knew the real ache of scornful words tossed at them in the marketplace. On their every page, the NT writings bear witness to the settings, the times and places, of their writing. Whatever else they are, these documents are the products of the cultural world within which they were written.

All this is to say that context is crucial for understanding the NT message. Accordingly, the articles in this volume are designed to give us a firmer grip on the NT world so that we may become more able interpreters of the NT Scriptures.

Behind this volume stands the Institute for Biblical Research (IBR),[2] a scholarly community that gave the impetus for this publication to provide an introduction to the background of the NT. The IBR is a community of evangelical biblical scholars from a variety of church backgrounds and theological traditions, who are committed to advancing biblical inquiry within the broad orthodox and evangelical traditions. Several authors in this volume are internationally known for their expertise in NT scholarship and have made significant contributions to the field of biblical scholarship. Others are newer to the field but have already begun to distinguish themselves. All possess specialized knowledge in various aspects of biblical inquiry. Most are IBR members, but some are not. We celebrate all of their contributions toward producing this useful resource for those who want a better understanding of the NT in its own contexts.

The editors express their appreciation to those who have contributed to this volume, sacrificing valuable time and effort to make this an important resource for students of the NT. We also express thanks to the editors and staff of Baker Academic; from early on they recognized the usefulness of this collection as a tool for biblical research for students and pastors alike and brought their own considerable expertise to the shaping of the volume. We are particularly grateful to Timothy Reardon, who prepared the indexes for this volume. The members of IBR have long appreciated their partnership with Baker Academic, and we are grateful for their taking on this project.

2. See http://www.ibr-bbr.org/.

2

New Testament Chronology

LEE MARTIN MCDONALD

Biblical scholars have long recognized the value of knowing the history and chronology of the NT for understanding its texts, but they also recognize the complexity of establishing reliable dates for the books and events mentioned in the NT. Outside of broad agreement that most if not all of it originated in the first century, scholars continue to debate the precise time when the NT documents were produced.

Establishing a reliable NT chronology is not an exact science, and there are many variables involved and many difficult choices to make. In antiquity, calendars and various chronologies were often rooted in the years of a king's rule or the tenure of governors, local rulers, or high priests—as we see in the NT itself (cf. Luke 1:5; 2:1–2; 3:1–2).

Dating NT events involves examining not only the NT writings but also a number of nonbiblical writings, whether Jewish, Christian, or Greco-Roman—writings roughly contemporary with the NT. For example, some persons mentioned in the NT, such as rulers and leading biblical personalities, are also mentioned elsewhere. An important resource for dating many NT events and persons was produced in the last quarter of the first century by Josephus, a Jewish general during the Jewish war against Rome who wrote *Jewish Antiquities* and *Jewish War*, as well as *The Life* and *Against Apion*. A second primary resource is Eusebius's *Ecclesiastical History* (fourth century), the first widely recognized reliable history of early Christianity, which shows considerable awareness of ancient sources and events from

7

the beginning of Christianity and its subsequent development. Along with these, those seeking to date events mentioned in the NT will find helpful the writings of Dio Cassius, Pausanius, Pliny, Suetonius, and Tacitus. Along with these and other classical writings, the context of early Christianity is also considerably clarified by examining the writings of Philo, the DSS (or more precisely, the Discoveries in the Judean Desert [DJD]), rabbinic writings (including the Mishnah, the Tosefta, the two Talmuds [Babylonian and Palestinian]), and the Jewish targumim (expanded Aramaic translations/interpretation of the Jewish Scriptures), as well as the early church fathers, especially Clement of Rome, Justin Martyr, Irenaeus, Tertullian, and Origen.

Although students will often find these and other ancient sources indispensable in establishing both the chronology and the context of early Christianity, we should not be surprised to find different dates for the same events in the ancient sources and, periodically, different dates for the same event in the same author. This can be seen in Josephus's dating of Herod's temple; in one place he writes that it was begun in the eighteenth year of Herod's reign (*Ant.* 15.380), while in another he refers to his fifteenth year (*J.W.* 1.401). Although we would be at a considerable loss without the writings of Josephus, we should read him with caution, as we do all ancient historians.

Dating the New Testament

Some of the more important NT dates have to do with the stories of Jesus and Paul, but other important and related persons and events are also significant in establishing a NT chronology. Often scholars can come within a year or two of the actual date by the use of nonbiblical sources. For example, the reference to the Roman emperor Claudius's expulsion of Jews from Rome—which consequently led Aquila and Priscilla to come to Corinth, where they met Paul (Acts 18:1–4)—has several nonbiblical references that allow us to date the event to around AD 48–49. In another instance, because of the discovery of an ancient inscription at Delphi, north of the Corinthian Sea in ancient Greece, we know that Gallio, the governor of the province of Achaia, resided there; the inscription even allows us to say with relative precision when he was governor. The book of Acts refers to him in conjunction with Paul's ministry in Corinth (Acts 18:12–17), and this allows us to date with some assurance when Paul was in Corinth. We will discuss both of these items below.

Biblical scholars regularly acknowledge that the dates they set forth for the writing of the NT books as well as the events to which they bear witness are at best approximate, even if some dates are more likely than others. When some ancient dates are relatively well established, scholars use them as benchmarks to produce a chronology of the NT era. For instance, scholars continue to debate the dating of the NT Gospels, though there is general agreement they were written in the last half of the first century.

Some of the More Established Dates

Some of the more important dates that are relatively certain relate to events pertaining to Jesus and Paul. The following examples are debated among scholars, but an assessment of them allows readers to draw responsible conclusions. They focus mostly on Jesus and Paul, but also on actions of others mentioned in the NT—for example, Claudius, Felix, and Festus. These examples will make clear the importance of using nonbiblical sources to date many NT events.

The Birth of Jesus

According to Matt. 2:1–21, Jesus' birth took place during the reign of Herod the Great. Josephus chronicled Herod's life and concluded that Herod the Great died shortly before April (or March) 12, 4 BC (*Ant.* 17.190–91; *J.W.* 1.665). Since Josephus says that Herod died in April of 4 BC, and if Jesus was born during Herod's reign, then he was born at least before April of 4 BC. If this is the case, then the traditional dating of the birth of Jesus in the year 0 (a year that does not even exist in traditional calendars) needs to be reconsidered. What complicates things is that Jesus' birth was not widely celebrated by Christians until the fourth century, so the keeping of such records was not high on the early church's agenda. If Herod, out of fear of a rival king in Israel, sought to kill all the male children in and around Bethlehem under the age of two (Matt. 2:16), and if he died in 4 BC, then it is reasonable to conclude that Jesus was born sometime around 6–4 BC.

Along with this, Luke dates the beginning of John the Baptist's ministry, Jesus' baptism, and the initiation of Jesus' ministry in the fifteenth year of Emperor Tiberius's reign (3:1–2). The first two years of Tiberius's reign (AD 12–14) reportedly overlapped with the last two years of the reign of Caesar Augustus (Octavius), who died in AD 14. By adding fifteen years to that time, to either AD 12 or 14, we arrive at a date of sometime around AD 27–29 for Jesus' baptism and the beginning of his ministry. Since Luke 3:23 indicates that Jesus was baptized when *about* age 30, we can go backward to *around* 4–3 BC for Jesus' birth.

Further, John's Gospel has a few references that allow us to conclude that the previous dating is likely. In the Gospel of John, Jesus says, "Destroy this temple, and in three days I will raise it up" (2:19). Jesus' critics respond that the temple has been in the making for forty-six years and question how Jesus could raise it up in three days (2:20). If the temple has been in the making for forty-six years, and if Josephus is correct in saying that construction of the temple began in the eighteenth year of Herod's reign (namely, in 20–19 BC; see *Ant.* 15.354, 380; cf. *J.W.* 1.401), then Jesus, at about the age of thirty during this encounter with his critics (AD 26), would have been born at least around 4 BC (for further discussion, see Finegan, *Chronology*, 346–49). It is true that Josephus offers an alternative date for the beginning of the construction of the temple—during the fifteenth year of Herod's reign (ca. 23 BC; see *Ant.* 15.354)—but the later date is more likely. If we add John's forty-six years to 19 or 20 BC, then Jesus' ministry began around AD 26 and possibly as late as 27.

Some references are unclear or too confusing to be used for dating Jesus' birth or the onset of his ministry—for example, Matthew's reference to the star in Bethlehem that identifies the location of Jesus after his birth (2:1–12) and the reference to Jesus' age in John 8:57. Both are vague and not easily aligned with the biblical story. We should also note that the dating of Jesus' birth during a registration or census for taxation ordered by Quirinius (Luke 2:1–2) is problematic since there is a significant difference between the dating of this census in nonbiblical sources and Luke's dating of this census. For example, Tacitus claims that Quirinius began his rule *after* Archelaus, the son of Herod the Great, was deposed in AD 6 (*Ann.* 6.41). This is similar to Josephus (*Ant.* 18.1–10; *J.W.* 7.253), who agrees with Tacitus that Quirinius ordered the census in AD 6–7 and that it led to a Jewish revolt (mentioned in Acts 5:37). Support for a double reign of Quirinius, namely, an additional one in 7–6 BC, is not supported by the external evidence. Nonbiblical sources do not support Luke's report of a census during Herod the Great's reign and during the rule of Quirinius of Syria, so some caution is in order. Stanley Porter has noted that there is separate evidence that a census was taken in Egypt in 4 BC, and he suggests that a similar one may have been taken in Judea. Roman censuses for tax purposes normally occurred every fourteen years, but some recently discovered evidence indicates that in Egypt the censuses were taken every seven years, and they can be established for the years 11–10 BC, 4–3 BC, AD 4–5, and AD 11–12. This does not mean that the same pattern prevailed in Judea, but it is suggestive (Porter, "Chronology," 202).[1]

In terms of the specific day of Jesus' birth, the familiar date of December 25 may be based on an ancient belief that the conception of Jesus took place on March 25, and that his birth took place precisely nine months later, namely, December 25 (see Finegan, *Chronology*, 320–28). There was considerable debate in the early churches over whether Jesus was born on December 25 or January 6. The later date was celebrated by Christians in the East as the day of Jesus' birth, but now most Christians celebrate the appearance of the magi or wise men coming from the East to visit Jesus in Bethlehem on January 6, twelve days after his birth. Matthew, however, suggests that Jesus may have been two years old at that time and in a house, not in a manger near animals (2:11); however, in Matthew it really is not clear how soon the magi came to the town where Jesus was born. The traditional "twelve days of Christmas" run, of course, between December 25 and January 6. Others have suggested that the celebration of the birth of Jesus on December 25 is rooted in the pagan celebration of the sun, the solstice, when the sun stands still briefly, after which days begin to lengthen. This is "Solis Invictus," the festival of the "Invincible Sun." Some early Christians thought that this parallel

---

1. Porter depends here on the work of R. S. Bagnall and B. W. Frier, *The Demography of Roman Egypt* (Cambridge: Cambridge University Press, 1994).

was a fulfillment of the prophecy in Mal. 4:2: "But for you who revere my name the sun of righteousness shall rise, with healing in its wings."

There is no mention of birth celebrations of Jesus by earlier Christian writers such as Irenaeus (ca. 130–200) or Tertullian (ca. 160–225).[2] Origen of Alexandria (ca. 165–264) even mocks Roman celebrations of birth anniversaries, dismissing them as "pagan" practices—a strong indication that Jesus' birth was not marked with similar festivities at that place and time (*Hom. Lev.* 8). Apparently, Christmas was not widely celebrated before the fourth century.

Clement of Alexandria (ca. 200) made reference to the date when Jesus was born, claiming that several different days had been proposed by various Christian groups, but he does not mention December 25. He writes:

> There are those who have determined not only the year of our Lord's birth, but also the day; and they say that it took place in the twenty-eighth year of Augustus, and in the twenty-fifth day of [the Egyptian month] Pachon [May 20 in our calendar]. . . . And treating of His Passion, with very great accuracy, some say that it took place in the sixteenth year of Tiberius, on the twenty-fifth of Phamenoth [March 21]; and others on the twenty-fifth of Pharmuthi [April 21] and others say that on the nineteenth of Pharmuthi [April 15] the Savior suffered. Further, others say that He was born on the twenty-fourth or twenty-fifth of Pharmuthi [April 20 or 21]. (Clement, *Strom.* 1.21; *ANF* 2:133)

The Ministry of Jesus

All four Gospels agree that Jesus began his ministry during John the Baptist's ministry, of which Luke writes:

> In the fifteenth year of the reign of Emperor Tiberius, when Pontius Pilate was governor of Judea, and Herod [Antipas] was ruler of Galilee, and his brother Philip ruler of the region of Ituraea and Trachonitis, and Lysanias ruler of Abilene, during the high priesthood of Annas and Caiaphas, the word of God came to John son of Zechariah in the wilderness. (Luke 3:1–2)

The date of the fifteenth year of the rule of Tiberius is roughly AD 26–27 (28–29 if his sole regency, that is, without the coregency with Caesar Augustus, is in mind). This date is confirmed by Josephus, who discusses Jesus' ministry during the time when Pilate was procurator of Judea (*Ant.* 18.63–64); although Josephus's text was likely later expanded in order to clarify Jesus' messiahship for a Christian audience, the original text almost certainly contained information about Jesus, and this provides an important, independent witness to the presence of Jesus as a teacher and miracle worker during the days of Pontius Pilate, as well as confirmation that his followers continued on even in the generation of Josephus.

2. For much of the content in this section, see Andrew McGowan, "How December 25 Became Christmas," *BAR Magazine*, http://www.bib-arch.org/e-features/christmas.asp#top.

The length of Jesus' ministry is often based on the number of Passovers mentioned in the Gospels. Each of the Synoptic Gospels refers to a single Passover (Matt. 26:17; Mark 14:1; Luke 22:1) during Jesus' ministry, but the Gospel of John refers to three (2:13, 23; 5:1 [possibly]; 6:4; 11:55). Christians have generally followed John here, but some scholars suggest that Jesus' tenure of ministry was somewhere between two and three years. Long ago, Ethelbert Stauffer claimed that the stories of John could not be fitted into the timeframe of the Synoptic Gospels, but that the Synoptic Gospels could easily be incorporated into John's.[3] If this is correct, then his ministry may have begun sometime between 26 (at the earliest) and 28 and lasted at least two and possibly slightly more than three years, that is, until around AD 29–31.

The Death of Jesus

Each of the four canonical Gospels provides detailed information about the time of Jesus' death, and all agree that his death took place on a Friday (Matt. 27:62; Mark 15:42; Luke 23:54; John 19:31, 42). According to John, Jesus was crucified just as the Passover lambs were being sacrificed. This would have occurred on the fourteenth of the Hebrew month of Nisan, just before the Jewish holiday that began at sundown (considered the beginning of the fifteenth day; in the Hebrew calendar, days both conclude and begin at sundown). In Matthew, Mark, and Luke, however, the Last Supper is held *after* sundown, on the beginning of the fifteenth (Matt. 27:62; Mark 14:12; Luke 23:54), unlike John, who places it the day before the Passover (19:14). All agree that Jesus was crucified the next morning, that is, on the fifteenth. All four Gospels place Jesus' death just prior to Passover and coordinate this event with the rules of Pilate as governor of Judea and Caiaphas as the high priest. Luke places Jesus' ministry in conjunction with John the Baptist, during the reign of Tiberius (Luke 3:1–2). Tiberius, as noted above, began his reign as the successor to Caesar Augustus (Octavian) during a two-year coregency in AD 10–12 or subsequently in AD 14. The fifteenth year would then be AD 25–27 or 29–30, and if Jesus had a two- to three-year ministry, then his death would likely be around AD 30–31.

The celebration of Easter, a much earlier development than the celebration of Jesus' birth, was simply the gradual Christian reinterpretation of the Passover in terms of Jesus' passion. Its observance could even be implied in the NT (1 Cor. 5:7–8: "For our paschal lamb, Christ, has been sacrificed. Therefore, let us celebrate the festival"); it was certainly a distinctively Christian feast by the mid-second century, when an apocryphal text, *Epistle of the Apostles (Epistula Apostolorum)* 15, says that Jesus instructed his disciples as follows: "And you therefore celebrate the remembrance of my death, which is the Passover."[4]

3. Ethelbert Stauffer, *Jesus and His Story* (New York: Knopf, 1960), 7; this comment is found in Finegan, *Chronology*, 351.

4. J. K. Elliott, *The Apocryphal New Testament: A Collection of Apocryphal Christian Literature in an English Translation* (Oxford: Clarendon, 1993), 565.

The Death of Herod Agrippa I

According to the Acts of the Apostles, Herod Agrippa I executed James the apostle and imprisoned Peter (12:1–3), and then he died suddenly and painfully following his pompous display of self-aggrandizement (12:18–23). This same story is reported by Josephus with several similarities and a few variants in the details (*Ant.* 19.344–52; see also 18.195–200, 237, 252), but it is sufficiently close to conclude that the broad details of this event are the same in both sources. Agrippa I was a close friend of the emperor Caligula, who succeeded Tiberius, and Caligula appointed Agrippa ruler over the tetrarchy of Herod Antipas. After the death of Caligula, and because Agrippa helped Claudius succeed Caligula as emperor, Claudius, who ruled from AD 41 to 54, made Agrippa I king over Judea and Samaria as well as the rest of the territory that Herod the Great had ruled, including Galilee, Transjordan, and the Decapolis. Josephus tells of Agrippa I's violent and painful death at the age of 54 after having ruled over all the territory of Israel from AD 41 to 44. Josephus dates this event at the time of the festival of dedication that was begun earlier by Herod the Great (*Ant.* 16.136–41) and in the year AD 44. Later Eusebius tells the story of Agrippa's death in Acts and brings it together with Josephus's account (*Eccl. Hist.* 2.10.1–10).

Paul's Conversion to Faith in Jesus Christ

Paul's conversion is more difficult to date with precision. However, Paul's brief chronology of his encounter with the risen Christ and early ministry (Gal. 1:11–2:10) gives us some dates with which to work. If one begins the chronology following his conversion (Gal. 1:18: "Then after three years"; 2:1: "Then after fourteen years"), then, combined with information obtained elsewhere, we can date Paul's conversion as early as 31 or as late as 36. In other words, we have either a total of fourteen years (if both dates mentioned are after his conversion) or seventeen (if they are sequential). Comparing Luke's reports (Acts 9:1–30; 22:3–16; 26:12–23) with Paul's own words, especially Gal. 1:13–2:10, Paul's encounter with the risen Christ (Gal. 1:16) gives us a time of AD 31–36. If Paul's visit to Jerusalem after his encounter on the Damascus road is the same as that mentioned in Acts 9:26–30, and the fourteen years came before the council recounted in Acts 15 (which was held almost assuredly sometime in AD 48 or 49), we have an early conversion date. This presumes a "South Galatian" destination of Galatians.[5] If, however, Paul's letter was written *after* the conference recounted in Acts 15, or during his second missionary journey (a North Galatian destination; see Acts 15:36–41), then it is possible that his conversion was later, though not much later than AD 35–36.

5. This debate and the arguments in favor of each position are conveniently summarized in F. F. Bruce, *The Epistle to the Galatians* (NIGTC; Grand Rapids: Eerdmans, 1982), 5–10; and in more detail in Richard N. Longenecker, *Galatians* (WBC 41; Nashville: Nelson, 1990), lxiii–lxxii.

The Expulsion of Aquila and Priscilla from Rome

According to Acts 18:2, Aquila and Priscilla came to Corinth from Rome following Claudius's edict expelling Jews from the city. Josephus describes this expulsion (*Ant.* 18.65, 80–84), and so does Tacitus (AD 55–120), who claims that the expulsion had to do with disputes over Jewish and Egyptian rites (*Ann.* 2.85). Suetonius (ca. 75–140) describes this event in his *Lives of the Caesars* but claims that the expulsion of Jews from Rome was because of problems among the Jews in the city over "Chrestus," a possible reference to Jesus, the Christ. He writes, "Since the Jews constantly made disturbances at the instigation of Chrestus,[6] he [Claudius] expelled them from Rome" (*Claud.* 15.4; LCL). Dio Cassius (ca. 150–235) also describes this event in his *Roman History* (57.18.5). Because these other sources date this event essentially the same, we can reasonably place it with some confidence in AD 49, although some scholars place it in AD 41. This also fits well with Paul's coming to Corinth in mid to late AD 49 and his meeting with Priscilla and Aquila.

Paul's Appearance at Corinth before Gallio

According to Acts 18:12, Paul was brought before the proconsul Gallio, who was governor of Achaia and resided in Delphi. His visit to Corinth came during Paul's eighteen-month ministry there (Acts 18:11) and more precisely in the late spring of AD 51. Gallio was the older brother of the well-known poet Lucius Annaeus Seneca (ca. 4 BC–AD 65; see Seneca's reference to Gallio in his *Epist. mor.* 104.1), and he is mentioned in several places in Roman writings. Gallio's full name was Lucius Junius Gallio Annaeus, and Pliny the Elder (AD 23–79) addresses him by that name (*Nat. Hist.* 31.31). Gallio is also mentioned in the now-famous first-century fragmented inscription discovered at Delphi in the province of Achaia, in Greece. It reads as follows:

> Tiberius Claudius Caesar Augustus Germanicus, Pontifex Maximus, Holder of the Tribunician Power for the twelfth time, Imperator for the twenty-sixth time, Father of the country, Counsel for the fifth time, and Censor to the city of the Delphians, greetings. For some time past I have been devoted to the city of the Delphians . . . and good will from the beginning; and I have ever observed the worshipping of the Pythian Apollo. . . . But as for the many current reports and those discords among the citizens, . . . just as Lucius Junius Gallio, my friend and proconsul of Achaia, wrote. . . . Therefore I am granting that you continue to enjoy your former. . . .[7]

---

6. Many scholars have suggested that "Chrestus" is a corruption of the word "Christ," a word unfamiliar to Suetonius. F. F. Bruce (*History*, 268) observes, however, that the name "Chrestus" actually means "useful" and was a common name for slaves. The question is whether a slave name fits the context adequately.

7. Everett Ferguson has highlighted the most important parts of this fragmented inscription as follows: "Tiberius [Claudius] Caesar Augustus Germanicus . . . In his tribunician] power [year 12. Acclaimed emperor the 26th time, father of the country . . . [Lucius] Junius Gallio my friend and [pro]consul [of Achaia wrote] . . ." (*Backgrounds of Early Christianity* [3rd ed; Grand Rapids: Eerdmans, 2003], 585). The text is also conveniently found and discussed in Adolf

Gallio's governorship can be discerned by the twenty-sixth acclamation of the emperor. According to another inscription, the twenty-fourth acclamation took place in the eleventh year of the tribunate, that is, in the eleventh year of the reign of the emperor Claudius, January 25 of AD 51 to January 24 of AD 52 (see *CIL* 3:1977). By means of these inscriptions and others (see *BCH* 11.306–7; *CIL* 6:1256), the Gallio inscription has been dated between January 25 and August 1 of the year AD 51. Since a proconsul's term or governorship normally lasted one year (January 25 to the following January 24), this means that Gallio was governor of Achaia from AD 51 to 52, which overlapped Paul's eighteen-month ministry in Corinth, when he stood before Gallio at the *bēma* (or council seat) in Corinth (Acts 18:12). Because of the inscription found at Delphi, scholars have been able to date Paul's ministry at Corinth as having likely begun in late AD 49 and lasting to 51 or 52.[8] As a result, by adding or subtracting the time mentioned in Acts and in Paul's Letters regarding his ministry before, during, and after Corinth, we are now able to date the beginning of Paul's missionary journeys mentioned in Acts from roughly 48–49 to approximately 58, a period of some ten years. Using the Delphic inscription, we are able to suggest approximate dates for several events related to Paul's ministry, including both before and after Paul's visit to Corinth.

Felix and Festus

According to the book of Acts, after Paul was arrested in Jerusalem, he was taken to Caesarea, where he was imprisoned for two years (21:27–26:32). Paul's time there overlapped the changing of the procurators Felix and Festus, and he stood before both (23:23–26:32), as well as before Agrippa II (26:1–32). Both Felix and Festus are mentioned by Josephus (*Ant.* 20.137–38, 142–44, 182; *J.W.* 2.247, 252–54, 271) and subsequently also in Eusebius, who describes Paul's arrest and imprisonment at Caesarea under Felix and Festus (*Eccl. Hist.* 2.19.1–22.8). Josephus's account of these two procurators fits well within the story in Acts, and similarly, they are also mentioned and dated by Tacitus (*Hist.* 5.9; *Ann.* 12.54). Because of these nonbiblical sources, we can safely date Paul's imprisonment at Caesarea to roughly AD 55–57.

The Death of Paul

Since Acts does not mention the death of Paul, the major hero in the book, some biblical scholars conclude that the Acts account was written prior to Paul's death. Since Acts follows the Gospel of Luke (see Acts 1:1–2; cf. Luke 1:1–4) and at its closing (Acts 28:23–31) Paul was in custody in Rome for two years but with

---

Deissmann, *Paul: A Study in Social and Religious History* (2nd ed.; trans. W. E. Wilson; New York: Harper, 1927), 261–86; and Finegan, *Chronology*, 391–95.

8. For discussion, see Lee Martin McDonald, "Acts," in *Acts–Philemon* (ed. Craig A. Evans; vol. 2 of *The Bible Knowledge Background Commentary*; Colorado Springs: Victor, 2004), 126–27; also Finegan, *Chronology*, 391–94. Finegan places the beginning of Paul's ministry in Corinth in December of AD 49, after his second missionary journey began in the spring of 49 (Acts 15:36–41).

relative freedom to continue his witness, it is unlikely that the death of Paul (likely in 62–64, as we will see) had taken place. If Paul died before the book of Acts was completed, it is difficult to understand why the death of its primary hero is missing from the story. Luke had no trouble mentioning the deaths of Stephen and James, so why not Paul's if it had already happened?

Clement of Rome (ca. AD 90) tells us that, after Paul had witnessed before rulers and reached the "limits of the West," he passed from this world (*1 Clem.* 5.7). Having said this, there is no clear indication that Paul was released from Rome after his first imprisonment and that he journeyed on to Spain and perhaps Crete and elsewhere.

Tertullian, after mentioning the death of Peter in Rome, claims that in Rome Paul won "his crown [see 2 Tim. 4:8] in a death like John's" (John the Baptist was beheaded; *Prescript.* 36.3; *ANF* 3:260). Eusebius later says that the death of Peter and Paul took place during the reign of Nero, noting that "Paul was beheaded in Rome itself, and that Peter likewise was crucified, and the titles of Peter and Paul" were "given to the cemeteries there" (*Eccl. Hist.* 2.25.5; *NPNF*[2] 1:129). Nero ruled from AD 54 to 68, and Eusebius claims that Nero's persecutions of Christians *began* in his eighth year (i.e., AD 62; see *Eccl. Hist.* 2.25.1; 2.22.1–8), so it is likely that the death of Paul took place sometime near AD 64 and no later than 68 (the year Nero was murdered).

The reference to Paul's "first defense," when no one stood with him (2 Tim. 4:16), suggests to some scholars that there was a second defense and that Paul was freed after the first defense for a time of ministry. Eusebius reports that Paul "spent two whole years" in Rome, was released with freedom to continue his ministry of preaching, but came a second time to Rome, whereupon he suffered martyrdom by Nero. Apparently citing 2 Tim. 4:16–17, Eusebius claims that the "first defense" came during his first imprisonment in Rome. Initially, Nero was apparently gentler with Christians, but according to Eusebius, at Paul's second defense Nero was "advanced toward reckless crime" and "the Apostles were attacked along with the rest" (*Eccl. Hist.* 2.22.1–8; *NPNF*[2] 1:123–25). After describing the atrocities carried out by Nero against the Christians, Eusebius reports that "Paul was beheaded in Rome itself, and that Peter likewise was crucified," adding that both apostles were martyred at the same time (*Eccl. Hist.* 2.25.1–8; *NPNF*[2] 1:129–30).

Those who claim that Paul wrote the Pastoral Epistles have difficulty fitting them into the chronology presented in the book of Acts or harmonizing them with Paul's other epistles. The ecclesiology appears more advanced in them, and several of Paul's major themes (reconciliation, eschatology, Christology, and pneumatology) are largely missing from these books. If Paul wrote the Pastoral Epistles, and this is debated, it is best to place them after Paul's first imprisonment and before a second.

James, the Brother of Jesus

James the brother of Jesus is mentioned in several NT passages (Mark 6:3; Matt. 13:55; Acts 12:17; 15:13–21; 21:18; Gal. 1:19; 2:9; 1 Cor. 15:7; and, if he was the author, in the Letter of James). After Peter's departure from Jerusalem (Acts 12:17), James became the leading spokesperson for the church (Acts 15:13–21; 21:18–26; Gal. 2:9–10). A NT letter attributed to him was written before AD 62–64, when, according to Josephus, Ananus the high priest in Jerusalem executed James (*Ant.* 20.197). Josephus says that James was well known and respected among the Jews, and he tells how Ananus, during the interim between the proconsuls Festus and Albinus in Judea in AD 62, "convened the judges of the Sanhedrin and brought before them a man named James, the brother of Jesus who was called the Christ, and certain others. [Ananus] accused them of having transgressed the law and delivered them up to be stoned. Those inhabitants of the city who were strict in observance of the law were offended at this" (*Ant.* 20.197, 199–201 LCL; see *J.W.* 2.166). The priesthood of Ananus lasted only three months; because of his action against James, Agrippa II removed Ananus from office, because he had convened the Sanhedrin without permission. We can therefore reasonably date the death of James, the brother of Jesus, during the high priesthood of Ananus at AD 62. Eusebius retells this same story and adds additional details (*Eccl. Hist.* 2.23.20–24), but less convincing is his report of the Hegesippus account (*Eccl. Hist.* 4.22.4).

Conclusion

The chronology of NT events is complex, but some events and persons can be reasonably dated. We can also approximate dates for some of the NT materials. The chart at the end of this chapter contains some of the most reliable dates for the context and background of the NT, but there is still some uncertainty about some of the listed dates. The chart begins with Alexander the Great, who had a significant impact on the land of Israel for several centuries and whose cultural agenda influenced the social context of early Christianity.

Bibliography

Bruce, F. F. *History of the New Testament.* Garden City, NY: Doubleday, 1972. A dated but still useful volume that synthesizes a considerable amount of biblical and nonbiblical information and adds to our understanding of the history, chronology, and context of early Christianity and the NT writings.

Evans, Craig A., ed. *The Bible Knowledge Background Commentary.* 3 vols. Bible Knowledge Series. Colorado Springs, CO: Victor, 2004–5. This collection of individual scholars' treatments of the Greco-Roman and Jewish backgrounds to the NT is an excellent resource for students wanting to see nonbiblical parallels to events and persons mentioned in the NT.

Finegan, Jack. *Handbook of Biblical Chronology.* Rev. ed. Peabody, MA: Hendrickson, 1998. An excellent resource for understanding the chronology of the Old and New

Testaments. Although some of the dates Finegan offers are contested, this volume gathers a wealth of information found nowhere else. This is a good place to start with any question related to biblical chronology.

Hoehner, Harold W. *Chronological Aspects of the Life of Christ*. Grand Rapids: Zondervan, 1977. A useful resource that is excellent in what it reports.

————. *Herod Antipas: A Contemporary of Jesus Christ*. Grand Rapids: Zondervan, 1983. Those interested in the Herodian story and the dating of various events in Herod's life can find no better resource than this one. Though dated, it still contains a wealth of useful information.

Porter, Stanley E. "Chronology, New Testament." *DNTB* 201–8. A succinct and reliable discussion of the most important dates of the NT related to Jesus and Paul; includes references to many nonbiblical sources.

Reicke, Bo. *The New Testament Era: The World of the Bible from 500 B.C. to A.D. 100*. Philadelphia: Fortress, 1968. This older resource is a valuable collection of well-recognized dates, historical information, biblical and nonbiblical resources, and helpful diagrams and charts of the historical development of early Christianity.

Schürer, Emil. *The History of the Jewish People in the Age of Jesus Christ (175 BC–AD 135)*. Revised and edited by Geza Vermes, Fergus Millar, and Martin Goodman. Revised English ed. 3 vols. in 4 parts. Edinburgh: T&T Clark, 1987. This collection of historical data is one of the best ever produced for the period identified in the title.

Chronology of Major Events Related to the Study of the New Testament

334 BC	Alexander the Great assumes power after the assassination of his father, Philip of Macedon, and begins his conquest of the Persian Empire.
332–330 BC	Alexander the Great conquers Palestine and initiates a long Greek occupation of the land.
323 BC	Alexander the Great dies. Control of the conquered lands, including the land of Israel, is divided among his successors (*diadochoi*). Israel is first under the control of Ptolemy, headquartered in Alexandria.
281–100 BC	Origins of the Septuagint (LXX), the translation of the Pentateuch into Greek (ca. 281 BC), and subsequently other OT and apocryphal books.
198–142 BC	Seleucid control of Palestine passes from the Ptolemies following the defeat of Ptolemy V at Pan (Banias) by Antiochus III (called "the Great").
169 BC	Antiochus IV (called Antiochus Epiphanes) invades Egypt; he ruthlessly subjugates Palestine, including attempting to force the Jews to offer sacrifices to pagan deities.
168–167 BC	Mattathias Maccabeus, a Jewish priest, leads Jews in their revolt against the Seleucid dynasty.
165 BC	Religious freedom is won by Judas Maccabeus, "the Hammer," who inherited from his father, Mattathias Maccabeus, leadership of the Jewish revolt against the Seleucid dynasty.
159–142 BC	Jonathan Maccabeus succeeds Judas Maccabeus as leader of the rebellion against the Greeks.

150–125 BC	Possible time of establishment of the Essene community at Qumran. The Pharisee party comes into prominence.
142 BC	Jewish political independence is secured from Seleucid dynasty under the leadership of Jonathan and Simon Maccabeus.
142–134 BC	Simon Maccabeus establishes the Hasmonean dynasty, which continues in leadership in Israel until the time of Herod the Great (37 BC). He is both king and high priest.
134–104 BC	John Hyrcanus I succeeds Simon and extends the borders of the nation beyond the limits of the territory controlled by Solomon.
104–103 BC	Aristobulus has short rule as Hasmonean king.
103–76 BC	Alexander Jannaeus rules the Jewish people.
76–67 BC	Salome Alexandra succeeds her husband as ruler of the Jewish people, but without the title and role of high priest.
67–63 BC	Aristobulus II rules the Jewish people until Rome invades the nation and the Hasmonean dynasty loses power.
63 BC	Pompey invades Jerusalem.
63–40 BC	Hyrcanus II rules a part of the Jewish people, but with little power.
63–43 BC	Cicero flourishes.
58–44 BC	Julius Caesar flourishes. In 44 BC he is assassinated by Brutus and Cassius.
42–41 BC	Octavian, along with Mark Antony, defeats Brutus and Cassius at Philippi in Macedonia. At this time, the land of Israel comes under the control of Mark Antony.
40 BC	The Parthians invade Syria and help the Hasmoneans struggle in Jerusalem to retain political power.
40–35 BC	Aristobulus III serves as high priest until Herod the Great has him drowned at Herod's spa in Jericho (see Josephus, *Ant.* 15.50–56 and *J.W.* 1.437). This ends the threat of Hasmonean leadership among the Jews.
37 BC	Herod the Great captures Jerusalem and begins his reign as king.
32–31 BC**	Octavian defeats Mark Antony at Actium and unites the Roman Empire. Octavian becomes Caesar Augustus. Herod offers allegiance to Octavian and survives as king over the Jews.
30 BC–AD 10	Two leading rabbis, Shammai and Hillel, emerge and have considerable influence on the religious life of Jews from the late first century BC onward.
20–19 BC	Herod begins rebuilding the temple in Jerusalem.
10 BC–AD 40	Philo of Alexandria flourishes.
6–4 BC**	Jesus of Nazareth is born.
4 BC**	Herod the Great dies in April, and his kingdom is divided among his surviving sons: Archelaus, Herod Antipas, and Herod Philip.

4 BC–AD 39	Herod's sons (Archelaus, Antipas, and Philip) rule Palestine.
AD 6**	Augustus (Octavian) deposes Archelaus as ruler of Judea and establishes governors, or proconsuls, in Judea.
AD 12–14**	Coregency of Caesar Augustus and his son Tiberius.
AD 14**	Beginning of Tiberius's reign as sole Roman emperor.
AD 26–27**	Beginning of John the Baptist's ministry.
AD 26–36**	Pontius Pilate serves as procurator or governor of Judea.
AD 26/27–29	Jesus' ministry in Galilee and Judea.
AD 29–30 **	Jesus' death in Jerusalem.
AD 31–32	Stephen becomes the first Christian martyr (Acts 7:54–60).
AD 32–36	The conversion of the apostle Paul (see Gal. 1:13–2:1).
AD 33–44	Paul is in Tarsus for some ten years after his conversion, then he goes to the church in Antioch with Barnabas (Acts 11:25).
AD 40–65	Seneca of Rome flourishes.
AD 41–44**	Herod Agrippa I becomes king of Samaria and Judea. After he dies suddenly, Judea is ruled again by a Roman proconsul.
AD 44**	Peter is imprisoned in Jerusalem; James the apostle is beheaded.
AD 46–48	Paul begins his first missionary journey with Barnabas (Acts 13–14).
AD 48–49**	Jews are expelled from Rome (Acts 18:1–2).
AD 48–49	The Jerusalem Council (Acts 15:1–29).
AD 49–51**	Paul has an eighteen-month ministry in Corinth (Acts 18:11). His Letter to the Romans is produced here, on his second missionary journey (see Rom. 15:24–29).
AD 49–52	Paul's second missionary journey begins (Acts 15:36–41) and ends (Acts 18:20–22).
AD 49–62	Possible period of Paul's correspondence with his churches and coworkers in Christian mission.
AD 52–55	Paul's third missionary journey begins (Acts 18:23).
AD 53–55	Paul is in Ephesus (origin of his Letters to the Corinthians; see 1 Cor. 16:8).
AD 54–68	Nero is Roman emperor. His persecution of Christians begins ca. AD 62.
AD 55–57/58	Paul's arrest in Jerusalem and imprisonment at Caesarea and Rome.
AD 58–60	Paul goes to Rome as a prisoner for at least two years (Acts 28).
AD 60–69	Possible period of production of the Gospels of Mark and Luke.
AD 62	Peter goes to Rome.
AD 62**	James the brother of Jesus is martyred in Jerusalem.

AD 62–64**	Because of the outbreak of persecution against Christians in Rome, some persecuted Christians leave Jerusalem and settle in Pella, east of the Jordan.
AD 62–64**	Peter and Paul die in Rome under Nero's persecution (end of apostolic era).
AD 64**	Rome is burned, probably by Nero, and Christians are blamed. Persecution of Christians follows in Rome.
AD 65–95	Post- or [sub]apostolic era begins with the deaths of the primary apostles (James the brother of Jesus, Peter, and Paul).
AD 66–73**	The First Jewish War with Rome. Jewish rebellion against Rome ends with the destruction of Jerusalem and the temple in 70. Skirmishes continue until the last stronghold (Masada) is destroyed in 73. Temple worship is concluded, along with animal sacrifices.
AD 68–69	Turmoil in Rome and year of four Roman emperors.
AD 70–95	Sometimes called the "Tunnel Period," since not much is known of events during this time. Likely period during which the Gospels of Matthew, possibly Luke (see also AD 60–69 above), and John are written. Pharisaism and the rabbis emerge as the dominant expressions of Judaism. Likely time of the production of the *Didache*.
AD 70–90	Jews meet at Jamnia (Yavneh) to deal with the reformation of Judaism, especially Judaism without its temple cultus. A rabbinical academy is established there by Rabban Johanan ben Zakkai, son of Rabban Gamaliel (cf. Acts 5:34).
AD 75	Josephus writes *Jewish War*.
AD 81–96	Domitian rules the Roman Empire. Between 85 and 95, outbreaks of persecution against Christians emerge in Asia Minor.
AD 90–95	Rise of docetic heresy (see 1 John 4:1–3).
AD 93	Josephus writes *Antiquities of the Jews*.
AD 95–100	Clement of Rome writes *1 Clement*.
AD 100	Josephus dies in Rome.
AD 115–117	Epistles of Ignatius and his martyrdom.
AD 117–138	Hadrian reigns as Roman emperor.
AD 132–135	Second Jewish War: Bar Kochba rebellion is put down by Rome; Hadrian expels the Jews from Jerusalem and renames it Aelia Capitolina, after his mother.
AD 135	Gnosticism flourishes.
AD 140	*Shepherd of Hermas* likely written.
AD 140–160	Marcion and Valentinus begin their teaching. Marcion writes *Contradictions* and *Prologues*.
AD 156–185	Montanus begins ministry in Phrygia. Montanist controversy emerges.

AD 160	Justin Martyr writes *Apologies* and *Dialogue with Trypho*.
AD 175–180	Tatian produces the *Diatessaron*, a harmony of the Gospels.
AD 178	Celsus writes *True Reason*, the first known major reasoned attack against the Christian faith.
AD 180–185	Irenaeus writes *Against Heresies*, challenging the major heresies of his day.

Note: Dates with a double asterisk (**) behind them are generally recognized as most reliable, but few dates of events in antiquity are uncontested.

PART 1

SETTING THE CONTEXT

Exile and the Jewish Heritage

Foundational to Christian faith are its Jewish heritage and roots. It is no exaggeration that Jesus and his contemporaries cannot be adequately comprehended without familiarity with that tradition.

The early Jesus movement, beginning with Jesus and his disciples and continuing with the apostolic mission, arose within a context shaped by centuries of religious reflection and practice within Israel, God's people. In the period leading up to the birth of Jesus of Nazareth, Israel's history was marked by turmoil from without and from within. As a people in exile, the people of Israel were subjected to the changing winds of military and political conquests. And as a people in exile, they struggled to maintain their particular identity as God's people. Chapters in this section help set the stage for NT study by delineating the broad contours of the Jewish heritage assumed by the major personages of the NT era.

3

Exile

NICHOLAS PERRIN

A t its most basic level, the term "exile" refers to either one or both of two signal events in Israel's history: the deportation of the northern kingdom at the hands of the Assyrians in 722 BC (2 Kings 15–17) and, the more common reference, the subsequent removal of the southern kingdom by the Babylonians in 587 BC (2 Kings 24–25; 2 Chron. 36:17–20). Whereas the ten tribes of the northern kingdom never came back from the land of their captivity, the Scriptures speak of the return of—at least in some measure—the two tribes of the southern kingdom in 539 BC under the Persian king Cyrus. Critical scholarship continues to explore the degree of correspondence between the historical events of the exile and the scriptural reflection on the same. Although some have regarded the biblical treatment of exile more as a mythographical construct than as a reflection of historical realities, there is broad agreement that the concept of exile remained an integral element of postexilic Jewish theology. Whether and to what extent the concept of exile had a theologically generative function in early Christian thought remains debated.

On any reckoning, exile certainly had *some* kind of function within the earliest Christian writings. A reader cannot pass the first page of the NT without noticing that Matthew organizes his genealogy (Matt. 1:1–17), a programmatic element within the Gospel, around the historical milestones of exile. Mark's interest in exile surfaces not only through his initial invocation of the exodus (Mark 1:2–3) but also through his strategically deployed parable of the sower (4:1–20), a parable that is unpacked with reference to Isaiah's warning of impending exile (v. 12; cf.

Isa. 6:9–10; on exile in Luke see Fuller, *Restoration*; in John, see Brunson, *Psalm 118*, 62–83). In Paul, exilic undercurrents have been detected in such classic Pauline passages as Gal. 3–4 (Scott, "Works of the Law") and Rom. 8. The concept of exile has also come to fuller light in 1 Peter (Mbuvi, *Temple*), whose introduction, charged with exilic imagery, is very close to that of James (1 Pet. 1:1; cf. James 1:1). Skimming the surface of the NT, we would not be going too far to say that the motif of exile is quietly rampant.

As becomes apparent on review of the OT literature, the concept of exile was pliable, referring not only to the specific time period during which the southern kingdom endured geographical displacement (Jer. 29:10; Ezek. 4:6; 2 Chron. 36:20–23; Ezra 1:1–3) but also to a more general condition in which God's elect were made to suffer marginalization, oppression, or deprivation. Because exile was regarded as the culminating punishment for covenantal disobedience (Lev. 26:14–46; Deut. 28:15–68), and was therefore closely associated with a litany of curses (including marginalization, oppression, and deprivation), this conceptual expansion was perhaps inevitable. The fact that the literal and metaphorical application of the motif continued well into the Second Temple period (and beyond) in turn raises questions relevant to the study of the NT. Assuming that the NT authors' appropriation of exilic texts and terms depended, at least in part, on a theological framework already operative in Palestinian Judaism, it remains to be asked whether this implied a simple analogy of experiences or something more. If something more, how exactly does the use of the exile metaphor contribute to our understanding of the NT? By exploring the metaphor of exile as it was employed in Second Temple Judaism, one might identify recurring thought patterns that could then shed light on how the authors of the NT understood themselves and their audiences within the scope of redemptive history.

Precisely because the meaning of exile in Second Temple Judaism has proved so controversial in recent decades, and because even a brief account of the motif as NT background can hardly be undertaken apart from some initial awareness of the issues at stake in contemporary scholarly discussion, it seems best to look first at the various interpretive lenses that contemporary scholars bring to bear on this topic. Thus I begin not with a review of relevant historical data as contained in the primary sources but with a brief survey of the relevant secondary literature. This is followed by an analysis of representative Second Temple texts, namely, the Apocrypha, Pseudepigrapha, and Qumran texts, and finally some summarizing remarks.

Contemporary Research into Exile as a Background to the New Testament

In the field of OT studies, given such programmatic studies as that of Julius Wellhausen's *Prolegomena to the History of Ancient Israel* (1957) and Peter R. Ackroyd's *Exile and Restoration: A Study of Hebrew Thought of the Sixth Century*

BC (1968), there was little chance that twentieth-century scholars of the Hebrew Scriptures would allow the concept of exile to fall by the wayside. For whatever reason, academic interest in exile was almost entirely restricted to the HB. This relative neglect of exile outside the OT canon, however, began to change slowly with such seminal publications as Odil H. Steck's *Israel und das gewaltsame Geschick des Propheten* [Israel and the Violent Fate of the Prophets] (1967),[1] Ralph Klein's *Israel in Exile: A Theological Interpretation* (1976), and in the same year, Michael A. Knibb's article "The Exile in the Literature of the Intertestamental Period." By the last quarter of the twentieth century, the stage had been set for more thorough explorations of exile as a theological category beyond the OT.

As it turned out, the main impetus for the most recent discussions of exile was a short treatment of the subject offered by N. T. Wright (*People of God*, 268–72) in his account of Christian origins, only later to be developed further in volume 2 of the same series (*Victory of God*, xvii–xviii, 246–51, 576–77). Wright's shaping influence, notwithstanding the brevity of his initial case, is perhaps as much a tribute to his originality as a thinker as it is to his ingenuity in integrating the data within a compelling, heuristically rich account. According to Wright, "Most Jews of this period, it seems, would have answered the question 'where are we?' in language which, reduced to its simplest form, meant: we are still in exile. They believed that, in all the senses which mattered, Israel's exile was still in progress" (*People of God*, 268–69).

For Wright, first-century Jews would have found clear evidence of their exiled status in two incontrovertible facts: Israel remained subjugated to the gentiles (e.g., Neh. 9:36–37; CD 1.3–11), and Yahweh had not visibly returned to Zion (Ezek. 43:1–7; Isa. 52:8–11). True, Israel had been sent into exile on account of its sin, but there is more to the redemptive equation than may meet the eye:

> If her sin has caused her exile, her forgiveness will mean her national re-establishment. This needs to be emphasized in the strongest possible terms: the most natural meaning of the phrase "the forgiveness of sins" to a first-century Jew is not in the first instance the remission of *individual* sins, but the putting away of the whole nation's sins. And, since the exile was the punishment for those sins, the only sure sign that the sins had been forgiven would be the clear and certain liberation from exile. (*People of God*, 273, italics original)

As Wright gladly acknowledges, this proposal is not entirely new: other scholars (notably Knibb, "Exile"; Scott, "Works of the Law") have made a similar case beforehand and in greater detail. What seems to be new, however, is the crucial role that Wright has assigned to exile in his account of first-century Judaism and early Christianity.

1. Odil H. Steck, *Israel und das gewaltsame Geschick des Propheten: Untersuchungen zur Überlieferung des deuteronomistischen Geschichtsbildes im Alten Testament, Spätjudentum und Urchristentum* (WMANT 23; Neukirchen-Vluyn: Neukirchener Verlag, 1967).

Although Wright's understanding of exile has resonated with a good number of scholars (notably Evans, "Aspects of Exile"; idem, "Continuing Exile"; and the majority of contributors to Scott, *Exile*; idem, *Restoration*), not everyone has been equally impressed. Criticism of the Knibb-Scott-Wright line—issued mostly through responses (e.g., Casey, "Wright"; Downing, "Exile"; Bryan, *Jesus*) to Wright's second volume of *Christian Origins and the Question of God*, focusing on the historical Jesus—has recurred on a handful of points. First, critics have questioned whether it is legitimate to ascribe a kind of metanarrative status to the exile-restoration schema on the basis of so few—and in some cases highly sectarian—sources. This criticism becomes more acute when we recognize that certain other ancient texts, rather than harboring a critical view of the Second Temple (ca. 516 BC–AD 70), actually assume that the then-current cultus was both highly functional and indeed the stage for Yahweh's long-awaited reestablishment of the theocratic order. Second, Wright's "ongoing exile" model is charged with imposing an overly tidy view of history onto the highly complex set of historical realities, replete with countless epicycles of victories and setbacks. It is difficult, in the words of Bryan, to imagine "a straight-line trajectory from exile to restoration" (*Jesus*, 14). As critics of the "ongoing exile" thesis seem to ask, would it not be closer to the mark to imagine the first-century Jewish outlook revolving around not the singular twofold event of Exile and Restoration (uppercase, as it were) but the experience of exile occurring alongside countless previous exiles and restorations (lowercase), all anticipating the eventual eschatological consummation?

Within the context of this debate, the crucial question is one of definition: What did the first-century Jew mean by "exile"? The logic of the Knibb-Scott-Wright line may be summarized as follows: For the first-century Jew (1) return from exile was a necessary and sufficient condition of the promised restoration, and (2) they had not yet experienced restoration; (3) therefore, the typical first-century Jew would reason, return from exile had not (truly) taken place. On this approach, exile was principally not a geographical reality but, through synecdoche (whereby one or more presenting symptoms of exile represents the whole idea) a theological and political reality. The Casey-Downing-Bryan model, maintaining that return from exile had already occurred some centuries beforehand, operates by a different set of historical judgments: Whereas return from exile was a necessary condition for full restoration, the former did not logically entail the latter. On this view, exile did indeed principally refer to Israel's removal from the land. The debate may also be reframed from a different angle. Was the return from exile conceived of as one stepping-stone among many to restoration (Casey-Downing-Bryan)? Or was it conceived of as the bridge, logically and temporally inseparable from other markers of divine restoration (Knibb-Scott-Wright)?

Three published dissertations centrally concerned with exile—all published within the past decade—have joined the conversation even as they have provided fresh points of departure. Simultaneously commending and criticizing Wright for having "the *right insight* but the *wrong exile*" (Pitre, *Jesus*, 35), Brant Pitre maintains that first-century Jews were indeed looking for a geographical return but one that involved not just the return of the two southern tribes but the ten tribes of the northern kingdom as well (*Jesus*, 35–38). Interestingly, this view introduces a mediating position in the debate, aligning not only with the Knibb-Scott-Wright line in its insistence that return from exile had not yet occurred but also with the Casey-Downing-Bryan approach, which adheres to the geographical tenor of exile. Like Pitre, Michael Fuller also has sympathies with Wright's proposal but maintains that Wright does not do justice to the motif's complexity and contingency (*Restoration*, 10–11). According to Fuller, the authors of Tobit, Sirach, and 2 Maccabees did not think of return from exile as properly having taken place; return could only finally occur when the population of the Diaspora had also moved back to their land (*Restoration*, 25–48). Other understandings of exile are also teased out (including Qumran, *4 Ezra*, and Philo); each of these has its own separate way of integrating the notion of exile with other theological commitments. Similarly, Martien Halvorson-Taylor's study of the exile concept in certain OT texts seeks to emphasize the flexibility of the term. She helpfully writes:

> By accommodating a variety of different metaphors that described it, exile laid the groundwork for its own metaphorization. When exile was rendered by other systems of association, it took on increasing conceptual depth. Now participating in, as Ricoeur would call it, "a whole array of intersignifications," exile was absorbed into a nexus of associations that included death, sterility, bodily and emotional pain, and servitude. (*Enduring Exile*, 202–3)

Halvorson-Taylor concludes that such metaphorization afforded a "compelling motif within early Judaism" (*Enduring Exile*, 203), contributing in particular to apocalyptic and messianic speculation. Such "increased conceptual depth" may well explain the seemingly contradictory portrait of exile that has come down to us in the most relevant Jewish sources. To those sources we now turn.

Exile in Later Postexilic Judaism

Whereas a full-length survey of exile (as a background to the NT) would normally require treatment of texts from the whole range of Israel's history (preexilic, exilic, and postexilic writings), space here requires limiting the range of inquiry to texts closest to the time of the first century. For discussion of OT materials, the reader is directed to the respective commentaries (see also Ackroyd, *Exile and Restoration*; Fuller, *Restoration*; Halvorson-Taylor, *Enduring Exile*). For the purposes of this essay, I have restricted myself to a representative sampling of some of the more significant texts.

Apocrypha

Tobit (second or third century BC) is a novelistic tale set in the Diaspora, likely written for a Diaspora readership. More than a source of entertainment, the book concerns itself with issues of divine justice and morality. In short, Tobit asks, What does it mean to live as a faithful Jew? Designed to provide its own answer to this question, the narrative closes with a final benedictory prayer on the lips of the main character, part of which reads as follows:

> Acknowledge him before the nations, O children of Israel; for he has scattered you among them. He has shown you his greatness even there. . . . He will afflict you for your iniquities, but he will again show mercy on all of you. He will gather you from all the nations among whom you have been scattered. . . . In the land of my exile I acknowledge him, and show his power and majesty to a nation of sinners: "Turn back, you sinners, and do what is right before him; perhaps he may look with favor upon you and show you mercy." (Tob. 13:3–6)

Impressed by the elaborate nature of the prayer, related apocalyptic material in 13:16–17, and Tobit's later forecasting that the exiles "will return from their exile and will rebuild Jerusalem in splendor" *after* the initial return from exile (14:5), some scholars (Knibb, "Exile," 264–68; Wright, *People of God*, 270; Evans, "Continuing Exile," 82–83) see the book as providing solid evidence that the author regarded postexilic Israel as existing in a state of continued exile. On the other hand, it has been countered that this inference involves an overreading of the text; the prayer was not necessarily relevant to the situation of the audience, for Tobit is, after all, a textually problematic *novel* set in the seventh century BC, one that looks forward to restoration in a more generalized sense (e.g., Jones, "Disputed Questions," 402). Similar arguments, both for and against the notion of continuing exile, have also been made in regards to Bar. 3:6–8, a text of roughly the same time period.

Another instance of exile language surfaces in the text of 2 Maccabees (late second or early first century BC). Here Jonathan offers a prayer similar to that which Nehemiah offered (cf. Neh. 9:36–37): "Gather together our scattered people, set free those who are slaves among the Gentiles, look on those who are rejected and despised, and let the Gentiles know that you are our God. Punish those who oppress and are insolent with pride. Plant your people in your holy place, as Moses promised" (2 Macc. 1:27–29).

Although the incorporation of exilic theology in Jonathan's prayer is certainly of interest, not least because he casts his ongoing struggle with the opposing Seleucids in exilic terms, this point must be brought alongside indications within the same book that the regnant priesthood is stamped with divine approval (2 Macc. 2:17; see Jones, "Disputed Questions," 402–3). The juxtaposition of the two sentiments raises the possibility that Jonathan's talk of exile reflects a fairly complex understanding. Moreover, one may ask, if 2 Maccabees does presume a condition of exile continuing well into the second century BC, how does this square with the quasi-messianic accolades accorded to Simon in 1 Macc. 14, the prequel of 2 Maccabees?

Pseudepigrapha

Two of the earliest examples of the genre of ancient Jewish apocalypse are the Apocalypse of Weeks (*1 En.* 93.1–10; 91.11–17; ca. 180 BC) and the Animal Apocalypse (*1 En.* 85–90; ca. 164 BC). As Knibb ("Exile") has underscored in his now-classic study (see also VanderKam, "Exile," 96–100), the authors of both texts seem to have attached strikingly little theological significance to the historical return from exile. The Apocalypse of Weeks is a short text that divides the course of history into ten "weeks," at the conclusion of which a new and eternal heaven of righteousness displaces the old order. According to the Apocalypse of Weeks, those who live in the sixth week remain blinded, having forsaken all wisdom, a situation that results in the destruction of the "house of dominion" and the dispersal of the "whole race of the chosen root" (*1 En.* 93.8)—an obvious allusion to the Assyrian and Babylonian exiles. This is immediately followed by the seventh week, which, although retaining the eventual prospect of an established righteous remnant, is characterized for most of its duration by grim apostasy (*1 En.* 98.9–10). Since scholars broadly agree that the author of the Apocalypse of Weeks locates himself and his milieu within the sixth week, it follows that his assessment of Israel's history, from 587 BC down to his own time, is essentially negative. Geographical return from exile remains unmentioned, seemingly because it neither reflects nor engenders a substantive change in Israel's disposition or covenantal standing.

The Animal Apocalypse, an allegory assigning animal characters to various historical groups, is even darker in its reading of postexilic history. Following a reference to the sixth-century BC destruction of the temple (*1 En.* 89.66–67), there is a description of the sheep being handed over to the wild beasts (the gentiles) for destruction, all under the oversight of shepherds (angels?). The shepherds are guilty of allowing more sheep to be devoured than is divinely prescribed (89.69–70), but the Lord of the sheep (Yahweh) only notes this injustice for future reference (89.70–71). Then three of the sheep return to build the house anew; despite resistance from the wild boars, they succeed in building a tower (the temple) along with a table, but, significantly, the bread on the table (the temple showbread) is unclean and impure (89.72–73). From the time of the building of the Second Temple, the allegory indicates, matters only become worse: the sheep remain blind, the shepherds continue to exceed their punitive remit, and the Lord of the Sheep remains unmoved throughout (89.74–77). As the narrative unfolds the course of postexilic history, the gentiles continue to feast on the sheep in even greater gory detail (90.1–6), while the sheep come to be characterized not simply as blind but also as "exceedingly deafened and . . . dim-sighted" (90.7; *OTP* 1:69). For the author of the Animal Apocalypse, the return from exile was, at its worse, an integral element of Israel's downward spiral and, at its best, of no consequence whatsoever. Although it is impossible to know whether the same author would have considered Israel to be in a technical state of exile as of the second century BC (if such a way of putting the question was even possible), clearly the author understood the covenantal curses associated with exile to be in even greater force in his own day than when the temple was destroyed.

Retelling biblical events as they occurred from creation to Sinai, the second-century BC text of *Jubilees* belongs to the genre of the "rewritten Scripture." The text begins with—and is therefore framed by—an encounter between Yahweh and Moses, in which Yahweh anticipates the apostasy and exile of Israel (*Jub.* 1.13–18). Although drawing largely on Deut. 28, the writer departs from familiar scriptural language by inserting mention of calendrical error as one of the besetting sins facing future Israel (*Jub.* 1.14); apparently the practice of misdating holy days had crept in, together with forgetfulness of God's law, during the time of exile. On the assumption that this point was intentionally added toward refuting (mis)construals of the calendar current in the day, it seems the author of *Jubilees* thought of Israel as still experiencing at least certain residual (as well as deleterious) effects of the exile. To what extent this constituted a continuation of exile depends in part on how one interprets Yahweh's stated intent to "gather them [i.e., the exiles] from the midst of all the nations" (1.15, OTP 2:53). From the vantage point of the author, this return from exile may refer to a future moment, marking the onset of the eschatological age (VanderKam, "Exile"), in which case, again so far as the author of *Jubilees* is concerned, God's people are certainly still in exile. Alternatively, this gathering may instead refer to the historical return from Babylon, which would mean that the author sees Israel as having taken only the first step in what amounts to a three-step process: (1) return from Babylonian exile, (2) earnest seeking after God, and (3) the onset of the eschaton (Halpern-Amaru, "Exile," 140–41). In either case, if return from exile has occurred for the author of *Jubilees* (a point that remains unclear), the true design of that return has yet to be realized.

A rather different perspective on exile seems to surface in the *Testament of Moses* (early first century AD). Explaining to Joshua important events as they will transpire, Moses looks ahead to the exile and lingers on the pious response of the captives (*T. Mos.* 3). Duly recognizing their plight and their sin, the tribes together call out to Yahweh, invoke the Abrahamic covenant (with added emphasis on the land), and wait for their God to respond. The author of the *Testament* through the mouthpiece of Moses then goes on to say that "they will be slaves for about seventy-seven years" (3.14, OTP 1:929). Since exile was tantamount to slavery (Ezra 9:9; Neh. 9:36; Jer. 25:11; 2 Macc. 1:27), this means that Moses anticipates a fixed seventy-seven-year exile (an unusual duration, but cf. Matt. 18:22; Gen. 4:24). For the same author, the Babylonian exile seems to have fulfilled redemptive purposes: those who are not able to return to offer sacrifices at the reestablished cultus grieve out of a holy longing; meanwhile, the northern kingdom is described as flourishing among the nations despite its dislocation (*T. Mos.* 4.6–9). Even if the exile is followed by intensified suffering in subsequent chapters, the historical exile not only is finite but also appears to have successfully achieved its divine purpose.

Like the *Testament of Moses*, the post-temple text of *2 Baruch* (ca. AD 100) is also relatively sanguine in its understanding of the redemptive value of the deportation (cf. *4 Ezra*). Judah's rebellion is heinous, and so the Lord foretells, "Behold, therefore, I shall bring evil upon this city and its inhabitants. And it will be taken away from before my presence for a time. And I shall scatter this people among the nations that they may do good to the nations. And my people will be chastened, and the time will come that they will look for that which can make their times prosperous" (*2 Bar.* 1.4–5; *OTP* 1:621).

In contrast to some of the above-cited texts, *2 Baruch* finds redemptive value in Israel's exile. But judging by the Apocalypse of the Clouds (53.1–74.4) within the text, an allegory that summarizes Israel's history as symbolically alternating between dark and brightly lit waters, it is to be inferred that the author saw exile as cyclical reality. For better or worse, his audience is indeed in exile but stands to be restored once again per their obedience (85.3–5).

Qumran

The literary witness of the Qumran community consistently attests to a community that saw itself in exile in some sense. This much becomes clear on examination of only one of its charter texts, the *Damascus Document* (CD). Here one finds the repetition of the phrase *šby yśr'l* as a sobriquet or nickname for the covenanteers (CD 2.4–5; 3.19–4.3; 6.2–7); the Hebrew phrase has been variously translated as "repentant of Israel," the "returnees of Israel," or, better yet, the "captives of Israel." Most likely they are "captives" in the sense of being exiles who "went out of the land of Judah" (CD 4.2–3; 6.5). The text of CD begins as follows:

> For when Israel abandoned Him by being faithless, He turned away from them and from His sanctuary and gave them up to the sword. But when He called to mind the covenant He made with their forefathers, He left a remnant for Israel and did not allow them to be exterminated. In the era of wrath—three hundred and ninety years from the time He handed them over to the power of Nebuchadnezzar king of Babylon—He took care of them and caused to grow from Israel and from Aaron a root of planting to inherit His land and to grow fat on the good produce of His soil. They considered their iniquity and they knew that they were guilty men, and had been like the blind and like those groping for the way twenty years. But God considered their deeds, that they had sought Him with a whole heart. So he raised up for them a teacher of righteousness to guide them in the way of His heart. (CD 1.3–11)[2]

2. In this chapter, all translations of the Qumran material are from Michael Wise, Martin Abegg Jr., and Edward Cook, *The Dead Sea Scrolls: A New Translation* (San Francisco: HarperSanFrancisco, 2006).

The faithful sectarians identify themselves as standing in the trajectory of the faithful remnant, the embodiment of the Isaianic "blind, . . . groping for the way" (cf. Isa. 42:16), who, according to the biblical prophet, will experience deliverance from exile (Isa. 42:1–43:9). Meanwhile, the Qumran covenanteers affirm that God has taken notice of their piety and has responded accordingly by granting them a Teacher of Righteousness "to guide them in *the way*," which exegetically is one and the same as "the way" (back from exile) heralded in Isa. 40:1–3 (cf. Isa. 40:14; 43:16, 19; Acts 9:2; 19:23). Isaiah 40, focusing on a vision of return from exile, was undoubtedly a defining text for the Qumran sectarians (1QS 8.12–14; 9.18–20; cf. 4Q258 frg. 3 3.4; 4Q259 frg. 1 3.19), as it would later be for John the Baptizer and the early Christians (Matt. 3:1–3; Mark 1:2–4; Luke 3:3–6; John 1:23; Rom. 11:33–34).

The numerical calculations in CD 1.3–11 should not go unobserved. The 390-year "era of wrath" derives from Ezek. 4:5, a text in which Yahweh informs the prophet that such will be the length of Israel's captivity. The failure on the part of the Qumran author to mention any return from exile in the period between the sack of Jerusalem and the termination of the nearly four-century period suggests that his community saw the return under Cyrus as incidental to a much more dominant trend of disobedience and wrath. It is improbable that this 390-year term, together with the extra twenty years of groping about, held merely symbolic or ideal value. Counting 410 years from the destruction of the temple, we arrive at 176 BC, not an unlikely time for the formation of the Qumran sect. This same window of time is *roughly* corroborated by a separate calculation in 4Q390 1.7–8, where the end of exile is promised at the "seventh jubilee" (343 or 350 years) after "the destruction of the land." If the founder of the Qumran community derived theological significance from his being forced into geographical exile by his enemies (1QHᵃ 12.8–9; 4Q177 frgs. 5–6 1.7–10), this point must have only paled in comparison with the implications of their numerological exegesis: Yahweh was about to exhaust the term of the exile in the very generation of Qumran's founding.

Other important Qumran texts likewise cast the sect's self-identity against the backdrop of exile and restoration. According to the *War Scroll*, for example, the eschatological battle between "the exiles of the Sons of Light" (1QM 1.3) and the Sons of Darkness was to be waged on the warrior-priests' return from the "Wilderness of the Peoples"—a certain reference to Ezek. 20:35, foretelling a moment in which divine judgment is executed and Yahweh gathers his people from the nations to which they have been scattered (20:34). The Qumran sect saw itself as taking on the identity of true Israel in exile, enduring eschatological wrath for the sake of procuring national atonement (4Q504 2.7–17). All those who resisted their teachings would fall prey to a renewed captivity or, perhaps more precisely, the same captivity that befell Israel in 587 BC (4QMMT C18–22; it is difficult to stipulate this point). In any case, the Qumran corpus gives us some of the clearest evidence of a Second Temple Jewish community that saw exile as continuing and indeed climaxing in its own day.

Conclusion

The most recent scholarship on exile has issued a salutary reminder of the necessity of a nuanced understanding of exile in antiquity. Given the diverse ways in which various Second Temple Jewish texts employ the motif, it now becomes difficult to make unqualified generalizations regarding ancient Judaism's understanding of exile. Certain Jewish communities of the period seem to have cast their own difficult situations in exilic terms for both rhetorical reasons and theological reasons, the latter usually as an outworking of the conviction that their suffering could be usefully mapped onto a broader redemptive-historical timeline. Although some texts envisage exile as an event of finite duration in the past, others seem to assume an ongoing exile. Likewise, alongside indications of exile and return as being nonrepeatable events within a unilinear timeline, one also finds ascriptions that are more cyclical in nature. In short, for pious Jews exile was a lens through which to interpret their own experience within the ambit or scope of Yahweh's mysterious providence. The meaning of that experience and providence varied according to each community's theological commitments, religio-political situation, understanding of Israel's national history, and so on. Notions of exile were as variegated as Judaism itself.

This neither proves nor disproves the assumption that exile and return were fundamental categories for the NT writers. However, precisely because exile was put to such widespread and wide-ranging use in Second Temple Jewish texts, we have some reason to expect something similar in the texts of the NT. Each NT book should be understood on its own terms and with its own unique theology of exile. At the same time, since the authors of the NT held certain core convictions in common, there is reasonable warrant for teasing out family resemblances between these exilic theologies. One such family resemblance, difficult to dispute, is the sense in some NT texts that return from exile has already occurred in Christ even as, paradoxically, a condition of exile still endures. Much like the kingdom of God (at least as it is now commonly though not universally understood), exile retains an already-but-not-yet aspect. This makes sense inasmuch as return from exile is a highly allusive and rich way of describing the coming of the kingdom; it provides not only an eschatological framework but also conceptual handles for coming to terms with the "present evil age" (Gal. 1:4), the existence from which believers have been redeemed.

Bibliography

Ackroyd, Peter R. *Exile and Restoration: A Study of Hebrew Thought of the Sixth Century BC*. Philadelphia: Westminster, 1968. Perhaps the modern classic exposition of exile as a central category within the OT.

Brunson, Andrew C. *Psalm 118 in the Gospel of John: An Intertextual Study on the New Exodus Pattern in the Theology of John*. WUNT 2/158. Tübingen: Mohr Siebeck, 2003.

Seeks to demonstrate the importance of Ps. 118 for Johannine theology; includes a brief but nonetheless valuable discussion of exile and its relevance to the Fourth Gospel (pp. 62–83).

Bryan, Steven M. *Jesus and Israel's Traditions of Judgement and Restoration*. SNTSMS 117. Cambridge: Cambridge University Press, 2002. Arguing for the historical Jesus' identity as a restorationist prophet, the author offers a concise yet well-conceived critique of Wright's view of exile (pp. 12–20).

Casey, Maurice. "Where Wright Is Wrong: A Critical Review of N. T. Wright's *Jesus and the Victory of God*." *JSNT* 69 (1998): 95–103. One of the earliest critiques of Wright on exile.

Downing, F. G. "Exile in Formative Judaism." Pages 148–68 in *Making Sense in (and of) the First Christian Century*. JSNTSup 197. Sheffield: Sheffield Academic Press, 2000. Though sometimes idiosyncratic, Downing offers counterarguments to Wright's thesis for "ongoing exile."

Evans, Craig A. "Aspects of Exile and Restoration in the Proclamation of Jesus and the Gospels." Pages 263–94 in *Jesus in Context: Temple, Purity and Restoration*. Edited by Bruce Chilton and Craig A. Evans. AGJU 39. Leiden: Brill, 1997. With his characteristic attention to historical detail, Evans makes a thorough case for ongoing exile as an important backdrop for the ministry of the historical Jesus.

———. "Jesus and the Continuing Exile of Israel." Pages 77–100 in *Jesus and the Restoration of Israel: A Critical Assessment of N. T. Wright's Jesus and the Victory of God*. Edited by Carey C. Newman. Downers Grove, IL: InterVarsity, 1999. Somewhat similar to Evans, "Aspects of Exile," but less technical; includes some fresh materials and enters the fray of the Casey-Wright debate as it was beginning to pick up steam.

Fuller, Michael F. *The Restoration of Israel: Israel's Re-gathering and the Fate of the Nations in Early Jewish Literature and Luke-Acts*. BZNW 138. Berlin: de Gruyter, 2006. Though sometimes overstated, this study is as wide ranging and impressive in scope as its title intimates. In addition to undertaking a careful study of Luke-Acts and exile, the author emphasizes the variegated nature of convictions of exile within the Jewish setting.

Halpern-Amaru, Betsy. "Exile and Return in Jubilees." Pages 127–44 in *Exile: Old Testament, Jewish, and Christian Conceptions*. Edited by James M. Scott. JSJSup 56. Leiden: Brill, 1997. Argues that the postexilic author of *Jubilees* transposes the definition of exile in such a way so as to minimize the importance of land and maximize the importance of true piety.

Halvorson-Taylor, Martien A. *Enduring Exile: The Metaphorization of Exile in the Hebrew Bible*. VTSup 141. Leiden: Brill, 2011. Well written and well argued; claims that the seeds for the metaphorization of exile were already present in the most important OT texts.

Jones, Ivor H. "Disputed Questions in Biblical Studies: 4, Exile and Eschatology." *ExpTim* 112 (2001): 401–5. Seeks to challenge Wright's "ongoing exile" thesis; includes some good points but is not a model of clarity.

Klein, Ralph W. *Israel in Exile: A Theological Interpretation*. Minneapolis: Fortress, 1976. Among the vanguard of contemporary treatments of the exile.

Knibb, Michael A. "The Exile in the Literature of the Intertestamental Period." *HeyJ* 17 (1976): 253–72. Knibb has been highly influential for Wright's perspective; it remains one of the most frequently cited treatments of exile in the Second Temple literature.

Mbuvi, Andrew M. *Temple, Exile and Identity in 1 Peter*. LNTS 345. London: T&T Clark, 2007. Seeks to demonstrate the temple was the driving theme of 1 Peter; exile is also—more convincingly—highlighted.

Pitre, Brant. *Jesus, the Tribulation, and the End of the Exile: Restoration Eschatology and the Origin of the Atonement*. WUNT 2/204. Tübingen: Mohr Siebeck, 2005. Repr., Grand Rapids: Baker Academic. An important work on the historical Jesus; sees return from exile as central to Jesus' aims.

Scott, James M., ed. *Exile: Old Testament, Jewish, and Christian Conceptions*. JSJSup 56. Leiden: Brill, 1997. Essential reading for anyone seeking to delve further into the topic.

———. "'For as Many as Are of Works of the Law Are under a Curse' (Galatians 3.10)." Pages 187–220 in *Paul and the Scriptures of Israel*. Edited by James A. Sanders and Craig A. Evans. JSNTSup 83. SEJC 1. Sheffield: JSOT Press, 1992. A good example of how the concept of exile has been persuasively brought to bear on exegesis of Paul.

———, ed. *Restoration: Old Testament, Jewish, and Christian Perspectives*. JSJSup 72. Leiden: Brill, 2001. Less relevant to the question of exile; overall, the quality of the essays is not as strong as that found in the companion 1997 volume, *Exile*.

VanderKam, James C. "Exile in Jewish Apocalyptic Literature." Pages 89–109 in *Exile: Old Testament, Jewish, and Christian Conceptions*. Edited by James M. Scott. JSJSup 56. Leiden: Brill, 1997. An expert in apocalyptic literature provides a highly capable and balanced overview of the primary literature.

Wright, N. T. *Jesus and the Victory of God*. Vol. 2 of *Christian Origins and the Question of God*. London: SPCK; Minneapolis: Fortress, 1996. The sequel to vol. 1 develops the idea of exile much more thoroughly with reference to the historical Jesus.

———. *The New Testament and the People of God*. Vol. 1 of *Christian Origins and the Question of God*. London: SPCK; Minneapolis: Fortress, 1992. The plank to his life's project and a future classic, Wright's first volume has proved highly influential in igniting debates over the role of exile in Second Temple Judaism; pages 268–72 provide a launchpad for his exploration of exile.

4

The Hasmoneans
and the Hasmonean Era

LARRY R. HELYER

From 167 BC until 36 BC, the remarkable family known as the Hasmoneans led an armed struggle for religious and political independence and then exercised national leadership. In the process, they transformed Jewish life and culture, etching an indelible impression that persists to this day. As major players in the larger arena of Middle Eastern politics, they had influence that extended far beyond the traditional boundaries of ancient Israel.

Sources

Two problems hinder the study of this era. First, the primary sources are skewed because the anonymous authors of 1–2 Maccabees and Flavius Josephus (*Jewish Antiquities* and *Jewish War*) narrate the story from the perspective of the leading figures. Lacking are accounts describing daily life among the common people, who appear only as background props. This article mentions some of the available archaeological evidence that illuminates more mundane aspects of Jewish life during the Hasmonean era.

Second, the authors were not unbiased. The author of 1 Maccabees was an ardent supporter of the Hasmoneans, whereas the author of 2 Maccabees admired only Judas Maccabeus, not his successors. Furthermore, both books mention Jews who were unenthusiastic or even hostile to the nationalistic agenda of the Hasmoneans, and many Jews joined their cause only when religious rights were at stake. The Hasmoneans were as much at war against Hellenizing Jews, who advocated assimilation and supported the Seleucid agenda to turn Judea into a Greek temple state, as against the Seleucids.

Although Josephus does not conceal the flaws of the later Hasmonean priest-kings, his account generally reflects pride in their achievements. A close reading of his works, however, also reveals dissenting voices that scarcely get a hearing. Consequently, one must read all four primary sources with discernment. Despite these caveats, they remain indispensable and tell us much about the era (Hayes and Mandell, *Jewish People*, 60–62; Tomasino, *Judaism before Jesus*, 137–40).

History of the Hasmoneans

Josephus traces Mattathias's genealogy back three generations to a priestly family belonging to the course of Joarib and descending from a man named Asamon or Hashmon, a resident of Jerusalem (*Ant.* 12.265; cf. 1 Chron. 24:7)—although it is possible that the name is toponymic (a place name), not patronymic (a family name). Mattathias had five sons: John, Simon, Judas, Eleazar, and Jonathan. The third son, Judas, was given the nickname "Maccabeus," meaning something like "the hammer" or "mallet head," a fitting epithet for a man who delivered violent blows against Hellenizing Jews and the Seleucid dynasty. This essay focuses on the Hasmonean family, often called the Maccabees, and their descendents to the sixth generation.

Revolt and Rise to Power

According to 1 Maccabees, when the family burst on the national scene, the aged priest Mattathias was living in Modein (also spelled Modiin/Modin; modern Ras Medieh), a Jewish settlement located about seventeen miles northwest of Jerusalem (1 Macc. 2:1). The occasion was a religious persecution unleashed by the Seleucid king Antiochus IV Epiphanes (ruled from 175 BC to 164 BC). After being forced to withdraw from Egypt under threat of war with Rome (Polybius, *Hist.* 29.27; cf. Dan. 11:18, 19) and receiving reports of armed revolt in Jerusalem (2 Macc. 5:11), Antiochus wreaked havoc on the city and launched an unprecedented anti-Judaism campaign. Besides his pique at the constant upheaval in Jerusalem over the high-priestly succession and joy over rumors that he was dead (2 Macc. 5:5–6), Antiochus was worried about Roman expansionism. Since many Jews were still fiercely devoted to their ancestral faith, which forbade the worship of other gods and observed strict ritual purity laws, restricting interaction with gentiles, this presented a problem. At the critical land bridge of his empire lay a Jewish enclave not fully espousing the Seleucid dynasty's ideological and religious ethos. Antiochus decreed that the Jews of Judea cease practicing their religion and become fully cooperating, Hellenistic citizens of the Seleucid Empire.

To this end, Antiochus unleashed draconian measures to ensure this "conversion." The author of 1 Maccabees provides a capsule summary of this "first known religious persecution in history" (Aharoni et al., *Atlas*, 142):

> Then the king wrote to his whole kingdom that all should be one people, and that all should give up their particular customs. All the Gentiles accepted the command of the king. Many even from Israel gladly adopted his religion; they sacrificed to idols and profaned the sabbath. . . . [They were] to leave their sons uncircumcised. They were to make themselves abominable by everything unclean and profane, so that they would forget the law and change all the ordinances. He added, "And whoever does not obey the command of the king shall die." (1 Macc. 1:41–43, 48–50)

In this hour of crisis, Mattathias, like Phinehas of old (Num. 25:6–13), stood up to defend the Torah of Moses. The specific occasion was an official delegation from the king that arrived at the village of Modein to enforce the new edict (167 BC). Citizens were called on to demonstrate their new loyalty by offering a pagan sacrifice. Mattathias and his sons, being foremost citizens, were invited to lead the way, but Mattathias steadfastly refused, and when another Jew came forward to do so, Mattathias killed both him and the king's delegate and tore down the altar (1 Macc. 2:15–26). He then issued a summons: "Let every one who is zealous for the law and supports the covenant come out with me!" (1 Macc. 2:27). This act of rebellion was the opening round of a prolonged struggle, first for religious freedom, then national liberation; twenty-five years later (142 BC), this struggle eventuated in an independent state, headed by Mattathias's second son, Simon.

Judas Maccabeus (167–161 BC)

The Hasmonean brothers fled to caves in a wilderness area called the Gophna Hills, which became a haven for similar-minded Jews. These refugees, especially a group called the Hasideans ("the pious ones"), swelled the ranks and gradually evolved from a guerrilla force into a formidable militia (1 Macc. 2:42–43). Initially, they punished apostate Jews, striking fear into the hearts of would-be defectors. Sons were forcibly circumcised, pagan altars torn down, and Torah scrolls rescued (1 Macc. 2:44–48; 2 Macc. 8:5–7).

The resistance movement inevitably led to armed conflict with the Seleucid regime. After Mattathias's death, Judas assumed command of the insurgents. Against superior numbers and weaponry, Judas, relying on stealth, courage, and intimate knowledge of the terrain, scored four stunning victories over the Seleucid forces (1 Macc. 3–4; Aharoni et al., *Atlas*, 142–43; Rainey and Notley, *Sacred*

Bridge, 308–11). This momentarily allowed Judas to reoccupy Jerusalem and take control of the temple mount—with the exception of the Akra, a Seleucid fortress overlooking the temple area. In the midst of great rejoicing, Judas cleansed and rededicated the temple and reinstituted proper worship. On the twenty-fifth day of Chislev (November–December) in 164 BC, a great celebration—henceforth called Hanukkah, meaning "dedication" (cf. John 10:22)—was instituted: "At the very season and on the very day that the Gentiles had profaned it, it was dedicated with songs and harps and lutes and cymbals" (1 Macc. 4:54; cf. Dan. 7:25). Josephus even says that Judas functioned as the high priest during this time, although he omits Judas's name from a list of high priests (cf. *Ant.* 12.414, 434; 20.224–51).[1]

Judas soon realized that religious liberty under the Seleucids would be insufficient to ensure the continued viability of the Jewish people in their ancestral homeland, given the intense hostility of their gentile neighbors. Forced to rescue Jewish communities threatened with annihilation in Hebron, Gilead, Galilee, and the coastal plain, Judas transitioned to a struggle for political independence (1 Macc. 5:3–13, 24–56). A key diplomatic move illustrating this new agenda was the forging of an alliance and mutual defense pact with Rome (1 Macc. 8). This doubtless sent shock waves through the Seleucid regime and foreshadowed the decisive role that Rome would eventually play in this part of the world. Ironically, what began as a courtship dance ended as a dance of death in the two revolts against Rome (AD 66–73, 132–135).

Wearied with lack of success in taking the temple mount and threatened by a rival claimant to the throne, Antiochus V, successor of Antiochus IV, opted for negotiations: "Let us agree to let them live by their laws as they did before; for it was on account of their laws that we abolished that they became angry and did all these things" (1 Macc. 6:59). Thus ended the first phase of the war of liberation.

Hostilities continued, however, and abandoned by many former supporters— many of the Hasideans appear to have been content with achieving religious freedom—Judas fell in battle at Elasa (1 Macc. 9:5–18). He was buried in the ancestral tomb at Modein (1 Macc. 9:19) and lionized in a stirring tribute by the author of 1 Maccabees (1 Macc. 9:20–22; cf. 13:25–30).

Jonathan (High Priest from 152 to 143 BC)

Jonathan succeeded Judas as leader of the insurgents and carried on the protracted struggle. Though clearly a formidable military leader, Jonathan achieved more to secure political independence through skillful diplomacy. After inflicting a decisive defeat on the Seleucid regent Bacchides and forcing him to return home (1 Macc. 9:62–69), Jonathan quickly sued for peace, and Bacchides accepted (1 Macc. 9:70–73). This left Jonathan in virtual control of Judea.

1. See Hayes and Mandell, *Jewish People*, 76–78; James C. VanderKam, *From Joshua to Caiaphas: High Priests after the Exile* (Minneapolis: Fortress, 2004), 241–44.

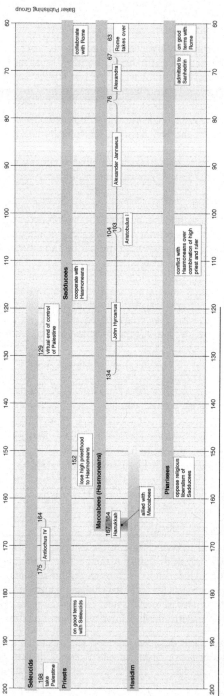

4.1. Time line of Seleucid and Hasmonean rule in Palestine.

In 153/52 BC Alexander Balas, who claimed to be the son of Antiochus IV, occupied Ptolemais and prepared to overthrow the incumbent, Demetrius I. A bidding war for Jonathan's services as an ally and friend resulted, ironically, in Jonathan's appointment as general and governor of Judea, and high priest of the Jerusalem temple. He was also able to extract a number of significant concessions, tax exemptions, and territorial acquisitions. An army was recruited and equipped, and captives were released from the Akra. The freedom fighters of the early days morphed into the strongest military force in Israel (Aharoni et al., *Atlas*, 150).

The struggle, however, was far from over. Fearing the growing power of Jonathan, Demetrius II twice sought to rein in this upstart, but both campaigns resulted in resounding victories for Jonathan. Another claimant to the Seleucid throne, however, was able to take him down, not by force of arms, but by treachery. Tryphon brought a large force to attack the Jews, and the two armies faced off at Beth-shean. Realizing he could not defeat Jonathan militarily, Tryphon held out a carrot, promising to turn over the important seaport of Ptolemais to Jewish control. He induced Jonathan to leave behind most of his army and accompany him to Ptolemais with only a thousand troops. The people of Ptolemais, in league with Tryphon, closed the city gates behind Jonathan and took him prisoner. Unable to defeat the Jewish forces now under Simon's command, Tryphon returned to Syria, but not before executing Jonathan (1 Macc. 12:39–13:24). Simon recovered the body and reburied it with great honors at the family tomb in Modein, which he adorned by a monument and seven pyramids (1 Macc. 13:25–30).

Simon (High Priest from 143 to 135 BC)

After Jonathan's death, Simon assumed the mantle of leadership. A landmark achievement was the declaration by Demetrius II that the Hasmonean state was released from paying tribute, all previous land grants remained valid, and the crown tax was cancelled (1 Macc. 13:35–42). At long last, "the yoke of the Gentiles was removed from Israel" (1 Macc. 13:41). The Jewish people acclaimed Simon "the great high priest and commander and leader of the Jews" (1 Macc. 13:42). The date was 142 BC, which marked a watershed in Jewish history. Documents were dated in reference to this event, and coins were struck to commemorate it.

All in all, it was a stunning achievement for a guerilla movement that began in the Gophna Hills fifteen years earlier. A final reminder of Hellenistic interference in the internal affairs of Judea was erased in 141 BC when, after a long siege, the hated Akra surrendered and the fortress was razed. Simon also commenced the construction of massive city walls circling the entire perimeter of Mount Zion (the western hill) and strengthened the walls around the ancient city of David. The temple mount itself was extended to the south and protected by a fortress. In 140 BC, in a public assembly and on bronze tablets, Simon's supporters declared his appointment as high priest to be "forever, until a trustworthy prophet should

Hasmonean High Priests and Qumran

The Hasmonean rejection of dyarchy (government shared by two rulers, in this case, political and religious; cf. Hag. 1:1; Zech. 4:3) elicited strong resistance in some circles. It is widely held that the antipathy stemmed from the fact that the Hasmoneans were not Zadokites, a priestly family from the days of David and Solomon claiming exclusive right to the high priesthood (T. H. Lim, *EDSS* 2:973–75 [974–75]). Other scholars, however, think it likely that the Hasmoneans were Zadokites[a] and that the opposition was prompted by resentment of rival priestly families over exclusive national and religious leadership.

Many scholars see in the Hasideans the precursors of the Essenes and Pharisees (e.g., Hengel, *Judaism and Hellenism*, 1:175–218). The Essenes rejected the temple cult and established their own communities throughout the country. At some point, a charismatic leader, called "the Teacher of Righteousness," himself a high priest, claimed to be the recipient of divine guidance in matters of correctly interpreting the pentateuchal laws. His followers withdrew to the site of Qumran and bound themselves to his particular halakah (interpretation and application of Torah) as the touchstone of what it means to be the true Israel (M. A. Knibb, *EDSS* 2:918–21).

Six passages from the sectarian literature of Qumran contain tantalizing references to a "Wicked Priest" who persecuted and pursued the "Teacher of Righteousness" (1QpHab 8.8–13; 8.16–9.2; 9.9–12; 11.4–8; 11.12–15; 12.2–10; 4QpPs[a] [4Q171] 4.7–12). Many scholars believe the Wicked Priest is either Jonathan or Simon (the so-called standard view).[b] The celebrated 4QMMT (4Q394–399) mentions twenty ritual purity issues in dispute between two parties, probably the Jerusalem priesthood and the Qumran community. This document may be earlier than the Habakkuk commentary since it is less combative in tone. The suggestion is that over time the disagreements intensified and resulted in mutual excommunication (L. H. Schiffman, *EDSS* 1:558–60; but see M. G. Abegg Jr., *DNTB* 709–11).

Other scholars believe that the evidence, especially 4QpNah (4Q169), better supports the view that the Wicked Priest was John Hyrcanus II (who sided with the Pharisees under the influence of his queen mother, Alexandra) and that the Qumran community actually applauded the crucifixion of some eight hundred Pharisees by the Hasmonean priest-king Alexander Jannaeus (Jonathan).[c] Still others hold that the Wicked Priest is an appellation for successive high priests (S. B. Tzoref, *EDEJ* 1050–55 [1053]). The identity of the Wicked Priest and the Teacher of Righteousness remains a contentious issue.

[a] James C. VanderKam, *From Joshua to Caiaphas: High Priests after the Exile* (Minneapolis: Fortress, 2004), 270n90.
[b] See, e.g., James C. VanderKam, *The Dead Sea Scrolls Today* (rev. ed.; Grand Rapids: Eerdmans, 2010), 130–32; Rajak, "Hasmonean Dynasty," 73–75.
[c] See Michael Wise et al., *Dead Sea Scrolls: A New Translation* (San Francisco: HarperSanFrancisco, 1996), 26–34.

arise" (1 Macc. 14:25–49; quote from v. 41). Like his brothers, however, Simon met a violent death (134 BC), when his ambitious son-in-law assassinated him in a vain attempt to seize power (1 Macc. 16:11–24).

The Dynasty of Hasmonean Priest-Kings

Simon's son John Hyrcanus, having assumed power as high priest and ruler, finally brought the decades-long struggle for political independence to an end.

John Hyrcanus I (135–104 BC)

The era of the third generation, under John Hyrcanus I, did not begin auspiciously, nor was it a time of peace. Difficulties with the Seleucid Empire continued, and Antiochus VII, still smarting from his failure to seize control of Judea in the days of Simon and deeming it essential to reclaim the important land bridge of Israel, invaded the coastal area, taking Joppa and Gazara (Gezer). He then proceeded to besiege Jerusalem for more than a year. In these dire circumstances, Hyrcanus was nonetheless able to negotiate a settlement with Antiochus VII, though the terms were grievous. Heavy indemnity and tribute was levied, arms were surrendered, the walls of Jerusalem were razed, and hostages—including Hyrcanus's son—were handed over (Josephus, Ant. 13.236–48). The successes of Jonathan and Simon were seemingly undone in one blow.

Hyrcanus's fortunes, however, quickly took a dramatic turn for the better. Antiochus VII was killed in battle against the Parthians in 129 BC, and Demetrius II was released and sought to reestablish his control over the Syrian Empire. The ensuing power struggle left Hyrcanus with a free hand in Judea, and he quickly reasserted Jewish sovereignty. Of special importance was the renewal of an alliance and mutual defense pact with the Romans. Syria was warned not to interfere in the internal affairs of Judea; consequently, Hyrcanus stopped all tribute payments. The final victory over the Seleucids was at last achieved (Josephus, Ant. 13.259–66).

Hyrcanus then engaged in a series of military campaigns aimed at territorial expansion. He first conquered areas in the Transjordan, wresting these away from the Nabateans and thereby gaining control of the important King's Highway linking Damascus with the Gulf of Elath (or Aqaba). He then turned his attention to Samaria, which had long separated Judea from the northern Jewish settlements in lower Galilee. Shechem and the Samaritan temple on Mount Gerizim were destroyed in 128 BC (Josephus, Ant. 13.254–56), as confirmed by archaeological excavations (I. Magen, NEAEHL 2:484–87). In the south, Adora and Marisa were conquered, and the Idumeans were given an ultimatum: either convert to Judaism (involving circumcision) or face expulsion. They chose the former, which in effect provided a buffer zone on the southern frontier (Josephus, Ant. 13.257–58).

The sweeping changes brought about by Hyrcanus's conquests were reflected in a first: coins minted in his name. Hyrcanus's thirty-year reign was the longest of the Hasmonean dynasty.

Aristobulus I (104–103 BC)

The fourth generation of Hasmonean rule began ominously. Aristobulus I, not content with being merely high priest, sought to be a Hellenistic monarch. Accordingly, he assumed the title of king and a diadem, the first Hasmonean leader to do so. In the process, however, he starved his mother to death in prison and treacherously executed his brother. His primary accomplishment was annexing and Judaizing the region of Iturea, located between the Lebanon and Anti-Lebanon mountains (Josephus, *Ant.* 13.301–19). Few lamented his premature death after a reign of one year, and "in many respects . . . his life resembled a Greek tragedy" (Rainey and Notley, *Sacred Bridge*, 329).

Alexander Jannaeus (103–76 BC)

During the reign of Alexander Jannaeus (also called Jonathan), the policy of territorial expansion reached its zenith, equaling the territory once ruled by David and Solomon. However, internecine conflict between religious and political parties intensified, sowing the seeds of self-destruction. Jannaeus, like Aristobulus, executed one of his brothers, whom he feared as a rival (Josephus, *Ant.* 13.323; *J.W.* 1.85). This was a harbinger of unprecedented bloodshed to follow.

Jannaeus annexed more territory in Galilee and Transjordan and occupied the entire coastline from Carmel to Rhinocorura (Rainey and Notley, *Sacred Bridge*, 331–32). Shrewd diplomacy, especially his dealings with Cleopatra III of Egypt and her estranged son Ptolemy Lathyrus, played a key role in his successes.

Jannaeus's later years were marked by civil war. He aligned himself with the Sadducees against the Pharisees, and in a "day of infamy," he crucified eight hundred of his Pharisaic opponents and executed their wives and children before their eyes (Josephus, *J.W.* 1.97; *Ant.* 13.380). This inhumane treatment is almost certainly referred to in the Qumran document 4Q169 frgs. 3–4 1.2–8. Many Jews detested Jannaeus.

Alexandra the Queen and Hyrcanus II the High Priest (76–67 BC)

Queen Shelamzion Alexandra succeeded her husband, Alexander Jannaeus, and became sole monarch (Ilan, *Silencing the Queen*, 50–58). Probably the influence of Ptolemaic Egypt, in which there were several queens, prompted this deviation. Alexandra's primary contribution was twofold: a period of relative peace with neighboring powers and a strategic switch of allegiance to the party of the Pharisees, in keeping with her husband's deathbed counsel. This apparently was more in tune with the sympathies of the majority. She had two sons: the firstborn, Hyrcanus II, whom she appointed high priest and regent, and Aristobulus II (Josephus, *Ant.* 13.405–32).

War between Aristobulus II and Hyrcanus II (67–64 BC)

In the fifth generation, deadly animosity once again arose between two brothers, setting the stage for the demise of the dynasty. The ambitious Aristobulus II wrested control from Hyrcanus II. The coup, however, did not go uncontested. Into the picture emerged another powerful family, of Idumean descent, that dramatically altered the course of Jewish history: the family of Antipater, father of Herod the Great. Antipater urged Hyrcanus to regain control from Aristobulus and enlisted the support of the Nabatean king Aretas.

Aristobulus was besieged in Jerusalem. At this point, Rome intervened and called a halt to the siege. In the stalemate that followed, both claimants made a beeline to Pompey, the Roman proconsul in Syria, to argue their case. A Jewish delegation also appeared before Pompey and emphatically rejected both contenders (Josephus, *Ant.* 14.41). After disobeying Pompey's direct order to stay put and wait for his decision, Aristobulus fled to Jerusalem. When his supporters refused to yield and fortified themselves on the temple mount, Pompey constructed a siege wall around it and, after a three-month siege, crushed all resistance (63 BC). He reinstated Hyrcanus as high priest and ethnarch, and he sent Aristobulus to Rome as a prisoner (Josephus, *Ant.* 14.57–79). In the ensuing power struggle between Julius Caesar and Pompey, Caesar dispatched Aristobulus to fight against Pompey, but Pompey's partisans poisoned Aristobulus before he arrived on the scene. In the meantime, Antipater served as the real power behind the throne, having installed his sons, Phasaelis and Herod, as governors in the land. Hasmonean hegemony existed in name only.

Mattathias Antigonus (40–37 BC)

Unexpectedly, one last Hasmonean prince, from the sixth generation, momentarily seized power. The powerful Parthian Kingdom (Iran) invaded and placed Mattathias Antigonus, son of Aristobulus II, on the throne. Coins were minted on which he appears as both high priest and king. Hyrcanus II's ear was cut off, rendering him unfit to serve as high priest. Antigonus's reign was short lived, however, because Antipater's son Herod managed by heroic measures to escape to Rome and plead his case. The Roman Senate conferred upon Herod the title of king and provided assistance (40 BC). For three years he fought a brutal war to subdue his new realm, at the end of which he took Jerusalem. Antigonus was captured alive and taken to Antioch, where he was beheaded. As for Hyrcanus II, Herod eventually sentenced and executed him in order to eliminate any possible uprising on his behalf (30 BC). The Hasmonean dynasty was over.

Hasmoneans during the Herodian Dynasty

Several Hasmoneans of the sixth through the eighth generations played unhappy roles in the drama of Herod's reign. Mariamme, whom Herod passionately loved, fell victim to his insane jealousy and was executed (29 BC). Mariamme's mother, Alexandra, was also executed by Herod (28 BC). Herod had already dispatched Aristobulus III, the seventeen-year-old brother of Mariamme, who was greatly admired by the populace in his role as high priest, in a "drowning accident" at Jericho (35 BC). After a drawn-out affair, Herod's two sons by Mariamme—Alexander and Aristobulus—were finally sentenced and strangled at Sebaste (Samaria)—ironically, where Herod had married her. In short, Herod eliminated all possible rivals belonging to the Hasmonean family.

Hasmonean Descendents in the New Testament: Ninth and Tenth Generations

Mariamme's son Aristobulus fathered three children, two of whom, along with a grandson and granddaughter, appear in the NT:

1. Herod Agrippa I was appointed king of the Jews from AD 37 to 44. He persecuted the early church, arrested Peter, and died at Caesarea (Acts 12; Josephus, *Ant*. 19.343–52). His son Herod Agrippa II was king of the Jews from AD 50 to 100 and listened to Paul's defense at Caesarea (Acts 25–26).

2. Herodias was the wife of Herod Antipas, tetrarch over Galilee (4 BC–AD 39; Luke 3:1). Her daughter, called Salome by Josephus (*Ant*. 18.136), and whose dancing captivated Antipas, requested the head of John the Baptist on a platter (Matt. 14:1–12; Mark 6:17–29).

Achievements of the Hasmoneans

The Hasmonean dynasty pulled the Jewish state into the orbit of Hellenism. At the same time, it preserved Jewish ideas and values that persist to this day.

Hellenization of the Heartland

The Hasmoneans, who initially resisted the inroads of Hellenism in the heartland of Israel, actually contributed to its acceleration and influence. The founding of Hellenistic cities along the Palestinian coast had already begun before the conquests of Alexander the Great (332 BC). Shortly before the Hasmonean revolt, Jason and Menelaus, rival claimants to the high priesthood, championed the adoption of a Greek way of life and enthusiastically sponsored the building of a gymnasium in the shadow of the Jerusalem temple. Athletic contests in the Greek tradition were eagerly attended and participated in by Jewish young men, some of whom even sought to hide evidence of their circumcision by an operation called *epispasm*.

By the time of Simon, Hellenistic influence was clearly present, not least in architecture and city planning. Cities were laid out in the Greek hippodamic style (a grid pattern), and grand walls and towers of hewn masonry replaced earlier mud-brick construction. Besides fortresses and palaces, even rural farmsteads began appearing in a style similar to Hellenistic sites in Asia Minor. Although archaeological evidence for imported ware and glass is meager until the Herodian era, Hasmonean sites (such as et-Tell [Bethsaida]) provide some good examples. Clearly, the Hasmoneans ushered in an era of economic growth and a rise in the standard of living. The capture and resettling of the seaport town of Joppa opened a gateway to the sea lanes of the Mediterranean with its far-flung commercial markets. Indeed, Simon's "capture of the city was celebrated as the crown of all his honors" (F. E. Udoh, *EDEJ* 557–61 [559]; cf. 1 Macc. 14:5). Jürgen Zangenberg (*EDEJ* 201–35 [206]) captures the transformation:

> Hasmonean restoration did not mean the end of Hellenization. It was during the Hasmonean period that Judaism developed a distinct variant of eastern Hellenistic material culture. Hellenism became indigenous to Jewish Palestine, embedded in its culture and in the self-definition of its ruling dynasty. Symptomatic of that process is how Simon Maccabee (high priest and ethnarch 142–134 B.C.E.) integrated elements of Greek architecture into his renovated family tomb in Modein (1 Macc. 13.23–30; Josephus, *Ant.* 13.210–12).

Unfortunately, the Hasmonean leaders also began to conduct themselves like the despotic Seleucid monarchs they displaced. Ironically, little tolerance was granted to people groups who came under their military control, leading to forcible conversions, expulsions, and in some cases, massacres.

The above observations should not, however, be taken to mean that Hellenism completely replaced the traditions of the ancestral faith. Especially in the hinterlands, where the majority of Jewish inhabitants lived, Hebrew traditions remained intact. Most Jews adapted to Hellenism but did not assimilate.

Restoration of Jewish Nationalism

The Maccabean era resembles the rise of King David and the transformation of the tribal federation into a united kingdom possessing military prowess and economic clout. The author of 1 Maccabees imparts to his work a Davidic typology fulfilled in the Hasmonean leaders. A classic example is when Judas takes the sword of vanquished Apollonius and uses it in his ensuing battles (1 Macc. 3:12), recalling David's use of Goliath's sword in battle (1 Sam. 17:51; 21:9). Later, Jonathan retreats to the wilderness of Tekoa and operates like David of old as the leader of a guerilla band, successfully evading the pursuit of the Seleucid forces (1 Macc. 9:28–49). In 2 Maccabees (1:20–2:23), Judas is "depicted as the 'successor' to Nehemiah, who, it was argued, had restored the original fire upon the rebuilt Jerusalemite altar and founded a library housing the sacred books" (Hayes and Mandell, *Jewish People*, 74). The Herodian dynasty was a bitter pill for many Jews, and two disastrous revolts against Rome testify to an intense longing for "the good old days" of Hasmonean autonomy. The rebirth of the modern state of Israel bears striking similarities to the rise of the Hasmonean dynasty and, not surprisingly, in our post-Holocaust world, the Maccabean ethos has reemerged in the ongoing struggle between the Israelis and their Arab neighbors.

Religious Legacy

The Hasmonean era initiated an age of diversity in Judaism. The old consensus forged by the leadership of the Judean temple state under the Persians fractured and led to the formation of rival parties, each offering its own response to the challenge of Hellenism. The NT reflects this diversity by the presence of Herodians, Sadducees, Pharisees, zealots, and inferentially, Essenes. Most scholars suspect there were other, lesser-known groups and movements whose presence is not documented. This diversity was supplanted, though never completely, by the ascendance of rabbinic Judaism in the aftermath of the two revolts against Rome. But in the wake of the Enlightenment, modern Judaism once again fragmented and now reflects the discordant diversity of the Hasmonean age.

In the end, however, the greatest contribution of the Hasmoneans lay in preserving monotheism in the face of Hellenistic pressure to assimilate. The courage of the second generation of Hasmoneans, leading to the death of all five brothers in defense of the ancestral faith, left a lasting legacy to the three great monotheistic faiths. The story of the martyrdom of a Jewish mother and her seven sons, the centerpiece of 2 Maccabees (chaps. 5–8), has inspired Christian martyrs down through the ages. Especially in Eastern and Latin Christianity the exploits of the Maccabees live on.

Bibliography

Aharoni, Yohanan, Michael Avi-Yonah, Anson F. Rainey, and Ze'ev Safrai. *The Macmillan Bible Atlas*. 3rd rev. ed. New York: Macmillan, 1993. Highly recommended resource for studying the historical-geographical background of the Bible (including the Second Temple period) and relevant extrabiblical sources.

Cohen, Shaye J. D. *From the Maccabees to the Mishnah*. 3rd ed. Louisville: Westminster John Knox, 2006. Highly readable and informative synthesis of this nearly four-hundred-year period of Jewish history.

Eshel, Hanan. *The Dead Sea Scrolls and the Hasmonean State*. SDSSRL. Grand Rapids: Eerdmans, 2008. A leading authority on the archaeology, history, and literature of Qumran places the DSS in the context of Hasmonean history.

Gafni, Isaiah M. "Hasmoneans." *EDSS* 1:329–33. An overview written by a recognized authority on Jewish history with special reference to the contribution of the DSS.

Goldstein, Jonathan A. "The Hasmonean Revolt and the Hasmonean Dynasty." Pages 292–351 in *The Hellenistic Age*. Vol. 2 of *The Cambridge History of Judaism*. Edited by W. D. Davies and Louis Finkelstein. New York: Cambridge University Press, 1989. Standard treatment of the era by an acknowledged authority.

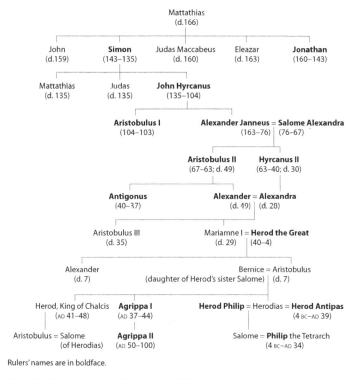

4.2. Family tree of the Maccabees and the Hasmoneans (167 BC–AD 100). From Harold Hoehner, "Hasmoneans," *ISBE* 2:622.

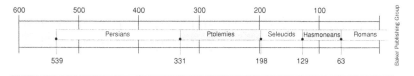

4.3. Time line of the final rules in Palestine.

————. *1 Maccabees.* AB 41. Garden City, NY: Doubleday, 1976. Detailed commentary on this important primary source written by an acknowledged expert.

————. *2 Maccabees.* AB 41A. Garden City, NY: Doubleday, 1983. Sequel to his commentary on 1 Maccabees, reflecting the fruit of many years spent studying both works.

Grabbe, Lester L. *Judaism from Cyrus to Hadrian.* 2 vols. Minneapolis: Fortress, 1992. Highly technical treatment and often skeptical of the reliability of the primary sources; incorporates a wide range of extrabiblical sources having some bearing on the history of this period.

Hayes, John H., and Sara R. Mandell. *The Jewish People in Classical Antiquity.* Louisville: Westminster John Knox, 1998. Treatment reflecting considerable skepticism about the reliability of the sources at various points, but useful in providing fresh perspectives and new insights.

Hengel, Martin. *Judaism and Hellenism: Studies in their Encounter in Palestine during the Early Hellenistic Period.* Translated by J. Bowden. 2 vols. Philadelphia: Fortress, 1974. Classic study by an internationally recognized scholar, identifying the Hasideans as the precursors of the Essenes and Pharisees.

Hoehner, Harold W. "Hasmoneans." *ISBE* 2:621–27. Still-valuable treatment by a leading authority on the historical backgrounds of the NT.

Ilan, Tal. *Silencing the Queen: The Literary Histories of Shelamzion and Other Jewish Women.* Tübingen: Mohr Siebeck, 2006. Specialized study distinguishing Shelamzion Alexandra from Salome Alexandra, wife of Aristobulus I, and identifying her with the woman called Shelamzion in two Qumran fragments.

Mendels, Doron. *The Rise and Fall of Jewish Nationalism.* Grand Rapids: Eerdmans, 1992. Thematic treatment of various aspects of Hasmonean nationalism. Fine introduction to the political history of this period.

Murphy, Frederick J. *Early Judaism: The Exile to the Time of Jesus.* Peabody, MA: Hendrickson, 2002. Excellent synthesis of the Hasmonean era written by a recognized scholar on the Second Temple period.

Netzer, Ehud. *The Palaces of the Hasmoneans and Herod the Great.* Jerusalem: Yad Ben Zvi, 2001. Masterful study by one of the world's leading archaeologists and historians of the Second Temple period. Excellent plans and reconstructions of Hasmonean architecture and construction.

Rainey, Anson F., and R. Steven Notley, eds. *The Sacred Bridge.* Jerusalem: Carta, 2006. This is the definitive Bible atlas and magnum opus of the leading scholar (and his student) on the historical geography of the Holy Land. Highly recommended.

Rajak, Tessa. "Hasmonean Dynasty." *ABD* 3:67–76. Skillful synthesis of the history and background of the Hasmonean era. Highly recommended.

Schwartz, Daniel R. *2 Maccabees.* New York: de Gruyter, 2008. The most up-to-date commentary in English on 2 Maccabees by a leading expert in the field of Second Temple Judaism.

Sievers, J. "Hasmoneans." *DNTB* 438–42. Excellent summary of the Hasmoneans by a leading authority.

————. "Hasmoneans." *EDEJ* 705–9. The most up-to-date digest of the Hasmonean dynasty available. Highly recommended for an overview.

Stern, Ephraim, ed. *New Encyclopedia of Archaeological Excavations in the Holy Land.* 5 vols. New York: Simon & Schuster, 1993. The most comprehensive treatment of archaeological work in the Holy Land available. Updated in supplementary volumes.

Tomasino, Anthony J. *Judaism before Jesus: The Events and Ideas That Shaped the New Testament World*. Downers Grove, IL: InterVarsity, 2003. An engaging and informative study that admirably serves as an introduction to NT backgrounds.

Zangenberg, Jürgen. "Archaeology, Papyri, and Inscriptions." *EDEJ* 201–35. Current summary of the archaeological evidence illuminating the period of the Hasmoneans.

5

The Herodian Dynasty

EVERETT FERGUSON

The Herodian dynasty provides the chronological framework for Palestine in NT times, from before the birth of Jesus under Herod the Great (d. 4 BC) until the death of Agrippa II in AD 100. The dynasty's interconnections with the Hasmoneans and the Romans provide the political context for the beginnings of Christianity. No other eastern client king's family is as well known as Herod's, thanks in large part to the Jewish historian Josephus.

Origins

Josephus identifies Herod's father, Antipater, as "an Idumaean by race" (*J.W.* 1.123),[1] but Idumea was more a geographical than an ethnic identification. From their homeland east and south of the Dead Sea, the Edomites had been displaced by the Nabatean Arabs and migrated to the west of the Dead Sea, so that Idumea in the late Hellenistic period comprised parts of what had been southern Judah, the northern Negev, and inland Phoenicia. Its inhabitants, therefore, comprised Jews, Arabs, Phoenicians, and Greeks in addition to Edomites. John Hyrcanus (ruled 134–104 BC) conquered Idumea for the Hasmonean Kingdom, and the inhabitants were converted, either forcibly or in some cases voluntarily, to Judaism.

---

1. Translations in this chapter are from LCL unless otherwise noted.

Among these converts was Herod the Great's grandfather, whom Alexander Jannaeus made governor of Idumea. Thus Herod was a third-generation proselyte. Herod's father, Antipater, advanced the family fortunes further. Josephus introduces him as a supporter of Hyrcanus II in the context of the struggle between the Hasmoneans Hyrcanus II and Aristobulus II in the early 60s BC. Josephus pays Antipater several compliments: "on account of his ancestry, wealth, and other advantages" he was at the forefront of his nation (*J.W.* 1.123); he was "distinguished for piety, justice, and zeal for his country" (*Ant.* 14.283, author's translation).

Nicolas of Damascus, the court historian for Herod the Great, invented a Jewish ancestry from Babylon for the family in order to make Herod more acceptable to his Jewish subjects, but Josephus rightly discounts this claim (*Ant.* 14.9). On the other hand, the indication of Edomite ancestry may be only a supposition. That the Hasmonean Antigonus called Herod a "half-Jew" because he was an Idumean (Josephus, *Ant.* 14.403) is not a clear reference to Edomite ancestry and may be simply derogatory and not literal. Later Christian sources assign to the family a connection with Ascalon, whose population was Hellenized Phoenicians (Kokkinos, *Herodian Dynasty*, 100). Regardless of Antipater's ancestry, he was a man of energy, resourcefulness, military effectiveness, and negotiating skills.

Antipater consistently supported Hyrcanus against Aristobulus and his son Alexander, and in turn Hyrcanus gave to Antipater the greatest part in the military and financial administration of his kingdom (Josephus, *Ant.* 15.177). Antipater cultivated good relations with the king of the Arabs, and he married Cyprus, from the Arab nobility. By her he had four sons: Phasael, Herod, Joseph, and Pheroras, and one daughter, Salome (Josephus, *J.W.* 1.181; *Ant.* 14.121).

It was especially to the Romans that Antipater hitched his star. On the death of Pompey, Antipater went over to Julius Caesar. He assisted Caesar in Egypt (Josephus, *Ant.* 14.127–39), and for his valor and service Caesar granted Antipater Roman citizenship, exemption from taxes, and formal friendship (Josephus, *J.W.* 1.194). Later Caesar confirmed Hyrcanus as high priest against the claims of Antigonus, the other son of Aristobulus, and appointed Antipater procurator (*epitropos*) of Judea (*J.W.* 1.199; *Ant.* 14.143). Antipater made Phasael governor (*stratēgos*) of Jerusalem and Herod governor of Galilee (*J.W.* 1.203; *Ant.* 14.158).

By skillfully serving the interests of the Roman governors of Syria, of the triumvirs Crassus, Pompey, and Caesar, and successively of Cassius and Mark Antony, Antipater laid the foundation for his son Herod's prominence. His ability to change sides in the changing fortunes of Rome's civil wars in the mid-first century BC was a skill inherited by Herod.

According to Josephus, the Jews honored Antipater as if a king, but he remained loyal to Hyrcanus (*Ant.* 14.162). Some Jews, however, accused Antipater before Hyrcanus because Antipater and his sons were becoming so powerful (Josephus, *Ant.* 14.163–67). Antipater finally met his end when Malichus (a Jewish noble) had Hyrcanus's butler poison him (Josephus, *J.W.* 1.226; *Ant.* 14.281).

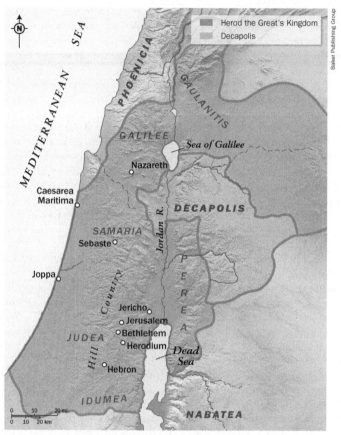

5.1. The kingdom of Herod the Great.

Herod the Great (73–4 BC)

Herod's early career showed his ability and resourcefulness but was hardly indicative of his future greatness. The conventional designation of him as "the Great" came later and was not applied to him by his contemporaries. Josephus uses the epithet only in *Jewish Antiquities* (see 18.130, 133, 136), where it appears to mean "the older" to distinguish him from descendants of the same name. Herod's official designation was "friend and ally of the Roman people" (Jones, *Herods*, 62). He exemplified the social diversity of his time: by birth an Idumean, by ancestry perhaps Phoenician, in citizenship Roman, in culture a Hellenist, and in religion officially Jewish (Kokkinos, *Herodian Dynasty*, 350–51).

Lee Martin McDonald

5.2. Herod the Great built this aqueduct to bring fresh water to Caesarea from the springs at Shuni (more than twenty miles north). It was extended further in the second century AD by Hadrian.

Josephus gives various characterizations of Herod, mostly negative: "He was a man who was cruel to all alike and one who easily gave in to anger and was contemptuous of justice. And yet he was as greatly favored by fortune as any man has ever been" (*Ant.* 17.191; cf. 19.329). Herod's faults included ruthlessness, murder of rivals and potential rivals, and a suspicious temperament. On the other side were his strong family affection (except when overridden by fears for his rule), untiring energy, and generous benefactions. As an example of the last, Herod generously used his own resources in relief of the effects of a severe drought (*Ant.* 15.299–316). His accomplishments included military ability (using a well-trained army of mostly foreign mercenaries) and personal investments that permitted vast expenditures yet left a full treasury and a prosperous country (Jones, *Herods*, 151–55). Josephus also comments on Herod's physical strength—irresistible in combat, a skilled horseman, a hunter accurate with the javelin and the bow (Josephus, *J.W.* 1.429–30). Josephus offers his own estimate that both Herod's magnanimous benefactions and his harsh punishments of even his closest relatives resulted from his love of fame and honors (*Ant.* 16.150–56).

As governor of Galilee, Herod suppressed brigands, capturing one of their chiefs, Ezekias, and putting many to death (Josephus, *J.W.* 1.204; *Ant.* 14.159–60). His enemies goaded Hyrcanus II to summon Herod to trial for killing persons without a trial or permission from the king, but the governor of Syria, Sextus Caesar, secured his acquittal (*J.W.* 1.208–15; *Ant.* 14.165–70).

Following the death of Julius Caesar, Herod won the friendship of Cassius, one of the conspirators (Josephus, *J.W.* 1.218–21; *Ant.* 14.274), and with Cassius's approval, Herod arranged the assassination of Malichus in revenge for the murder of Antipater (*J.W.* 1.227–35; *Ant.* 14.288–93).

After Cassius fell at the battle of Philippi in 42 BC, Mark Antony made Phasael and Herod tetrarchs over Judea (Josephus, *J.W.* 1.242–44; *Ant.* 14.326). When supporters of the Hasmonean Antigonus with Parthian support plotted against the brothers, Herod placed his family in the fortress of Masada and fled to Petra. Phasael was captured and according to one report killed himself by dashing his head against a rock so as to avoid torture (*J.W.* 1.263–72; *Ant.* 14.367–69). Malchus, king of Arabia, refused to help Herod (*J.W.* 1.274–76; *Ant.* 14.370–73), so Herod made his way to Egypt and from there, in the urgency of his situation risking travel in winter, to Rome (*J.W.* 1.277–79; *Ant.* 14.374–80).

Antony, recalling the hospitality shown him by Antipater, welcomed Herod, as did Octavian (later Augustus). The Senate unanimously approved Antony's proposal to make Herod king of the Jews (40 BC). Antony and Octavian left the Senate house with Herod between them (Josephus, *J.W.* 1.282–85; *Ant.* 14.381–89; Strabo, *Geogr.* 16.765; Tacitus, *Hist.* 5.9). From the Roman viewpoint, Herod made the ideal client king—loyal, an efficient administrator, and as a Jew presumably able to manage the religious affairs of his people (Jones, *Herods*, 66). A client king had considerable freedom in managing internal affairs of his realm, but he was not to pursue an independent foreign policy, and he was to supply soldiers and money at Rome's request. The position was personal, and on a king's death the kingdom returned to Rome.

In Judea, however, the Parthians had crowned Antigonus king. Hence, Herod had to win his kingdom against Antigonus, other Jews who opposed him, and Parthian troops in the region. On his return to Palestine, Herod gathered an army and, after relieving the siege of Masada, proceeded to take over Samaria and Idumea and drive out the resistance in Galilee (Josephus, *J.W.* 1.290–94; *Ant.* 14.394–98). While Herod led troops to assist Antony in the latter's siege of Samosata near the Euphrates, he left his brother Joseph in charge of the realm with instructions not to engage Antigonus until he returned. Joseph ignored these orders, however, and marched on Jericho with troops newly recruited in Syria and supplied by the Roman general in the east. Antigonus's soldiers routed the inexperienced soldiers, and Joseph was killed and beheaded (*J.W.* 1.323–25; *Ant.* 14.438, 448–50). Herod finally succeeded in taking Jerusalem, which he saved from pillaging and violation of the temple by the Roman troops through liberal gifts to the soldiers and officers (*J.W.* 1.349–57; *Ant.* 14.478–86). Antigonus was captured, carried in chains to Antony at Antioch, and beheaded (*J.W.* 1.357; *Ant.* 14.488–90; 15.9, quoting Strabo; Dio Cassius, *Hist.* 49.22). Herod now in 37 BC had secured the kingdom awarded him three years before.

The year 31 BC was a low point for Herod but saw another dramatic change in fortunes for him. Antony had sent him to war against the Nabatean Arabs, who initially defeated him (but after this setback, he was victorious and was chosen by them as their protector; Josephus, *J.W.* 1.385; *Ant.* 15.159); an earthquake rocked his kingdom (*Ant.* 15.121); and he lost his patron Antony, defeated by Octavian at Actium (Richardson, *Herod*, 168). Herod had to follow his father's policy of changing allegiance with the change in Roman ruler. He met Octavian at Rhodes, where he freely acknowledged his loyalty to Antony and laid down his diadem, only asking "that the subject of inquiry will be not whose friend, but how loyal a friend, I have been" (Josephus, *J.W.* 1.388–90; *Ant.* 15.187–93). Octavian was won over; he placed the diadem on Herod's head and confirmed him as king (*J.W.* 1.391–93; *Ant.* 15.194–96). Herod's original kingdom granted in 40 BC comprised Judea, Galilee, Perea, and Idumea. After the deaths of Antony and Cleopatra, Octavian returned the lands Cleopatra had appropriated and added the cities of Gadara, Hippos, Samaria, Gaza, Anthedon, Joppa, and Strato's Tower (*J.W.* 1.396–97; *Ant.* 15.217). Later, as Augustus, he progressively added to Herod's realm Samaritis, Hulitis, Gaulanitis, Batanea, Auranitis, and Trachonitis, resulting in a kingdom for Herod rivaling David's and Solomon's. These grants were based on Herod's loyalty to Augustus, his ability to govern the Jews effectively, and his commitment to Rome's policies (Richardson, *Herod*, 131, 145; cf. Josephus, *J.W.* 1.400). After 30 BC Herod was preeminent in the eastern Mediterranean, with no significant rivals (Richardson, *Herod*, 173).

5.3. Herod the Great's bathhouse at his winter palace in New Testament Jericho.

Herod, nevertheless, had to struggle to maintain peace and order in his realm. Government spying on its subjects is not a new phenomenon, for the suspicious

Herod "both in the city and on the open roads" had "men who spied upon those who met together" (Josephus, *Ant.* 15.366). He had Hyrcanus executed (different versions of the circumstances appear in *Ant.* 15.164–82). His pagan subjects disliked him because he was a Jew; Jews disliked him because he was not a Jew and because he was a vassal of Rome (Jones, *Herods*, 71).

Herod had even less success in resolving family conflicts. He had ten wives (Josephus, *J.W.* 1.562–63; *Ant.* 17.19–22 names the last nine as simultaneous, making Herod the only named polygamous person of the time), fifteen children, twenty grandchildren of whom we know, thirteen great-grandchildren, eight great-great-grandchildren, and two great-great-great-grandchildren (Kokkinos, *Herodian Dynasty*, 144; 363–66 lists in alphabetical order 144 individuals in the Herodian family tree; cf. Josephus, *Ant.* 18.130–42). He chose his wives for their beauty and, with one exception, not for their status or his political advantage; "His first wife was a Jewess [from Jerusalem] of some standing, named Doris, by whom he had a son Antipater" (Josephus, *J.W.* 1.241).

Herod's Wives and Children
(based on Kokkinos, *Herodian Dynasty*, 206–45)

Wives	Children
Doris, Jewess of Jerusalem	Antipater II
Mariamme, daughter of Alexander (son of Aristobulus II)	Alexander, Aristobulus, unnamed son, Salampsio, Cyprus II
Mariamme II, daughter of Simon (a high priest)	Herod III
A niece	none
A cousin	none
Malthace of Samaria	Archelaus, Antipas II, Olympias
Cleopatra of Jerusalem	Herod IV, Philip
Pallas	Phasael III
Phaedra	Roxanne
Elpis	Salome II

After he secured the throne in 37 BC, Herod dismissed Doris and, probably in part to give more legitimacy to his rule in the eyes of the Jews, married Mariamme (also spelled Mariamne), a Hasmonean, daughter of Alexander and granddaughter of both rivals Aristobulus II and Hyrcanus II. By Mariamme he had five children—Alexander, Aristobulus, another son, and two daughters. Herod was passionately in love with her, but, writes Josephus, "her hatred of him was as great as was his love for her" (*J.W.* 1.436). She plotted on behalf of her two older sons, demeaned Herod's family, and was constantly at odds with his sister Salome. Herod had Mariamme's brother Aristobulus drowned out of jealousy for the popular enthusiasm he aroused, perceived as a threat to his own rule (Josephus, *Ant.* 15.51–56). On two occasions (or are the stories duplicates? see Richardson, *Herod*, 216–20) when Herod had to be away in circumstances of danger, he left Mariamme under the charge of another (his sister Salome's husband, Joseph [or Herod's uncle Joseph], when he went to Antony [Josephus, *J.W.* 1.441–42]; his steward Joseph and Soemus the Iturean when he went to meet Octavian [Josephus, *Ant.* 15.185–86]) with instructions that if he did not return, Mariamme was to be killed lest someone else marry her. The guardian confided this information to Mariamme as a proof of Herod's love for her, but she did not take it this way. On Herod's safe return and learning that Mariamme knew the secret, he suspected adultery, a suspicion confirmed by Salome. In a rage, Herod ordered Mariamme put to death, but afterward his love returned, and for a long time he refused to believe she was dead (*J.W.* 1.438–44; *Ant.* 15.64–87; different circumstances in 15.218–43).

There was continued friction with Mariamme's sons, Alexander and Aristobulus, and as antagonism grew, Herod brought back Doris's son Antipater, who fostered suspicions of his half brothers. Herod's sister Salome and brother Pheroras sided with Antipater because Alexander's wife Glaphyra (daughter of Archelaus of Cappadocia) taunted Salome and Herod's wives for their low birth. Archelaus of Cappadocia, acting on behalf of his son-in-law, mollified Herod's attitude for a time.

Calumnies against the brothers as plotting against their father continued, intensified by Salome and Pheroras and by their older half brother Antipater after his recall. Herod, "his patience exhausted," imprisoned Alexander and Aristobulus and referred the case to Augustus by letter. Augustus recommended a trial, which Herod held at Beirut. As a result of the inquiry, Herod sent the brothers to Sebaste (Samaria), where he ordered them to be strangled (Josephus, *J.W.* 1.550–51; *Ant.* 16.392–94).

Other wives of Herod by whom he had children enter our story: a second Mariamme (mother of another Herod), Malthace of Samaria (mother of sons Archelaus and Antipas and a daughter Olympias), and Cleopatra of Jerusalem (mother of another Herod and of Philip).

Friction at court extended to Herod's brother Pheroras, whose wife stirred up contention. Herod tried unsuccessfully to convince Pheroras to divorce his wife and finally banished them both (Josephus, *J.W.* 1.578). When Pheroras fell ill, Herod went to him and tended to him until his death; nonetheless, there were rumors that Herod poisoned him (Josephus, *J.W.* 1.580–81; *Ant.* 17.58–59; for various rumors, see 17.61–67, 68–77).

Herod had designated Antipater, his eldest son, his successor. But Antipater had stirred up the suspicions about Alexander and Aristobulus and now plotted against his father. Widely disliked, Antipater found few friends when a plan to have his father poisoned was uncovered. Herod summoned Antipater from Rome to face trial before Varus, governor of Syria (6–4 BC): "The king had Antipater put in irons and dispatched messengers to the emperor to inform him of the catastrophe" (Josephus, *J.W.* 1.640; cf. *Ant.* 17.133). Five days before his death,

Herod, on receiving permission from Augustus, had Antipater executed (*J.W.* 1.664; *Ant.* 17.187).

Now seriously ill, Herod changed his will, naming Antipas king, passing over the older sons Archelaus and Philip; he bequeathed one thousand talents and other gifts to the emperor and assigned large tracts of territory and considerable sums of money to members of his family, honoring Salome with the most magnificent gifts of all (Josephus, *J.W.* 1.646; 17.146–47). Changing his will once again, he bestowed the kingdom on Archelaus and designated Antipas tetrarch of Galilee and Perea and Philip tetrarch of Trachonitis and neighboring districts (Josephus, *J.W.* 1.668–69; *Ant.* 17.188–89).

5.4. Recent restoration of the inside of the southeast corner of the temple mount, near the Triple Gate.

Herod's illness grew steadily worse. From the afflictions detailed by Josephus (*J.W.* 1.656; *Ant.* 17.169) various diagnoses have been put forward, from a cancer of the bowels to syphilis. Herod had gone to Jericho to seek relief in the healing baths of Callirrhoe across the Jordan, and at Jericho he died in 4 BC. To ensure mourning at his death, Herod had commanded the notable Jews to be gathered in the hippodrome at Jericho and gave orders to Salome and her husband, Alexas, to have them killed when he breathed his last; but before the death of the king became generally known, Salome and Alexas dismissed those who had been summoned to the hippodrome (*Ant.* 17.174–81, 193). Archelaus orchestrated a sumptuous funeral procession to Herodium, where Herod had planned for his burial (*J.W.* 1.671–73; *Ant.* 17.196–99).

Herod deserves the designation "Great" as the great builder (Netzer, *Architecture*; see the list in Richardson, *Herod*, 197–202). He refurbished and expanded Hasmonean fortresses—including the tower of Antonia overlooking the temple (named for Antony; Josephus, *J.W.* 1.402; 5.238–45), Alexandrium (Josephus, *Ant.* 14.419), Masada (*J.W.* 7.285–303), and Machaerus (*J.W.* 7.171–77); and he built others— Herodium (named for himself; *J.W.* 1.419–20; *Ant.* 15.323–25) and Cyprus, overlooking Jericho (named for his mother; *J.W.* 1.417; *Ant.* 16.143). Some of these served as residences as well; his palaces primarily for residences were in Jerusalem (*J.W.* 5.176–82; *Ant.* 15.318), guarded by three towers (named Hippicus, Phasael, and Mariamme; *J.W.* 5.161–72), Jericho (*J.W.* 1.407), and Caesarea. Cities he founded or refounded included Antipatris (named for his fa-

ther; *J.W.* 1.417; Acts 23:31) and Sebaste (Samaria, now named for Augustus; *J.W.* 1.403; *Ant.* 15.292–96). Herod demonstrated loyalty to Rome by building temples to Augustus and Roma at Paneas (*J.W.* 1.404–6; *Ant.* 15.363), Sebaste (*J.W.* 1.403), and Caesarea (*J.W.* 1.414).

Herod's building projects extended to cities outside his realm. Notable were the Pythian temple at Rhodes, public buildings at Nicopolis, and a principal street in Antioch of Syria (Josephus, *Ant.* 16.146–48; 15.326–30). Furthermore, he provided an endowment for the Olympic Games (Josephus, *J.W.* 1.426–28; *Ant.* 16.149). These benefactions were primarily at cities with sizable Jewish populations, but the benefactions were not directly for them or any segment of the population but for the cities as a whole (Richardson, *Herod*, 94, 174–76, 272).

The most spectacular of Herod's foundations was the city of Caesarea built on the site of Strato's Tower (Holum et al., *Herod's Dream*). Employing the newly developed material of concrete, Herod's engineers constructed underwater breakers to create the largest harbor in the eastern Mediterranean, rivaling in size Piraeus, the port of Athens. In addition to the palace and the temple to Augustus with statues of Augustus and Roma, Herod's builders constructed warehouses at the harbor, a theater, a hippodrome, and civic buildings (Josephus, *J.W.* 1.408–15; *Ant.* 15.331–41). Caesarea became a center of commerce and government during the NT period and for subsequent centuries.

For the Jews the greatest of Herod's building projects was the reconstruction at his own expense of the temple in Jerusalem. Priests were trained as masons and carpenters so there would be no impurity attached to the work, and arrangements were made so there would be no disruption in the daily rituals. "The expenditure devoted to this work was incalculable, its magnificence never surpassed" (Josephus,

J.W. 1.401). Josephus devotes long sections in each of his major writings to describing the work (*J.W.* 5.184–227; *Ant.* 15.380–425). An innovation of the new temple complex, sections requiring progressive degrees of holiness were clearly demarcated. A large outer court, today called the Court of the Gentiles, was a public area. A stone balustrade with inscriptions warning foreigners to proceed no farther separated the area open to Israelites alone, itself with a separate section for women. The third, inner court was open only to priests and contained the altar for the daily burnt offering. The sanctuary itself contained a holy place (with the incense altar, table of showbread, and menorah) and a most holy place (or holy of holies), into which the high priest entered annually on the Day of Atonement. The magnificence and beauty of the temple was something on which Josephus and the rabbis agreed: "He who has not seen the temple . . . has never seen a glorious building in his life" (*b. Sukkah* 51b).

Herod's appointments of high priests abandoned the precedent of inheritance by the Hasmonean family (with the exception of Aristobulus, grandson of Hyrcanus II) and the policy of life appointment. His choices came from undistinguished priestly families, and he changed the holder of the office frequently, eight during his thirty-three year reign (Richardson, *Herod*, 243).

Herod's relation to Judaism remains ambiguous. The building of pagan temples in his realm was a standard expression of loyalty to Rome and outside his realm a customary form of benefaction, and these must be set alongside the far grander temple in Jerusalem. He generally respected the aniconic convictions of Jews, but he did set up a golden eagle on the temple, which aroused a violent reaction near his death (Josephus, *J.W.* 1.648–55; *Ant.* 17.151–63). His establishment of pagan athletic contests, chariot races, and wild-beast combats in Jerusalem greatly offended many Jews (*Ant.* 15.267–76). When a marriage was arranged between a

5.5. Herodium fortress and palace and the Roman swimming pool, located east of Bethlehem and destroyed during the First Jewish Revolt against Rome.

non-Jew and a female member of his family, he insisted on circumcision (*Ant.* 16.225), but the motive is not clear.

Herod enters the NT in connection with the birth of Jesus (Matt. 2:1–18). The "slaughter of the innocents" in Bethlehem has no independent attestation, but skepticism about its historicity is unwarranted. The story fits the character of Herod, who had his own children and other members of his family killed and particularly in his last years was filled with paranoia, and there was no reason for observers to take special notice of the killing of a few children in an obscure village in Judea.

Archelaus (Ethnarch 4 BC–AD 6)

Archelaus was born to Herod and Malthace about 23 BC. He and his brother Antipas were educated in Rome (Josephus, *Ant.* 17.20), as was Herod's custom with his male children. Archelaus married another Mariamme, but he divorced her to marry Glaphyra, widow of Archelaus's half brother Alexander and divorced wife of King Juba of Mauretania (Josephus, *J.W.* 2.114, says Libya; *Ant.* 17.341 points out that it was contrary to Jewish law to marry the wife of a brother by whom she had borne children).

In the rioting during Passover after the death of Herod, Archelaus was convinced that it was "impossible to restrain the mob without bloodshed," so he let loose his entire army against the rioters "busy with their sacrifices" at the temple and killed about three thousand mostly innocent people, a deed used against him in Rome by his enemies (Josephus, *J.W.* 2.13, 30, 32; *Ant.* 17.218, 237, 239, 313).

Archelaus went to Rome to present his case for succeeding his father as king (Josephus, *J.W.* 2.14; *Ant.* 17.219), but Antipas also went to present his case (*J.W.* 2.20; *Ant.* 17.224). Herod's family took the side of Antipas, "not out of goodwill to him but because of their hatred of Archelaus" (*Ant.* 17.227; cf. *J.W.* 2.22). Antipas's spokesman argued that Herod's codicil was made when he was not in his right mind due to illness (*J.W.* 2.31). Nicolas of Damascus spoke for Archelaus, making the argument that since Herod's codicil referred the final decision to Augustus, "one who was sane enough to cede his authority to the master of the world was surely not mistaken in his selection of an heir" (*J.W.* 2.34–36; cf. *Ant.* 17.240, 244). This event may be reflected in Jesus' parable in Luke 19:11–27, but in Archelaus's case he did not receive the kingdom, and he killed people before he left for Rome (although Varus, the Roman governor of Syria, did later kill others in suppressing the revolts; Richardson, *Herod*, 299–300).

Augustus's decision basically followed Herod's last will in dividing the kingdom, with the exception that he designated Archelaus ethnarch rather than king (holding out the prospect of his becoming king if he proved worthy); the money Herod bequeathed to Augustus was also distributed to Herod's family (Josephus, *J.W.* 2.94–98; *Ant.* 17.317–23; Tacitus, *Hist.* 5.9).

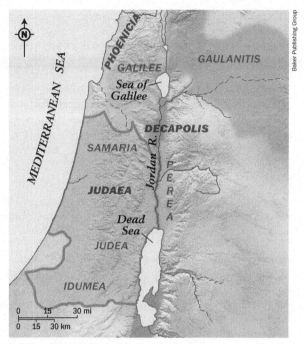

5.6. The divisions of Herod the Great's kingdom.

One of the few items that Josephus reports concerning Archelaus's decade in office is that he followed his father's practice of not appointing high priests from the Hasmonean family (*Ant.* 20.249). Popular distrust and fear of Archelaus is reflected in Matt. 2:19–22.

Animosity to Archelaus remained strong, increased by his brutality. "In the tenth year of Archelaus's rule the leading men among the Jews and Samaritans, finding his cruelty and tyranny intolerable, brought charges against him before" the emperor (Josephus, *Ant.* 17.342; cf. *J.W.* 2.111). Augustus banished him to Vienne in Gaul and confiscated his property (*Ant.* 17.344). His territory was made a province under a Roman governor (*J.W.* 2.117; *Ant.* 17.355), who appointed the high priest and had control of the temple. Antipas and Philip continued to rule their tetrarchies (*J.W.* 2.167).

Herod Antipas (Tetrarch 4 BC–AD 38)

Herod Antipas was born about 21 BC to Herod and Malthace. Estimates of Antipas vary from the "ablest of Herod's sons" (Jones, *Herods*, 176) to not "remarkable either in deeds or misdeeds" (Jensen, *Herod Antipas*, 100). His title of "tetrarch" is correctly given in Matt. 14:1 and Luke 9:7. The title "king" in Mark 6:14, rather than being an error, may reflect a popular view, may be Mark's deliberate paralleling him with the cruelty of his father, or may have been a translation issue, for the Aramaic *malkā'* was used in a broad sense beyond "king" (Jensen, *Herod Antipas*, 40). His realm of Galilee and Perea meant that both he and his territory often enter the Gospel narratives.

> ## The Herodian Dynasty
>
> Antipater, procurator of Judea (55–43 BC)
> Herod the Great (40/37–4 BC), married to Mariamme I (d. 29 BC), granddaughter of Hyrcanus II
> Herod Archelaus over Judea, Samaria, and Idumea (4 BC–AD 6)
> Herod Antipas over Galilee and Perea (4 BC–AD 38)
> Herod Philip over Batanea, Auranitis, and Trachonitis (4 BC–AD 33/34)
> Herod Agrippa I over Galilee (AD 40) and later over all Israel (AD 41–44)
> Herod Agrippa II over the territory of his father from ca. AD 49/50 to 100

The residents of Galilee were largely newcomers from Judea after the Hasmonean takeover under Aristobulus (Jensen, *Herod Antipas*, 6). This circumstance would account for Joseph's being from Bethlehem but living in Nazareth (Luke 2:4). The extent of Hellenization in Galilee is much debated. Archaeological finds indicate that in the early Roman period Galilee possessed a Jewish culture similar to that of Judea and the level of urbanization was not comparable to Caesarea Maritima and Scythopolis (Jensen, *Herod Antipas*, 8, 45). The villages that have been excavated indicate that Galilee flourished in the first half of the first century AD (Jensen, *Herod Antipas*, 178).

The few surviving coins issued by Antipas feature only floral decorations with Greek legends. The wider contacts of Antipas are indicated by an inscription from Cos: "Philon, son of Aglaos, but by birth son of Nikonos erected the (statue) in honor of Herod, son of Herod the King, tetrarch, his guest and friend" (Jensen, *Herod Antipas*, 203–4, 210).

Antipas founded two cities, Tiberias and Sepphoris. The building of Tiberias antagonized the Jews, because it was built over tombs (Josephus, *Ant.* 18.36–38). Antipas built his palace there (Josephus, *Life* 65), and Tiberias served as the capital of Galilee until Sepphoris became the capital under Nero (*Life* 37). Remains from the first century AD are sparse (Jensen, *Herod Antipas*, 135–49). Extensive excavation has been carried out at Sepphoris, located a short distance from Nazareth. Antipas fortified it to be "the ornament of all Galilee" (Josephus, *Ant.* 18.27), but most of what is visible now is post–AD 70 (Jensen, *Herod Antipas*, 149–62).

Antipas's first wife was the daughter of Aretas IV, king of Nabatea in Petra. When visiting his half brother, he fell in love with his wife, Herodias, daughter of their brother Aristobulus and sister to Agrippa I. Herodias agreed to marry him if he divorced his wife, which he agreed to do. His wife escaped to her father, who had other reasons to quarrel with Antipas, and war ensued. The army of Aretas destroyed Antipas's troops (Josephus, *Ant.* 18.109–15).

In this account Josephus gives the name of the half brother of Antipas as Herod, but Mark 6:17 and Matt. 14:3 give the name as Philip. Later Josephus expands on the family relationships: "Herodias was married to Herod, the son of Herod the Great by Mariamme. . . . They had a daughter Salome, after whose birth Herodias, taking it into her head to flout the way of our fathers, married Herod, her husband's brother by the same father, who was tetrarch of Galilee; to do this she parted from a living husband" (*Ant.* 18.136). It is generally assumed that the Gospels give the name incorrectly as Philip, or an attempt is made to reconcile the accounts by postulating that the person bore both names, Herod and Philip (Hoehner, *Herod Antipas*, 131–36); another possibility is that Josephus is confused and that Herodias was first married to Herod, son of the second Mariamme, by whom she had Salome, but had left him for the tetrarch Philip (Kokinnos, *Herodian Dynasty*, 237, 265–69).

"To some of the Jews the destruction of Herod's army seemed to be divine vengeance, and certainly a just vengeance, for his treatment of John, surnamed the Baptist" (Josephus, *Ant.* 18.116)—with those words Josephus introduces his account of John the Baptist. In some respects his account agrees with that in the Gospels (moral message of John), in other respects it differs (purpose of baptism, Herod's fear that John's preaching could lead to sedition), and in yet others it supplements the Gospels (the information that the imprisonment and execution of John occurred at the fortress of Machaerus; *Ant.* 18.119).

Followers of Jesus included family members of Herod's staff (Luke 8:3; Acts 13:1). Conflict between Jesus and Herod must have gone beyond what the Gospels explicitly tell us (Mark 8:15; Luke 13:31), probably because Herod associated Jesus with the followers of John the Baptist (Luke 9:7–9). Jesus' designation of him as a "fox" (Luke 13:32) likely indicates an insignificant or base person (Hoehner, *Herod Antipas*, 343–47). At the trial of Jesus, Pilate referred his case to Herod because Jesus was from Galilee (Luke 23:6–16); Herod would have had no jurisdiction in Jerusalem, but Pilate sought a second opinion and perhaps thought he could get Jesus off his hands if Herod would take him back to Galilee.

When Pilate dedicated golden votive shields at the royal palace in Jerusalem, the Jews in protest sent a delegation to him headed by four sons of Herod the Great, which would have included Antipas, who was perhaps the spokesman, and sent letters to Tiberius. The result was that the shields were transferred to the temple of Augustus at Caesarea (Philo, *Legat.* 299–300, 303–5).

After successful negotiations for peace between Tiberius and the Parthian king Artapanus, Antipas gave a feast in a luxurious pavilion that he constructed on a bridge across the Euphrates, where the Roman commander Vitellius (proconsul of Syria) and Artapanus met (Josephus, *Ant.* 18.101–2), an indication that Antipas must have been a key figure in the negotiations. In a misstep afterward Antipas sent the news to Tiberius before Vitellius filed his official report. This angered

Vitellius and made another enemy for Antipas that he did not need when he later came before Gaius Caligula.

Herod Antipas had cultivated good relations with the emperor Tiberius, but when Gaius came to the throne, the situation changed. The appointment of Herodias's brother Agrippa as king of Judea prompted her to goad her husband to seek the same title (Josephus, *Ant.* 18.240–46). Despite his reluctance, at her insistence Antipas set sail for Rome, accompanied by Herodias (*Ant.* 18.247). There he discovered that Agrippa had sent letters of accusation against him (*Ant.* 18.247–51). Gaius, accepting the charges by Agrippa, banished Antipas to Lugdunum (Josephus, *J.W.* 2.181–83, says Spain, and there was a Lugdunum on the border of Spain, but *Ant.* 18.252 corrects this to Lugdunum in Gaul). Since Herodias was Agrippa's sister, Gaius offered her the opportunity to keep her property and not go into exile, but she stood by her husband (*Ant.* 18.254–55). Herodias's pestering Antipas to ask for kingship fits well with Matthew and Mark's account of her relationship with her husband in the execution of John (Jensen, *Herod Antipas*, 123). Antipas's tetrarchy was given to Agrippa (Josephus, *Ant.* 18.252).

Interpreters have presented two pictures of Antipas: either a ruler who brought a peaceful reign with economic prosperity and served as a buffer against excesses of Roman rule, offsetting the disadvantages of a Hellenistic style monarchy; or a passive, indecisive ruler whose realm seethed with political and economic conflict. The evidence is too limited to support either picture of Antipas and his reign (Jensen, *Herod Antipas*, 252–59).

Philip (Tetrarch 4 BC–AD 33/34)

Philip was born about 20 BC to Herod and Cleopatra of Jerusalem (Josephus, *J.W.* 1.562). Like his brothers he was brought up in Rome (Josephus, *Ant.* 17.21). Antipater's slanders turned his father against Philip, at least for a time (*Ant.* 17.80, 146). Philip appears to have been close to Archelaus, who, when he went to Rome to claim the kingship, left him to look after affairs (*J.W.* 2.14; *Ant.* 17.219). At the urging of Varus, governor of Syria, Philip too went to Rome to support Archelaus's cause and if that failed to seek his share of Herod's estate (*J.W.* 2.83; *Ant.* 17.303).

The tetrarchy assigned to Philip by Augustus covered the regions north and east of the Sea of Galilee—Batanea, Trachonitis, Auranitis, the neighborhood of Paneas, Gaulanitis, and Iturea (Josephus, *J.W.* 2.95; *Ant.* 17.189, 319; Luke 3:1). When Jesus withdrew from the territory of Antipas, he went into Philip's realm (Richardson, *Herod*, 301–5). The majority of the population of Philip's territory was non-Jewish.

According to Josephus, Philip married Herodias's daughter Salome (*Ant.* 18.137)—if this is not a mistake on Josephus's part (Kokkinos, *Herodian Dynasty*, 266–67). Philip died childless at Bethsaida (Josephus, *Ant.* 18.108).

Philip's poorer territory did not permit the building programs of his father or even Antipas, but he did rebuild Caesarea in the district of Paneas (Caesarea

Philippi; Matt. 16:13; Mark 8:27) and Bethsaida Julias (Josephus, *J.W.* 2.168; *Ant.* 18.28). The coins he issued reflected his realm's non-Jewish population by carrying a human image and depicting the facade of a temple (Jensen, *Herod Antipas*, 198–200). An anecdote about how he proved the true source of the Jordan River shows his scientific curiosity (Josephus, *J.W.* 3.512).

5.7. Ruins of a portion of Herod Philip's and Herod Agrippa II's palace at Caesarea Philippi, first century AD.

Josephus acknowledges that Philip ruled well: "In his conduct of the government he showed a moderate and easygoing disposition. Indeed, he spent all his time in the territory subject to him" (*Ant.* 18.106). Philip carried his throne with him as he traveled about his territory, and when a petitioner approached him, he set up the throne and gave judgment (*Ant.* 18.197).

On Philip's death, Tiberius annexed his tetrarchy to Syria (Josephus, *Ant.* 18.108), but Gaius then gave it to King Agrippa I (*Ant.* 18.237), and eventually Claudius assigned it to Agrippa II (*Ant.* 20.138).

Herod Agrippa I (King AD 37–44)

Aristobulus, son of Herod the Great and Mariamme and so with Hasmonean blood, and Berenice, daughter of Herod's sister Salome, had five children: Herodias (who married Antipas), Mariamme, Agrippa I, Herod of Chalcis, and Aristobulus II (Josephus, *J.W.* 1.552). When Agrippa was three, his father and his father's brother were executed, and his mother took him and his siblings to Rome, where she was close to Antonia the Younger, daughter of Mark Antony and mother of the future emperor

Claudius. Agrippa grew up with Drusus the Younger (Tiberius's son) and Claudius (Schwartz, *Agrippa I*, chap. 2.1; Kokkinos, *Herodian Dynasty*, 264, 271). With his wife, Cyprus, granddaughter of Herod's brother Phasael, Agrippa had five children—a son who died young, Agrippa II, and three daughters, the last of whom was Drusilla (Josephus, *J.W.* 2.220; *Ant.* 20.104; Kokkinos, *Herodian Dynasty*, 276–77).

According to Josephus, "Agrippa was naturally noble in spirit and lavish in giving" (*Ant.* 18.144). After Berenice died, his extravagances reduced him to poverty, and he left Rome to return to Judea (*Ant.* 18.145–47). Despondent, he considered suicide, but his wife deterred him (*Ant.* 18.147–48). In response to an appeal from her, Herodias and Antipas gave him the position of commissioner of markets in Tiberias (*Ant.* 18.149). Finding the taunts of his brother-in-law concerning his dependent status unbearable, Agrippa went to live with the governor of Syria, with whom he had been close in Rome (*Ant.* 18.150–51).

The governor of Syria broke off his friendship with Agrippa, who in dire financial difficulties returned to Rome. A generous loan from Antonia rescued the spendthrift Agrippa (Josephus, *Ant.* 18.155–66), who now cultivated friendship with her grandson Gaius. Agrippa expressed the desire that Gaius would soon succeed Tiberius as master of the world (Josephus presents two different circumstances in which the wish was expressed, in *J.W.* 2.179 and *Ant.* 18.168). The remark was reported to Tiberius, who indignantly imprisoned Agrippa (*J.W.* 2.180; *Ant.* 18.169, 186–90).

When Tiberius died six months later (AD 37), Gaius Caligula released Agrippa; in a stunning reversal of fortunes he appointed Agrippa king over the former tetrarchies of Philip and Lysanias and gave him a gold chain of equal weight to his iron one (Josephus, *J.W.* 2.181; *Ant.* 18.237).

Returning to the East the following year to take up his kingdom, Agrippa passed through Alexandria. There the anti-Jewish elements in the population made fun of the king, even dressing up a well-known lunatic as a king and addressing him as "lord" in Aramaic. The prefect Flaccus indirectly if not openly encouraged the insults. Agrippa left the city, but riots ensued, with many calling for the setting up of images in the synagogues (Philo, *Flacc.* 25–43).

The banishment of Antipas in AD 39 resulted in Agrippa's returning to Rome to receive from Gaius Caligula an enlargement of his territory to include Galilee and Perea (Josephus, *J.W.* 2.183; *Ant.* 18.252). On passing through Alexandria again on his journey east, Agrippa received and transmitted the petition of the Alexandrian Jews to Gaius (Philo, *Flacc.* 103), thus playing a significant role in Flaccus's downfall while showing himself an advocate of Jews in the Diaspora (as did his grandfather; Schwartz, *Agrippa I*, chap. 3.2).

Agrippa soon had another opportunity to defend the rights of Jews to Gaius, this time in Jerusalem. The emperor had the mad idea of having a statue of himself set up in the temple. Two wildly different versions of Agrippa's role in the episode (Josephus, *Ant.* 18.289–301; Philo, *Legat.* 261–333) agree that the Jewish king through his friendship with Gaius had a decisive influence in Gaius's withdrawing the plan and thereby averting what could have provoked a Jewish uprising a generation earlier than it occurred in AD 66 (Schwartz, *Agrippa I*, chap. 3.3, who offers a third scenario of what happened). Gaius Caligula's death ended the episode (Tacitus, *Hist.* 5.9).

Sources presumably coming from Agrippa's court circles give him an exaggerated and unlikely part in the accession of Claudius. Agrippa, still in Rome, is presented as the mediator between Claudius and the Senate (Josephus, *J.W.* 2.206–13), persuading Claudius to take the crown (Josephus, *Ant.* 19.236) and not to attack the Senate (*Ant.* 19.265). Claudius confirmed Agrippa's kingship and his brother Herod as king of Chalcis, enlarging Agrippa's kingdom to include Judea, Samaria, and other territories to equal the lands ruled by his grandfather (*J.W.* 2.214; *Ant.* 19.274–75), and bestowed on him the rank of consul and on Herod the rank of praetor (Dio Cassius, *Hist.* 60.8.2).

Agrippa went to Jerusalem to take over his kingdom, and he dedicated at the temple the gold chain that Gaius Caligula had given him "that it might serve as a proof both that greatness may sometime crash and that God uplifts fallen fortunes" (Josephus, *Ant.* 19.292–96). Agrippa began to surround Jerusalem with an outer wall (Josephus, *J.W.* 2.214; described in 5.147–55), but when rumors of revolt arose, Claudius ordered him to desist (*Ant.* 19.326–27). On another occasion Agrippa aroused suspicions by Roman authorities: he entertained five eastern client kings (including his brother Herod of Chalcis) at Tiberias, but the new governor of Syria thought such a meeting was not in Roman interests and ordered each of the kings to return to his own territory (*Ant.* 19.338–42).

Josephus designates Herod Agrippa "the Great" (*Ant.* 18.110, 142), but in the context of other family members, this may indicate only his seniority over Agrippa II. Josephus compares him with his grandfather Herod the Great as being of gentler disposition and more of a benefactor to the Jews, in contrast to his grandfather's "evil nature, relentless in punishment and unsparing . . . against the objects of his hatred" (*Ant.* 19.328–30).

Agrippa's coins minted in Jerusalem retain features of Jewish coinage, but those minted elsewhere continue pagan style, including his own head (Jensen, *Herod Antipas*, 201–2). In inscriptions Agrippa is called "king" and "friend of the emperor"; he is called "great" on his coins and in inscriptions. Inscriptions give his full Roman name, Marcus Julius Agrippa (Richardson, *Herod*, 209–10).

Josephus reflects the favorable Jewish opinion of Agrippa, no doubt exaggerating: "He scrupulously observed the traditions of his people. He neglected no rite of purification, and no day passed for him without the prescribed sacrifice" (*Ant.* 19.331). King Agrippa became a "stock figure" in rabbinic literature. The anecdotes about him have little historical value but are important as reflecting the estimate of him as a prudent ruler, willing to give up some of his usual privileges but thereby receiving greater praise. The rabbinic literature supports Josephus's view of him as "loving honor" but not his picture of Agrippa as an observant Jew, for he is linked only with the "showy externals of the Temple cult" (Schwartz, *Agrippa I*, chap. 6.4). Caligula's estimate of his seeking to please the Jews (reported by Philo, *Legat.* 332) matches Acts 12:1–3. The use of "Herod" for him in Acts 12:1, 21, contrary to the usual designation "Agrippa," is likely Luke's linking him with his grandfather's cruelty in suppressing dissent and with his gruesome death.

The account in Acts 12:20–23 of Agrippa's being hailed as a god and then struck down and eaten by worms is told more fully in Josephus. Both accounts attribute his death to his accepting divine honors from his gentile subjects (Schwartz, *Agrippa I*, chap. 6.1). Josephus elaborates on his radiant garments, his not rebuking the flattery of him as "more than a mortal," and especially his painful death (*Ant*. 19.343–50), which occurred in mid-AD 44 (Kokkinos, *Herodian Dynasty*, 378–80). Reasonable guesses of the medical cause of death are clotting of the blood supply to the abdominal organs or a gastric/duodenal ulcer (Schwartz, *Agrippa I*, appendix 10).

> ### Herod Agrippa's Death
>
> "[In Caesarea] he celebrated spectacles in honor of Caesar. . . . On the second day of the spectacles, clad in a garment woven completely of silver, . . . he entered the theatre at daybreak. There the silver, illumined by the touch of the first rays of the sun, was wondrously radiant and by its glitter inspired fear and awe in those who gazed intently upon it. Straightway his flatterers raised their voices from various directions, . . . addressing him as a god. . . . He felt a stab of pain in his heart. He was also gripped in his stomach by an ache that he felt everywhere at once and that was intense from the start. . . . Exhausted after five straight days by the pain in his abdomen, he departed this life in the fifty-fourth year of his life and the seventh of his reign." (Josephus, *Ant*. 19.343–45, 346, 350)

On Agrippa's death Judea was placed under procurators, and authority over the temple, holy vessels, and selection of the high priest was given to Herod of Chalcis (Josephus, *Ant*. 20.15), but custody of the high priest's robe was turned over to the Romans (*Ant*. 15.405).

Agrippa II (King AD 49/50–100)

Because of his youth at Agrippa I's death, Agrippa II did not succeed his father (Josephus, *Ant*. 19.360–62). Claudius gave the territory of Herod of Chalcis (died in AD 48) to him in 49 (*Ant*. 20.104). In AD 53 Claudius transferred him from Chalcis to the territory of Philip and Lysanias (Josephus, *J.W.* 2.247; *Ant*. 20.138). Nero added four cities to his realm, including Tiberias (Josephus, *J.W.* 2.252; *Ant*. 20.159; *Life* 38).

Being pro-Roman but regarded by the Romans as an expert on Jewish affairs thrust Agrippa II into an ambiguous role. His kingdom was a mixed population of Jews and Syrians (Josephus, *J.W.* 3.57). Josephus describes Agrippa II and all his family as "persons thoroughly conversant with Hellenic culture" (*Life* 359). He was given responsibility for overseeing religious affairs at the Jerusalem temple. He appointed high priests (Josephus, *Ant*. 20.179, 213), and he deposed Ananus for the stoning of James the brother of Jesus (*Ant*. 20.200–203). Thus he maintained a palace in Jerusalem (*Ant*. 20.189–93). He embellished the pagan cities of

Paneas (*J.W.* 3.514) and Beirut, in the latter case angering the Jews because of his expenditures there (*Ant.* 20.211–12). Yet he supplied the materials for enlarging the Jerusalem temple, a project interrupted by the revolt in 66 (*J.W.* 5.36).

Agrippa II gave his sister Drusilla in marriage to the king of Emesa, who consented to circumcision (Josephus, *Ant.* 20.139). She left him to become the wife of Governor Felix (Acts 24:24). There were rumors that Agrippa II lived in an incestuous relationship with his older sister Berenice (Juvenal, *Sat.* 6.157–58; Kokkinos, *Herodian Dynasty*, 321–22). They were together when they met Paul in Acts 25:13–26:32. Agrippa II left no children.

During the First Jewish Revolt of 66–73 Agrippa II consistently supported the Romans while trying to protect Jews not involved in the revolt. Josephus records a long speech by the king at Jerusalem to dissuade the Jews from war (*J.W.* 2.344–407), no doubt Josephus's own composition. Agrippa II, "anxious that the Romans should not lose the Jews nor the Jews their temple and mother city," sent troops to aid the pro-Roman element in the population (*J.W.* 2.241), but the insurgents prevailed. He also supplied troops to assist Cestius, governor of Syria, in putting down the revolt and personally accompanied Cestius to guide him (*J.W.* 2.500, 502). Agrippa II attempted a parley with the rebels, but the insurgents assaulted the king's embassy (*J.W.* 2.523–26).

Agrippa II sent auxiliaries with Vespasian, whom he entertained at Caesarea Philippi (Josephus, *J.W.* 3.68, 443). Out of regard for Agrippa II, Vespasian forbade his troops to pillage Tiberias (*J.W.* 3.461). For his part, Agrippa II induced some cities not to revolt (*J.W.* 4.4).

When Titus, representing his father, Vespasian, left for Rome to salute Nero's successor Galba, Agrippa II accompanied him. Galba was assassinated, so Titus turned back, but Agrippa II went on to greet Otho. Titus was now the lover of Berenice, but social and political pressure in Rome forced him to send her away (Kokkinos, *Herodian Dynasty*, 329–30).

Agrippa II's army followed Titus for his final attack on Jerusalem in AD 70 (Tacitus, *Hist.* 5.1.2). Later Josephus presented Agrippa II a copy of his history of the Jewish war (Josephus, *Life* 362; *Ag. Ap.* 1.5). He claimed that Agrippa II wrote letters testifying to his accuracy (*Life* 364–66).

Agrippa II died in AD 100 (Kokkinos, *Herodian Dynasty*, 396–99), and with him died the place of the Herods in the world of the NT.

Bibliography

Charlesworth, Martin Percival. *Five Men: Character Studies from the Roman Empire*. Martin Classical Lectures 6. Freeport, NY: Books for Libraries, 1936. The first of these lectures (pp. 3–30) by a noted classical historian takes Agrippa I as an example of a "native ruler."

Grant, Michael. *Herod the Great*. New York: American Heritage Press, 1972. Eminent numismatist and classicist, Grant wrote several popular biographies of figures from ancient history for educated lay readers. Herod was a shrewd and consummate politician who became paranoid.

Hoehner, Harold W. *Herod Antipas: A Contemporary of Jesus Christ*. Cambridge: Cambridge University Press, 1972. Repr., Grand Rapids: Zondervan, 1980. A standard biographical treatment, conservative in its conclusions on NT texts.

Holum, Kenneth G., et al. *King Herod's Dream: Caesarea on the Sea*. New York: Norton, 1988. A history of Strato's Tower/Caesarea through Crusader times and its modern excavation with stunning color photographs. Chapters on Herod's city and on Roman Caesarea.

Jensen, Morten Hørning. *Herod Antipas in Galilee*. 2nd ed. WUNT 2/215. Tübingen: Mohr Siebeck, 2010. Brings more recent archaeological discoveries and sociological models to bear on the circumstances in Galilee in the first century. Also gives a literary analysis of how Josephus organized and presented his material.

Jones, A. H. M. *The Herods of Judaea*. Oxford: Clarendon, 1938. Covers Antipater through Agrippa II. Contains a chronological chart and a foldout chart of the Herodian family.

Knoblet, Jerry. *Herod the Great*. Lanham, MD: University Press of America, 2005. A well-researched but uncritical and popularly presented life, which includes a defense of the historicity of Luke 2:1–3 and the slaughter of the infants at Bethlehem (Matt. 2:1–23). Appendixes present the Herodian family, a chronology of Herod's life, and an evaluation of Josephus, seeing him as biased in favor of Herod.

Kokkinos, Nikos. *The Herodian Dynasty: Origins, Role in Society and Eclipse*. JSPSup 30. Sheffield: Sheffield Academic Press, 1998. Kokkinos writes as a classical historian using literary and nonliterary sources, emphasizing the extent of Hellenization of the Herodian family. Concentrates on the lesser-known family members.

Mahieu, B. *Between Rome and Jerusalem: Herod the Great and His Sons in Their Struggle for Recognition; A Chronological Investigation of the Period 40 BC–39 AD, with a Time Setting of New Testament Events*. Louvain: Peeters, 2011. Provides altered dates for Herod the Great and his sons, placing the birth and death of Jesus a few years later than is commonly accepted. He shows that the Roman impact on the East was substantial, as was Hellenistic influence on local cultures.

Netzer, Ehud. *The Architecture of Herod the Great Builder*. Tübingen: Mohr Siebeck, 2006. Repr., Grand Rapids: Baker Academic, 2008. Presents Herod's major building projects—including Masada, Jericho, Samaria, Caesarea Maritima, the temple in Jerusalem, and Herodium—and a topical discussion of the planning of palaces, temples, sport and entertainment facilities, and cities. Chapters consider architectural influences from the Greco-Roman world and Herod's personal involvement in the projects.

Perowne, Stewart. *The Later Herods: The Political Background of the New Testament*. New York: Abingdon, 1958. The subtitle gives the main content of the book. The descendants of Herod tried to achieve a *modus vivendi* between the Jews and the Romans but failed.

———. *The Life and Times of Herod the Great*. New York: Abingdon, 1956. Upholds a positive appreciation of Herod's outstanding ability, loyalty to his family and Roman friends, and achievements, and places his negative qualities in the contexts of a brutal and violent age, the effects of his illness in his last years, and his own insensitivity to Jewish spirituality.

Richardson, Peter. *Herod: King of the Jews and Friend of the Romans*. Columbia: University of South Carolina Press, 1996. Repr., Minneapolis: Fortress, 1999. Takes seriously both roles of Herod expressed in the subtitle, which set up the tension in which he and his family lived. Incorporating insights from social history and archaeology, Richardson offers a "somewhat more generous assessment" than is often given.

Schürer, Emil. *The History of the Jewish People in the Age of Jesus Christ (175 BC–AD 135).* Revised and edited by Geza Vermes, Fergus Millar, and Martin Goodman. Revised English ed. 3 vols. in 4 parts. Edinburgh: T&T Clark, 1987. A long standard history for its thoroughness, now brought up to date as of the time of publication, this work gives important treatments of each of the major Herodians as part of the larger history.

Schwartz, Daniel R. *Agrippa I: The Last King of Judaea.* Tübingen: Mohr Siebeck, 1990. A principal concern is Josephus's sources and how he used them. By differences in viewpoint and vocabulary, Schwartz identifies hypothetical sources employed by Josephus and uses these to reconstruct the story of Agrippa, who was probably instrumental in showing the Romans that Christians were not Jews and whose major contribution to Jewish existence as a tolerated religion came despite himself in leading to Judaism as a religion and not a political state.

6

Monotheism

NATHAN MACDONALD

The Jewish religion, as Greek and Roman observers were aware, was distinctive within the ancient world. The Roman senator and historian Tacitus (AD 56–117) succinctly describes the peculiarities as follows: "The Jews acknowledge one God only, of whom they have a purely spiritual conception" (*Hist.* 5.5).[1] In a world where the worship of numerous deities was otherwise universal, outside observers were astonished by these two features of Jewish worship. First, Jews believed that their God was unique, and second, they rejected representing him by an image. Jewish writers of the same period were equally insistent about their distinctive religious perspective. The *Letter of Aristeas* (ca. second century BC), for example, describes how Moses "taught that God is one" and "beginning from these premises he went on to shew that all other men except our nation consider that there are many gods" (*Let. Aris.* 132–35).[2] This worship of many gods is equated with the worship of images (*Let. Aris.* 135–38). So distinctive were such views that Jewish apologists sometimes had to deny accusations that these beliefs made them antisocial and atheistic (e.g., Tacitus, *Hist.* 5.4–5).[3] These basic and

---

1. Translation according to *Tacitus: The Histories* (trans. W. H. Fyfe and D. S. Levene; Oxford World's Classics; Oxford: Oxford University Press, 1997).
2. Translation according to H. St. J. Thackeray, *The Letter of Aristeas* (London: SPCK, 1917).
3. For other Greco-Roman perspectives on Judaism, see M. Whittaker, *Jews and Christians: Greco-Roman Views* (Cambridge: Cambridge University Press, 1984).

nonnegotiable characteristics of Jewish religion during this period can be labeled as "monotheism" and were an essential part of the Jewish heritage that the early Christians presupposed.

The Term "Monotheism"

Although the term "monotheism" captures this essential distinctiveness of Jewish belief in the ancient world, recent scholarship has insisted that the term must be used with care. The word itself was coined only in 1660, by the Cambridge theologian and philosopher Henry More. The use of a modern word to describe ancient religious belief is not in itself a problem, but since it was first used the term has been at the center of philosophical and religious discussion, as it continues to be in the present. Whether used of rational and universal religion in the Enlightenment or discussed in the recent angst about the relation between religious belief and extremist violence, the word "monotheism" often brings associations far removed from the world of first-century AD Judaism. There is a need to be hermeneutically aware when using the word and contemplating its possible associations. Two particular difficulties are worth noting. First, the dictionary definition of the term, "the belief in only one God," tends to emphasize theological conceptuality to the detriment of religious practice. Second, the term "monotheism" is often taken to exclude the existence of other semidivine beings, such as angels. Used in this way the term "monotheism" would exclude virtually everyone in the ancient world.[4]

Although some scholars have argued that the term "monotheism" is no longer usable in the study of early Judaism and Christianity, the term has some value as a way of speaking about the distinctiveness of early Judaism. When the term "monotheism" is used of ancient religious beliefs and practices, however, its meaning must be determined by a careful examination of what ancient writers said and did. In this respect we should also bear in mind that monotheism was not a fixed concept; monotheistic belief and practice could and did change over time. Different groups and individuals understood its moral, social, and political entailments in diverse ways.

Monotheism and Ancient Israel

First-century Jews were heirs of a long history of religious development and change. Over the last thirty years OT scholarship has emphasized that the emergence of monotheism in ancient Israel was not a sudden event, the result of an intuitive insight or external influence, but the product of many centuries of indigenous religious development. Although the biblical texts attribute the Ten

---

4. See esp. the essays by R. W. L. Moberly and Nathan MacDonald in Stuckenbruck and North, eds., *Early Jewish and Christian Monotheism*.

Commandments—including the prohibition of the worship of other gods and the making of idols—to God's revelation to Moses, many OT scholars hold that something akin to monotheism appeared only in the Babylonian exile many centuries later, in the sixth century BC. Whereas Yhwh was the principal deity in preexilic Israel, archaeological finds (e.g., the inscriptions from Kuntillet ʿAjrud) and the biblical text (e.g., 1–2 Kings) show that worship of other deities took place among Judahites and Israelites and that the worship of Yhwh was not always of a kind that would later be considered orthodox. A number of modern scholars have argued that a minority "Yhwh-alone party" began in the ninth century BC as a response to the introduction of Phoenician religious practices during the Omride dynasty. This group achieved some political success in the late Judean Kingdom, especially during Josiah's reign, which saw some of the Yhwh-alone agenda put into practice. It was during the disaster of the exile, however, that the decisive breakthrough to monotheism was achieved, probably by the exilic prophet who wrote Isa. 40–55, although Ezekiel and the author of Deut. 4 have also been proposed.[5]

In this critically reconstructed history the emphasis on Yhwh as unique occurs only toward the end of what is typically thought of as Israel's history. Our perspectives on Israel's history tend to be influenced by the canonical portrayal such that we think of Israel's history largely in terms of the period between Moses and the fall of Jerusalem, that is, the time marked out between the books of Exodus and 2 Kings. This might lead us to think that only a small proportion of the OT literature is characterized by the perspective of monotheism. Such a view might appear to find confirmation in the relatively small number of explicitly monotheistic statements in the OT. It is increasingly being recognized, however, that the vast proportion of the OT literature was composed, collected, and edited after the Babylonian exile, during the Persian period. The OT, therefore, reflects the belief in Yhwh's uniqueness throughout its different parts. This is not to say, however, that scholars cannot detect earlier material with a somewhat different religious perspective from the literary context in which they now belong.

The expressions of monotheism in the OT are by no means unified, and we can identify at least four distinguishable strands.[6] First, there are texts strongly informed by Deuteronomistic conceptuality, such as Deuteronomy, the historical books from Joshua to 2 Kings, Jeremiah, and Isa. 40–55. Israel's unique relationship to Yhwh is emphasized, especially as it has been realized through covenant and Israel's history. There is a vigorous rejection of the worship of other gods and an

---

5. For two recent presentations of Israel's religious development from two different perspectives, see Smith, *Biblical Monotheism*; and Sommer, "Monotheism." The overview of scholarship in Robert Karl Gnuse, *No Other Gods: Emergent Monotheism in Israel* (JSOTSup 241; Sheffield: Sheffield Academic Press, 1997), is useful, even if Gnuse's overall framing of the issues is sometimes problematic.

6. See Fritz Stolz, *Einführung in den biblischen Monotheismus* [Introduction to biblical monotheism] (Darmstadt: Wissenschaftliche Buchgesellschaft, 1996).

emphasis on Yhwh's incomparability. Second, there are texts that reflect a priestly provenance, such as the priestly document discernible in Genesis to Leviticus and in Ezekiel. The reconstructed priestly document offers a more inclusivist vision, portraying God as the creator of humanity in his image and structuring history around various dispensations characterized by the names God revealed. At the center of God's world is the Israelite cult, through which God makes himself present to Israel and, by extension, the rest of humanity. Third, there are wisdom texts. Conveniently for their Israelite reception, the ANE wisdom traditions had always couched their instructions in relation to divinity in general, rather than to specific deities. This international culture of wisdom writings was appropriated within Israelite circles and at some point was placed into a Yahwistic framework (e.g., Prov. 1–9). Finally, apocalyptic thinking was a distinctive development within the prophetic tradition. It emphasized Yhwh's control of history and portrayed evil as a necessary means to expose and destroy the wicked and, at the same time, to test and vindicate the righteous. In apocalyptic writings, the uniqueness and sovereignty of Yhwh could be held alongside the belief in numerous other divine beings.

These different monotheistic theologies appropriated and responded to earlier Israelite traditions in different ways. Thus, whereas angelic messengers appear occasionally in the historical books from Joshua to 2 Kings, they are rather more prominent in the nonpriestly stories of Genesis and even more so in later prophetic and early apocalyptic literature. Additionally, these four main strands should be regarded as neither an exhaustive list nor independent of one another. Already within the OT there is evidence of mutual influence and partial integration. Two examples may suffice. First, in the final form of the Pentateuch, Deuteronomic and priestly theologies are brought together, especially in the Holiness Code (Lev. 17–26) and the book of Numbers. Second, the polemic against idols that is characteristic of Deuteronomy and especially Isa. 40–55 is incorporated into the wisdom tradition (see Wis. 13–15).

The partial integration of these monotheistic theologies is part of the strong textual consciousness, or intertextuality, that developed within Israel. From at least the late seventh century BC, authoritative writings and a tradition of scribal interpretation and rewriting existed within Israel. This text-consciousness increased with time and would eventually lead to a closed list of canonical books. It is within this growing consciousness of a scriptural canon that both the monotheism of the OT that we have already examined and subsequent developments within Jewish monotheism should be seen. Later readers wrestled with the diversity of texts that had authoritative claim on their communities within the challenges of their own historical and social contexts. Whatever the complex history of those texts and the origins of monotheism in Israel, ancient Jews lacked any sense of this religious development. They understood all of their sacred Scriptures as an account of the activities of the one God, his relationship to his people, and his instructions for how to behave. They consequently sought to understand the diversity of ancient witnesses to Israel's God as a coherent revelation. Various exegetical techniques developed that allowed the texts to be read as a unity and to have application beyond their original context of composition. The complexity of subsequent Jewish belief about God—and the controversy among Jews and between Jews and Christians—can in large part be related to the multifaceted nature of their authoritative Scriptures.

The Hellenistic and Roman Periods

Some of the developments that we have described, such as the initial steps within prophecy toward apocalypticism and the integration of different monotheistic theologies, continued into the early Hellenistic period. For more than a century after Alexander the Great's conquest of Palestine (333–332 BC), the replacement of the Persian imperial power with a Greek one appears to have posed no significant difficulties for Jews. Our sources for this period are limited, but they tend to suggest that the penetration of Greek culture and ideas was slow, if persistent, and that the new overlords were not felt to be any more threatening than those that had preceded them. For some Jews it was possible to describe Israel's supreme deity in terms reminiscent of Zeus, the high god of the Greek pantheon, just as earlier Jews and the Persian authorities shared the language of "the God of heaven" (e.g., Ezra 7:12).[7] However, the attempt by the Seleucid monarch Antiochus IV Epiphanes (175–164 BC) to suppress Judaism and assimilate Judea to Hellenistic culture provoked the Maccabean revolt and produced a stronger emphasis on the uniqueness of Israel's God. The rejection of Hellenization starkly defined Judaism as an exclusive commitment to Yhwh alone and his law.

In the first century AD the commitment to Yhwh and his law was expressed most especially through the regular recital of the Shema from Deuteronomy: "Hear, O Israel, Yhwh our God, Yhwh is one. So, you shall love Yhwh your God with all your heart, all your soul, and all your strength" (Deut. 6:4–5, author's translation). The subsequent instructions require that the commandments are "to be upon your hearts," taught to children, and the topic of regular conversation (vv. 6–7). The requirement that the commandments be bound on the hands, before the eyes, and placed on the doorposts and gates (vv. 8–9) was realized through the use of *tefillin* and *mezuzot* (small leather boxes and cases containing verses from Torah). The daily recital of the Shema was accompanied by prayers. The commandments that the Shema enjoined to be repeated are most obviously the Ten Commandments (Deut. 5), but in a wider sense the whole of the Mosaic Torah. Israel's belief in one God was expressed in obedience to Torah. This was particularly the case with the distinctive markers of Jewish religion that had been so contentious during the

7. For discussion, see James K. Aitken, "The God of the Pre-Maccabees: Designation of the Divine in the Early Hellenistic Period," in *The God of Israel* (ed. Robert P. Gordon; UCOP 64; Cambridge: Cambridge University Press, 2007), 246–66.

reign of Antiochus IV. All males were circumcised on the eighth day. The biblical purity laws were followed, not least the dietary laws. The Sabbath was kept, and Jews met together at the synagogue for study and prayer.

Jewish devotion to God focused especially around the Jerusalem temple. A single site of cultic worship was thought to be concomitant with belief in one deity (Philo, *Spec.* 1.67; Josephus, *Ant.* 4.200–201). God was believed to manifest his presence there, and particular care was taken for the ritual purity of worshipers. Whereas temples for other gods could be tolerated elsewhere, even within the boundaries of Palestine, there were particular sensitivities about Jerusalem, as also for the presence of images in the city.

It has been plausibly argued that one of the most defining features of Jewish monotheism was its restriction of cultic worship, including animal sacrifices, to the one God of Israel alone (Hurtado, *One God*; idem, *Lord Jesus Christ*). A belief in angels, demons, and even gods was not excluded—it was arguably demanded by scriptural texts that referred to these divine beings—but they were not to receive cultic worship. Divine agents, such as high angels and even exalted human beings, could receive veneration from humans. They received honorific titles and prayers; and literary texts portray human beings prostrating themselves before divine agents. The line between veneration and worship is notoriously thin, not only for modern scholarship, but also for ancient Jewish writers. The challenge of maintaining this distinction was expressed in a common literary motif where a human mistakes an angelic messenger for God himself and begins to offer worship. The angel refuses this and directs the human to worship God (e.g., Tob. 12:16–22; *Apoc. Zeph.* 6.11–15). The potential for confusion thus offers an opportunity to affirm the uniqueness of Israel's God. Although early Christian worship of Jesus of Nazareth has been explained by analogy to the devotion that angels or exalted humans received, there is considerable debate about whether this is the correct precursor, or whether the worship of Jesus is a unique development comparable only to the worship of the one God.

Since Jewish monotheism did not exclude the existence of other divine beings, but rather insisted that Israel's God was unique and alone deserving of worship, there was considerable scope for metaphysical speculation about the existence and nature of angels, demons, and the heavenly realm. Such speculations can be found in a variety of literature, not least in apocalyptic texts. Many of the ideas, though not all, can be seen to derive from biblical exegesis as writers of the Second Temple period wrestled with authoritative texts, whose content, as we have seen, was often complex and opaque.[8] Similar speculations also arose around the biblical references to God's spirit, word, name, glory, and so forth. These sometimes appear to have been viewed as quasi-independent or even fully independent beings.

---

8. See, e.g., Saul M. Olyan, *A Thousand Thousands Served Him: Exegesis and the Naming of Angels in Ancient Judaism* (TSAJ 36; Tübingen: Mohr Siebeck, 1993).

Pagan Monotheism

The importance of Jewish monotheism as the matrix for the development of the distinctive Christian devotion and theology should not cause us to neglect the presence of what some have called "pagan monotheism." Recent study has emphasized that the rise of Christianity and decline of paganism was not a simple story of monotheism versus polytheism. Since the pre-Socratics (sixth–fifth centuries BC) there had been philosophical speculation about the ultimate principle of reality that lay behind the world of the gods, or about the highest god. These monotheistic tendencies are probably better described as a form of henotheism and were mostly restricted to certain intellectual circles. Nevertheless, they seem to have become increasingly more important, and in the first few centuries AD, at the earliest, such trends began to be expressed in religious practices. For some Jewish thinkers, these philosophical beliefs provided an attractive point of commonality and became part of their attempts to explain Jewish beliefs to their pagan contemporaries. Similar moves can also be discerned among later Christian apologists (see Athanassiadi and Frede, *Pagan Monotheism*; Mitchell and van Nuffelen, *One God*).

Bibliography

Athanassiadi, Polymnia, and Michael Frede, eds. *Pagan Monotheism in Late Antiquity*. Oxford: Clarendon, 1999. Examines pagan monotheism, focusing particularly on the philosophical tradition.

Bauckham, Richard. *Jesus and the God of Israel: God Crucified and Other Studies on the New Testament's Christology of Divine Identity*. Grand Rapids: Eerdmans, 2009. Explores what it means to refer to Jesus as "divine."

Hurtado, Larry W. *Lord Jesus Christ: Devotion to Jesus in Earliest Christianity*. Grand Rapids: Eerdmans, 2003. Examines the worship of Jesus Christ from AD 30 to 170.

———. *One God, One Lord: Early Christian Devotion and Ancient Jewish Monotheism*. Philadelphia: Fortress, 1988. An earlier, influential work.

Mitchell, Stephen, and Peter van Nuffelen, eds. *One God: Pagan Monotheism in the Roman Empire*. Cambridge: Cambridge University Press, 2010. Attempts to move beyond Athanassiadi and Frede's *Pagan Monotheism in Late Antiquity* by considering pagan monotheism as a religious phenomenon.

Newman, Carey, et al., eds. *The Jewish Roots of Christological Monotheism: Papers from the St. Andrews Conference on the Historical Origins of the Worship of Jesus*. JSJSup 63. Leiden: Brill, 1999. Attends to the veneration of mediator figures in Judaism and the early worship of Jesus.

Smith, Mark S. *The Origins of Biblical Monotheism: Israel's Polytheistic Background and the Ugaritic Texts*. New York: Oxford University Press, 2000. An account of the development of monotheism within ancient Israel that reflects the different perspective that has emerged in OT studies since 1980.

Sommer, Benjamin D. "Monotheism and Polytheism in Ancient Israel." Pages 145–74 in *The Bodies of God and the World of Ancient Israel*. Cambridge: Cambridge University Press, 2009. An account of monotheism in ancient Israel that engages the newer perspective on monotheism in ancient Israel but argues that monotheism is a meaningful category for discussing preexilic Israelite religion.

Stuckenbruck, Loren T., and Wendy E. Sproston North, eds. *Early Jewish and Christian Monotheism*. JSNTSup 263. London: T&T Clark, 2004. A collection of essays together with a select bibliography on early Jewish and Christian monotheism.

7

The Scriptures
and Scriptural Interpretation

LIDIJA NOVAKOVIC

For many readers, the terms that appear in the title of this chapter are synonymous with "the Bible" and "biblical interpretation." Both sets of designations are certainly appropriate for the postcanonical period—that is, for the time when the books that compose the HB were universally recognized as uniquely authoritative and binding. Before the second century AD, however, the designations "Bible" and "biblical" would be anachronistic: there was no closed canon of Jewish Scripture. In order to avoid imposing a canonical label on precanonical literature, then, most scholars today prefer the terms "Scripture" and "scriptural" when they discuss the Second Temple period.

The choice of proper terminology, however, is not the only problem we encounter when we examine early Jewish literature. Another, even more complicated issue is a distinction between Scripture and scriptural interpretation. "Scripture" typically refers to the writings that are considered sacred and authoritative by a particular religious community, whereas "scriptural interpretation" includes various activities—oral or written—whose purpose is to explain, elucidate, or make relevant the text of Scripture. This differentiation, which is quite suitable for the postcanonical period, becomes problematic when we try to apply it to the Second Temple literature. The text of Scripture was not fixed, and several text

85

types were in circulation, sometimes even within the same community. The level of scribal interventions into sacred texts varied, from minor explanatory comments to the creation of new compositions. Some of these interpretive writings, such as the book of Chronicles, which rewrites the Deuteronomistic history in the books of Samuel and Kings, were eventually included in the Jewish canon, while others, such as the book of *Jubilees*, which rewrites the narrative of Gen. 1–Exod. 14, were not.

The fluidity of Scripture and the difficulty of distinguishing text from interpretation notwithstanding, a conceptual distinction between Scripture and scriptural interpretation is still a convenient starting point. It allows us to examine, on the one hand, the writings whose scriptural status was acknowledged by most Jewish groups, and on the other hand, the various ways those authoritative traditions were interpreted in Jewish and Christian literature, as well as the level of authority ascribed to them in a particular setting.

The Scriptures

Several references in early Jewish and Christian writings indicate that certain books achieved scriptural status in the late Second Temple period. The prologue to the Greek translation of the Wisdom of Ben Sira, dated to the late second century BC, mentions "the Law and the Prophets and the other books" (see NRSV translation note). According to the *Rule of the Community* (1QS), a foundational Qumran document, the instructor's task is to teach the members of the community to "seek God with a whole heart and soul, and do what is good and right before Him as He commanded by the hand of Moses and all His servants the Prophets" (1QS 1.1–3).[1] The *Halakic Letter* (4QMMT), another Qumran document dated to the second century BC, contains the following statement: "[And] we have [written] to you so that you may study (carefully) the book of Moses and the books of the Prophets and (the writings of) David" (C 10).[2] Luke-Acts frequently mentions the Law and the Prophets (Luke 16:16, 29, 31; 24:27; Acts 26:22; 28:23) and once also the Psalms (Luke 24:44). There are also several references to the number of the sacred writings: *4 Ezra* (14.44–47) mentions ninety-four books (twenty-four public and seventy hidden), for example, and Josephus (*Ag. Ap.* 1.37–43) mentions twenty-two "justly accredited" books (five books of Moses, thirteen prophetic books, and four books of hymns and precepts).

In addition to general references concerning the authority of the Law, the Prophets, and some of the Writings, more than two hundred scriptural manuscripts, commonly labeled "biblical," were discovered in the Judean Desert caves.

---

1. Unless otherwise indicated, English translations of the Qumran documents are from Geza Vermes, *The Complete Dead Sea Scrolls in English* (rev. ed.; New York: Penguin, 2004).
2. Elisha Qimron and John Strugnell, *Miqṣat Maʿaśe ha-Tôrâ* (DJD 10; Oxford: Clarendon, 1994), 58–59.

The Qumran collection includes multiple copies of each of the five pentateuchal books and four scrolls that combine two of them together. The prophetic books are also well represented—for example, Joshua (two copies), Judges (three copies), Samuel (four copies), Kings (three copies), Isaiah (twenty-one copies), Jeremiah (six copies), Ezekiel (five copies), and the Book of the Twelve (eight copies from Qumran and two copies from Naḥal Ḥever and Murabbaʿat). The Psalms were undeniably the most popular books among the Writings, as we can see from the thirty-seven copies of the Psalms found at Qumran, two at Masada, and one at Naḥal Ḥever. The scriptural status of many of these books is additionally substantiated through other compositions that quote or refer to them as works bestowed with special authority. The pentateuchal books are not only frequently quoted in the *Damascus Document* and other Qumran writings but are also the subject of implicit exegesis in various compositions classified as rewritten Scripture. The prophetic books and Psalms are explicitly quoted and commented on in the Qumran pesharim (pl. of *pesher*, "interpretation").

On the basis of this evidence we can conclude that all Jewish groups in the late Second Temple period accepted the Torah, or Pentateuch, as Scripture. It seems that most of the prophetic books, now found in the second division of the HB, were also regarded as authoritative Scripture. (The Samaritans did not accept the prophetic books as authoritative.) The status of the books that now constitute the third division of the HB, the Writings, is much less certain. Many Jews probably viewed the Psalms, Proverbs, and Job as authoritative. The authority of other writings is difficult to determine. On the basis of the fact that no copies of Esther were found among the DSS, we can perhaps conclude that this book did not have scriptural status at Qumran. At the same time, the Qumran community apparently ascribed scriptural authority to some of the writings that did not become part of the Jewish canon, such as the *Apocryphon of Joshua* (4QTestimonia [4Q175] quotes a passage from the *Apocryphon of Joshua* after citations from Exodus, Numbers, and Deuteronomy) and *Jubilees* (cf. CD 16.1–3, which mentions "the Book of the Divisions of the Times").

Textual Pluriformity of Scripture

Qumran biblical manuscripts have also enhanced our knowledge of the transmission process of Scripture in Second Temple Judaism. The date of the copies of scriptural scrolls ranges from the mid-third century BC until the second half of the first century AD. The dominant view before, and for some time after, the Qumran discoveries was that the MT, which provides the basis for the rabbinic canon, became a dominant text form already in the Hasmonean period. As a result, numerous textual disagreements with the MT, which characterize the Qumran biblical manuscripts, were labeled "sectarian" or "vulgar." Eugene Ulrich, however, has shown that "there is nothing in the biblical texts to suggest that they are specific to Qumran or to any particular group within Judaism"

(*Dead Sea Scrolls*, 9). Textual pluriformity at Qumran was not an exception but a common feature of the Second Temple milieu. What is surprising, however, is the preservation of the variant readings of the scriptural books within the same community. No evidence suggests that the Qumranites saw the presence of textual variants as a problem or that the group had a preference for a particular textual tradition. For example, 4Q175 contains a quotation of a passage from Exodus in the pre-Samaritan tradition and a quotation of Deuteronomy in the tradition of the Septuagint and 4QDeut[h]. It seems that, for the scribe of this document, both text types were equally authoritative. Such a pluriformity of textual versions indicates that it was a particular book, and not its textual form, that was considered authoritative (Ulrich, *Dead Sea Scrolls*, 93).

The study of various text forms of scriptural manuscripts has led to the recognition of not only their diversity but also the common features that are shared by some, but not all, manuscripts, which allows grouping them into several text types. Frank Moore Cross has distinguished three textual families on the basis of their geographic provenance: the MT from Babylonia, the Samaritan Pentateuch from Palestine, and the LXX from Egypt (Cross and Talmon, *Qumran*, 193–95). Emanuel Tov, in contrast, divides all texts into two major categories based on their textual characteristics: proto-Masoretic and pre-Samaritan. Tov also acknowledges the group of texts that are close to a presumed Hebrew source of the LXX as well as those that cannot be neatly classified into any of the major categories (E. Tov, *EDSS* 2:833–36).

The proto-Masoretic (or proto-rabbinic) group of texts includes the precursors of the textual forms that were eventually accepted as canonical in the rabbinic period. What binds them together is not a specific set of common textual features but only the fact that they contain the textual antecedents of the rabbinic "received text." The textual history of each individual book is different and must be studied on its own (Ulrich, *Dead Sea Scrolls*, 113–15).

The pre-Samaritan group of texts is characterized by various harmonizations, which occur when a scribe imports the elements from certain passages, typically from Deuteronomy, to the parallel texts in Exodus and Numbers. Harmonization reflects the conviction that different parts of Scripture are in perfect agreement with each other, which is brought to the fore through the production of harmonized, expanded, and sometimes highly repetitive texts. This exegetical technique can be seen as an early form of *gezerah shawah*, a midrashic technique of relating two different scriptural passages based on their common vocabulary or theme.

Canonization of Scripture

It is frequently assumed that the canonization of the Hebrew Scriptures, which took place in the rabbinic period, represents an outcome of the stabilization of the pluriformity of text types that characterized Second Temple Judaism. There is, however, no evidence that the rabbis engaged in a critical evaluation of the existing variants and made a conscious selection of a single version of a scriptural book that would become part of the canon. Their deliberate decisions seem to have been limited to the choice of the texts written in Hebrew rather than those written in or translated into Greek, which were preferred by the early Christians, and the choice of the texts written in "square" script rather than in the Paleo-Hebrew script that was used by the Samaritans. It is therefore more accurate to conclude with Eugene Ulrich that "the text was more 'frozen' than 'stabilized.'"[3] And the closure of the Hebrew canon should not be ascribed to the decisions made by the council of Jamnia (Yavneh) but to the ongoing discussions among the rabbis about the authority of some of the books that make up the third division of the HB.

The Septuagint

The translation of the Hebrew Scriptures into Greek, commonly called the Septuagint (LXX), made the sacred texts accessible to Greek-speaking communities. The LXX was regarded as authoritative Scripture in Hellenistic Judaism and the early church. The name "Septuagint" is a Latin term for "seventy," which derives from the tradition preserved in the *Letter of Aristeas*, a Hellenistic composition from the second century BC. According to this tradition, seventy-two (or seventy) Jewish scholars came from Jerusalem to Alexandria and translated the Torah from Hebrew to Greek for Ptolemy II Philadelphus, who ruled Egypt in the first half of the third century BC. The Aristeas story is also repeated by the Jewish philosopher Philo (*Mos.* 2.25–44) and by Josephus (*Ant.* 12.11–118). Although the accuracy of this tale was questioned as early as the sixteenth century, its historical core probably includes traditions about the chronological priority of the translation of the Pentateuch and its Egyptian provenance. The term "Septuagint" was eventually extended to the Greek translations of all books that compose the HB and of several additional writings, and to a number of original Greek compositions.

There is a considerable variation in quality and style of the Greek translations of the books that are included in the LXX. Some translators closely followed their Hebrew source, while others took various interpretive liberties, including paraphrasing or spiritualizing religiously objectionable concepts, such as anthropomorphic or anthropopathic expressions that seem to assign human attributes or emotions to God. There is also a significant diversity in the text types of the Hebrew (or Aramaic) sources. Some Greek translations are based on the proto-Masoretic text type, while others reflect other Hebrew variants. Not surprisingly, then, older translations were continually revised as readers detected discrepancies between the presumed Hebrew original and the Greek translation. The three best-known revisions (or recensions) are those by Theodotion, Aquila, and Symmachus, dated between the first century BC and the third century AD.

3. Eugene Ulrich, "The Notion and Definition of Canon," in *The Canon Debate* (ed. Lee M. McDonald and James A. Sanders; Peabody, MA: Hendrickson, 2002), 31n34.

Jewish Scriptural Interpretation

The main purpose of Jewish scriptural interpretation was to make the text of Scripture intelligible and relevant to its readers. A distinction between pure and applied exegesis, introduced by Geza Vermes, is especially helpful here. Pure exegesis, he claims, seeks to solve the problems related to the text, such as unclear vocabulary, lack of details, apparent contradiction, or an unacceptable meaning. Its purpose is "to render every word and verse of Scripture intelligible, the whole of it coherent, and its message acceptable and meaningful to the interpreter's contemporaries."[4] Applied exegesis seeks to provide scriptural justification for the problems arising from everyday life or contemporary customs and practices, that is, for problems external to the text itself. It should be kept in mind, however, that a differentiation between pure and applied exegesis is only a helpful analytical tool. For most ancient interpreters, the two types of exegesis were probably inseparable.

Jewish exegetical literature is characterized by diversity, in terms of both literary genres and exegetical techniques. This literature demonstrates, on the one hand, that sacred texts were the primary objects of study among many Jewish groups and, on the other, that there were manifold ways of interpreting the authoritative traditions embodied in the scriptural texts. Overall, exegetical texts can be divided into two major categories: writings that intertwine text and interpretation (implicit exegesis) and writings that formally separate text and interpretation (explicit exegesis). The works that use implicit exegesis do not explicate exegetical reasoning behind a particular interpretation, while the works that use explicit exegesis provide such explanations. In the former case, the reader is given greater freedom to reconstruct the motivations for and the goals of specific exegetical decisions; in the latter case, the reader is guided and helped in this process by the interpreter. The emergence of explicit exegesis is sometimes linked to the canonization of Scripture, because the distinction between the scriptural text and the commentary presumes that the former was seen as fixed and authoritative. Such a linear shift from implicit to explicit interpretation, however, cannot be justified in light of the Qumran library, which contains examples of both types of exegesis. The presence of rewritten scriptural texts alongside the explicit scriptural quotations in the *Damascus Document* and the pesharim—as well as the presence of some documents, such as 4QCommentary on Genesis A (4Q252), that combine implicit and explicit exegesis—shows that both interpretive systems belong to the late Second Temple milieu.

The following review of Jewish exegetical literature is meant to be representative rather than exhaustive. Broadly speaking, every Jewish text of a religious nature interacts with Scripture in some way or another. Attempting to cover such a vast amount of literature, however, is counterproductive. We will limit our discussion to rewritten Scripture, the pesharim, Philo's allegorical commentaries, rabbinic midrash, and the targumim.

4. Geza Vermes, *Post-Biblical Jewish Studies* (SJLA 8; Leiden: Brill, 1975), 59–91 (80).

Rewritten Scripture

The method of rewriting scriptural texts includes various forms of scribal interventions into the sacred (base) texts, such as conflation, harmonization, modifications, and additions, for the purpose of making them relevant for contemporary Jews. The degree of scribal intervention varies, from sporadic alterations of the base text to the creation of entirely new works. This exegetical tradition, which blends text and interpretation, is a prime example of implicit exegesis. It is comparable to the interpretive rewriting of the books Exodus and Numbers by the book of Deuteronomy and the rewriting of the Deuteronomistic History by Chronicles (sometimes referred to as "inner biblical exegesis").

The recognition of exegetical literature that employs this type of interpretive strategy is usually credited to Geza Vermes, who in 1961 coined the label "rewritten Bible."[5] In view of recent discussions about the anachronistic connotations of the term "Bible" within the Second Temple context, a more appropriate term might be "rewritten Scripture." What is less clear, however, is whether this designation refers to a literary genre or a textual strategy. If it refers to a literary genre, the term can be used to distinguish a group of texts that share certain formal features and seek to accomplish similar compositional goals. If it indicates a textual strategy, the term can be used to explain similar techniques of modifying the text of Scripture that appear in different literary genres and not only in the compositions that engage the scriptural text in a sequential and systematic fashion.

Even more difficult is the question of the relationship between the compositions that are classified as rewritten Scripture and their base texts. Although the former are not created to replace the latter, they frequently make claims to authority comparable to the authority of Scripture. What are the boundaries between Scripture and scriptural interpretation if one group's "rewritten Bible" could very well be another's "biblical text"?

One way of dealing with this problem is to place the rewritten scriptural works on a spectrum with regard to the degrees of rewriting (Crawford, *Rewriting Scripture*, 13–14). The closest to its base text is the group of manuscripts known as the *Reworked Pentateuch* (4Q364, 4Q365, 4Q366, 4Q367, and 4Q158), which are characterized by harmonistic editing and various scribal insertions of outside material into the text of the Pentateuch. With the exception of two longer insertions in 4Q365, scribal interventions are relatively minor. Other rewritten compositions, however, contain more extensive scribal modifications of the base text. The book of *Jubilees* retells the narrative of Gen. 1–Exod. 12 in order to validate some polemical issues, such as the solar calendar, antiquity of the Jewish law, righteousness of Israel's ancestors, the Levitical priestly line, and eschatology. This work claims divine authority by presenting itself as divine revelation to Moses at Sinai mediated through an angel. The *Temple Scroll* contains a rewritten version of various pentateuchal laws pertaining to the temple, festivals, purity, and other

---

5. Geza Vermes, *Scripture and Tradition in Judaism* (StPB 4; Leiden: Brill, 1961).

legal matters. It claims divine authority by presenting itself as God's revelation to Moses at Sinai. The *Genesis Apocryphon* retells the stories of Noah, the flood, and Abraham by combining the traditions of Genesis, *Jubilees*, and *1 Enoch*. This new composition, written in Aramaic, lies on the farthest end of the spectrum with regard to its closeness to the scriptural text and the inherent claims to authority.

Josephus's *Jewish Antiquities* 1–11, a Hellenized version of Jewish history until the death of Alexander the Great, and Pseudo-Philo's *Liber antiquitatum biblicarum*, a revised account from Adam to Saul, could also be ascribed to the category of rewritten Scripture. Both works follow the general order of scriptural narratives in that they retell and employ various exegetical techniques that are typical for implied exegesis, such as additions, conflations, omissions, correlation of scriptural episodes, and paraphrasing.

The Pesharim

Pesharim are Qumran sectarian commentaries on the text of Scripture. Some of them, called "continuous pesharim," are the running commentaries on the selected prophetic books and the Psalms. There are six commentaries on Isaiah (3Q4, 4Q161, 4Q162, 4Q163, 4Q164, 4Q165), two on Hosea (4Q166, 4Q167), two on Micah (1Q14, 4Q168), one on Nahum (4Q169), one on Habakkuk (1QpHab), two on Zephaniah (1Q15, 4Q170), and three on the Psalms (1Q16, 4Q171, 4Q173). Others, called "thematic pesharim," juxtapose scriptural quotations and interpretations that pertain to a certain theme. The best-known manuscripts in this group are 11QMelchizedek (11Q13), 4QFlorilegium (4Q174), 4QCatena[a] (4Q177), and 4QCatena[b] (4Q182). (Some scholars also add the third group, called "isolated pesharim," which use pesher methods and [sometimes] pesher terminology but appear in a text of a different literary genre.) A distinctive characteristic of both types is a quotation of Scripture (lemma) followed by a commentary that is introduced with the formulas that include the term *pesher* ("interpretation"). The "citation plus comment" form indicates that the pesharists were aware that their comments should not be confused with the authoritative base text. Such a reverent attitude toward Scripture, however, did not prevent them from using the variant readings of some passages or from modifying the wording of Scripture if that suited their interpretive needs.[6]

In the pesharim, scriptural quotations are linked to specific commentaries through a series of identifications, which link individual words or short phrases in the citations to the contemporary experience of the Qumran community on the basis of their linguistic features or allegorical potential. Exegetical techniques include wordplays, allegorization, and atomization. In most cases, individual components of the scriptural passages are applied to the contemporary situation without regard to their original literary and historical contexts.

6. Timothy H. Lim, *Pesharim* (London: Sheffield Academic Press, 2002), 54–63.

The events related to the past, present, and future of the Qumran community are read in light of Scripture as fulfilled prophecies. For example, "the wicked" from Ps. 37:32 is interpreted as "the Wicked Priest" from the Qumran experience (4QpPsᵃ [4Q171] 4.8). The prophetic critique in Hab. 2:8a, "You have plundered many nations," is applied to "the last Priests of Jerusalem, who shall amass money and wealth by plundering the peoples" (1QpHab 9.4–5). Only one interpretation of a given verse is offered. This does not mean that the pesharists always ascribed one meaning to the same scriptural word. In some cases, the same term is used to designate different referents. For example, 4Q169 frgs. 3–4 1.1–2 identifies "the lion" from Nah. 2:12b as Demetrius. A few lines down, the pesharist equates "the lion" from Nah. 2:13a with Alexander Jannaeus (4Q169 frgs. 3–4 1.4–8).

To an outsider, the correspondence between the scriptural text and Qumran experience must have looked strained and arbitrary. To an insider, however, it was plausible and probably authoritative. Its authority was based on the authority of the sect's founder, the Teacher of Righteousness, and the shared belief that God had revealed the secret meaning of the prophetic texts only to him. This core belief is most clearly expressed in 1QpHab 7.1–5: "And God told Habakkuk to write down that which would happen to the final generation, but He did not make known to him when time would come to an end. And as for that which He said, That he who reads may read it speedily: interpreted, this concerns the Teacher of Righteousness, to whom God made known all the mysteries of the words of His servants the Prophets." This type of exegesis could be called "revelatory and inspired" because it presumes that only a select few are capable of conceiving and understanding it. Since it is based on the assumption that the only truth is the revealed truth, it does not have the ambition of persuading the outsiders. Such interpretation is typical for sectarian groups whose experience has been shaped by the separation and alienation from a larger group. Its primary task is to justify their existence and their sectarian worldview.

Philo's Allegorical Commentaries

Philo's expositions of Scripture, composed in the first half of the first century AD, offer us a glimpse into the exegetical traditions of Jews living in Alexandria. For Philo, Scripture has a twofold meaning, the literal and the allegorical, but only the latter reveals the true sense of the sacred texts, which is hidden below the surface. Allegorical meaning, which is available only to the initiated, can be discovered by paying close attention to the smallest details in the text, such as grammar and spelling. Philo frequently introduces his allegorical interpretations by referring to the "rules of allegory" (*Abr.* 68; *Spec.* 1.287; *Somn.* 1.73, 102), but he never explains what they are. On the basis of the Philonic corpus, Carl Siegfried long ago compiled a list of twenty-three rules that indicate when, though not how, an interpreter should engage in allegorical interpretation.[7] They

7. Carl Siegfried, *Philo von Alexandria als Ausleger des Alten Testaments* (Jena: Dufft, 1875), 165–68.

include doubling of a word or phrase; superfluous words or facts; synonymous words or phrases; wordplay; unusual words or spelling; the presence of particles or adverbs; inseparable prepositions; small modifications of a word that convey different meaning; the gender of a noun; unusual statements; numbers, objects, and names that can be interpreted symbolically; and so on.

Philo's actual practice of finding the allegorical meaning of scriptural passages was influenced by both his Jewish heritage and his philosophical ideas, such as Pythagoreanism, Middle Platonism, and Stoicism. Instone Brewer has suggested, "The main assumption underlying Philo's exegesis is that the whole of Scripture is inspired prophecy, and that its interpretation and translation must be equally inspired" (*Techniques and Assumptions*, 208). Philo's occasional references to other allegorists (*Cher.* 48; *Spec.* 1.214) point to a vibrant interpretive community in Alexandria, which shared ideas and cultivated the allegorical approach to the written text.

Rabbinic Midrash

Midrash is an exegetical practice documented in the rabbinic writings.[8] The term "midrash" comes from the Hebrew verb *darash* ("to seek," "to search out," "to interpret") and can be used to designate a type of literature or an exegetical technique. As a type of literature, midrash "stands in direct relationship to a fixed, canonical text, considered to be the authoritative and the revealed word of God by the midrashist and his audience, and in which this canonical text is explicitly cited or clearly alluded to."[9] The standard division of midrashic literature into halakah (interpretation pertaining to Jewish law) and haggadah (nonjuristic interpretation) is not always helpful given the significant overlap between these two categories. Many haggadic passages are based on legal principles or have practical application. As an exegetical technique, "midrash" refers to a creative explication of Scripture with the help of certain interpretive mechanisms, such as etymology, wordplay, catchwords, analogy, and so forth. Its primary purpose is not to determine the plain meaning of the text, called *peshat* ("simple"), but to seek knowledge that can be gained through logical inferences, analogies, combinations of different passages, and the like. According to Ithamar Gruenwald, the goal of midrash "is not the mere act of understanding texts, but the creation of the meaning that is attached to them."[10]

Midrashic techniques atomize the text of Scripture to a greater degree than do other hermeneutical methods. The occasion for midrash can be an unusual word,

8. Some authors apply the term "midrash" to any exegetical activity that presumes the existence of an authoritative base text.

9. Gary Porton, "Defining Midrash," in *The Study of Ancient Judaism* (ed. Jacob Neusner; 2 vols.; New York: Ktav, 1981), 1:55–92 (62).

10. Ithamar Gruenwald, "Midrash and the 'Midrashic Condition': Preliminary Considerations," in *The Midrashic Imagination: Jewish Exegesis, Thought, and History* (ed. Michael Fishbane; Albany: State University of New York Press, 1993), 6–22 (7).

an apparent redundancy, an unexpected turn in the narrative, or even an apparent contradiction between two passages. Midrashic activity is frequently guided by certain hermeneutical principles, or *middot*, that developed over time. The first list of seven principles is attributed to Hillel (*t. Sanh.* 7.11), followed by a list of thirteen principles attributed to Ishmael. (See the introduction to *Sipra* [W.1a–b]. For the most part, the thirteen middot attributed to Ishmael are an expanded version of the seven arrributed to Hillel.) A list of thirty-two middot is attributed to Rabbi Eliezer ben Yose ha-Gelili.[11] Two most common procedures are *qal wahomer* (inference from minor to major) and *gezerah shawah* (the principle of analogy based on identical wording in distinct scriptural passages).

Midrashic exegesis presumes the existence of a closed, revealed text that needs to be elucidated for a contemporary audience. The sacred text embodies the will of God but is not identical with it. As an independent entity, it can be interrogated to answer all kinds of religious questions. Midrash creatively combines two contrasting principles: the fixedness of the text and the plurality of its meanings. The concept of a fixed text did not prevent the rabbis from using textual variants to support a particular interpretation (cf. Instone Brewer, *Techniques and Assumptions*, 172–73). With the help of midrash, the closed canon of Scripture is actualized through the (almost) endless combinations of individual elements. The deliberate use of interpretive principles and the high level of sophistication of midrashic interpretations display the reliance on reason and logic to disclose the truth of Scripture.

Targumim

Targumim are interpretive Aramaic translations of the Hebrew Scriptures. They reflect the synagogue practices of providing oral translations of the portions of the Torah and Prophets into Aramaic by translators, called *mĕtûrgĕmānîm*. The origin of this practice is debatable. Some scholars trace it back to Ezra's reading of the Torah to the postexilic community in Jerusalem, which the Levites simultaneously translated into Aramaic (Neh. 8:1–8). There is, however, no evidence in the Second Temple literature that Aramaic translations accompanied the reading of the Torah and the Prophets during synagogue worship. The only pre–AD 70 targumim are the Qumran fragments of the Aramaic translations of Leviticus (4Q156) and Job (11Q10 and 4Q157), but they provide no information about their actual use.

The Mishnah and other early rabbinic writings provide the earliest evidence for the liturgical use of the targumim.[12] The public reading of each verse from the Torah and up to three verses from the Prophets was to be followed by an oral

---

11. See Hyman G. Enelow, ed., *The Mishnah of Rabbi Eliezer or the Midrash of Thirty-Two Hermeneutic Rules* (New York: Bloch, 1933).

12. For the pre-rabbinic, even pre-Christian dating of the interpretive traditions found in the Palestinian Targum to the Pentateuch, see McNamara, *Targum*, 139–252.

rendering of the Hebrew text into Aramaic (*m. Meg.* 4.4). These oral translations were eventually written down and were probably stored in the synagogues.
There are several indicators that the distinction between the targumim and the
sacred texts was preserved. In the liturgical setting, only the scriptural text was
read from the scroll while the Aramaic rendering had to be delivered orally, even
after the targumim were written down. Aramaic translation represented an activity accompanying the reading of the Hebrew Scriptures, never a replacement
for it. In a scholastic setting, in which some of the written targumim might have
been used, they served as the supplementary rather than the primary material
for scriptural study.

The main purpose of a targum was to interpret the Hebrew text for the unso-
phisticated audiences that, even if some of them were bilingual, needed help in
comprehending Scripture. Targumic activity frequently extended beyond the mere
translation to include various halakic (legal) and hagaddic (narrative) expansions
that supplied explanations for the more difficult or obscure passages, applied the
rules and regulations from the sacred texts to contemporary circumstances, and
used the scriptural text as a pretext to convey homiletical lessons, traditional
sayings, and legendary material. The earliest targumim from the rabbinic times
are dated not before the third century AD. There are considerable differences
among them with regard to the correspondence between the Hebrew text and
the Aramaic translation, as well as the scope of accompanying expansions. *Targum Onqelos* to the Pentateuch and *Targum Jonathan* to the Prophets follow the
Hebrew text more closely, even if they contain many nonliteral translations. Two
Palestinian targumim to the Pentateuch, *Targum Neofiti* and especially *Targum
Pseudo-Jonathan*, are more paraphrastic and contain numerous expansions. (For
a helpful introduction to all extant targumim, see McNamara, *Targum*, 253–329.)

Although targumim share some similarities with other types of Jewish exegetical
literature, they represent a distinct group of texts with their own characteristics.
Unlike the works of rewritten Scripture, targumim are not new compositions and
make no claims to special authority. They are primarily concerned with conveying
the meaning of the Hebrew base text, which they follow closely, in new linguistic and cultural settings. Unlike the pesharim, targumim do not use technical
terms to distinguish the scriptural text from interpretation and do not interpret
the scriptural text as fulfilled prophecies. Unlike Philo's commentaries, they do
not prioritize allegorical interpretation. Unlike rabbinic midrashim, they neither
provide multiple interpretations of individual scriptural passages nor associate
different scriptural texts together.

The Interpretation of Israel's Scripture in the New Testament

In 1 Cor. 15:3–4, Paul reiterates one of the earliest Christian confessions "that
Christ died for our sins in accordance with the scriptures, and that he was buried,

and that he was raised on the third day in accordance with the scriptures." The repeated expression, "in accordance with the scriptures," suggests the primacy of engagement with the Scriptures in theological reflection. From the beginning, Israel's Scriptures provided the most fundamental conceptual categories for the understanding of Jesus' life, death, and resurrection. Only through dialogue with the sacred texts were early Christian interpreters able to express the meaning and significance of Jesus' person and ministry.

Formally, the NT writings are quite different from rewritten Scripture, the pesharim, Philo's allegorical commentaries, midrashic literature, and the targumim. They do not rewrite the text of Scripture with the help of implicit exegesis. They do not contain continuous or thematic commentaries on the scriptural books. They do not interpret the Scriptures following the rules of allegory. They do not offer a variety of interpretations of a single verse. And they do not provide paraphrastic translations of the Hebrew Scriptures. Behind the formal differences, however, lie striking similarities. The NT authors sometimes revise scriptural narratives to make them more readily applicable to the career of Jesus or to the life of the church (e.g., Acts 7:2–34). On other occasions, they claim that certain events in Jesus' life directly fulfill ancient prophecies (e.g., Matt. 1:22–23; 2:15, 17–18, 23; 12:17–21). They sometimes interpret the sacred texts allegorically (e.g., Gal. 4:22–31). In some cases, they develop sophisticated scriptural arguments that disclose a surprising confidence in human rationality (e.g., Acts 2:25–36; 13:32–37). And they are occasionally more interested in the explanation of Scripture than in the literal rendering of the base text (e.g., John 12:39–41).

Jewish interpretive strategies therefore provide the most important backdrop for understanding early Christian exegetical practices. Early Christian interpreters did not use hermeneutical methods that differed from the methods of their Jewish contemporaries, but they interpreted Scripture from a different standpoint. The same interpretive technique could yield different outcomes depending on the interpreter's viewpoint. What differentiated Christian exegetical endeavors was their unique perspective on Jesus and his career, which represented the main vantage point for Christian interpreters as they were searching the Scriptures. The conviction that the entirety of Scripture testifies about Jesus not only provided a christocentric lens for understanding the sacred texts but also led to what George Brooke calls "a minimalist approach" to Scripture. Although scriptural texts themselves set the agenda for Jewish exegetical compositions, Christian exegetes focused only on the passages that were consistent with "the early Christian experience kerygmatically formulated."[13]

Scholarly discussions on early Christian interpretations of Israel's Scriptures— or, to use a better-known though slightly anachronistic idiom, the NT's use of the OT—focus on three questions: (1) In what ways do NT authors use Scripture? (2) Which textual versions are utilized? (3) How are scriptural passages interpreted?

13. George J. Brooke, *The Dead Sea Scrolls and the New Testament* (Minneapolis: Fortress, 2005), 56–57 (57).

The first question involves the definition of terminology that is applied to various forms of the use of Scripture in the NT. The most common categories are direct quotations, allusions, and echoes, although other categories that appear in scholarly literature include formal quotations, indirect quotations, allusive quotations, paraphrase, reminiscence, intertextuality, type-scenes, and scriptural summaries. Each of these terms, however, has to be carefully defined in order to avoid confusion and enable comparison and discussion of various categories.[14] Recognition of direct quotations is based on formal correspondence between the citation and the actual words that appear in the text of Scripture. What is less clear, however, is how many identical words would qualify as a quotation, and whether they need to be introduced with an explicit quotation formula. Allusion could be understood as "the nonformal invocation by an author of a text (or person, event, etc.) that the author could reasonably have been expected to know."[15] Echoes, in contrast, are not necessarily conscious authorial acts but the resonances of various scriptural texts that readers—both ancient and modern—might hear in the NT. Richard Hays, who devised a list of seven tests for identifying scriptural echoes in the Letters of Paul, explains that "later readers will rightly grasp meanings of the figures that may have been veiled from Paul himself" (see Hays, *Echoes*, 29–33).

The second question requires careful study of the extant textual variants in order to determine which one was quoted or referred to. Many scriptural quotations in the NT follow the LXX, but it is not always clear which Greek recension was used. In some cases, early Christian interpreters appear to have provided their own translations of the Hebrew text (see Matthew's translation of Isa. 53:4 in Matt. 8:17), but it is sometimes difficult to determine which specific variant they used. Some scriptural renderings are influenced by targumic traditions (see the interpretation of Deut. 30:12–14 in Rom. 10:5–10, which might have been influenced by the rendering of Deut. 30:12–13 in *Targum Neofiti*), while others incorporate deliberate modifications for interpretive purposes, as we see in the replacement of the phrase "of our God" with "his" at the end of the quotation of Isa. 40:3 in Mark 1:3 and parallels.

The third question pertains to the interpretive strategies used by early Christian interpreters to explicate the meaning of Scripture. Although many scholars continue to compare Christian interpretive procedures with Jewish exegetical practices, some consider the influence of Greco-Roman rhetorical strategies or investigate Christian hermeneutics with the methods of modern literary criticism. Relevant questions include not only technical issues, such as particular exegetical techniques and the influence of specific interpretive traditions, but also theological issues, such as the view of Scripture, the understanding of salvation history, and

14. See Stanley E. Porter, "The Use of the Old Testament in the New Testament: A Brief Comment on Method and Terminology," in Evans and Sanders, *Scriptures of Israel*, 79–96.
15. Porter, "Use of the Old Testament," 95.

the role of revelation and inspiration vis-à-vis interpretive endeavors of early Christian communities.

Conclusion

Most Jewish groups in the late Second Temple period regarded the Pentateuch, Prophets, and some of the Writings as the authoritative Scriptures. This era was also characterized by textual pluriformity, but that disappeared with the emergence of the rabbinic canon based on the proto-Masoretic text. Linguistic needs in Hellenistic Judaism led to the emergence of the LXX and its acceptance as the authoritative Scriptures by Greek-speaking Jewish communities and the early church.

The main purpose of Jewish scriptural interpretation was to make Scripture comprehensible and applicable to particular communities. Jewish exegetical writings include works that intertwine text and interpretation (rewritten Scripture) and works that formally separate text and interpretation (pesharim, Philo's allegorical commentaries, and rabbinic midrash). Works classified as rewritten Scripture belong to the stream of tradition that integrates interpretation into the development and the transmission of the text. Scriptural commentaries that separate text and interpretation presuppose a fixed, unchangeable text. Targumim, which translate the Hebrew Scriptures into the vernacular, blend text and interpretation while clearly distinguishing the sacred text written on the scroll from its oral rendition.

From the beginning, Israel's Scripture provided the language and key theological concepts for understanding the career of Jesus and the experience of the early church. The main difference between Christian interpreters and their Jewish contemporaries should be sought not in a different exegetical methodology but in a different theological perspective. By reading the Scriptures through the christocentric lens, NT authors were able to construe scriptural arguments that helped them understand the meaning of Jesus' life, death, and resurrection within the overall scheme of God's relationship to Israel and to the world.

See also "The Dead Sea Scrolls"; "Josephus and the New Testament"; "Philo and the New Testament"; "Rabbinic Literature and the New Testament."

Bibliography

Crawford, Sidnie White. *Rewriting Scripture in Second Temple Times*. Grand Rapids: Eerdmans, 2008. An examination of exegetical techniques, claims to authority, and theological tendencies in various rewritten scriptural texts found at Qumran.

Cross, Frank Moore, and Shemaryahu Talmon, eds. *Qumran and the History of the Biblical Text*. Cambridge, MA: Harvard University Press, 1975. A collection of essays, written by major specialists in the field of Qumran studies, examining the transmission of the scriptural texts in the light of Qumran discoveries.

Evans, Craig A., and James A. Sanders, eds. *Early Christian Interpretation of the Scriptures of Israel: Investigations and Proposals*. JSNTSup 148. Sheffield: Sheffield Academic Press, 1997. A collection of essays focusing on various issues related to the interpretation of Israel's Scripture in early Christianity, from the questions of methodology to the use of Scripture in specific passages from the Gospels, Acts, Epistles, and Revelation.

Falk, Daniel K. *The Parabiblical Texts: Strategies for Extending the Scripture in the Dead Sea Scrolls*. London: T&T Clark, 2007. A detailed study of the extension and interpretation of Scripture in the *Genesis Apocryphon*, the *Reworked Pentateuch*, and 4QCommentary on Genesis A–D.

Fishbane, Michael, ed. *The Midrashic Imagination: Jewish Exegesis, Thought, and History*. Albany: State University of New York Press, 1993. The first part of this book addresses some methodological issues related to midrashic hermeneutics. The second part explores midrashic creativity through mythmaking and parables. The third part examines midrashic interpretation in the Middle Ages.

Hays, Richard. *Echoes of Scripture in the Letters of Paul*. New Haven: Yale University Press, 1989. This study explores the role of Israel's Scripture in the formation of Paul's writings with the help of the concept of intertextuality, which is used to identify and interpret scriptural echoes. The thesis of the book is that Paul's reading of Scripture is ecclesiocentric (church centered) rather than christocentric (Christ centered).

Hengel, Martin. *The Septuagint as Christian Scripture: Its Prehistory and the Problem of Its Canon*. Translated by Mark E. Biddle. Edinburgh: T&T Clark, 2002. An investigation of the LXX as a collection of writings claimed by Christians, the later consolidation of the Christian "Septuagint Canon," the origin of the Jewish LXX, and the origin of the "Christian Septuagint" and its additional writings.

Instone Brewer, David. *Techniques and Assumptions in Jewish Exegesis before 70 CE*. TSAJ 30. Tübingen: Mohr Siebeck, 1992. An examination of exegetical technique and assumptions in the scribal traditions preserved in rabbinic literature that are likely to have originated before AD 70, comparing them with those of their predecessors and contemporaries.

Juel, Donald. *Messianic Exegesis: Christological Interpretation of the Old Testament in Early Christianity*. Philadelphia: Fortress, 1988. An exploration of the relationship between Jewish modes of exegesis and the NT. The central thesis is that the confession of Jesus as Messiah stands at the beginning of Christian scriptural interpretation.

Kraus, Wolfgang, and Glenn R. Wooden, eds. *Septuagint Research: Issues and Challenges in the Study of the Greek Jewish Scriptures*. SBLSCS. Atlanta: Society of Biblical Literature, 2006. A collection of essays that addresses various methodological issues in septuagintal research, thematic and book-centered studies focused on the Old Greek Septuagint translations, the use of these translations in the NT, and the theologies of the LXX.

McNamara, Martin. *Targum and Testament Revisited: Aramaic Paraphrases of the Hebrew Bible; A Light on the New Testament*. 2nd ed. Grand Rapids: Eerdmans, 2010. The first part of this book examines the origin, transmission, and date of the targumim to the Pentateuch and the Prophets. The second part investigates the possible relationship between the NT and targumic tradition. The appendix provides a helpful outline of all extant targumim of the rabbinic tradition.

Popovic, Mladen, ed. *Authoritative Scriptures in Ancient Judaism*. JSJSup 141. Leiden: Brill, 2010. A collection of essays that discusses the canonical process, the status of Scripture, transmission process, and other issues related to the authoritativeness of Scripture in Second Temple Judaism.

Porter, Stanley E., ed. *Hearing the Old Testament in the New Testament*. MNTS. Grand Rapids: Eerdmans, 2006. A collection of essays that address various methodological issues and offer specific illustrations about the use of the OT in the NT.

Ulrich, Eugene C. *The Dead Sea Scrolls and the Origins of the Bible*. SDSSRL. Grand Rapids: Eerdmans, 1999. An examination of various aspects of the complex development of the ancient texts that eventually came to form the OT.

PART 2

SETTING THE CONTEXT

Roman Hellenism

Christianity emerged within a Greco-Roman context, and, to varying degrees, the NT writings both assume and engage with these cultural features.

The beginnings of the Jesus movement and the story of the apostolic mission are located at the confluence of two great traditions. The one is marked by centuries of religious reflection and practice within Israel, God's people, especially as this was shaped by exile (part 1). The second comprises the cultural streams of Hellenism and life in the Roman Empire. The immediate experience of empire, first under the Greeks and then under the Romans, exercised significant influence on the formation of the Jewish people and, therefore, on the thought forms, institutions, and challenges of the early church.

Unfortunately for readers of the NT, this pivotal influence generally appears more in the background of the NT books than in the foreground. Apart from a few passages here and there, we do not typically see in the NT explicit treatment of the worship of the emperor, candid reflection on the institution of slavery, or

103

overt discussion of the status of children in the Mediterranean world. Introduction to these and related issues, then, helps us to read the NT materials more as "insiders." That is, these chapters give us a greater sense of what people of the NT era simply took for granted in their day-to-day lives. Reading with the insight that comes from this background material helps us to see where and how the NT writers actually were engaging, and sometimes challenging, the everyday assumptions of the world around them.

8

Greek Religion

MOYER V. HUBBARD

The conquests of Alexander the Great (334–323 BC) and the expansion of Hellenistic culture and thought had a significant influence on the religious climate of the ancient world. Although no dramatically new beliefs were introduced into conquered territories (with the possible exception of the development of ruler cults, treated in the chapter "The Imperial Cult"), there was a notable expansion of traditional Greek religious conceptions, together with the inevitable cross-fertilization of ideas that such monumental social collisions entail. The result was the emergence of a panhellenic religious framework that continued to honor the classical pantheon of ancient Athens, yet without excluding the multitude of regional deities, local mythologies, and wide spectrum of beliefs and practices among the scores of ethnic groups that composed Hellenistic antiquity. Although understanding this diversity is important, it is also possible to identify enough unifying features and broad commonalities to recognize one basic religious system. The focus of this chapter will be on the panhellenic religious system of the Hellenistic and early Roman era (from the third to the first century BC), with an eye to beliefs and practices that illumine the NT.

Before we further delineate the main features of Greek religion of this period, it will be beneficial for the contemporary reader to keep in mind what Greek religion was not (see also Garland, *Religion*, ix):

- It was not exclusive. Many divinities could be worshiped by any individual or community; this was both expected and encouraged.

- There was no need for conversion from one faith or deity to another, nor were there proselytizing or evangelistic tendencies.

- It was primarily concerned not with ethics—how one *ought* to live—but with how to earn material blessings from the gods and how to avoid their wrath.

- There was no centralized cult, temple, or priesthood with translocal authority, nor were there sacred texts to study for training in "orthodox" dogma.

- It was not experienced as a personal faith, in the modern sense, deeply affecting the emotional life or character development of the worshiper.

In short, ancient Greek religion (and Roman, for that matter) was very different from what most moderns are acquainted with, particularly in Europe and North America. Moreover, the lack of any canonical sacred texts means that historians must draw on a wide variety of sources as they attempt to present synthetic accounts of Greek religion.

Sources for the Study of Greek Religion

Denizens of the ancient world were born into societies with rich and often variegated religious traditions. With little, if any, formal religious education, people heard stories about the gods, retold fables, frequented shrines, participated in festivals, and acquired a sufficient knowledge of the divine world to get on in life. Modern-day historians, sifting through the remains of these ancient cultures, typically divide the evidence into three categories: literary, epigraphic, and archaeological. The literary evidence for the religious conceptions of the Greek world includes the epic literature of Homer and Hesiod (both ca. eighth century BC); popular playwrights such as Sophocles (fifth century BC), Euripides (fifth century BC), and Aristophanes (fifth–fourth century BC); the musings of philosophers; and various other historians and orators whose works have survived. Although some of these sources significantly predate the Hellenistic era, much of this literature was seminal and perennially popular, establishing the core mythology for subsequent centuries. Even as late as the first century AD, the philosopher Dio Chrysostom remarks of the educational system of his day that "Homer comes first, middle, and last" (*Or.* 18.8). Epigraphic evidence refers primarily to inscriptions—everything from coinage to official dedicatory inscriptions to curses etched in lead and tossed into a well. Archaeological remains include temples, statuary, frescoes, household altars, funerary remains, and a great variety of other religious artifacts unearthed from the rubble of antiquity.

This threefold classification of material is important not only as a means of organizing the data but also for gaining a full comprehension of the subject matter. For example, the writings of Homer depict a divine family with petty rivalries and character flaws—not unlike most human families—whose interest in mortals extends little beyond using them as pawns to settle their own squabbles or for satisfying their lusts. The nonliterary papyri and epigraphic evidence, on the other hand, reveal a vast world of intermediary divine beings who, if the correct ritual is performed, could be invoked to persuade a hesitant suitor or to ruin the business of a competitor. In contrast to both of these stand the lofty conceptions of the philosophers, who tended to reject the base notions of popular literature and recast the gods in line with their own high-minded ideals. For example, Plato (fifth–fourth century BC) argues (through Socrates) that the stories of Homer and Hesiod are simply falsehoods that should not be repeated: "If we want the guardians of our city to think that it is shameful to be easily provoked into hating one another, we must not allow any stories about gods warring, fighting, or plotting against one another, for they are not true" (*Rep*. 378b–c).[1] Temples represent the most noteworthy and easily identifiable archaeological witness to the public expression of ancient religion. They typically occupied the most prominent place in the *polis* (Greek, "city") and represented an enormous physical endeavor as well as a significant civic expenditure (often supported by wealthy benefactors). Their sometimes grand architecture, granite columns, marbled altars, muraled walls, and so on remind us how seriously the ancients took religion. Each of these sources illumines facets of Hellenic religion and will be drawn upon in the portrayal that follows. We begin with perhaps the most obvious and fundamental reality of religious belief in antiquity: polytheism.

A World of Gods

A time traveler from the twenty-first-century West visiting ancient Corinth, Ephesus, or Athens would face considerable adjustments, including packed streets, cramped accommodation, and the complete absence of any conveniences of modern life: electricity, cell phones, prepackaged food, aspirin—the list goes on. One item, however, our fictitious tourist would have in abundance: gods. In the ancient Greco-Roman world, gods were everywhere. There were gods for lovers, gods for poets, gods for bakers, gods for farmers, gods for travelers, gods for protecting the hinges on one's door, and many others. An inscription from Corinth mentions "the gods of the beehive."[2] Many divinities are known from only a single inscription or an obscure literary reference. Of course, the divine world of the ancient Greeks was not a democracy, nor were all gods created equal.

The Olympian Deities

The traditional pantheon of Athens was considered the council of supreme deities that were worshiped in one form or another throughout the Greek-influenced world. In literature they are pictured residing at the peak of Mount Olympus,

1. *Plato: Complete Works* (ed. John M. Cooper; Indianapolis: Hackett, 1997).
2. John Harvey Kent, *Corinth: The Inscriptions, 1926–50* (Princeton, NJ: American School of Classical Studies at Athens, 1966), no. 68.

but in epigraphic remains they are frequently addressed as if they dwell in the temples dedicated to their worship. The twelve main Olympic deities (Zeus, Hera, Athena, Apollo, Artemis, Poseidon, Aphrodite, Hermes, Ares, Demeter, Dionysus, and Hephaestus) formed a family, with Zeus at its head, joined by his wife (and sister), Hera—normal boundaries of sexual propriety do not apply to the Olympians. The gods were eternal and ageless, but not self-existent. They came into being at a point in time and remained frozen at the age of their initial creation: Zeus and Poseidon were always middle-aged and bearded, Aphrodite was forever at the peak of womanly beauty, Persephone would remain eternally a young maiden. The gods were powerful and endowed with distinctive gifts (e.g., Apollo specialized in music and prophecy, Hephaestus in metallurgy) or spheres of authority (e.g., Ares was the god of war, Poseidon ruled the sea, Hestia watched over the home), but none, not even Zeus, was omnipotent. Zeus himself gained the throne on Olympus by overthrowing his father, Cronus, and the mythological lore abounds with tales of one god thwarting another in their various escapades. Nor were the gods omniscient—they were often tricked by each other—or even particularly perceptive: Rhea duped Cronus—who was attempting to eat their sixth son (Zeus)—by feeding him a rock. In short, the portrayal of the gods in literature, archaeology, and art was highly anthropomorphic. In physique they were depicted in an idealized form of perfection and beauty, while in character, often as not, they were deeply flawed.

Principal Panhellenic Deities

Aphrodite	Goddess of beauty, sexual love, and fertility
Apollo	God of music, prophecy, healing, and archery
Ares	God of war
Artemis	Goddess of fertility, the wilderness, and hunting
Asclepius	God of healing
Athena	Patron deity of Athens; goddess of wisdom, arts and crafts, and war; helper of heroes
Demeter	Goddess of grain
Dionysus	God of wine, merriment, and nature
Eros	God of love
Hades	God of the underworld and the dead
Hecate	Goddess of the underworld and sorcery; also associated with crossroads
Hephaestus	God of fire; blacksmith of the gods; disfigured and banished from Olympus
Hera	Goddess of marriage; wife of Zeus

Hermes	Messenger of the gods; helper of travelers and merchants
Hestia	Goddess of hearth and home
Persephone	Daughter of Zeus and Demeter; queen of the underworld; associated with spring and the fruits of the field
Poseidon	God of the sea and earthquakes
Uranus	God of the sky; father of the Titans
Zeus	Ruler of the gods

The Olympic deities appear in innumerable forms throughout the ancient Mediterranean. Very commonly epithets are attached to their name, almost resembling a surname. For example, in Corinth we find Aphrodite Melainis ("the Black," perhaps in connection with the underworld); in Messenia (Western Greece), Artemis Nurser of Children was worshiped; in Sumnia (near Athens) we find Poseidon Soter ("Savior"); the seaman embarking on a voyage would pour a libation to Zeus Limenoskopos ("Watcher of Havens"). Usually these epithets can be construed as a specific attribute of the god in question (as we see throughout Homer's works) or as a means of claiming the god for a particular city through connecting them to a local legend. For example, according to legend Athena aided Bellerophon, the storied hero of Corinth, by taming Pegasus. Hence, the Corinthians honored Athena Chalinitis, "the Bridler."

The Olympian gods, along with their predecessors, the Titans, produced scores of offspring. These were fully divine but not as powerful as their forebears. Some of these divine offspring were personifications of the cosmos or natural order: Aither ("Light"), Hemera ("Day"), Thalassa ("Sea"), Potamoi ("Rivers"), Thanatos ("Death"). Others were personifications of virtue: Eukleia ("Good Repute"), Euphemia ("Praise"), Hedones ("Pleasure"), Dike ("Justice"), Eirene ("Peace"), Aglaia ("Beauty"). The nymphs were a class of lesser divinities, nature goddesses, who were associated with all manner of natural phenomena, such as caves, flowers, fields, winds, trees, rocks, or sand. Some were immortal, while others expired along with the element of nature they represented, as when a tree dies or a breeze subsides. In many ways the mythology of the ancient Greeks represents a kind of primitive animism organized in a hierarchy and presented with a genealogy.

Regional Deities

In addition to serving up the traditional Olympic deities with a little local flavor, municipalities also offered worshipers a selection of provincial divinities. Sometimes the traditional gods of a region were fused with an Olympian deity with similar attributes. For example, in North Africa from the Ptolemaic period (332–320 BC) onward we frequently find Zeus and Serapis merged into one god (Zeus-Serapis).

Many examples of regional deities could be given (there were thousands), but it might be more useful to take a closer look at one example with a direct bearing on the NT.

Acts 16:16–19 describes a curious incident during Paul's first visit to Philippi, where the apostle exorcises a spirit from a young prophetess. The girl trails Paul and his companions around Philippi, shouting, "These men are servants of the Most High God, who proclaim to you the way of salvation [*sōtēria*]" (16:17 ESV). For those familiar with the OT, the expression "Most High God" sounds like a reference to the one true God (Gen. 14:18; Ps. 78:35; Dan. 5:18), but Luke tells us that Paul becomes "greatly annoyed" (Acts 16:18 ESV) at her proclamation. It appears unlikely that the prophetess intends a reference to the God of the Jews, and even more doubtful that residents of Philippi would interpret her words in this way. In fact, archaeological work has uncovered an abundance of evidence in this area attesting to the worship of a pagan deity known as Theos Hypsistos, "Most High God," the same terminology used by this prophetess. Dedicatory inscriptions to this deity have been found all throughout Macedonia (sometimes referred to as "Zeus Hypsistos"), and the high concentration of epigraphs in this region leads some historians to conclude that this cult originated here. For example, in Philippopolis, north of Philippi, a certain Gaius Mailios Agathopus inscribed a dedication to Zeus Hypsistos "on behalf of the health [*sōtēria*]" of his patron. Given this background, Paul's annoyance becomes more comprehensible. Not only is the apostle wary of having a pagan prophetess as his publicity agent, but he also understands the confusing and highly ambiguous nature of her press release.

Heroes

Heroes were a class of semidivine beings, many of whom, particularly by the time of the Hellenistic era, were virtually indistinguishable from the gods. In ancient Greece heroes were mortals who had displayed great courage and accomplished remarkable feats in both their life and their death and so became immortal spirits upon death. Although a few gained panhellenic fame, like Theseus, Heracles, and Perseus, most were associated with a specific locale and were unknown outside that area. They aided mortals in a variety of ways, particularly as protectors of the towns and cities with which they were connected, almost as patron deities. Since every municipality claimed at least one, if not several, legendary heroes as its own, the heroes constituted a large caste of intermediary divinities. Their principal shrines where ritual practices occurred were the legendary burial place of the hero, known in Greek as the *hērōon*. Although they should be distinguished from the Olympian deities, by the Hellenistic era their cult and related worship often differed little from that of the gods.

Daimones

Another very large group of spiritual beings constituted the *daimones* (sg. *daimōn*), or "spirits." In Hesiod's writings (*Works and Days* 107, 235) and other ancient sources, *daimones* are sometimes described as the spirits of great men who died, or even as a circumlocution for the gods themselves. Plato depicts a *daimōn* as a person's guardian spirit who watches over the individual in life and escorts them to Hades at death (*Phedr.* 107d–e; *Rep.* 617d–e). In the Hellenistic period the *daimones* were conceived as intermediary spiritual powers of either a benevolent or a malevolent nature. They populated the earth in great numbers and could be called on for help or to cause harm to an enemy. The *daimones* were increasingly perceived as unpredictable and dangerous, and they figured prominently in popular superstition (see below). The common view of Plutarch's day (ca. AD 46–120) was that a *daimōn* was the most harmful being in the universe (*Mor.* 153A). In the NT and early Christian literature the *daimones* are always described negatively as evil spirits or demons. Philo, Paul's Jewish contemporary in Alexandria, looks at the multitude of deities and intermediary beings of Greek religion and reasons that what the gentiles call gods, "the sacred Word calls angels" (*Somn.* 1.141, author's translation). Other Jewish writers, such as the author of *1 Enoch* and the apostle Paul, are less generous: they say that the gods of the gentiles are demons (cf. 1 Cor. 10:20–21; see also *1 En.* 19; 2Q23 frg. 1 line 7; *L.A.B.* 25.9; Ps. 95:5 LXX).

Public Expressions of Religion

Temple and Cult

Temples constituted the most noteworthy physical expression of religion in antiquity. Every city, township, and village had multiple temples, although they varied significantly in size. Large cities and provincial capitals had grand temples with extensive precincts located at the center of the city or on a point of raised elevation within the city, known as the acropolis. Most temples, however, were far more modest. Visitors to Corinth's central market area in Paul's day would find themselves surrounded by temples: to Hermes, Poseidon, Heracles, Apollo, the Pantheon, Tyche, the imperial cult, and others. Numerous shrines and smaller sanctuaries would be scattered throughout a typical city, and rustic memorials would also be found along the roads leading to the city and would be dotted across the countryside. The book of Acts depicts Paul as becoming deeply distressed as he strolls through Athens and observes that the city is "full of idols" (17:16), which reflects the humdrum reality of the religious clutter in the urban landscape of an ancient Greek city.

With the exception perhaps of some mystery religions, temples were not used for regular worship gatherings in the modern sense. The temple would house statuary and images of the god and would provide facilities for sacrifices, feasts, and other ritual practices. The sacrificial altar normally stood outside the temple, often on a raised platform in the front of the temple, where sacrifices would be most visible and which would allow for adequate drainage of blood from animal sacrifices. Although animal sacrifices (sheep, goats, pigs, cattle) are most commonly depicted in literature

8.1. Temple of Apollo at Delphi, Greece, from the sixth to the fourth century BC.

and artwork, sacrifices of grain, fruit, and other produce were also made. Portions of the sacrificial meat were burned as an offering to the god, and other portions were distributed among participants or sold in the market (cf. 1 Cor. 10:25–30). Sacrifices were made for four principal reasons: (1) to honor the god (particularly during religious festivals), (2) to give thanks to the god for some kind of material blessing (e.g., an abundant harvest, victory in an athletic competition, a safe journey), (3) to appease the god (in the case of a ritual infraction or a perceived punishment from the deity), or (4) in conjunction with a petition for help from the god.

More common than sacrifices, which could be costly, were votive dedications. The worshiper would offer a token of his or her possessions to the god as means of securing a favor, or simply to build up goodwill. Almost anything could serve as a dedicatory offering, from articles of clothing or utensils to more valuable items: bronze platters, ornamented vases, plunder from a military campaign, and so on. Temples could be bulging with such items. In Troezen (southern Greece), every maiden dedicated a lock of her hair to the hero-god Hippolytus before her marriage (Pausanias, *Descr.* 2.32.1). Those in need of healing would offer a clay representation of the affected body part, often sold by vendors outside the temple precincts.

Temples were staffed by locals, usually citizens of rank, who were elected or chosen by lot to serve as priests. Male priests served male gods and female priests served female gods. A priesthood was connected with a specific temple or sanctuary and did not carry citywide responsibility or authority. This was a civic honor and sometimes came with the expectation of financially supporting the temple

A Sacrifice to Apollo

"Then Chryses lifted up his hands, and prayed aloud for them: 'Hear me, [Apollo], god of the silver bow; . . . fulfill for me this my desire: ward off now from the Danaans the loathly pestilence.' So he spoke in prayer, and Phoebus Apollo heard him. Then, when they had prayed, and had sprinkled the barley grains, they first drew back the victims' heads, and cut their throats, and flayed them, and cut out the thighs and covered them with a double layer of fat, and laid raw flesh thereon. And the old man burned them on stakes of wood, and made libation over them of gleaming wine; and beside him the young men held in their hands the five-pronged forks. But when the thigh-pieces were wholly burned, and they had tasted the entrails, they cut up the rest and spitted it, and roasted it carefully, and drew all off the spits. Then, when they had ceased from their labor and had made ready the meal, they feasted, nor did their hearts lack anything of the equal feast. But when they had put from them the desire for food and drink, the youths filled the bowls brim full of drink and served out to all, first pouring drops for libation into the cups. So the whole day long they sought to appease the god with song, singing the beautiful paean, the sons of the Achaeans, hymning the god who works from afar; and his heart was glad, as he heard." (Homer, *Iliad* 1.450–74, LCL)

facilities and activities. There was no formal religious training involved, nor (in the Hellenistic context) did the priests of a municipality form a fraternity. Priests officiated at civic ceremonies and other special events but otherwise continued in their civilian professions, although important temples in large cities would have some full-time staff. Temple upkeep was the responsibility of the local citizenry, especially those who benefited from temple commerce. In Magnesia, south of Ephesus, property owners and businesses were required to contribute to the upkeep of the temple of Artemis, under the threat of a curse:

> And it is good for the owners of houses or for those who have built workshops to provide according to [their] means for the decorations of the altars before the [temple] entrance, and for those who make inscription[s] for Artemis Leukophryene Nikephoros. And if someone should fail to accomplish [these things], it will not be good for him. (*SIG* 695)[3]

In addition to their strictly religious functions, temples also served as banks, taking deposits and extending loans. They displayed artwork and statuary related to the cult and became objects of civic pride, attracting tourists visiting the city. One such ancient tourist, Pausanias, took extensive notes on his travels to various cities in Greece, and his diary provides a virtual catalog of the artwork and attractions of the temples he visited. It is no surprise, then, that robbing temples

---

3. Cited in Richard Ascough, "The Completion of a Religious Duty: The Background of 2 Cor. 8:1–15," *NTS* 42 (1996): 597.

was a perennial problem in the ancient world and even warrants mention by Paul (Rom. 2:22). Some temples had sacred groves attached, which functioned almost as city parks do today. The sanctuary of Demeter and Kore in Corinth included a theater that seated approximately one hundred people. Temples provided dining facilities for private parties, local guilds, and political associations (cf. 1 Cor. 8:10; 2 Cor. 6:14–7:1). Schoolteachers might hold their classes in the shaded porticoes of a temple, philosophers or rhetoricians would situate themselves on the steps to gain a better hearing, and all manner of vendors could be found outside the temple precincts, selling food, crafts, and religious paraphernalia.

Even this brief and incomplete listing of temple life in the Greek city reveals an institution deeply embedded within the social and economic structure of the ancient world. In fact, perhaps the most noteworthy confrontation between the early Christian movement and a civic cult was not primarily ideological, mono-theism versus polytheism, but economic. Consider the riot of the silversmiths in Ephesus. In the words of the silversmith Demetrius, rallying his fellow artisans to oppose Paul: "You know, my friends, that we receive a good income from this business. And you see and hear how this fellow Paul has convinced and led astray large numbers of people here in Ephesus and in practically the whole province of Asia. He says that gods made by human hands are no gods at all" (Acts 19:25–26 NIV). The kind of large-scale conversion to Christianity that Luke describes in Acts 19 would have had a significant impact on a local economy, because in Hel-lenistic antiquity religion and economy were tightly intertwined.

Festivals and Competitions

Temples occupied a central role in the social and economic life of a commu-nity; this issues from the fact that religion was more of a communal concern in the ancient world than it is in many modern societies, especially modern societies with a carefully delineated separation between "church" and state. The ruling magistrates of the Greek *polis* or other townships in Hellenistic antiquity saw themselves charged with ensuring that their ancient contract with the gods was fully executed. The obligation on the part of the city was to celebrate, reverence, and honor the gods; the obligation on the part of the gods was to protect, bless, and enrich the city. One of the most important ways the community fulfilled its responsibility was by regularly honoring the gods through festivals and sport. Each city had a festal calendar that specified the dates on which the various gods were celebrated, usually on an annual basis. Important gods warranted lengthier, more elaborate festivals, some lasting nearly a week. Athens had nearly sixty days allot-ted to festal veneration, though most of these would consist of a simple sacrifice in the temple of the deity. Major festivals began with a grand procession winding through the significant quadrants of the city and, depending on the deity and the precise nature of the cult, sometimes involved representatives of the local citizenry: children, young men and women, military figures, politicians, members of local guilds and businesses, and others. The procession would end at the temple of the god or goddess and climax with a sacrifice.

Competitions often accompanied a festival and would draw spectators from all over the Greek world. The competitions included many athletic events familiar to a modern audience (boxing, running, wrestling, javelin, etc.), as well as musical and theatrical arts. The Panathenaic festival, in honor of Athena, included competitions and prizes for singers, flute players, dancers, and poets. Sacrifices and libations to the gods were an important feature of these competitions, in many cases being performed by the competitors before each event.

The most important point to grasp from this synopsis of the most significant public expressions of Hellenistic religion is the pervasive nature of civic religion in antiquity. In fact, religion and society were so fully integrated in the Greco-Roman world that it is hard to imagine participating meaningfully in community life without also participating in the religious life of that community. This becomes particularly apparent in the Corinthian correspondence, where in three different contexts the apostle Paul has to take the Corinthians to task for continuing to frequent pagan temples (1 Cor. 8:1–13; 10:1–30; 2 Cor. 6:15–7:1). In 1 Cor. 8 and 10 Paul expresses his concern candidly, but by the time he writes 2 Corinthians his patience has worn thin and his approach is more confrontational: "What harmony is there between Christ and Belial? Or what does a believer have in common with an unbeliever? What agreement is there between the temple of God and idols? . . . 'Come out from them and be separate, says the Lord'" (6:15–17 NIV).

> ### A Festal Procession at Ephesus Honoring the Local Hero-God Habrocomas and Heroine-Goddess Anthia
>
> "The local festival of Artemis was in progress with its procession from the city to the temple nearly a mile away. All the local girls had to march in procession richly dressed, as well as the young men of Habrocomas' age. He was around sixteen, and already a member of the ephebes and took first place in the procession. There was a great crowd of Ephesians and visitors alike to see the festival, for it was the custom at this festival to find husbands for the girls and wives for the young men. So the procession filed past, first the sacred objects; the torches, the baskets and the incense; and horses, dogs, hunting equipment, some for war, most for peace. . . . Each of the girls was dressed as if to receive a lover. Anthia led the line of girls."[a]
>
> [a] Simon Price, *Religions of the Ancient Greeks* (Cambridge: Cambridge University Press, 1999), 30.

Domestic Expressions of Religion

The expression of religion in the domestic setting took many different forms in the Hellenistic milieu. A full description of the rituals and practices of religion in the Greek household could fill several volumes and would have to be nuanced according to region, city, and tribe. In what follows I offer a generic depiction of the most typical elements of domestic and familial religion, drawing on material from various regions, loosely organized around the themes of household gods, familial rituals, and domestic décor.

Virtually every Greek home, be it a rural farmhouse, a small urban flat, or a larger domicile, would have at least some space devoted to a household deity, although the household altar was not a permanent architectural feature until the late Hellenistic era. Perhaps the most common household deity was Hestia, the goddess of the hearth. The hearth was the center of domestic life—associated with warmth, dining, and food preparation—and many family rituals would be enacted in front of the hearth. For example, a newborn was carried around the hearth—the symbolic representation of the goddess—to signify his or her acceptance into the family. While Hestia presided over family life, Zeus Herkeios ("of the enclosure/fence") protected boundaries of the household, often in the form of an altar or statuette in the courtyard. Zeus Ktesios ("of the property") and Apollo Agyieus ("of the street") might also be stationed at prominent points around the property, warding off intruders. The Cynic Epistles report that every home in Cyzicus (northern Asia Minor) bore an inscription invoking the strength of Heracles: "The son of Zeus, the gloriously triumphant Heracles, lives here. Let no evil enter" (*Epistles of Diogenes* 36.1)[4]. In addition to these (more or less) universal household deities, scores of other gods were associated with the home in various regions: Hermes, the triple Hecate, the Dioscuri, Zeus Katabasis ("who comes down"), and Zeus Meilichios ("gracious"), among others. Finally, mention should be made of the Agathos Daimon ("Good Spirit"), who was often represented as a snake painted on a wall inside a domicile and who brought good fortune and prosperity to the household.

Homage was paid to these gods in a variety of ways, principally through prayers, offerings, and libations. A woman might offer a prayer to Hecate before leaving the home or embarking on a journey (cf. Aristophanes, *Lysistrata* 64). Apollo Agyieus was commonly anointed with oil and fillets. Sometimes portions of a meal would be set out for the household god, or libations poured on the floor or at the base of the god's statue. The Agathos Daimon was regularly offered a few drops of unmixed wine at the end of the day.

In addition to the routine rituals that punctuated the daily life of a Hellenistic household—morning and evening offerings, libations and prayers before a dinner party, and so on—religious rites accompanied all the major events of family life: rites of passage (male puberty rites); the entrance of a child, bride, or slave into the home; marriage; death and burial; the cycles of nature (spring and harvest in particular); and others beside. What was true on the civic level also applied to

---

4. Abraham J. Malherbe, *The Cynic Epistles: A Study Edition* (Sources for Biblical Study 12; Missoula, MT: Scholars Press, 1977).

the household: piety toward the gods was the obligation of the family and tribe in order to secure the favor of the gods and avoid their wrath.

Religion also influenced domestic décor, sometimes significantly. In addition to statuary and household altars (which were fixed architectural features by the NT era), a Greek home tended to mirror the mythology of the culture in many other ways. Vases commonly depicted mythological characters and events (Zeus seated with Hera, Heracles battling the Hydra, etc.). Many household utensils and furnishings incorporated aspects of religion and superstition (see below) into their design: a serving tray with the muses as the pedestal, a lamp in the shape of a phallus to ward off evil, a ladle etched with a magical symbol, a comb engraved with Aphrodite's likeness—such items were commonplace. Muraled walls, frescoed courtyards, and tiled floors also frequently depicted popular religious motifs. This becomes more significant when we remember that the primitive Jesus movement was centered in the local home and multiplied through establishing household assemblies.

Individual Expressions of Religion

When we moderns think of ancient Greek religion, our thoughts probably dwell on the major deities of the pantheon. Many of us have visited the impressive remains of their temples, marveled at their statuary in museums, and probably read a bit of Homer, or at least seen some of the popular cinematic representations of his stories. It is arguable, however, that for the ancients themselves, more energy was expended not on practices that were related to the organized religion of civic cults, or even to deeply ingrained domestic traditions, but on activities voluntarily undertaken by individuals to ward off evil, procure benefits, or discern what would happen tomorrow: oracles, divination, astrology, and magic.

Wikimedia Commons

Divination

Knowledge of the future has ever been the fascination of mortals, and the Hellenistic world had a long and venerated tradition of oracles and divination. The major oracular centers were at Delphi (honoring Apollo), Dodona (honoring Zeus and Dione), Epidaurus

8.2. This omphalos ("navel") stone preserved in the Delphi museum reflects the legend that Delphi was the center of the earth and the place where two eagles released by Zeus met. Two golden eagles likely stood over this conical marble stone. At Delphi, oracles stood on a stone and delivered prophetic messages interpreted by prophets. Acts 16:16 speaks of a female oracle who has a spirit of *python*; the earliest name of Delphi was Python.

(honoring Asclepius), and Corinth (honoring Apollo). Here the oracle would receive questions from individuals, usually mediated through a priest or priestess, and give a reply. The supplicant would pay a fee, of course, and also perform preparatory rites before the query would be received. Although the oracles were sometimes consulted by officials of state seeking direction on issues of national importance (military ambitions, stemming the outbreak of a plague, etc.), usually the clients were individuals concerned with more mundane matters, as this sampling illustrates: "Shall I receive the allowance?" "Am I to be sold?" "Am I to be reconciled with my offspring?" "Shall I become a senator?" "Am I to be divorced from my wife?"[5] In the later Hellenistic era, mediums and diviners had become common fixtures in the marketplaces and alleyways of Greek towns and villages. The casual references in the literature to street-corner seers and peripatetic prophets reveal a world where, not unlike today, psychic hotlines were readily available. Haruspicy (examining the entrails of animals), augury (studying the flight patterns and eating habits of birds), and the observation of unusual natural phenomena (earthquakes, floods, swarming bees, animals born with deformities, etc.) were common techniques of divination, but there were many others besides, including astrological predictions and especially dreams.

According to Homer, "dreams come from Zeus" (*Iliad* 1.63, LCL); this perspective represents the conventional wisdom of the ancients. Plutarch (ca. AD 46–120), for example, calls dreams "the most ancient and respected form of divination" (*Mor.* 159A, LCL). Philo's *On Dreams* is a lengthy apologetic work on the divine origin of dreams. Biblical literature, too, recounts divine encounters through dreams, from Joseph to Daniel to the apostle Paul. In the ancient world mediums were sometimes consulted to clarify the meaning of nocturnal revelations, though always for a price. The interpretation of dreams was always the risky part, as this letter reveals:

> Apollonius to Ptolemaeus his father: Greetings.
>   I swear by the god Serapis that if I had not a little compunction you would never see my face again; for you utter nothing but lies, and your gods likewise, for they have plunged us into a deep mire in which we may die, and when you have a vision that we are to be rescued, then we sink outright! . . . Never again can I hold up my head in Tricomia for shame that we have given ourselves away and been deluded, misled by the gods and trusting in dreams!
>   Farewell![6]

Superstition and Magic

In addition to these more quantifiable practices were a whole host of other beliefs and activities that can be loosely categorized as superstition and magic.

5. P.Oxy. 1477; *Select Papyri*, 193 LCL.
6. P.Par. 47; *Select Papyri*, 100 (revised) LCL.

While the philosophers waxed eloquently on the grandeur and perfection of the gods, and while priests and civic officials organized festivals to celebrate beneficence of their patron deities, the butcher scratched a curse in lead on his competitor, the courtesan buried a frog at a crossroads to prevent a fever, the traveler tucked a talisman into his cloak to ensure safe passage to his destination, and a young maiden purchased an incantation that, if properly enacted, would guarantee a good marriage and many offspring. In fact, the townsfolk, merchants, and magistrates of Hellenistic antiquity were deeply superstitious and envisioned the universe as brimming with supernatural beings—be they heroes, nymphs, gods, or spirits (*daimones*)—who could be invoked to help oneself or harm others. Moreover, even the most insignificant events could portend disaster: a donkey braying in the distance, a shoe gnawed by a mouse, or even a sneeze.

The belief that supernatural powers could be summoned to aid mortals gave rise to a prolific industry producing charms, talismans, amulets, and incantations, along with the various types of sorcerers and spiritists who trafficked in magical paraphernalia and soothsaying. Numerous stories are told of charlatans and purveyors of snake oil who preyed on the phobias of the gullible and sometimes made a handsome profit.[7] In fact, peddlers of the paranormal were so commonly associated with rank profiteering that the Greek word for "sorcerer" (*goēs*) came to be a simple synonym for "swindler."

The principal forms of magic in antiquity were protective magic (from enemies, illness, evil spirits), imprecatory magic (invoking a curse on a foe or rival), and love magic (compelling affection in another). The common denominator in each of these is the belief that spirits and supernatural powers could be manipulated to do one's bidding through the correct execution of secret rites and incantations. Philo deplores the hordes of magical practitioners in Alexandria, and the scene he describes here would have been typical of most cities of the Hellenistic and NT era:

> But there is a counterfeit of this [true magic], most properly called a perversion of art, pursued by charlatan mendicants and parasites and the basest of the women and slave population, who make it their profession to deal in purifications and disenchantments and promise with some sort of charms and incantations to turn men's love into deadly enmity and their hatred into profound affection. The simplest and most innocent natures are deceived by their bait. (*Spec.* 3.101, LCL)[8]

The NT contains numerous references to diviners, exorcists, and other practitioners of the magical arts, particularly in the book of Acts. Luke tell us of Simon Magus ("the magician"), the duplicitous sorcerer who tried to purchase the power of the Spirit like any other magical incantation (Acts 8:9–25); of Bar-Jesus,

---

7. Lucian of Samosata took particular delight in exposing religious frauds. See his *Alexander the False Prophet*; *Lover of Lies*; *The Ship*; *Menippus, or Descent into Hades* and scattered references throughout his writings.

8. Compare Horace's description of Rome in *Sat.* 1.6.111–15; 1.8.17–22.

another sorcerer, who attempted to dissuade the Roman governor Sergius Paulus from accepting the message of Paul and Barnabas (13:4–12); of a prophetess in Philippi (16:16–18), exorcists in Ephesus (19:13–16), and a bonfire of magical texts and paraphernalia in Ephesus (19:18–20). What is remarkable about the magical bonfire is that it was *believers* who became convicted of their clandestine sorcery and who turned over their scrolls for burning. Even more astounding is that the value of this material, estimated by Luke, was fifty thousand pieces of silver. Such a colossal figure implies a large number of Ephesian believers with an enormous investment in the dark arts.

Mystery Religions

Alternative systems of religion were also practiced, most notably the mystery cults. Mystery religions were voluntarily undertaken by individuals for a variety of reasons: one person might be attracted to the promise of a blissful eternal life, another to the religious community, or another to the more personal expression of religion that these groups offered. Mystery religions are so designated because each involved secret rites of initiation that could not be revealed to outsiders. The ancient Greek mysteries included Orphism, Dionysian mysteries, the Cabiri at Samothrace, the Andanian mysteries, and most important, the Eleusinan mysteries. In the later Hellenistic and Roman era the mysteries of Isis, Cybele, and Mithras became extremely popular.

Because of the secretive nature of these mystery religions, we lack any detailed description of the rites undertaken by the initiate, though the accounts that have survived mention rituals of purification, sacrifices, the recitation of oaths, sacred vows, rituals involving the symbolic death and rebirth of the initiate, and sacred meals. These rites have prompted comparisons between Christianity and the mysteries. The most readily available primary sources discussing the mysteries include the *Homeric Hymn to Demeter* (sixth century BC), Plutarch's *Isis and Osiris* (late first century AD), and Apuleius's *Metamorphoses* (second century AD).

The cults of the mysteries often sponsored public festivals and parades (most famously depicted in Apuleius, *Metam.* 11) and created close-knit communities of initiates. Their conception of the deity—particularly devotees of Isis—was more personal and affectionate than how the gods were perceived in the civic cults. Historians frequently speculate that this feature of the theology of mystery religions, together with their promise of a blissful afterlife, was particularly important in attracting followers.

The Afterlife

Few areas of ancient Greek religious conceptions offer more confusion and contradictions than their thoughts on the afterlife. This is largely due to the fact that Hellenistic religion—itself quite diverse—had no canonical texts to teach "orthodox" dogma on any point, and hence coming to terms with Hellenistic conceptions of the afterlife essentially amounts to cataloging and organizing a broad range of disparate popular beliefs and images.

The Homeric tales popularized the idea of Hades, the cheerless underworld where faceless souls wandered drearily after death. Plato taught that the soul of the noble philosopher would survive death and attain perfect knowledge (*Phaedo*). Elysium (or the Elysian Fields) was the peaceful repose for initiates into the mysteries, heroes, and other favorites of the gods, while astral transformation (becoming a star in the galaxy) and reincarnation were also popular in the imagination of the ancients. Epicureans were known for their metaphysical materialism and their absolute denial of any kind of postmortem existence. In the words of Epicurus (341–270 BC): "Death is nothing to us; for the body, when it has been resolved into its elements, has no feeling, and that which has no feeling is nothing for us" (Epicurus, *Principal Doctrines* 2; in Diogenes Laertius, *Lives* 10.139 LCL). The notion of complete extinction surfaces in other forms as well, quite apart from Epicurean influence. Stoics—one of the most popular philosophies of the late Hellenistic and early Roman era—believed in an endless cycle of cosmic conflagration, after which the entire history of the cosmos would be repeated in exactly the same sequence. Usually this involved the temporary extinction of the soul until the next cosmic cycle.

Funerary monuments and burial practices also reveal other notions, including the primitive but enduring belief that the dead somehow continued to live in the tomb. For example, the deceased are often depicted as reclining on a couch, alert and peaceful. In Corinth and elsewhere, we find tombs with openings so that food and drink could be supplied. Others were equipped with clothing and items for meal preparation; some were stocked with charms to ward off evil. Gravestones in Macedonia portray the deceased as a mythic horseman (a Thracian Rider) ascending to immortality and sometimes contain references to the departed as joining the divinized heroes. When Paul assures the Thessalonians that believers among them who have died are not in any sense disadvantaged with respect to the Lord's return, and so the Thessalonians need not grieve like those "who have no hope" (1 Thess. 4:13), his thought is not that those outside the Christian faith entertain no prospects for an afterlife. Rather, the cacophony of perspectives that bombarded residents of a typical Greco-Roman city like Thessalonica allowed little room for certainty and was a stark contrast to the clear proclamation and teaching of Paul and his fellow apostles.

We could add other popular conceptions to this list—ghost stories, references to punishment in the afterlife, and so on—but the general picture should be clear enough. It is important to remember, however, that all of these beliefs were united on at least one point: their denial of a bodily resurrection. In fact, the idea of a postmortem physical rejuvenation was distasteful to most Greeks, particularly in light of their disparagement of the physical component of personhood as a useless husk that needed to be discarded. Thus it is no surprise that the apostle Paul's preaching of the resurrection was greeted with open skepticism in Athens (Acts 17:32) and derision in Corinth (1 Cor. 15).

Conclusion

Greek society, as the apostle Paul observed of Athens, was indeed "very religious" (Acts 17:22 NIV). Religion was integral to community life, family life, and the private aspirations of individuals. Most civic celebrations contained overtly religious elements, as did the grand ceremonies of state. Family traditions, along with the mundane duties of daily life, were performed under the watchful eyes of the household gods, and if calamity struck the family or the city, the first order of business was to determine which of the gods had been offended and what must be done to appease him or her. Christianity entered this milieu and made some rather startling claims. In contrast to the conventional religious conceptions of the day, the followers of Jesus claimed that there was only one God, who created everything. This God cared about humanity to the point of sending his own Son in the flesh to atone for their sins. Even more preposterous, this atoning self-sacrifice took place though the shameful spectacle of crucifixion—a death reserved for slaves, criminals, and enemies of the state. The figure of Jesus was certainly an oddity in the religious smorgasbord of antiquity. Amid the plethora of divinities being worshiped in the first century, it is remarkable that anyone would dare to add a crucified Jewish peasant to this list, and even more remarkable that the primitive Jesus movement would snowball into an empire-wide phenomenon.

Bibliography

Burkert, Walter. *Ancient Mystery Cults.* Cambridge, MA: Harvard University Press, 1989. A careful comparison of five major mystery religions, discussing their rituals, membership, structure, and propagation.

———. *Greek Religion.* Oxford: Wiley-Blackwell, 1991. The most comprehensive one-volume treatment of Greek religion available in English and the standard textbook. Although no treatment of this vast topic can claim to be exhaustive, Burkert covers all the important topics in detail, with copious reference to primary and secondary sources.

Easterling, P. E., and J. V. Muir, eds. *Greek Religion and Society.* Cambridge: Cambridge University Press, 1985. A collection of topflight classicists offering brief but informative essays on most of the topics treated in this chapter. Particularly useful are the chapters by Paul Cartledge on "The Greek Religious Festival" and by Simon Price on "Greek Art and Religion."

Evans, Craig A., and Stanley E. Porter, eds. *Dictionary of New Testament Backgrounds.* Downers Grove, IL: InterVarsity, 2000. A useful compendium of articles covering all areas of NT background. Entries are succinct, informative, and written by specialists.

Particularly relevant to the topic of this chapter are B. W. R. Pearson, "Civic Cults," 217–20; S. E. Porter, "Festivals," 368–70; B. W. R. Pearson, "Polytheism, Greco-Roman," 815–18; and N. C. Croy, "Religion, Personal," 926–31.

Garland, Robert. *Religion and the Greeks*. London: Duckworth, 2001. Concise and highly readable.

Graf, Fritz. *Magic in the Ancient World*. Cambridge, MA: Harvard University Press, 1997. An in-depth look at sorcery, divination, and magic in antiquity. Sources range from the classical period to the third century AD.

Klauck, Hans-Joseph. *The Religious Context of Early Christianity*. Minneapolis: Fortress, 2003. The standard text for understanding the religious context of the first century and early Christianity.

Mikalson, John D. *Ancient Greek Religion*. Oxford: Blackwell, 2005. A mid-length treatment of the topic that specifically aims to incorporate perspectives and practices from various social classes. Includes a chapter on the Hellenistic era.

Rice, David G., and John E. Stambaugh. *Sources for the Study of Greek Religion*. Corrected ed. Atlanta: Society of Biblical Literature, 2009. An ample selection of primary sources relating to Greek religion, each briefly introduced by the editors.

9

The Imperial Cult

NICHOLAS PERRIN

For the greater part of the history of modern NT scholarship, the first-century practice of emperor worship was considered of secondary importance to our understanding of the background to early Christianity. Traditionally, classicists believed that the ancient Roman world rolled its collective eyes at the pretensions of deified emperors and that the associated cult, hardly anything more than a recurring case of overly enthusiastic imperial propaganda, had little connection with early Christian persecution. Along these lines it has also been suggested that Rome's alleged role in persecuting Christians and perhaps even the persecutions themselves—as described, for example, in Revelation—must have been born more of early Christian imagination than of reality. In the past several decades, however, closer attention to Roman imperial ideology, the emperor worship's integration within this ideology, and the related NT texts themselves has changed this assessment. Much recent scholarship is appreciating anew the fact that the early Christians lived in a world dominated by the Roman imperial cult. As such, a better understanding of the imperial cult is prerequisite to a better understanding of the NT itself.

Octavian and the Origins of the Emperor Cult

Octavian's Rise to Political Power

The genesis of the emperor cult must be understood against the political backdrop that helped give it rise. The story begins with the assassination of Julius

Caesar (100–44 BC). On Caesar's death, the great Roman leader's inheritance fell to his great-nephew Octavian (63 BC–AD 14), who by virtue of Caesar's will was adopted as his son. Soon thereafter, Octavian formed an uneasy alliance with Mark Antony (83–30 BC) and Marcus Aemilius Lepidus (ca. 88–ca. 12 BC). Together, on November 26, 43 BC, the three formed what is now known as the Second Triumvirate, in effect a three-man dictatorship. It was a moment that marked the end of the Roman Republic. All the same, all three leaders were well aware that it would be in their best interests to maintain as much as possible the nostalgic appearance of republican days.

Eventually, the instability of the triumvirate became manifest. After a poorly timed attempt to usurp power in Sicily in 36 BC, Lepidus was unilaterally removed from office. Several years later, tensions between Octavian and Antony came to a head, especially in connection with the latter's romantic liaison with the Egyptian Cleopatra VII (69–30 BC). On Octavian's encouragement, the Senate declared war on Antony, who—following a devastating setback at the battle of Actium (31 BC) as well as a further defeat at Alexandria (30 BC)—committed suicide along with Cleopatra. For all intents and purposes, Octavian at that point became the unchallenged ruler of the Roman Empire. Thus was soon to begin his role as princeps (technically meaning the leading senator) and the era historians call the Roman Principate (27 BC–AD 284).

Mark Antony's demise did not bode well for the province of Asia (modern-day western Turkey), which had not only supported him against Octavian but took the extra measure of deifying him as the New Dionysus, an ascription that Antony apparently did not resist. Responding quickly to the turn in political tides, the council of Asia's representative elders (the *koinon*) made an overture to Octavian in the winter of 29 BC, in which they requested permission to establish a cult in his honor in Pergamum (Dio Cassius, *Hist.* 51.20; Tacitus, *Ann.* 4.37). Around the same time, a similar request came on behalf of the city Nicea in the province of Bithynia. Unfortunately, the ancient sources do not clarify the motivation for the *koinon*'s request. In *Rituals and Power*, S. R. F. Price has argued that the local leadership issued the petition as part of an attempt to render Roman rule in symbolic terms that would be sensible to the Asian mind. The weakness of this explanation lies in its inability to explain the increasingly widespread enthusiasm for the imperial cult in succeeding decades (see Witulski, *Kaiserkult*, 15). Of course there was an element of self-serving expediency in the *koinon*'s request (Friesen, *Twice Neokoros*, 7–8); given the province's previous allegiance to Octavian's failed rival, it was only the better part of political wisdom for the local leadership to show that it could be just as subservient to the newly established princeps. However, the bid does not seem to have been simply a matter of political calculation. In a display of military prowess, Octavian had finally brought peace and therefore some measure of prosperity to the East. This fact alone seems not only to have impressed the Asian cities but also to have prompted a spirit of genuine gratitude mixed with deep admiration.

Sources reflecting on Octavian's response to the *koinon*'s request indicate a note of hesitancy. This is understandable, for the new ruler must have been keenly aware that many Romans regarded his ascension as a mixed blessing; this is because it effectively spelled the end of the republic as the Roman citizens had known it. Octavian knew that if he were to accrue too much power (or too much glory) too quickly, this would cause more than a few senators to second-guess their support for his leadership. In the end, he acceded to the request from Asia, but on two conditions—first, that the cultic worship be directed to him alongside the goddess Roma, the deified embodiment of the republic; and second, that the cities of Nicea and Ephesus also erect separate sanctuaries to *Dea Roma* and *Divus Iulius* (the spirit of his illustrious predecessor, who had been deified by Senate decree in 42 BC), presumably to serve Roman citizens inhabiting those cities. To what extent the counterproposal issued from Octavian's personal discomfort with such high accolades is impossible to know. Of this we can be sure: Octavian's counterproposal reflected not only his sensitivity to the differentiated socioreligious composition of the Asian province but also his political shrewdness. Although expatriate Romans would have preferred to continue worshiping the dead hero Julius Caesar alongside Roma (whose cult was already well established) in traditional republican style, local Greeks would now have opportunity to worship Augustus (the name given Octavian by the Roman Senate) himself but not apart from his symbolical embodiment of Roman power. By allowing the Greeks to establish a cult in his name, he was cementing and indeed institutionalizing their loyalties to him as a ruler; by allowing the Romans to continue worshiping Julius Caesar, whose temple he himself had just dedicated months earlier on his victorious return from Egypt, he was consolidating his base as Caesar's heir among traditional Roman republicans.

Two years later, on January 16, 27 BC, after Octavian signaled his intention of returning full authority to the Senate, including a substantial degree of power Octavian had retained over the provinces and the armies, the ruling body rewarded the gesture by declaring him princeps and *Augustus* (Greek *Sebastos*). The latter term, meaning "illustrious one" or "venerable one," had strong religious overtones. Seeking to stabilize an empire that had been racked by violent civil war, in which Octavian himself played no small part, the Senate saw it best to make a clean break with Rome's recent bloodied past and set their ruler on new footing. As acclaimed Augustus, Octavian would be lord not simply of the Roman Empire but also, in some respects, of the whole realm of nature.

The implications of Augustus's religious role have remained a matter of some dispute. Prior to Price (*Rituals and Power*), classical and NT scholarship generally thought of language pertaining to Augustus's religio-theological significance as more a matter of exaggerated pious rhetoric than of actual belief. That is, the emperor's religious claims were thought to be mere window dressing for his political claims, not statements that spoke meaningfully to metaphysical realities. More recent scholarship, however, has pointed out that this scholarly account has depended on the application of modern and therefore anachronistic conceptual categories to the study of the cult. Today the ascribed split between Roman religion and Roman politics can no longer be convincingly sustained.

This shift in scholarly opinion has in turn opened up new vistas of study, involving an integrated account of Roman ideology and emperor worship. Allen Brent, for example, seeks to show that the myth of the imperial cult drew on a Stoic philosophy of order so as to cast Caesar Augustus as the empire's new *augur*, that is, the one duly appointed on behalf of mortals to interpret the will of the gods (*Imperial Cult*). If the chronic instability of earlier years was a sign of the wrath of the gods, it now fell to Augustus to achieve Rome's destiny by securing the *pax deorum* ("peace of the gods") on earth. This would suggest that even though Augustus did not officially acquire the office of Pontifex Maximus (the priestly "greatest bridge builder" between the gods and mortals) until 13 BC, his office was equally political and religious from the start.

As surviving statuary makes clear, Augustus was not simply a model for emulation (though he was that, as evidenced by Roman men adopting Augustus's hairstyle), but also the human incarnation of those virtues that up to that point had been personified only within the pantheon of Roman gods. Thus it is not so much the case—as is commonly stated—that the Romans had a waning interest in the traditional gods and that this created a vacuum that the emperor cultus filled; rather, it was the expansion of the emperor's public persona, a correlate of his suddenly expanded political power, that began to make these gods redundant. All of this meant that any challenge to the religious supremacy of the emperor could be perceived as an act of political subversion—a dynamic that would prove challenging for the early church.

Precedents to the Imperial Cult

Although it is sufficient on one level to assert that the origins of the Roman imperial cult can be traced to the initiative of the Asian *koinon*, this hardly answers the question as to how the cultic sites established for Octavian relate to preexisting religious practices. Amid the various backgrounds that have been adduced for the emperor cult, leading experts on the subject have reminded us that caution is in order. In particular, we can no longer assume that the Romans simply and without residue modeled their imperial cult on the Hellenistic practice of worshiping rulers and heroes (Price, *Rituals and Power*, 25–40). History is better served if it admits elements of both continuity and discontinuity between the imperial cult and Hellenistic practices.

Although the deification of deceased mortals was not entirely uncommon in the West, according the same honor to living human beings was comparatively rare, though not unheard of. According to Duris of Samos (350–281 BC), the first recorded instance of a deified living human being comes in the case of the fifth-century BC Spartan general Lysander, who received divine honors upon his victorious return to Samos. Plutarch (*Dion* 46.1) also attests that Dion of Syracuse

(408–354 BC) accrued similar honors, but this is disputable. More clear-cut is the case of Alexander the Great (356–323 BC), who was reported at various points and by different ancient historians as having received worship from his conquered. Alexander also seems to have implied his divine self-identity in a variety of ways, not least through his having erected a star-laden canopy over his throne (Plutarch, *Alex.* 37.7). When one of Alexander's later successors, the Macedonian Demetrius I (337–283 BC), also donned a robe displaying the twelve signs of the zodiac, thereby symbolically intimating mastery over the cosmos, he was undoubtedly following Alexander's lead.

Self-identification with the divine and use of divine imagery continued sporadically down into the NT era. In his account of the death of King Herod Agrippa I, the Jewish historian Josephus (*Ant.* 19.343–50) links the resplendence of the king's robes, tailored to reflect the sun's intensity, with the crowd's acclamation of him as a god (cf. Acts 12:20–23). David Aune ("Influence") observes that Nero wore a robe similar to that of Demetrius I, and he constructed a lavish banquet hall engineered to revolve as the heavens, which makes the intriguing suggestion that the astral imagery of Rev. 1:16 was meant to parody imperial pretensions. The history of Hellenistic kingship is crowded with other figures who by various means—the receiving of *proskynēsis* ("prostration"), hymns, and golden crowns—accepted ascriptions of divinity. The NT era appears to be no exception to this rule. However, interestingly enough, on Augustus's rise to power, the Eastern practice of offering cultic honor to military or political personages outside the emperor or his family did fall off markedly. Given Caesar's unsurpassable authority, it was likely considered neither wise nor appropriate to divert honor from the one who was deemed most worthy of homage. So on one level, Roman emperor worship fits in well with the established practices of paying high homage to Hellenistic kings.

But again, most scholars are now wary of drawing too tight a connection between this context and the cult launched early in the Principate. First, some have supposed a categorical difference between Hellenistic king worship and the Roman imperial cult. To be sure, even though Hellenistic society was predicated on reciprocal (i.e., patron-client) relationships, and one might explain the imperial cult as excessive homage of this type, nevertheless the phenomenon of emperor worship seems to reflect not simply a difference in degree (that is, in intensity) but also a difference in kind.

Second, as a general rule, cultic honor that the Greeks paid to the politically empowered leaders tended to be both temporary (lasting only as long as their political tenure) and relatively unattached to designated sacred space. The case remains different on both counts when it comes to emperor worship. For example, the above-mentioned temple dedicated to the worship of Octavian Augustus continued to flourish even a century after Octavian's death.

Third, Steven Friesen draws a distinction between Hellenistic king worship and the imperial cult in that while the former was often directed to the king's dynasty as whole and thereby retained a largely institutional focus, the latter was more fundamentally oriented to the emperor as an individual (*Twice Neokoros*, 9).

Fourth, taking a position that is somewhat at odds with the above critiques but no less convincing, Ittai Gradel denies any sort of influence from Hellenistic practice (*Emperor Worship*). He proceeds by arguing (1) that Roman worship was not unprecedented in the republican era (there are solid reasons for believing that Julius Caesar received such worship in his last days) and (2) that the rise of the imperial cult was less a function of Eastern religious influence than of the sociopolitical reordering that transpired at the close of the republic, leaving Octavian in a position of unprecedented social and political power. That there is continuing debate regarding the origins of the emperor cult suggests that a new consensus has yet to be formed.

The Development of the Imperial Cult

One of the standard, popular-level misconceptions regarding the imperial cult is that it was launched as a kind of top-down initiative, a propaganda device for the politically empowered to secure the support of the masses. Two facts in particular give lie to this notion. First, as mentioned above, the initiative for the very first imperial cult issued not from Rome but from the leading cities of one of its eastern provinces. Second, as will be made clear below, the cult's growing popularity does not seem to be traced to imperial initiative so much as to largely spontaneous enthusiasm of the people on a local level. The growing fervor that attended the cult and Augustus's steadily increasing honorary status are reflected in the historical sources.

This burgeoning enthusiasm was evident very early on. Writing only a handful of years after the establishment of the Principate, Nicolaus of Damascus, a biographer of Augustus and friend to Herod the Great, speaks to the significance of Octavian's acquisition of the title "Augustus." He writes, "Because humankind address[es] him thus (as Augustus) for this esteem of his honour, they revere him with temples and sacrifices over islands and continents, being organised both by cities and peoples, repaying the greatness of his virtue and his benefaction to them" (trans. and cited in Hardin, *Galatians*, 27). True, given Nicolaus's position in Herod's court, we cannot expect him to issue a fully detached assessment of Augustus's position in Roman society. However, even if we were to allow for exaggeration, it seems difficult to resist the conclusion that the emperor cult had spontaneously and quickly spread across the Mediterranean world.

Further evidence of Augustus's exalted status comes by way of decree issued from Mytilene (located on the island of Lesbos just off the northwest coast of modern-day Turkey). The decree dates to a time between 27 and 11 BC and is found on an inscription set on two sides of a stele (an upright stone slab). In keeping with a tradition of offering cultic honors to foreign rulers, Pompey and Julius Caesar among them, the city of Mytilene apparently sent a delegation with this decree to Augustus in order to request permission to establish a cult for him. The civic leaders also requested that they be allowed to hold regular athletic contests in Augustus's honor and to celebrate his birthday every month along with sacrifices of animals raised on the provision of public funds. In what might perhaps be considered an audacious move, they further suggested that the details of their initiative be published throughout the Roman Empire, in the public spaces of the major cities and even in Augustus's very home. One section of the decree is worth quoting:

> For there is to be an oath . . . with the ancestral gods, and Sebastos . . . the image [*eikona*] of God. . . . That on the altar . . . every month on his birthday and . . . as the same sacrifices, as are offered to Zeus. . . . That is consistent with the typical greatness of his mind and takes note that there are those things which by fate and by nature are humbler and can never attain equality with those who secure a heavenly reputation and possess the station and power of gods. But if anything is discovered in later times more glorious than these decrees, then let not the zeal and the piety of the city come up short in those things that can deify [*theopoiein*] him all the more. (my translation)

Similarly effusive expressions of honor are not hard to find. For example, in a decree from the League of Asia (Prienne, 9 BC), we read as follows:

> Since Providence, which has divinely disposed our lives, having employed zeal and ardor, has arranged the most perfect culmination for life by producing Augustus, whom for the benefit of mankind she has filled with excellence, as if she had granted him a savior for us and our descendants, a savior who brought war to an end and set all things in peaceful order; and since with his appearance Caesar exceeded the hopes of all those who had received glad tidings [*euangelia*] before us, not only surpassing those who had been benefactors before him, but not even leaving any hope of surpassing him for those who are to come in the future; and since the beginning of glad tidings [*euangeliôn*] on his account for the world was the birthday of the god. (trans. and cited in Harrison, "Paul," 85)

Consistent with the Mytilene inscription, the Prienne inscription envisages Augustus as "savior" and the author of universal peace. His birthday is reckoned as the source of "glad tidings," or "gospel." Similar ascriptions and titles, including "son of God" and "God Sebastos," are not uncommon in other inscriptions and coinage. One inscription even states that Augustus has "outstripped even the Olympian gods" (trans. and cited in Hardin, *Galatians*, 29). Unless history has misled us, such attributions clearly exceed the level of honor accorded to any previous Hellenistic ruler. For this reason, it would perhaps be no overstatement to say that up to that point in Western history, no human figure had been accorded a status equal to that of Caesar Augustus.

Despite the citation that Augustus "outstripped even the Olympian gods," it is unlikely that first-century Greeks or Romans put the princeps in exactly the same category as the pantheon of gods. Friesen is probably right to maintain that with respect to the population of mortals, Octavian was indeed a god (*Twice Neokoros*). But, in respect to the gods, the ruler of the empire remained a mortal, notwithstanding the fact that his honors excelled those of any gods. On his death, Augustus might have expected to undergo full apotheosis in the same way that Julius Caesar was said to have done (evidenced by the enduring nocturnal appearance of a comet during the course of a weeklong games held in his honor [Pliny the Elder, *Nat. Hist.* 2.93–94]), but this expectation would have also entailed a future, postmortem change of status. Ascriptions of divinity were nuanced. Indeed, Augustus and Tiberius (42 BC–AD 37) after him probably did not think of themselves as receiving worship directly. The worship of the people was to be directed to their *genius* ("spirit"), inherited from Julius Caesar, even if this theoretical distinction might have made little difference in practice. In this connection, Price offers an explanation worth quoting at length:

> Death is one of the major problems facing any monarchy. The human frailty of the ruler and the anxious transition from reign to reign are cruces that have to be resolved by any royal system. The power of the living king demanded attention, but to have given heroic honours in his lifetime would have laid an undesirably explicit emphasis on the mortality of the king. On the other hand heroic honours after death would have made more difficult the association of the rule of the king with the rule of the gods. The offering of divine honours avoided these difficulties. If they were given in the lifetime of the rule they served to veil the awkward fact of death, which could be seen merely as a change of state. Divine honours after death and the glorification of death as a "transferral to the gods," as with the Attalids of Pergamum, or as an apotheosis, as in Rome, established a link with the gods and also made it possible to give prominence to the collectivity of the royal ancestors. (*Rituals and Power*, 35)

For the modern student, the divine status of the emperor must perhaps remain ambiguous. Precise thinking here is exacerbated when we impose a modern Western framework that tends to define deity in ontological terms, terms that would have been quite foreign to the first-century devotees of Caesar Augustus. The ancient Romans certainly distinguished mortals from gods, but the boundaries between the two categories were more fluid than our own.

In due course, the imperial cult thrust itself to the forefront of public consciousness by occupying prominent public space. In Ephesus, the image of the emperor soon crowded the local forum, occupying central public venues throughout the city (see Friesen, *Twice Neokoros*). This was fairly representative of cultural practice elsewhere in the Roman world. Countless imperial temples have survived (seventy-seven in Asia Minor alone, almost half of which were built before the close of the first century); likewise, statues of the emperor were omnipresent throughout the empire. All such projects seem to have been driven on a grassroots level. Only toward the end of the Principate was there any substantive evidence that such visible images of the emperor were monitored by Rome. As a rule, local architecture and artwork dedicated to the emperor, engendered by popular-level enthusiasm for the cult, dominated the cities' public visual-arts culture.

If the emperor cultus redefined public space, the same could be said for public time. On the suggestion of the proconsul Paullus Fabius Maximus, Asia adopted a new calendar that set the first day of its year as September 23, Augustus's birthday. Although many towns continued to use local calendars (see Oakes, *Philippians*, 139–40), the urban centers had essentially caused time to revolve around the person of the emperor. Eventually an increasing number of festivals and games were entered into a public calendar shared across the empire, all held in honor of the emperor himself. If Justin Hardin is right, this phenomenon provided the occasion for Paul's chiding the Galatian believers for observing "days, and months, and seasons, and years" (Gal. 4:10; Hardin, *Galatians*, 116–47). This postcolonial-style conflict over the Augustan calendar finds historical analogy in early Protestant resistance to the Gregorian calendar, the implementation of which was initially seen—in political terms—as the imposition of the Church of Rome.

The newly introduced Augustan calendar was only a subset of a much broader Roman vision that saw Augustus as ushering in a kind of eschatological age of peace (see, e.g., Virgil, *Aen.* 1.286–96; 6.789–807). Early Christians were forced to pit their own vision of history against that which was promulgated through Rome (see esp. Harrison, "Paul"). When the NT writings were produced, the imperial cult had already infiltrated every aspect of Roman life. Even if the very first generation of Christian believers were not necessarily forced to participate in the imperial cult, the cult as a religious expression of Romanocentric ideology remained a force with which to reckon.

As rulers changed, so too did the terms of the cult. As noted above, Octavian willingly but sheepishly accepted a cultus in his honor. His successor, Tiberius (ruled AD 14–37), who was relatively retiring by nature, was said to have been even more reluctant but was persuaded by his political advisers to accede to this homage. With the ascension of the third emperor, Caligula (AD 12–41), this humble posture suddenly changed. According to Dio Cassius (*Hist.* 59.26–28), Caligula was forthright in insisting on worship, something that Dio Cassius also notes even the commoners found to be exceedingly crass. When the Julian-Claudian line came to an end with Nero's suicide (AD 68), the Roman Empire suddenly found itself in a destabilized position, which seemed to raise the political stakes of any actions that implied either support or nonsupport for the regnant emperor. This may help explain why, by the end of the first century, there is evidence in the NT itself that the emperor cultus was making increasingly high sociopolitical demands on the Christian movement.

Conclusion

Christianity was born into a world firmly under the political control of Rome—that much is a commonplace observation in introductory NT reference works.

It is also true that this political control had religious entailments. Contemporary scholarship is still coming to terms with those entailments for devotees of Caesar as well as for the early Christians. Although a number of questions remain, it is nonetheless clear that the early Christians on some level would have had to accommodate themselves to the often grim realities of Roman rule, much as Jesus himself had done. At the same time, one detects throughout the NT a consistent undercurrent of dissent. On Jesus' death and resurrection, Jesus' followers came to declare that the risen Jesus himself was Lord and Savior of the universe. It is difficult to do proper justice to the NT without realizing that what is "good news" for the Christians is religious *and* political deviancy for the Romans.

Bibliography

Aune, David E. "The Influence of Roman Imperial Court Ceremonial on the Apocalypse of John." *BR* 28 (1983): 5–26. A wide-ranging article that both offers a helpful consideration of human deification in antiquity and passes along highly stimulating insights into any study of Revelation.

Brent, Allen. *The Imperial Cult and the Development of Church Order: Concepts and Images of Authority in Paganism and Early Christianity before the Age of Cyprian.* VCSup 45. Leiden: Brill, 1999. In addition to affording a succinct overview of the imperial cult, this monograph seeks to explore the two-way interface between Roman religion and early Christianity.

Carter, Warren. *Matthew and Empire: Initial Explorations.* Harrisburg, PA: Trinity Press International, 2001. Explores ways in which Matthew responds to a sociopolitical environment deeply influenced by the imperium.

Friesen, Steven J. *Twice Neokoros: Ephesus, Asia and the Cult of the Flavian Imperial Family.* Leiden: Brill, 1993. A well-researched monograph that helpfully synthesizes textual and material history to investigate the impact of the imperial cult on Asia.

Gradel, Ittai. *Emperor Worship and Roman Religion.* OCM. Oxford: Clarendon, 2002. A student of S. R. F. Price, Gradel presents a stimulating monograph that both responds to Price and builds on him. Gradel seeks to interpret emperor worship as an expression of homage in a benefaction social system.

Hardin, Justin K. *Galatians and the Imperial Cult: A Critical Analysis of the First-Century Social Context of Paul's Letter.* WUNT 237. Tübingen: Mohr Siebeck, 2008. Building on some recent studies of the setting of Galatians, Hardin seeks to understand the more difficult passages in Paul's letter against the background of the imperium.

Harland, P. A. "Imperial Cults within Local Cultural Life: Associations in Roman Asia." *Ancient History Bulletin* 17 (2003): 85–107. Having written extensively on associations in the first-century world, the author here explores the role of such associations in emperor worship, in particular how such groups relied on cultic participation as a way of integrating themselves within the fabric of Roman society.

Harrison, J. R. "Paul, Eschatology and the Augustan Age of Grace." *TynBul* 50 (1999): 79–91. Focusing on two passages from Romans, the author argues that Paul is self-consciously contrasting his own eschatology with the utopian vision of Roman ideology.

Horsley, Richard A., ed. *Paul and Empire: Religion and Power in Roman Imperial Society*. Harrisburg, PA: Trinity Press International, 1997. An anthology consisting of papers offered by leading scholars, this book not only is highly informative but has also proved significant in having freshly forced the issue of Paul and the imperium to the forefront of scholarly discussion.

―――, ed. *Paul and Politics: Ekklesia, Israel, Imperium, Interpretation: Essays in Honor of Krister Stendahl*. Harrisburg, PA: Trinity Press International, 2000. Like the earlier 1997 volume, this collection of essays is fairly technical, but nonetheless thought provoking.

Kim, Seyoon. *Christ and Caesar: The Gospel and the Roman Empire in the Writings of Paul and Luke*. Grand Rapids: Eerdmans, 2008. This book is ideal for anyone interested in an alternative voice to most writing on the imperial cult today. Kim argues that the case for a political reading of Paul and Luke ultimately fails to be sustained by the evidence.

Kraybill, J. Nelson. *Imperial Cult and Commerce in John's Apocalypse*. JSNTSup 132. Sheffield: Sheffield Academic Press, 1996. Investigates the creeping tie between the imperial cult and Roman commerce—a must-read for anyone seeking to understand Revelation against the background of the cult.

Kreitzer, L. Joseph. *Striking New Images: Roman Imperial Coinage and the New Testament World*. Sheffield: Sheffield Academic Press, 1996. Marshals numismatic evidence so as to draw fascinating connections with the biblical text.

Oakes, Peter. *Philippians: From People to Letter*. SNTSMS 110. Cambridge: Cambridge University Press, 2001. Applying a thorough knowledge of civic and social backgrounds (many of which relate directly or indirectly to the imperial cult), the author offers a close reading of certain passages from Philippians.

―――. "Re-mapping the Universe: Paul and the Emperor in 1 Thessalonians and Philippians." *JSNT* 27 (2005): 301–22. A model of scholarly balance, this article provides a good exegetical case study for how the apostle Paul conceived of the cult.

Price, S. R. F. *Rituals and Power: The Roman Imperial Cult in Asia Minor*. London: Cambridge University Press, 1984. Insisting on the close tie between religion and politics in Roman society, this book constitutes a turning point in classical scholarship on the imperial cult.

Tellbe, Mikael. *Paul between Synagogue and State: Christians, Jews, and Civic Authorities in 1 Thessalonians, Romans, and Philippians*. ConBNT 34. Stockholm: Almqvist & Wiksell, 2001. This book explores the delicate and often complex triadic relationship between imperium, synagogue, and the fledgling church.

Witulski, Tomas. *Kaiserkult in Kleinasien: Die Entwicklung der kultisch-religiösen Kaiserverehrung in der römischen Provinz Asia von Augustus bis Antoninus Pius*. NTOA, SUNT 63. Göttingen: Vandenhoeck & Ruprecht; Fribourg: Academic Press, 2007. For any German readers, this book is certainly worthwhile. It is the first work to explore the diachronic development of the cult from Augustus up to the mid-second century.

Wright, N. T. *Paul: In Fresh Perspective*. Minneapolis: Fortress, 2005. One of the leading popularizers of the thesis that Paul sought to engage the Roman world head-on offers a brisk, eminently readable account of how this political theology ties in with the apostle's larger program.

10

Greco-Roman
Philosophical Schools

JOHN T. FITZGERALD

Modern philosophy often differs in key respects from ancient philosophy. Early twentieth-century analytic philosophy, for example, tended to neglect both ethics and religion, two of the subjects emphasized by most philosophical schools during the Hellenistic and Roman periods. Yet the Greco-Roman emphasis on these subjects differed from the focus of philosophers in archaic Greece, who were primarily concerned with physics and the cosmos. Indeed, as Aristotle (*Metaph.* 1.2.9) once observed, it was a sense of "wonder" (*to thaumazein*) about the world that prompted the inquiries of the first Greek philosophers, who, profoundly curious about nature (*physis*) and the physical universe, gave attention to the sun, moon, and stars, including such phenomena as eclipses, and concentrated on cosmogony (that is, the origins of the cosmos), the basic substance underlying all things, and the coherence of things as a whole.

The Term "Philosophy" and Its Significance in Antiquity

The pursuit and cultivation of wisdom was a notable feature of many societies in the ancient Mediterranean world, including those in Egypt, Mesopotamia, and Israel. The same endeavor was present in archaic Greece, which produced the Seven Sages and numerous others who were renowned for their wisdom. In this context, it was common for various thinkers, experts, and lawmakers to call themselves "wise" (*sophos*) and to be referred to in this manner, with their "wisdom" (*sophia*) serving to distinguish them from others who were less discerning. It was in this context, according to an ancient tradition that is at least as old as Heraclides Ponticus (fourth century BC), that the terms "philosophy" (*philosophia*) and "philosopher" (*philosophos*) were first coined. The person credited with the creation of these newly coined words was Pythagoras, who wanted to distinguish sagacity as an attribute belonging to an individual from the quest for wisdom as something ardently to be desired. Pythagoras believed that "wisdom" was properly used only of the divine, that "no one is wise but God alone" (Diogenes Laertius, *Lives* 1.12, author's translation; cf. Mark 10:18: "No one is good but God alone"). In contrast to his predecessors, therefore, Pythagoras humbly eschewed the term *sophos* ("wise") and called himself only a *philosophos*, or "lover of wisdom" (Cicero, *Tusc.* 5.8; Quintilian, *Inst.* 12.1.19; Iamblichus, *Vit. pyth.* 8.44; 12.58; Clement of Alexandria, *Strom.* 1.14.61.4). In doing so, he wished to make clear that he did not regard himself as already having attained wisdom but rather that he was simply someone who loved (*philos*) and valued wisdom and was assiduously seeking it. Pythagoras's reticence to make claims for himself in regard to the attainment of wisdom was not always followed, but it was influential in later centuries, especially among Stoics of the Roman Empire, who generally venerated their philosophic predecessors but refrained from saying that they had achieved the highest perfection of human nature (Quintilian, *Inst.* 12.1.18; Plutarch, *Stoic. rep.* 1048e).

Pythagoras believed that "philosopher" was sufficient to distinguish the minority who devoted themselves to the contemplation and discovery of nature from the majority who gave themselves to other pursuits. In a conversation with Leon, ruler of a Greek city, he compares human life to a festival with games attended by crowds of people who have three different motives for coming. Some (the athletes) come in pursuit of glory, others (merchants) come to hawk their wares and to make money, but the best are the third group, the spectators, who come to observe all that is going on, such as the athletic contests, the craftsmen's creations, and the speeches given, noting not only what is done but also how it is done. These three groups of people, he says, represent three types of human life and endeavor—the quest for victory and the fame that goes with it, the pursuit of wealth through acquisition and financial gain, and the search for wisdom. Whereas the vast majority of people are slaves of either fame or money, there are a few individuals who, counting all else as nothing, closely scan the nature of things in pursuit of truth and wisdom. These people, Pythagoras says, call themselves "philosophers" (Cicero, *Tusc.* 5.9; Diogenes Laertius, *Lives* 8.8; Iamblichus, *Vit. pyth.* 12.58–59).

There at are least two aspects of this narrative about the beginnings of "philosophy" as a particular, named human endeavor that are important for its subsequent history in antiquity. First, philosophy in a formal sense was never the arena for more than a small minority of individuals. Even among the educated of the Greco-Roman period, rhetoric was studied and practiced far more often than philosophy. At the same time, some philosophical notions and terms had a broad cultural currency, so that they became part of ancient popular culture and literature. Like the various Jewish sects in first-century Palestine, the philosophers had far greater influence on their society than their small number of professional practitioners might suggest.

Second, ancient philosophy was not simply the pursuit of wisdom and the development of various intellectual notions about reality. It was also a way of life, a manner of living that was characterized by the pursuit of truth and the observation of the world and of the things within it, and a mode of thinking and acting in accordance with certain convictions about cosmic and human nature. Philosophy as a way of life was seen already in Pythagoras's metaphor about the three types of human life (*bios*), and it became extremely widespread in later centuries, owing especially to Plato's use of this tripartite classification (*Rep.* 581c) and its influence on subsequent philosophy, though sometimes in altered form. Aristotle (*Eth. nic.* 1095b.14–19), for example, identifies three types of life—the life of enjoyment, characterized by the pursuit of pleasure; the life of politics, with its concern for civic honor and virtue; and the contemplative (*theōrētikos*) life, which is philosophy's purview. Aristotle's word *theōrētikos* is cognate with the verb *theōrein* ("to look at," "to observe," "to be a spectator at the games and festivals") and picks up Pythagoras's comparison of philosophers to "spectators" (*theatai*) at festival games.

The precise kind of life led by philosophers varied in keeping with their diverse convictions, but all philosophies had this salient feature of being a mode of living, including the Skeptics (Sextus Empiricus, *Pyr.* 1.17). In one of his works, the satirist Lucian of Samosata depicts Zeus as putting various philosophers up for sale, as though they were slaves to be purchased in the marketplace. A common modern title of that work, popularized by its use in the Loeb Classical Library, is *Philosophies for Sale*, but the manuscript title is literally *The Sale of Lives*, with that title used to indicate that Lucian is distinguishing different types of philosophical life. Of all the philosophical schools, the Pythagoreans and the Cynics were especially known for their way of life. Both Aristoxenus of Tarentum (b. ca. 370 BC) and Iamblichus of Chalcis (ca. AD 245–ca. 325) wrote works with the titles *On the Pythagorean Way of Life* (*De vita pythagorica*), highlighting some of the distinctive features of Pythagorean lifestyle (such as rejecting meat and living as vegetarians). Similarly, when the Letter to the Colossians rails against "philosophy" (2:8), it is combating not only teachings about "the elemental spirits of the universe" (2:20) but also directives concerning lifestyle and conduct (2:16, 20–23). Ancient philosophy thus combined thought with life, and however theoretical and technical philosophy could become in its relentless probing of reality, it usually retained an eminently practical grounding in human life and in the need to live prudently in the face of life's challenges and demands. Indeed, it was because

Cynics so emphasized their endeavor as a way of life and deemphasized the more intellectual aspects of philosophy that critics debated whether it was actually a philosophy or simply a way of life (Diogenes Laertius, *Lives* 6.103).

Because philosophy was not understood as an ivory-tower intellectual exercise devoid of significance for daily life, its practical implications were accentuated. In keeping with this vital link between thought and action, great emphasis was placed on the lives of philosophers as demonstrating and exemplifying the principles they espoused. Above all, both their students and their critics looked to see whether their words and deeds conformed to the principles that they taught (Pseudo-Diogenes, *Ep.* 15; Julian, *Or.* 7.214b–d; Lucian, *Icar.* 29–31), which was also a widespread concern of early Christian communities (Matt. 23:3; Rom. 2:1, 21–23; 2 Cor. 10:11; 1 John 3:18; *1 Clem* 30.3; Ign. *Eph.* 15.1).

The Term "School" of Philosophy

The standard Greek word for a "school" or "sect" of philosophy was *hairesis*. As a term, it was derived from the verb *haireomai* in the sense of "to take for or to oneself," "to take in preference to," and so "to prefer" or "to choose." Use of the term thus called attention to the choice that people voluntarily made in regard to which of the competing principles and doctrines (*dogmata*) they preferred and which of the distinctive ways of life they elected to lead. Similarly, the term could be used of assent to the teaching or doctrinal rule of a particular school, adherence to the school's *dogmata* (Sextus Empiricus, *Pyr.* 1.16), or the choice of a way of life made by an individual or a community (Sextus Empiricus, *Pyr.* 1.145), and advocates of these philosophical opinions, principles, and modes of conduct were occasionally called *hairetistai* (Diogenes Laertius, *Lives* 9.6). As one might anticipate, the same term was used to describe the various schools of medicine, such as the Empiricists, the Rationalists (Dogmatists), and the Methodists, all of which espoused different methodological approaches to healthcare. Galen's work *On Sects for Beginners* provides a useful introduction to these medical schools and their debates.

The same complex of terms occurs in Hellenistic Jewish writings and in early Christian literature to describe the different Jewish sects and their adherents, which were active during the Hasmonean and early Roman periods of Jewish history. Josephus, for example, uses *hairesis* in regard to the Pharisees, Sadducees, and Essenes as schools (*Ant.* 13.169) and *hairetistai* of their adherents (*J.W.* 2.119). It is therefore not surprising that he also refers to these groups as those who are "philosophizing among the Jews" (*J.W.* 2.166), compares the Pharisees to the Stoics (*Life* 12) and the Essenes to the Pythagoreans (*Ant.* 15.371), and depicts the Sadducees as Jewish Epicureans (*J.W.* 2.164–65; *Ant.* 13.173; 18.16).

Similarly, the NT not only uses *hairesis* of both the Sadducees (Acts 5:17) and the Pharisees (Acts 15:5; 26:5) but also indicates that already at an early stage outsiders used the term to describe the Christians (Acts 24:5, 14; 28:22). This characterization of Christianity in terms of a *hairesis*, or "school," was fundamentally descriptive and neutral as a category, not pejorative. It was not the term itself but rather the outsider's evaluation of Christianity that determined whether the depiction was positive or negative. Given the frequent animosity toward the early Christians, however, the characterization could be quite derogatory (e.g., "a godless and lawless school sprung from a certain Jesus, a Galilean deceiver" [Justin Martyr, *Dial.* 108.2; see also 17.1]).

Major Genres for Reconstructing the History of Ancient Philosophy

Greek philosophers were acutely conscious that they were not operating in an intellectual void, and they developed their thoughts by comparing them with those of their predecessors and contemporaries. Attempts to link the ideas of thinkers to their poetic predecessors and to classify opinions are probably as old as the Sophists, but it was Aristotle who made such endeavors a standard component of philosophical inquiry, beginning his *Metaphysics* with an evaluative sketch of his predecessors' theories before expounding his own views as well as writing treatises on individual philosophers and schools. His concern for situating his own thought within the history of discourse about a topic was continued by his successor Theophrastus, who collected various kinds of biographical and doxographical information about early Greek philosophers (esp. for his works *On the Senses* and *On the Tenets of Natural Philosophy*). The history of philosophy as an integral part of ancient philosophy thus began with Aristotle and Theophrastus, and treatments of this history soon spread beyond their school to become a widespread intellectual activity during the Hellenistic period, with six main genres employed as part of this endeavor. (The following genres are different from the genres, such as the dialogue and *erōtapokriseis* ["questions and answers"], that philosophers used to articulate their own thoughts.)

The first genre was biography, with Aristoxenus of Tarentum, Hermippus of Smyrna (fl. third century BC), and Antigonus of Carystus (fl. 240 BC) among the most important Hellenistic contributors. Examples of philosophical biographies from the Roman period include Philostratus's *Life of Apollonius of Tyana* and Porphyry's *Life of Pythagoras*.

The second genre was doxography, or collections of the *doxai* ("tenets," "views," "opinions") of philosophers and/or the schools associated with them. The term "doxography" is modern, having been coined by Hermann Diels (1848–1922), a German classicist particularly interested in pre-Socratic philosophy. The most important early example of this genre was Aëtius's *Placita* (*Doctrines*), probably dating from the late first or early second century AD. This work is lost, but it can be partially reconstructed (see Diels's *Doxographi graechi*) from three later sources that made use of it: Pseudo-Plutarch, *On the Doctrines of the Philosophers*; John

Stobaeus, *Eclogae (Selections)*; and Theodoret of Cyrus, *Cure for the Diseases of the Greeks.*

The third genre was summaries of the main doctrines of the philosophical schools, such as those given by Hippobotus (late third–early second centuries BC) and Clitomachus (187/86–110/9 BC) in their works titled *On Philosophical Schools.* Another work belonging to this same genre was compiled by Arius Didymus, one of Augustus's teachers (Suetonius, *Aug.* 89), on whose behalf Augustus spared Alexandria (Plutarch, *Ant.* 80.1). Arius's work is especially valuable as a compendium of Stoic and Peripatetic ethics, with an epitome of it preserved by Stobaeus. A subgenre of these multischool summaries focused on the teachings of one school; these treatises functioned either as a comprehensive introduction to the thought of a particular school or as a synopsis of one school's teaching on one of the three principal fields of ancient philosophy: physics, ethics, and logic. The *Didaskalikos (Handbook of Platonism)* of Alcinous (second century AD) is a Middle Platonic example of the former, and Hierocles's *On Appropriate Acts* (= *On Duties*) contains a second-century AD summary of Stoic ethics on obligations toward the gods, one's homeland, parents, friends, and relatives.

The fourth genre was collections of the sayings attributed to different philosophers. For example, the *Principal Doctrines (Kyriai doxai = Ratae sententiae)* are a collection of forty moral maxims of Epicurus, with another collection of his shorter sayings known as *Sententiae vaticanae* (known also as *Gnomologium vaticanum* because it is preserved in the fourteenth-century codex Vaticanus Graecus 1950). The *Pythagorean Sentences* provide a neo-Pythagorean example of such a collection.

A fifth genre was "refutations," that is, polemical attacks by a member of one philosophical school on the tenets and doctrines of another school. Plutarch, a Middle Platonist, wrote several such treatises against the Stoics, including his *On Stoic Self-Contradictions.* A well-known Christian example of this same basic genre is Hippolytus's *Refutation of All Heresies,* a valuable source not only for the theological views of Hippolytus's Christian opponents but also for pre-Socratic thought.

The sixth and final genre was "successions" (*diadochai*), which purported to provide the lineages of teachers and students in the various philosophical schools, often focusing on which person succeeded the other as head of a particular school. Sotion of Alexandria, a Peripatetic philosopher active in the early second century BC, was apparently the originator of this genre, with later examples including Philodemus's *History of the Academy (Index academicorum)* and *History of the Stoics (Index stoicorum),* both of which were originally part of his *History of Philosophy (Syntaxis philosophorum),* and Diogenes Laertius's *Lives and Maxims of Those Who Have Distinguished Themselves in Philosophy and the Doctrines of Each School* (also called *Lives of Eminent Philosophers*), which is the most valuable of the surviving works of this genre.

There were other genres, such as "questions" (*zētēmata*) and commentaries. The former had been developed to address questions and problems that arose in interpreting particular passages in Homer, and they were sometimes used in hermeneutical efforts to interpret the works of philosophers from the classical period. Plutarch's *Platonic Questions* is one such work. Yet it was not Plato's works but rather those of Aristotle that most frequently became the subject of commentaries. Thanks to the editorial work of Andronicus of Rhodes in the first century BC, the Aristotelian corpus attracted the comments of scholars such as Alexander of Aphrodisias and Simplicius the Neoplatonist. Although all of these genres are important sources for the philosophical schools of the Greco-Roman world, it is the successions of philosophers that provide the basic narrative, with that of Diogenes Laertius the most important. It is to a basic exposition of his narrative that we now turn.

Diogenes Laertius on the Origin and History of the Greek Philosophical Schools

In the first half of the third century AD, when Diogenes Laertius set out to write the history of Greek philosophy, he posited a twofold origin for the enterprise (*Lives* 1.13), one lying geographically to the east of mainland Greece and one to the west. The idea of a bipartite genesis of philosophy was not original with him but had already been used as an organizing principle in *Succession of the Philosophers* by Sotion of Alexandria, who may have derived the idea of two parallel lines of development from hints in Aristotle (*Metaph.* 1.3.5; 1.5.15). For the eastern origins of Greek philosophy, Diogenes begins his history with Thales of Miletus (fl. ca. 585 BC), the man with whom Plato began his list of the seven sages of ancient Greece (*Prot.* 343a). One of Thales's students was Anaximander of Miletus (d. ca. 546 BC), who had as one of his students his fellow Milesian Anaximenes (fl. ca. 546–525 BC). Because all three were from Miletus, the southernmost of the major Greek city-states of Ionia on the coast of Asia Minor, Diogenes Laertius (*Lives* 1.13, 122) refers to this school of philosophy as "Ionian," and he credits its inception with Thales and Anaximander. The distinguishing mark of this Ionian school at the beginning was a concern with physics (which in antiquity included metaphysics), and this concern with physics is not only reflected in the fact that Thales was credited with accurately predicting an eclipse that took place in 585 BC but also seen in Anaximander's being the first to write a Greek philosophical prose treatise, known as *On Nature*.

Diogenes (*Lives* 1.14) traces this Ionian school through Socrates, whom he credits with introducing ethics into the study of philosophy (1.14, 18). At that point, according to Diogenes (1.14–15), the Ionian school trifurcates and forms three distinct branches. The first branch is that of Plato's Academy. It goes from Plato (ca. 429–347 BC) to Clitomachus in the second century BC, and it constitutes the history of Plato's school down to the New Academy. The second branch is the Cynic-Stoic branch; the Cynic line goes from Socrates's associate Antisthenes to

Diogenes and his disciple Crates, and down to Menedemus in the third century BC; the Stoic line goes from Zeno of Citium (ca. 334/33–262/61 BC) to Chrysippus (ca. 280–207 BC). The third branch is that of Aristotle's school, which Diogenes ends with Lyco in the late third century BC. Diogenes treats the first branch in books 3 and 4 of his *Lives*, the second branch in books 6 and 7, and the third branch in book 5.

For the Western origins of Greek philosophy, Diogenes Laertius (*Lives* 1.13) looks to Pythagoras, whom he connects with Pherecydes of Syros (fl. ca. 544 BC), a mythographer and theogonist who was regarded as one of archaic Greece's ancient sages. Although Pythagoras was born in Samos, an island in the eastern Aegean, around 530 BC he migrated to Croton, an Achaian colony in Magna Graecia on the coast of Italy. Because Pythagoras spent most of his life as a philosopher in Italy, Diogenes Laertius calls the school of philosophy founded by him "Italian." He traces this school through the Eleatics Parmenides and Zeno, who are said by Plato (*Parm.* 127a–c) to have met Socrates when they came to Athens. This same Zeno is credited with the invention of dialectic (Diogenes Laertius, *Lives* 1.18; 8.57) because of his epistemological elevation of logic and rational proof over sense experience. Diogenes Laertius (1.15) continues the succession in the Italian school through the atomists Leucippus and Democritus, ending it with Epicurus, the most famous of the ancient atomists. The Italian school thus goes from Pythagoras to Epicurus and is discussed in books 8–10 of Diogenes's work, but in books 8 and 9 he also includes some pre-Socratics, such as Epimenides of Crete (quoted in Titus 1:12), some "sporadics" (philosophers who did not found successions), and several important Skeptics, such as Pyrrho.

As should be immediately clear from the preceding summary, Diogenes does not continue the history of the schools down to his own time in the third century. He does not narrate the history of Epicureanism beyond its founder Epicurus; Middle Platonism and Neoplatonism are omitted, as is neo-Pythagoreanism. Cynics of the Roman period are similarly not covered. How much of the Stoa he covered is unknown, for the extant manuscripts break off with Chrysippus; so, even if he extended his coverage to the Middle and Roman Stoa, that information is lost. The latest philosopher he mentions is a second-century AD Pyrrhonian Skeptic named Saturninus. In short, his coverage of philosophy in the Greco-Roman period is valuable for the earlier part of the Hellenistic period but becomes sparser or nonexistent for the later Hellenistic and Roman periods. There is also another factor. In the early Hellenistic period philosophy was Athens-based, and narratives of successions in the schools were focused on Athens. During the later Hellenistic period, and especially following Sulla's partial sack of Athens in 86 BC, philosophy became radically decentralized, with many other locales becoming centers for philosophical inquiry. To write a true narrative of successions for the later periods not only would have been difficult but also would have left out many important contributors. In short, in the first few centuries of the Roman Empire, philosophy was geographically a widespread endeavor, so that the study of Greco-Roman schools requires scholars to make use of the other genres mentioned in the preceding section, and, of course, the writings of the philosophers themselves, as well as, in some cases (such as Epictetus), their students' records of their lectures.

Six Major Greco-Roman Philosophical Schools

The School of Plato

Plato's school was known as the Academy, and it passed through several distinct phases. The first was the Old Academy (347–267 BC), during which Plato's early successors continued many of his interests and sought to systematize his thought. The two most important in terms of ethics were Xenocrates and Polemon; the story of the latter's conversion to philosophy became a staple of later narratives about the power of philosophy to transform lives. This emphasis on practical morality is seen in Crantor's treatise *On Grief*, which became highly influential in works devoted to consolation. Plato's school began to take a completely different approach when Arcesilaus became head of what is sometimes called the New Academy (267–80 BC), in which skepticism became the hallmark. Socrates's relentless questioning was taken as the model for inquiry, with suspension of judgment (*epochē*) viewed as the necessary consequence of the impossibility of knowledge (*akatalēpsia*). The two most important representatives of the skeptical phase of the Academy were Carneades and Clitomachus, but one of its most influential individuals was Philon of Larissa, perhaps its last scholarch (ca. 128–ca. 79 BC), to whom Cicero is frequently indebted in his main philosophical works. With Antiochus of Ascalon (ca. 130–ca. 68 BC)—another Academic who strongly influenced Cicero—Middle Platonism (ca. 80 BC–ca. AD 250) begins. During this period Platonism became more dogmatic and eclectic, with various representatives drawing heavily on the thought of other schools, especially those of the Stoics, Peripatetics, and Pythagoreans. Major Middle Platonic figures include Albinus, Alcinous, Apuleius, Atticus, Eudorus, Maximus of Tyre, Numenius, and especially Plutarch. Middle Platonism proved highly influential, as can be seen in the writings of Philo of Alexandria, Clement of Alexandria, and Origen, with Middle Platonic ideas also reflected in Hebrews and in Paul's contrast between the "inner" and "outer" person (2 Cor. 4:16). The final phase of the Academy was Neoplatonism, which was introduced by Plotinus (AD 204–269) and continued by such individuals as Porphyry, Iamblichus, Sallustius, Julian the Roman emperor, Macrobius, and Proclus. Patristic thought in Late Antiquity was almost always heavily indebted to Neoplatonism.

The School of Aristotle

Aristotle founded his school in 335 BC in the Lyceum, a gymnasium located near a sanctuary dedicated to Apollo Lykeios. Later tradition, represented by

Hermippus, had Aristotle make use of its walkway (*peripatos*) as a place for his teaching, and others suggested that Aristotle used to "walk about" (*peripatein*) there as he spoke. Both of these traditions are etiological attempts to explain the name associated with Aristotle's philosophy—the Peripatetic School. In reality, the term "Peripatos" probably derives from the public walk where the school met in the time of Aristotle's successor, Theophrastus, whose *Characters* contains sketches of various distinctive types of human behavior, such as that associated with *deisidaimonia* (cf. Acts 17:22; 25:19). According to ancient testimony (Plutarch, *Sull.* 26.1–2; Strabo, *Geogr.* 13.1.54, 608), when Theophrastus died he willed his and Aristotle's library to Neleus, at which point their works passed into oblivion. In the first century BC, however, the books were brought to Rome, where Amisus began and Andronicus of Rhodes completed an edition of Aristotle's esoteric works, plus some by Theophrastus. Whatever the historical credibility of these accounts, they function to explain the relative insignificance of Aristotle and his school for much of the Hellenistic period as well as the Aristotelian renaissance that began as a consequence of this edition and reached a pinnacle with the appointment of Alexander of Aphrodisias to a chair in Aristotelian philosophy between AD 198 and 209.

The School of Epicurus

A native of Samos, Epicurus (341–270 BC) moved to Athens in 307/6 and purchased a house with a garden, where he and his followers resided. Consequently, his school became known as "the Garden." Although Epicurus was a prolific writer, only a few of his works survive—three letters, fragments of his *On Nature*, and two collections of his sayings. Epicurus's works, plus those of his three chief associates (Hermachus of Mytilene, Metrodorus of Lampsacus, and Polyaenus of Lampsacus), formed the classical authoritative texts for generations of Epicureans. Knowledge of his school and of particular Epicureans (such as Colotes of Lampsacus, Carneiscus, Polystratus, and Demetrius of Laconia) has been greatly expanded in recent years with the publication of critical editions and translations of many of the papyrus scrolls found in the library of the Villa of the Papyri at Herculaneum. These scrolls demonstrate that the school was characterized by much greater intellectual diversity than had been previously thought. The most important Epicureans from the late Hellenistic and Roman periods were Zeno of Sidon, his student Philodemus of Gadara, Lucretius, and Diogenes of Oenoanda. Famous for their quietism and cultivation of friendship, the Epicureans advocated imperturbability (*ataraxia*) as the ideal and sought to cure humanity's fear of the gods, pain, and death by applying the "fourfold remedy" (*tetrapharmakos*), which consists in the knowledge that "god presents no fears," "death occasions no worries," "the good can be easily attained," and "pain can be readily endured." Philodemus's work *On Frank Criticism* provides insight into the Epicurean practice of psychagogy (the guidance of souls), which entailed the confession of one's faults to other members of the community and the use of frank speech (*parrēsia*) to correct shortcomings and to promote moral progress.

The Cynics

The two traditional founders of Cynicism were Antisthenes (ca. 446–366 BC) and Diogenes of Sinope (ca. 412/403–ca. 324/321 BC), with the name for adherents of this sect deriving from the latter, whose nickname was "the Cynic," that is, "the Dog." Infamous for their verbal "barking" and "biting" and occasional "doggish" behavior, the Cynics saw themselves as society's watchdogs who, rejecting logic and physics as indispensable components of philosophy, believed that their austere manner of life and simple dress were in accordance with nature, and that their freedom from the conventions and values of aristocratic Greco-Roman society provided a conspicuous model of self-sufficiency that functioned as a shortcut to virtue and happiness. There was a strong revival of Cynicism during the early empire, so that early Christ believers such as Paul were well aware of Cynic traditions and adapted them to express their own self-understanding and to address issues within their churches. The most important documents produced by later Cynicism were the Cynic Epistles, which were pseudonymous letters attributed to Socrates and famous earlier Cynics, such as Crates.

The Stoics

Zeno of Citium, the student of Crates, was the founder of Stoicism, so called because he lectured near the Athenian agora in the "Painted Colonnade" (*stoa poikilē*). Zeno, Cleanthes (author of a famous "Hymn to Zeus"), and Chrysippus (the greatest of the Stoic thinkers) were the most important members of the Old Stoa, but Aratus of Soli, one of Zeno's students, wrote a Stoicizing textbook on astronomy titled *Phaenomena*, which is quoted in Acts 17:28. Diogenes of Seleucia (Babylon), one of the last members of the Old Stoa, stimulated interest in Stoicism when he visited Rome in 156–155 BC and appears to have initiated changes in the formulation and presentation of Stoic doctrines that came to fruition in the work of his student Panaetius (ca. 185–109 BC), usually regarded as the founder of the Middle Stoa, who shifted the focus of Stoic ethics from the sage (*sapiens*) to those "making progress toward wisdom" (the *proficientes*) and emphasized the duties of civic leaders. His ideas were appropriated by Cicero for his own treatise *On Duties*. But the undisputed Middle Stoic par excellence was Posidonius (ca. 135–ca. 51 BC). The fact that his school was in Rhodes rather than Athens illustrates the decentralization of philosophy that was occurring in the first century BC. Unfortunately, no complete work from the Old and Middle Stoa has survived; that situation changes with the Late Stoa (ca. 31 BC–ca. AD 200), also known as Roman Stoicism (and occasionally Neostoicism). It was the most influential school of philosophy during this time period, with some of its most important representatives being Cornutus, Dio Chrysostom (who also reflects Cynic ideas),

Epictetus, Hierocles, Marcus Aurelius, Musonius Rufus, and Seneca. The Stoics attached great importance to the ancient practice of spiritual exercises, which were a source for Christian monasticism (see Hadot, *Philosophy*), and their ideas influenced writers as diverse as Lucan, the author of 4 Maccabees, and Clement of Alexandria. Stoic tenets also appear in works such as the *Tabula of Cebes*, a work of popular philosophy that also utilizes Cynic terms and neo-Pythagorean imagery.

The School of Pythagoras

Although this school was founded by Pythagoras (ca. 570–490 BC) and thus was the oldest of the Greco-Roman schools of philosophy, it is virtually impossible to narrate the history of this school, with Aristoxenus stating that it had disappeared by his time (the late fourth century BC), and Cicero claiming that his friend Nigidius Figulus (d. 45 BC) had revived this sect and its ascetic discipline. The combination of these two ideas has led to the modern myth of Pythagoreanism as extinct for more than two centuries. The existence of Hellenistic Pythagorean texts (see Thesleff, *Pythagorean Texts*) provides literary evidence that Pythagoreanism did not entirely disappear, though it undoubtedly declined in popularity. There was indeed a marked resurgence in the early empire, and the school during this period is known as neo-Pythagoreanism. Its chief representatives include Moderatus of Gades, Nicomachus of Gerasa, Numenius of Apamea, and Apollonius of Tyana, whose life and exploits were vividly depicted by Philostratus. Of particular interest are the Pythagorean sayings collections, with the *Golden Verses* the best-known example.

There were other Greco-Roman philosophical schools, such as the Skeptics (with Pyrrho, Aenesidemus, and Sextus Empiricus the chief representatives), and various eclectics (such as Cicero) who drew on ideas from numerous schools to formulate their own thought. Both Hellenistic Jews and early Christians did the same, which is one of the reasons why philosophical concepts and terms appear in their writings and why both Rabbinic Judaism and early Christianity frequently resembled schools of philosophy.

Bibiliography

Algra, Keimpe, et al., eds. *The Cambridge History of Hellenistic Philosophy*. Cambridge: Cambridge University Press, 1999. A first-class collection of essays dealing with various issues in and aspects of philosophy in the Hellenistic period, including sources, chronology, organization and structure of the philosophical schools, logic, language, epistemology, physics and metaphysics, cosmology, theology, determinism and free will, medicine and science, politics, psychology, social and political thought, and ethics.

Arnim, H. F. A. von, ed. *Stoicorum veterum fragmenta*. 4 vols. Leipzig: Teubner, 1921–24. Although dated in certain respects, this indispensable set remains the most complete collection of Stoic fragments.

Branham, R. Bracht, and Marie-Odile Goulet-Cazé, eds. *The Cynics: The Cynic Movement in Antiquity and Its Legacy*. Berkeley: University of California Press, 1996. A valuable and cutting-edge treatment of the Cynics and their literary, philosophical, and cultural significance.

Diels, Hermann. *Doxographi graeci*. Berlin: Reimer, 1879. Until quite recently, this book was the standard treatment in the ancient doxography of physics, and it is still indispensable.

Engberg-Pedersen, Troels. *Paul and the Stoics*. Louisville: Westminster John Knox, 2000. A major discussion of Paul's indebtedness to Stoic ideas, with an emphasis on the comparative function of these two systems of thought.

Hadot, Pierre. *Philosophy as a Way of Life: Spiritual Exercises from Socrates to Foucault*. Edited with an introduction by Arnold I. Davidson. Translated by Michael Chase. Malden, MA: Blackwell, 1995. The most accessible treatment of spiritual exercises in English.

Inwood, Brad, ed. *The Cambridge Companion to the Stoics*. Cambridge Companions. Cambridge: Cambridge University Press, 2003. A collection of essays on a wide array of topics pertinent to the Stoics.

Inwood, Brad, and Lloyd P. Gerson, trans. *Hellenistic Philosophy: Introductory Readings*. 2nd ed. Indianapolis: Hackett, 1997. A valuable translation of basic Epicurean, Stoic, and Skeptic texts from the Greco-Roman world.

Long, A. A. *Hellenistic Philosophy: Stoics, Epicureans, Sceptics*. 2nd ed. Berkeley: University of California Press, 1986. Traces the main developments in Greek philosophy from the death of Alexander the Great to the end of the Roman Republic, highlighting the Stoics, Epicureans, and Skeptics.

Long, A. A., and D. N. Sedley, eds. and trans. *The Hellenistic Philosophers*. 2 vols. Cambridge: Cambridge University Press, 1987. The most important collection of the principal sources for the study of Hellenistic Pyrrhonism, Epicureanism, Stoicism, and Academic philosophy, with the original text, English translations, and commentary.

Malherbe, Abraham J., ed. and trans. *The Cynic Epistles: A Study Edition*. SBLSBS 12. Missoula, MT: Scholars Press, 1977. Texts and translations of the pseudonymous Cynic Epistles, including those attributed to Anacharsis, Crates, Diogenes, Heraclitus, Socrates, and the Socratics.

———. *Moral Exhortation: A Greco-Roman Sourcebook*. LEC 4. Philadelphia: Westminster, 1986. An excellent collection of sources dealing with moral instruction by Greco-Roman philosophers, with attention given to the social settings of instruction, the teacher's aims and character, methods and means of instruction and nurture, hortatory styles, literary and rhetorical conventions, and *topoi* (conventional subjects).

Sedley, David N., ed. *The Cambridge Companion to Greek and Roman Philosophy*. Cambridge Companions. Cambridge: Cambridge University Press, 2003. Covers the entire range of Greek and Roman philosophy, including the pre-Socratics, Socrates, and Aristotle, but also with solid treatments of Hellenistic, Roman, and Late Antique philosophy, plus chapters dealing with the relationship of philosophy to literature, science, and religion.

Sharples, R. W. *Stoics, Epicureans, and Sceptics: An Introduction to Hellenistic Philosophy*. London: Routledge, 1996. A comprehensive account of the principal Hellenistic philosophical doctrines, arranged by topic rather than school.

Sterling, Gregory E. "Hellenistic Philosophy and the New Testament." Pages 313–58 in
   Handbook to Exegesis of the New Testament. Edited by S. E. Porter. Leiden: Brill, 1997.
   A sagacious treatment of the relationship of Hellenistic philosophy to the texts of the NT.

Thesleff, Holger, ed. *The Pythagorean Texts of the Hellenistic Period*. Acta Academiae
   Abonesis, Series A, Humaniora 30.1. Åbo: Åbo Akademi, 1965. The standard collection
   of Pythagorean texts deriving, or alleged to derive, from the Hellenistic period rather
   than later.

Timothy, H. B. *The Tenets of Stoicism Assembled and Systematized from the Works of
   L. Annaeus Seneca*. Amsterdam: Hakkert, 1973. Useful thematic collection of various
   topics treated by the Roman Stoic Seneca.

Zeyl, Donald J., ed. *Encyclopedia of Classical Philosophy*. Westport, CT: Greenwood, 1997.
   An extremely useful one-volume reference work, with articles devoted to almost all of the
   important ancient philosophers and schools of philosophy, and with useful bibliography.

11

Civic and Voluntary Associations in the Greco-Roman World

MICHAEL S. MOORE

The purpose of this essay is to review the history and primary attributes of the civic and voluntary associations operating in the Mediterranean world of late antiquity in order to help readers develop a clearer understanding of (1) how the Jesus movement interacts with this world, and (2) how such interaction contributes to the shape and substance of the NT. This is a difficult but necessary task. Its difficulty rests in the multiplicity of disciplines on which it draws, the paucity and perplexity of the primary data (both epigraphic and literary), and the remarkable breadth of published opinion on how to interpret this data. Even though we cannot exhaustively address the subject here, all serious students of the NT need to develop at least a rudimentary understanding of the Mediterranean *polis* ("city") as well as the voluntary associations with which it habitually interacts, especially those *ekklēsiai* later called "churches."

Public-Private Polarity

However difficult it is for us to conceptualize the political dynamics of Greek history, our investigation starts off on the wrong foot whenever we rigidly segregate our analysis of the activities of private voluntary associations from our analysis of the activities conducted under the auspices of the *politeia* ("government"). Exceptions occur, of course, but unlike many modern writers, ancient writers tend to imagine this polarity in symbiotic rather than oppositional terms. Plutarch's account of Aristides's decision to forego private club membership, for example, shows that even the most popular politician can be penalized for such a decision. Here Plutarch contrasts Themistocles's decision to join a political "party" (*hetaireia*)—thereby enveloping himself in a protective political "fence" (*problēma*)—with Aristides's decision to "walk his own path to statesmanship," thereby avoiding the path of engaging in "wrongdoing with club-brothers" (*Arist.* 2.4–5).[1] Moreover, Plato's account of Socrates's decision to "neglect what most men care for—money-making and property, military offices, public speaking, and the various 'offices' [*archōn*], 'factions' [*staseōn*], and 'clubs' [*synōmosiōn*]"—intentionally tries to explain the group dynamics responsible for *his* fate (Plato, *Apol.* 36b). Aristotle presumes a similarly symbiotic approach in his *Athēnaiōn politeia* (1–21), a chronicle designed (1) to show how oligarchical tyranny (exemplified by Peisistratos and his sons) inevitably runs aground, and (2) to show how the Athenian *polis* inevitably and repeatedly throws itself into "factional dissonance" (Aristotle, *Ath. pol.* 20.1), and thereby (3) to justify Cleisthenes's decision to hand over the reins of power to the *plēthos* ("multitude"; Aristotle, *Ath. pol.* 20.1). Keenly aware of the gravity of this moment, Aristotle deftly refocuses it to show that "democracy" is a viable political ideology able to address the weaknesses perpetually characterized by oligarchical tyrannies, but also that the modus operandi of the *hetaireiai* ("private clubs") who "gang up" (*hēttōmenos*; Aristotle, *Ath. pol.* 20.1) on Cleisthenes is hardly unusual. Should this be an accurate recounting of Greek political history,[2] then three points follow about private voluntary associations: (1) they symbiotically work alongside public civic organizations from a very early time (see Aristotle, *Eth. nic.* 1160a.4: "all associations are parts, as it were, of the political process"), (2) they provide the best-known traditionalist regimen for training Greek leadership, and (3) their modus operandi shows no hesitation before the prospect of clothing irrational prejudice in the garb of manipulative secrecy.

These last two points resonate most with early Christian thinking about leadership, particularly those sections of the Pastoral Epistles that focus on questions about what to look for in the character of leaders within the *ekklēsia tou Christou* ("church of Christ"). Christian leaders, for example, must demonstrate the character trait of "hospitality" (*philoxenos*, literally "stranger-lover"; 1 Tim. 3:2), a term Aristotle uses to describe one of the characteristics of the Free Man (Aristotle, *Virt. vit.* 1250b.34)—that is, the exact opposite of the club brother always in

---

1. This and all other translations in this chapter are by the author.
2. Some question the historicity of *Ath. Pol.*, but most find it to be a carefully researched chronicle in that it avoids (unlike other *Politeiai*) the adulteration of history with elements rooted in mythopoeic fantasy. See G. Huxley, "On Aristotle's Historical Methods," *GRBS* 13 (1972): 157–69; D. Toye, "Aristotle's Other *Politeiai*: Was the *Athenaion Politeia* Atypical?" *CJ* 94 (1999): 235–53.

need of reassurance and validation from other club brothers. Moreover, Christian leaders must possess a "good testimony [*martyria*] from those outside" (1 Tim. 3:7)—again, the exact opposite of the *hetairos* ("club brother") whose character and reputation depends only on the "testimony" of other *hetairoi*.

Civic Life

Exactly what constitutes an ancient "city" (Akkadian *ālu*; Hebrew *'ir*; Greek *polis*; Latin *urbs*; Arabic *medīna*) can be difficult to ascertain. Various definitions focus on various factors, including population size and density, religious status, educational accomplishment, military preparedness, and socioeconomic status. From Aristotle's perspective, the basic unit of society is the *oikos* ("house"), composed as it is of individuals who share the same "meal-tub" (*homosipyos*; Aristotle, *Pol.* 1252b.14). By way of comparison, Spartans and Cretans participate in public "mess-halls" (*sussitia*; earlier called *andreia*, "men's messes"; Aristotle, *Pol.* 1272a), and Qumran covenanters share in "the pure food of the many" (*ṭhrt hrbym*; 1QS 6.16–17, 25; 7.3, 18, 21). Neither attribute in and of itself holistically defines the Greco-Roman *polis*. The *polis* is much more complex and includes at least the following components: "farmers" (*hoi geōrgoi*), whose job is to provide a stable food supply (Aristotle, *Pol.* 1328b.6, 20); "craftsmen" (*technitai*, literally "technicians"), whose job is to provide the "many tools needed for life" (Aristotle, *Pol.* 1328b.7, 21; see also Heb. 11:10); "soldiers" (*machimos*, literally "warrior"), whose job is to protect citizens from internal rebellion and external invasion (Aristotle, *Pol.* 1328b.8–9, 22; see also Xenophon, *Cyr.* 5.4.46); "wealthy benefactors" (*euporos*, literally "well endowed") to fund whatever the citizens of the *polis* need to survive and prosper (Aristotle, *Pol.* 1328b.23; see also Thucydides 2.64.3); "priesthoods" (*hiereis*) to maintain the religious shrines and temples (Aristotle, *Pol.* 1328b.13, 23); and "judges," whose job is to arbitrate conflicts between citizens, a *polis* component Aristotle calls "most necessary" (*anankaiotētos*; Aristotle, *Pol.* 1328b.13). Centuries later, Pausanias idealistically asserts that no settlement can be a *polis* without a "gymnasium" (*gymnasion*; Pausanias, *Descr.* 10.4.1), "theatre" (*theatron*; Pausanias, *Descr.* 10.4.1), "public square" (*agora*; Pausanias, *Descr.* 10.4.1), "public well" (*krēnē*; Pausanias, *Descr.* 10.4.1; the "Superintendent of Wells" is an important municipal position [Aristotle, *Ath. pol.* 43.1]), or "town-hall" (*archeion*, housing the office of the *archōn*, "mayor/chief magistrate"; Pausanias, *Descr.* 10.4.1; see also Aristotle, *Ath. pol.* 17.1; Matt. 9:18). Why? Because without these components the *polis* cannot be *autarkēs* ("self-sufficient"; Aristotle, *Pol.* 1328b.15–19).

As "East" and "West" collide and coalesce into what soon becomes a Greek-speaking empire, the *polis* transforms into something much more ethnically, linguistically, religiously, and socioeconomically diverse. In Egypt, for example, the Ptolemaic *polis* of Alexandria divides into separate "quarters": one for Greek rulers, one for native Egyptians, one for Cretans and other foreigners (*Papyrus Tebtunis* 32.17 [second century BC]), and one for the large Jewish population. Following the death of Alexander, his generals create pyramidical, inefficient, sycophantic, and highly corruptible regimes as the empire-versus-city polarity slowly replaces the *autarkēs* ideal of the old Greek *polis*. Pergamum, for example, begins to govern itself via *astynomoi*, "city managers" working under the aegis of a board of "governors" (*stratēgoi*), who in turn answer to a bank of bureaucrats embedded within the imperial court (*OGIS* 483; Plato, *Leg.* 759–66; Aristotle, *Ath. pol.* 50.2; Herodotus, *Hist.* 5.38.2, contrasts old-order *tyrannoi* ["tyrants"] with new-order *stratēgoi* ["governors/generals"]). Thus

> the transition from the Hellenic polis to the Hellenistic metropolis, and thence to the Alexandrian megalopolis, was marked by no sudden changes; for the institutions and forms of the latter had already been prefigured in the commercial cities of Asia Minor, and until Rome put a final quietus upon the struggle, the polis fought a long, desperate, rear-guard action, which continued, even after Demosthenes' defeat, to preserve its existence and restore the values that had made it great.[3]

With the arrival of the Romans, the Mediterranean *polis* submits to a much more aristocratic form of imperialistic tyranny, especially in districts where the Roman bureaucracy oppressively taxes the populace to fund the building of gaudy religious temples dedicated to the deification of the latest patrician emperor.

Voluntary Associations

Against this richly textured backdrop two things occur: (1) voluntary associations of various shapes and sizes experience phenomenal growth, thereby creating (2) a much greater level of interaction with Mediterranean civic government at the municipal (*politeia*), federal (*koinon*), and imperial (*basileia*) levels. The data describing these developments have been variously assessed. Frederick Danker, for example, subdivides these associations into two broad types: (1) "those sanctioned by the state" and (2) "a broad range of private associations, many . . . composed of members engaged in a common craft" (F. Danker, *ABD* 1:501–3). Edwin Judge, in a pioneering study, more expansively speaks of (1) the social institutions of the "city-state" (*politeia*), (2) the "household" (*oikonomia*), and (3) the voluntary association (*koinōnia*).[4] Helmut Koester summarily distinguishes between (1) the associations that help fulfill the needs of the whole community (like the

3. L. Mumford, *The City in History: Its Origins, Its Transformations, and Its Prospects* (New York: Harcourt, Brace, & World, 1961), 183.

4. E. A. Judge, *The Social Pattern of Christian Groups in the First Century: Some Prolegomena to the Study of New Testament Ideas of Social Obligation* (London: Tyndale, 1960). Where Plato links *koinōnia* to *philia* ("friendship," *Gorg.* 507e), Paul links it to the Holy Spirit (Phil. 2:1), the privilege of serving the saints (2 Cor. 8:4), and the passion of the Christ (Phil. 3:10).

gymnasia), (2) the professional associations (guilds, unions, cartels), (3) the social clubs (*hetaireiai*, *synōmosiai*), and (4) the religious associations (*thiasoi*).[5] And in a particularly influential study, Wayne Meeks extrapolates from the data four sociological "models": (1) the "household," (2) the "voluntary association," (3) the "philosophical school," and (4) the "synagogue."[6]

Where Meeks seizes on the synagogue as the "natural model" most responsible for shaping the socioreligious identities of the earliest Mediterranean *ekklēsiai*, Richard Ascough accuses Jonathan Smith of criticizing this approach for too quickly appealing "to the Jewish roots of Christianity," presuming that this assessment "insulates formative Christianity from its so-called pagan surroundings."[7] Sensitive to this critique, John Kloppenborg (re)classifies the voluntary associations of the Greco-Roman world into three basic "types": (1) funerary associations, (2) professional associations, and (3) religious associations.[8] Two of his students, Richard Ascough (*Macedonian Associations*) and Philip Harland (*Associations*), have attempted to build newer superstructures on these heuristic foundations, but others, concerned that the Judaism-Hellenism pendulum may have swung too far to the Hellenistic side of the spectrum, refocus attention on the "Judean economic and cultural context," particularly as exemplified in the puritan sect of the Essenes (Capper, "Community of Goods," 61n1). To Hans Dieter Betz's belief that "the movement initiated by Jesus of Nazareth is anti-Hellenistic" (*ABD* 3:127–35 [130]), scholars like Ascough challenge readers to transcend any and all approaches that focus too much attention on Christianity's "Jewish roots" (*Macedonian Associations*, 1), to which other scholars respond by questioning any and all attempts to focus on "Greco-Roman practice external of Palestine" (Capper, "Community of Goods," 61n1). Others more holistically respond to this pendulum-swinging debate (and the reductionism it generates) by carefully analyzing the impact of *both* worlds on the fledgling Jesus movement.

Ekkehard Stegemann and Wolfgang Stegemann, for example, avoid most extremist sandtraps by focusing on (1) the basic socioeconomic situation of the first-century Mediterranean world, (2) the socioeconomic situation of Hellenized Palestine within this world, (3) the social histories of Christ-confessing *ekklēsiai* operating within urban centers of this world, and (4) the social roles enacted by women within these particular *ekklēsiai*. Thus, of all the studies so far discussed on this complex question, the Stegemann study comes most highly recommended.

5. H. Koester, *History, Culture, and Religion of the Hellenistic Age* (vol. 1 of *Introduction to the New Testament*; Berlin: de Gruyter, 1982), 68.

6. W. A. Meeks, *The First Urban Christians: The Social World of the Apostle Paul* (2nd ed.; New Haven: Yale University Press, 2003), 75–84.

7. Meeks, *First Urban Christians*, 80; Ascough, *Macedonian Associations*, 1, interacting with J. Z. Smith, *Drudgery Divine: On the Comparison of Early Christianities and the Religions of Late Antiquity* (Chicago: University of Chicago Press, 1990), 83.

8. J. Kloppenborg, "*Collegia* and *Thiasoi*: Issues in Function, Taxonomy, and Membership," in *Voluntary Associations in the Graeco-Roman World* (ed. J. Kloppenborg and S. Wilson; London: Routledge, 1996), 18–22.

Concluding Remarks

Any serious investigation of the NT should be highly critical of any attempt to understand its message apart from the socio-literary context in which it first came to life. To ignore this context is to misinterpret the holistic impact of Christian *ekklēsiai* on the Greco-Roman world, an impact one ancient observer summarizes as follows:

> They dwell in cities of Greeks and barbarians, . . . yet the constitution of their own government [*politeia*], which they regularly proclaim, is marvelous, even though it contradicts expectation [*paradoxos*]. They reside in their own country, but only as aliens [*paroikoi*]. They participate in everything as citizens [*politeia*], yet tolerate everything as foreigners [*xenoi*]. (*Diogn.* 5.4–5)

Bibliography

Ascough, Richard. *Paul's Macedonian Associations*. Tübingen: Mohr Siebeck, 2003. Interfacing with a variety of inscriptional sources, this book argues that the Philippian church is analogous to a religious voluntary association, whereas the Thessalonian church is analogous to a professional voluntary association.

Capper, Brian G. "Jesus, Virtuoso Religion, and the Community of Goods." Pages 60–80 in *Engaging Economics: New Testament Scenarios and Early Christian Reception*. Edited by B. Longenecker and K. Liebengood. Grand Rapids: Eerdmans, 2009. This essay suggests that the Reformers' summary rejection of religious orders denies to readers of biblical scholarship an accurate understanding of its importance in the life of voluntary virtuoso religious communities like those in which Jesus and his disciples participated. Because of this, many (particularly Protestants) fail to recognize the precedent set by these ancient virtuoso religious communities for validating the work of contemporary Christians seeking to renounce property and practice a community of goods in service to the poor.

Crook, Zeba A. *Reconceptualising Conversion: Patronage, Loyalty, and Conversion in the Religions of the Ancient Mediterranean*. Berlin: de Gruyter, 2004. Paul expresses his conversion in terms of a call or commission, but this book argues that this language is the language of patronage/benefaction: Paul invokes the Greco-Roman example of the call of the divine patron-benefactor ("conversion") and the call of the Hebrew prophets at the same time. Paul's conversion is not unique but follows the general pattern of conversion found throughout the Mediterranean world.

Gardner, Gregg. "Jewish Leadership and Hellenistic Civic Benefaction in the Second Century BCE." *JBL* 126 (2007): 327–43. An important element of Greek culture and politics, *euergetism* (i.e., private beneficence for public benefit) helps us understand the behavior of the early Hasmoneans. For Hyrcanus, it serves to promote his image and country on the international stage. For Simon Maccabee, however, it is restructured to invent an acceptable formula for the conferral of the high priesthood, one that relies on widespread public support instead of simple genetic succession.

Harland, Philip A. *Associations, Synagogues, and Congregations: Claiming a Place in Ancient Mediterranean Society*. Minneapolis: Fortress, 2003. Investigates how diverse associations, synagogues, and congregations find places for themselves within the *polis* under Roman rule, focusing predominantly on the *poleis* of Asia Minor.

Hays, Christopher M. *Luke's Wealth Ethics: A Study in Their Coherence and Character*. Tübingen: Mohr Siebeck, 2010. Four strategies have been proposed for interpreting Luke's teaching about money—bivocational, literary, personalist, and interim—yet the personalist and bivocational strategies come closest to conveying the single coherent principle underlying Luke's Gospel message, namely, that nobody can be considered Jesus' disciple who is unwilling to renounce all possessions.

Joubert, Stephan. *Paul as Benefactor: Reciprocity, Strategy, and Theological Reflection in Paul's Collection*. Tübingen: Mohr Siebeck, 2000. Investigates the Pauline correspondence from the perspective of the social convention of benefit exchange. Considering various forms of benefit exchange within the Greco-Roman world, it tries to determine the basic interpretive framework for understanding the Pauline literature, giving special attention to the nature of the reciprocal relationship between Paul and the Jerusalem community, especially their reception of Paul's collection.

Marshall, Jonathan. *Jesus, Patrons, and Benefactors: Roman Palestine and the Gospel of Luke*. Tübingen: Mohr Siebeck, 2009. Concerned that current attempts to apply models of "patron-client" relations in social-scientific Gospel studies have confused rather than clarified the different types of reciprocity employed within the Greco-Roman world, this book tries to discern the historical picture of early Roman Palestine, specifically the adoption, rejection, and/or modification of *patrocinium* and benefaction by Jesus and his disciples.

Stegemann, Ekkehard W., and Wolfgang Stegemann. *The Jesus Movement: A Social History of Its First Century*. Minneapolis: Fortress, 1999. This book is an encyclopedic summary focused on four areas of concern: (1) the economic and social stratification of eastern Mediterranean society; (2) the economic and socioreligious developments *in Israel* in the first century AD (focusing on the Jesus movement and the Matthean and Johannine communities); (3) the social history of Christian communities in the cities of the Roman Empire; and (4) the social roles of women, in both Roman society and the church.

Winter, Bruce W. *Seek the Welfare of the City: Christians as Benefactors and Citizens*. Grand Rapids: Eerdmans, 1994. This book describes the challenges, difficulties, and necessary adjustments involved in being a Christian in Greco-Roman society, arguing (contra Meeks) that the earliest Christians were not ambivalent toward the *polis* but sought its welfare as benefactors committed to enhancing the quality of life in the *poleis* where they lived.

12

Economics, Taxes, and Tithes

DAVID J. DOWNS

In contemporary discourse, the word "economy" typically refers to a system for the production, distribution, and consumption of scarce resources (i.e., goods and services). The cognate term "economics," therefore, designates the study of economies and economic activity. The modern English word "economy" derives from the ancient Greek word *oikonomia*, a term that in antiquity usually designated household management or, more generally, the activity of "organization" or "administration" (cf. Luke 16:1–4). The ancient concept of *oikonomia* is thus far more expansive than the modern understanding of an "economy," for ancient writers did not view economic activity as distinct from other aspects of political and social life, including estate and household management. Xenophon's fourth-century BC work *Oeconomicus*, for example, is a Socratic dialogue that covers topics such as wealth, agriculture, household administration, and marital relations. Individuals and groups in the ancient world no doubt engaged in activities that would today be assigned to an "economic" sphere, including agricultural production, trade and commerce, manufacturing, tax collection, and minting of coins. Ancients, however, did not view these activities as separate "economic" endeavors, for behaviors and discourses that moderns would classify as "economic" were in antiquity embedded in other social structures.

The Economy of the Roman Empire

The economy of the Roman Empire, spanning roughly the second century BC until the fifth century AD, has offered economic historians an excellent opportunity to

156

study the economic structures and performance of a relatively unified political entity that exerted considerable control and influence over a specific geographical region, namely, the Mediterranean basin. A significant debate has characterized the work of contemporary historians on the ancient economy, however. This dispute has largely centered on the extent to which, if at all, the structures and performance of "the ancient economy" (or various ancient econom*ies*, including those of classical Greece and imperial Rome) resembled medieval, early modern, or modern economies.

On the one hand, the so-called modernist camp (represented in the work of scholars like Eduard Meyer and Mikhail Rostovtzeff) has stressed trade and market enterprise as keys to urbanization and the development of early capitalism in the ancient world, even while acknowledging that "archaic" economies did not reach levels of production similar to modern, industrialized economies. Rostovtzeff, for example, declares, "The modern [economic] development . . . differs from the ancient only in quantity and not in quality. The ancient world witnessed the creation of a world-wide trade and the growth of industry on a large scale. . . . In a word, the ancient world experienced, on a smaller scale, the same process of development which we are experiencing now."[1]

On the other hand, "primitivists," led by Moses Finley, the leading historian of classical economics in the twentieth century, have contended that the structures of the ancient economy severely constrained its performance. Drawing especially on the substantivist economic theory of Karl Polanyi, Finley argues that, in a traditionally agrarian context, economic activity was limited both by social values that discouraged practices such as lending, trade, and integrated market development and by technological confines that made interregional trade cost-prohibitive, apart from some items such as wine, oil, and certain luxury goods. Concentration of wealth in the hands of a small number of landowners stunted the growth of integrated markets, for the vast majority of the population lived at, near, or below subsistence level and therefore did not possess the buying power to stimulate large-scale market expansion. Since economic activity in antiquity was embedded in other social customs and institutions, modern economic theory is not useful in the analysis of the ancient economy.

The Finleyan perspective on economic sociology remains prominent in studies on the Roman economy. Many would concur that the economy of the Roman Empire was characterized by considerable disparity in wealth distribution, that significant economic growth was constrained by social values, that cities tended to be centers of consumption rather than production, and that financial and trade systems were relatively undeveloped (esp. when compared with the growth of trade in early modern Europe, for example). Yet even if the main contours of this picture offer the most influential heuristic model for understanding the

---

1. Mikhail Rostovtzeff, *The Orient and Greece* (vol. 1 of *A History of the Ancient World*; Oxford: Clarendon, 1926), 10.

structure and performance of the ancient economy, the resulting image has not gone unchallenged. A number of Finley's own students, including especially Keith Hopkins, have suggested that the primitivist representation of the ancient economy garnered from literary sources does not easily square with material evidence that suggests an increase in trade and nonagricultural production in the first two centuries AD.[2] As a result, several scholars of the Roman economy have offered more positive assessments of economic performance and growth during the Roman imperial period, with some suggestions of modest per capita economic growth between 200 BC and AD 200 (see Mattingly and Salmon, *Economies*).

More recent work on the economic conditions of the Roman Empire has also emphasized the need to move beyond a single model to explain "*the* ancient economy," since factors such as the climate, geographical location, population, political context, and redistributive mechanisms of various regional economies might indicate that Finley's primitivist model is too static to account for the diversity of economic activity and conditions in Greco-Roman antiquity (see esp. Horden and Purcell, *Corrupting Sea*). The theoretical model remains powerful, but it must also account for evidence that suggests higher levels of production, performance, and trade than the model allows. The discussion of the Roman economy is also shifting to include more attention to the relationship between economic performance and human well-being, a movement with parallels in the field of development studies, where terms like "poverty" are now frequently defined with reference to multidimensional categories such as financial resources, education, access to healthcare, nutrition, and so on.[3]

The question of wealth distribution, which has factored prominently in discussions of economic growth and performance in antiquity, offers an example of how a macroeconomic perspective can shape interpretation of specific evidence. Elite authors in antiquity tend to paint economic stratification in binary terms, often as a distinction between the few privileged *honestiores* (including senatorial, equestrian, and curial orders) and the vast majority of the poor *humiliores*. Although modern authors have occasionally accepted this binary division—with elites constituting 1 percent (or less) and "the poor" constituting 99 percent (or more) of the population (so Meggitt, *Paul*)—recent scholarship has generally moved away from this binary division toward more highly stratified models of wealth distribution. In an important article published in 2004, for example, Steven Friesen offers a seven-tiered "poverty scale" of the Roman imperial economy as a heuristic device for considering questions of wealth distribution in the early Christian movement ("Poverty"):

2. See, e.g., Keith Hopkins, "Introduction," in *Trade in the Ancient Economy* (ed. P. Garnsey et al.; Berkeley: University of California Press, 1983), ix–xxv.

3. See esp. a number of publications by Walter Scheidel, e.g., "Physical Well-Being," in *The Cambridge Companion to the Roman Economy* (ed. W. Scheidel; Cambridge: Cambridge University Press, 2012), 321–33.

Poverty Scale (PS) Level	Description	Representative Groups	Percentage of Population
PS1	Imperial elites	Imperial dynasty, Roman senatorial families, a few retainers, local royalty, a few freedpersons	0.04%
PS2	Regional or provincial elites	Equestrian families, provincial officials, some retainers, some decurial families, some freedpersons, some retired military officers	1.00%
PS3	Municipal elites	Most decurial families, wealthy men and women who do not hold office, some freedpersons, some retainers, some veterans, some merchants	1.76%
PS4	Moderate surplus resources	Some merchants, some traders, some freedpersons, some artisans (esp. those who employ others), and military veterans	7%?
PS5	Stable near subsistence level (with reasonable hope of remaining above the minimum level to sustain life)	Many merchants and traders, regular wage earners, artisans, large shop owners, freedpersons, some farm families	22%?
PS6	At subsistence level (and often below minimum level to sustain life)	Small farm families, laborers (skilled and unskilled), artisans (esp. those employed by others), wage earners, most merchants and traders, small shop/tavern owners	40%
PS7	Below subsistence level	Some farm families, unattached widows, orphans, beggars, disabled, unskilled day laborers, prisoners	28%

More recently, Friesen and Walter Scheidel have attempted to establish the gross domestic product of the Roman Empire in the mid-second century AD, using this number as a means of outlining a model of income distribution and inequality. The numbers are slightly different, but the overall picture is quite similar: "We conclude that in the Roman Empire as a whole, a 'middling' sector of somewhere around 6–12 percent of the population, defined by a real income of between 2.4 and 10 times 'bare bones' subsistence or 1 to 4 times 'respectable' consumption levels, would have occupied a fairly narrow middle ground between an élite segment of perhaps 1.5 percent of the population and a vast majority close to subsistence level of around 90 percent" (Scheidel and Friesen, "Economy," 84–85). Others have argued for a slightly larger middling group, perhaps as high as 15 percent of the urban population (so Longenecker, *Remember the Poor*), but the emerging picture moves beyond the binary division of ancient authors and earlier modern scholarship. Although these models are abstractions and do not account for regional and even slight chronological differences, they do shed light on the destitution experienced by the vast majority of inhabitants of the Greco-Roman world, who lived "at or near subsistence level, whose primary concern it [was] to obtain the minimum food, shelter, and clothing necessary to sustain life, whose lives [were] dominated by the struggle for physical survival" (Garnsey and Woolf, "Patronage," 153). This picture forms an important background for discussing the social context of the early Christian movement, reminding readers of the NT that subsistence existence and poverty would have been the norm for the vast majority of contemporaries of Jesus and his earliest followers.

The Economy of Roman Palestine

Although much research has been done on the structure of the Palestinian agrarian economy, a lack of primary sources before the destruction of Jerusalem in AD 70 often forces scholars to rely upon later archaeological and literary evidence, along with comparative studies from other (allegedly) similar societies, to make judgments about economic performance in Palestine in the first century.

An Agrarian Economy

It is generally agreed that the economy of Roman Palestine, like most of classical antiquity, was agrarian in nature. Particularly influential in discussion of the Palestinian economy has been the macrosociological perspective of Gerhard Lenski, whose work has often been used by NT scholars to label Roman Palestine as an "advanced agrarian society." According to this perspective, advanced agrarian societies are characterized by "*marked social inequality*, . . . [and] *institutions of government are the primary source of social inequality*" (*Power and Privilege*, 210). Lenski offers eight levels of social stratification characteristic of advanced agrarian economies: (1) ruler, (2) governing class, (3) retainer class, (4) merchants, (5) priests, (6) peasants, (7) artisans, and (8) unclean, degraded, and expendables. Crucial to this model is the assertion that political systems are central to social inequality. With regard to the Palestinian economy, the claim is made that wealth and power, including land ownership, were concentrated in the hands of urban elites (particularly in Jerusalem), whereas the vast majority of the peasant population in Judea and Galilee worked the land and paid taxes that supported the comfortable lifestyles of the wealthy. Often there is the following assumption that, beginning in the Herodian period, the political economy forced more land to come under the control of elites through high taxation and debt mechanisms, leaving most peasants landless and hopeful for tenancy agreements or, worse, occasional work as day laborers: "Thus, the powerful kept peasants and villages under a constant barrage of demands and obligations—perennially in debt, if possible" (Hanson and Oakman, *Palestine*, 111).

There is no doubt that economic activity in Roman Palestine centered on agricultural production, with the harvest of grain for food, olives for oil, and grapes for wine the primary crops (Josephus, *Ag. Ap*.1.60). It is debatable, however, whether the theoretical model of an "advanced agrarian society," and the political economy that such a model entails, adequately explains the available data. For example, there is little archaeological and/or literary evidence for large-scale displacement of peasants through the aggregation of land ownership in the hands of private estates in Palestine in the first century. Although Herod and his sons did own significant private lands (Josephus, *J.W.* 1.418; *Ant.* 17.147), there is no justification for the claim that during the Herodian period "polycropping and self-sufficiency on family farms gave way to monocropping on estates and royal lands and to an asymmetrical exchange of goods."[4] Instead, the structure of land ownership was not significantly altered under Herod, and most of the land in Judea and Galilee seems to have been owned and farmed by freeholding peasants (cf. Mark 10:29// Matt. 19:29). The theoretical model of an advanced agrarian society must be tested by material evidence.

A Trade Economy

The extent of trade in Palestine has also been a flashpoint of debate, for it is a topic closely related to the issue of economic production. According to some pessimistic assessments, cities in Palestine's "political economy" had a parasitic relationship with agrarian villages. Resources were funneled from rural to urban areas through debt mechanisms such as rent and taxation, and trade among nonelites was severely limited. As Douglas R. Edwards summarizes this view, "By bureaucratic, military, commercial, or fiduciary means, [cities] became the centers of control, primarily over land use and raw materials, and thereby determined the conditions under which all other parts of the system operated."[5] This negative view of trade in Roman Palestine is often strengthened by appeal to Josephus's statement that Jews do not inhabit "a maritime country; neither commerce nor the intercourse which it promotes with the outside world has any attraction for us. Our cities are built inland, remote from the sea; and we devote ourselves to the cultivation of the productive country with which we are blessed" (*Ag. Ap.* 160).

There is undoubtedly some truth to Josephus's assertion. Yet by the time of Herod the Great the ports of Joppa, Anthedon/Agrippias, and (esp.) Caesarea Maritima facilitated international trade (Josephus, *Ant.* 15.333–40). Moreover, the extent of local and regional trade in Palestine in the Second Temple period— often without the engagement of the urban elite—is frequently underestimated.

---

4. John Dominic Crossan and Jonathan L. Reed, *Excavating Jesus: Beneath the Stones, Behind the Texts* (San Francisco: HarperSanFrancisco, 2002), 100.

5. Douglas R. Edwards, "Identity and Social Location in Roman Galilean Villages," in *Religion, Ethnicity and Identity in Ancient Galilee* (ed. J. Zangenberg et al.; WUNT 1/210; Tübingen: Mohr Siebeck, 2007), 357–74 (362).

Archaeological evidence in Galilee, for example, suggests regional trade in clay pottery, basalt, millstones, and olive oil. Non-elite trade was an important aspect of economic production in Roman Palestine and throughout the economy of the Roman imperial period, indicating that the economy was not merely controlled by elites. Again, the theory of minimal non-elite trade—a theory based on a substantivist view of the ancient economy—does not do justice to the complexity of material evidence that indicates the existence of diverse, integrated regional markets.

Tithes

We turn now to several structures related to the distribution and consumption of goods and services in the Palestinian economy. The practice of tithing—that is, giving one-tenth of one's income or harvest to the state or temple—is frequently attested in ANE literature.[6] Yet it does not appear that tithes were consistently set at one-tenth in Israelite tradition, nor is it evident that they were always compulsory. The OT evidence captures this ambiguity. In Hebrew, the noun *ma'ăśēr* ("one-tenth") and its verbal cognate *'āśar* ("to give a tenth") sometimes denote voluntary gifts (Gen. 14:20; 28:22; Amos 4:4). At other times this terminology suggests obligatory payments. In legal texts, for example, tithing is presented as a compulsory activity (e.g., Deut. 14:22–29; 26:12; cf. Num. 18:20–32; Lev. 27:30–33; Neh. 10:35–38), although the prophetic indictment of Mal. 3:8 ("'How are we robbing [God]?' In your tithes and offerings!") suggests that this obligation was not always met.

Moreover, the OT offers a variety of tithe regulations: (1) the Deuteronomic tradition of a yearly tithe consumed in Jerusalem by the one who offers it (Deut. 14:22–27); (2) a tithe offered every three years to provide for the Levites, resident aliens, orphans, and widows (Deut. 14:28–29); and (3) a tithe designed to finance the sacrificial system in the sanctuary (Lev. 27:30–33) and its attendants, the Levites (Num. 18:21–32). Attempts in the Second Temple period to harmonize the various OT traditions include Tobit's offering of fourteen tithes in a six-year cycle (a yearly tithe to Levites and a yearly tithe in Jerusalem, and two tithes to the poor in the third and sixth years; Tob. 1:6–8; cf. Josephus, *Ant.* 4.68, 205, 240) and the twelve-tithe system advocated in *Jub.* 32.1–15 (with no mention of the poor tithe).

Tithing is explicitly mentioned in the NT only a few times. First, in the context of a discussion about washing before meals with a Pharisee who has invited Jesus to eat with him, Jesus in Luke 11 pronounces a series of woes upon the Pharisees, including the first: "But woe to you Pharisees! For you tithe mint and rue and herbs of all kinds, and neglect justice and the love of God; it is these you ought to have practiced, without neglecting the others" (Luke 11:42). In the Matthean parallel, a similar series of woes upon scribes and Pharisees also includes an indictment of

6. See Erkki Salonen, "Über den Zehnten in Alten Mesopotamien" [Concerning the Tithe in Ancient Mesopotamia], *StudOr* 43 (1972): 1–65.

those who "have neglected the weightier matters of the law: justice and mercy and faith. It is these you ought to have practiced without neglecting the others" (Matt. 23:23). In both of these sayings, the phrase "without neglecting the others" likely indicates that Jesus does not condemn tithing itself; it is the adherence to the law without concomitant attention to justice and love to which Jesus objects. Second, in the Lukan parable of the Pharisee and the tax collector (18:10–14), the Pharisee mentions in his prayer both fasting and tithing as signs of his piety (Luke 18:12). Again, it is not these pious deeds that Jesus regards as objectionable; it is instead the self-exultant attitude of the Pharisee, whose boasting in virtuous behavior is contrasted with the humility of the tax collector. Finally, Heb. 7:1–10 refers to the narrative in Gen. 14 of Abram giving one-tenth to Melchizedek after Abram's defeat of the four kings who captured Lot. The citation of this narrative in the context of Hebrews is not directly related to economic praxis, serving instead to strengthen the author's claim that Jesus' priesthood in the order of Melchizedek is superior to the Levitical priesthood: (1) Melchizedek's priesthood is sui generis and eternal (Heb. 7:3), and (2) Levi himself, who was in the loins of his ancestor Abraham, paid tithes to Melchizedek (Heb. 7:9–10).

Tributes and Taxes

If tithing is generally voluntary, tributes and taxes are usually viewed as the conscription of private goods by the state. In the first century, Rome exerted its power and raised funds to support its military activities through levies on conquered peoples. A distinction between tributes and taxes can be made between payments to foreign powers (i.e., tributes) and to local authorities (i.e., taxes). Thus, Jewish leaders in Palestine were obligated to pay tribute to foreign powers, first the Ptolemies in Egypt, then the Seleucids in Syria, followed by Rome. Jewish authorities also collected taxes from inhabitants of Palestine and other Jews throughout the Mediterranean Diaspora.

The Roman tribute (Greek *phoros*) was instituted in Judea when the region came under Roman control in 63 BC. The Roman tribute was initially collected by *publicani*, individuals contracted by the Roman Senate for the right to gather these funds. Collection in this period, however, was likely irregular and unsystematic (Cicero, *Flac.* 69; *Prov. cons.* 5.10; Dio Cassius, *Hist.* 39.56.6). According to Josephus, in response to their support during the Alexandrian War, Julius Caesar made a "treaty of friendship and alliance" with the Jews in 47 BC, a pact that resulted in a reduction of the tribute and an exemption from the tribute during the sabbatical year (*Ant.* 14.190–95, 200–210).

It is sometimes claimed that taxation under Herod the Great was crippling for inhabitants of Palestine, since taxes raised for Herod's own reign were combined with the Roman tribute, the Jerusalem temple tax, and tithes for priests and festivals—all of these conscriptions resulting in an extremely high tax burden for the Jewish peasantry. Such an oppressive fiscal situation is far from certain, however. In fact, there are several indications that the tax burden under Herod and his sons was not inordinately high. There is no evidence in Josephus that Herod was compelled to pay annual tribute to Rome, nor is there any indication that Herod's sons Archelaus, Antipas, and Philip were forced to render proceeds from taxes gathered in their territories to Rome as a tribute after their father's death (cf. Josephus, *Ant.* 18.108, for an indication that funds from Philip's tetrarchy were kept on deposit and not given to Rome upon his death, and on the imposition of a census for tax assessment purposes in AD 6 *after* Rome's annexation of Judea). In fact, as descendants of the Roman citizen Antipater (Josephus, *Ant.* 14.137), Herod, his heirs, and their territories would have been exempt from Roman tribute. Far more likely is a situation in which Herod imposed or, when politically expedient, reduced a variety of taxes—including land taxes on property value or agricultural yield (Josephus, *Ant.* 15.189, 303), tolls (Josephus, *J.W.* 2.287), and perhaps limited sales taxes on market activity (Josephus, *Ant.* 17.205). As Fabian Udoh has argued, Herod's notable building projects were likely financed by his own significant personal wealth and by funds raised from tolls and duties on trade—not by a heavy tax burden upon Jewish peasants (*Caesar*, 180–206).

When Herod's son Archelaus was deposed by Rome as ruler of Judea in AD 6, the territory became a Roman province ruled by imperial officials and subject once again to Roman tribute. The reorganization of Judea as a province was accompanied by a census in both Judea and Syria, overseen by Quirinius, governor of Syria (Josephus, *Ant.* 18.1–9; cf. Luke 2:1–5). Josephus implies that the goal of Quirinius's census was "the registration of property" (*tēn epi tais apographais*) instead of a counting of persons (*Ant.* 18.3); this property registration, for the purpose of accurate land tax collection, met with some Jewish resistance (*Ant.* 18.4–10).

Payment of the Roman tribute is an issue in the conversation between Jesus and a contingent of Pharisees and Herodians in Mark 12:13–17 (cf. the parallels in Matt. 22:15–22 and Luke 20:20–26). When asked, "Is it lawful to pay taxes to the emperor [*exestin dounai kēnson Kaisari*], or not? Should we pay them, or should we not?" (Mark 12:14–15), Jesus asks for a denarius. There is some debate about whether reference to this tax should be counted as evidence for Jewish payment of a "poll tax" after the Roman census in AD 6, especially given Mark's use of the word *kēnsos*, which has been viewed as a loanword from the Latin *census*. In the parallel version in the Third Gospel, the author of Luke employs the Greek word *phoros* in the question posed to Jesus, indicating more clearly that the debate centered on the Roman tribute. Either way, Jesus' response to the query is somewhat cryptic.

Writing to the community of Jesus' followers in Rome in the middle of the first century, the apostle Paul advocates payment of taxes (Rom. 13:6–7). This passage, too, has been read as an implicit critique of imperial power, particularly in light of the countercultural ethical position Paul encourages in the immediate literary context (cf. Rom. 12:1–2; 13:11–12). On the other hand, Paul's statements about the ruling authorities in Rom. 13:1–7 (cf. 1 Tim. 2:1–2; 1 Pet. 2:13–17) can be seen as particular and pragmatic counsel for the believing community in Rome, the capital city of the empire, to avoid controversy by paying taxes to the civil powers, advice penned in a context of increasing frustration with Roman tax policy (cf. Tacitus, *Ann.* 13.50–51; Suetonius, *Nero* 10.1).

Tolls

Tolls represent a tariff on the transportation of goods, and these levies constituted a significant source of funds for Jewish leaders in Roman Palestine. As mentioned earlier, Roman *publicani* had been involved in the collection of the Roman tribute in Palestine before these tax companies were abolished in Judea by Julius Caesar. Tolls on transit trade were a significant source of profit for both the Hasmoneans and Herod. Unlike most other forms of taxation, tolls and duties would mostly have been paid in cash rather than in kind.

With the resumption of the Roman tribute in Judea in AD 6, some Jewish officials—including village leaders and members of the Sanhedrin (Josephus, *J.W.* 2.405–7)—seem to have been involved in the collection of funds for the tribute and payment of these dues to the Roman governor. Other agents of tax collection included "toll collectors" (Greek *telōnai*), individuals contracted to extract tolls at transit and trade points. It is generally agreed that these toll collectors were responsible for gathering local tolls (Greek *telē*) levied by cities (*CIS* 3913), including duties on agricultural produce sold in Jerusalem (Josephus, *Ant.* 18.90), although they may also have played a part in the collection of tithes and the Roman tribute (*Ant.* 20.181, 206–7).

In the Synoptic Gospels, Jesus frequently encounters or mentions these *telōnai* (Matt. 5:46; 9:10–11; 10:3; 11:19; 18:17; 21:31–32; Mark 2:15–16; Luke 3:12; 5:27–32; 7:29, 34; 15:1; 18:10–14). All three Synoptics record Jesus' commissioning of a disciple who is a toll collector at his tollbooth, although he is called Levi in both Mark (2:14) and Luke (5:27) and Matthew in Matthew (9:9; cf. 10:3). The NT Gospels capture the disdain with which these toll collectors were viewed, which was likely because of their ability to exploit the duty system for their own profit: they are frequently grouped with "sinners," that is, violators of Jewish law (*hamartōloi*: Matt. 9:10–11; 11:19; Mark 2:15–16; Luke 5:30; 7:34; 15:1; cf. prostitutes in Matt. 21:31–32); in Matt. 18:15–20 a sinful member of the *ekklēsia* who will not listen to the congregation is to be treated "as a pagan and a toll collector" (*hōsper ho ethnikos kai ho telōnēs*); and in the parable in Luke 18:10–14, the narrative turns on the status contrast between the pious Pharisee and the humble toll collector.

Temple Tax

Given the close relationship between civic and religious institutions throughout the ancient Mediterranean world—and in Palestine in particular—it is problematic to draw a sharp distinction between state and religious taxation. Nevertheless, the Jerusalem temple can helpfully be discussed separately, since its cultic apparatus was subsidized by the taxation of Jews in Palestine and throughout the Mediterranean Diaspora.

Most adult Jewish males in the early Roman period, whether they lived in Palestine or in the Diaspora, paid a yearly half-shekel tax to the Jerusalem temple. Although the origins of this postexilic practice are unclear, yearly contributions for the cultic apparatus and maintenance of the Jerusalem temple seem to have been rooted in interpretations of Exod. 30:11–16 (cf. the voluntary contributions to the temple in Neh. 10:32–39). Roman policy allowed Jews to transport funds to Jerusalem without hindrance (Cicero, *Flac.* 28.67–69; Josephus, *Ant.* 14.225–27; 16.162–65; Philo, *Spec.* 1.77–78; *Legat.* 156–57, 216, 311–16). Since it received a consistently large influx of money, the temple in Jerusalem was regarded as one of the wealthiest institutions in the Roman world (Philo, *Spec.* 1.76). After the destruction of the temple in AD 70, the Roman emperor Vespasian required the yearly payment of the *fiscus Iudaicus*, a poll tax of two drachmas, by Jewish males to the temple of Jupiter Capitolinus as a replacement for the temple tax (Josephus, *J.W.* 7.218). In an exchange that may reflect later debates about the temple tax (or its successor, the *fiscus Iudaicus*) between followers of Jesus and other Jews, in Matt. 17:24–27, Peter is asked by the collectors of the temple tax (*hoi ta didrachma lambanontes*) if Jesus pays the tariff.

Bibliography

Atkins, Margaret, and Robin Osborne, eds. *Poverty in the Roman World*. Cambridge: Cambridge University Press, 2006. An excellent collection of essays that explores understandings of and responses to poverty across a wide range of Roman sources.

Finley, Moses I. *The Ancient Economy*. 2nd ed. Berkeley: University of California Press, 1999. The most influential twentieth-century monograph on the Greek and Roman economies, this book presents a "primitivist" reading of ancient economic activity.

Friesen, Steven J. "Poverty in Pauline Studies: Beyond the So-Called New Consensus." *JSNT* 26 (2004): 323–61. Using the recent history of scholarship on the social status of Paul and the churches of his mission as an entry into the topic, this article constructs a "poverty scale" and then employs this scale to assess wealth among the Pauline assemblies.

Garnsey, Peter, and Greg Woolf. "Patronage of the Rural Poor in the Roman World." Pages 153–70 in *Patronage in Ancient Society*. Edited by Andrew Wallace-Hadrill. London: Routledge, 1990. An instructive essay that explores the dynamics of patronage and kinship as models of resource distribution among the rural poor in Roman society.

Hanson, K. C., and Douglas E. Oakman. *Palestine in the Time of Jesus*. 2nd ed. Minneapolis: Fortress, 2008. As a popular-level introduction to the social context of Jesus' mission, this book adopts a Lenskian model of Palestine's "political economy."

Harland, Philip A. "The Economy of First-Century Palestine: State of the Scholarly Discussion." Pages 511–27 in *Handbook of Early Christianity*. Edited by Anthony Blasi et al.

Walnut Creek, CA: AltaMira, 2002. A clear and concise summary of recent scholarship on the economy of Roman Palestine.

Horden, Peregrine, and Nicholas Purcell. *The Corrupting Sea: A Study of Mediterranean History*. London: Wiley-Blackwell, 2000. A groundbreaking and much-lauded history of the Mediterranean world that synthesizes an impressive array of historical, geographical, social, economic, and archaeological data.

Jensen, Morten H. *Herod Antipas in Galilee*. 2nd ed. WUNT 2/215. Tübingen: Mohr Siebeck, 2010. A detailed and carefully researched study of the literary and archaeological evidence for Herod Antipas's influence in Galilee that is particularly attentive to the socioeconomic dimensions of Herod's reign.

Lenski, Gerhard. *Power and Privilege: A Theory of Social Stratification*. New York: McGraw-Hill, 1966. This work by one of the leading sociologists of the twentieth century has frequently been employed by NT scholars in discussions of first-century Palestinian society.

Longenecker, Bruce W. *Remember the Poor: Paul, Poverty, and the Greco-Roman World*. Grand Rapids: Eerdmans, 2010. A compelling challenge to the notion that the apostle Paul had little concern for the poor, the book also engages recent work on economic stratification in Greco-Roman antiquity.

Longenecker, Bruce W., and Kelly D. Liebengood, eds. *Engaging Economics: New Testament Scenarios and Early Christian Reception*. Grand Rapids: Eerdmans, 2009. A collection of essays devoted to the economic dimensions of the NT writings and the reception of those scriptural texts in patristic interpretation.

Mattingly, David J., and John Salmon, eds. *Economies beyond Agriculture in the Classical World*. London: Routledge, 2001. A challenge to the Finleyan orthodoxy, this collection of essays considers material evidence for activities such as textile production, mining, and building construction in order to argue that the economies of ancient Greece and Rome were more developed and integrated than is assumed by the "primitivist" model.

Meggitt, Justin J. *Paul, Poverty and Survival*. Edinburgh: T&T Clark, 1998. A controversial monograph that offers a binary description of Roman society in terms of a very small minority (1 percent or less) of elites and a vast majority (99 percent or more) living in destitution, with the additional conclusion that Paul and all the members of his assemblies lived in poverty.

Scheidel, Walter, et al., eds. *The Cambridge Economic History of the Greco-Roman World*. Cambridge: Cambridge University Press, 2007. Currently one of the best resources for consideration of a plethora of evidence and questions related to the economies of the ancient Mediterranean world, especially useful for issues of economic growth and localized economies.

Scheidel, Walter, and Steven J. Friesen. "The Size of the Economy and the Distribution of Income in the Roman Empire." *JRS* 99 (2009): 61–91. This innovative article employs several strategies for estimating the gross domestic product of the Roman Empire in the second century AD and then considers the implications of the size of the economy for the distribution of resources.

Stegemann, Ekkehard W., and Wolfgang Stegemann. *The Jesus Movement: A Social History of Its First Century*. Minneapolis: Fortress, 1999. This social history of early Christianity offers an excellent introduction to twentieth-century debates about the ancient economy and how those debates relate to the interpretation of the NT and the activities and beliefs of the earliest followers of Jesus.

Udoh, Fabian. *To Caesar What Is Caesar's: Tribute, Taxes, and Imperial Administration in Early Roman Palestine, 63 B.C.E.–70 C.E.* Providence, RI: Brown Judaic Studies, 2005. This revised dissertation offers a careful and reasoned evaluation of the evidence for the tributes and taxes paid by Jews in the Second Temple period. It is often critical of works that offer sweeping generalizations about Judaism or the Jesus movement based more on theory than on historical evidence.

Veyne, Paul. *Bread and Circuses: Historical Sociology and Political Pluralism.* London: Penguin, 1992. The classic study of Greco-Roman "euergetism" (i.e., private beneficence for public benefit) by a leading French historian.

13

Slaves and Slavery
in the Roman World

S. SCOTT BARTCHY

Orientation: How Slavery Fundamentally Shaped Roman Society and Culture

Sometime early in the history of human society, enslaving one's vanquished enemies became preferred to killing them in hand-to-hand combat. As slaves, these human beings were subjected to the absolute power of their owners and experienced a kind of "social death." They were separated from their families, tribes, identities, sense of honor and dignity, self-determination over their bodies and time, capacity to forge new kinship bonds through marriage alliance, and the legal protections enjoyed by free persons (see Patterson, *Slavery*, 17–76). The ancient Greeks and Romans independently transformed this long-established and widespread dehumanizing practice into the foundation for a genuine slave economy. That is, the large-scale employment of slave labor in both the countryside and the cities became absolutely essential to maintain Greco-Roman culture and society (see Finley, *Ancient Slavery*, 67–92).

In the patriarchal and highly stratified societies of ancient Greece and Rome, owning human beings who could be used as property (chattel slavery) became not only economically indispensable and elaborately regulated by law but also morally justified and regarded as normal. Slaves were owned not only by individuals and

169

families but also by various corporations, such as religious temples, voluntary associations, communities and municipalities, and even the state. The leisure the ancient Greeks exploited to create their greatly admired and imitated culture was made possible only by the labor of the enormous number of human beings they had enslaved, who bore the burden of the drudgery of daily life for everyone as well as produced a substantial surplus for commerce.

Aristotle had defined a Greek slave as "a living tool" and insisted that the robust anatomy of some human bodies made their enslavement appropriate, that is, they were "slaves by nature" (*Pol.* 1252a–55b). In contrast, Romans regarded slavery as contrary to nature but argued that every society they were aware of practiced it (*ius gentium*, a law common to all peoples); were slaves not the legitimate spoils of war? Slaves thus owed their entire existence to the victor who had saved them from death, which also explains why enslaved persons retained no rights even to their own names. Becoming a slave—by capture, birth, sale by impoverished parents, or self-sale—was usually simply the result of bad luck (see Seneca, *Dial.* 9.10.3; *Epist. mor.* 47).

In his essay *That Every Good Person Is Free*, Philo observes that the adverse blows of fortune could result in even the most virtuous freeborn person becoming enslaved, so that no one makes such slavery the subject of investigation (*Prob.* 18). As a slave, a human being was bodily and totally subjected to the practically unlimited power of an owner and the owner's heirs. As such, this slavery should be distinguished from other forms of exploitation of human labor or from dependence of any kind, financial or otherwise (e.g., day laborers, free gladiators, wagon drivers, contract workers, those paying off loans, and the like).

Ancient authors showed little interest in discussing slavery as a social institution. Even the first-century Stoic-Cynic philosopher Epictetus, who had been raised in slavery himself, seems to have regarded the existence of physical slavery as economically inevitable. He focused his concern rather on becoming free from mental and spiritual slavery—on "inner freedom" (*Diatr.* 4.1.1–5 LCL). For Epictetus, what made even a free person a spiritual slave was living with self-deception, fear, grief, envy, pity, and a lack of personal discipline, including nurturing desires for unattainable things. The result of this perspective is the fact that very little of our data comes from slaves themselves, and historians disagree on the most adequate ways to integrate what we do know from literature (written by and for the elite, i.e., slaveholders), various inscriptions, gravestones, and business documents (primarily papyri).

Historians estimate that as many as twelve million people were enslaved in the Roman Empire (16–20 percent of the entire population of at least sixty million) during the first century of our era (see Harris, "Slave Trade," 117–40; Joshel, *Slavery*, 7–9). An additional large percentage had been slaves earlier in their lives and had been made freedmen and freedwomen by their owners, who then became their patrons, usually with expectations that their new clients would continue to provide at least some of their former services (*obsequium* and *operae*, respectful behavior and services). Huge numbers of slaves were used extensively in rural areas. For example, Caius Caecilus Isidorus, a freedman of a leading Roman family, could plow his huge farm (*latifundia*) with 3,600 pair of oxen because he owned 4,116 slaves (Pliny the Elder, *Nat. Hist.* 33.47; see Wiedemann, *Greek and Roman Slavery*, 99–100). The labor of field slaves provided their owners' primary income, supporting a large number of domestic slaves who were trained to provide a wide range of personal services. In the urban areas as well, the number and quality of slaves one owned were critical factors in determining the owner's reputation and social status; more than one senatorial household included more than four hundred slaves (see Pliny the Elder, *Nat. Hist.* 7.12; Apuleius, *Apol.* 93).

The children of slaves became slaves themselves at birth. It was not unusual for free parents—Greek, Roman, and Judean—to sell their older children into slavery because they could not support them, to pay pressing debts, or even to improve the child's future situation (see Philostratus, *Vit. Apol.* 8.7; *Code of Theodosius* 3.3.1). As Jewish historians have pointed out, creditors frequently forced Judean fathers to sell their (premenstrual) daughters.

Without question, Roman culture was shaped by the institution of slavery and the values that justified it. Rome was a warrior state that became an empire on the backs of its fearless soldiers and its hundreds of thousands of vanquished prisoners of war, who, as slaves, generated the wealth needed to fund an empire. Violence characterized Roman history: civil wars, riots, provincial revolts, and foreign conquests. Public rituals and massive monuments glorified war and the subjection of those the Romans defeated. Physical violence against slaves by their owners was regarded as right and proper. Slaves were subjected to beatings, torture, and death (by burning or crucifixion) to reinforce social hierarchy and to make clear that they did not belong to the fully human, rational community. Slaveholders routinely suspected that without fear of punishment their slaves would become lazy and disobedient, even rebellious. Pliny the Younger writes, "Slaves are ruined by their own evil natures" (*Ep.* 3.1). Seneca reports a common saying, "You have as many enemies as you have slaves" (*Epist. mor.* 47), to which he objects: "More correctly, by cruel and inhuman treatment, we make them enemies."

Yet slaves were usually regarded as valuable property (e.g., an unskilled adult male was worth about four tons of wheat) and were treated as such. Large-scale slave revolts took place between 140 and 70 BC, instigated by recent prisoners of war such as Spartacus, during a period of rapid Roman conquest and expansion. The goal of these rebels was to regain their identity as free men, not to challenge the institution of slavery as such. There were no significant rebellions in the early Roman Empire, although fear of possible revolts from within households influenced Roman attitudes and policy. Wiedemann concludes that, while many scholars continue to be fascinated by slave rebellions, "this emphasis on violent resistance runs the risk of masking the fact that most slaves, most of the time, accepted their situation" (*Slavery*, 44–45).

The Same and Not the Same: How to Avoid Anachronism

Historians identify five societies in world history that have had true slave economies: Greece, Rome, Brazil, the Caribbean Islands, and the southern United States. Most readers of this article bring some knowledge about slavery in the New World, which can be misleading if they assume that they are thus prepared to understand what slavery was like in the Roman Empire.

Perhaps the greatest challenge for the twenty-first-century reader is to learn about the inhumanity and aura of terror surrounding Roman slavery and at the same time to reflect on the apparent inability of anyone, including most NT writers, to imagine an economic and societal reality without slaves. Entering the everyday world of the Roman Empire is difficult not only because of the distance in time but also because of widespread admiration for the architectural, artistic, legal, and philosophical products of Greco-Roman culture.

To be sure, ancient and modern slavery are significantly similar in that slavery itself is defined by the "social death" of the enslaved person, whose owner enjoys total control over the slave's body, including practically unrestricted brutal treatment and sexual exploitation. Yet awareness of the differences will influence how the reader of the NT will interpret passages that directly or indirectly deal with slavery. Here, then, are some guidelines for comprehending this central aspect of life in the Roman Empire.

1. In radical contrast to slavery in the New World, neither skin color nor ethnic/racial origins indicated slave status in the population of the Roman Empire. Moreover, rarely could one identify a slave by distinctive clothing or other aspects of appearance (except if marked by a tattoo, or a collar—the evidence is primarily post-Constantinian—or branding as a "runaway").

2. Thus slaves who escaped from their owners could seek to make themselves "invisible" among urban crowds or in remote rural areas, while risking severe punishment if caught. In contrast to the situation in nineteenth-century America, there was no free North to which Roman slaves might flee. As Joshel notes, "What slaves knew of the world outside their households or farms helped or hindered them" (*Slavery*, 154).

Not infrequently, knowledgeable slaves left their owner's control temporarily to hide from an angry owner and wait for tempers to cool, perhaps hoping to find an advocate to intervene on the slave's behalf. Others took off to visit their mothers (*Dig.* 21.1.17.4–5). According to Proculus, the foremost Roman jurist in the early first century, such a slave emphatically did not become a *fugitivus* (*Dig.* 21.1.17.4). In light of this legal opinion, the fact that Philemon's slave Onesimus did not take off for parts unknown but rather fled to Paul in prison strongly suggests that it is incorrect to regard Onesimus as a runaway slave (see Byron, *Paul and Slavery*, 116–37).

3. Both the enslaved and their owners shared the dominant cultural values, social codes, and religious traditions, even when most slaves yearned to become their own masters—and then as freedmen and freedwomen to own their own slaves.

4. Indeed, even while they were slaves, they could own property, and some already owned their own slaves. They could accumulate a fund, called a *peculium*, which they might then use to purchase their own freedom (manumission) from their owners. On the other hand, the enslavement of debtors by their creditors was a well-known practice among Greeks and Romans as well as Judeans; it was the primary source of slaves in Israel in the Second Temple period.

5. Again in distinct contrast to New World slavery, the education of slaves was encouraged, which generally increased their value. Rescuing and educating children whose parents had abandoned ("exposed") them in public places could be a profitable business (note that Greco-Roman moralists do not seem to have commented on this practice, nor do any NT writers). Some slaves were better educated than their owners, who had purchased them to carry out important functions outside and inside the home, to educate the owner's children, and to add to the owner's public reputation. Rome's cultural leadership in its empire largely depended on educated non-Italians who had been enslaved.

6. Thus many slaves functioned in highly responsible and sensitive positions, such as managers of large farms, of households, of business enterprises and workshops, as well as physicians, accountants, personal secretaries, tutors, sea captains, and even municipal officials. An important minority among the slaves enjoyed considerable influence and social power, depending on the status of their owners, even over freeborn persons of lesser status than that of these slaves' owners. For example, powerful Roman landowners used bands of slaves to enforce the obedience of their free tenants (see Wiedemann, *Slavery*, 44–45).

Perhaps most surprising is the power exercised by the emperor's personal slaves and freedmen, the *familia Caesaris*, who were given top administrative positions, a practice that dismayed both Tacitus (*Ann.* 12) and Pliny the Younger (*Ep.* 8.6). Claudius drew from his more than twenty thousand slaves and freedmen to create an imperial bureaucracy. In Acts 8:27, we meet a high-ranking black eunuch from Nubia, just outside the Roman Empire, who was most likely Queen Candace's slave. Because of their extreme social marginality, having no offspring or romantic attachments, eunuchs were used by political rulers in highly sensitive positions as the "ultimate slaves" (see Patterson, *Slavery*, 315–31).

7. Although slave status was universally despised and slaves had no honor, slaves as a group were not at the bottom of the socioeconomic pyramid. Rather, impoverished free persons, who had to seek work as day laborers with no guarantee of being hired, made up the lowest level. Some of them actually sold themselves into slavery in order to obtain job security, food, clothing, and shelter. Some sold themselves into slavery to pay off debts (see Dio Chrysostom, *Or.* 15.23), to climb socially (into the household of a prestigious owner), or to obtain special governmental positions, usually with hope of future manumission.

For example, a certain Erastus, identified as the city treasurer of Corinth who had become a Christ-follower there (Rom. 16:23), most probably had to sell himself to the city (as a form of "bonding insurance"?) to be appointed to this responsible position. Holding this office in a Roman provincial capital most likely made Erastus the most socially distinguished member of the congregation in Corinth. Also, in an action that displays some Christians' astonishing compassion, "many gave themselves into bondage that they might ransom others [from slavery]. Many sold themselves into slavery and provided food for others with the price they received for themselves" (*1 Clem.* 55.2).

8. Roman slaves, who came from a wide variety of ethnic, social, and educational backgrounds, had no consciousness of being a social class as such. Because they were owned by persons across a wide range of social and economic levels, they developed no sense of suffering a common plight. They usually derived their sense of identity from that of their respective owners, as the gravestones of freed slaves frequently testify. Thus, even though the Romans created an extensive body of law to regulate the institution of slavery, no laws were needed to hinder public assembly of slaves, such as were passed in the New World.

9. In contrast to lifelong slavery as practiced in the New World, a large number of domestic and urban slaves in the early Roman Empire could anticipate being set free, often by the age of thirty. The frequency with which slaveholders were manumitting slaves at the beginning of the empire provoked Augustus to set legal limits to the number of slaves who could be manumitted in a Roman citizen's will: half in a household of three to ten slaves; a third if more than ten and fewer than thirty; a quarter if more than thirty and fewer than a hundred; a fifth if more than a hundred, with a maximum of a hundred (see the lex Fufia Caninia of 2 BC).

Although some slaves were manumitted as a reward for good and faithful work or because a vain slave owner sought to become known for his generosity, the majority of slaves were freed because it served directly the owners' other personal, financial, and legal interests (see Bartchy, *Slavery*, 87–91). Innumerable ex-slaves throughout the empire were ample proof that enslavement was not a permanent condition (see Bradley, *Slaves*, 81–112). To be sure, condemned criminals who were sentenced as slaves of the state to work in the mines or on galley ships had no hope of manumission and were worked to death. Rural slaves also seem rarely to have been manumitted.

Manumission changed a slave's legal status to that of "freedman" or "freedwoman," which might either distinctly improve or sometimes decrease their actual social and economic position (see Patterson, *Slavery*, 209–96). Since the act of manumission was entirely in the hands of the slaveholder, slaves had no possibility of remaining in slavery against the will of the owner. Thus those translations of 1 Cor. 7:21 that read "even if you can gain your freedom, make use of your present condition more than ever" (so the NRSV) display ignorance of the actual options open to a manumitted slave (see Bartchy, *Slavery*, 96–98; Harrill, *Manumission*, 126–28, 194). Note also that the "synagogue of the Freedmen" mentioned in Acts 6:9 was apparently a congregation founded by former Roman slaves (perhaps captured by Pompey's forces during the Roman attack on Jerusalem in 63 BC) who had been able to move back to Jerusalem.

Quite often slaves of Roman citizens became full Roman citizens themselves when manumitted, a fact that astonished many ancient Greek commentators (see Dionysius of Halicarnassus, *Ant. rom.* 4.22.4–23.7). A high-status example of such a freedman is Marcus Antonius Felix (see Acts 23–25), the Roman governor of Judea (AD 52–58), who had been a slave until Antonia, the Emperor Claudius's mother, manumitted him (see Suetonius, *Claud.* 52; Tacitus, *Hist.* 5).

How Slaves Were Treated

The centralization of power as the Roman Republic became an empire resulted in the state taking control of slaveholders' treatment of their slaves, which had earlier been solely in the hands of individual owners and patrons. For example, in addition to his limiting the number of slaves an owner could manumit in his will, Augustus set the conditions for such manumission, including a minimum age of thirty, except in special circumstances (see the lex Aelia Sentia of AD 4). Augustus allowed freed slaves to gain honor by serving in the Roman navy as commanders and in the prestigious fire brigades in Rome, seven thousand freedmen strong. Financially successful freedmen attained honor by membership in the Augustales, religious and social associations, common in the cities of the western Roman Empire, dedicated to veneration of the emperor and to public improvement in their cities (Petronius, *Sat.* 30; see Joshel, *Slavery*, 69–72). Emperor Claudius I (AD 41–54) ordered that sick slaves abandoned by their owners be manumitted if they recovered (see Suetonius, *Claud.* 25).

Another law passed before AD 79 prohibited slaveholders from forcing their slaves to face death by wild beasts in the arena unless these owners had persuaded the local magistrate that such punishment was appropriate (lex Petronia). At the end of the first century, Domitian banned castrating slaves for commercial use, and several later emperors limited prostituting of female slaves. Early in the second century Hadrian (AD 117–138) prohibited the use of slave prisons (*ergastula*) and forbade the sale of slaves to pimps and gladiatorial suppliers and trainers, unless a judge approved such a punishment (see the edictum perpetuum Hadriani; Joshel, *Slavery*, 69–72).

Later in the second century, Antoninus Pius made slave owners liable for homicide if they killed any of their own slaves without just cause, just as they were guilty if they killed another person's slave (Gaius, *Inst.* 1.531). From the time of Augustus, these imperial limitations on an owner's absolute control of his or her slaves included encouraging slaves to inform against their owners not only in cases of treason (*maiestas*) but also in cases of adultery (lex Julia de adulteriis coercendis; see Wiedemann, *Slavery*, 24).

These and other imperial protections of slaves influenced earlier historians to emphasize an increasing humanitarian concern for the enslaved. Yet, as more recent historians have stressed (see Finley, *Ancient Slavery*; Bradley, *Slaves*; Glancy,

Slavery), the benevolent legislation that various emperors ordered had little effect on improving the daily life of slaves. All these measures serve to highlight the inhumane treatment of slaves that had been taken for granted prior to such imperial proclamations. There is no evidence for any imperial interference with slaveholders' total physical domination of their slaves (even torture and killing were justified for sufficient cause) or with the owners' sexual use of their own slaves. An owner usually based good treatment of slaves on the desire to gain a reputation for generosity rather than on insight into a slave's inherent equality as a human being.

Conclusion

Without a solid knowledge about slavery in the Roman Empire, readers of the NT can make major errors in interpretation. A clear grasp of how one was made a slave, the wide range of responsibilities carried by slaves, how one was treated as a slave, and what hope those enslaved nurtured regarding their future freedom provides insight into many NT passages that are otherwise quite puzzling. For example, in his letters, Paul of Tarsus not only refers to enslaved Christ-followers (see, e.g., 1 Cor. 1:11; 7:21; 16:15; Philemon) but also frequently employs metaphors taken directly from the experience of slavery in his world. Three keywords in Paul's vocabulary—"redemption," "justification," and "reconciliation"—draw directly on the process and results of manumission from slavery, which releases the believer from the slavery to sin and alienation (and from "social death," if a slave) and elevates the Christ-follower to the status of "son" or "daughter" and a "brother" or "sister" (see Patterson, *Slavery*, 70).

Bibliography

Bartchy, S. Scott. *First-Century Slavery and the Interpretation of 1 Corinthians 7:21*. Missoula, MT: Scholars Press, 1973. Repr., Eugene, OR: Wipf & Stock, 2003. This "classic" was based on the best classical scholarship at the time of writing, according to which the relative humaneness in the treatment of slaves in the Roman Empire was emphasized. Since then, ancient historians have highlighted the brutality of Roman enslavement and the rampant sexual exploitation of the enslaved, calling into question the earlier consensus. This book's presentation of the exegetical, legal, and theological context of 1 Cor. 7:21 remains important (e.g., the NRSV version is legally impossible); and the philological conclusions regarding the key Greek word *klēsis* in 7:20 have been greatly strengthened by recent research.

Bradley, Keith R. *Slaves and Masters in the Roman Empire: A Study in Social Control*. New York: Oxford University Press, 1984. Bradley's many articles and books have largely shaped the current understanding of Roman slavery and historians' debates about it. With an emphasis on the harsh realities of Roman slavery, Bradley gives close attention to the family life of slaves, to the possibilities for their manumission, and to the general climate of violence and fear that surrounded them.

Byron, John. *Recent Research on Paul and Slavery*. Sheffield: Sheffield Phoenix Press, 2008. A survey of two hundred years of scholarship, focusing on the last thirty-five years, with attention to African American responses to Paul, Paul's slavery metaphors, 1 Cor. 7:21, and the Letter to Philemon.

Finley, Moses I. *Ancient Slavery and Modern Ideology*. New York: Viking, 1980. This prominent social historian of Greece and Rome points out the different types of servile labor in antiquity and emphasizes the utter powerlessness and social isolation of the vast majority of ancient slaves, while sharply criticizing the apologetic treatment of ancient slavery in Western classics scholarship.

Glancy, Jennifer A. *Slavery in Early Christianity*. New York: Oxford University Press, 2002. Focusing on the importance of the human body in the thought and practice of Roman slavery, and especially on the sexual exploitation of slaves, Glancy argues that scholars have consistently underestimated the pervasive impact of slavery on the institutional structures, ideologies, and practices of the early churches and individual Christians.

Harrill, Albert. *The Manumission of Slaves in Early Christianity*. HUT 32. Tübingen: Mohr Siebeck, 1995. This detail-packed monograph has persuaded many interpreters that in 1 Cor. 7:21 Paul urges enslaved Christ-followers to grasp freedom should they have an opportunity to do so (versus the NRSV). Although Harrill exaggerates the amount of control slaves could exercise regarding their legal situation, he correctly emphasizes that a person could not choose to remain in slavery against the will of the owner and thus that it would have made no sense for Paul to have urged a Christ-follower to stay in slavery if set free by the owner.

Harris, William V. "Toward a Study of the Roman Slave Trade." Pages 117–40 in *The Seaborne Commerce of Ancient Rome: Studies in Archaeology and History*. Edited by J. H. D'Arms and E. C. Kopff. Memoirs of the American Academy in Rome 36. Rome: American Academy in Rome, 1980. A thorough discussion of the issues involved in calculating the percentage of the population in Roman slavery.

Horsley, Richard A. "The Slave Systems of Classical Antiquity and Their Reluctant Recognition by Modern Scholars." Pages 19–66 in *Slavery in Text and Interpretation*. Edited by A. D. Callahan et al. Semeia 83/84. Atlanta: Society of Biblical Literature, 1998. This excellent article is one of this volume's many challenging presentations of fresh perspectives regarding Roman slavery, including Horsley's own "Paul and Slavery: A Critical Response to Recent Readings" (pp. 153–200), with an insightful response by Stanley K. Stowers (pp. 295–311).

Joshel, Sandra R. *Slavery in the Roman World*. Cambridge Introduction to Roman Civilization. Cambridge: Cambridge University Press, 2010. Up to date and readable, with good maps, tables, and illustrations. Chapters focus on the practices of slaveholders and the lives of slaves, the sale of slaves, slaves at work, and slavery in the Roman social order. Especially recommended for readers having little familiarity with Roman antiquity.

Patterson, Orlando. *Slavery as Social Death: A Comparative Study*. Cambridge, MA: Harvard University Press, 1982. A monumental landmark in the study of slavery, comparing more than sixty tribal, ancient, premodern, and modern societies. Patterson draws on pertinent social-scientific theory that he applies in historical societal contexts, and his analysis is especially strong when situating Roman slavery in the context of Roman imperial culture.

Wiedemann, Thomas E. J. *Greek and Roman Slavery.* London: Routledge, 1981. An excellent collection of the Greek and Latin primary sources in English translation, with brief introductions. Extensive cross-references and a detailed index greatly increase this book's usefulness.

————. *Slavery: Greece and Rome.* Oxford: Clarendon, 1987. A fascinating summary treatment of major issues by the highly esteemed founder of the International Centre for the History of Slavery (ICHOS, now called the Institute for the Study of Slavery [ISOS]) at the University of Nottingham.

14

Women, Children, and Families in the Greco-Roman World

LYNN H. COHICK

Families and Fathers in the Greco-Roman World

The family in the Greco-Roman world valued the community over the individual and promoted corporate honor and fortune. Those living in the *domus* ("home") included parents and children, and perhaps extended family, such as adult siblings, cousins, and grandparents, as well as slaves, freedmen, and freedwomen. Each individual had a specific status within the home, and each family member deemed the social status of the family, including its wealth and social prestige, as of equal or greater value than their personal happiness. Idealized portraits of the Roman family are preserved in artwork and public monuments. For example, domestic landscape paintings often depict a mother and daughter standing by the sea, presumably waiting for their husband and father to return. Most commonly, mothers and daughters are presented in a religious context, before an altar or shrine. Boys are never painted with their mother, unless they are quite young. Instead, they are shown with their father in public scenes, doing business, for example (Fuchs, "Ancient Landscape"). Public imperial art on monuments, columns, and coins conveys a similar theme. Roman families are designated with a father and his child (son or daughter). Non-Roman families are depicted as a mother and her children, without a father and in postures of submission. These scenes serve to promote the ideals of the Roman elite that fathers are involved with their children's well-being, and children represent the potential of Rome (Uzzi, "Roman Art," 64). The separation between Roman and non-Roman children in art does not reflect the reality that free children often slept in the slave room with their wet nurse and played with their family's slave children (e.g., Soranus, *Gyn.* 2.19–20).

The father held the highest social and legal standing in the family and possessed power over his children and property. Scholars have used the Latin term *paterfamilias* to describe this all-encompassing power; however, the definition of "paterfamilias" has been challenged (Saller, "*Pater Familias*," 191). The term is found predominantly in legal documents and reflects primarily the running of an estate; thus a man can be a paterfamilias yet unmarried and without children. The term is almost never used in describing a father; instead, the ideal Roman father is characterized as beneficent, that is, using his power in the patriarchal system to help the family (e.g., Cicero, *Cat.* 4.12; see Severy, *Augustus*, 9–10). The feminine form of the term, "materfamilias," conveyed a woman of virtue, modesty, and sterling character.

In the homes of the wealthy, public and private space were divided primarily by status rather than by gender. That is, no rooms were restricted to be used only by women or only by men. Moreover, slaves served every area of the home. The paterfamilias would invite his peers (i.e., men of high status) to private areas such as the dining room or small rooms adjacent to the dining room that served as bedrooms at night. Here business contracts were struck and political alliances were made, as men did much of their work in the home. Women were patronesses in their own right, owning property and slaves, having clients and business concerns. The materfamilias would oversee the operations of the home, which could include the commercial production of goods, for example, from looms located in the house. Roman custom included the materfamilias at the evening dinner party (*convivium*), but the guests were predominantly male, and the meal focused on male socializing and politicking. In Greek homes, the women of the family did not participate in the evening dinner party (*symposium*) if men unrelated to the family were present (e.g., Cicero, *Verr.* 2.1.26).

The most common house style for Jewish families in Roman-period Palestine was a single-room structure with a courtyard in front or in back, and access to the roof with an exterior staircase (Meyers, "Domestic Architecture," 45). Most of the family's production activities, both men and women's work,[1] took place in the home or in its adjacent courtyard (Meyers, "Domestic Architecture," 58–60).

The Roman household venerated the *Lares*, or household deities of the father's ancestors, and the *genius* ("divine spirit") of the paterfamilias. Families participated in religious rites, including regular, repeated festivals, prayers, and sacrifices as

1. This included food preparation, sewing, carpentry, and other essential tasks. See E. M. Meyers, J. F. Strange, and C. L. Meyers, *Excavations at Ancient Meiron* (Cambridge, MA: ASOR, 1981), 23–44.

part of their civic and social duties to their families and the state. Both men and women served as priests, depending on the specific beliefs of a given cult. They participated together in most cults, although occasionally a particular festival was reserved for either men or women. Pilgrimages, votive offerings, prayers for health and safety—women and men sought the gods' favor in these acts of piety (e.g., Ovid, *Fast.* 2.645–54; *LSAM* 48).

Women as Wives and Mothers in the Greco-Roman World

Most men and women married in the ancient world; many women experienced widowhood, while fewer experienced divorce (e.g., Babatha Letters [P.Yadin 10, 17, 18, 19];[2] Dio Cassius, *Hist.* 56.3). Often women were defined in relation to their male relatives—their father, husband, or son (e.g., Plutarch, *Conj. praec.* 33; Valerius Maximus, *Fact. dict. mem.* 8.3.3). Moreover, society reinforced for women the ideals of modesty, industry, and *pietas*, or fidelity to family, the state, and the gods. All these virtues were captured in the widely portrayed image of the chaste matron working her wool at the loom (e.g., the epitaph from a husband praising the virtues of his deceased wife, *Laudatio Turiae*; *ILS* 8393). The picture of seclusion gives the unfortunate and unhistorical impression that women led private lives with little or no public engagement. In fact, women worked in market shops, hired out as wet nurses, studied philosophy, and served as patronesses of trade guilds, to name but a few activities (Cohick, *Women*, 225–55). Most women were poor, working long and hard to feed themselves and their children. Some women were slaves, charged with watching children, carrying out domestic tasks, and working in the sex trade (e.g., Horace, *Carmina* 3.6; *CIL* 6:3482).

Women married first in their mid- to late teens, while men usually married at age twenty-five to thirty (Laes, *Children*, 30). The couple was considered married if both agreed to live as husband and wife. Most families celebrated the marriage with a wedding ceremony based on local customs. No official state body gave marriage certificates; the legal document of the event was the dowry contract. Marriages were identified as *sine manu* ("without hand") if the wife remained legally a member of her father's family rather than under her husband's hand, or power. She brought with her a dowry, which her husband could invest or spend as he saw fit. If either party requested a divorce, the husband was legally obligated to return his wife's dowry, though he could keep any interest or profit gained from his investments. If the wife predeceased her husband, her will often required that her dowry be used to support their children. If her husband predeceased her, the wife might elect to remain unmarried, and thus have only one husband (*univira*), reflecting a first-century AD social ideal demonstrating perpetual honor to her

2. Naphtali Lewis, Yigael Yadin, and Jonas C. Greenfield, eds., *The Documents from the Bar Kokhba Period in the Cave of Letters* (Judean Desert Studies 2; Jerusalem: Israel Exploration Society, Hebrew University, Shrine of the Book, 1989).

dead husband. Usually, however, the widow remarried, especially if she was of childbearing years (e.g., Babatha, a second-century AD Jew, and Berenice, the great-granddaughter of Herod the Great).[3] Marriages were established in part to produce children to carry on the family line. However, a childless marriage was not necessarily grounds for divorce, especially among Romans, for whom adoption was a respectable option. Wives who were Roman citizens and produced three children were given a special privilege under the Augustan laws, namely, that they were free from the oversight of a guardian (tutor) in their business and legal affairs; a freedwoman who had four children was granted the same privilege (lex Julia, lex Papia Poppaea).

People might marry for pragmatic reasons, for example, to strengthen the family's social standing, but it was also hoped that the couple would live together harmoniously. Divorce did not have a social stigma attached unless it was on account of adultery, and elite families especially used divorce and remarriage to align their family to better political advantage. Poor couples likely divorced less often, but the data on this, as with most other areas of a poor family's life, is slim. Greeks and Romans did not recognize bigamy (marriage to two people at the same time); however, we have some evidence that Jews practiced polygyny (two or more wives). Wives were restricted to sexual intercourse with only their husbands, but men were charged with adultery only if they had intercourse with another man's wife.

Motherhood generally accompanied marriage. Mortality in childbirth was high and affected both rich and poor women, but especially mothers in their early teens. Women often delivered with a birthing stool and the aid of a midwife. Although a few strong rhetorical voices emphasized the importance of the mother nursing her child, in reality, many families feared the added strain of nursing would be too difficult for the mother. Additionally, wealthy families might hire a wet nurse (or buy a wet-nurse slave) to reinforce their high status that allowed for leisure. However, evidence survives of low status and poor families using a wet nurse (*nutrix*) and nurse (*nutritor*), which might indicate that the social values of the upper class were influential among those of lower status (Bradley, *Roman Family*, 63). Slave owners might encourage unions between slaves and would raise their children as additional slaves in the household (e.g., Columella, *De re rustica* 1.8.19).

Mothers with some means tended not to be involved in the daily care of their child; these tasks were done by a wet nurse, and subsequently by a *paedagogus* (Latin, "household slave"; see below). Mothers involved themselves more directly in the later education of their children. In wealthy homes, mothers were expected to be educated themselves and oversee their child's education, especially as related to religious matters and philosophical virtues (Cohick, *Women*, 144). When the

---

3. Ross Kraemer, "Typical and Atypical Jewish Family Dynamics: The Cases of Babatha and Berenice," in *Early Christian Families in Context: An Interdisciplinary Dialogue* (ed. David L. Balch and Carolyn Osiek; Grand Rapids: Eerdmans, 2003), 130–56.

child reached adulthood, the mother was influential in establishing marriages and forwarding her son's career with her personal funds. Mothers were expected to train their daughters in domestic duties, including the religious practices of the home (e.g., Quintilian, *Inst.* 1.1.6).

Women at Work in the Greco-Roman World

Households were the place of production in rural settings. Women worked the farm, chopped firewood, prepared meals, and taught their children these tasks, especially in cases where their husbands were away at war or on business. In cities, men and women labored in shops or worked in trades. Women were shopkeepers, blacksmiths, or tailors, for example, and they often worked alongside their husbands in a family business. Women with means traded goods and lent money; however, they could not stand as surety for another's debt or pay another person's debt. A few women published poetry, studied philosophy, or painted or carved artwork, usually under the tutelage of their husband or father. Indeed, few jobs were done only by men, namely, holding political office and serving in the military. Yet in distinction to men, women drew their social esteem not from their work but through their virtues. Slave women, likewise, experienced slavery differently than did their male counterparts inasmuch as the slave woman's sexual honor was compromised. Moreover, the slave woman usually lacked marketable skills, which limited her ability to earn her freedom. It is not accidental that the image of the slave woman symbolized defeat and despair in the Greco-Roman world.

Children in the Greco-Roman World

The modern Western experience of bearing and raising children shares little in common with the assumptions, conventions, and experiences of the Greco-Roman world. Perhaps the most striking difference is the fact that today in the West we have developmental models of childhood and tightly organized stages of development; these were almost entirely lacking in the ancient world. Instead, children were valued as they contributed to the larger social whole. Moreover, their social class and physical maturity were the markers used to determine age-appropriate behavior and occupation. There was little sentimentalism about childhood itself, little interest in discovering the world through a child's eye.

A second important difference is that a child's parents were often not the primary caregivers. This fact has led some modern readers to assume a general lack of compassion or love by ancient parents. More-recent scholarship suggests that modern bias failed to appreciate the evidence for genuine care for children, shown by employing nurses, educators, and *paedagogi* or by sending the youngster away for a few years to apprentice in a trade. Additionally, having several people involved in raising the child might provide a slight and necessary emotional distance between parent and child, given the high infant mortality rate. These caregivers reinforced the social network between family members; children were not the private possession of their father or mother but were important to the viability of the larger family group. In this sense, children were highly valued for their potential contribution to the family (e.g., Valerius Maximus, *Fact. dict. mem.* 4.4).

A third difference is the role that wealth and status played in the child's life. With no middle class, the majority of children grew up in poverty or at a subsistence level. This resulted in vastly different childhood experiences between the child connected with Caesar's household, for example, and the child born in a small village in northern Italy.

A fourth crucial difference between childhood today in postindustrial countries and in the Greco-Roman period is the level of violence and social disruption experienced by ancient societies. Public executions and torture were not off-limits for children's viewing, and beatings by schoolmasters and within the family were quite common. Moreover, life expectancy was short, and losing a parent or sibling was sadly familiar. Terms such as "stability" and "safety" cannot be used to describe a child's life in the Hellenistic and early imperial periods.

Parents in the ancient world eagerly anticipated and were greatly anxious about the birth of their child. Although there might be a slight preference for sons, epitaphs for children (most of which were commissioned by parents) reveal a similar love for daughters (e.g., one mother writes that her deceased daughter must have been envied by some god and thus taken from her; *ILLRP* 971). The birth itself was fraught with danger for the mother and infant; the mortality statistics are alarming. About 30–35 percent of all newborns did not survive their first month, and 50 percent of children died by the age of ten (Laes, *Children*, 26). Some estimate seventeen maternal deaths out of a thousand births. (In Western countries today, the risk is one-tenth per thousand; in Bangladesh today the average is as in ancient Rome, seventeen in a thousand [Laes, *Children*, 50n2].) A woman who survived to fifty years of age probably gave birth to six children, with perhaps two or three living to adulthood (Laes, *Children*, 50). If the newborn seemed strong and healthy to the midwife, she would present the child to the father for acceptance or rejection. If the father embraced the newborn laid before him, the child was raised in the house; if the father rejected the child, he or she was put out. Jews did not practice infanticide.

The newborn would be swaddled, and perhaps not fed for up to two days (Soranus, *Gyn.* 2.17–19), since it was thought the baby needed to rest. On the ninth day after birth, the Roman male child was named in an elaborate purification service that involved the maternal aunt and uncle. The female baby was named on the eighth day in a similar ceremony. Another celebration took place on the fortieth day after birth, which marked this milestone. The baby was fed breast milk until five months, and then cereal or bread moistened with milk, honey, or wine might be introduced to supplement breast milk. The average age for weaning was two to three years. Young children's diets were often lacking in nutrition, especially protein and vitamins A and D, contributing to the high death rate among children less than five years of age (Garnsey, *Food and Society*, 52–53). Infants were often swaddled until two years old, since their limbs were understood to be quite weak. Most people believed children should begin talking between the ages of two and three. Not until age five were children considered capable of working at those chores and functions that enabled the survival of the family. During the ages from birth to about five or seven years, the child would be under the care of the wet nurse and nurse. In the main, women served in this role, but male *nutritores* ("nurses") also looked after both male and female children.

Once children lost their baby teeth, at approximately age seven, they were considered physically ready to begin schooling or learning a trade. The literature consistently describes this training period as characterized by beatings. Such violence was in part typical of the period, but it was also based on the assessment that children, as irrational beings, must be strongly disciplined to develop rationality and self-control. The ancients knew nothing of modern developmental psychology, and they viewed childhood as a social category (Laes, *Children*, 99). A *paedagogus* accompanied the child to school; most of these servants were male, but a few inscriptions commemorate females (Laes, *Children*, 115). These attendants taught rudimentary academic lessons and also moral lessons in character, socializing the child. Male and female slaves (of any age) were sexually available to their owners, who might also prostitute them. Pederasty (sexual relationship between an older man and a young boy) was ubiquitous; however, violating a free Roman boy was considered a crime (lex Julia; Laes, *Children*, 244).

Children began working alongside adults before their teen years. Most sons learned the trade of their father or were apprenticed to learn a skill. Boys (slave and free) from ages thirteen to fifteen might learn weaving of cloth and carpet, jewelry making, embalming, or playing the flute, spending on average two to three years learning the trade. Female slaves apprenticed primarily in weaving. Rarely did free girls leave the parental house to live at the craftsman's home, suggesting that free girls learned their craft at home. Based on skeletal remains from Herculaneum, children as young as seven years old showed signs of upper-body injuries caused by repetitive motions such as rowing or manual farming (Laes, *Children*, 153–54). Children, especially slaves, were often assigned tasks of table service, including bringing food and drink to the guests or helping the latter remove their shoes. Young male slaves served as messengers, taking documents and letters across the city. In rural areas, children often took care of their younger siblings, gathered wood, cleaned the house, helped in the fields, or watched over the animals.

Conclusion

Having a more complete picture of the family in the Greco-Roman world, especially relating to women and children, enables the NT reader today to better appreciate the NT's teachings and descriptions of the family. For example, Elizabeth (John the Baptist's mother) and Mary the mother of Jesus likely faced their pregnancy and labor with some trepidation, knowing the dangers involved. The circumcision and naming of John (Luke 1:57–63) and the dedication of Jesus at the Jerusalem temple highlights the joy that accompanied a healthy baby (Luke 2:21–22). Turning to Jesus' interaction with families, we find that when Jesus teaches in homes, children might be present (Matt. 18:1–5; Mark 9:35–37; Luke 9:46–47). Statistics show that life was precarious, and Jesus' healing of Jairus's daughter (Matt. 9:18–26; Mark 5:22–43; Luke 8:41–56), the demon-possessed boy (Matt. 17:14–20; Mark 9:14–29; Luke 9:37–43), and the raising of the widow's son (Luke 7:11–17) links his story to that fact. Notice that the parents welcome with great joy their restored children. As we turn to the house churches, widows and orphans were an all too present reality, explaining the frequent mention of these groups (James 1:27; 1 Tim. 5:9–16). In the early house churches, we find that both children and slaves of all ages are expected to hear and know the Christian message (Eph. 5:21–6:9; Col. 3:18–4:1). Paul spoke in homes with young people present (Acts 20:7–12) and baptized entire households, presumably including children and slaves (Acts 16:34).

Bibliography

Bradley, Keith R. *Discovering the Roman Family: Studies in Roman Social History.* Oxford: Oxford University Press, 1991. A series of studies exploring childcare and child labor, as well as familial relationships in dynamic family structures that included remarriage and expanding kin networks.

Cohick, Lynn. *Women in the World of the Earliest Christians: Illuminating Ancient Ways of Life.* Grand Rapids: Baker Academic, 2009. Examines the life of the Greco-Roman woman as daughter, wife, mother, laborer, religious devotee, and patroness. Where appropriate, Cohick distinguishes the gentile and Jewish woman's experience.

Fuchs, Michel E. "Women and Children in Ancient Landscape." Pages 95–107 in *Children, Memory, and Family Identity in Roman Culture.* Edited by Véronique Dasen and Thomas Späth. Oxford: Oxford University Press, 2010. Presents papers from the Fifth Roman Family Conference (2007) on "Secret Families, Family Secrets." Several chapters address issues of memory in forming identity or preserving tradition, and six essays deal directly with marginalized children, including slaves and the sick.

Garnsey, Peter. *Food and Society in Classical Antiquity.* Cambridge: Cambridge University Press, 1999. Examines the diet of the Greco-Roman world, noting what was and was not eaten, and the economic and social factors of food production and consumption.

Laes, Christian. *Children in the Roman Empire: Outsiders Within.* Cambridge: Cambridge University Press, 2011. History of Roman childhood that begins with current research on childhood in antiquity and the Roman family. Laes follows the child from birth to coming of age, focusing on Roman attitudes toward children and childhood, as well as the child's experiences of work, school, and introduction to sexuality.

Meyers, Eric M. "The Problems of Gendered Space in Syro-Palestinian Domestic Architecture: The Case of Roman-Period Galilee." Pages 44–69 in *Early Christian Families in Context: An Interdisciplinary Dialogue*. Edited by David L. Balch and Carolyn Osiek. Grand Rapids: Eerdmans, 2003. The chapters in this volume reflect an interdisciplinary dialogue between scholars of the NT, early Christianity, early Judaism, and the Roman family. Topics range from the archaeological evidence of ancient homes to the situations of women, slaves, and children in the ancient household and the theological implications of these findings for Christianity.

Saller, Richard P. "*Pater Familias, Mater Familias* and the Gendered Semantics of the Roman Household." *Classical Philology* 94 (1999): 182–97. Analyzes the use of "paterfamilias" in ancient texts, concluding that the term speaks not of familial relationships but of estate ownership.

Severy, Beth. *Augustus and the Family at the Birth of the Roman Empire*. New York: Routledge, 2003. Traces the development of Augustus's family as it became intertwined with his political pursuits, and discusses the role of women in the elite Roman family.

Uzzi, Jeannine Diddle. "The Power of Parenthood in Official Roman Art." Pages 61–81 in *Constructions of Childhood in Ancient Greece and Italy*. Edited by Ada Cohen and Jeremy B. Rutter. Athens: The American School of Classical Studies in Athens, 2007. Explores the artistic representation of children and childhood from the classical Greek through the imperial Roman periods, and includes numerous color and black-and-white photographs and sketches.

Wallace-Hadrill, Andrew. "Engendering the Roman House." Pages 104–15 in *I, Claudia: Women in Ancient Rome*. Edited by Diane E. E. Kleiner and Susan B. Matheson. New Haven: Yale University Art Gallery, 1996. Uses visual Roman art from the public, domestic, and funerary realms to explore the lives of Roman women.

15

Education in the
Greco-Roman World

BEN WITHERINGTON III

The study of ancient education has become more complex over the last half century and more sophisticated. This is due in part to advances in the studies of orality, oral cultures, rhetoric, and the way education and texts actually functioned in the NT world. However, the matter has been complicated by the lack of hard data in regard to ancient literacy, as well as debates about what counts as literacy.

If literacy is defined narrowly, as the ability to both read and write, then estimates that only 10–15 percent of the population of the first-century Greco-Roman world were literate might be accurate. Writing, however, was largely a specialized task in antiquity, the province of the few who were educated to do it and had scribal training. But sources suggest that many more people than scribes could read: for example, they might read road signs, brief letters, inscriptions, honorific columns, business documents, or tax collectors' notes.

Accordingly, both literary and archaeological evidence should have led to caution about such claims as "Jesus and his original disciples were likely illiterate and could be described as peasants," or "Paul was an extreme exception in levels of education and literacy when it comes to the early Christians and their communities." Were these claims true, it is hard to explain not merely why we have so many early Christian documents, both canonical and otherwise, but also why their authors seem to assume audiences that have a significant modicum of literate persons. Indeed,

188

they assume some listeners were not merely literate but also, in some cases, learned when it comes to the Hebrew Scriptures. It is also hard to explain the evidence that Jesus himself could read Hebrew scrolls (cf. Luke 4:16–20) if one goes with the illiterate-peasant paradigm. Here, then, is a cautionary word: one should not take for granted that literacy, education, and texts in ancient oral cultures can be evaluated the same way such things are evaluated today.

Oral Texts and Rhetorical Contexts in Ancient Cultures

All ancient peoples, whether literate or not, seem to have preferred the living word, that is, the spoken word. Texts were enormously expensive to produce: papyrus was expensive, ink was expensive, and scribes were ultraexpensive. Serving as a secretary in Jesus' and Paul's age could be a lucrative job indeed.

Few if any documents in antiquity seem to have been intended for "si-

Papias and the Living Word

Writing early in the second century, Papias, bishop of Hierapolis, wrote a five-volume *Expositions of the Sayings of the Lord*, a work that survives only in fragments in the writings of Irenaeus and Eusebius. In the following citation, he describes how he gathered his information:

> If, then, any one came, who had been a follower of the elders, I questioned him in regard to the words of the elders,—what Andrew or what Peter said, or what was said by Philip, or by Thomas, or by James, or by John, or by Matthew, or by any other of the disciples of the Lord, and what things Aristion and the presbyter John, the disciples of the Lord, say. For I did not think that what was to be gotten from the books would profit me as much as what came from the living and abiding voice. (*NPNF*[2] 1:171)

lent" reading, and only a few were intended for private individuals to read. Rather, they were be to read aloud, usually to a group of people. For the most part, they were simply necessary surrogates for oral communication. This was particularly true of ancient letters.

In fact, most ancient documents, including letters, were not really *texts* in the modern sense at all. They were composed with their aural and oral potential in mind, and they were intended to be orally delivered when they arrived at their destination. Thus, for example, when one reads Eph. 1 (after the prescript), loaded as it is with aural devices (assonance, alliteration, rhythm, rhyme, and various rhetorical devices), it becomes clear that no one was ever meant to hear this in any language but Greek; furthermore, no one was ever meant to read this silently. It needed to be heard.

There was a further reason it needed to be orally delivered. Because of the cost of making documents, a standard letter in Greek would have been written in *scriptio continua*, a script written continuously with no separation of words, sentences, paragraphs, or the like; little or no punctuation; and all capital letters. Imagine having to sort out a document that begins as follows:

PAULASERVANTOFCHRISTJESUSCALLEDTOBEAN
APOSTLEANDSETAPARTFORTHEGOSPELOFGOD

The only way to decipher a string of letters like this was to sound them out, out loud. Recall the famous anecdote, in which Augustine said that Ambrose was the most remarkable man he had ever met, because he could read without moving his lips or making a sound.

Clearly, an oral culture is a different world from a largely literate, text-based culture, and texts function differently in such a world. Education functions differently as well. All sorts of texts were surrogates for oral speech, and this statement applies to many of the biblical texts themselves.

It is too seldom taken into account that the twenty-seven books of the NT reflect a remarkable level of literacy, and indeed of rhetorical skill, among the inner circle of leaders of the early Christian movement. Early Christianity was not, by and large, a movement led by illiterate peasants or the socially deprived. The leaders of the movement mostly produced the texts of the movement, and NT texts reflect a considerable knowledge of Greek, of rhetoric, and of general Greco-Roman culture. This skill and erudition can only seldom be attributed merely to scribes, except in cases where scribes such as Tertius or Sosthenes (cf. Rom. 16:22; 1 Cor. 1:1) had joined the Christian movement.

> **Augustine, on Ambrose the Reader**
>
> "But while reading, his eyes glanced over the pages, and his heart searched out the sense, but his voice and tongue were silent. Ofttimes, when we had come (for no one was forbidden to enter, nor was it his custom that the arrival of those who came should be announced to him), we saw him thus reading to himself, and never otherwise; and, having long sat in silence (for who durst interrupt one so intent?), we were fain to depart, inferring that in the little time he secured for the recruiting of his mind, free from the clamour of other men's business, he was unwilling to be taken off."
> (Augustine, *Confessions* 6.3.3; *NPNF*[1] 1:91)

Given that the division between a speech and an orally performed text was more like a thin veil than a thick wall separating literary categories, it will come as no surprise that oral conventions shape the so-called epistolary literature of the NT more than epistolary conventions do, and with good reason. This was not only because of the dominant oral character of the culture but also, more important, because the Greco-Roman world of the NT period was a rhetorically saturated environment; the influence of literacy and letters was far less widespread.

The rise to prominence of the personal letter used as something of a vehicle for instruction or as a treatise of sorts was a phenomenon that took root in the Greco-Roman milieu with the letters of Cicero shortly before the NT era. Contrast this with the long history of the use of rhetoric, going back to Aristotle. Rhetoric was a tool useable with the educated and uneducated, with the elite, and also with the ordinary; and most public speakers of any ilk or skill in antiquity knew they had to use the art of persuasion to accomplish their aims. Not only were there schools of rhetoric throughout the Mediterranean world, but rhetoric was also part of elementary, secondary, and tertiary education. There were no comparable schools of letter writing, not least because it was a rather recent art, just coming to prominence in the first century AD.

Education in the Greco-Roman World

The study of education in antiquity has been hampered to a considerable degree because of the paradigms used to approach the issue. Too often, the focus has been on *formal* education with famous teachers or at famous schools. When this has been the focus, the corollary has understandably been that education was the privilege of the few, the socially elite. When one investigates the empirical evidence, formal education tells only part of the story. Consider Acts 4:13: "Now when they saw the boldness of Peter and John and realized that they were uneducated and ordinary men, they were amazed and recognized them as companions of Jesus." This text does not tell us that Peter and John were illiterate fishermen but rather that the well-trained scribes and officials in Jerusalem were amazed at "the boldness [*parrēsia*]" and rhetorical effectiveness of the apostles' speech, even though they had never studied formally in Jerusalem. *Agrammatoi* (NRSV: "uneducated") signifies not having been formally trained by a *grammateus* ("instructor," "scribe"); it does not necessarily imply anything about literacy per se. Similarly, *idiōtēs* (NRSV: "ordinary") refers to someone who has not been initiated into formal education—that is, into formal training within the circles the Jewish officials inhabited. Hence, we might capture the point of Acts 4:13 as follows: "How can these men speak like this when they didn't come to Jerusalem for formal education?" In antiquity, though, education began not with schools but at home, and in Jewish settings it was augmented by training in synagogues.

David Aune claims that *propaideia* ("preliminary education") occurred in the home and was provided by parents, or in a more elite home by an educated slave.[1] The fact that there were many literate and educated slaves who served as instructors or helpers in the educational process in the Greco-Roman world should remind us that the dictum "social status determines education" or "education can only be assumed for the socially elite" is patently false. Indeed, the Greek term

1. David Aune, "Education," in *The Westminster Dictionary of New Testament and Early Christian Literature and Rhetoric* (Louisville: Westminster, 2003), 143.

paidagōgos, which refers to a slave who is a child's guardian and helps the child get back and forth to school and assists with lessons, reminds us of the frequent presence of educated slaves in antiquity.[2] What did this elementary education in the home look like? In the first instance it involved learning how to form letters (Greek or Latin ones, or in the Jewish context Hebrew or Aramaic ones) and beginning to learn to read. Writing would apparently come later, and with higher levels of education, even outside home education. The evidence suggests that classic texts like Homer's *Odyssey* or, later, Virgil's *Aeneid* or the Hebrew Scriptures were used to help children begin to recognize their letters and read a text written in *scriptio continua*.

We must bear steadily in mind that all education in the Greco-Roman world, including Jewish education, was indebted to the spread of Hellenism. Greek forms of education, including the learning of philosophy and rhetoric, formed the basic building blocks of education throughout the Mediterranean crescent. Greek was the lingua franca of that world, and not surprisingly Greek approaches to education were adopted throughout the Roman Empire, with modifications for local subcultures. By early in the first century AD, if not earlier, rhetoric had become the primary discipline to be learned, particularly in Roman education.[3] Indeed, even the elementary *progymnasmata* exercises included learning to form a *chreia* (a short pithy saying or act, attributed to someone, and regarded as useful for living) and to do *synkrisis* (rhetorical comparison), among other things. Rhetoric was a part of every level of ancient education, whether one was educated in Tarsus, Pergamum, Athens, Alexandria, or even Jerusalem.

> **The *Chreia***
>
> The *chreia* was basic to education in the Greco-Roman world and is one of the several varieties of rhetorical exercises described in the rhetorical handbooks of the ancient world. Here is an example of a *chreia*: "Diogenes the philosopher, on being asked by someone how he could become famous, responded: 'By worrying as little as possible about fame.'"[a] Examples abound in the NT Gospels, including this one: "Now after John was arrested, Jesus came to Galilee, proclaiming the good news of God, and saying, 'The time is fulfilled, and the kingdom of God has come near; repent, and believe in the good news'" (Mark 1:14–15).
>
> [a] ET in Duane F. Watson and Alan J. Hauser, *Rhetorical Criticism of the Bible: A Comprehensive Bibliography with Notes on History and Method* (Leiden: Brill, 1994), 117.

2. Bear in mind that slaves in antiquity were often newly conquered, formerly socially elite people from non-Roman subcultures. The story of Tiro, Cicero's personal slave and scribe, who is credited with inventing the system of shorthand (see, e.g., Plutarch, *Cato the Younger* 23.3), should caution us against assuming education was possessed only by the elite and the free and the patricians.

3. See S. F. Bonner, *Education in Ancient Rome from the Elder Cato to the Younger Pliny* (Berkeley: University of California Press, 1977); D. L. Clark, *Rhetoric in Greco-Roman Education* (New York: Columbia University Press, 1957); Clarke, *Higher Education*.

It was indeed one of the major cultural goals that all free persons would strive for *paideia*, which was the term for education beyond the preliminary level, referring more technically to education outside the home, that is, to the beginnings of more formal education. The elite child, usually a boy, would attend a local school, and often would have a slave, a *paidagōgos*, to help with his lessons, in lieu of the parent's bearing the main burden of higher education. The rhetorical and philosophical education begun in the home and carried forward in secondary education outside the home might be brought to completion in the tertiary level of education. This level "concentrated on rhetoric and philosophy, both of which thrived on debate. This tertiary level of Greco-Roman education (where the student could 'major' in either rhetoric or philosophy) required texts on rhetorical theory and practice."[4]

Although there were no universal standards for ancient education, Greek rhetoric was an essential part of that education since the time of Aristotle, drawing on handbooks and treatises by Aristotle and his successors. Training in letter writing of a more-than-mundane sort (the letter essay) was only beginning to become a part of general education in the first centuries BC and AD. That is, the primary paradigm for understanding ancient education involved rhetoric and philosophy, not training in letter writing. Indeed, it was the *grammateus*, a secondary-school instructor, who taught writing in general, arithmetic, reading of Greek poets, and the like, but rhetoric was found at all three levels of ancient education, especially at the tertiary level. The reason for this was twofold: (1) these were oral cultures that placed a premium on the ability to speak well and persuade, whether one was a philosopher, a businessman making a sale, a teacher, or a politician; and (2) the key to advancement in a nondemocratic society like the Roman Empire involved persuasion and reciprocal relationships of various kinds. This was especially crucial for Greco-Roman persons trying to climb the *cursus honorum* (Latin, "course of offices," a sequence of administrative positions of gradually increasing responsibility and status), the ancient equivalent of the ladder of political and social success.

Quintilian wrote his handbook on rhetoric, the *Institutio oratoria*, in the late first century AD. In this work, he sums up the whole trend of the age toward the increasing use of rhetoric to get ahead in life and thus marks the first century AD as a rhetoric-saturated age. Accordingly, the vast majority of persons in the Roman world were either producers or avid consumers of the art of persuasion, that is, rhetoric. Orators were lionized in books like Athenaeus's *Deipnosophists* or Philostratus's *Lives of the Sophists* and became some of the wealthiest members of ancient society. There were rhetoricians in every major city, and rhetorical training was on offer in places both great and small in the Greco-Roman world. This was because the living word, the oral word, was preferred, and the oral art of persuasion was the key to education and advancement, whether for the free or the freedman, whether for the *paidagōgos* or the actual pedagogue.

4. Aune, "Education," 143.

Bibliography

Clarke, M. L. *Higher Education in the Ancient World*. London: Routledge & Kegan Paul, 1971. This is still the standard textbook on this subject.

Gamble, H. Y. *Books and Readers in the Early Church*. New Haven: Yale University Press, 1997. Valuable resource on texts and the beginning of book culture in these largely oral cultures.

Tapia, J. E. *Rhetoric and Centers of Power in the Greco-Roman World: From Homer to the Fall of Rome*. Lanham, MD: University Press of America, 2009. Resource on literacy and rhetoric in the ancient world.

Witherington, Ben, III. *New Testament Rhetoric: An Introductory Guide to the Art of Persuasion in and of the New Testament*. Eugene, OR: Cascade Books, 2009. This basic introduction to rhetoric for beginners is on education in general in the Greco-Roman world.

PART 3

THE JEWISH PEOPLE IN THE CONTEXT OF ROMAN HELLENISM

Roman Hellenism powerfully influenced the social and religious institutions of the Mediterranean world, including those in Israel. The variegated expressions of Judaism in the first century owe their differences in part to their varied responses to the influence of Hellenistic culture and Roman rule.

Without a grasp of the great traditions that gave rise to Second Temple Judaism, our understanding of Jewish beliefs and practices of Jesus' day and thus our understanding of Jesus himself and his followers would be anemic. These great traditions include centuries of religious reflection and practice within Israel, God's people, especially as this was shaped by exile (part 1) and the cultural streams of Hellenism and life in the Roman Empire (part 2). The question that confronts us in this section is how the various forms of Judaism in the period just before and during the NT era framed what it would mean to remain faithful to Yahweh in the context of massive upheavals politically and militarily, and in the context of major challenges socially, economically, and religiously.

16

Temple and Priesthood

DAVID INSTONE-BREWER

History and Buildings

The so-called Second Temple period (516 BC–AD 70) spans the history of two temple complexes: the first built by Zerubbabel and the completely new construction built by Herod that could properly be called the "third temple."

During this period there were also two Jewish temples in Egypt: on the island of Elephantine near Aswan in the fifth century BC, until it was destroyed in the fourth century; and the temple of Onias in Leontopolis in the second century BC, which offered sacrifices when the Jerusalem temple was desecrated by Antiochus and probably continued to do so until it was destroyed at about the same time as the Jerusalem temple on the orders of Vespasian.

We know very little about the physical size and nature of Zerubbabel's temple, except the measurements that are recorded in Ezra 6:3, which says that sixty cubits was both the height and the width of the building. This is considerably larger than Solomon's temple, which had a central hall of twenty by sixty cubits and was thirty cubits high (1 Kings 6:2). This is partly resolved by assuming Ezra's width is the external measurement, which included the thirty rooms arranged in three stories along the sides of the temple building, and by assuming that the height is the maximum point of a facade or some other tall structure. It is clear that the disappointment felt by those who compared Zerubbabel's temple with Solomon's (Hag. 2:3–9) was due more to the lack of gold than to the lack of stature.

16.1. Model of Herod's temple, from the north.

The temple was probably extended and improved many times. Simon II (ca. 218–215 BC) is praised for repairs, fortifications, and extensions to the enclosure (Sir. 50:1–3). It fell into disrepair after Antiochus Epiphanes desecrated it by sacrificing a pig on the altar in about 168 BC and removing all the gold vessels and furniture. When Judas Maccabeus restored the temple in 164 BC, he had to replace all the altars, sacred vessels, veils, and doors, and he even had to rebuild the priests' quarters.

Herod's Temple

Herod's rebuilding was based on the same pattern and size as the predecessors but with much greater magnificence and with greatly extended courtyards. In order to produce an extended area, he had to build up the hillsides surrounding the temple into a vast elevated platform. The so-called Wailing Wall consists of the remains of the edge of this elevation, and the huge size of the individual stones found there shows what an ambitious engineering project this was.

Herod promised he would replace the temple itself as quickly as possible to minimize the interruption of the offerings. Remarkably he succeeded in demolishing the old temple, laying new foundations, and building the new temple in eighteen months. Unfortunately, the work on the foundations was insufficient for the weight of the temple, which consequently started to sink and had to be repaired during Nero's reign (Josephus, *Ant.* 15.389–91, 421).

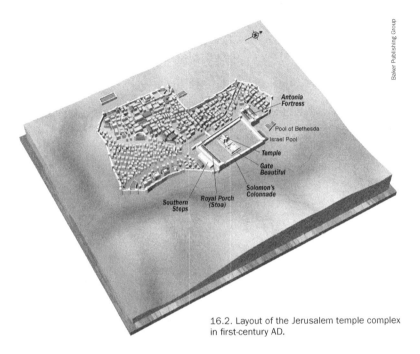

16.2. Layout of the Jerusalem temple complex in first-century AD.

The general layout and internal size was based on Solomon's temple, which emulated the standard four-section pattern of tenth-century BC temples in Palestine: a courtyard with altar and purification vessels; a porch bound by pillars but no door; a door leading into a sanctuary containing a lampstand, a table for bread, and an incense altar; and an inner sanctuary that was empty but would have contained the ark with cherubum if this had not been lost during the exile.

Hebrew and Greek terminology for these different sections is varied. The whole complex is the "house" (Hebrew *bayit*; Greek *oikos*) or "sanctuary" (*miqdāš*; *hagios*); the whole building is the "temple" (*hêkāl*; *hieron*); the two internal sanctuaries are also called *hêkāl* in Hebrew but generally *naos* in Greek; the outer and inner sanctuary are literally known as "holy [place]" and "holy of holies," respectively, in both Hebrew and Greek. A few other terms are also used.

The extended courtyards of Herod's temple were bounded by a double portico on three sides and a taller treble "royal" portico on the south side. This large area was divided into three concentric areas: for Jewish men; for Jewish men and women; and for anyone, including gentiles. Periodic signs warned gentiles not to transgress this boundary; some of these signs have survived. However, a secret tunnel from the Fortress of Antonia, overlooking the courtyards from the north, led straight to the eastern gate of the inner courtyard, at the entrance to the temple itself, so Roman soldiers could erupt into the center of any disturbance (Josephus, *Ant.* 15.424). The priestly vestments were also kept in the fortress, released by the Romans at festivals to remind the high priest that the Romans were in charge (*Ant.* 15.403–8).

Two veils adorned Herod's temple, one separating the holy place from the holy of holies, and one covering the outer door of the holy place. Until the first century AD, the two veils were distinguished by different terminology (inner and outer, respectively, were *pārōket* and *māsak* in Hebrew and *katapetasma* and *epispastron* in Greek), so that the temple could be called "the house of the veil" (singular *katapetasma* in Sir. 50:5). However, Josephus referred to them both as *katapetasma* (*J.W.* 5.211–19), and Hebrews refers to the inner veil as the "second" *katapetasma* (Heb. 9:3). They were probably identical, as implied by their original description (Exod. 26:36; 36:35–38), so Josephus described the outer one, which was visible: "Babylonian tapestry, embroidered with blue, fine linen, scarlet, and purple, a wondrous piece of artistry . . . a panorama of the whole heavens" (*J.W.* 5.211–14, Thackeray LCL).

16.3. Southern steps entering the temple mount in Jerusalem, from the first century BC/AD.

The Synoptic Gospels report that a veil was torn during Jesus' crucifixion (Matt. 27:51; Mark 15:38; Luke 23:45); this may have been the outer veil. Although the inner one might have more symbolic value, no one would have know it had been torn. The veil of Christ's flesh in Heb. 10:19–20 could refer to either veil because it admits believers into the "holies" (*hagiōn*), a term that is used in the LXX for both the holy of holies and the holy place (cf. Lev. 16:2; 2 Chron. 5:9).

Priesthood

Priests were descended from the family of Aaron, which was part of the tribe of Levi. At some point, probably during the reign of David, the Zadokite family became a particularly important family for the high priesthood, and their gene-alogy may have been changed when this happened. Priests were divided into twenty-four courses (as specified in 1 Chron. 24:1–19) that were still recognized in Qumran and early rab-binic literature. Each course was on duty for two weeks each year, plus the major festivals, when all the courses attended the temple to help with the large number of people bringing of-ferings (*m. Sukkah* 5.7).

Jewish High Priests
Joazar son of Boethus (4 BC)
Eleazar son of Boethus (4 BC–?)
Jesus son of See (?–?)
Annas (AD 6–15)
Ishmael son of Phiabi (AD 15–16)
Eleazar son of Annas (AD 16–17)
Simon son of Camithus (AD 17–18)
Iosephus Caiaphas son in-law of Annas (AD 18–36)
Jonathan son of Annas (AD 36–37)
Theophilus son of Annas (AD 37–?)
Simon Cantheras son of Boethus (AD 41)
Matthias son of Annas (AD 41–44)
Elionaeus son of Cantheras (AD 44–46)
Ananus son of Annas (AD 62)

The hereditary high priesthood en-visioned in the Pentateuch ended with Onias III in 174 BC, when his brother Jason bribed Antiochus Epiphanes to make him high priest. Menelaus (who was not even a Levite) gained the post with a similar bribe three years later, and when he was accused of pilfering temple gold, Alcimus was appointed. Onias III was murdered in 171 BC, so his son was the Onias (IV) who went to Egypt and founded the rival temple in Leontopolis (2 Macc. 4:33; contrary to Josephus, *J.W.* 1.1). In Jerusalem, the temple sacrifices and priesthood lapsed until Judas Maccabeus, of the priestly Hasmonean family, led a revolt and restored the temple in 164 BC. This family retained the combined high priesthood and secular kingship until Antigonus was beheaded by Herod the Great in 37 BC. The high priesthood then became a political appointment super-vised by Rome, with about thirty individuals holding the post before it lapsed with the destruction of the temple in AD 70.

Many priests lived outside Jerusalem, including a large number at Jericho, and traveled in when they were on duty. At these times they could share the sacred portions that could be eaten only by priests and their families in a state of cultic purity. These included portions of offerings made in the temple and the "heave offerings" that consisted of about one-twenty-fourth of all produce grown in the country. Priests who were farmers were exempt from this tax. By the first century, the sacred tithe of one-tenth of all produce, which Mosaic law called the tithe for the Levites, was probably distributed only among the priests.

Although most priests were Sadducees, the Pharisees had enjoyed much political and religious influence during at least part of the Hasmonean period, from about

76 BC under Queen Alexandra (whose brother was the Pharisee leader Simeon ben Shetah) and perhaps her son Hyrcanus. Even in the first century a few priests were Pharisees, and the title "Rabbi" may have originally indicated a priestly teacher; at least five of the six individuals consistently given this title before AD 70 were priests.

Later rabbinic traditions suggest that the Pharisees instructed the priests how to carry out their duties properly, but this is unlikely. It is possible that the high priests did indeed need help on the Day of Atonement, because most of them were political appointees with no experience (cf. *m. Yoma* 1.6; 5.1), but there is nothing to substantiate the later rabbinic assertions that the priests acted in accordance with Pharisaic rulings (e.g., *t. Kipp.* 1.8; *b. Yoma* 19b). Indeed, the later rabbis complained that the priests acted against Pharisaic teaching (e.g., *m. Pesaḥ.* 5.8).

Worship

Although worship at the temple of Zerubbabel was interrupted only for three and a half years by Antiochus Epiphanes, this began a serious decline from which that temple never really recovered. The building of the temple at Leontopolis roughly coincided with this interruption, which gave legitimacy to the rival temple and demonstrated that Jews could survive without sacrifices at Jerusalem.

The Jerusalem temple lost further legitimacy with the disruption of the hereditary priesthood and the adoption of a new calendar in the second century BC (as implied by the calendar discussions in *Jubilees* and *1 Enoch*). Some Jews broke away, including those who went to live at Qumran. They still respected the temple's sacrifices but thought that the festivals were celebrated on the wrong dates and that the rites were imperfect due to wrongly appointed high priests.

However, even those who were disaffected with the temple calendar did not attempt to set up a separate worship center. It is possible that the priesthood helped to accommodate those who used a different calendar. They were willing, for example, to accept a Passover offering that was brought on the "wrong" date and treat it as a peace offering, because this was processed in exactly the same way (*m. Pesaḥ.* 5.2; *m. Zebaḥ.* 1.1, 3).

Little is known about actual prayers or songs in the temple. Although the OT frequently mentions Levitical singers, there is little or no evidence of them in the first century AD, though Ben Sirach mentions them in the second century BC (Sir. 50:18). The fact that prayers did not have any fixed wording before the destruction of the temple (*m. Ber.* 4.4) suggests that they were not prayed publicly by the temple priests. A possible exception is the Eighteen Benedictions, since this was said at the time of morning and evening sacrifice, with an extra one on Sabbaths at the time of the afternoon offering (*minḥâ*); accordingly, it is likely that this was originally associated with temple worship. However, the only wording that was fixed by the first century was the one-line benediction at the end of each of the eighteen sections.

16.4. *Mikveh*, or purification pool, situated on the southern steps of the temple mount in Jerusalem.

Perhaps a priest ended each section of communal private prayer with a benediction, possibly accompanied by a trumpet blast or prostrations (cf. Sir. 50:16–21).

Finances

Like many ancient temples, the Second Temple had more money than it could use, and this made it a target for conquest. Antiochus Epiphanes stole all the temple's gold vessels and emptied the treasury in 167 BC (Josephus, *Ant.* 12.248–50); yet, a hundred years later, when Pompey conquered Jerusalem in 63 BC, the temple had already accumulated two thousand talents (about six million shekels) and many new gold vessels that he magnanimously left there (Josephus, *Ant.* 14.72). This money came mainly from offerings.

Every Israelite male was expected to pay a half-shekel annual temple tax, except for priests (which annoyed some rabbis; *m. Šeqal.* 1.3b–5). Those who did not travel to Jerusalem could pay at booths set up once a year in the provinces. Qumran Jews argued that this tax should be paid only once per lifetime because they did not think that 2 Chron. 24:5 should overturn the Torah (4Q159 frg. 1 2.6–7). It is possible that others agreed, because Peter was asked if his rabbi, Jesus, paid the tax, as though this was not a foregone conclusion (Matt. 17:24).

Other money was also collected in the thirteen "trumpet chests"—probably named after trumpet-like horns for funneling coins into small holes. These received freewill offerings or payment in lieu of burnt offerings or sin offerings.

The half-shekel tax theoretically paid for public sacrifices made on behalf of everyone, but in practice only a tiny proportion of the money was used this way, and worshipers tried to make sure their coins were used for this purpose (*m. Šeqal.* 3.1–3). The debates about what the temple authorities did with the excess money suggest that the finances were completely nontransparent, but not even the later rabbis were willing to consider that fraud occurred (cf. *m. Šeqal.* 4.2–4).

Destruction

It is difficult to imagine the feeling of loss when the temple was destroyed. Daily worship to God, which was offered on behalf of every Jew, had stopped. Hence, individuals felt the burden to replace this worship by other means. Family gatherings, which included a temple visit (such as Passover and celebrations after a birth) felt incomplete. The second tithe—a kind of holiday tax that was spent on enjoying oneself in Jerusalem—was redundant. Sins that required sin offerings and serious sins that awaited the Day of Atonement now remained unforgiven. Those with corpse impurity could be purified only by the ashes of the red heifer, and because it was transmitted by touch, the whole nation gradually became impure.

For some decades, many Jews followed policies that lived in expectation of a new temple. They accumulated the second tithe in the hope that they could one day

16.5. Southwestern corner of the temple mount. A portion of Robinson's arch is visible, protruding from the wall. The arch formed an entrance into Herod's temple, which the Romans destroyed in AD 70.

Lee Martin McDonald

spend it in Jerusalem (*t. Ma'aś. Š.* 3.13–14; *b. Pesaḥ.* 7a; *b. Sanh.* 30a). They continued to discuss the administration of temple offerings in the hope that the discussion itself was a substitute for carrying them out, or perhaps because they wanted to be ready to reinstate the system. The second century saw increased interest in offerings that were "put to pasture till they are blemished"—which in temple times had been done to offerings that could not be offered because (for example) they were the wrong gender (e.g., *m. Pesaḥ.* 9.6–8; *m. Zebaḥ.* 8.1–3). Perhaps this was another way they coped with no longer being able to sacrifice offerings.

The half-shekel tax became voluntary after AD 70 (*m. Šeqal.* 8.8), and Josephus assumed that it stopped completely (*J.W.* 7.218) because Vespasian had replaced it with the *fiscus Iudaicus*—a tax of the same value paid to the cult of Jupiter in Rome. However, it is likely that people continued to put money aside for some time in the hope of taking it to a new temple. The rabbis certainly continued to discuss the half-shekel tax until the Bar Kokhba revolt, but there is relatively little interest in it thereafter. The tractate concerning it is hardly discussed in the Talmud, which may indicate that they had accepted their long-term loss of the temple.

Yohanan b. Zakkai, who in many ways rescued Judaism after the destruction of the temple, argued that sacrifices could be replaced by almsgiving, echoing Jesus' quotation, "I desire mercy, not sacrifice" (*'Abot R. Nat.* 4.5; Matt. 9:13; cf. 12:7—both quote Hosea 6:6). He also pragmatically ended the rite of *Sôṭâ* (the test of an adulteress) when the dust of the temple floor was no longer available (*m. Sotah* 9.9); he allowed the *lulav* (the palm branch plus citrus fruit) to be waved outside Jerusalem throughout the Feast of Tabernacles (*m. Sukkah* 3.12); and he let the New Year *shofar* be blown at every town with a court (*m. Roš. Haš.* 4.1). These reforms helped Judaism to continue without a physical temple or sacrifices, and gradually Jewish theology found ways to continue Jewish life and worship without a temple.

Temple and Priests in the New Testament

The NT does not disparage the temple, and Jewish Christians continued to use it and brought offerings (Matt. 5:23–24; Acts 2:46; 3:1; 5:42; 21:26). When it was destroyed, there was little consternation among Christians, because the temple had been largely appropriated into their theology as a spiritual dwelling place of God. On earth, this spiritual temple consisted of the body of God's people (1 Cor. 3:16; 6:19; 2 Cor. 6:16; Eph. 2:21), while in heaven it represented the presence of God, into which Jesus had entered, and where Christian worship reaches God's attention (Heb. 6:19; 8:2; 9:11, 24; 10:20).

In Revelation the temple is found solely in heaven and is inhabited by (and perhaps partly made up of) believers who have died (3:12; 7:15). Revelation envisions a new temple in Jerusalem, but its worship is tainted, and it is contrasted with the true temple in heaven (11:1–2, 19). When, at the end, a new Jerusalem is built on earth, it pointedly does not contain a temple (21:22).

Jewish priests were still respected in the NT—they are not criticized when consulted concerning Scripture and rites (Matt. 2:4; 8:4 par.) or performing temple rites (Luke 1:9), and the office of high priest is regarded with respect (Acts 23:5). However, almost all of the many references to "high priest" are negative, in both the singular (referring to the current holder of the office) and the plural (usually translated "chief priests" and referring to a class of ruling priests, not merely to former holders of the post of high priest).

Bibliography

Grabbe, Lester L. *Judaic Religion in the Second Temple Period: Belief and Practice from the Exile to Yavneh*. London: Routledge, 2000. A minimalist history concentrating on the sources.

Hayward, C. T. R. *The Jewish Temple: A Non-biblical Sourcebook*. London: Routledge, 1996. All of the primary sources are conveniently collected with brief insightful commentary.

Instone-Brewer, David. *Feasts and Sabbaths: Passover and Atonement*. Traditions of the Rabbis in the Era of the New Testament 2A. Grand Rapids: Eerdmans, 2011. Early rabbinic sources with brief commentary on dating, Jewish context, and NT application.

Shanks, Hershel. *Jerusalem's Temple Mount: From Solomon to the Golden Dome*. New York: Continuum, 2007. Beautiful and historically informed illustrations and text.

17

Jews and Samaritans

LIDIJA NOVAKOVIC

"Jews do not share things in common with Samaritans," explains the author of John's Gospel (4:9). This statement is consistent with other sources that speak about strained Jewish-Samaritan relations in antiquity. Yet the exact nature and the cause of the separation between these two groups are far from clear. The evidence from Jewish and Samaritan literature is frequently biased, unreliable, or both. According to the Jewish sources, which are generally hostile to Samaritans, the latter were semipagans who rejected the Jerusalem temple and regarded Mount Gerizim as the exclusive legitimate place of worship. According to the Samaritan sources, most of which come from Byzantine and medieval times, Samaritans were true Israelites who stood in unbroken continuity with the religion of ancient Israel. The self-designations of the Samaritans, who have survived until today as a tiny community of approximately seven hundred people living in Holon and on Mount Gerizim, include terms such as "guardians of the Torah," "guardians of the land of Israel," and "Israelite Samaritans." Should, then, the Samaritans be regarded as a Jewish sect, especially in view of Judaism's variegated character before AD 70, or as an independent form of Yahwism? The matter is further complicated by numerous similarities in the beliefs, practices, and sacred texts of both groups, which suggest close relations over a long period of time. If so, when exactly did the final parting of the ways between the Jews and the Samaritans take place?

Historical reconstructions of Jewish-Samaritan relations have unfortunately suffered from ambiguous and inconsistent terminology. Until about forty years ago, most scholars made no distinction between the inhabitants of the political district of Samaria and the Samaritan religious community. Since then, it has been customary to apply the term "Samaritans" only to the Yahweh-worshipers whose religious center was Mount Gerizim and the term "Samarians" to other inhabitants of Samaria.

Literary and Archaeological Evidence

According to 2 Kings 17, after the Assyrians deported most of the citizens of the northern kingdom, they populated the towns of Samaria with pagan immigrants. When some of the new settlers were killed by lions because of their ignorance of "the law of the god of the land" (vv. 26–27), the Assyrian king sent one of the exiled northern priests to teach them how to worship the God of Israel. Consequently, the inhabitants of Samaria accepted Yahwism but also continued with their former religious practices. The account concludes with a condescending statement: "To this day their children and their children's children continue to do as their ancestors did" (v. 41).

The polemical character of this report significantly reduces its historical reliability. Scholars generally recognize that the numbers of Israelites who were taken into exile and of the foreign immigrants who were settled in Samaria were relatively small. Moreover, although 2 Kings 17:29 contains the term šōmrōnîm, which does not occur anywhere else in the HB, the original account most likely referred to the Samarians—that is, the syncretistic population of Samaria. The pagan origin of the inhabitants of Samaria is also presumed in the Ezra-Nehemiah cycle about the adversaries of the Jewish returnees from the Babylonian captivity who opposed the rebuilding of the Jerusalem temple and the reconstruction of the city walls (cf. Ezra 4:1–16; Neh. 4:1–8). Yet none of the biblical writings mention a rival cult associated with Shechem and Mount Gerizim. Moreover, both references to Mount Gerizim in the MT of Deuteronomy (11:29; 27:12) present it in a positive light.

One of the earliest references to the Samaritans appears in Sir. 50:25–26, an early second-century BC text that describes them as "the foolish people that live in Shechem" (v. 26). The condescending tenor of the passage is unmistakable, but it is unclear whether the author refers to the Samaritans as a distinct ethnic group comparable to other pagan nations or merely as an objectionable religious community. What can be said with more certainty is that by the second century BC, the Samaritans were identified through their association with Shechem and perceived as "foolish." This association is supported by Josephus's comment that Shechem was located on Mount Gerizim and served as the Samaritans' capital (Ant. 11.340). The reasons for such a derogatory assessment are not provided, however, and there is no mention of the Gerizim temple.

Second Maccabees, usually dated to the last quarter of the second century BC, contains two passing references to the Samaritans. In 2 Macc. 5:22–23, the group associated with Mount Gerizim is included in the Jewish people. According to 2 Macc. 6:1–2, Antiochus IV Epiphanes renamed the Jerusalem temple as "the temple of Olympian Zeus" and the Gerizim temple as "the temple of Zeus-the-Friend-of-Strangers." Neither passage displays an explicit hostility toward the Samaritans.

In 1979 two inscriptions, dated respectively from the third to second and from the second to first centuries BC, were discovered on the island of Delos. The dedicators of these inscriptions call themselves "the Israelites in Delos who make offerings to hallowed *Argarizein*" (see Pummer, *Samaritans*, 16). Since these people presume the sacredness of Mount Gerizim, most scholars identify them as Samaritans. They clearly perceive themselves as Israelites. Since, however, the context of these inscriptions is unknown, nothing else can be said about this community.

The NT contains several passages that provide some information about Jewish-Samaritan relationships in the first century AD. In Matt. 10:5–6, Jesus instructs his disciples not to enter any town of the Samaritans but to go rather to the lost sheep of the house of Israel. Regardless of whose view is reflected in this text, that of the historical Jesus or of the Matthean church, it clearly presumes that Samaritans are not Israelites. According to Luke 9:51–53, the residents of one Samaritan village refused to show hospitality to Jesus because he was on his way to Jerusalem. In the parable of the good Samaritan (Luke 10:25–37), however, a Samaritan who shows mercy to an injured Jew becomes a model of neighborly love. Similarly, Luke 17:11–19 singles out a Samaritan among the ten lepers who have been healed by Jesus as the only one who has shown gratitude. The last two passages, like the account of the Samaritan mission in Acts 8:4–25, not only betray a sympathetic view of the Samaritans but also portray them as devoted observers of the Torah. The most instructive NT passage about Jewish-Samaritan relations in antiquity is the story of Jesus' encounter with the Samaritan woman in John 4:4–42, which mentions a disagreement between the Jews and the Samaritans with regard to the proper place of worship and the Samaritan expectation of a messianic figure. Nevertheless, like other NT references, this text does not offer any specific information about the appearance of the Samaritans as a distinct religious community.

In contrast to these sporadic references to the Samaritans, the writings of Josephus contain several lengthy passages that discuss their origin and relationship to the Jews. The following survey includes only some of the most significant passages in Josephus (more fully, see Pummer, *Samaritans*, 67–285). This does not mean that Josephus had firsthand knowledge of Samaritans. He never describes their beliefs and customs and shows no familiarity with the Samaritan Pentateuch. He was also apparently unaware of the existence of the Dositheans, a Samaritan sect that regarded a certain Dositheus as the prophet like Moses, foretold in Deut. 18:15–18 (Isser, *Dositheans*, 163–64). Most of Josephus's accounts are derived from Scripture and other literary (or oral) sources, which he utilizes for his own purposes (Pummer, *Samaritans*, 66). In *Jewish Antiquities*, where Josephus mentions the Samaritans most frequently, he regularly presents them as a foil for the Jews in order to commend the latter to his Roman audience. Josephus's more neutral portrayal of the Samaritans in *Jewish War* better reflects the actual relationship between Jews and Samaritans in the first century AD, which was not as antagonistic as it is sometimes assumed (see Pummer, *Samaritans*, 282).

In *Ant.* 9.288–91 and 10.183–85, Josephus offers his interpretation of 2 Kings 17:24–41. He firmly links this biblical passage to the Samaritans of his day by emphasizing the ethnic discontinuity between the northern Israelites and the new inhabitants of Samaria. The latter are, he says, called Cutheans in Hebrew (after their Persian and Median countries of origin) and Samaritans in Greek (after their new settlement in Samaria; see *Ant.* 9.290; 10.184). Josephus regularly emphasizes the foreign origin of the Samaritans (cf. *J.W.* 1.63; *Ant.* 11.302; 13.255–56). In all of these instances, he uses the terms "Samaritans" and "Cutheans" as synonyms, regardless of whether his sources made such an identification or not.

At the same time, however, Josephus underscores the religious sincerity of these new converts to Yahwism and presents them as genuine proselytes. Yet he also adds that the Samaritans are opportunists in their dealings with the Jews. When the Jews prosper, the Samaritans behave as though they are their relatives, but when the Jews are in difficulties, the Samaritans deny any association with them (*Ant.* 9.291; for similar accusations of opportunism, see *Ant.* 11.341; 12.257).

Josephus is the only ancient author that provides an account of the building of the Samaritan temple on Mount Gerizim (*Ant.* 11.302–47). He reports that during the campaign of Alexander the Great against the Persian king Darius, Manasseh, the brother of the high priest Jaddua, married a daughter of Sanballat, the governor of Samaria who was of Cuthean origin. The elders of Jerusalem, however, coerced Jaddua to ask Manasseh to divorce his non-Jewish wife or resign from his sacerdotal duties. When Sanballat learned that Manasseh would rather dissolve his marriage than relinquish his priestly privileges, he promised to build him a temple on Mount Gerizim like the one in Jerusalem if he remained married to his daughter. Sanballat was able to fulfill this promise with the help of Alexander the Great, to whom he pledged unreserved allegiance. In the meantime, however, Jaddua also secured Alexander's goodwill by predicting the latter's victory over the Persians. When the Samaritans heard that Alexander had sacrificed to Israel's God in the Jerusalem temple, they opportunistically declared that they too were Jews and invited Alexander to bestow a similar honor on their temple on Mount Gerizim. He promised to do so on his return but was prevented by his premature death. Josephus closes his report by remarking that the religious community at Shechem welcomed those Jews who claimed to have been unjustly accused by the citizens of Jerusalem of eating unclean food, breaking the Sabbath commandment, or other similar transgressions.

Josephus's narrative about Jaddua, Manasseh, and Sanballat resembles a similar account in Neh. 13:28–29, which mentions one of the sons of Jehoiada, son of the high priest Eliashib, who was the son-in-law of Sanballat the Horonite. Whether

Josephus's account expands Neh. 13:28 or represents an independent account, it is clear that he presents the Samaritan temple and its priesthood in a negative light: the Gerizim temple was built with the help of a foreign king, and its first high priest was a Jewish renegade married to a foreign woman. This narrative also offers an alternative interpretation of the origin of the Samaritans. Unlike those passages that portray them as descendants of the Medes and Persians, they are presented here, for the most part, as apostate Jews. Such diverse accounts most likely reflect the ambiguous attitude toward the Samaritans that Josephus shared with his Jewish contemporaries.

Josephus's other reports about the Samaritans in the pre-Roman period include accounts of their cowardly compliance with the decrees of Antiochus IV Epiphanes (*Ant.* 12.257–64), of quarrels between Jews and Samaritans in Egypt about whether the temple in Jerusalem or the one on Mount Gerizim had been built according to the Mosaic law (*Ant.* 12.7–10; 13.74–79), and of the capture of Shechem and the destruction of the Gerizim temple by John Hyrcanus I (*J.W.* 1.62–63; *Ant.* 13.254–56). His accounts about the Samaritans in the Roman period include the stories of a group of Samaritans who scattered human bones in the temple area (*Ant.* 18.29–30), of a Samaritan prophet during Pilate's procuratorship who misled a band of followers by promising to show them the sacred vessels buried at Mount Gerizim (*Ant.* 18.85–87), of a violent incident between the Samaritans and the Galileans during Cumanus's procuratorship (*J.W.* 2.232–46; *Ant.* 20.118–36), and of a Roman massacre of the Samaritans on Mount Gerizim (*J.W.* 3.307–15).

Two major groups of post-Josephan literary sources about the Samaritans are the rabbinic texts[1] and the Samaritan chronicles.[2] For the rabbis, the Samaritans were both Jews and non-Jews (cf. *t. Ter.* 4.14; *y. Demai* 25d; *y. Git.* 43c; *m. Ber.* 7.1; *y. Ber.* 11b; *y. Ketub.* 27a; *b. Qidd.* 75b; *b. Sanh.* 85b; *b. Nid.* 56b). The Samaritan chronicles, in contrast, offer insights into the Samaritan self-understanding, which could provide a needed counterbalance to the antagonistic presentation of the Samaritans in the Jewish sources. They trace the origin of the Samaritans back to the eleventh century BC, when the wicked priest Eli allegedly moved Israel's cultic center from Shechem to Shiloh. The Samaritans were those Israelites who stayed in Shechem and remained faithful to the worship of the God of Israel, thus avoiding the paganism of the northern kings and the heresy of the Judeans.[3] Most scholars, however, are hesitant to use these documents for historical reconstructions because they embody many late traditions that cannot be substantiated.

1. See Lawrence H. Schiffman, "The Samarians in Tannaitic Halakhah," *JQR* 75 (1984–85): 323–50; Sacha Stern, *Jewish Identity in Early Rabbinic Writings* (AGJU 23; Leiden: Brill, 1994), 99–105.

2. Paul Stenhouse, "Samaritan Chronicles," in *The Samaritans* (ed. Alan D. Crown; Tübingen: Mohr Siebeck, 1989), 218–65.

3. John Macdonald, *The Samaritan Chronicle No. II (or: Sepher Ha-Yamim): From Joshua to Nebuchadnezzar* (BZAW 107; Berlin: de Gruyter, 1969), 111–23, 157–59.

Archaeological excavations at Mount Gerizim, which began in the 1980s, led to a discovery of the remains of the sacred precinct surrounded by a large city. According to the excavator, Yitzhak Magen, the Gerizim temple was originally built in the mid-fifth century BC (Persian period) and was later enlarged in the second century BC (Hellenistic period).[4] Magen believes that this evidence invalidates Josephus's dating of the building of the Samaritan temple in the time of Alexander the Great; Josephus apparently confused the erection of the city around the sacred area in the late fourth century BC with the building of the temple itself.

The Origin of the Samaritans

It is not easy to reconstruct the origin of the Samaritans on the basis of the evidence surveyed above, which is frequently ambiguous and inconsistent. Many scholars still give more weight to Jewish perspectives on Samaritan origin,[5] but there is a growing interest in the Samaritans' own claims.[6] One way of integrating both viewpoints is to regard the Samaritans as a Jewish sect that had its roots in northern Yahwism.[7] For lack of a better term, many scholars still use the designation "sect," despite its anachronistic insinuation of a normative Judaism, because it conveys the idea that the Jews and the Samaritans were two intrinsically related groups that shared many similarities, such as strict monotheism, Sabbath observance, circumcision, synagogue worship, and celebration of the festivals prescribed in the Pentateuch. The unique feature of the Samaritan religious community, which differentiated them from all other Jewish groups, was the Gerizim temple. There were other religious communities, such as the Qumran covenanters and the early Christians, who were critical of the Jerusalem temple, but they did not build alternative temples for themselves. Also, two other Jewish temples—Elephantine and Leontopolis—were built outside Palestine. There is no doubt that the building of the Gerizim temple on the Palestinian soil, regardless of when it actually took place, was met with disapproval by the Jews. What is less clear, however, is whether this affair also led to a definitive rift between the two groups. The available evidence points not only to periods of hostility but also to periods of intense

4. Yitzhak Magen, "The Dating of the First Phase of the Samaritan Temple on Mount Gerizim in Light of the Archaeological Evidence," in *Judah and the Judeans in the Fourth Century B.C.* (ed. Oded Lipschits et al.; Winona Lake, IN: Eisenbrauns, 2007), 157–211; idem, *A Temple City* (vol. 2 of *Mount Gerizim Excavations*; JSPub 8; Jerusalem: Staff Officer of Archaeology—Civil Administration for Judea and Samaria; Israel Antiquities Authority, 2008).

5. See James Alan Montgomery, *The Samaritans, the Earliest Jewish Sect: Their History, Theology and Literature* (Philadelphia: Winston, 1907).

6. For recent trends in Samaritan scholarship, see Ingrid Hjelm, "What Do Samaritans and Jews Have in Common? Recent Trends in Samaritan Studies," *CBR* 3 (2004): 9–59.

7. Reinhard Pummer, "Samaritanism—a Jewish Sect or an Independent Form of Yahwism?," in *Samaritans: Past and Present; Current Studies* (ed. Menachem Mor and Friedrich V. Reiterer in collaboration with Waltraud Winkler; Berlin: de Gruyter, 2010), 16–17.

communication by means of trade, travel, migration, and scribal interactions. This suggests that the separation was not a sudden occurrence but a gradual process.

The dominant view in scholarship is still a so-called two-episode paradigm (Hjelm, *Samaritans*, 30). It presumes that there was an initial split between the Jews and the Samaritans, usually associated with the erection of the Gerizim temple (either in Persian or Hellenistic times), followed by a final schism in the second to the first century BC (Hasmonean time). An alternative view is that Samaritanism developed from Judaism's formative period, beginning with the third century BC, as one among several Jewish factions that had disagreements about cult, beliefs, and society, until it finally split from rabbinic Judaism in the present era (Coggins, *Samaritans and Jews*, 163). Regardless of whether one considers the destruction of the Samaritan temple by John Hyrcanus I in 128 BC to be the decisive event that caused the definitive breach between Jews and Samaritans, there is no doubt that it significantly contributed to their eventual separation. From that time onward the Samaritans sought to legitimate their independent existence by establishing their own identity as the true Israel over against the Jewish community. They firmly rejected all claims to the primacy of Jerusalem, which might have intensified in the Hasmonean period. Mount Gerizim, even without the actual temple on it, continued to be regarded as the only legitimate place of worship. One of the most significant means of validating Samaritan religious claims was the adaptation of certain passages from the Pentateuch to create a sectarian version known as the Samaritan Pentateuch.

The Samaritan Pentateuch

Since the Samaritans could not find support for their beliefs and practices in the prophetic and other writings that emphasize the centrality of Jerusalem, they accepted only the Pentateuch as Scripture. The Samaritan Pentateuch is, apart from several variations in wording and slightly different orthography, identical to the Jewish Torah. Since, however, the Torah as a unified work is a postexilic Jewish product, the Samaritan Pentateuch, and thus the emergence of the Samaritans as a distinct religious group, could not have predated the fifth century BC. The discovery of the pre-Samaritan harmonizing versions of the Pentateuch among the biblical fragments from Qumran has significantly contributed to our understanding of the history of the Samaritan Pentateuch. The most complete forms of this textual type are found in the texts of Exodus (4QpaleoExod^m) and Numbers (4QNum^b). These texts are called "harmonizing" because they introduce textual blocks, typically from Deut. 1–9, into the parallel passages in Exodus and Numbers and thus "harmonize" both versions of the same event. Qumran documents demonstrate that the harmonizing texts of the Pentateuch, none of which reflect a specifically Samaritan ideology, were in circulation in Palestine in the last two centuries BC (Purvis, *Samaritan Pentateuch*, 69–87). One of these harmonizing texts was later adapted by the Samaritans to emphasize the sacredness and centrality of Mount Gerizim. Harmonizing versions of the Pentateuch were probably chosen either because of their widespread use or because of their tendency to resolve scriptural inconsistencies through harmonization.

Samaritan sectarian adaptations of the Pentateuch are usually dated from the second to the first century BC. The Samaritans, however, did not suddenly decide to accept the Pentateuch of the Jews in the south. Rather, as Reinhard Pummer argues, "When the Samaritan 'sectarian' changes were made, they were made in texts that had circulated among Yahwistic Samarians long before the breach in the 2nd/1st century B.C."[8] Moreover, the Samaritan scribes modified the received text with the help of the same exegetical techniques that were used by other Jewish scribes at the time. The main characteristic of this exegetical tradition is scribal freedom to manipulate the received text to make it more compatible with existing beliefs and practices.

The first group of changes in the Samaritan Pentateuch involves the replacement of all allusions to Jerusalem as the central place of worship with references to Mount Gerizim (*hargarizim*, usually spelled as one word). Moreover, the Samaritan Decalogue includes a new commandment about the building of the altar on Mount Gerizim, which is created through the addition of Deut. 11:29a; 27:2b–3a, 4a, 5–7; and 11:30 after Exod. 20:17 in the Exodus version of the Decalogue and after Deut. 5:18 in the Deuteronomy version of the Decalogue. The total number of the commandments is still ten, because the first commandment is considered to be an introduction to the Decalogue. The Exodus version of the Decalogue has two additional expansions that are not motivated by sectarian interests but reflect the expansionistic, harmonizing tendencies typical for the pre-Samaritan textual type: (1) Deut. 5:24–27 is added after Exod. 20:18, and (2) Deut. 5:28b–29; 18:18–22; and 5:30–31 are added after Exod. 20:21. Another unique feature of the Samaritan Pentateuch is the reading of "Gerizim" in Deut. 27:4 for "Ebal" in the MT, which is also used in the construction of the tenth commandment of the Samaritan Decalogue. Yet whether this textual variant represents a sectarian adaptation is less certain. In this case, the Samaritan Pentateuch may have preserved the older version of the text.

The second group of changes involves a consistent replacement of the formula "the place that the LORD your God will choose," which appears twenty-one times in Deuteronomy (12:5, 11, 14, 18, 21, 26; 14:23, 24, 25; 15:20; 16:2, 6, 7, 11, 15, 16; 17:8, 10; 18:6; 26:2; 31:11), with the formula "the place that the LORD your God has chosen." In this way, the Deuteronomistic predictions about the future election of Jerusalem—from the standpoint of the wandering Israelite tribes—are turned into declarations that God had already chosen Shechem/Gerizim.

8. Reinhard Pummer, "The Samaritans and Their Pentateuch," in *The Pentateuch as Torah: New Models for Understanding Its Promulgation and Acceptance* (ed. Gary N. Knoppers and Bernard M. Levinson; Winona Lake, IN: Eisenbrauns, 2007), 237–69 (264).

The Samaritan Pentateuch thus provides scriptural proof for the Samaritan claim that it was they, and not the Jews, who worshiped God in accordance with the most ancient Israelite traditions. It validates the sanctity of Mount Gerizim by confirming that God chose this mountain as the exclusive place of worship, beginning with Abraham, who built the first altar at Shechem (Gen. 12:6–7).

Conclusion

The view of the Samaritans as the syncretistic semipagan neighbors of the Jews cannot be justified, because it is based on the uncritical acceptance of antagonistic presentations of the Samaritans in Jewish sources, especially in the writings of Josephus. The main difference between the Jews and the Samaritans was not their ethnicity or religiosity but the location of their cultic center. The erection of the Gerizim temple and its eventual destruction by John Hyrcanus I significantly contributed to the gradual partition and the eventual separation of these two groups. The production of the Samaritan Pentateuch, which in light of the Qumran pre-Samaritan harmonizing texts could not have taken place before the second century BC, was an important step in this process and allowed the Samaritans to legitimate their independent existence vis-à-vis Jerusalem-oriented Judaism. In this sense, perhaps, we can talk about the Samaritans as a Jewish sect, or as a variety of Judaism. This, however, does not mean that the former "broke away" from an "orthodox" version of Judaism. Rather, Samaritanism was but one among many expressions of Yahwism that developed around the turn of the era.

Bibliography

Anderson, Robert T., and Terry Giles. *The Keepers: An Introduction to the History and Culture of the Samaritans*. Peabody, MA: Hendrickson, 2002. An introductory volume written for a general readership that offers a reconstruction of the history of the Samaritans from antiquity to the present.

Coggins, Richard J. *Samaritans and Jews: The Origins of Samaritanism Reconsidered*. Growing Points in Theology. Oxford: Basil Blackwell, 1975. An influential study of Samaritanism that proposes a late final split between the Samaritans and the Jews.

Crown, Alan David, ed. *The Samaritans*. Tübingen: Mohr Siebeck, 1989. A comprehensive collection of articles dealing with various questions related to Samaritan history, literature, language, theology, rituals, customs, calendar, and music.

Crown, Alan David, and Reinhard Pummer. *A Bibliography of the Samaritans*. 3rd ed. ATLA Bibliography 51. Lanham, MD: Scarecrow, 2005. The most comprehensive bibliography of the Samaritan studies to date.

Hjelm, Ingrid. *The Samaritans and Early Judaism: A Literary Analysis*. JSOTSup 303. Copenhagen International Seminar 7. Sheffield: Sheffield Academic Press, 2000. An examination of Samaritan, Jewish, Christian, and Hellenistic literature that argues that Samaritanism and Judaism were two competing traditions that developed independently.

Isser, Stanley Jerome. *The Dositheans: A Samaritan Sect in Late Antiquity.* SJLA 17. Leiden: Brill, 1976. An investigation of material about the Dosithean sect of the Samaritans provided by Josephus, patristic writers, and Arabic sources, including the Samaritan chronicles.

Macdonald, John. *The Theology of the Samaritans.* NTL. London: SCM, 1964. One of the first reconstructions of the theology of the Samaritans based on their own literature. It argues that Samaritans should be considered not a Jewish sect but original Israelites.

Mor, Menachem, and Friedrich V. Reiterer. *Samaritans: Past and Present; Current Studies.* Berlin: de Gruyter, 2010. A collection of papers presented at two recent meetings devoted to the Samaritans (in 2004 and 2007), which discuss Samaritan history, the Samaritan Pentateuch, Samaritans in the Talmudic period, and Samaritans in modern times.

Nodet, Étienne. *A Search for the Origins of Judaism: From Joshua to the Mishnah.* JSOTSup 248. Sheffield: Sheffield Academic Press, 1997. A reconstruction of early Judaism that differs from Josephus's. The author argues that the Samaritans preserved an Israelite tradition associated with Joshua that was independent of the Mosaic law.

Pummer, Reinhard. *The Samaritans in Flavius Josephus.* TSAJ 129. Tübingen: Mohr Siebeck, 2009. A comprehensive study of all references to the Samaritans in the writings of Josephus within the context of his work as a whole. The goal is not to reconstruct the history of the Samaritans but to discover the literary and theological aims that guided his portrayal of the Samaritans.

Purvis, James D. *The Samaritan Pentateuch and the Origin of the Samaritan Sect.* HSM 2. Cambridge, MA: Harvard University Press, 1968. This book argues that the formation of the Samaritan Pentateuch, which took place at about the same time as the destruction of the temple by John Hyrcanus I, marks the definitive split between Jews and Samaritans.

18

Pharisees, Sadducees, and Essenes

MICHELLE LEE-BARNEWALL

The Pharisees, Sadducees, and Essenes represent perhaps the three most important Jewish movements for understanding the background of the NT. We see Jesus and the early church frequently facing opposition from the Pharisees and the Sadducees over the law. The Essenes were also a prominent Jewish sect at that time, and scholars have speculated on their influence on the teachings on the NT, although they are not mentioned directly in the NT.

The three groups appear to have emerged, or at least been most active, during the Hasmonean era. Josephus mentions these three "philosophies" as being prominent during the reigns of the Hasmonean Jonathan (152–142 BC; *Ant.* 13.171–73) and of Archelaus (4 BC–AD 6; *J.W.* 2.119). Some have argued that they had earlier roots, from as early as the third century BC or even the time of Ezra and Nehemiah. The return from exile and the Hellenization program initiated by Alexander the Great led to an increased concern over who was a "true Jew" and how to follow the law. These groups, in their various stages of formation, represented different responses to these issues.

The task of reconstructing the teachings and historical situation of the groups faces several challenges. For example, the theory that the Qumran documents are from an Essene group has come under question. There is the difficulty of assessing the various tendencies or prejudices of the available sources and what impact these biases might have had, especially regarding their accuracy. Josephus has been seen as being biased toward the Pharisees, since he claims to have once been a Pharisee (*Life* 10–12). Josephus also emphasizes the disagreements between the Pharisees and the Sadducees, whereas in the Gospels the two groups are often united in their opposition against Jesus. Despite these challenges, what emerges from the literature is consistent enough that we can attempt to make some careful conclusions regarding these Jewish sects.

Pharisees

Origins

The name "Pharisee" appears to go back to the Hebrew *pāraš* and may mean "one who is separate." It is uncertain whether the term has positive or negative connotations, and whether the Pharisees first used the term to describe themselves or whether they were labeled as such by their opponents. It is also not clear from what or whom they were separated, although the name may relate to their deep concern for separation from impurity or even all pagan practices.

The origins of all three groups may be from the time of the Maccabean revolt. The threat of Hellenization under Antiochus Epiphanes led to the formation of the Jewish resistance movement led by the Hasmoneans (1 Macc. 2:1–28) and the Hasideans (1 Macc. 7:12–13) and included "many who were seeking righteousness and justice" (1 Macc. 2:29). However, the coalition did not last long. Since it was believed that the victory was due to the keeping of the Torah (e.g., 1 Macc. 2:45–46; 3:5, 46–60; 2 Macc. 8:26–27), in line with a Deuteronomistic mind-set, the issue became how the entire people—not just the priests—could keep the law so that the nation could receive blessings instead of curses. This led to the question of how the people, as a nation and as individuals, would keep the commandments.

The Pharisees may have arisen from the Hasideans, with their ties to the scribes, as the ones who emphasized the study of the law and obedience to the command-ments. However, their roots may go back to the postexilic era, which also saw a strong Deuteronomistic mind-set with increased focus on following the law. The return from exile could have been a catalyst for values and practices that led to the rise of the Pharisees.

Influence

Josephus and the NT portray the Pharisees as the most influential of the three sects in Palestinian Judaism. Josephus reports that they were the most popular among the people since they had "the support of the masses" (*Ant.* 13.298) and were "extremely influential" among the people (*Ant.* 18.15 LCL). In the Gospels the Pharisees emerge as the most significant opponents of Jesus and the early church, frequently initiating conflicts with him over matters of ritual purity and observance of the law. However, the extent of the Pharisees' influence on society is debated. It is possible that Josephus, since he claimed to have been a Pharisee, may have exaggerated the extent of their impact (*Life* 12), and some scholars argue that the Sadducees were more influential.

According to Josephus, the Pharisees' power rested primarily on their broad base of support among the people. He states that the Pharisees maintained the support of the majority of the people (*Ant.* 13.296). Acts 5:34 reflects this sentiment when it describes the Pharisee Gamaliel as being "respected by all the people." Josephus records that they were influential during the reign of John Hyrcanus (134–104 BC), who was originally a student of the Pharisees. However, Hyrcanus changed his allegiance to the Sadducees after a Pharisee, Eleazar, asserted that he should lay down the high priesthood and be a secular governor only, and Hyrcanus suspected that this was the sentiment of the entire group (*Ant.* 13.288–99).

The Pharisees clashed with the rulers at other times. They were among the thousands killed during Alexander Jannaeus's reign (103–76 BC) for opposing him (Josephus, *J.W.* 1.88–92; *Ant.* 13.372–76). But before he died, he advised his wife, Alexandra, to give some power to them so that they would "dispose the nation favourably to her." He argued that they would be able to do so because of their influence among the Jews, since they "had the complete confidence of the masses" (Josephus, *Ant.* 3.400–404 LCL). Josephus then records that during her reign they essentially became the "real administrators" of the state (*J.W.* 1.111 LCL).

We find a prominent role played by the Pharisees in the NT. Acts 23:6 states that some were members of the Sanhedrin, along with some Sadducees. Most of all, the Pharisees are the primary opponents of Jesus and the early Christian movement. The Essenes are never mentioned, and while the Sadducees and Pharisees may appear united at times in their opposition to Jesus (e.g., Matt. 16:1), it is more often the Pharisees who come to dispute, sometimes accompanied by the scribes (e.g., Matt. 9:11, 34; 12:2, 38; Mark 7:5; 8:11; Luke 6:7). Their disputes with Jesus are primarily in areas of external piety, such as tithing, fasting, purity, and keeping the Sabbath.

If the Pharisees were the most prominent group in Judaism, it may have been due to their reputation as accurate interpreters of the law. Although all three sects emphasized the importance of the Torah, Josephus particularly cites the Pharisees as being the ones who are seen to be "unrivaled experts" in the law (*Life* 191 LCL; *J.W.* 2.162; 1.110) and who pride themselves as such (*Ant.* 17.41). They have the reputation of being the most observant of the Jews (*J.W.* 1.110). Paul describes himself as a Pharisee who was "educated strictly according to our ancestral law" (Acts 22:3) and belonged "to the strictest sect of our religion" (Acts 26:5). Several Qumran texts identify a group described as those who seek "smooth things" (CD 1.18–19; 4Q169 frgs. 3–4 3.3, 6–7),[1] a negative statement on the impact of the Pharisees' interpretation in that it seduces the people and ultimately leads them astray.

1. Translation from Geza Vermes, *The Complete Dead Sea Scrolls in English* (New York: Penguin Press, 1997).

18.1. *Mikveh* baths at the southern end of the temple mount were used for ceremonial cleansing.

The Pharisees' opposition to Jesus' activities on the Sabbath is a prime example of this emphasis on the strict observance of the law. For the Pharisees, Jesus' healings violate God's prohibition against doing work on the Sabbath (Matt. 12:9–14//Mark 3:1–6//Luke 6:6–11; Luke 14:1–6; John 9:1–41). Jesus challenges them with an alternative interpretation of the Torah, arguing that what is lawful to do on the Sabbath is to do good and to save a life (Mark 3:4; Matt. 12:10–11). When the Pharisees confront Jesus over ritual purity regarding cups and dishes and the cleanness of one's hands, Jesus responds that people are defiled not by what goes into a person but by the things that come out, and that one should clean the inside rather than the outside (Matt. 15:1–20//Mark 7:1–23; Matt. 23:25–26//Luke 11:37–44). Thus Jesus proclaims that it is not external conformity to the law and being justified in the sight of others that counts but internal piety and the matters of the heart (Luke 16:15). Jesus' conflicts with the Pharisees also involve tithing and fasting (e.g., Matt. 23:23; Mark 2:18–20; Luke 18:9–14).

Doctrines and Practices

As opposed to the Qumran community, which withdrew from society, the Pharisees emphasized practicing holiness within society. Josephus records that Pharisees were known for their "virtuous conduct" and that the people perform "worship, prayers, and sacrifices" according to their direction (*Ant.* 18.15 LCL). Their halakah guided the people in the pursuit of holiness in everyday life.

The Pharisees accepted a tradition in addition to the written law of Moses, which is referred to as the "tradition of their fathers" (Josephus, *Ant.* 13.408 LCL) or the "tradition of the elders" (Mark 7:5) and probably consisted of interpretation and application of the law. This tradition, which was rejected by the Sadducees

(Josephus, *Ant.* 13.297), may have arisen out of the desire to be as observant as possible in following the written law.

Although the Pharisees believed in divine providence, according to Josephus they also held that the ability to do what was right or wrong was within the capacity of every person, so that fate cooperated with human free will (*J.W.* 2.162–63; *Ant.* 18.13). Thus, according to Josephus, they held a position in between the Essenes, who believed that all events are ascribed to God's will (*Ant.* 18.18), and the Sadducees, who rejected fate entirely (*J.W.* 2.164–65; *Ant.* 13.173). The Pharisees believed in the resurrection of the dead and in an afterlife in which people would be rewarded or punished according to their actions in this life—as opposed to the Sadducees, who believed that the soul perished at death, and the Essenes, who believed only in the immortality of the soul (*J.W.* 2.162–65; *Ant.* 18.15–18). In Acts 23:8 we read that the Pharisees believed in angels and spirits, whereas the Sadducees denied their existence.

According to Josephus, the Pharisees were opposed to the Jewish revolt against Rome and tried to stop it (*J.W.* 2.411–12). Their political realism and deep concern to preserve the religion of their forefathers may have helped them survive the destruction of Jerusalem in AD 70. Their beliefs are generally seen to have formed the basis for rabbinic Judaism, and many Pharisaic teachings are seen in early rabbinic texts, such as the Mishnah.

Sadducees

A second major group within Palestinian Judaism during this time was the Sadducees. In the Gospels they are sometimes unified with the Pharisees in their opposition to Jesus.

Origins

The name "Sadducee" may be derived from Zadok, the Davidic high priest (2 Sam. 8:17; 15:24), who was himself descended from Aaron (1 Chron 24:3). Ezekiel 40:46 states that Zadok and his descendants were the only Levites who could be high priests. The Sadducees could have been these descendants or perhaps merely sympathizers to the Zadokites, who were deposed in 172 BC.

Another theory concerning the origins of the Sadducees connects them with the Qumran community. Lawrence Schiffman has argued that this community was founded by a breakaway group of Sadducees who were unwilling to compromise with the Hasmoneans, who replaced the Zadokite priesthood with their own priests and favored the Pharisees.[2] Schiffman has compared the laws in the DSS manuscript 4QMMT (the *Halakic Letter*) with those in the Mishnah and the

2. Lawrence H. Schiffman, "The Significance of the Scrolls," *BRev* 6 (1990): 18–27; idem, "The New Halakhic Letter (4QMMT) and the Origins of the Dead Sea Sect," *BA* 53 (1990): 64–73.

Talmud and has concluded that the views of the writers of the text were similar to those attributed to the Sadducees and the views of their opponents were those of the Pharisees. A Saducean origin may also explain why the group frequently referred to themselves as "Sons of Zadok."

Numerous elements make this theory unlikely. Although there are agreements between the Sadducees and the writer of 4QMMT, many can be explained by the shared priestly roots of the Sadducees and the Essenes. There are also some significant differences that would seem to exclude the Sadducees as the primary influence. For example, the manuscript teaches the importance of fate, whereas the Sadducees opposed a predestinarian theology and instead emphasized free will and human responsibility. The concern about purity would fit the Pharisees better, since they were known for their strict adherence to purity laws.[3] However, although it may be difficult to identify the Qumran community as Saducean, documents such as 4QMMT may shed light on Saducean halakah.

Influence

The main sources for information on the Sadducees are the NT, Josephus, rabbinic texts such as the Mishnah, and some Qumran documents such as *Pesher on Nahum* and possibly 4QMMT. The Sadducees appear less often in the NT and Josephus than do the Pharisees, perhaps reflecting a lesser influence among the general population. Josephus mentions that the Sadducees "are able to persuade none but the rich, and have not the populace obsequious to them," in contrast to the Pharisees, who have the confidence of the people (*Ant.* 13.298 LCL). However, some scholars assign a more influential role to the Sadducees. E. P. Sanders, for example, argues for a greater influence because the Romans would have expected the high priests (some of whom were Sadducees) and the aristocrats (which all Sadducees would have been) to have sufficient control over the people that the people would have generally heeded them (*Judaism*, 316–40).

In the NT, the Sadducees are closely associated with the high priest (Acts 5:17). Josephus identifies one Sadducee who was a high priest, Ananus (*Ant.* 20.198–99). Along with the Pharisees, the Sadducees were members of the Sanhedrin, the Jewish high court (Acts 23:6–7).

According to the Gospels and Acts, the Sadducees played a key role in the history of the early church. They appear with the Pharisees in the Gospels as opponents of Jesus (e.g., Matt. 16:1–12). The Sadducees, along with the high priest, have the apostles arrested (Acts 4:1–22; 5:17–18). Since Jesus spoke against the temple (e.g., Mark 11:15–19; 14:57–58; 15:29), the Sadducees' actions may reflect a concern for the temple.

---

3. William A. Simmons, *Peoples of the New Testament World* (Peabody, MA: Hendrickson, 2008). For a more detailed discussion of the differences between the Sadducees and the Qumran community, see also James C. VanderKam, "The People of the Dead Sea Scrolls: Essenes or Sadducees?," *BRev* 7 (1991): 42–47.

Doctrines and Practices

Because the Sadducees left no written documents of their own, the only record of their doctrines is from other sources. We read in the NT that they denied the resurrection, instead believing that the soul died with the body (Matt. 22:23; Mark 12:18; Luke 20:27; Acts 23:8). In Acts, Paul uses this knowledge to provoke division between the Sadducees and the Pharisees, who do hold to the doctrine (23:6–10). Josephus mentions that the Sadducees also denied the immortality of the soul and the idea of future punishment and rewards in Hades (*J.W.* 2.165; *Ant.* 18.66). Acts 23:8 records that they did not believe in angels or spirits. The Sadducees also rejected fate and believed in free will, that good and evil actions are simply a matter of human choice (Josephus, *J.W.* 2.164–65; *Ant.* 13.173). The Sadducees accepted only the written law, and so, in contrast to the Pharisees, rejected the traditions of the elders (*Ant.* 13.297; 18.16). However, this may mean not that they accepted only the law of Moses as Scripture but rather that they accepted only that as authoritative in legal matters. The Mishnah reflects disagreements between the Pharisees and Sadducees regarding purity (e.g., *m. Yad.* 4.6–8, over the uncleanness of hands).

Although the Sadducees were considered to be less strict in their interpretation of the law than were the Pharisees, they were apparently more severe in punishing offenders. Josephus records that the Sadducees were the most rigid among all the Jews in judging offenders (*Ant.* 20.199; 13.294). In the NT it is the Pharisee Gamaliel who convinces the Sanhedrin not to kill the apostles (Acts 5:33–39).

Although Josephus emphasizes the conflicts between the Sadducees and the Pharisees, in the NT they often appear united in their opposition to Jesus. The only conflict between them comes in the dispute Paul starts over the resurrection. The difference in the portrayals may be explained because of the essential agreement both groups, along with the Essenes, found in the centrality of the Torah, which contrasted them with the Christians, who replaced the Torah with Christ as the main principle. Thus, while the Jewish groups differed in interpretation of the law, they could still have found themselves united in their opposition to a group that subordinated the Torah to Christ.

The Sadducees disappeared from the scene following the destruction of Jerusalem, perhaps because their base of power in the temple was destroyed and they did not have a popular following like the Pharisees did.

Essenes

The third major sect is the Essenes. They are described by the Jewish authors Josephus and Philo and also by the Roman historian Pliny. Although they may have survived the destruction of the Jerusalem temple, there is no evidence to confirm their continued existence after AD 70. They are widely believed to be the group that established the community at Qumran, and the DSS are often seen to have been an Essene library.

Doctrines and Practices

Josephus gives little information on the beliefs of the Essenes. However, he does present extensive descriptions of their practices. Josephus relates how one could be admitted to the sect. For the first year, the novice was to remain outside the community while following their way of life. For the second and third years, one could be a "partaker of the waters of purification" but still not be admitted to the community. At the end of this period, the initiate could be admitted after taking "tremendous oaths," which included pledges to "practice piety toward the Deity," "observe justice toward men," and "hate the unjust and fight for the battle of the just" (*J.W.* 2.137–42 LCL).

Josephus reports that the Essenes numbered about four thousand (*Ant.* 18.20). Both he and Philo explain that the Essenes lived throughout the cities and villages in Judea (Josephus, *J.W.* 2.124; Philo, *Hypoth.* 11.1; Philo also mentions in *Prob.* 76 that they avoided cities because of the lawlessness of the inhabitants). According to Pliny the Elder, they lived on the west side of the Dead Sea (*Nat. Hist.* 5.15.73). It is possible that there was a main settlement near the Dead Sea, with smaller groups scattered throughout Judea.

The Essenes held their property in common (Josephus, *J.W.* 2.122; *Ant.* 18.20; Philo, *Prob.* 85–87), did not own slaves (Philo, *Prob.* 79), and practiced frugality and moderation (Philo, *Hypoth.* 11.11). According to Josephus, Philo, and Pliny, the Essenes were male and did not marry (Josephus, *Ant.* 18.21; *J.W.* 2.120; Philo, *Hypoth.* 11.14–17; Pliny, *Nat. Hist.* 5.73). However, Josephus also mentions another group of Essenes who did marry for the purpose of "the propagation of the race" (*J.W.* 2.160 LCL).

The Essenes were extremely devoted to the law, revering Moses as second only to God himself (Josephus, *J.W.* 2.145), and they were very dedicated to the study of "the writings of the ancients" (*J.W.* 2.136 LCL). Josephus records that they were more strict than any other Jews in observing the Sabbath (*J.W.* 2.147).

In regard to the afterlife, Josephus says that the Essenes, like the Greeks, believed in the immortality of the soul and that the body is like a prison from which the soul is set free at death (*J.W.* 2.154–58). However, Hippolytus says that they believed in the resurrection of the body (*Haer.* 9.22), although it is unclear if he has added this to make it more in line with his own Christian beliefs or if his account is simply more trustworthy than Josephus's. They held a deterministic view and would "leave everything in the hands of God" (Josephus, *Ant.* 18.18; also Philo, *Prob.* 84), although they believed in rewards and punishments after death (Josephus, *J.W.* 2.154–58; *Ant.* 18.18).

Purity played an important role in the sect. The Essenes considered oil to be a defilement (Josephus, *J.W.* 2.123). Every day all except the novices clothed themselves in white veils and participated in purification baths in cold water (*J.W.* 2.129). Senior members were considered superior to junior members, and seniors who had contact with a junior were required to wash "as after contact with an alien" (*J.W.* 2.150).

They also engaged in communal meals. Josephus records that after the baths they would go into the dining room, "as to some sacred shrine" (*J.W.* 2.129). They did not offer sacrifices in the temple but performed their own sacrifices using their own purification ritual (Josephus, *Ant.* 18.19).

The Essenes and the Qumran Community

Many scholars have connected the Essenes with the community at Qumran, since the DSS describe a community that seems very similar to the Essenes. Pliny says the Essene settlement was on the west side of the Dead Sea, above Engedi (*Nat. Hist.* 5.73). According to the archaeological evidence, the Qumran community probably existed from the mid-second century BC until the First Jewish Revolt. This corresponds with Josephus's chronology of the Essenes: he first mentions them during the time of Jonathan Maccabeus (*Ant.* 13.171) and claims to have spent time with the sect (*Life* 10–12).

There are several significant correspondences between the Qumran documents and the testimonies of Josephus and Philo. Both Josephus and the DSS text the *Rule of the Community* (1QS) describe a similar process of admission, consisting of a two-year candidacy period within the community following an initial preparatory period spent outside the group (1QS 6.13–23). The Qumran community also had common ownership of property (1QS 1.11; 6.18–22). Like the Essenes, they believed in fate, or predeterminism (1QS 3.15–16, 21–23; 1QS 1.7–8; 9.23–24; 1QM 17.5). They both had common meals, from which novices were excluded (Josephus, *J.W.* 2.139; 1QS 6.16–19). There are even interesting correspondences on trivial details, such as a prohibition against spitting in the assembled congregation (Josephus, *J.W.* 2.47; 1QS 7.13).

On the other hand, there are some important differences, and the Qumran-Essene hypothesis has not gone without challenges, including the possible connection of the Qumran community with the Sadducees instead. Pliny, Philo (*Hypoth.* 11.14–15), and Josephus (*J.W.* 2.120) assert that the Essenes were ascetics, but excavations at Qumran have revealed skeletons of women and children as well as men. However, Josephus also records that there was another order of Essenes who did marry (*J.W.* 2.160–61). Thus, we run into a discrepancy among the sources themselves, along with the possibility that they may be describing the community at different stages in their development. However, even if the Qumran community cannot be positively identified as Essene, its members resemble the sect more than any other group in antiquity.

Influence on the New Testament

If we assume that the Qumran community was Essene, it is still difficult to assess the direct influence of the sect on the NT. There has been some speculation that John the Baptist could have been an Essene, given factors such as his asceticism, the possibility that his ministry could have brought him near Qumran (VanderKam,

Dead Sea Scrolls, 208), and similarities between his baptism and the Essene/Qumran community's daily purification baths. However, his onetime, public baptism contrasts with the Essene/Qumran community's daily washing, which was limited only to the members of the sect, and the Essenes were certainly not the only ascetics.

There are some similarities between the early NT church and the Essene/Qumran community, such as a communal sharing of goods (Acts 2:44–45; 4:32). There are similarities in their teachings as well. Both looked to a resurrection of the dead (4Q521) and spoke of a dualism of light and darkness (e.g., 1QS 3.18–21; 1QM; John 1:5; 2 Cor. 6:14–7:1; 1 John 2:9–10). However, many of these concepts are not unique to either the Essenes or the NT and can be found in other places, including the OT.

Although we may not be able to discern a direct influence of the Essenes on the writers of the NT, a greater knowledge of the group enhances our understanding of the NT world and sheds light on some of the tendencies present in the larger environment that saw the beginning of the Christian movement.[4]

See also "The Dead Sea Scrolls."

Bibliography

Baumgarten, Albert I. *The Flourishing of Jewish Sects in the Maccabean Era: An Interpretation*. Leiden: Brill, 1997. Baumgarten examines why Jewish sects became prominent during the period of the Second Temple. He concludes that disappointment with the Hasmonean leaders in their attitude toward Hellenism was one of the key factors that led to the flourishing of the sects.

Beall, T. *Josephus's Description of the Essenes Illustrated by the Dead Sea Scrolls*. SNTSMS 58. Cambridge: Cambridge University Press, 1988. Examines Josephus's testimony about the Essenes in light of the DSS, as opposed to the reverse, which has been the norm in scholarship, and concludes that Josephus gives a generally trustworthy account. Useful especially for the examination of the parallels between Josephus and the DSS.

Deines, Roland. "The Pharisees between 'Judaisms' and 'Common Judaism.'" Pages 443–504 in *Justification and Variegated Nomism: The Complexities of Second Temple Judaism*. Edited by D. A. Carson et al. Grand Rapids: Baker Academic, 2001. Defends the traditional position of the threefold division of Judaism and the identity of the Pharisees as the most influential movement from the time of the Hasmoneans to the destruction of Jerusalem.

Neusner, Jacob. *The Rabbinic Traditions about the Pharisees before 70*. 3 vols. Leiden: Brill, 1971. An extensive study on the Pharisaic-rabbinic traditions.

Neusner, Jacob, and Bruce D. Chilton, eds. *In Quest of the Historical Pharisees*. Waco: Baylor University Press, 2007. Summarizes current scholarship on the Pharisees, focusing mostly on major primary sources.

4. For a summary of scholarship on the DSS and the NT, including the different views on the relationship between Jesus and the DSS, see George J. Brooke, *The Dead Sea Scrolls and the New Testament* (Minneapolis: Fortress, 2005), 3–26.

Pate, C. Marvin. *Communities of the Last Days: The Dead Sea Scrolls, the New Testament and the Story of Israel*. Downers Grove, IL: InterVarsity, 2000. A helpful comparison of the DSS and the NT that argues that they shared the same metanarrative, the story of Israel (sin-exile-restoration), and that they reworked the tradition by redefining its symbols, rituals, and beliefs.

Saldarini, Anthony. *Pharisees, Scribes and Sadducees in Palestinian Society*. Grand Rapids: Eerdmans, 2001. An influential work that first appeared in 1988, it utilizes a sociological approach to analyze the three groups. Saldarini focuses on social roles, status, and so forth, rather than on beliefs.

Sanders, E. P. *Judaism: Practice and Belief; 63 BCE–66 CE*. London: SCM, 1992. Concentrating on the Judaism of ordinary Jews, Sanders calls into question a number of prevailing views, including those regarding the true extent of the influence of the Pharisees.

Stemberger, Günther. *Jewish Contemporaries of Jesus: Pharisees, Sadducees, Essenes*. Minneapolis: Fortress, 1995. Focusing on the primary documents, Stemberger advocates a cautious approach in drawing historical conclusions about the three groups.

VanderKam, James C. *The Dead Sea Scrolls Today*. 2nd ed. Grand Rapids: Eerdmans, 2010. Written by a member of the DSS editorial committee, this book is an excellent introduction to the Scrolls, including their possible connection with the Essenes and how they impact our understanding of Judaism.

Vermes, Geza, and Martin D. Goodman, eds. *The Essenes according to the Classical Sources*. Sheffield: JSOT Press, 1989. A collection of primary sources about the Essenes in Greek with English translation. This slim volume also includes texts from the DSS and a discussion of the possible relationship between the Essenes and the Qumran community.

19

The Dead Sea Scrolls

C. D. ELLEDGE

Since their discovery in 1947, the Dead Sea Scrolls (DSS) have contributed some of the most significant resources for understanding Palestinian Judaism during the period of Christian origins. Preserving approximately nine hundred compositions, the Scrolls range in date from about 250 BC to the first century AD, an era of crucial concern for NT backgrounds. An ongoing problem since the discovery has been the identity of those who placed the Scrolls in the eleven caves that ran along a north–south axis surrounding *Khirbet Qumran*, an archaeological site overlooking the northwest coast of the Dead Sea.

Identity of the Qumran Movement

The "Qumran-Essene hypothesis" identifies the community of the DSS as a group of Essenes, a Jewish religious movement referenced in both pagan (Pliny the Elder, *Nat. Hist.* 5.73; Synesius, *Dio* 3.2) and Jewish writers (Philo, *Prob.* 75–80; *Contempl.* 1–3; *Hypoth.* 11; Josephus, *J.W.* 2.119–61; *Ant.* 18.18–22; *Life* 2). By correlating the contents of the Scrolls with such evidence from ancient writers, the hypothesis identifies shared property, predeterminism, pure meals, and initiatory practices as among the more convincing intersections between the Scrolls and the Essenes. Although these correlations are not always precise, the hypothesis has withstood ardent criticism and remains, in spite of its shortcomings, the most

19.1. Ruins of the Qumran community, including the scriptorium (where the scrolls were copied) and storage rooms.

commonly accepted identification of those who preserved the Scrolls. A few comparisons illustrate the logic of the hypothesis.

The Scrolls portray a movement that formed a community of goods, a popular practice among Essenes. According to the *Rule of the Community*, a disciplinary code for the Qumran community, everyone who enters as a full member "shall have his property merged" with the larger movement (6.23–24).[1] Analogous customs are also attested of Essenes: "Those entering into their movement must devote their property to the order . . . there is a single commonwealth in which the possessions of each man are mixed together" (Josephus, *J.W.* 2.122, author's translation).[2]

Admission into the community was strictly supervised by a formal initiation. According to the *Rule*, an extended novitiate involves initial examination, which allows prospective members a year of provisional membership. After another examination, a prospective member is allowed access to pure meals alone for an additional year; then finally, a successful initiate is granted full membership, access to the pure drink of the community, and the incorporation of their property (1QS 6.14–24). Differing in some details, Josephus also reports that Essenes admitted members through a three-year initiation (*J.W.* 2.137–42).

1. Translations of the DSS in this chapter follow Vermes, *Dead Sea Scrolls*.
2. My translation has been published in C. D. Elledge, *The Bible and the Dead Sea Scrolls* (Archaeology and Biblical Studies 14; Atlanta: Society of Biblical Literature, 2005), 48.

The *Rule* also offers stridently predeterministic teaching regarding the deity's creation of the world: "From the God of Knowledge comes all that is and shall be. Before ever they existed He established their whole design . . ." (3.15–16). Josephus, likewise, distinguishes Essenes by their predeterministic theology: "The teaching of the Essenes is fond of admitting all things to the care of God" (*Ant.* 18.18).

The most significant information about this community, of course, emerges from the Scrolls themselves, as its authors tell the story of their own movement. Both Pliny and Dio Chrysostom, for example, situate an Essene community in the same general locale as Qumran in the Judean wilderness; yet the Scrolls themselves reveal much more about the community's understanding of its geographical setting. According to the *Rule*, the members of the Qumran community viewed themselves as fulfilling the prophecy of Isa. 40:3: "they shall separate from the habitation of unjust men and shall go into the wilderness to prepare there the way of Him; as it is written, *Prepare in the wilderness the way of [the* LORD*], make straight in the desert a path for our God.* This (path) is the study of the Law which He commanded by the hand of Moses, that they may do according to all that has been revealed from age to age, and as the Prophets have revealed by His Holy Spirit" (1QS 8.13–16). Finding in themselves the fulfillment of Isaiah's prophecy, the community attached profound meaning to its wilderness vocation. Through their legal observances and worship, they were preparing the path for God's future redemption of Israel.

19.2. Cave 4 at Qumran is the site of the largest discovered collection of Dead Sea Scrolls.

Although no manuscripts were discovered at the particular archaeological site of Qumran, numerous details point toward an active association between the site and the manuscripts found in nearby caves. First, the dates of occupation at Qumran roughly correspond to the dates of the Scrolls. Qumran may have been utilized sometime after 140 (de Vaux, *Archaeology*) or just after 100 (Magness, *Archeology of Qumran*) BC; portions were destroyed and reoccupied by the Romans during the First Jewish Revolt in AD 68. Second, fragments of the relatively rare cylindrical pottery types in which seven scrolls were preserved in Cave 1 were also discovered at the Qumran site itself, thus linking Qumran to the caves and to the Scrolls themselves. Third, the architecture of Qumran suggests that it would have been a fitting locale for the kinds of religious practices described in the *Rule of the Community*. For ritual lustrations, for example, Qumran offers at least six stepped bathing pools; for communal meals, it offers a long, narrow room approximately twenty-two meters long, with an accompanying chamber in which over a thousand pottery vessels were stored. Moreover, the Qumran site rests in a centrally located position relative to the eleven caves in which scrolls were found.

Centering on an anonymous figure, called the "Righteous Teacher" (or "Teacher of Righteousness"), the Scrolls further situate the origins of their religious movement in conflicts between the Teacher and the Jerusalem priesthood in the second century BC. The chronology of the *Damascus Document*, for example, situates the coming of the Teacher to a fledgling group of penitents sometime after 177 BC during a time of great religious darkness: "He raised for them a Teacher of Righteousness to guide them in the way of His heart" (CD 1.10–11). Elsewhere in the Scrolls, the coming of the Teacher is heralded as a fulfillment of scriptural prophecy. The *Pesher on Habakkuk*, for example, reveals that the "vision" of Hab. 2:1–4 is fulfilled, not in the days of the prophet, but in the advent of the Righteous Teacher, "to whom God made known all the mysteries of the words of His servants the Prophets" (1QpHab 7.3–5). The Teacher's authority as the chosen mediator of scriptural revelation came into direct conflict with a certain "Wicked Priest." This anonymous epithet seems to refer to the priestly rulers of Jerusalem's Hasmonean dynasty, which controlled the high priesthood from 152 to 63 BC (1QpHab 8.3–17; 11.4–7, 13–14; 12.8–9). Qumran would define its own origins in the advent of the Righteous Teacher and his powerful—yet ultimately rejected—revelation of the proper interpretation of Israel's law and prophecy, even in writings that were copied a century after his own activity had ceased.

When the reports of ancient historians, the relationships between Qumran and the Scrolls, and the internal evidence for the origins of the community are considered together, they yield the portrait of a religious movement of Essenes, pure religious communalists who rejected the authority of the Hasmonean priesthood and separated from other Jews in what they perceived to be an apocalyptic era of corruption. Inspired by the struggle of the Righteous Teacher, they turned to Qumran as the wilderness landscape in which they would "prepare the way of the LORD" through their exclusively pure observance of Jewish law, living out this vocation in a highly structured community maintained by strong boundaries, shared property, pure meals, scriptural study, and a disciplinary code. It is likely that the Scrolls represent the remains of the religious library collected by this movement over approximately two centuries of its history.

The Contents of the Scrolls

The DSS represent a diverse range of literary compositions. Nevertheless, some of the most frequently encountered categories of literature include scriptural manuscripts and commentaries, rules and legal writings, hymns and prayers, and writings concerned with apocalyptic and sapiential themes.

Scriptural Manuscripts and Their Interpretations

Among the remains of the Qumran library, the most abundantly attested kind of writing includes scriptural texts. Just over two hundred manuscripts from the eleven Qumran caves—approximately 25 percent of the entire collection—are copies of the same books that now appear in the canonical Jewish Scriptures. The Scrolls thus provide remarkably rich and detailed insights into the varied nature of Scripture texts during the period of Christian origins. The most frequently attested of these is the "proto-Masoretic" type, which represents the same kind of text that would ultimately factor into Judaism's official scriptural version, the Masoretic text. Additionally, however, Qumran also preserves scriptural copies that resemble the Samaritan Pentateuch; still others represent the text type that underlies the LXX. Yet other manuscripts exhibit a style that seems unique to Qumran itself, while others align with none of these categories (Tov, *Textual Criticism*). Since Qumran provides evidence that the same religious movement preserved multiple text types, this has advanced the possibility that the phenomenon of "textual plurality" prevailed within Judaism of the Second Temple period. While later Judaism would follow the Masoretic text as its official version, Qumran poses an earlier moment in which Jews studied multiple versions of scriptural books as authoritative writings.

Moreover, Qumran exhibits a relatively different understanding of "authoritative literature" than would prevail within Judaism in later times. The Scrolls certainly attest to a strong reception for the books of the Torah and the Prophets, as well as a comparatively smaller collection of the Writings (the three divisions of the Hebrew Bible). Other compositions from among the Apocrypha and the Pseudepigrapha, however, feature so prominently in this community's collection that one may venture the possibility that they functioned with a measure of authority equal to that of "canonical" books. These include *Jubilees*, which registers fourteen to fifteen copies at Qumran, a number surpassed only by Genesis, Exodus, Deuteronomy, Isaiah, and Psalms. As for *1 Enoch*, the community preserved at least eleven copies. A range of modified

19.3. Replicas of
the clay jars in which
the Dead Sea Scrolls
were discovered in
caves beside the site
at Qumran, on the
northwest side of the
Dead Sea.

scriptural texts also flourished among the Scrolls. Scriptural "anthologies," like
the *Testimonia* and *Consolations*, edit a series of select scriptural passages that
converge upon common themes. Perhaps the most protean category of modified
scriptural texts exhibits the practice of "rewriting" Scripture. Utilizing a diverse
range of compositional methods, the *Temple Scroll*, *Reworked Pentateuch*,
Apocryphon of Joshua, and *Pseudo-Ezekiel* (along with many other texts) actively rewrite the language of earlier Scriptures while also subtly interweaving
their authors' interpretive viewpoints. In such cases, the boundaries between
Scripture and rewritten Scripture, between text and interpretation, are often
difficult to discern. Since both the *Apocryphon of Joshua* and *Jubilees* (itself a
rewriting) are actually quoted as scriptural authorities in other scrolls, it seems
likely that rewritten Scriptures could function as authoritative literature for the
Qumran community.

The authors of the Scrolls also devised distinctive practices of scriptural interpretation that legitimated their own religious movement as the locus of prophetic
fulfillment. A group of formal scriptural commentaries, organized by explicit
citation and interpretation styles, offers interpretations of prophetic literature and
the Psalms. These commentaries title their interpretations with the Hebrew word
pesher (plural: *pesharim*), a word used in earlier dream-interpretation literature

(e.g., Dan. 2:4–6, 24–26; 5:15–16; 7:16). A pesher is literally an "unloosening," a "solution," of the mysteries of prophetic revelation. In the Qumran pesharim, such interpreted mysteries from Scripture find their fulfillment in the prior history of the Righteous Teacher's conflicts with the Wicked Priest, in the present political circumstances of Judea under the rule of the *Kittim* (a probable reference to the Romans), and in the future glorification of the community in the latter days, when "God will execute the judgment of the nations by the hand of His elect" (1QpHab 5.4–5).

Rules and Legal Writings

As part of a movement disciplined by specific communal structures, the community at Qumran preserved a number of writings that it classified by the title *Serek*, or "rule," documents. These include twelve copies of the *Rule of the Community*, a disciplinary code for a group of Jewish males who enter into a covenant community, or *yaḥad*, defined by a strict process of initiation, pure meals, liturgical guidelines, and dualistic teachings. The community organized by these principles describes itself as "Sons of Light" in the midst of a cosmic conflict between Truth and Falsehood. Representing the last vestiges of Truth in a divided cosmos, the community suffers trial as it awaits God's final apocalyptic triumph over evil. Another remarkable way in which this community describes its own vocation is in its crucial role of atoning for the sins of the entire land of Israel (1QS 8.3–10; 9.3–6). In this way, the community seems to have regarded its own practices—and not those of the Jerusalem temple or its leadership—as the divinely sanctioned means of removing guilt from Israel.

Alongside the *Rule of the Community*, other documents called "rules" are also attested. Edited together within the *Rule* scroll from Cave 1, for example, are two additional rules. The *Rule of the Congregation* describes the proper configuration of Israel for a latter-day procession and feast "when [God] leads forth the Messiah with them" (1QSa 2.11–12). The accompanying *Rule of the Blessings* concludes the great *Rule* scroll with a series of benedictions upon various figures who will emerge in the latter days, including an ideal assembly of Zadokite priests and a "Prince of the Congregation," who will govern Israel justly.

The *Damascus Document*, present in ten copies, represents yet another rule. It is written for communities of righteous Jews, both men and women, who have entered into a "new (or renewed) covenant" (CD 6.5, 19) that was originally devised in the land of Damascus. The *Damascus Document* views the community's struggle to live by the laws of God within a dualistic conflict between good and evil; and it is highlighted by extended legal expositions that range from oaths and offerings to the proper practices of bearing witness, keeping the Sabbath, ritual lustrations, and dietary laws. Finally, the *War Scroll* spells out the proper military code for the last days, when Israel and the nations will clash in an apocalyptic holy war.

In addition to these rule documents, Qumran preserved a larger range of legal expositions that charted the proper practice of Jewish law. In the *Halakic Letter*, an exposition of over twenty points of legal interpretation, is introduced with the declaration "These are some of our words . . . " (4QMMT B1–3). It is imperative that the priests direct these rulings faithfully; otherwise, they will "lead the people into sin," defiling Jerusalem and its temple. The authors plead diplomatically with their opponents, suggesting that "these are the latter days," when Israel will now turn to the true interpretation of the Torah. It has often been conjectured that the *Halakic Letter* represents the legal conflicts that originally animated Qumran's rejection of the present temple leadership. Perhaps the work may even express the views of the Righteous Teacher himself, making his diplomatic appeals to the Wicked Priest and explaining the community's rationale for why "we have separated ourselves from the multitudes of the people" (section C 7). The dates of actual copies of the *Halakic Letter* in the first century BC suggest that, whatever its origins, this legal exposition continued to guide the community's reading of the Torah long after those conflicts had emerged.

In the *Temple Scroll*, a vast rewriting of passages of the Torah reveals its authors' judgments regarding the temple's sacred artifacts and altars (11QTᵃ 3.1–13.8), sacrifices and offerings (13.9–29.8), the architecture of the larger temple complex (29.8–40.6), and laws of purity (45.7–51.10), concluding with a paraphrase of Deut. 17–26 (51.11–66.17). Contemporary reflection on the *Temple Scroll* continues to explore its possible functions within the Qumran community. One theory regards the scroll as a kind of reformist, eschatological Torah that Israel would follow in a new era when "I shall create my sanctuary, to establish it for myself for all time" (29.9–10).

Alongside many other legal expositions, the *Halakic Letter* and the *Temple Scroll* are important reminders that the character of the Qumran community was forged not only by its eschatological expectation or by political conflicts within the priesthood. It was equally charged by legal concerns over the proper interpretation of the Torah. Such legal devotion was further expressed within a larger cosmic, apocalyptic framework in which Truth and Falsehood conflicted within a period of latter-day affliction. Qumran's legal opponents were deceived by powerful supernatural beings, while the community itself strived to represent the last vestiges of truth in a fallen world.

Ardon Bar Hama/Wikimedia Commons

19.4. A portion of the great Isaiah scroll found in Cave 1 at Qumran. This scroll, containing the complete text of the book of Isaiah, is called "great" (i.e., complete) to distinguish it from a second Isaiah scroll found at Qumran, which preserves only 75 percent of the biblical text.

Liturgical and Hymnic Writings

Qumran's religious devotion is also expressed in the form of hymnic writings, which provide some of the most sophisticated poetic compositions from this era. In the *Thanksgiving Hymns* (*Hodayot*, 1QH^a), worshipers offer blessings to the deity with the typical form of introduction, "Blessed are you, O Lord, because. . . . " The many reasons for praising the deity range from personal redemption to enlightenment in the mysteries of divine wisdom. Likewise, another text, *Bless, O My Soul*, praises the deity for having mercy on the destitute and atoning for the sins of the speaker. In the *Angelic Liturgy*, a collection of hymns is sequenced with the offering of the Sabbath sacrifice and describes the heavenly worship of angelic beings within the celestial realms. The *Words of the Luminaries* praises the deity through a reminiscence on the history of Israel, in which the deity has remained faithful in spite of Israel's transgression: "You remembered your covenant, for you redeemed us from among the nations and did not abandon us among the nations" (4Q504 16.9–11). One of the more prominent claims among these writings is that the members of the Qumran movement worship in the presence of angelic beings of supreme holiness (*Angelic Liturgy*; *Blessings*); as the *Rule of the Community* states, God "has joined their assembly to the Sons of Heaven" (1QS 11.8), as though the lines separating heaven and earth have diminished in Qumran's pure worship.

Wisdom and Apocalyptic Writings

The Scrolls also attest the flourishing of Jewish wisdom and apocalyptic traditions in the late Second Temple period. In addition to copies of Proverbs, Ecclesiastes, and Job, as well as a *Targum of Job* and portions of Ben Sira, the Qumran community preserved several previously unknown wisdom compositions. These include writings like *Sapiential Work A*, which explores topics ranging from creation to anthropology and eschatology in pursuit of "the mystery that is yet to be" (see also *Book of Mysteries*). Other poetic compositions, like *Beatitudes*, extol the blessedness of pursuing Lady Wisdom: "Happy is the man who has attained wisdom, and walks by the law of the Most High, and fixes his heart on her ways, and gives heed to her admonitions" (4Q525 frg. 2 2.1–4; trans. Harrington, *Wisdom Texts*); while still others malign the ways of folly and seduction (*Wiles of the Wicked Woman*).

Although the Scrolls have not unearthed a large number of new literary apocalypses, they have provided an extensive resource for the flourishing of apocalyptic ideas within early Judaism. Daniel became a popular writing at Qumran within a generation of its composition (assuming a second-century date for this work), with eight copies attested; *1 Enoch* also featured prominently. Among previously unknown writings, at least six copies of an apocalyptic tour of the heavenly Jerusalem offer a detailed description of how the holy city will be renewed in the eschatological age; *New Jerusalem* thus unveils the kinds of apocalyptic traditions that Rev. 21 has reactualized in its portrait of the holy city. Other eschatological traditions, like the *Messianic Apocalypse* and the *Aramaic Apocalypse*, offer significant evidence for the nature of Jewish messianism prior to the era of Christian origins. Apocalyptic thought pervaded multiple aspects of the community's self-awareness, worship, and legal piety. The presence of apocalyptic teaching in the community's rule books (1QS 3.13–4.26; CD 1.1–2.1) strongly indicates that Qumran's self-understanding and religious behaviors were intensively shaped by apocalyptic currents in early Jewish thought.

Contributions to New Testament Research

The DSS emerged from the same historical and cultural context as Jesus and his earliest followers. Yet the precise methods of interpreting the NT in light of the Scrolls have remained a matter of ongoing investigation. Three categories that have traditionally been explored include Qumran's relevance for understanding (1) actual persons in the NT, (2) the communal structures of the early church, and (3) the religious ideas found in the NT. Taken together, these areas of inquiry have gradually enhanced modern awareness of how Jesus and his earliest followers did—and did not—fit into the religious landscape of Palestinian Judaism. Attempts to show that Qumran functioned as a more direct religious progenitor to the church have proved inconclusive. Instead, the Scrolls' contribution to NT study is to be found in the ways they have expanded our understanding of the diverse context of religious thought and practices that existed within first-century Judaism, a context within which both Qumran and Christian origins flourished—each in its own way.

Persons in the New Testament

The NT figure most likely to resemble the community members at Qumran remains John the Baptist. Although proposals that Jesus or other early Christian figures had some relation to the community have not been successful, the striking comparisons that can be made between John and the Qumran members require more careful examination. The issues at stake in such a connection are profound. If John bore any connection to Qumran, then it would follow that the historical Jesus himself stood at least that much closer to the community's activity. Both John and the Qumran community seem to have been active at the same time and in the same region (Matt. 3:1; Josephus, *Ant.* 18.116–19). Both insisted that rituals of purification in water were only efficacious when accompanied by a life of ethical repentance (Mark 1:4; Luke 3:7–14; Josephus, *Ant.* 18.117; 1QS 3.8–9). Both are further associated with the explicit fulfillment of Isa. 40:1–3 (Mark 1:1–4; 1QS 8.13–16). Together with other commonalities, including references to the "Holy Spirit's" eschatological cleansing of humans and to strict matrimonial laws, these parallels have sometimes led to the conclusion that John the Baptist could have had some earlier connection to Qumran (or to Essenes more generally).

Even so, differences between the two are equally intriguing, suggesting that even if John had somehow associated with Qumran, he must ultimately have broken away from them in a bold new direction. For the community at Qumran, the Jordan held no sacred significance; their rituals of purification were daily, yet John's baptism may have been a final eschatological cleansing. The social dynamics of the two movements also differ; John is never associated with a community of goods or with a novitiate. John's wilderness preaching was also public in a way that Qumran's more introverted piety was not. However one concludes the matter, it is at least clear that the wilderness setting offered a sacred landscape for religious renewal that held mutual appeal for Qumran, John, and Jesus.

19.5. The walls of the scriptorium in the ruins of Qumran. The view is toward the Dead Sea.

Communal Structures in the Early Church

Another comparison frequently made between Qumran and the NT emerges in the form of communal structures in the early church. The book of Acts, for example, suggests that the Jerusalem church practiced a community of goods, in which "all who believed were together and had all things in common; they would sell their possessions and goods and distribute the proceeds to all, as any had need" (Acts 2:44–45). Qumran attests yet another Jewish union in which members devoted their property to the worshiping community. As Acts describes this phenomenon primarily among the Jewish believers in Jerusalem (Acts 4:32–35), scholars have been willing to consider the possibility that the early Jerusalem church may have shared the popular religious option of shared property, a practice also attested in contemporary Judaism at Qumran. Like the Matthean community (Matt. 18), Qumran also provided in its *Rule* a disciplinary code for admonishing and restoring errant members of its movement (1QS 5.24–6.1).

Religious Ideas in the New Testament

Finally, the greatest contributions that Qumran has made to the writings of the NT center on the religious ideas attested in the Scrolls. An excellent example concerns the very notion of messianism itself. At the center of Qumran's messianic teaching seems to have been the expectation of dual messiahs, one royal and one priestly. This form of expectation is directly attested in the *Rule of the Community*: "They . . . shall be ruled by the primitive precepts in which the men of the Community were first instructed until there shall come the Prophet and the Messiahs of Aaron and Israel" (1QS 9.10–11). Since the expectation of dual messiahs seems further to be reinforced in other Qumran writings (CD 12.23; 14.19; 19.10–11; 20.1; 4QFlor 1.10–12; 4QTest 9–20), this "diarchal messianism" appears to have stood as the core messianic vision of the Qumran community. This expectation of dual messiahs cuts subversively against the wider political realities of Qumran's own social setting, where the Hasmonean priests also reigned as kings; in Qumran's ideological vision, God would restore these roles in the future between two separate, anointed rulers.

Alongside this core messianic vision, the Scrolls also preserve other, more diverse expressions of messianism. In the *Rule of the Congregation*, a single "Messiah of Israel" is portrayed as proceeding in a holy congregation of all Israel, preeminent among the people, yet equally guided by priestly authorities (1QSa 2.11–22). The *Commentary on Genesis A* envisions a "Messiah of Righteousness," who will be like David (4Q252 frg. 6 5.1–4). The *Melchizedek* document further expects a "Messiah of the Spirit," one whose prophetic anointing will fulfill the expectations of Isa. 52:7 (11Q13 2.15–20). An *Aramaic Apocalypse* at Qumran also depicts one who is called "Son of God," an apocalyptic figure modeled on the "son of man" prophecy of Dan. 7. A "messiah" with universal rule in "heaven and earth" headlines the expectations of the *Messianic Apocalypse*, a writing that envisions how God will restore the fortunes of the suffering righteous, healing the wounded, reviving the dead, and proclaiming good news to the poor (4Q521 frgs. 2+4 2.1–13). Finally, several scrolls anticipate a "Prince of the Congregation," a charismatic warrior who will exercise violent power against Israel's enemies in the military conflicts that will characterize the latter days (*Rule of Blessings*, *Rule of War*, *Moses Apocryphon*[b], *Commentary on Isaiah*[c]; cf. CD 7.20).

When the early church called Jesus "Messiah" and "Son of God," it appears to have appealed to a number of traditional messianic ideals, while also dramatically reinterpreting them in light of the distinctive features of Jesus' own activity. Today NT scholars note, in particular, the surprising commonality between the description of the messianic era in the Qumran *Messianic Apocalypse* and the Q sayings material attested in Matt. 11:2–6//Luke 7:18–23. Both sources share the common tradition, perhaps inspired by mutual reflection upon Isa. 61, that in the time when the messiah is revealed, the wounded will be healed, the blind will receive sight, the dead will be raised, and the poor will have glad tidings proclaimed to them. Likewise, the *Aramaic Apocalypse* has deepened understanding of how the title

"Son of God" functioned as a messianic term in Judaism prior to Christianity. The messianism of the *Aramaic Apocalypse* emerges through the author's heavy reliance on the scriptural context of Dan. 7–12, a tendency also reflected in the messianism of the Synoptic Gospels (Mark 13:24–27; 14:61–62 par.). Since the *Aramaic Apocalypse* utilizes the very words "he will be called [gr]eat and will be designated by his name. He shall be called Son of God, and they will call him Son of the Most High, . . . his kingdom will be an eternal kingdom," some scholars have even considered the possibility of a more direct literary relationship between this writing and Luke 1:32–33, where the coming of the messiah is anticipated in strikingly similar language (Collins, *Scepter*). Whether direct literary reliance can be certified, Qumran has revealed the extent to which NT literature reflects popular messianic traditions that had an extended history in earlier Judaism.

Beyond the specific question of messianism, the Scrolls offer a deep reservoir for understanding the history of other ideas of crucial concern in the NT, including teaching on divorce and remarriage (11QT^a 57.15–19), the Sabbath (CD 10.15–11.18), resurrection and the afterlife (*Messianic Apocalypse, Pseudo-Ezekiel*), demonology and exorcism (*Songs of the Sage, Apocryphal Psalms, Incantation Formula*), the beatitudes (*Beatitudes*), dualism (1QS 3.13–4.26; CD 1.1–8.21), and criticism of Jerusalem and its temple authorities (*Halakic Letter, Damascus Document, Commentary on Habakkuk*). The result of such deepening historical awareness has been an unprecedented recognition of the diversity of early Jewish thought in the age of Christian origins, a diversity within which Jesus and his earliest followers forged their own paths of devotion. Neither Qumran nor the Jesus movement aligned themselves with the kind of Judaism represented by the Jerusalem priestly aristocracy or the Pharisaic-rabbinic stream that would prevail after the temple destruction; yet both of them faithfully reinterpreted Israel's faith in their own ways and even utilized, at times, common traditions as they addressed the predominant religious concerns of Judaism in the first century.

Bibliography

Critical editions of most of the DSS in Hebrew, Aramaic, and Greek may be studied, together with accompanying photographic plates, in the volumes of the Discoveries in the Judaean Desert (DJD) series (Oxford: Clarendon, 1955–). A comprehensive list of individual scrolls and their publication data is provided by Emanuel Tov, "Appendix F: Texts from the Judean Desert," in *The SBL Handbook of Style for Ancient Near Eastern, Biblical, and Early Christian Studies* (ed. P. Alexander et al.; Peabody, MA: Hendrickson, 1999), 176–233. Updated editions of nonbiblical scrolls, without photographic plates, are often published in the volumes of *The Dead Sea Scrolls: Hebrew, Aramaic, and Greek Texts with English Translations* (ed. J. Charlesworth; PTSDSSP; Tübingen: Mohr Siebeck, 1994–). A series of six volumes presents brief editions of nonbiblical scrolls in *The Dead Sea Scrolls*

Reader (ed. D. Parry and E. Tov; Leiden: Brill, 2004); and a more abbreviated edition of most of the scrolls has been provided by Florentino García Martínez and Eibert J. C. Tigchelaar in *The Dead Sea Scrolls Study Edition* (2 vols.; Leiden: Brill; Grand Rapids: Eerdmans, 2000). *The Dead Sea Scrolls Electronic Reference Library* (ed. E. Tov et al.; rev. ed.; Leiden: Brill, 2006) provides electronic images and texts of nonbiblical scrolls, together with analytical and search tools.

Collins, John J. *The Scepter and the Star: Messianism in Light of the Dead Sea Scrolls.* 2nd ed. Grand Rapids: Eerdmans, 2010. A treatment of messianism in the DSS and other literature.

Harrington, Daniel J. *Wisdom Texts from Qumran.* LDSS. New York: Routledge, 1996. A translation and interpretation of wisdom literature in the DSS.

Magness, Jodi. *The Archaeology of Qumran and the Dead Sea Scrolls.* SDSSRL. Grand Rapids: Eerdmans, 2006. A revised interpretation of Qumran archaeology, which argues that the community of the DSS may have inhabited Qumran only after 100 BC.

Tov, Emanuel. *Textual Criticism and the Hebrew Bible.* 2nd rev. ed. Minneapolis: Fortress, 2001. An analysis of manuscripts of the HB, with special attention to the DSS.

VanderKam, James C. *The Dead Sea Scrolls Today.* 2nd ed. Grand Rapids: Eerdmans, 2010. An updated introduction to the DSS, their dating, the Qumran movement, and its relevance for understanding the Old and New Testaments.

Vaux, Roland de. *Archaeology and the Dead Sea Scrolls.* London: Oxford University Press, 1973. De Vaux's interpretation of the archaeology and history of Qumran and related sites in the Judean wilderness.

Vermes, Geza. *The Complete Dead Sea Scrolls in English.* New York: Penguin, 1998. Translations of the DSS, with brief scholarly introductions.

20

Prophetic Movements and Zealots

JAMES D. G. DUNN

"Prophetic movements and Zealots" refers primarily to a sequence of movements that emerged in Judea in the buildup to the Jewish revolt against Rome (AD 66–70) and that contributed decisively to the revolt itself. In both cases, prophetic movements and Zealots, our information comes almost exclusively from Josephus in his history the *Jewish War* and in his subsequent larger account of Israel's history, *Jewish Antiquities*. The movements emerged in the period following the death of Herod Agrippa, who, under Emperor Claudius's patronage, had been granted the same degree of sovereignty previously enjoyed by Herod the Great (Josephus, *J.W.* 2.214–17; *Ant.* 19.274–75). Prior to that, the only serious unrest in Palestine under Roman rule had been in the period immediately following the death of Herod the Great in 4 BC, including the messianic pretenders Simon and Athronges (*J.W.* 2.10–79; *Ant.* 17.206–18, 250–98). The intervening period, including the (probably) three years of Jesus' mission, had been relatively quiet. The Roman historian Tacitus indeed reports that "under Tiberius [AD 14–37] all was quiet" (*Hist.* 5.9 LCL; see Schürer, *History*, 1:330–35).

Agrippa, however, had evidently used his short period of kingship (AD 41–44) to demonstrate his Jewish piety (Josephus, *Ant.* 19.293–94), to win favor with the Jerusalemites (*Ant.* 19.299), to stoke the fires of resentment at Roman rule (*Ant.* 19.300), and to strengthen Jerusalem's defenses (Josephus, *J.W.* 2.218; *Ant.* 19.326). In so doing, he presumably intended to strengthen Israel's self-identity and to heighten its nationalistic hopes for a restoration of Judea's sovereignty, lost a century earlier with Pompey's conquest of Palestine in 63 BC. Agrippa also developed alliances with other client kings in the region, which aroused the Roman governor's undoubtedly justifiable suspicions (*Ant.* 19.338–42). Whatever plans or hopes Agrippa had cherished, they were cut short by his unexpected death in AD 44 (Josephus, *Ant.* 19.343–50; Acts 12:20–23). Josephus also reports that the Caesareans and Sebastenes (Samaria) received the news of Agrippa's death with riotous pleasure (*Ant.* 19.356–59), which strongly suggests that the stirrings of Judean nationalism and possible revolt under Agrippa were regarded with understandable trepidation by the Hellenistic cities around Judea's borders (Schürer, *History*, 1:442–54).

> **Messianic Claimants around the Time of Jesus**
>
> Judas of Sepphoris, son of Hezekiah, the "brigand chief" (4 BC)
> Simon of Perea (4 BC)
> Athronges the shepherd of Judea (4–2 BC)
> Menahem (grand)son of Judas of Sepphoris (AD 66)
> John of Gischala, son of Levi (AD 67–70)
> Simon bar Giora of Gerasa (AD 68–70)
> Lukuas of Cyrene (AD 115)
> Simon ben Kosiba/Bar Kokhba (AD 132–135)

Following the death of Agrippa, the restoration of Rome's direct rule, badly mishandled by a series of incompetent procurators (Josephus, *J.W.* 2.223–44), or so Josephus leads us to believe, no doubt added to the flames of increasing resentment and thoughts of revolt (Schürer, *History*, 1:455–70). It was in this context of mounting unrest and disquiet that the prophetic movements and Zealots emerged.

Prophetic Movements

Theudas, the Egyptian, and Sign Prophets

Josephus characterizes two of the movements that emerged in Judea in the late 40s and 50s as prophetic, focusing on the leadership of two individuals explicitly named as "prophets." Both evidently intended to reenact miracles of the entry into the promised land.

Josephus narrates that during the procuratorship of Cuspius Fadus (AD 44–46), "a certain imposter [*goēs*] named Theudas persuaded the majority of the masses to take up their possessions and to follow him to the Jordan River. He stated that he was a prophet and that at his command the river would be parted and would provide them an easy passage [that is, presumably to cross back into the promised land]. With this talk he deceived many" (*Ant.* 20.97–98). The NT contains a complementary report, though Acts 5:36 numbers Theudas's followers at only about four hundred. According to Josephus, Fadus sent against them a squadron of cavalry, which caught the would-be revolutionaries/pilgrims unexpectedly, slew many of them, and took many prisoners. Theudas himself was captured and peremptorily executed, and his severed head was taken to Jerusalem.

A second prophetic movement, during the procuratorship of Felix (AD 52–60), featured an "Egyptian," designated by Josephus as a "false prophet, a charlatan [*goēs*]." He had gathered about thirty thousand followers (Josephus calls them "dupes") and led them by a circuitous route from the desert to the Mount of Olives. According to Josephus, his intention had been to force an entrance into Jerusalem, assuring his followers that at his command the walls would fall down (as they had at Jericho). After overpowering the Roman garrison, he planned to set himself up as a tyrant of the people. Felix confronted him with a heavy force of Roman infantry, supported by the population, says Josephus, and killed and took prisoner most of the Egyptian's followers. The Egyptian himself escaped with a few of his followers, and the rest dispersed and sneaked back to their homes (Josephus, *J.W.* 2.261–63; *Ant.* 20.167–72). Acts also refers to "the Egyptian," since, according to Luke, the tribune who arrested Paul in the temple at first assumed that he was "the Egyptian who recently stirred up a revolt and led the four thousand assassins out into the wilderness" (Acts 21:38).

The differences in numbers should not occasion any surprise, since the numbers of large crowds are still notoriously hard to estimate, and there is a natural tendency of the victors to exaggerate the size of the forces defeated. The figures in Acts are more sober and probably nearer the mark, which only serves to highlight both the fear that even a small prophetic protest movement occasioned in the Roman authorities and the ruthlessness of their response. Also interesting is the fact that both movements started with a return to the desert, presumably as part of a purifying ritual, a return to the priorities and discipline that had initially secured the promised land.

Jewish Prophets around the Time of Jesus

John the Baptist (late AD 20s)
The "Samaritan" (ca. AD 26–36)
Theudas (ca. AD 45)
The "Egyptian" Jew (ca. AD 56)
An anonymous "impostor" (ca. AD 61)
Jesus son of Ananias (AD 62–69)
Jonathan the Weaver, refugee of Cyrene (ca. AD 71)

Josephus also refers to others who promised "signs of deliverance" (*J.W.* 2.258–60 [= *Ant.* 20.168]; 6.285–7 ["many prophets"]; 7.437–41; *Ant.* 20.188), and though he does not describe them all as prophets, the recent practice of classifying them all as "sign prophets" is quite justified (particularly Barnett, "Sign Prophets"; Gray, *Prophetic Figures*, 112–44). This data, together with that relating to John the Baptist, provides sufficient evidence that the category of "prophet" was still viable at the time of Jesus.[1]

---

1. It is now generally recognized that the idea of the prophetic Spirit's having withdrawn (with reference to the variegated evidence of Ps. 74:9; Zech. 13:2–3; 1 Macc. 4:45–46; 9:27; *2 Bar.* 85.1–13) has been much exaggerated; see particularly J. Levison, "Did the Spirit Withdraw from Israel? An Evaluation of the Earliest Jewish Data," *NTS* 43 (1997): 35–57.

Jesus and the First Christians as a Prophetic Movement

Jesus was seen as a prophet during his mission. The testimony of the Jesus tradition is both quite widespread and consistent across its breadth.

1. Jesus emerged from the circle around John the Baptist. The Synoptic Gospels make some attempt to cloak this fact. For example, Mark delays his account of the beginnings of Jesus' mission until after the Baptist has been arrested and removed from the scene (1:14); and Matthew tries to explain why Jesus, the son of David, submitted to a baptism of repentance at the hands of the Baptist (Matt. 3:14–15). But John makes it clear that two of Jesus' closest followers were drawn from the ranks of the Baptist's disciples (John 1:35–39) and indicates that Jesus' early mission paralleled that of the Baptist (3:22–26). So it is entirely relevant to note that the Baptist was seen as a prophet. According to John 1:21, he was asked whether he was "the prophet." The overtones of John as an Elijah-type figure may well have deeper roots than Christian apologetic, that is, as more than an attempt to legitimize Jesus' messianic claims by identifying John the Baptist as the forerunner prophesied by Mal. 4:5. And both the report of John's popularity in Q (Matt. 11:7–9//Luke 7:24–26) and the argument about Jesus' authority (Mark 11:27–33 par.)[2] assume that John was widely seen as a prophet. Josephus does not call the Baptist a "prophet," but that may well be because Josephus regarded the category as dubious ("sign prophets"), whereas he respected John. If the Baptist was thought to be a prophet, then it would be natural for the same speculation to be voiced in regard to Jesus.

2. Mark 6:15 and parallels, as well as 8:28 and parallels, specifically report rumors or speculation that Jesus was John the Baptist, Elijah, or a prophet. Such reports are certainly part of the developed form in which these stories were told. In the one case, they are attributed to Herod Antipas; in the other, such inadequate rumors serve as a foil for Peter's confession of Jesus as "the Messiah" (8:29). But the variations in these reports (a prophet, one of the old prophets, Jeremiah) likely attest the range of rumors that circulated (and continued to circulate) within Palestine regarding Jesus.

3. That the question was voiced whether Jesus was a prophet, or even *the* prophet, is attested more widely. Notice that in Matt. 21:10–11, when asked, "Who is this?" the crowds reply, "This is the prophet Jesus from Nazareth of Galilee" (cf. 21:46; see also Luke 7:16, 39; 24:19). And the references in John's Gospel, though drawn fully into John's dramatic presentation, confirm that Jesus as (the) prophet was a possibility debated among those intrigued by the reports of Jesus' mission (John 6:14; 7:40, 52 [in John 7:52 "the prophet" is the reading of two early manuscripts, $\mathfrak{P}^{66}$ and $\mathfrak{P}^{75}$]). That various miracles reported of Jesus seemed to

---

2. Opinion is divided on the historical value of the passage; see, e.g., J. A. Fitzmyer, *The Gospel according to Luke* (2 vols.; AB 28; New York: Doubleday, 1981–85), 2:1272–73; W. D. Davies and D. C. Allison, *The Gospel according to Saint Matthew* (3 vols.; ICC; Edinburgh: T&T Clark, 1988–97), 3:157–58.

parallel those attributed to Elijah and Elisha would presumably not have escaped notice. Compare particularly Mark 5:22–34 with 1 Kings 17:17–24 (Elijah) and 2 Kings 4:18–37 (Elisha). The account of Jesus being mocked as a failed prophet (Mark 14:65 par.) should also be given some weight.

4. It would appear that Jesus himself was by no means unwilling to refer to himself as a prophet (Mark 6:4 par.; Luke 13:33). And if indeed he did regard Isa. 61:1–2 as setting out the program for his own mission—as is explicitly claimed in Luke 4:17–21 (and implicit in Luke 6:20–21//Matt. 5:3–6 and Matt. 11:5//Luke 7:22)—that essentially describes a prophetic figure and role (Dunn, *Jesus Remembered*, 655–66). Many of those who study the historical Jesus think that Jesus is best characterized in terms of the "eschatological prophet" (Dunn, *Jesus Remembered*, 666n244).

5. That political implications were readily attached to the belief that Jesus was a prophet is indicated by the sequence of John 6:14–15: the Galilean crowd thought Jesus was indeed a prophet and intended to "take him by force to make him king." Particularly notable also is the sad confession of Cleopas and his companion on the road to Emmaus, following Jesus' execution: "Jesus of Nazareth, who was a prophet mighty in deed and word before God and all the people. . . . We had hoped that he was the one to redeem Israel" (Luke 24:19, 21). The argument has been made several times, indeed, that Jesus was charged with leading people astray and false prophecy, though the Gospels know nothing of this; however, Luke does refer to a charge of political agitation (Luke 23:2; see Stanton, "Jesus," 175–80).

6. It is true that the thought of Jesus as the prophet like Moses (Deut. 18:15, 18) is given some mileage in early Christianity (esp. Acts 3:22–23; 7:37). But otherwise the evaluation of Jesus as a prophet is usually noted, only to be left on one side to be superseded by higher christological claims. The most notable of these is the confession at Caesarea Philippi: others say Jesus is a prophet, Peter says he is the Messiah, Jesus says the Son of Man (Mark 8:28–31 par.). Cleopas says he is "a prophet mighty in deed and word," but does so in an encounter with the risen Christ (Luke 24:19). For John, Jesus as the prophet like Moses is far transcended by Jesus as the one who gives and is the living bread from heaven (John 6:25–58). Overall, there is no indication whatsoever that the first Christians regarded themselves as a prophetic movement gathered around the prophet Jesus.[3]

7. However, the first Christians can be properly characterized as a prophetic movement. Acts begins the story of Christianity with the outpouring of the Spirit on the day of Pentecost (Acts 2). And in quoting Joel 2:28–32 (3:1–5 MT), Luke repeats the promise that those who receive the Spirit "shall prophesy" (Acts 2:17–18). Thereafter, prophecy is depicted as a regular feature of early-church gatherings (11:27–28; 13:1; 15:32; 19:6; 21:9–10). Paul too regards prophecy as a regular feature of his churches' worship and ranks prophecy as the most valuable of the Spirit's gifts (see Rom. 12:6; 1 Cor. 12:28; 14:1–5, 39). It is notable, however, that prophecy is regarded as an in-house gift, for building up the church. There is no

3. See James D. G. Dunn, *Christology in the Making* (2nd ed.; London: SCM, 1989), §19.1.

hint of what is commonly regarded as "prophetic" speech—that is, of critical social or political comments addressed to civic or political leaders, as was often the case with OT prophets. The one exception is the book of Revelation, which exalts its own prophetic role (1:3; 19:10; 22:7, 9–10, 18–19), including prophecy "about many peoples and nations and languages and kings" (10:11). A notable role is given to the mysterious two prophets who take a leading part in the confrontation with the beast in all the wickedness of its political power and who are killed by it (11:3, 7–10; 16:6). This is as near as first-century Christianity comes to being a prophetic movement like that of Josephus's "sign prophets."

8. Prophecy continued to be a major factor in early Christian worship into the second century, with the accompanying concern over the danger of false prophecy (1 John 4:1–6; *Did.* 11–13; *Herm. Mand.* 11). And prophetic movements continued to feature in Christianity through the following centuries, although the Montanist movement, which flourished in the latter decades of the second century, left a suspicion of enthusiasm and heresy that has haunted all subsequent expressions of Christian prophecy.

Zealots

The Zealots

For most of those with knowledge of the period, the name "Zealots" refers at once to the violent revolutionaries who emerged in Jerusalem as major players in the revolt against Rome (Josephus, *J.W.* 2.651) after its initial phase (winter of AD 66–67). They were one of the ruthless groups that fought for control of Jerusalem when the revolt sank into chaos and internecine warfare as hope to defeat the military might of Rome became increasingly unrealistic. For a flavor of the period, it is worth quoting at length a passage from Josephus, who as himself a former leader of the Jewish revolt in Galilee understandably regarded the final acts in Jerusalem with unmitigated horror. In the final section of his history of the revolt, he castigates unmercifully, but justifiably, those bent on tyranny and on violence and plundering the property of the wealthy.

> The Sicarii were the first to set the example of this lawlessness and cruelty to their kinsmen, leaving no word unspoken to insult, no deed untried to ruin, the victims of their conspiracy. Yet even they were shown by John [of Gischala] to be more moderate than himself. For not only did he put to death all who proposed just and salutary measures, treating such persons as his bitterest enemies among all the citizens, but he also in his public capacity loaded his country with evils innumerable, such as one might expect would be inflicted upon men by one who had already dared to practice impiety even towards God. . . . Again there was Simon son of Gioras: what crime did he not commit? Or what outrage did he refrain from inflicting upon the persons of those very freemen who had created him a despot? What ties of friendship or of kindred but rendered these men more audacious in their daily murders? . . . Yet even their infatuation was

outdone by the madness of the Idumeans. For these most abominable wretches, after butchering the chief priests,[4] so that no particle of religious worship might continue, proceeded to extirpate whatever relics were left of our civil polity, introducing into every department perfect lawlessness. In this the so-called Zealots excelled, a class which justified their name by their actions; for they copied every deed of ill, nor was there any previous villainy recorded in history that they failed to emulate. And yet they took their title from their professed zeal for virtue, either in mockery of those they wronged, so brutal was their nature, or reckoning the greatest evils good. (Josephus, *J.W.* 7.262–70)

The Zealots were evidently a distinct faction, though their alliances with John of Gischala and the Idumeans against the more moderate Ananus makes for a somewhat confused story (Josephus, *J.W.* 4.193–216, 224–32, 305–13, 326). John is represented as breaking away from the larger Zealot body in aspiration for sole leadership (*J.W.* 4.389–95) and as leading Zealots in warfare against the Idumeans (*J.W.* 4.566–70). It was in response to the mayhem thus caused that Simon ben Giora was given entry to the city and confined John and the Zealots to the stronghold of the temple (*J.W.* 4.574–84; 5.527–30). Subsequently Eleazar formed a new faction of the Zealots and took control of the inner courts of the temple, leaving John in control of the outer courts and Simon in control of the upper city and a large part of the lower city (*J.W.* 5.5–10, 248–57). Josephus obviously regards these as circles of intensifying fanaticism.

Zealots are sometimes linked or identified with the Sicarii, a band of extremists whose name was taken from the curved dagger (Latin *sica*) that they concealed in their garments and used to stab opponents in crowds. They were probably the first of the extremist groups to emerge (during the procuratorship of Felix; Josephus, *J.W.* 2.254–57; *Ant.* 20.185–87). Josephus says of them: "The Sicarii were the first to set the example of this lawlessness and cruelty to their kinsmen, leaving no word unspoken to insult, no deed untried to ruin, the victims of their conspiracy" (*J.W.* 7.262). Nevertheless, they seem to have dropped out of the Jerusalem factions, focusing their energies in the defense of Masada, which they had previously captured (*J.W.* 4.400, 516; 7.253, 275; see further Schürer, *History*, 2:602–6).

In his description of the various subgroups within Second Temple Judaism, which for apologetic purposes he denotes as "philosophies" (Pharisees, Sadducees, and Essenes), Josephus also seems to identify the Zealots with "the fourth philosophy" (*Ant.* 18.23). This is significant, since he describes the fourth philosophy as established by Judas the Galilean, in reaction to the census carried out by the Roman governor Quirinius in AD 6 or 7, and thus seems to indicate a coherent political body that existed from that time (Hengel, *Zealots*, 89). It is certainly the case that Judas's descendants were active in the two decades before the revolt, in the capture and defense of Masada and in the beginnings of the internecine rivalry in Jerusalem (Schürer, *History*, 2:600–601). However, Josephus himself seems to make a point of not using the term "Zealot" for a faction or party until

---

4. The chief priests Ananus and Jesus (Josephus, *J.W.* 4.314–17); Josephus dates the final overthrow of the city and the downfall of the Jewish state from the day of their murder (*J.W.* 4.318).

the revolt itself (see Horsley, "Zealots"; Schwartz, "Zealots").[5] According to Josephus, the fourth philosophy agreed with the Pharisees in all respects, "except that they have a passion for liberty that is almost unconquerable, since they are convinced that God alone is their leader and master" (*Ant.* 18.23). So "the fourth philosophy" is probably a general title for the more extreme views that bubbled below the surface until they began to come to expression in the two decades before the revolt and climaxed in the several factions that brought the revolt to its disastrous climax in AD 70.

Christian Zealots?

Too little noticed is the fact that, apart from his regular references to the Zealots in the *Jewish War*, Josephus also uses the term "zealot" more broadly. In *Antiquities* he never refers to the "Zealots" and uses "zealot" only in the sense of someone completely committed to his religious traditions and praxis (10.49; 6.271; 20.47). He also describes himself as a "zealot" in his search for the right philosophy for his own life (*Life* 11) and even ranks Pythagoras as a "zealot" in his attitude to Israel's law (*Ag. Ap.* 1.162–65; cf. also Philo, *Migr.* 62; *Somn.* 1.124; 2.274; *Abr.* 22, 33, 60; *Mos.* 1.160–61; 2.55, 161, 256).

Here we should recognize that the "Zealots" took their name from a long tradition within Second Temple Judaism that prized "zeal" as an expression of ardent commitment to maintain and defend the unique relationship (covenant) that Israel believed God had established with Israel alone. In the expression of such zeal, these zealots would believe that they were taking their lead from God himself. For "zeal" (*qn'*) also means "jealousy" and is so used to describe Yahweh's "zeal/jealousy" in insisting that Israel must not worship any other gods but must remain dedicated to him alone. So, classically, God's jealousy is described in Exod. 20:5: "You shall not bow down to them [other gods] or worship them; for I the LORD your God am a jealous God" (see also Exod. 34:14; Deut. 4:23–24; 5:9; 6:14–15; 32:21; Hengel [*Zealots*, 146] notes that the adjectives are applied only to God). Notably in the Greek translation of these passages, it is God himself who is described as a "zealot" (Exod. 20:5; 34:14; Deut. 4:24; 5:9; 6:15).

The great hero of "zeal" was Phinehas, who, when an Israelite brought a Midianite woman into his tent (into the congregation of Yahweh), forthwith slew them both "because he was zealous for his God" (Num. 25:6–13); it is no surprise that in Num. 25:11 Phinehas's zeal is understood as a direct reflection of Yahweh's. For this single deed he was often recalled and his zeal praised (cf. Ps. 106:28–31; Sir. 45:23–24; 1 Macc. 2:26, 54; 4 Macc. 18:12), and he became the model and inspiration both for the Maccabean rebels against Syrian overlordship and for the later

---

5. Josephus's earlier uses of the term (*J.W.* 2.444, 564) are best translated in some way other than as "Zealots," and in *J.W.* 2.651 he refers to "those called Zealots" in Jerusalem at the beginning of the war, evidently conscious of the fact that they were being so named in his history for the first time. See also D. Rhoads, *ABD* 6:1043–54.

Zealots (Hengel, *Zealots*, chap. 4). Other "heroes of zeal" were Simeon and Levi, "who burned with zeal for you [God] and abhorred the pollution of their blood" (Jdt. 9:4), referring to their slaughter of the Shechemites after the seduction of their sister Dinah by the son of Hamor (Gen. 34). Notice that in *Jub.* 30 the avenging of Dinah's defilement (30.4–5) and protection of Israel's holiness from gentile defilement (30.8, 13–14) were counted to them for righteousness (30.17). Elijah's zeal for the Lord was most fully expressed in his victory over (and execution of!) the prophets of Baal (see 1 Kings 18:40; 19:1, 10, 14; Sir. 48:2–3; 1 Macc. 2:58). The prophets of Baal would at least include fellow Israelites who had taken service in the worship of Baal (see also Exod. 32:26–29; 2 Kings 10:16–28). And Mattathias sparked the revolt against the Syrians when, burning "with zeal for the law, just like Phinehas," he executed a Syrian officer and a fellow Jew who was going to apostatize by offering a forbidden sacrifice (1 Macc. 2:23–26). Mattathias rallied the rebellion by crying out, "Let every one who is zealous for the law and supports the covenant come out with me!" (2:27; cf. Josephus, *Ant.* 12.271), and his deathbed testimony is a paean in praise of zeal and the heroes of Israel (1 Macc. 2:50–60).

All this is relevant to the question of whether we can speak of Christian "zealots." One of Jesus' disciples is referred to as Simon "the zealot" (Luke 6:15; Acts 1:13). We should certainly not translate this as "Simon the Zealot," or conclude from the use of the term, as some have suggested, that Jesus had chosen a "freedom fighter" or "terrorist" as one of his disciples. As we have already noted, the extremist faction who called themselves "Zealots" did not emerge until the beginning of the First Jewish Revolt, nearly forty years later. But we can certainly infer that Simon ardently maintained the belief that Israel had a commitment to worship only the God of Israel. That Jesus chose such an intensely religious person, possibly with strong political views about Rome's domination of Israel, is itself significant.

A more obvious candidate for a Phinehas-like zeal is Saul of Tarsus, who is described in Acts as "zealous for God" (Acts 22:3) and who describes his pre-Christian religious intensity as being "zealous for the traditions of my ancestors" (Gal. 1:14). More strikingly, he attributes his persecution of the church to this same "zeal" (Phil. 3:6; cf. Gal. 1:13–14). His zeal had characteristics similar to those of Phinehas, in that he was prepared to use violence against his fellow Jews, presumably because, like Phinehas and the other "heroes of zeal," he thought it necessary to resist by force what he regarded as a threat to Israel's holiness (its set-apartness) to God alone. The degree to which his zeal foreshadowed that of the Zealots, even if only to a small degree, is one of the most embarrassing features of the biography of the great apostle to the gentiles. Of course, the Paul who admits to this "zeal" does so as an act of confession and repentance for what his conversion has convinced him was a totally unjustified and wrong attitude and policy. That, despite such repentance, Paul continues to use the term "zeal" as a positive term (2 Cor. 7:7; 9:2; 11:2; Col. 4:13 [variant reading]) is a reminder that the basic concept is a positive one and that the Zealots are to be condemned not so much for their zeal as for the abuse and extremist expression of their zeal.

Were Christians involved in the Jewish revolt? That is a question that can never be given a final answer, since our knowledge of Galilean and Judean churches during the period of AD 40–70 is so thin. As for the Jerusalem church itself, the only tradition relating to the outbreak of the war is what is known as "the flight to Pella" tradition, to the effect that early in the war the main body of Christians in Jerusalem fled from Jerusalem across the Jordan to the Perean city of Pella, one of the cities of the Decapolis (see Eusebius, *Eccl. Hist.* 3.5.3; Epiphanius, *Pan.* 29.7.2–8). The tradition is much questioned, but it does provide what seems to be a likely link between the traditionalist Jewish Christianity in Jerusalem (Acts 21:20) and the later Ebionites, which cannot be lightly dismissed.[6] The point here, however, is that the only tradition available to us about the Jerusalem Christians in the course of the Jewish revolt indicates the unlikelihood that the bulk of the Jerusalem Christians were caught up in the revolt itself, and it is far less likely that they or any of their number could be ranked with the Zealots.

All, then, that can be attributed to the first Christians is a recognition that zeal can be pressed to extremes, but a readiness to recognize too that zeal for other people's welfare and good is something to be affirmed and commended.

Bibliography

Barnett, P. W. "The Jewish Sign Prophets (AD 40–70): Their Intentions and Origin." *NTS* 27 (1981): 679–97.

Dunn, James D. G. *Beginning from Jerusalem*. Grand Rapids: Eerdmans, 2009.

———. *Jesus Remembered*. Grand Rapids: Eerdmans, 2003.

Gray, Rebecca. *Prophetic Figures in Late Second Temple Jewish Palestine: The Evidence from Josephus*. Oxford: Oxford University Press, 1993.

Hengel, Martin. *The Zealots*. Edinburgh: T&T Clark, 1989.

Horsley, Richard A. "The Zealots: Their Origin, Relationship and Importance in the Jewish Revolt." *NovT* 28 (1986): 159–92.

Schürer, Emil. *The History of the Jewish People in the Age of Jesus Christ (175 BC–AD 135)*. Revised and edited by Geza Vermes, Fergus Millar, and Martin Goodman. Revised English ed. 3 vols. in 4 parts. Edinburgh: T&T Clark, 1987.

Schwartz, Daniel R. "On Christian Study of the Zealots." Pages 128–46 in *Studies in the Jewish Background of Christianity*. WUNT 60. Tübingen: Mohr Siebeck, 1992.

Stanton, Graham N. "Jesus of Nazareth: A Magician and a False Prophet Who Deceived God's People?" Pages 164–80 in *Jesus of Nazareth: Lord and Christ*. Edited by J. B. Green and M. Turner. Grand Rapids: Eerdmans, 1994.

---

6. C. Koester, "The Origin and Significance of the Flight to Pella Tradition," *CBQ* 51 (1989): 90–106; J. Carleton Paget, "Jewish Christianity," in *The Early Roman Period* (ed. E. Horbury et al.; vol. 3 of *The Cambridge History of Judaism*, ed. W. D. Davies and L. Finkelstein; Cambridge: Cambridge University Press, 1999), 731–75 (747–48).

21

Apocalypticism

LARRY R. HELYER

Apocalypticism permeates the NT, and many scholars interpret early Christianity as an apocalyptic movement. At the very least, serious readers of the NT need a basic understanding of this complex, socioreligious phenomenon. Despite continuing terminological ambiguity, there is an emerging consensus on matters of definition, characteristics, and function. Debate still continues concerning its origins, social location, and significance for the NT.

Definition

At the outset, one must distinguish between several related terms. The noun "apocalypticism" and the adjective "apocalyptic" are transliterations of the Greek adjective *apokalyptikos*, meaning "revelatory," and are related to the Greek verb *apokalyptō*, "to unveil, disclose, or reveal." Typically, the content of what is unveiled deals with events leading up to and including the consummation of God's redemptive plan for individuals and the cosmos, matters traditionally designated as "eschatology" (i.e., the study of last things). Occasionally, the focus falls on the secret, inner workings of the cosmos, especially its celestial realms.

To the above terms should be added the Greek cognate noun *apokalypsis*, transliterated into English as "apocalypse" and denoting a divine disclosure or revelation. Scholars apply this term to a literary genre that purports to disclose eschatological and cosmological secrets. The following is a widely accepted definition:

> Apocalypse is a genre of revelatory literature with a narrative framework, in which a revelation is mediated by an otherworldly being to a human recipient, disclosing a transcendent reality which is both temporal, insofar as it envisages eschatological salvation, and spatial, insofar as it involves another, supernatural world. (J. Collins, "Morphology," 9)

The seer communicates his or her visionary experience using a fairly standard stock of literary devices. All apocalypses known to us are pseudonymous (i.e., written under a false name), with the exception of Zech. 1–6 in the OT, the book of Revelation in the NT, and *Shepherd of Hermas* in the Apostolic Fathers. Typically, an apocalypse implicitly invokes the authority of a revered figure from the past. Whether the seer has actually experienced the ecstatic, visionary state described in an apocalypse is debated, though some recent study has taken more seriously the role of religious experiences (and particularly altered states of consciousness) that might give rise to visions of this kind. Probably a combination of intense visionary experience augmented by literary embellishment best accounts for the finished product.

To the uninitiated reader, apocalypses appear to be written in secret code. On closer inspection, however, one generally finds a reasonably reliable interpretive key in canonical apocalyptic prototypes: Isa. 24–27; 65:17–25; 66:22–24; Ezek. 38–48; Joel 2:28–3:21; Zech. 1–6; Dan. 7–12. The "source code" of apocalypses features a wide assortment of domestic and wild animals representing human or superhuman antagonists and protagonists. Liturgical, military, scribal, and numerical imagery and symbols abound, and angelic beings of various ranks, orders, and moral dispositions populate the world of apocalypse. Apocalypses blend ANE and Hellenistic mythological creatures (serpents, dragons, demons) and concepts (cosmology, primeval combat, paradise and Hades) with a wide array of Greco-Roman cultural features (cities, imperial cult, warfare, trade and commerce). The result is akin to a cartoonlike depiction of reality, such as one might experience in a vivid nightmare. It follows that the key to understanding an apocalypse lies in recovering as much as possible the symbolic world of the seer rather than importing one's own contempoary context. The indispensable starting point is the canonical background mentioned above.

The NT book of Revelation is a classic example of an apocalypse, even employing the term "apocalypse" as a self-description in its opening lines: "The revelation [*apokalypsis*] of Jesus Christ, which God gave him to show his servants what must soon take place; he made it known by sending his angel to his servant John, who testified to the word of God and to the testimony of Jesus Christ, even to all that he saw" (Rev. 1:1–2). Some scholars also use the term "apocalypse" for eschatological passages inserted into another genre, such as a Gospel or an epistle

(Mark 13//Matt. 24//Luke 21 ["the little apocalypse"]; 2 Thess. 2:1–17 ["the Pauline apocalypse"]), but, strictly speaking, these are instances of apocalyptic eschatology.

"Apocalyptic eschatology" describes "neither a genre, nor a socio-religious movement, nor a system of thought, but rather a religious perspective, a way of viewing divine plans in relation to mundane realities, . . . a perspective which individuals or groups can embrace in varying degrees at different times" (Hanson, "Apocalypticism," 29). Many scholars also use the term "apocalyptic" as a noun to refer to both the basic ideas and the social movement that produced them. The resulting semantic confusion has led some scholars to urge a clear distinction between the noun "apocalypticism" and the adjective "apocalyptic" (Kreitzer, "Apocalyptic," 57). Nonetheless, the two terms are still used interchangeably.

In summary, apocalypticism is essentially a "worldview expressed in apocalypses and embodied in social movements." Apocalyptic eschatology is "governed by a worldview in which the revelation of divine secrets is constitutive of salvation from an alien or threatening world" (Nickelsburg, "Apocalyptic Texts," 29). An apocalyptist is thus one who manifests an apocalyptic viewpoint or exhibits behavior typical of apocalypticism.

Overview of Sources

Apocalyptic literature, usually expressed in a specific literary genre called "apocalypse," flourished in the period of about 200 BC to AD 200. Included in this corpus are some thirty-seven extant documents, fourteen Jewish and twenty-three Christian (Kreitzer, "Apocalyptic," 58). In addition to apocalypses, there are other genres—such as the "rewritten Bible" *Jubilees*, the oracular work *Sibylline Oracles*, and a number of testamentary writings (e.g., *Testaments of the Twelve Patriarchs*, *Testament of Moses*)—that contain apocalyptic sections or passages. Perhaps the single most formative noncanonical Jewish work to significantly influence both Jewish and Christian apocalyptic thought is *1 Enoch*, a composite document consisting of five distinct works and dating from the mid-third century BC to the first century AD. It displays the features of at least three major genres: testament, apocalypse, and epistle. In this regard, one finds an interesting parallel in the book of Revelation, which combines the genres of epistle, prophecy, and apocalypse. The Jewish apocalypses (often with Christian redaction and interpolations) are accessible in an edition by James Charlesworth (*Old Testament Pseudepigrapha*). One may consult the Christian apocalypses (often incorporating or influenced by Jewish traditions) in J. K. Elliott's *Apocryphal New Testament*.

Origins

Jewish apocalypses do not suddenly appear without precedent; precursors in OT canonical literature, especially Dan. 7–12, prepared the way. But what is the taproot of this distinctive worldview? The majority view, especially among English-speaking scholars, understands apocalyptic literature as a historical development of OT prophecy. The national crisis confronting the Jewish people in the collapse of the first commonwealth (587 BC) and intensified during the Hellenistic era (ca. 323 BC to AD 63), especially during the onslaught of Antiochus IV Epiphanes (167 BC) against their ancestral faith (1 Macc. 1:10–6:16), served as the catalyst for apocalypticism.

The magnitude of this unprecedented suffering challenged traditional understandings of God and his relationship to the world. Apocalyptists concluded that evil was so entrenched and cosmic in scale that only divine intervention could rectify the situation. But God was not unmindful of this catastrophic eruption of evil; all was foreseen, all was predestined. For the present, the faithful must persevere. Soon God will act decisively to destroy evil and evildoers. Apocalypticism in all its diversity gives expression to this unshakable conviction: God will triumph over the forces of evil and reward the righteous. Apocalyptic texts adapt imagery and themes found in OT prophetic texts to make this point and in so doing implicitly appeal to their authority.

Not all scholars agree with this postulated development of apocalypticism. Dismissing the direct link with the OT prophetic tradition, the German OT scholar Gerhard von Rad famously located the roots of apocalypticism in the OT wisdom tradition. He questioned whether the prophetic traditions could adequately explain the combination of determinism, dualism, radical transcendence, and esotericism (i.e., the mysterious and impenetrable). Furthermore, in both the wisdom and apocalyptic traditions, the sages and seers refer to themselves as "the wise" and commit their teachings to writing (Eccles. 12:9–12; Sir. 38:34–39:11; 51:23–28; Dan. 12:3; Rev. 1:11; 10:8–11; 13:18; 14:13; 22:18–19), and the sense of order and fascination with the cosmos more likely stems from wisdom circles interacting with Hellenism. Despite its eloquence, von Rad's narrowly framed thesis has failed to convince most scholars.

Some history-of-religions scholars argue that Iranian dualism and eschatology played a major role in shaping Jewish apocalypticism. Given the long period during which Jews resided in Persia, this cannot be discounted. On the other hand, the proposal has encountered resistance, not least because of the notorious problem of dating: the extant Iranian materials are considerably later than the Jewish apocalyptic texts. Furthermore, a close reading of the respective literatures reveals fundamental differences. Anders Hultgård therefore concludes, "There was no direct and general borrowing of the Iranian apocalyptic eschatology as such by Judaism and Christianity. Instead, the influence exerted itself in an indirect way but was of no less importance."[1]

---

1. Anders Hultgård, "Persian Apocalypticism," in *The Origins of Apocalypticism in Judaism and Christianity* (ed. John J. Collins; vol. 1 of *The Encyclopedia of Apocalypticism*; New York: Continuum, 1998), 39–83 (80).

An emerging consensus recognizes that an either/or solution misses the mark. Wisdom traditions, ANE mythology, Hellenism, and perhaps even Iranian thought all contributed to the genesis of apocalypticism. A majority, however, still gives priority to the OT prophetic traditions (which themselves evidence borrowing from ANE traditions).

Characteristics of Apocalyptic Literature

There is general agreement on certain distinguishing features of apocalyptic litera- ture. There is less agreement on how best to integrate these into a coherent whole.

Dualism

All researchers agree that apocalypticism is marked by pronounced dualism, a dualism operating on three different axes or planes.

1. A *temporal dualism* exists between the present and the future. Two juxta- posed eras—the present, evil age and the future, glorious age to come—frame apocalyptic thought. In Jewish apocalypticism, the present age is demarcated by creation and the climactic day of the Lord. The age to come follows and lasts forever. This is classically expressed in the first-century AD apocalyptic work 2 Esdras (*4 Ezra*): "But the day of judgment will be the end of this age and the beginning of the immortal age to come, in which corruption has passed away" (7:43 [113] RSV; cf. 2 Esd. 7:47, 50; 8:1).

Temporal dualism frames the NT master narrative with one, all-important modification: some of the blessings of the age to come are already being experi- enced by believers at the close of the present age (Heb. 6:5; Col. 3:1–4). The cross and resurrection of Jesus, providing forgiveness of sins (Rom. 3:21–26; 8:1–4) and guaranteeing the resurrection of believers at the parousia (1 Cor. 15:12–28), and the outpouring of the Holy Spirit (Acts 2:17–36) inaugurate the age to come. For this reason, some scholars prefer the expression "inaugurated eschatology" to distinguish this Christian concept from its Jewish predecessor. The reality is nicely summarized in the catchphrase "now but not yet." At the parousia (i.e., Christ's second coming), the present age drops away and the consummation of God's saving plan arrives in all its glory. In short, apocalyptic eschatology, whether Jewish or Christian, is essentially linear: history is moving inexorably toward a crisis climaxed by divine intervention. Consequently, apocalypticism displays a short-term pessimism but a long-term optimism. This linear movement, conceived in terms of a horizontal dualism between present and future, is fundamental to apocalypticism.

2. A second axis may be expressed in spatial terms: a *vertical dualism* exists between the above and the below, between a heavenly, transcendent realm and an earthly, finite realm. The temporal and spatial axes of apocalypticism are integrally related in that the earthly and heavenly realms parallel each other in the present

age until the crisis point, when God supernaturally intervenes in judgment. Then the earthly realm disappears (or is destroyed), and the new order characterizing the glorious, transcendent realm appears and endures forever. The Jewish apocalypse that most clearly emphasizes spatial dualism is 2 *Baruch* (cf. 2 *Bar.* 4.1–7; 32.1–7; 44.4–15; 51.1–16, esp. v. 8). Precisely such a spatial dualism also figures significantly in the NT and, in addition to Revelation (Rev. 4–5), is most clearly seen in Heb. 8–10 (cf. Col. 3:1–4; Eph. 1:20–22; 2:19–21).

3. The preceding two axes intersect with a third: *anthropological dualism.* Humanity falls into two clearly demarcated entities: the righteous and the wicked. Some scholars prefer to label this as an ethical dualism, reflecting a cosmic arena in which the righteous are pitted against not only the wicked on the earthly plane but also heavenly powers of darkness (Eph. 2:1–7; 6:12). Paul even attributes unbelief to the fact that "the god of this world has blinded the minds of the unbelievers" (2 Cor. 4:4; cf. 2 Cor. 11:14; Eph. 2:2). On the other hand, John and Paul are confident that the gospel is winning the long-term struggle against the powers of darkness (1 John 2:8, 14, 28; 4:4; 5:4–5, 18; Rom. 16:20; 1 Cor. 15:24), just as their Lord has promised (Mark 3:27; Matt. 16:18; Luke 10:18).

In some apocalyptic circles, the basis for ethical dualism is predestined; that is, human beings are foreordained either to be saved or to be condemned. This type of dualism surfaces, for example, in the Qumran writings generally assigned to the Jewish sect known as the Essenes (CD 2.7–8; 1QS 3.13–4.26).[2] Though clearly accepting an anthropological dualism, 2 Esdras lays the blame at the feet of those who disobey God's revealed truth in the law. In other words, human choice rather than divine decree determines the dualism. Precisely this tension between divine sovereignty and human freedom manifests itself in the pages of the NT (e.g., Rom. 8–11).

Angelic Mediators

Angelic mediation is a typical feature of apocalyptic literature in which an angel serves as a guide or informant for a visionary. This is seen already in Ezekiel: an angel transports the prophet, in a visionary state, from his refugee camp in Babylon (modern Iraq) to the Jerusalem temple (Ezek. 8–11). The angel guides him on a temple tour and intermittently asks him what he sees; Ezekiel replies with detailed descriptions of the abominations he witnesses. The medium of an angelic informant is developed further in Dan. 7–12 in that the seer now asks questions of the angel (Dan. 10:16–17) and makes requests (Dan. 10:19). Later apocalyptic literature takes this even further and often features extended dialogue back and forth between informant and recipient (as in 1 *Enoch* and 2 Esdras).

2. See Jonathan Klawans, "The Dead Sea Scrolls, the Essenes, and the Study of Religious Belief: Determinism and Freedom of Choice," in *Rediscovering the Dead Sea Scrolls: An Assessment of Old and New Approaches and Methods* (ed. M. L. Grossman; Grand Rapids: Eerdmans, 2010), 264–83.

The book of Revelation displays this dialogical format (5:5; 7:13–17; 10:8–11; 17:6–18; 19:9–10; 22:8–11).

In connection with angelic mediation, a heavenly ascent regularly serves as the locus of revelation. Once again, 1 Enoch is paradigmatic for this revelatory experience (1 En. 14.8). In neither Ezekiel nor Daniel does the seer ascend into the heavenly realm; rather, the revelation is revealed on the earthly plane ("In the vision I was looking and saw myself in Susa the capital, in the province of Elam"; Dan. 8:2). The opening three chapters of Revelation, reflecting the OT prophetic pattern, likewise feature a terrestrial revelation, on the island of Patmos (1:9–11), before switching to the apocalyptic mode and transporting the seer to the heavenly realms (4:1–2), where he receives celestial visions concerning "what must take place after this" (4:1). The apostle Paul mentions his extraordinary throne-room visit in 2 Cor. 12:1–13.

Revelation of Divine Secrets

We come to what many deem the essential core of apocalypticism, namely, the notion of revealing previously hidden information. Larry Kreitzer observes that "this is perhaps the only one [feature] which might gain a general agreement as essential to any definition of the literature as a whole" ("Apocalyptic," 62). In the book of Daniel, the sage/seer is commanded: "Go your way, Daniel, for the words are to remain secret and sealed until the time of the end" (12:9). The book of Revelation, on the other hand, after identifying itself in its opening line as a "revelation of Jesus Christ" (1:1), concludes with an angelic command: "Do not seal up the words of the prophecy of this book, for the time is near" (22:10). In the case of Daniel, the end was perceived as distant; in the case of John of Patmos, the end is imminent (Rev. 1:1; 22:7, 12, 20). Only the Qumran community displays a sense of imminence comparable to what characterizes the NT (Collins, "Eschatology," 257–59).

Christian apocalypticism proclaims open secrets. This stands in stark contrast to Hellenistic mystery religions and the writings of the sectarians of Qumran, in which divine mysteries are closely guarded secrets (1QS 5.10–16; 9.16–17). New Testament apocalypticism revels in revealing God's saving secrets (Rom. 11:25; 16:25–26; 1 Cor. 15:50–58; Eph. 1:9–10; 3:3–13; 6:19–20; Col. 1:26–27; 2:2–7; 4:3–4; Rev. 1:20; 10:7; 17:5–18). Although Jesus limited his mission to Israel during his lifetime (Mark 4:10–12; Matt. 11:25–27; 13:51–52), he anticipates a time in which the "good news of the kingdom will be proclaimed throughout the world, as a testimony to all the nations; and then the end will come" (Matt. 24:14; cf. Mark 13:10). Certainly, the postresurrection Great Commission makes no allowance for an elite circle of the enlightened: "teaching [all nations] to obey everything that I have commanded you" (Matt. 28:20; cf. Acts 1:8). To be sure, the apostle Paul can speak of reserving wisdom for the mature (1 Cor. 2:6–7), but this occurs in a highly ironic and sarcastic context, in which he chastises his readers, who ought to be mature, spiritual people but were still "infants in Christ" (1 Cor. 3:1–4).

The major content of these unveilings concentrates on eschatology, that is, the end times. How will human history conclude, and what eternal destiny is in store? But this is not the sole content. The inner workings of the cosmos are occasionally the subject of an unveiling of hidden secrets as well. The prime example is *1 En.* 72–82, the Astronomical Book, featuring a lengthy (if a bit tiresome!) tour of the celestial luminaries and a mechanical explanation for various weather phenomena. A closer reading of the text, however, suggests that even this digression into cosmological clockwork grows out of a deeper dispute over the proper calendar rather than fascination with the workings of the cosmos. In short, a solar calendar rather than a lunar calendar should be followed, and the tedious explanation for how it all works is part of a demonstration for the correctness of the solar option, which in turn significantly influences Enoch's eschatology. Seen in its larger context, such cosmological passages actually appear to be secondary to the primary focus on revealing eschatological secrets.

A primary focus of apocalyptic literature centers on the fate of the righteous and the wicked. Heaven and hell are matters of perennial interest to human beings, and in this regard apocalyptists do not disappoint. For example, extensive tours of heaven and hell feature in *1–2 Enoch*, and the book of Revelation itself concludes with a terrifying glimpse of the lake of fire and a grand tour of the new Jerusalem (chaps. 20–22). But also figuring prominently in apocalyptic texts are ascents to the majestic throne room of God. The Enoch traditions (*1 En.* 14) and the book of Revelation (chaps. 4–5) highlight throne-room scenes as a centerpiece of their respective revelations. The sovereignty of God is thus visually reinforced by picturing the entire cosmos in orbit around God's throne.

Jewish apocalyptic eschatology falls into two general types. On the one hand, some eschatological scenarios conceive the future in this-worldly terms. What will be is a greatly enhanced version of what has been: the end recapitulates the beginning. The end times involve a return to the pristine times of the primeval world. Redeploying ancient creation mythology, apocalyptic eschatology envisions a return to the garden of Eden. The best example of this imagery is the book of Revelation where the motifs of Gen. 1–3 reappear (Rev. 21–22). Such a patterning of human history is a standard feature of apocalyptic thought. If the Davidic dynasty disappointed by its covenant unfaithfulness and descent into degradation, the future kingdom fully actualizes the aspirations of prophet and poet for an ideal king and ideal age, a sort of Jewish Camelot (Amos 9:11–15; Isa. 2:1–5; 11:1–16; 32:1–8; Pss. 2; 72; 89).

Most often, Jewish apocalyptic literature demonstrates a radical break with the prophetic vision of the future and reimages it in transcendental terms: "Evil was so monstrous and entrenched that a mere restoration was not sufficient. Nothing short of transformation could eradicate the damage done" (Helyer, *Jewish Literature*, 119). This eschatological escalation is already adumbrated in Isa. 65:17, wherein the prophet envisions "new heavens and a new earth." Isaiah's new earth, however, is still recognizably continuous with the present world order.

To this should be compared *2 Baruch*, in which the age to come displays radical discontinuity with the present age. The NT emphasizes an other-worldly eschatology in 2 Pet. 3:10–13, where fire dissolves the present heavens and earth before the new heavens and a new earth appears. And in John's vision of the end, "the first heaven and the first earth had passed away, and the sea was no more" (Rev. 21:1). Paul simply affirms "the glory about to be revealed" (Rom. 8:18) and a time that brings "unity to all things in heaven and on earth under Christ" (Eph. 1:10 NIV).

Social Location and Function of Apocalypticism

Perhaps the most problematic issue concerns the specific social environment that produced and nurtured apocalypticism. Attempts to trace this complex movement back to a particular socioreligious group from the Second Temple period—such as the Pharisees, Essenes, Sadducees, or Zealots—have failed to win consensus. As a default position, many are content to postulate various anonymous apocalyptic groups whose existence is only inferred from the surviving apocalyptic literature. Though plausible, the highly subjective basis for this view is not always forthrightly acknowledged, with the results that supposition often becomes axiomatic and nondocumented apocalyptic sects tend to proliferate.

It is widely held that apocalypticism arises within groups who are oppressed and marginalized. But even this generalization has been called into question. It is conceivable that an apocalyptist could emerge from socially elite circles if for some reason that person became deeply disillusioned with the status quo. For example, although Leo Tolstoy was by no means an apocalyptist, he radically turned away from his aristocratic roots and identified with the poor and downtrodden peasants. Such may also have been the case for some who identified with apocalypticism. In spite of this caveat, modern sociological research on apocalyptic communities suggests a disenfranchised minority as the most likely locus for such thinking.

In this regard, the DSS have played a leading role in the debate over the social location of apocalypticism. Despite continuing challenges, a majority of scholars identify the Essenes as the community responsible for the distinctive sectarian literature emanating from the Qumran caves. Based on the number of copies found, the book of *1 Enoch* appears to have been a favorite of this community, as was the book of Daniel. In addition, fragments of previously unknown writings reflecting apocalyptic ideas were discovered in the Qumran library. The sectarian scrolls reveal a group of Jewish dissidents who were harassed by the Jerusalem temple priesthood. They bitterly condemn their opponents and articulate a well-defined scenario for the end time, which has either begun or is imminent. In short, they constitute a socioreligious group displaying characteristics that modern sociologists associate with an apocalyptic sect (see further A. Collins, "Apocalypses").

On the other hand, Pharisaism cannot be ruled out as another legitimate location for the rise of apocalypticism. Although it is true that in the aftermath of the Jewish revolts against Rome (AD 66–73, 132–135) the successors of Pharisaism (the Tannaim of ca. AD 20–200) distanced themselves from apocalypticism, its presence prior to this national disaster seems fairly certain. A prime witness is none other than the apostle Paul, a self-identified Pharisee (Phil. 3:5; cf. Gal. 1:14; see also Acts 23:6), whose eschatological views, especially affirming bodily resurrection (cf. Acts 23:6–10), were surely influenced by his Pharisaic roots (e.g., 1 Cor. 15; cf. 2 Maccabees; see Helyer, *Jewish Literature*, 163–64).

The function of apocalyptic literature is a by-product of its social location. In many ways, these writings are tracts for hard times in which the faithful are exhorted and encouraged to hang on in the midst of opposition and persecution. Appeal to the sovereign God, whose plan for the end is certain and imminent and involves reward for the faithful and punishment for the wicked, is a primary theme of this insider literature. Revelation provides a classic example, with repeated exhortations to patient endurance (1:9; 2:9–11; 13:9–10; 14:12–13; 16:15; 21:6–8).

Bibliography

Allison, Dale C., Jr. "The Eschatology of Jesus." Pages 267–302 in *The Origins of Apocalypticism in Judaism and Christianity*. Edited by John J. Collins. Vol. 1 of *The Encyclopedia of Apocalypticism*. Edited by John J. Collins, Bernard McGinn, and Stephen J. Stein. New York: Continuum, 2000. Written by a recognized authority on historical Jesus research, this essay locates Jesus squarely within Jewish apocalypticism.

Aune, David E. *Apocalypticism, Prophecy, and Magic in Early Christianity*. Grand Rapids: Baker Academic, 2008. Collected essays on various aspects of apocalypticism in the NT, with special attention given to the book of Revelation.

Aune, David, T. J. Geddert, and C. A. Evans. "Apocalypticism." Pages 45–58 in *Dictionary of New Testament Background*. Edited by Craig A. Evans and Stanley E. Porter. Downers Grove, IL: InterVarsity, 2000. Perhaps the best introduction to the topic of apocalypticism and the NT.

Charles, R. H., ed. *Apocrypha and Pseudepigrapha of the Old Testament in English*. 2 vols. Oxford: Clarendon, 1913. Classic but dated introduction to and translation of the known sources prior to the discovery of the DSS and related finds.

Charlesworth, James H., ed. *Apocalyptic Literature and Testaments*. Vol. 1 of *The Old Testament Pseudepigrapha*. New York: Doubleday, 1983. Standard English translation of the relevant Jewish apocalyptic literature.

Collins, Adela Yarbro. "Apocalypses and Apocalypticism: Early Christian." *ABD* 1:288–92. Helpful discussion of the apocalyptic passages in the NT, the apocalypse of John, and the later, postapostolic Christian and gnostic apocalypses.

Collins, John J. "Apocalyptic Literature." Pages 40–45 in *Dictionary of New Testament Background*. Edited by Craig A. Evans and Stanley E. Porter. Downers Grove, IL: InterVarsity,

2000. Concise treatment of terminology, background, and description of Jewish and Christian apocalyptic literature.

————. "Apocalyptic Literature." Pages 345–70 in *Early Judaism and Its Modern Interpreters*. Edited by R. A. Kraft and G. W. E. Nickelsburg. Philadelphia: Fortress, 1986. Masterful survey and description of the corpus of apocalyptic literature.

————. "Eschatology." Pages 256–61 in vol.1 of *Encyclopedia of the Dead Sea Scrolls*. Edited by Lawrence H. Schiffman and James C. VanderKam. 2 vols. New York: Oxford University Press, 2000.

————. "From Prophecy to Apocalypticism: The Expectation of the End." Pages 129–61 in *The Origins of Apocalypticism in Judaism and Christianity*. Edited by John J. Collins. Vol. 1 of *The Encyclopedia of Apocalypticism*. Edited by John J. Collins, Bernard McGinn, and Stephen J. Stein. New York: Continuum, 2000. Important essay surveying the history of Jewish apocalypticism, emphasizing the importance of the OT prophetic tradition as the primary factor in its genesis.

————. "Towards the Morphology of a Genre." *Semeia* 14 (1979): 1–20. Introduction to a collection of essays reporting on the work of the Apocalypse Group of the Society of Biblical Literature Genres Project.

Collins, John J., Bernard McGinn, and Stephen J. Stein, eds. *The Encyclopedia of Apocalypticism in Judaism and Christianity*. 3 vols. New York: Continuum, 2000. Definitive dictionary by an interdisciplinary team of scholars addressing the ancient, medieval, and modern phenomena of apocalypticism. A wealth of information and a required resource for those who wish to study apocalypticism in depth. Highly recommended.

Collins, John J., and Daniel C. Harlow, eds. *The Eerdmans Dictionary of Early Judaism*. Grand Rapids: Eerdmans, 2010. Concise, up-to-date treatment of early Judaism, including an important article on apocalypticism. Highly recommended.

Elliott, J. K., ed. *The Apocryphal New Testament: A Collection of Apocryphal Christian Literature in an English Translation Based upon M. R. James*. Oxford: Clarendon, 1993. Standard resource for the Christian apocalypses.

Hanson, Paul D. "Apocalyptic Literature." Pages 465–88 in *The Hebrew Bible and Its Modern Interpreters*. Edited by D. A. Knight and G. M. Tucker. SBLBMI 1. Philadelphia: Fortress, 1985. Classic essay that describes and defines apocalyptic literature and argues that OT prophecy was the formative factor in its rise.

————. "Apocalypticism." Pages 28–34 in *The Interpreter's Dictionary of the Bible: Supplementary Volume*. Edited by Keith Crim. Nashville: Abingdon, 1976.

Helyer, Larry R. *Exploring Jewish Literature of the Second Temple Period*. Downers Grove, IL: InterVarsity, 2002. Entry-level textbook that discusses the relevance of apocalyptic literature for reading the NT.

————. *The Witness of Jesus, Paul and John: An Exploration in Biblical Theology*. Downers Grove, IL: InterVarsity, 2008. Entry-level textbook in which apocalypticism is discussed as a formative factor in understanding NT theology.

Jokiranta, Jutta. "Social-Scientific Approaches to the Dead Sea Scrolls." Pages 246–63 in *Rediscovering the Dead Sea Scrolls*. Edited by Maxine L. Grossman. Grand Rapids: Eerdmans, 2010. Examines the contribution of social-scientific methods for understanding the apocalypticism of the community responsible for the DSS.

Kreitzer, L. J. "Apocalyptic, Apocalypticism." Pages 55–68 in *Dictionary of the Later New Testament and Its Developments*. Edited by Ralph P. Martin and Peter H. Davids. Downers Grove, IL: InterVarsity, 1997. Highly recommended overview of the leading issues necessary for understanding apocalypticism and the NT.

Ladd, George E. "Apocalyptic Literature." *ISBE* 1:151–61. Classic and still valuable treatment that defines, describes, and surveys the Jewish apocalyptic sources.

———. *The Presence of the Future: the Eschatology of Biblical Realism*. Grand Rapids: Eerdmans, 1974. Classic statement of inaugurated eschatology by a leading evangelical scholar.

Nickelsburg, George W. E. "Apocalyptic Texts." *EDSS* 1:29–35. A leading authority examines the fragments of *1 Enoch* and Daniel from Qumran and contrasts them with the Ben Sira texts, calling into question any indebtedness to OT wisdom traditions in the genesis of apocalyptic literature.

Russell, D. S. *Divine Disclosure: An Introduction to Jewish Apocalyptic*. London: SCM, 1992. An internationally recognized authority provides a useful overview of apocalyptic literature.

VanderKam, James. "Messianism and Apocalypticism." Pages 193–228 in *The Origins of Apocalypticism in Judaism and Christianity*. Edited by John J. Collins. Vol. 1 of *The Encyclopedia of Apocalypticism*. Edited by John J. Collins, Bernard McGinn, and Stephen J. Stein. New York: Continuum, 2000. A leading expert on the DSS discusses messianism in Jewish apocalyptic sources. Provides important comparative material for NT messianism.

Wright, Benjamin G., III, and Lawrence M. Wills, eds. *Conflicted Boundaries in Wisdom and Apocalypticism*. Atlanta: Society of Biblical Literature, 2005. Symposium focused on exploring the complex origins of apocalypticism. Open to the influence of the OT wisdom traditions as a factor in its genesis.

Wright, N. T. *Jesus and the Victory of God*. Minneapolis: Fortress, 1996. An internationally known NT scholar seeks to explicate Jesus' mission against the backdrop of Jewish apocalyptic thought. His approach differs significantly from that of Dale Allison.

22

Synagogue and Sanhedrin

KENNETH D. LITWAK

Information concerning the two institutions of synagogue and Sanhedrin, both of which have important roles in the NT, comes from multiple sources, both literary and archaeological. In addition to the NT itself, we have Jewish sources in Greek, including Philo and Josephus; rabbinic literature, especially the Mishnah and the Talmud; the OT Apocrypha and Pseudepigrapha; and numerous inscriptions. Rabbinic sources provide the most information on synagogues and the Sanhedrin, but they must be used cautiously. This is because rabbinic works probably portray the Second Temple Sanhedrin and synagogues the way later rabbis thought these two institutions should be, not as they actually were. Therefore, rabbinic texts are most helpful when they are corroborated by Second Temple sources. In addition to literary sources, evidence from inscriptions and buildings contribute to our knowledge of Second Temple synagogues. Ongoing scholarly debate about both of these institutions reflects in part differing assessments of the significance of what the pre–AD 70 sources do not tell us.

The Synagogue

The synagogue, as a place for Jews to gather especially on the Sabbath day, appears numerous times in the NT, Josephus, and Philo. Jesus both taught and performed mighty deeds in synagogues, such as his programmatic statement about the nature

264

of his ministry in terms of Isa. 61:1–2 in the synagogue of Nazareth (Luke 4:16–30) and the casting out of a demon in a synagogue in Capernaum (Mark 1:21–27). According to the book of Acts, Paul sought out synagogues whenever he went to a new city or town to begin preaching the gospel (e.g., 13:14; 14:1; 17:1).

Terminology

The Greek term *synagōgē*, carried over into English as "synagogue," refers to a gathering together and is used both for a place (e.g., Matt. 9:35) and for a gathering of people (James 2:2), which is the primary sense of the word in the Septuagint. The NT generally uses *synagōgē* in a literal way, but metaphorical uses also occur (e.g., Rev. 2:9; 3:9). *Proseuchē* was commonly used by Jews (e.g., Philo) for a building, a "prayer house," to which Jews went for Sabbath activities and thus likely refers to a synagogue. It may have referred also to an informal gathering place for prayer. Acts 16:13 and 16 are the only references to a *proseuchē* as a place of prayer in the NT. Some commentators suggest that the *proseuchē* in Philippi was an informal place for prayer because there were fewer than ten Jewish males in Philippi, the minimum for a synagogue, but this deduction may depend too heavily on a later rabbinic tradition.

Some argue that most NT references to a *synagōgē* can be understood as referring to either a building or a gathering of Jews. Although this is technically correct in most cases, the main usage was probably when referring to a building (cf. Luke 7:5). For example, using similar wording, Mark 1:21 speaks of Jesus entering a *synagōgē* and 1:29 of Jesus entering a house. Jesus' entering a *synagōgē* and encountering a man possessed by a demon in the *synagōgē* (Mark 1:23–28) makes more sense if *synagōgē* refers to a building.

Second Temple literature also appears to use synagōgē to refer to an assembly of Jews, which is generally in a building, but that building need not have been built specifically for religious purposes. Some scholars have asserted that there were no pre–AD 70 synagogue buildings, but both the literary and archaeological evidence strongly challenge this claim.

Origin

The origin of the synagogue as a place for Jews to gather for Sabbath activities is unclear. The synagogue may have originated after the return from the Babylonian exile or perhaps in Egypt as a way to promote the Jewish community. With the change to Hellenistic-style cities (beginning around 300 BC), which had no city gate (the usual place of meeting for commerce, legal matters, and public assemblies for Jews; cf. 2 Kings 7:1; Neh. 8:1), city-gate functions appear to have moved indoors to the synagogue. The references to a *proseuchē* in third-century BC inscriptions and papyri in Egypt are the earliest clear evidence for the existence of synagogues for Sabbath activities. For example, an inscription dated to 246–221 BC states, "On behalf of King Ptolemy, son of Ptolemy, and Queen Berenice, his wife, and his sister, and their children, the Jews of Crocodilopolis dedicated the prayer hall

22.1. Fourth-century AD synagogue at Capernaum, the center of Jesus' ministry in Galilee. This synagogue was built on top of a basalt foundation, which may have been the location (or near the location) of the synagogue where Jesus taught (Mark 1:21–28).

[*proseuchē*]" (Runesson, *Source Book*, 193, no. 150 = CPJ 3:1532a). Note that it is dedicated on behalf of the king and queen, not to them. Jews explicitly or implicitly dedicated a *proseuchē* "to God most high," as in an inscription found at Attribis, dated in the range of the second to first century BC (Runesson, *Source Book*, 193, no. 151 = CIJ 2:1443). Although *proseuchē* refers to "prayer," in several texts it is clear that it is used of a building for prayer, likely a synagogue. For example, Philo speaks of statues being placed in the *proseuchai* (the plural of *proseuchē*; *Flacc.* 41) and of the destruction of the *proseuchai* (*Flacc.* 45).

Functions

The synagogue served multiple purposes, such as Sabbath activities, social gatherings, legal proceedings, and political meetings in primarily Jewish cities and towns (cf. Josephus, *Ant* 2.235, 258, 259–61; *J.W.* 1.180, 277, 293; Philo, *Legat.* 156).

Although the formal synagogue liturgy described in rabbinic texts might not have been practiced in Second Temple synagogues, Sabbath activities included public prayer and the reading and study of the Torah, as stated by Josephus (*Ag. Ap.* 2.176), Philo (*Legat.* 156), and the NT (e.g., Acts 15:21). Luke-Acts show that the Prophets were read in synagogues in the first century AD (cf. Luke 4:17; Acts 13:15), a practice that is otherwise unknown outside the NT until after the destruction of the Jerusalem temple in AD 70. Second Temple sources also make it clear that, after the Torah was read, someone would offer a sermon or interpretation of the biblical passage (cf. Philo, *Prob.* 80–84; *Legat.* 311; Luke 4:16–30; Acts 13:15–41 [specifically after the reading of the Law and the Prophets]). Synagogues had leaders, an *archisynagōgos* (cf. Mark 5:22, 35, 36, 38; Luke 13:14; Acts 13:5; 18:8, 17)—a term that appears primarily in the NT and inscriptions in the Second Temple period. This person probably officiated during religious meetings and may have been responsible for the building. At least one *archisynagōgos* oversaw the construction of a synagogue. The Theodotus inscription (found in Jerusalem and dated by L. Levine to the first century AD) reads, "Theodotus, son of Vettenus, a ruler of the synagogue [*archisynagōgos*], son of a ruler of the synagogue [*archisynagōgos*], and grandson of a ruler of the synagogue [*archisynagōgos*], built the synagogue for the reading of the Law and for teaching of the commandments" (Runesson, *Source Book*, 52, no. 26 = *CIJ* 2:1404).

What practices of Jewish worship were included in synagogues on the Sabbath, such as the communal singing of prayers (e.g., the Psalms), is a matter of considerable debate. For the most part, Second Temple literature does not speak of worship among those gathered on the Sabbath, but evidence from the DSS and from Pseudo-Philo indicates that there was worship on the Sabbath.

Archaeological Evidence

Several sites in Palestine and the Diaspora have been identified as synagogues from the Second Temple period, such as at Delos, Masada, Herodium, Kiryet Sefer, Gamla, and Modiin. Almost all the Palestinian synagogues excavated so far have similar architecture, including square benches arranged concentrically, plastered interior walls, and a central open space where a leader or a reader of Scripture could stand. Another common feature is a series of columns that interfere with seeing the central space (done perhaps in imitation of the Jerusalem temple, as visitors there were likely "left with the dominant visual experience of looking between columns to see the activity in any court" of the temple (Strange, "Ancient Texts," 41). This is visible in the Masada synagogue (see photo).

These pre–AD 70 structures, and indeed most buildings identified as synagogues, exhibit a similar architectural plan. Pre–AD 70 synagogues existed in the Diaspora also but generally did not follow the same design as those in Galilee or Judea. Fourth- and fifth-century AD synagogues have features not found in pre–AD 70 synagogues, particularly ornate mosaic floors and wall decorations that contain pictures of biblical scenes (e.g., Beth Alpha) and the twelve signs of the Zodiac (e.g., Dura Europa). This has led some to deny the existence of pre–AD 70 synagogue buildings; for example, the building at Gamla has been identified by some as a private house. However, those sites identified as pre–AD 70 synagogues are quite different in design when compared with private houses. The evidence suggests that the synagogue was a place where Jews gathered at least on the Sabbath for worship in the Second Temple period.

22.2. A synagogue at Masada.

The Sanhedrin

In the literature of Second Temple Judaism, the term "sanhedrin" (*synedrion*) might refer to a governing body, such as a town council (cf. Matt. 5:22?; 10:17), to that council's meeting place (cf. Luke 22:66?), or to the council meeting itself. In the NT, however, the term is used primarily with reference to the Sanhedrin in Jerusalem (e.g., Matt. 26:59), the ruling body for Jews in much of the Second Temple period. By far the most detailed descriptions of the Sanhedrin and how it functioned are in rabbinic literature, especially the *Sanhedrin* tractates in the Mishnah and Talmud. Josephus and the NT sometimes provide important information that differs from what later rabbinic materials assert. For example, Josephus and the NT speak of a single ruling council, whereas *m. Sanh.* 1.6 speaks of two with different jurisdictions. Acts shows the Sanhedrin as consisting of the high priest, Sadducees, and Pharisees (Acts 23:1–6), while *m. Sanh.* 4.3–4 indicates that the Sanhedrin consisted of sages and their disciples. Some scholars think the Mishnah provides a fairly accurate picture of how the Sanhedrin functioned in the first century AD (e.g., Mantel, *Sanhedrin*). Others deny all evidence that such an institution even existed (e.g., Goodman, *Ruling*, 113). Positions between these two extremes focus on the evidence in Josephus, the NT, and other Second Temple texts that portray a central Jewish judicial council, consisting primarily of Jerusalem aristocracy, at least during the time of the procurators (AD 6–66) and probably through most of the Second Temple period, though its status and functions probably varied over time.

Terminology

"Sanhedrin" is from a Hebrew term that transliterates the Greek word *synedrion* (cf. *m. Soṭah* 9.11), and it often refers to the primary Jewish governing body in Jerusalem or to local councils or governing boards (cf. Matt. 10:17; Mark 13:9). Josephus refers to a council (Sanhedrin) led by the high priest that met in Jerusalem and was responsible for legal decisions. For example, Josephus writes that if a local council cannot decide a case, the matter should be referred to the high priest, the prophet, and the "council of elders" in the "holy city," Jerusalem (*Ant.* 4.218). He uses the phrase "council of elders" in multiple ways but often equates this council with a supreme Jewish governing body that met in Jerusalem (Josephus, *Ant.* 13.166; *J.W.* 7.412). Although only rabbinic sources speak of the Great Sanhedrin, *Bet Din ha-Gadol* (literally "the great courthouse"), by the first century AD the term *synedrion* had become virtually synonymous with *the* Sanhedrin in Jerusalem, with final judicial authority in Jewish legal matters. Other terms refer to local councils or courts and to the Jerusalem Sanhedrin. *Gerousia* ("senate," "council of elders"), a term not commonly used of ruling bodies in Hellenistic cities, is mentioned in 2 Macc. 4:43–47 as having been established by Jason in Jerusalem. Josephus (*Ant.* 12.138) uses the term *gerousia* to designate a council of elders in Jerusalem during the reign of Antiochus (223–187 BC). The only NT occurrence of this term is in Acts 5:21, where it is found together with *synedrion*. One way to translate the phrase in question would be to take *gerousia* as an explanation for Luke's gentile readers of the Jewish term *synedrion*: "They called together the Sanhedrin, that is, the council of elders." The term is common in the Apocrypha (e.g., Jdt. 4:8; 2 Macc. 11:27) and Josephus (e.g., *Ant.* 13.166). *Boulē* is also used for the council or senate in Jerusalem (Josephus, *Ant.* 20.11; cf. Luke 23:50: Joseph of Arimathea was "a member of the council [*bouleutēs*]") and local courts. Luke also refers to the Sanhedrin as a "council of elders" (*presbyterion*; cf. Luke 22:66; Acts 22:5).

Origin

The origin of a ruling council of priests and other Jewish aristocrats is unknown. Part of the difficulty lies in knowing whether a Second Temple reference to a council refers to a local court or to the central Jewish court for legal matters in Jerusalem. It seems likely that the Sanhedrin as a Jewish supreme court did not exist before Hasmonean times and that before then, a number of local councils and courts existed. Herod the Great destroyed much of the power of the Sanhedrin, but under the subsequent rule of the Roman proconsuls, the council grew again in power, and the council was convened by the high priest as needed. Based on the evidence from Josephus and Acts, the Sanhedrin was made up of the high priest, the chief priests, Sadducees, and Pharisees (Acts 5:21, 34). The rabbinic picture of a scribe-led Sanhedrin, in which points of biblical interpretation were debated (cf. *m. Ḥag.* 2.2), reflects later conditions when the Mishnah was written and almost certainly does not reflect the pre–AD 70 Sanhedrin. From AD 6 to 66, the Sanhedrin met with the permission of the Roman procurators, and according to Acts 22:30, Roman officials could also order the Sanhedrin to convene.

Nature and Functions

The Mishnah and the Talmud describe the "Great Sanhedrin"—including its size (seventy-one members), where it met (the House of Hewn Stone), and the types of issues it ruled on (esp. capital punishment), as opposed to lesser councils that it created (cf. *m. Sanh.* 4.1). Some scholars, depending on rabbinic texts to the fullest extent, have developed complex pictures of at least two Sanhedrins, one with seventy-one members and one with twenty-three members. However, attempts to reconcile Second Temple sources with later rabbinic literature have generally proved to be unsatisfactory (see Grabbe, *Judaic Religion*). The depictions of the Great Sanhedrin in rabbinic works appear to be "ideal" descriptions of how the Sanhedrin *ought* to have functioned and therefore provide limited information about the Sanhedrin in the world of the NT.

As a result, in the main Greek sources—Josephus, the NT, and the Apocrypha—we should not expect to find literary portrayals of a Jewish supreme court that closely match rabbinic descriptions. For example, contrary to the Mishnah (cf. *m. Ḥag.* 2.2; *m. 'Abot* 1), the reigning high priest presided over the Sanhedrin. Roman procurators would not normally have involved themselves in Jewish religious questions, as in the case of the whole Sanhedrin's deciding whether Jesus had committed a crime against the temple or God (Matt. 26:59–66). According to Josephus, only the Sanhedrin could decide on capital punishment (but not carry it out, under Roman rule), and he records a communication with the Hasmonean king–high priest Hyrcanus in which Jews complained that Herod had killed someone without the Sanhedrin's approval (*Ant.* 14.167). Procurators, such as Pontius Pilate or Felix, depended on Jewish courts or councils to handle many administrative matters, such as the collection of taxes.

See also "Jesus Research and Archaeology."

Bibliography

Catto, Stephen K. *Reconstructing the First-Century Synagogue: A Critical Analysis of Current Research*. London: T&T Clark, 2007. Reviews the debate over the existence and nature of first-century AD synagogues and affirms the general value of the Luke-Acts depiction of synagogues.

Goodman, Martin. *The Ruling Class of Judaea: The Origins of the Jewish Revolt against Rome A.D. 66–70.* Cambridge: Cambridge University Press, 1987. Argues that *the* Sanhedrin did not exist during the Second Temple period.

Grabbe, Lester L. *Judaic Religion in the Second Temple Period: Belief and Practice from the Exile to Yavneh.* London: Routledge, 2000. Describes both the chronological history, mainly through canonical and extracanonical texts, and special topics, such as the temple, Scripture, and "messiahs."

Levine, Lee I. *The Ancient Synagogue: The First Thousand Years.* New Haven: Yale University Press, 2005. Detailed treatment of archaeological and literary information on synagogues in both Palestine and the Diaspora.

Mantel, Hugo. *Studies in the History of the Sanhedrin.* Cambridge, MA: Harvard University Press, 1965. Examines rabbinic and Greek sources on the Sanhedrin, understanding the institution primarily in terms of rabbinic portraits, which he sees as fairly reliable.

Mason, Steve. "Chief Priests, Sadducees, Pharisees, and Sanhedrin in Acts." Pages 115–77 in *The Book of Acts in Its Palestinian Setting.* Edited by Richard Bauckham. A1CS 4. Grand Rapids: Eerdmans, 1995. Describes the narrative presentation of the chief priests, Sadducees, Pharisees, and Sanhedrin in Luke-Acts and Josephus, concluding that there are several major points of agreement and shared assumptions, without claiming this as a historical reconstruction.

Runesson, Anders, et al., eds. *Ancient Synagogue from Its Origins to 200 C.E.: A Source Book.* AJEC 72. Leiden: Brill, 2007. Contains texts, from both literature and inscriptions, regarding synagogues. For each, it gives the original text, a translation, a likely date, and bibliography.

Sanders, E. P. *Judaism: Practice and Belief; 63 BCE–66 CE.* Philadelphia: Trinity Press International, 1992. Covers several areas of Jewish life and religion in the late Second Temple period.

Schürer, Emil. *The History of the Jewish People in the Age of Jesus Christ (175 BC–AD 135).* Revised and edited by Geza Vermes, Fergus Millar, and Martin Goodman. Revised English ed. 3 vols. in 4 parts. Edinburgh: T&T Clark, 1987. Covers a wide array of historical, cultural, and religious aspects of Jewish life in the Second Temple period, though at times overly reliant on rabbinic traditions.

Strange, James F. "Ancient Texts, Archaeology as Text, and the Problem of the First-Century Synagogue." Pages 27–41 in *Evolution of the Synagogue: Problems and Progress.* Edited by Howard Clark Kee and Lynn H. Cohick. Harrisburg, PA: Trinity Press International, 1999. Diverse essays on the development of synagogues throughout the Greco-Roman world. Authors take opposite positions, such as Kee (who denies that there were any pre–AD 70 synagogue buildings) and Strange (who affirms that there probably were at least four).

———. "Archaeology and Ancient Synagogues up to about 200 C.E." Pages 37–62 in *The Ancient Synagogue from Its Origins until 200 C.E.: Papers Presented at an International Conference at Lund University, October 14–17, 2001.* Edited by Birger Olsson and Magnus Zetterholm. Stockholm: Almqvist & Wiksell, 2003. A collection of several articles on many aspects of early synagogues, including architecture, artwork, and liturgy.

23

Jews in the Diaspora

DAVID A. DESILVA

The whole land and sea are full of Jews.

Sib. Or. 3.271

They have reached every town, and it is hard to find a place in the world
whither this race has not penetrated and where it has not obtained a hold.

Strabo, as quoted in Josephus, Ant. 14.115

In the first century AD, the majority of Jews lived not in the land of their ancestral tribes but in the lands of the gentile nations. Their geographic distribution is often referred to in the Jewish Scriptures and other Second Temple literature as a "scattering,"[1] whence the Greek label *diaspora*, a "dispersal." Many Jews were compelled to leave their homeland, exiled to resettle in the heartland of their conquerors. Many more chose to dwell in the Diaspora, whether because their parents

1. See, e.g., Lev. 26:33; Deut. 28:64; 30:3; Ps. 44:11; Jer. 9:16; 30:11; 31:10; Ezek. 22:15; 36:19; Tob. 13:3, 5; Sir. 48:15; Bar. 2:13; 3:8; James 1:1; 1 Pet. 1:1.

and parents' parents had built a life in a foreign land or because the prospects for making a better life for themselves and their families prompted new emigration. The latter impulse received fresh impetus with Alexander's unification of the lands from Macedonia to Babylon and back around to Egypt, the expansion of international trade and the infrastructure required to sustain the same, and the growth of Greek as a language potentially connecting people from such diverse regions. In this context it is important to remember that "Diaspora" is not an exclusively Jewish phenomenon: "The Jewish diaspora . . . met a Greek dispersion everywhere, from Sardis to Elephantine. There were similarly an Aramaic and a Phoenician diaspora in Egypt and surely elsewhere" (Bickerman, *Jews*, 37). Although the largest populations of expatriate Jews were to be found in a handful of major Diaspora centers like Alexandria, Syrian Antioch, and Babylon, Jewish communities were formed in cities across the Mediterranean in almost every region and province (see Acts 2:9–11; Philo, *Legat.* 214, 281–83; *Flacc.* 45–46; Josephus, *J.W.* 7.43; *Ant.* 14.115).

The Formation of the Jewish Diaspora

The Jewish Diaspora appears to have been born when part of the northern tribes of Israel was deported to Assyria (721 BC) and a large number of Judean elites and others were deported to Babylon (597 and 587 BC). What began under compulsion persisted by choice. When the opportunity to return to their ancestral homeland presented itself under Sheshbazzar and Zerubbabel (538 and 520 BC; see 2 Chron. 36:22–23; Ezra 1:1–4), many Jews elected to remain in Babylon and its environs. Babylon would remain a thriving Diaspora center, one that would exercise a strong influence over the practice of Judaism in the homeland itself (seen in the editing of the Torah in Babylon; the work of Ezra, Nehemiah, and Hillel; and the ascendancy of the Babylonian Talmud over the Jerusalem Talmud). There are signs that Jews exercised some level of self-governance under the auspices of the Babylonian and Persian rulers. Texts speak of "elders" or "elders of the exile" (Susanna; Jer. 29:1), while Neh. 11:24 refers to Petahiah, who "was at the king's hand in all matters concerning the people," a court official who oversaw the affairs of his people but reported to the king (Bickerman, *Jews*, 50).

A second major center of Jewish Diaspora was Egypt, particularly the seacoast metropolis of Alexandria. For the most part, the Egyptian Diaspora was formed voluntarily. The former "house of bondage" became a place of asylum for many refugees fleeing Judea in the time of Nebuchadnezzar's conquest of Judea (see Jer. 43:1–13). Jewish soldiers and their families were an important part of a military colony established in Elephantine by the pharaoh in the sixth or fifth century BC, enjoying their own temple for the practice of their sacrificial cult. There is some evidence of syncretism among these Jews—for example, swearing oaths by the God of Israel alongside other gods or sending money to support the cults of other gods. They also appear to have ignored some stipulations of the Torah, such as those regarding not lending at interest (though this was also true in Jerusalem; Bickerman, *Jews*, 44–45, 424).

Ptolemy I greatly added to the Jewish population of Egypt by bringing back tens of thousands of Jews as slaves and prisoners of war after the initial splitting of and skirmishing over Alexander's empire, though his successor, Ptolemy II, freed the majority of these (Tcherikover, *Hellenistic Civilization*, 269–73; *Let. Aris.* 12–14). Voluntary migration continued under their dynasty, with Egypt as a growing "land of opportunity," whose potential was avidly developed by its Greek pharaohs. Migration from Palestine was also fueled by the Hellenization crisis and Maccabean revolt. It was during this period (around 160 BC) that Onias IV, son of the murdered high priest Onias III, came to Leontopolis with his party, which built a temple where the displaced Onias IV could exercise his birthright (Modrzejewski, *Jews*, 121–33; Tcherikover, *Hellenistic Civilization*, 275–81). Jewish military involvement in internecine conflicts between claimants to the Ptolemaic throne led to a brief period of repression under Ptolemy VIII Euergetes; together with their later support of Roman forces moving into Egypt, this may be an important factor in the development of anti-Judaism in Egypt, especially in Alexandria, where it erupted in violent pogroms in AD 38 and 66 (Josephus, *Ant.* 13.65, 284–87, 349; *Ag. Ap.* 2.49–55; Smallwood, *Jews*, 223–24; Tcherikover, *Hellenistic Civilization*, 281–82). The majority of Egypt's Jews lived in Alexandria, concentrated in two of Alexandria's five districts (Philo, *Flacc.* 55), though gentiles lived within those districts as well, and Jews lived throughout the other districts. Jews were found in every occupation, from military and government service to agriculture, trade, commerce, and crafts (Tcherikover, *Hellenistic Civilization*, 334–42).

A Jewish presence was established in Cyrenaica (modern-day Libya) when Ptolemy I sent a large number of Jews into Cyrene, probably as military personnel. Nonindigenous soldiers could better serve the king's interests where native patriotism might give rise to conflicts of interests on the part of local recruits (Josephus, *Ag. Ap.* 2.44; Bickerman, *Jews*, 89–90; Smallwood, *Jews*, 120). By the time Strabo writes about this territory in the second century BC, the Jewish presence is strong enough for "Jews" to be named as a fourth group of inhabitants alongside "citizens, peasants, and resident aliens" (quoted in Josephus, *Ant.* 14.115). Military resettlement was also responsible for a significant migration of Jews into Asia Minor. After acquiring Lydia and Phrygia, Antiochus III resettled about two thousand Jewish families from Mesopotamia there to serve as a peacekeeping force on his behalf sometime between 210 and 205 BC, providing them with land grants and allowing the settlers to live by their ancestral laws (Josephus, *Ant.* 12.148–53; Bickerman, *Jews*, 92–93; Tcherikover, *Hellenistic Civilization*, 287). Continued, voluntary migration led to the expansion of Jewish communities in cities throughout those regions and beyond (Josephus, *Ant.* 12.125–28; 14.185–267; 16.6, 27–61, 160–78).

Jews settled in Syrian Antioch as early as the third century BC (Josephus, *Ant.* 12.119; *Ag. Ap.* 2.39), and the proximity of Syria to Judea encouraged migration throughout the region. As in Alexandria, anti-Jewish violence erupted on several occasions in Antioch as well (Josephus, *J.W.* 2.457–60, 477–79; 7.40–62). Less is known about the beginnings of Jewish migration to Greece, though Jewish communities were well established in many of its cities by the early Principate (Philo, *Legat.* 281–82; Acts 16:13; 17:1, 10, 17; 18:4).

Although the origins of the important Jewish community in Rome remain unknown, Rome already had a noticeable Jewish presence by the second century BC. One of the earliest incidents on record is the (temporary) expulsion of Jews from Rome in 139 BC (Valerius Maximus, *Fact. dict. mem.* 1.3.3; Smallwood, *Jews*, 128–30), apparently prompted by the conversion of Romans to the Jewish way of life, something on which the Roman government would continue to frown throughout the Principate. Pompey's military actions in Judea in 63 BC and other early Roman actions in Palestine led to large numbers of Jews being deported to Rome as slaves, though many were apparently manumitted within a generation (Philo, *Legat.* 155; Josephus, *Ant.* 14.70–71, 79, 85, 119–20). By the time of Augustus, the community had grown to such an extent that eight thousand Jews could gather to show support for the request brought by an embassy to Augustus from Judea (Josephus, *Ant.* 17.300). The Jews were once again expelled from Rome by Tiberius in AD 19, probably due to the conversion of some members of the senatorial class, whose defection to un-Roman, eastern superstitions could not be countenanced (Tacitus, *Ann.* 2.85; Josephus, *Ant.* 18.65–84; Dio Cassius, *Hist.* 57.18.5). The action appears to have been part of a larger crackdown on foreign cults and superstitions in the capital.

The banishment was either partial or short lived, for Jews were again present in Rome in large numbers under Caligula and Claudius—and again targets of imperial judicial actions. Sources speak of actions taken against Jews in both AD 41 and 49 (see discussions in Smallwood, *Jews*, 210–16; Barclay, *Jews*, 303–6). The first action, in AD 41, probably involved the banning of Jews' meeting together in Rome after some unrecorded provocation. This ban must have been short term. The second, in AD 49, involved expelling some portion of the Roman Jewish population on account of disturbances within the Jewish community over someone named "Chrestus," by which Suetonius (*Claud.* 25.4; see Acts 18:2) most likely meant "Christos" (mistaking the Greek title for a Latin personal name). In this instance, it seems that Jewish Christian missionaries, who would have occasioned dissension within the Jewish community and at the same time sought to convert good Romans to an eastern superstition, were the catalyst for the trouble. The expulsion could not have been total (Claudius was too fair minded for that), or permanent, as even Priscilla and Aquila were back in Rome by AD 58 (Rom. 16:3). The lingering intolerance for conversion of noble Romans to an eastern superstition and foreign cult appears again toward the end of the first century AD in Domitian's execution or banishment of a few high-ranking Roman converts to Judaism (the charge against them—"atheism"—is telling; Dio Cassius, *Hist.* 67.14.1–3).

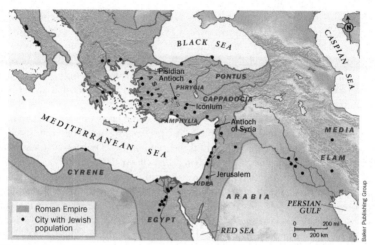

23.1. Locations of the highest concentrations of Jews in Roman provinces in the first century AD.

Diaspora Jews and the Homeland

Jews in the Diaspora remained connected with their ancestral homeland—and thus with one another and with their ethnic identity and distinctiveness—in several practical ways. All male Jews between the ages of twenty and fifty paid the required half-shekel tax in support of the sacrifices performed at the temple, often paying tithes as well (Philo, *Legat.* 156–57, 216, 291, 311–16; *Spec.* 1.77–78; Josephus, *Ant.* 16.162–72; 18.312–13). Far from regarding this as a burden, Diaspora Jews regarded it as a privilege and a duty to be guarded jealously.

Religious pilgrimage, particularly for the festivals of Passover, Pentecost, and Tabernacles (also called "Booths"), brought "innumerable companies of people from a countless variety of cities, some by land and some by sea, from east and west, from the north and from the south" (Philo, *Spec.* 1.69–70;[2] see also Acts 2:9–11). Such pilgrimages were opportunities for Diaspora Jews not only to reconnect with their ancestral land but also to connect with each other, recognizing their common bond and belonging wherever they might live in the known world (Philo, *Spec.* 1.69–70; Josephus, *Ant.* 4.203–4; Barclay, *Jews*, 423).

There was ongoing contact of other kinds as well, both official and informal. The two letters prefixed to 2 Maccabees (1:1–2:18) represent official communiqués from Jerusalem to Egyptian Jews, asking them to observe the newly established festival of Hanukkah (thus affirming their connection with the fortunes of the

2. Translation from C. D. Yonge, *The Works of Philo Judaeus, the Contemporary of Josephus: Translated from the Greek* (4 vols.; London: Henry G. Bohn, 1854–55).

homeland). The historical fiction called 3 Maccabees affirms, in narrative form, that the Diaspora Jewish community shares in the fortunes of the temple as fully and as surely as the native Judean population in 2 Maccabees. The prologue to Ben Sira opens a window on how a private citizen could bring the fruits of a Jerusalem wisdom teacher's career to Alexandria and make it available to any interested reader there. The connectedness of Jews in the Diaspora and in Judea is evident in their mutual interventions—for example, the support shown by Roman Jews for an embassy from Judea, the force with which Judean soldiers in both the Maccabean and Roman periods acted on behalf of Jewish communities in cities in neighboring gentile territories, and the demonstrations and appeal made by Jews throughout the eastern empire in response to Caligula's attempt to erect a cult image in the Jerusalem temple. The last example also shows the symbolic significance of the temple for Jews throughout the eastern Mediterranean, even those who might never see it firsthand.

Texts written by Jews living in Palestine or its environs tend to speak of Diaspora, appropriately from their geographical and historical perspective, as a calamity, a consequence of disobedience to the covenant and of failure to recognize or follow the wisdom of the Torah (e.g., Bar. 2:13–14, 29; 3:8, 10; Tob. 14:4b). They often pray to God to remedy it speedily and "gather" the tribes from the four winds, restoring them to their homeland (Bar. 4:36–37; 5:5–6; Sir. 36:13, 16; Tob. 13:5; 14:5; Pss. Sol. 8.28; 11.1–4; 17.44; 4 Ezra 13.39–48; 2 Bar. 78.7). By contrast, there is little indication that Jews living in the Diaspora regarded their location outside the homeland as a sign of experiencing God's disfavor or covenantal "curse." Josephus (Ant. 4.114–16) interprets the Diaspora as a sign of God's fulfillment of the promises given to Abraham that his descendants will be more numerous than the sands by the sea or the stars in the sky, such that one land will not be able to hold them. In addition to occupying the land promised to them, they "shall live on islands and every continent, numbering beyond the stars of heaven." Philo speaks of the Diaspora as the positive result of the Jewish nation's colonization of the inhabited world—an interesting perspective from a member of a (perpetually) colonized people!

> Jerusalem is the capital not of the single country of Judaea but of most other countries also, because of the colonies which it has sent out from time to time to the neighboring lands of Egypt, Phoenicia and Syria, . . . to the distant countries of Pamphylia, Cilicia, most of Asia as far as Bithynia and the remote corners of Pontus, and in the same way to Europe, to Thessaly, Boetia, Macedonia, Aetolia, Attica, Argos, Corinth, and most of the best parts of the Peloponnese. Not only are the continents full of Jewish colonies. So are the best known of the islands, Euboea, Cyprus and Crete. (Philo, Legat. 281–82)[3]

3. Translation from E. Mary Smallwood, Philonis Alexandrini: Legatio ad Gaium (Leiden: Brill, 1970).

Diaspora Jews continued to exhibit a high reverence for the homeland, internalized from the role of Jerusalem, Zion, and Judah in the sacred Scriptures. It was a kind of spiritual homeland for all Jews, who nevertheless remained at home in their local contexts. Jerusalem was still the Jews' "mother city" (*metropolis*), but the lands of their residence and their forebears' residence remained their "native lands" (*patrides*; Philo, *Flacc.* 45–46). They gave little indication of a longing to "return" to their mother city or of an ideological problem with living outside Israel, though some did appear to have relocated to Jerusalem. Acts 6:9, for example, attests to synagogues for repatriated Diaspora Jews in Jerusalem itself.

Despite their emotional and ideological connection with their homeland, Diaspora Jewish communities did not identify themselves with or support the cause of the revolutionaries in Judea and its environs during the First Jewish Revolt (AD 66–70). Nevertheless, the revolt gave a pretext for outbreaks of anti-Jewish violence in several major cities. Jewish residents of Caesarea Maritima were massacred by their neighbors in AD 66. This provoked reprisals by Jews in Palestine (already armed for war and ready for a fight) against Greek cities with Jewish communities in the coastlands and the Decapolis, which led, in turn, to counterreprisals against Jews throughout the cities of Syria (Josephus, *J.W.* 2.457–60; see also 2.559–61). In Syrian Antioch, an apostate Jew named Antiochus incited actions against the Jewish community there on the pretext of suspicion of planning arson (*J.W.* 7.46–62). In the aftermath of the war, refugee revolutionaries attempted to stir up anti-Roman actions in Alexandria and Cyrene, but the loyalty of the local Jewish authorities remained steadfastly with Rome (*J.W.* 7.409–19, 437–46).

In the wake of the Jewish Revolt and the destruction of the Jerusalem temple, Vespasian instituted the *fiscus Iudaicus* (Josephus, *J.W.* 7.218; Dio Cassius, *Hist.* 66.7.2). The temple tax, now expanded to include both men and women throughout the empire and extended from ages 20–50 to ages 3–62 (and perhaps beyond for men), was still to be collected but sent to Rome for the rebuilding and the maintenance of the temple of Jupiter Capitolinus (and no doubt to make up for the immense military spending involved in the suppression of the Jewish Revolt of AD 66–70; see Smallwood, *Jews*, 373–74; Barclay, *Jews*, 76–78). This was a bitter reminder of the fate of the homeland, as well as an ideological affront, forcing Jews to participate in the subvention of an idolatrous cult of a Roman god.

Local Organization and Legal Status of Diaspora Jews

An important institution within Judea and its surrounding regions, the synagogue (*synagōgē*), sometimes called a "place of prayer" (*proseuchē*; e.g., 3 Macc. 7:20; Philo, *Flacc.* 41, 45; *Legat.* 132; Josephus, *Ant.* 14.258; Acts 16:13), was essential for Diaspora Judaism. Multiple synagogues are attested in Alexandria (Philo, *Legat.* 132), in Middle Egypt, in Cyrene, Asia Minor, Greece, Rome, and elsewhere (see, e.g., Acts 9:2, 20; 13:5, 14; 14:1; 17:1, 17; 18:4, 19; 19:8). Although there are local differences among excavated synagogues, one generally finds some common elements: a prominent place for the storing of the Torah scrolls, a lectern for reading, and benches for attendees, as well as a "fellowship hall" for community functions. The synagogue served many purposes (Barclay, *Jews*, 414–18). It was the center for the Jewish community's regular study of the Torah, prayer, and worship each Sabbath (Josephus, *Ag. Ap.* 2.175; Philo, *Mos.* 2.215–16; *Spec.* 2.62–64). Jews also gathered there to celebrate the regular festivals of the Jewish liturgical calendar (in conscious distinction from the calendar of festivals observed by their neighbors in honor of their gods). It often served regulatory and administrative purposes as well, such as the settling of disputes internal to the Jewish community, the maintenance of records, and the safekeeping of the gathered temple tax and tithes. It also served as a kind of "community center" for social activities. Many of the distinctive features of Jewish life, as well as other community-binding activities, were practiced there. Each synagogue was under the direction (whether honorific or actual) of a synagogue leader (*archisynagōgos*), a title held by men and women (along with "mother of the synagogue," "elder," and the like). It is unclear whether the men and women who held such titles actually functioned as leaders in worship or were honored with such titles as benefactors of the Jewish community, but no differentiation is made between men and women in this regard (hence, what is deemed true of the one gender should be deemed true of the other; Rajak, "Jewish Community," 22–24). There is also no direct evidence that women and men were segregated in synagogues and certainly no evidence of seating women in the rear, behind a barrier.[4]

Larger Jewish communities in the Diaspora appear to have been organized as bodies of resident aliens with right of abode. The word *politeuma* is sometimes used to describe this political body, but it appears not to have been the technical term in the ancient world that modern scholars have sometimes assumed. The term is used in regard to Alexandrian Jews (see *Let. Aris.* 310) and in regard to Cyrenian Jews in two inscriptions (*CIG* 5361, 5362; Smallwood, *Jews*, 141). Jews enjoyed a certain amount of legal protection and tenure, as it were, in their city of residence, though it seems that Jews never *collectively* had the rights of Greek citizenship. Josephus's narratives on this topic have been found to be exaggerated or based on imprecise reports of imperial concessions (see *Ant.* 12.119; 12.125–26; *Ag. Ap.* 2.37–39; Tcherikover, *Hellenistic Civilization*, 318–25). Individuals, of course, could obtain citizenship (see Philo, *Legat.* 155–57; Acts 21:39). Nevertheless, it does appear that Jews were allowed to form a kind of intermediate-level political organization with certain authority for self-regulation, though always under the ultimate jurisdiction of the Greek or Roman authorities in the city. Contemporary sources speak of a number of official positions or bodies with Diaspora communities regulating community life, representing the interests of the Jewish community to the Greek and Roman authorities, and the like. In some

4. P. R. Trebilco and C. A. Evans, "Diaspora Judaism," *DNTB* 281–96 (287).

instances, these included an *ethnarch*, more often a council of elders (*gerousia*) with a leader (*gerousiarch*) or leaders (*archons*).

The Jews' practice of their ancestral laws and customs was generally tolerated and, in some periods and places, formally protected. Julius Caesar, for example, gave the Jews particular—and empire-wide—privileges that Augustus would later confirm (Philo, *Legat.* 311–16; Josephus, *Ant.* 14.241–46; 14.256–64; 16.162–65). These included the right to follow their ancestral laws where diet and Sabbath were concerned. Observing diet meant the ability to create their own markets; Sabbath observance meant exemption from conscription into military service (since a soldier could not decide whether to bear arms every seventh day) and from a summons to appear before a court on the Sabbath. They were also allowed to collect money for the support of the Jerusalem temple and transfer these considerable funds from their own provinces to Judea. Opportunistic governors and cities, loath to see such capital leaving their jurisdiction, sometimes tried to interfere with this particular right, but the Jews generally won in any appeal to Rome (Josephus, *Ant.* 16.27–60; 16.162–73). Of course, they were given the right to build synagogues and elect community officials. The Judean and Egyptian Jews' military support for Caesar in the civil war against Pompey (the violator of the temple in 63 BC!) was no doubt a factor in gaining such notable privileges (Smallwood, *Jews*, 135).

In some cities, the leaders of Jewish communities did seek to gain citizenship for the Jewish community as a whole. The Jewish quest to be enrolled as citizens of Alexandria became an important issue in the wake of Augustus's introduction of the *laographia* in Egypt (24 BC), a tax imposed on inhabitants of Egypt from which Greek citizens were exempt. Aside from the financial burden, the Jews were struck by the social stigma of being, for the first time, clearly and explicitly classed with the indigenous and often un-Hellenized (even illiterate) Egyptian peasants rather than with the Greek and Graecized citizens of the major cities, with whom they felt themselves to have much more in common in terms of social and cultural levels (Tcherikover, *Hellenistic Civilization*, 311–12; Smallwood, *Jews*, 231–32). The Greek citizens, however, not to mention the indigenous Egyptians, were already resentful of a body of resident aliens enjoying so many privileges and exemptions—in effect, being allowed, even encouraged, by Rome to persevere in their "atheistic" and antisocial manner of life in the midst of the Greek city. Apion's complaint (quoted in Josephus, *Ag. Ap.* 2.65) is not entirely without merit: "Why, if they are citizens, don't they worship the same gods as the Alexandrians?" Citizenship implied the highest degree of solidarity with the city and one's fellow citizens, but the Jews' general abhorrence of the city's gods and of table fellowship with their fellow citizens (and their gods) was incompatible with such solidarity. The Jews' desire to receive additional privileges without the accompanying obligations of being fully a part of the civic life fueled the fires of this resentment.

After decades, the issue gave rise, on the one hand, to complex litigation before the emperors Caligula and Claudius (Philo's *On the Embassy to Gaius* provides a firsthand account) and, on the other hand, to violent anti-Jewish pogroms throughout the city of Alexandria. These resulted in the demolition or desecration of synagogues throughout the city, the herding of Jewish residents into a single quarter as a ghetto (and consequent looting of the dispossessed), the public abuse and lynching of at least several dozen Jewish men and women, and the attempt to pass a measure declaring the Jews to be aliens *without* right of abode (Philo, *Flacc.* 25–57; *Legat.* 120–35). Claudius's decision confirmed the Jews' historic privileges and status as aliens with right of abode, but he also later responded to new outbreaks in Alexandria by speaking of the Jews as living "in a city not their own" and made a clear and sharp distinction between them and "Alexandrians," that is, Greek citizens of Alexandria (Josephus, *Ant.* 19.286–91; *CPJ* 2:153 [discussed in Smallwood, *Jews*, 247–50]).

Responses to Hellenization among Diaspora Jews

Alexander extended not only a political but also a cultural empire. Greek became the language that would allow people throughout the eastern Mediterranean and the Levant to interact with one another and was also the language of politics and international commerce. Greek culture became the body of knowledge, etiquette, and ideology shared by the "educated" or "civilized," regardless of an individual's original ethnicity. There were, therefore, powerful incentives—some quite practical, some more ideological—to "Hellenize," at least to a certain extent, throughout the territory ruled by Alexander and his successors (Judea not least of all).

We may speak of "Hellenization" as a process that took place in a number of arenas of life and experience (see Tcherikover, *Hellenistic Civilization*, 344–57; Barclay, *Jews*, 88–91). The first and most basic area of Hellenization was the acquisition of knowledge of, even facility in, the Greek language. This was prerequisite to all meaningful interaction between indigenous or transplanted people groups and the Greek elites or colonists in their midst. The degree to which large numbers of Jews in the Diaspora embraced the Greek language to the neglect and eventual loss of their native languages (Hebrew and Aramaic) is most dramatically seen in the production of Greek translations of the Jewish Scriptures (generally all referred to together under the rubric "Septuagint" [LXX]) as early as the mid-third century BC. The *Letter of Aristeas* is an early expression of the legend of the Septuagint's emergence. The act of translation brought the Jewish Scriptures more directly into conversation with the philosophies and ethics of the Greek world by rendering them in the same language and representing their key concepts with words that now resonated with Greek conversations about piety and virtue. If, on the one hand, the translation could be severely criticized by later rabbis for its departures from the exact meaning of the Hebrew, it was nevertheless essential as a way to keep the Scriptures accessible to many Diaspora Jews (and now their Greek-speaking neighbors as well).

Another area of Hellenization involved personal names. Those who wished to "blend in" more easily or make themselves more accessible to Greek persons or Greek speakers might take on Greek names or give Greek names to their children,

thus representing themselves as a part of the more international, Hellenized population, much as, for example, Chinese or Indian residents in America will often
adopt Western names or at least simplify their own. Learning the Greek language
opened up the possibility of reading Greek literature, attending Greek drama and
recitals of poetry, listening to philosophers promoting their ethics and ideals in the
public spaces, and even receiving a Greek education (including literature, rhetoric,
philosophy, religion, and other curricular subjects). Hellenization occurred not
only in the arena of cultural knowledge but also with regard to cultural practice
(e.g., dress, forms of entertainment, arrangement of homes, practices of dining);
participation in the civic, social, and religious life of the Greek city; and even
becoming politically enfranchised as a Greek citizen.

An individual might be Hellenized in each of these areas to extremely different
degrees. A high level of fluency in Greek did not by itself imply a high degree of
Hellenization in other areas. It is also important to discern carefully the use to which
particular Jews and Jewish communities put their knowledge of, and embeddedness
within, Greek language and culture. John Barclay has developed a helpful list of
"scales" on which to measure Hellenization and its ideological and social effects with
appropriate discernment and care (Barclay, *Jews*, 92–102). The first scale measures
assimilation, asking to what degree Jews were integrated into gentile society and in
what contexts (and to what degree the marks of differentiation between Jews and
their neighbors remained visible). The second scale is acculturation, asking about
the degree to which particular Jews acquired facility in, and familiarity with, Greek
language and culture (e.g., that body of knowledge and set of values to which the
educated Greek would have had access). The third scale measures accommodation, asking primarily about the use to which Jews put their acculturation (or lack
thereof). Did they foster antagonism against Greco-Roman society and culture,
foster understanding while retaining Jewish distinctiveness, or seek to hide or erase
their Jewish distinctiveness? In other words, did the particular Jew or Jews under
investigation build bridges or walls? Some Jews attaining a high degree of facility
in Greek and Greek culture and a high degree of integration into Greek society
ultimately chose to abandon the distinctive beliefs and practices of their Jewish
heritage in favor of a fully Graecized identity. One illustrious example is Tiberius
Julius Alexander, ironically the nephew of the staunchly loyal Jew Philo of Alexandria. Alexander traded in his Jewish observances for a notable career as procurator
of Judea and governor of Alexandria (Barclay, *Jews*, 105–6; Modrzejewski, *Jews*,
185–90). He showed no favoritism toward his fellow co-religionists when he served
on Vespasian's staff during the First Jewish Revolt (Josephus, *J.W.* 5.45–46, 205).
Similarly, a Jew named Antiochus apostatized, attained significant influence in his
city of Antioch, and became a potent enemy against his own people there (see *J.W.*
7.46–53). The response to apostates is consistently negative in Diaspora Jewish
literature. The author of 3 Maccabees indulges in fantasies of their execution by
pious Jews, while the Wisdom of Solomon vividly portrays the tension between
the more powerful apostates and the less powerful "righteous" (Wis. 1:16–2:24).

Many Jews, however, remained faithful to their ancestral way of life *and* were fully engaged in the lives of the cities in which they lived (to the extent that the Torah permitted) *as* Jews.

Advanced facility in Greek language, literature, philosophy, and rhetoric by no means implied any degree of relaxation of commitment to Jewish identity and heritage or to the particulars of Torah observance and the Jewish way of life. The writer of *Pseudo-Ezekiel* used his facility in Greek literary style to retell the Hebrew epic—the exodus story—in the form of a Greek tragedy, celebrating the foundational narrative of the Jewish people in the most noble style of the Greeks. Philo of Alexandria and the author of 4 Maccabees, both highly Hellenized writers, were also fully committed to living out the distinctive way of life prescribed by Torah as their duty and privilege before God. Philo was more thoroughly Hellenized than Paul in most areas, but his devotion to the practice of the Torah was never questioned, as was Paul's (Barclay, *Jews*, 91). These and similar writers (like the author of the *Letter of Aristeas*) used their acculturation to re-present Judaism as, essentially, a kind of ethical philosophy comparable to those promoted among the learned Greeks.

Philo interpreted the narratives and laws of Genesis and Exodus as instruction concerning the soul's journey from slavery to the passions to perfection in virtue. The author of 4 Maccabees sought to strengthen adherence to the ancestral Jewish way of life by explaining how it was in no way inferior to the practice of the gentiles and was, in fact, the way to attain the highest ideals prized even by them. The Torah was the God-given discipline that empowered the mind to rule over the passions (4 Macc. 1:15–17; 2:21–23) and that trained the adherent in justice, courage, temperance, and prudence, the cardinal virtues of Greek ethical philosophy (5:22–24). These writers desired to interpret even the most culturally distinctive elements (like circumcision and the dietary laws) in terms of the philosophical lessons such elements encode or the moral training they nurture. Some Jews, indeed, undertook such an enterprise to find a way to remain connected with the "essence" of their Jewish heritage while leaving behind its distinctive—and socially problematic and limiting—practices. In the case of Philo and 4 Maccabees, however, the purpose was not to facilitate departures from the ancestral law. Philo strongly disapproved of those who thought they could fulfill the "spirit" while neglecting the "letter" of these commandments (*Migr.* 89–93). Instead, Philo sought to encourage other Jews who were themselves familiar with Greek culture and ideals about the value of their own ancestral practice. He urged them to continue in practices that maintained distinctive Jewish identity and also equipped them with rationales for those practices that "worked" within an increasingly Greek mind-set.

Identity, Boundaries, and Ethnic Tension in the Diaspora

Jews were connected by an ethnic bond—the fact that their lineage could be traced, theoretically at least, to one family (the sons of Jacob) and to one native land.

Nevertheless, Jewish identity was not solely an ethnic matter: it involved a way of life (a set of customs) that could be left behind (e.g., by Tiberius Alexander) or taken up (e.g., by a gentile convert like Izates, the king of Adiabene [Barclay, *Jews*, 403]). Although belonging to a particular "race" or "nation" or "tribe" was part of the definition of a "Jew" held by both Jews and non-Jews alike, even more central to this working definition was the practice of a particular set of "ancestral customs" or "ancestral laws" (Barclay, *Jews*, 405–10). For those Jews who wanted to preserve their identity as part of the Jewish people, a number of practices emerged as centrally important. Indeed, the effectiveness of these practices for creating boundaries and differentiation between Jew and non-Jew allowed Jews to acculturate to the Greek environment to a high degree without fear of losing their distinctiveness as members of the historic people of the one God. The most central of these practices were avoidance of idolatry, observance of the dietary laws of Torah, observance of the Sabbath, and circumcision. That these were effective markers of identity and group boundaries is attested by the fact that, if gentiles knew anything about Jews at all, they knew that Jews followed at least these practices.

Rejection of idolatrous expressions of worship and of worship directed toward any god but the God of Israel was of central importance to living in line with the Jews' ancestral tradition. It also became a principal sign of the difference and distinctiveness of the Jew in the midst of a polytheistic, gentile world. Avoiding all rites directed toward another god also meant that Jews would associate with their gentile neighbors only in certain contexts and up to a certain point. This practice drew strong social boundaries that clearly marked Jews and non-Jews as different social bodies, with no danger of the latter swallowing up the former. The author of the *Letter of Aristeas* understood, in fact, that the more particular laws of the Torah were given specifically to help reinforce the boundaries and limit close association between the groups. Because the Jews *alone* had come to the knowledge of the one, living God and were surrounded by people whose religious knowledge was tainted by polytheism and iconic religion, "our lawgiver . . . fenced us about with impregnable palisades and with walls of iron, to the end that we should mingle in no way with any of the other nations, remaining pure in body and in spirit, emancipated from vain opinions, revering the one and mighty God above the whole of creation" (*Let. Aris.* 139).[5]

The dietary laws were especially well suited to prevent the close association between Jews and people of other nations that would lead eventually to the corruption of the Jews' pure religion. These laws did not merely prohibit the consumption of the meat of certain animals (like pigs, rabbit, crabs, and so forth) or the consumption of meat improperly prepared (like beef or lamb in which the blood of the animal has been allowed to sit and congeal). These laws also encouraged the

5. Translation from Moses Hadas, *Aristeas to Philocrates (Letter of Aristeas)* (New York: Harper & Brothers, 1951), 157.

Jews to create their own markets, keeping their food separate from the gentiles' from production through consumption. In addition, these laws were a constant reminder that the Jews have been set apart by God from all other peoples: when they distinguished between clean and unclean food, they mirrored God's action of distinguishing between Israel, as God's own nation (thus "clean" for God), and the unclean nations (so Lev. 20:22–26; deSilva, *Honor*, 269–71). The law also prohibited, however, the consumption of food that had been connected with the worship of other gods. Almost all meat in Greco-Roman society came from a pagan sacrifice, but libations and grain offerings made to other gods consecrated all the wine and bread in a house as well (Bickerman, *Jews*, 248–49). Eating with gentile neighbors who would not forsake their own expressions of piety for the sake of their Jewish guests would be difficult, if not impossible, for the conscientious Jew. These difficulties help us understand why some Jews would opt to leave behind their ancestral traditions in order to better connect with their neighbors and city. Tessa Rajak writes, "It is not inevitable that special dietary laws compel people to eat away from others. . . . All sorts of arrangements are feasible, where there is a social reason to make them" ("Jewish Community," 18). However true this may be in principle, the fact remains that most Greek and Latin writers commenting on the Jews in their midst (see below) bear witness to the latter's tendency to abstain from mingling at a common table. As a natural corollary, Jews tended not to marry non-Jews unless they became full converts, as in the story of *Joseph and Aseneth*, or unless the Jews became practical apostates.

Circumcision literally marked the Jewish male as a Jew. Although this sign of Jewishness would not be immediately visible in most contexts, it appears to have been prominent in Jewish self-awareness (witness the number of times the practice is mentioned, especially as a defining characteristic that distinguished Jews from non-Jews, in the HB, Apocrypha, and NT) as well as in gentile awareness of what distinguished a Jew from others. Sabbath observance was a far more visible and obvious sign. Jews gathered for worship together and observed holidays from business in rhythms completely different from the religious and holiday calendar of the people around them in their city. They rested on other people's business days; they stayed home when other people's establishments (and lawcourts and armies) were open for business.

It was evidently not easy for Jews to hold on to their convictions of monolatry (monotheism) while living in the midst of gentiles expressing their pious and heartfelt devotion to their gods. A good number of surviving texts bear witness to their authors' perception of the need to insulate their fellow Jews from the striking impression that gentile rites and liturgies made on the Jews living in their midst. The Letter of Jeremiah, for example, seeks to drill into its readers' minds that the nations' gods "are not gods; so do not fear them" (Let. Jer. 16, 23; similarly 29, 40, 44, 52, 56, 65, 69) by dwelling on the lifelessness and helplessness of the idols themselves. The tale of Daniel and Bel ridicules gentile religion on the same grounds. Wisdom of Solomon 13:1–15:17 employs both anti-idolatry polemics from the Jewish Scriptures and Greek explanations for the invention of idolatrous cults (and thus the perversion of rational religion) to stress the emptiness of the religious activity surrounding the Diaspora Jew.

This criticism extended to the practitioners of idolatry, whom Jewish authors accused of being empty headed, depraved in their thinking, and mired in every personal and social vice imaginable on account of their devotion to false gods and consequent ignorance of the law of the one God (see Wis. 14:12–14, 22–27; 3 Macc. 4:16; 5:12; 6:4–5, 9, 11). Diaspora Jews "needed the passions of contempt and hatred for the religion of their neighbors to protect their faith from the daily allure of paganism," and from neighbors who would have welcomed them into their temples (Bickerman, *Jews*, 256). Despite warnings about being sensitive to their neighbors' religious sentiments, seen dramatically in the LXX translation of Exod. 22:28 (where "You will not speak ill of God [Hebrew *'ĕlōhîm*]" becomes "You will not speak ill of gods [Greek *theoi*]"),[6] such contempt for their neighbors' cherished religious beliefs could not have gone unnoticed by outsiders.

That Diaspora Jews were largely able to maintain their identity and distinctiveness, and that distinctively Jewish practices were central to the task, is confirmed by reactions to Jews by their gentile neighbors. From outside, the Jews' avoidance of their neighbors' temples and rites, and no doubt the Jews' attitude toward their neighbors' gods, put them in the category of "atheists," those who disbelieve in the gods' existence. This was further understood as a sign of the Jews' injustice toward the gods on whom the life of the city depended. Gentiles were aware that the Jews' beliefs had social implications. In the words of Apollonius Molon (as cited in Josephus, *Ag. Ap.* 2.258 LCL), "The Jews do not accept people who have other views about God." Atheism, in his eyes, bred misanthropy (or at least xenophobia) on the Jews' part (see also Diodorus Siculus, *Lib. Hist.* 34–35). Jews were seen as extremely loyal to one another but not to the non-Jewish residents in the same cities. In avoiding all idolatrous settings, Jews cut themselves off from a major means of establishing fellowship and feelings of solidarity with their neighbors. It was "an act of unsociability that might have been condoned, on the grounds that the Jews were merely following the ways of their ancestors, but it was surely never understood" (Bickerman, *Jews*, 251).

The effectiveness of the dietary laws of Torah in reinforcing social cohesion among Jews and differentiation from gentiles was clear to the Jews' neighbors (Diodorus Siculus, *Lib. Hist.* 34.1.1–4; 40.3–4; Tacitus, *Hist.* 5.5.1–2; Philostratus, *Vit. Apol.* 33; 3 Macc. 3:3–7). In response to this, the Jews' dietary laws became an object of ridicule and criticism (Josephus, *Ag. Ap.* 2.137; Tacitus, *Hist.* 5.4.2–3; Juvenal, *Sat.* 6.160; 14.98–104; Plutarch, *Table Talk* 5.1 [*Mor.* 669E–F]). Their observance of the Sabbath was censured as a mark of laziness (Tacitus, *Hist.*

---

6. In the HB, the Hebrew word *'ĕlōhîm*, though plural in form, is used to refer to the one God of the Jews. The LXX reads it here as an actual plural and so translates it by the Greek plural form for "gods."

5.4.3; Juvenal, *Sat.* 14.105–6; Plutarch, *Superstition* 8 [*Mor.* 169C]). The practice of circumcision was denounced as a barbaric mutilation (Josephus, *Ag. Ap.* 2.137; Tacitus, *Hist.* 5.5.2; Juvenal, *Sat.* 14.104). Some Greeks, like Poseidonius, could admire Moses as a high-minded theologian and lawgiver, but they held that his pure religion degenerated into superstition as his followers added circumcision, dietary regulations, and Sabbath observance (Strabo, *Geogr.* 16.760–61). Such comments in Greek and Latin literature show just how clear and important precisely *these* boundary markers were to creating and sustaining the identity of the people in their midst that refused to assimilate. These prejudices, focused on the markers of Jewish distinctiveness, also served as the ever-glowing embers from which anti-Jewish riots were always ready to flare up.

But gentiles could also be attracted to this distinctive way of living practiced by the Jews in their midst. Varro, the first-century BC Roman philosopher, approved of the Jews' rejection of iconic representations of divinity, criticizing his own people for abandoning the original, pure, Roman practice of not representing deity in physical form (quoted in Augustine, *Civ.* 4.31). Gentiles could also be attracted to the rigorous discipline of the Torah, the high-minded ethical principles therein taught and practiced by its adherents, and the social bond between Jews. Many gentiles showed their approval, and perhaps to some extent their adherence, by supporting local synagogues. An inscription in Aphrodisias lists fifty-some "fearers of God" (*theosebeis*), whether indicating formal adherents or gentile benefactors of the Jewish community.[7] Sometimes a gentile would take up the whole yoke of the law and accept circumcision. Jews were not active evangelists, but they did not turn away gentile inquirers.

Jewish hostility against their neighbors finally matched decades of gentile violence perpetrated against Diaspora Jews in the "Diaspora revolts" of AD 115–117 (see Eusebius, *Eccl. Hist.* 4.2.1–4; Dio Cassius, *Hist.* 48.32.1–2). Uprisings began in Cyrene and then flared up in Egypt as Jews attacked their Greek neighbors. Pagan temples appear to have been a favorite target for arson. The insurgents initially got the upper hand, but the emperor Trajan sent Marcius Turbo, a skilled general, with a sufficiently large army to suppress the rebellion. The effort took over a year, during which time the assault on Greek neighbors turned into an all-out revolt against Rome. The war took on messianic dimensions in Cyrene and Egypt and may have involved a plan to liberate Judea from Roman domination. Revolt eventually spread to the island of Cyprus. Tens of thousands of Jewish lives were lost, and gentile casualties also ran high, particularly in the early stages of the uprisings. Jewish communities in Egypt and North Africa appear never to have recovered their former prominence. Jews were forbidden even to land on Cyprus for at least a century.

In the wake of Trajan's conquest of Mesopotamia, Jews in that region also rebelled against the newly imposed Roman rule. This appears, however, to have

7. Trebilco and Evans, "Diaspora Judaism," 286.

been a part of a larger, regional resistance to Roman imperialism. After Trajan's death, Hadrian abandoned attempts to hold Mesopotamia within the Roman Empire, and the Diaspora revolts with their demands on the Roman military's time, energy, and resources may well have contributed to the failure of that attempt at expansion (Smallwood, *Jews*, 421).

See also "Synagogue and Sanhedrin."

Bibliography

Barclay, J. M. G. *Jews in the Mediterranean Diaspora from Alexander to Trajan (323 BC–117 CE)*. Edinburgh: T&T Clark, 1996. The single most valuable and comprehensive resource for the study of the Diaspora. Barclay provides extensive analysis of the history and circumstances of Jews in Egypt during the Ptolemaic and early Roman periods and of texts written by Egyptian Jews bearing witness to varying levels of acculturation and assimilation and varying degrees of openness to the gentile world. The second half of the book explores the growth of Diaspora communities in Cyrenaica, Syria, Asia Minor, and Rome and the literature of these communities and concludes with a synthetic sketch of Diaspora Judaism and Jewish identity.

Bickerman, Elias J. *The Jews in the Greek Age*. Cambridge, MA: Harvard University Press, 1988. Though focusing more on Palestine than the Diaspora, this book includes helpful treatments of the history of the Jewish Diaspora in Egypt before and during the Ptolemaic period (pp. 38–45, 81–90).

Cappelletti, Silvia. *The Jewish Community of Rome from the Second Century B.C.E. to the Third Century C.E.* Leiden: Brill, 2006. An advanced study of the history and material culture of the Jews in Rome, with a particularly useful reconstruction of the history of the community during the early Roman Empire (pp. 33–142).

Collins, John J. *Between Athens and Jerusalem: Jewish Identity in the Hellenistic Diaspora*. 2nd ed. Grand Rapids: Eerdmans, 2000. Approaches the question by means of careful analysis of individual texts written by Diaspora Jews as windows into the circumstances and challenges of maintaining Jewish identity. A comprehensive introduction to Diaspora Jewish literature.

deSilva, David A. *Honor, Patronage, Kinship and Purity: Unlocking New Testament Culture*. Downers Grove, IL: InterVarsity, 2000. Chapter 7 analyzes the significance of Jewish dietary laws, circumcision, and Sabbath observance (focal practices for Jewish identity in the Diaspora) within the comprehensive purity maps of ancient Israel and early Judaism.

———. *Introducing the Apocrypha: Message, Context, and Significance*. Grand Rapids: Baker Academic, 2002. An in-depth introduction to each of the books contained in the collection known as the OT Apocrypha/Deuterocanonicals as found in the NRSV, ESV, and CEB. The treatments of Greek Esther, Wisdom of Solomon, Letter of Jeremiah, Additions to Daniel, 3 Maccabees, and 4 Maccabees are especially attentive to what these texts reveal of their Diaspora setting and what they reflect of their authors' responses to Hellenism.

Feldman, Louis H. *Jew and Gentile in the Ancient World: Attitudes and Interactions from Alexander to Justinian*. Princeton: Princeton University Press, 1993. A comprehensive, balanced study of primary gentile and Jewish sources for prejudice against Jews and the attraction of Judaism among their gentile neighbors, as well as Jewish proselytism in the Roman imperial period.

Goodman, Martin. "Jewish Proselytizing in the First Century." Pages 53–78 in *The Jews among Pagans and Christians in the Roman Empire*. Edited by Judith Lieu et al. London: Routledge, 1992. Offers a careful assessment of the evidence for Jewish mission before and after the rise of the Christian movement.

Gruen, Erich S. *Diaspora: Jews amidst Greeks and Romans*. Cambridge, MA: Harvard University Press, 2002. A thorough study of Jewish life and communities in the Diaspora, especially helpful for further information on the Jews of Rome, Egypt, and Asia Minor; the relations between the Diaspora and the homeland; and civic and social organization of Jewish Diaspora communities.

————. "Judaism in the Diaspora." *EDEJ* 77–96. An excellent overview article of the extent and nature of Jewish life and community in the Diaspora.

Leon, Harry J. *The Jews of Ancient Rome*. Updated ed., with an introduction by Carolyn Osiek. Peabody, MA: Hendrickson, 1995. A classic study of the history and conditions of the Jewish community in Rome, particularly enhanced by Leon's attention to epigraphic and archaeological evidence for the life, status, and everyday involvements of Jews in the Roman capital.

Modrzejewski, Joseph M. *The Jews of Egypt from Ramses II to the Emperor Hadrian*. Philadelphia: Jewish Publication Society, 1995. An essential resource for the history of and problems facing the Jewish communities of Egypt, and of Alexandria in particular. Especially helpful are the author's reconstructions of the Jewish communities at Elephantine and Leontopolis, conditions under the Ptolemies, the tumults in Alexandria and the problem of citizenship, and the Diaspora revolt in Egypt.

Rajak, Tessa. "The Jewish Community and Its Boundaries." Pages 9–28 in *The Jews among Pagans and Christians in the Roman Empire*. Edited by Judith Lieu et al. London: Routledge, 1992. A careful study of practices marking Jewish identity and group boundaries in the later Roman imperial period, paying special attention to interactions between rabbinic Judaism and the Diaspora communities.

Safrai, S., and Menahem Stern, eds. *The Jewish People in the First Century*. CRINT 1.1. Assen: Van Gorcum; Philadelphia: Fortress, 1974. Especially helpful for further study are the essays by S. Applebaum, "The Organization of the Jewish Communities in the Diaspora"; idem, "The Legal Status of the Jewish Communities in the Diaspora"; S. Safrai, "The Synagogue"; idem, "Relations between the Diaspora and the Land of Israel"; and Menahem Stern, "The Jews in Greek and Latin Literature," which examines the literary evidence for ancient anti-Judaism, among other topics.

Silva, Moises, and Karen Jobes. *Invitation to the Septuagint*. Grand Rapids: Baker Academic, 2000. A comprehensive introduction to the origins of the Greek translations of the Jewish Scriptures, the transmission and reconstruction of the text, the history of Septuagint studies, and the importance of the Septuagint for the study of early Jewish biblical interpretation, including Christian interpretation of Scripture.

Smallwood, E. Mary. *The Jews under Roman Rule: From Pompey to Diocletian*. Leiden: Brill, 1976. A classic and thorough study of the history of the Jewish people during the late Roman Republic and the imperial period, both in Palestine and throughout the Diaspora. Especially important are the chapters on the Jews in Alexandria and the struggles over citizenship (pp. 227–50) and the treatment of the Diaspora revolts (pp. 389–427).

Tcherikover, Victor. *Hellenistic Civilization and the Jews*. Philadelphia: Jewish Publication Society, 1961. The second part of this classic and important work focuses on the Jewish Diaspora and its encounter with Hellenism. It is particularly helpful for its treatments of the processes of Hellenization itself, the organization of Jewish communities, the evidence concerning Jews' citizenship in Greek cities, privileges granted to the Jews under the Caesars, and anti-Judaism in the Hellenistic and Roman periods.

Trebilco, Paul R. *Jewish Communities in Asia Minor*. SNTSMS 69. Cambridge: Cambridge University Press, 1991. An in-depth study of the spread of the Jewish Diaspora throughout Asia Minor and the circumstances and challenges thereof. Trebilco (pp. 145–66) includes a helpful study on gentile adherents and the selectivity and range of their adoption of Jewish practices.

24

Noncanonical Jewish Writings

DANIEL M. GURTNER

The designation of a selection of ancient writings as both noncanonical and Jewish requires some explanation, particularly when used with respect to the so-called Apocrypha and Pseudepigrapha. These documents are sometimes referred to as "Old Testament" Apocrypha and Pseudepigrapha, respectively. This distinction is important because there are a plethora of "New Testament," or Christian, apocrypha, and even pseudepigrapha, though the latter category, as will be seen below, is more difficult to discern. In general, the designation employed here refers to texts that date from the Second Temple period, are discernibly Jewish in origin, and are not included in the Protestant Christian canon of Scripture.

Apocrypha

The term "apocrypha" derives from the Greek noun *apokrypha*, meaning "hidden." It is used in the LXX and NT of a secret thing, whether deliberately kept out of sight (1 Macc. 1:23; Isa. 45:3; Pss. 26:5 [27:5 ET]; 30:21 [31:20]; cf. Deut. 27:15; Isa. 4:6; Ps. 9:29 [10:8]; Mark 4:22; Luke 8:17); simply invisible; or not easily seen, without denoting intent (Sir. 23:19; 39:3; 42:9, 19; 48:25; Dan. [Theodotion] 2:22; Col. 2:3). The historical origin of the designation of these books as "apocrypha" is obscure. Perhaps the notion stems from apocalyptic traditions that view certain divine disclosures as lying hidden or sealed (cf. Dan. 8:26; 12:4,

9–11; *2 Bar.* 20.3–4; 87.1; etc.). More specifically, however, the term has been used since Jerome with reference to collections of books found in Greek codices of the Scriptures (and sometimes the Latin Vulgate) but not found in the (Hebrew) MT or the (Greek) NT.

The Books of the Apocrypha

Discerning which books belong to this categorization is difficult. The major Greek codices are not uniform in their inclusion of books. The collection in each codex is as follows:

Sinaiticus (fourth cent. AD)	Vaticanus (fourth cent. AD)	Alexandrinus (fifth cent. AD)
Greek Esther	Greek Esther	Greek Esther
Judith	Judith	Tobit
Tobit	Tobit	Judith
1 Maccabees		1 Maccabees
		2 Maccabees
		3 Maccabees
4 Maccabees		4 Maccabees
Wisdom of Solomon	Wisdom of Solomon	Wisdom of Solomon
Sirach	Sirach	Sirach
		Psalms of Solomon
1 Baruch	1 Baruch	
Letter of Jeremiah	Letter of Jeremiah	Letter of Jeremiah
	Susanna	Susanna
	Bel and the Dragon	Bel and the Dragon
		Prayer of Manasseh
		Additional psalms and odes

The list was by no means fixed, and modern collections often omit Psalms of Solomon and 3–4 Maccabees. Other works, such as 2 Esdras (2 Esd. 3–14 = *4 Ezra*) and the Prayer of Manasseh, are often included.

Though not present in the ancient texts themselves, the designations "apocryphon" and "apocryphal" have been applied among modern scholars for certain documents from the DSS whose existence was previously unknown. These include the *Genesis Apocryphon* (1Q20), *Apocryphon of Moses* (1Q22, 1Q29, 2Q21,

4Q375, 4Q376, 4Q408), and 11QApocryphal Psalms (11Q11), to name but a few. The DSS also attest to ancient manuscript evidence of better-known apocryphal books, such as Sirach, Tobit, Letter of Jeremiah, and Ps. 151. A broad and inclusive collection will be addressed here, and delineations of the inclusion or exclusion of various books by respective religious traditions are noted below. However one divides the corpus of documents, a variety of literary genres is represented among them, most of which date from the era of the completion of the last book of the Hebrew Scriptures to the early period of the NT canon.

The Content of Apocryphal Books

Tobit is a fourteen-chapter narrative probably composed between 200 and 168 BC. It tells the story of Tobit, an Israelite in exile in Assyria who faces persecution and hardships for his piety. Simultaneously, a relative, Sarah, experiences calamities of her own. God intervenes by sending his angel, Raphael, who through Tobias, Tobit's son, comes to the aid of both Sarah and Tobit. Tobias marries Sarah, who bears him sons. The book depicts the sufferings of righteous Israelites, the punishment of Israel for its sins, and the ultimate regathering and vindication of God's pious people, exhorting the reader to pursue piety and righteous living despite inevitable hardships.

The book of Judith is a narrative exhibiting God's power to aid the oppressed pious Israelite. Written around the middle of the second century BC, Judith's story is set in a national crisis for Israel. Nebuchadnezzar dispatches the general Holofernes against those who resist his dominance. Judith—stepping into the narrative with faith, wisdom, and cunning—entices and manipulates Holofernes to literally lose his head. Israel is saved and God is established as the true Lord, the champion of the meek and oppressed. Readers are reminded that Israel's strength is in its God, not its size.

Greek Esther, also called the Additions to Esther, is a collection of six expansions upon the biblical (Hebrew) book of Esther, preserved in Greek. All of the expansions were written prior to AD 70, but they may have been added at different times between the second and first centuries BC. Some modern editions place the additions at the end of the shorter Esther, but they are actually interspersed throughout the book in ancient Greek editions. The additions contain an alleged dream by Mordecai, the content of Artaxerxes's decree for the extermination of Israelites, prayers of both Mordecai and Esther, an expansive description of Esther before the king, Artaxerxes's decree in praise of the Jews, and an additional interpretation of a dream. Collectively, the additions serve to add theological depth to the work, supply the otherwise absent name of God, and underscore the piety (rather than courage) of Esther.

As its name suggests, the Wisdom of Solomon is Wisdom literature. It was likely written in Egypt in the first century BC or early in the first century AD. It exhibits a unique synthesis of Hellenistic rhetoric with facets of Jewish apocalypticism.

The text in part reads as a narration by King Solomon, expounding on wisdom based in the religious heritage of Israel, exhibiting the personification of Wisdom, and exhorting all rulers of the earth.

Sirach, or the Wisdom of Ben Sira, is a book of wisdom similar to Proverbs though considerably longer. It was written in Hebrew early in the second century BC by Joshua Ben Eleazar Ben Sira, a scribe in Jerusalem, and translated into Greek by his grandson. The book contains poetic acclamations of wisdom, a climactic doxology to God, and a song of praise for Israel's past heroes. Much of it, however, is instructive in nature, pertaining to such matters as the use of speech, familial relations, and wealth and poverty, to name but a few, with the instruction rooted in wisdom and Torah.

Baruch, or 1 Baruch, is ascribed to Baruch, the scribe of Jeremiah, and dates from the first or second centuries BC. It concerns the theme of exile and return and recounts a prayer, sapiential poem, and exhortation to Israel purportedly five years after the destruction of Jerusalem.

The Letter of Jeremiah was written before 100 BC and is extant only in Greek. In most manuscripts it is a final chapter in the book of Baruch. The letter is a polemic against idolatry, influenced by Jer. 10:2–15; 29:1–32. It offers a repetitious exhortation to avoid the folly of gentile idols, which are not gods but lifeless, impotent, and not to be feared.

The Additions to Daniel is a collection of three texts added to the canonical Dan. 1–12 that date between 165 and about 100 BC. The first addition to Daniel, the Prayer of Azariah and the Song of the Three Young Men, contains a prayer attributed to Abednego (also known as Azariah), in which he confesses Israel's sins and pleads for God's intervention. The Song of the Three Young Men is a hymn of thanksgiving. The second addition is Susanna, written by about 100 BC. This is a tale of a righteous woman conspired against by two wicked elders. Daniel rescues her, exposes the deceit of her adversaries, and vindicates her piety. The third addition, Bel and the Dragon, is a single chapter with two stories, both polemics against idolatry. The first describes how Daniel proves that it is the priests and not Bel, the idol, that eat the food presented to it. Daniel then destroys the idol. The second story is a narrative describing Daniel's destruction of a Babylonian idol in the form of a dragon or serpent.

The book of 1 Maccabees is a historical narrative recounting Israel's history from the death of Alexander the Great to the rule of John Hyrcanus the priest. The author affirms the validity of the Hasmonean high-priestly caste by celebrating the military accomplishments of Mattathias and his sons to rid Jerusalem and its temple of Hellenistic pollutions.

Second Maccabees is likewise a historical narrative chronicling events from 180 to 161 BC, condensing a now-lost, five-volume work by a certain Jason of Cyrene. Unlike 1 Maccabees, this book is more theological in orientation, discussing subjects like resurrection, martyrdom, and the miraculous. In a number of respects it overlaps with events of 1 Maccabees rather than continuing where that book finishes. Together 1 and 2 Maccabees provide the main source of historical material from the middle of the second century BC.

The book of 1 Esdras, also known as 3 Ezra, originated between 150 and 100 BC and recasts portions of 2 Chronicles, Nehemiah, and the book of Esther. Much of the new material is found in 1 Esd. 3–4 and describes events alleged to have occurred around the rise of the Second Temple. Second Esdras is a Christian document that contains a Jewish apocalypse (*4 Ezra*) within it (chaps. 3–14).

The Prayer of Manasseh is a penitential prayer attributed to Manasseh, king of Judah. The king allegedly repents of his idolatries (2 Kings 21) and is restored to his throne in Jerusalem from his captivity in Babylon (2 Chron. 33:12–13). The work was likely written in Greek, and whether it is Jewish or Christian in origin is debated. If the former, it may date from early in the first century AD.

The books of 3 and 4 Maccabees are sometimes classified with the Pseudepigrapha, but they are presented here among the Apocrypha, alongside 1 and 2 Maccabees. Third Maccabees deals with Diaspora Jews' maintaining their Israelite identity under Ptolemaic rule in Egypt and reflects Egyptian Judaism from the first century BC. It seems to be written in defense of Diaspora Judaism while maintaining boundaries between Jews and gentiles. The book describes the military advances of Ptolemy IV Philopator, his pollution of the Jerusalem temple, and his expulsion. God frustrates the intended revenge of Ptolemy, whose ultimate repentance further vindicates the faithful Israelites. Fourth Maccabees, written in Greek in the early to mid-first century AD, is largely a philosophical treatise affirming Torah and Jewish beliefs, exhorting Diaspora Jews, like martyrs before them (much from 2 Maccabees), to adhere to their traditional ways of life even in persecution by gentiles, who may find them peculiar. He sets out essential virtues that are achieved through the instruction of Torah.

Pseudepigrapha

The English term "pseudepigrapha" is the transliteration of a Greek word that refers to "falsely attributed writing," from *pseudēs* ("false") and *epigraphē* ("inscription, superscription"). The Greek term *pseudepigrapha* (sg. *pseudepigraphon*) occurs nowhere in biblical or Second Temple sources but is attributed to Serapion (ca. AD 191–211) with respect to writings falsely attributed to Christ's apostles and therefore rejected by the church (Eusebius, *Eccl. Hist.* 6.12.3). More generally, it is often used to designate works falsely attributed to, or in some way related to, prominent individuals. In the case of the so-called Old Testament Pseudepigrapha, works are attributed to or in some way associated with certain people featured in the body of literature contained in the Old Testament. The label was probably first used in biblical scholarship by Johann Albert Fabricius (1713). In practice, however, the term seems to be employed with respect to documents included in modern-language collections, such as that of James Charlesworth (*OTP*; see Reed,

"Modern Invention"). As opposed to the books contained in the Apocrypha, which are preserved in Greek and many of which stem from a Semitic original, a variety of documents designated as Pseudepigrapha are extant also in Latin, Syriac, Coptic, Ethiopic, and a number of other languages. Moreover, nearly all the documents in question are preserved exclusively in Christian traditions. Unlike the works of the Apocrypha, which date prior to the Bar Kokhba revolt (AD 132–135), the date of composition and even one's ability to ascribe a date for some of these pseudepigraphic documents are often debated. Indeed, it sometimes seems as if the term "OT Pseudepigrapha" is used merely as a category for writings not included among the Apocrypha or the Jewish or Christian canons, though there is some overlap with writings found among the DSS.

Pseudonymity

To some modern readers, the term "pseudepigrapha" implies the presumption of deceit. Although the practice of writing in the name of another was sometimes criticized, particularly in early Christianity, ancient responses to the books themselves were not uniform. Josephus, for example, seems to have regarded the apocryphal Additions to Daniel as sacred Scripture (*Ant.* 10.210; cf. 10.190–281; 11.337–38; 12.322). Others saw *1 Enoch* as Scripture and its ascription to Enoch as authentic (*Barn.* 4.3; 16.5–6; Tertullian, *Apparel* 3; *Idolatry* 4). Some held *1 Enoch* in high esteem, regardless of its origin (Irenaeus, *Adv. haer.* 4.16; Clement of Alexandria, *Eclogae propheticae* 2; 53; Anatolius of Alexandria, *Paschal Canon* 5; Ethiopic Orthodox tradition). Others rejected such works because of their pseudepigraphic origin (Tertullian, *Apparel* 3; cf. Origen, *Cels.* 5.54; Augustine, *Civ.* 18.38). Some scholars today suggest that the practice of producing pseudepigrapha was widely accepted and engaged in for a number of reasons.

Some libraries, such as the famous Alexandrian library, collected works of well-known writers. Therefore one may write in another's name to gain a place among well-known writers. This could be done to get a hearing for one's own views, whether to counter a false claim by (an) opponent(s) or draw the circumstances of the ancient figure into the context of the real author's setting. So, for example, the author of *4 Ezra* draws from the biblical Ezra. The book of Ezra is set in a context of the return from exile and reconstitution of the temple. *Fourth Ezra*, drawing from Ezra's narrative setting, is set after the destruction of the Herodian temple in AD 70, and "the affinities between biblical context and the time of writing were overwhelmed by the real author's pressing interests."[1] More recently scholars have contended that in antiquity writing in one's own name may have been perceived as unethical, whereas writing in the name of another is a more modest way of expressing one's indebtedness to a tradition. This suggests

---

1. Loren T. Stuckenbruck, "Apocrypha and Pseudepigrapha," *EDEJ* 143–62 (154).

that presumptions regarding the nature of a work because of its classification as pseudepigraphic should be held in check.

Provenance

Another pertinent problem with the Pseudepigrapha is determining the provenance of each of these writings: Is the document in question Jewish or Christian, and (how) can or (how) should such a distinction be made? This complicated question has relevance for the NT interpreter. Some scholars of the past presumed that if a document revering an OT figure was devoid of explicitly Christian content, it must necessarily be a Jewish document and appropriate for background to the NT. Yet if the document is actually Christian, one could unwittingly employ a *Christian* document for *Jewish* background to the NT. More recent scholarship has suggested a default position that, for some documents, presumes a Christian provenance influenced by Jewish Scriptures and traditions, such as the *Testaments of the Twelve Patriarchs*, the *Ascension of Isaiah*, *Lives of the Prophets*, *3 Baruch*, and *Joseph and Aseneth*.

The problem is exacerbated by the fact that nearly all of the so-called OT Pseudepigrapha were preserved not by Jews but by Christians. For some time, Robert Kraft ("Pseudepigrapha and Christianity"; "Pseudepigrapha in Christianity") has advocated understanding these documents in the Christian contexts in which they are preserved, at least initially. More recently, James R. Davila (*Provenance*) has called for a seemingly more objective set of criteria for discerning the origins of a pseudepigraphon. Davila isolates what he perceives to be "signature features," that is, common characteristics among indisputably Jewish texts. These include monotheism; acceptance of certain sacred books and a historical narrative drawn from them; adherence to their customs, laws, and rituals; support of the temple cult; self-identification as Jewish; used, valued, and read within a specific Jewish community; and recognition of Palestine as the Holy Land. A text need not have all these characteristics, and of course the identification of a text as Jewish depends at least to some extent on what description of Judaism one adopts. That is, what does one mean by "Jewish"? Richard Bauckham ("Continuing Quest") challenges this notion of documents' exhibiting a sort of "boundary maintenance," for it a priori marginalizes texts congenial toward Christianity, some of which are preserved in Christian contexts. Moreover, he suggests, one must be clear why such documents were preserved in Christian contexts and recognize that the document predates the manuscript in which it is preserved. In this view, a "default" position may be unwarranted. But the question does raise awareness among NT students of the difficulties in determining, let alone presuming, a "Jewish" provenance to a pseudepigraphon.

Where the provenance of an OT pseudepigraphon can be discerned, a diverse array of origins comes into view. Some texts, such as *1 Enoch* and *Jubilees*, are clearly Jewish, as their presence among the DSS attests. Others are Christian documents making use of Jewish traditions (*Lives of the Prophets*, *History of the Rechabites*), or simply Christian documents with little evidence of other influences at all (*Sib. Or.* 6–8; *Vision of Ezra*; *Apocalypse of Elijah*). Some texts may have originally been Jewish documents but, to some extent, have become essentially Christian documents over the course of transmission (*3 Baruch*, *Testaments of the Twelve Patriarchs*). Only in some instances are the interpolations by Christians evident. Some documents in this corpus give little indication of either Jewish or Christian influences (*Sentences of the Syriac Menander*). Again, the collection is rich and diverse and often defies simple categorization with respect to provenance.

The Books of the Pseudepigrapha

Which books are included among the so-called OT Pseudepigrapha is by no means uniform, even among published collections. The first such collection was that of Fabricius, whose *Codex pseudepigraphus Veteris Testamenti* (1713) included a number of Greek and Latin texts of this category (published in a second edition in 1722 and a second volume in 1723). Works from other languages, such as Ethiopic, were made available for the *Ascension of Isaiah* (1819) and *1 Enoch* (1821). The latter half of the nineteenth century saw the publication of still more books, such as *Jubilees*, *2 Baruch*, *3 Baruch*, *2 Enoch*, the *Apocalypse of Abraham*, and the *Testament of Abraham*. They were eventually published as collections of thirteen (Kautzsch, 1900 [German]), seventeen (Charles, 1913 [English]), twenty-five (Sparks, 1984 [English]), fifty (*Jüdische Schriften aus hellenistisch-römischer Zeit* [*JSHRZ*, 1973–, including Apocrypha [German]), sixty-one (Riessler, 1928 [German]), sixty-five (Charlesworth, *OTP* [English]), and nearly eighty (Bauckham, Davila, and Panayotov, 2013 [English]).[2] The latter collection (Bauckham et al.) contains fifty documents and nearly thirty fragments or quotations from other sources.

One could add to this a dizzying array of texts from the DSS that fall within this broad category. A selection of these include documents known about before the discovery of the DSS but attested among the Scrolls also, such as the Book of Watchers (*1 En.* 1–36; 4Q201–202, 204–206), the Animal Apocalypse (*1 En.* 85–90; 4Q204–207), and the Epistle of Enoch (*1 En.* 92.1–5; 94.1–105.2; 4Q204, 212). Also found were Hebrew texts from *Jubilees* (e.g., 1Q17, 1Q18, 2Q19, 2Q20) and Pss. 151, 154, 155 (11Q5). There were also documents attested at Qumran classified broadly as pseudepigrapha that were previously unknown, such as the

2. Emil Kautzsch, *Die Apokryphen und Pseudepigraphen des Alten Testaments* (Tübingen: Mohr, 1900); R. H. Charles, ed., *Apocrypha and Pseudepigrapha of the Old Testament in English* (2 vols.; Oxford: Clarendon, 1913); H. F. D. Sparks, *The Apocryphal Old Testament* (Oxford: Oxford University Press, 1984); H. Lichtenberger, W. G. Kümmel, et al., eds., *Jüdische Schriften aus hellenistisch-römischer Zeit* (many vols.; Gütersloh: Gütershloher Verlag-Haus Mohn, 1973–); Paul Riessler, *Altjüdisches Schrifttum ausserhalb der Bibel* (Augsburg: Filser, 1928).

Aramaic *Prayer of Nabonidus* (4Q242), *Four Kingdoms* (4Q552, 4Q553), and the *Testament of Jacob* (4Q537), to name but a few. Other works are attributed to the archangel Michael (4Q529), Obadiah (4Q380), Manasseh (4Q381), and perhaps Moses (1Q22, 2Q21, 4Q385a, 4Q387a, 4Q388a, 4Q389, 4Q390).

The Contents of Pseudepigraphic Books

The books classified as OT Pseudepigrapha are much too diverse to summarize all of them. Below is a list of the documents included in Charlesworth (*OTP*), the most diverse and inclusive edition currently in print. Charlesworth divides the texts according to genre. After this list, a brief description of a select few documents is provided.

1. Texts

Apocalypses: *1 Enoch, 2 Enoch, 3 Enoch, Sibylline Oracles, Treatise of Shem, Questions of Ezra, Revelation of Ezra, Apocalypse of Sedrach, 2 Baruch, 3 Baruch, Apocryphon of Ezekiel, Apocalypse of Zephaniah, Apocalypse of Abraham, Apocalypse of Adam, Apocalypse of Elijah, 4 Ezra, Greek Apocalypse of Ezra, Apocalypse of Daniel, Vision of Ezra*

Testaments: *Testaments of the Twelve Patriarchs, Testament of Job, Testament of Moses, Testament of Solomon, Testaments of the Three Patriarchs* (Abraham, Isaac, and Jacob), *Testament of Adam*

Expansions of OT and Legends: *Letter of Aristeas, Ladder of Jacob, 4 Baruch, Jannes and Jambres, History of the Rechabites, Eldad and Modad, History of Joseph, Jubilees, Martyrdom and Ascension of Isaiah, Joseph and Aseneth, Life of Adam and Eve*, Pseudo-Philo (*Liber antiquitatum biblicarum*), *Lives of the Prophets*

Wisdom and Philosophical Literature: *Ahiqar*, 3 Maccabees, 4 Maccabees, Pseudo-Phocylides, *Sentences of the Syriac Menander*

Prayers, Psalms, and Odes: *More Psalms of David*, Prayer of Manasseh, *Psalms of Solomon, Hellenistic Synagogal Prayers, Prayer of Joseph, Prayer of Jacob, Odes of Solomon*

Fragments of Judeo-Hellenistic Works: Philo the Epic Poet, *Orphica, Fragments of Pseudo-Greek Poets*, Demetrius the Chronographer, Eupolemus, Cleodemus Malchus, Pseudo-Hecataeus, Theodotus, Ezekiel the Tragedian, Aristobulus, Aristeas the Exegete, Pseudo-Eupolemus, Artapanus

2. Select Summaries

The documents in this corpus are diverse and complex. Here we will provide brief overviews of but a few documents from this collection that are widely regarded as both Jewish in origin and of sufficiently early date of composition (roughly prior to the Bar Kokhba revolt, AD 132–135) for background to the NT.

The book of *Jubilees* is a work probably composed in Hebrew in the second century BC. It was translated into Greek, and from there into Ethiopic. Today it is extant in its entirety only in Ethiopic. Throughout its fifty chapters, the book expands on the biblical accounts of Gen. 1–Exod. 19. It purports to contain a secret revelation given to Moses on Mount Sinai (*Jub.* 1.1). The narrative generally follows the biblical sequence and divides its time into forty-nine years, or jubilees. The author recounts the stories of Adam, Noah, Abraham, Jacob and his sons, and the bondage and deliverance from Egypt. The author is steeped in priestly concerns and recasts biblical figures in that light. For example, it is Levi who receives the blessing of Jacob (21.12–17) and inherits ancestral books (45.16). Adam (3.27), Enoch (4.25), Noah (6.1–4), and Abraham all offer sacrifices or incense (cf. 21.7–16). Repeated concerns for priestly matters, such as the consumption of blood (6.7–14; 7.31–32; 21.6), circumcision (15.25–34; 20.3), and distinction from the nations (22.16–18; 25.4–10) underscore the priestly bent.

The *Psalms of Solomon* is a collection of eighteen poetic writings dating from the first century BC, extant in Greek and Syriac but likely composed in Hebrew. Why Solomon's name is affixed to the collection is unknown, since there is nothing within it to make such a connection. It seems unlikely that a single individual wrote these psalms, but they share some uniformity in their collective outlook of Jews after the death of Pompey (48 BC). The *Psalms* make regular allusions to historical events from the era of their composition. For example, one text describes the sinner as entering Jerusalem and the foreigner as defiling the temple (*Ps. Sol.* 2.1–2), associated with the Roman general Pompey (ca. 63 BC; cf. Josephus, *Ant.* 14.57–79; *J.W.* 1.141–58; Dio Cassius, *Hist.* 42.5; see also *Pss. Sol.* 8.15–17; 17.11–13). The psalmists see themselves as pious and righteous (*Pss. Sol.* 2.33; 3.3; 9.3; 10.6; 11.1; 12.4), while others, whether gentiles or Israelites, are wicked sinners (4.8, 20, 23; 12.1, 5; 14.6; 17.20). Often the *Psalms* are associated with the Pharisees because of their affinities toward known Pharisaic concerns (Josephus, *J.W.* 2.162–66), such as resurrection (*Pss. Sol.* 3.12), interpretation of Torah (4.8), and free will (9.4–5). Yet such simplifications are tenuous. What seems clear, however, is the *Psalms'* polemic against a monarchy outside the Davidic line (17.6), where the Hasmoneans are clearly in view. The *Psalms* assert that, though Israel has fallen prey to a foreign power, God will send his messiah, the son of David, to set things right (*Pss. Sol.* 17).

The *Letter of Aristeas* is a fictitious epistle by Aristeas, allegedly a courtier of some standing with Ptolemy II Philadelphus (283–247 BC), to his brother Philocrates. It was actually written by a Jew, probably in Alexandria between 140 and 130 BC. In it Aristeas claims to recount the circumstances surrounding the translation of the Hebrew Torah into Greek. The translation is commissioned at Ptolemy's request to Eleazar, the high priest in Jerusalem. Eleazar readily agrees and sends seventy-two men to Alexandria for the task (*Let. Aris.* 41–51), where they enjoy a banquet before beginning the translation work (172–300). The seventy-two translators work for seventy-two days, and their translations are ratified by the Jewish community (308–11). The translators are sent home with praises and gifts from Ptolemy (317–21). Most scholars recognize the *Letter of Aristeas* as a fictional account of the origins of the LXX for its promotion as sacred writ among Greek-speaking Jews of Alexandria.

The book of *1 Enoch* is not a single book, per se, but a collection of writings dating from the fourth century BC to the turn of the era. It was originally written in Aramaic, as fragments from Qumran affirm, but it is extant in full only in Ethiopic, translated from a Greek text. All portions are associated with the biblical Enoch (Gen. 5:21–24). The first component is the Book of Watchers (*1 En.* 1–36), which dates from the latter half of the third century BC. It describes righteous Enoch's reception of heavenly visions, the rebellion of angels, or watchers, and the work of Azazel, the rebellion's leader. Enoch ascends to the heavenly throne room and is commissioned as a prophet of judgment. Accompanied by an angelic entourage, he travels throughout the earth and receives visions of judgment. The second component of *1 Enoch* is called the Similitudes, or Book of Parables (*1 En.* 37–71), and it dates between the last half of the first century BC and the late first century AD. This work too is a record of Enochic visions and angelic interpretations as the prophet travels through God's throne room and the universe. Aside from Enoch, the main figure here is an eschatological judge, mostly called "Chosen One," but also "son of man" and other titles. The Astronomical Book, or Book of the Heavenly Luminaries (*1 En.* 72–82), describes the role and structure of heavenly and earthly bodies and addresses the importance of the solar calendar of 364 days. The Book of Dreams (*1 En.* 83–90) contains two visions: The first (*1 En.* 83–84) contains a vision of the coming flood, followed by a prayer. The second (*1 En.* 85–90), also called the Animal Apocalypse, recounts an apocalyptic vision of human history, using animals to represent people and people to represent angels. The Epistle of Enoch (*1 En.* 91–108) dates from the end of the second to the middle of the first century BC. The letter is allegedly written by Enoch to subsequent generations and contains an Apocalypse of Weeks, giving a visionary account of human history from the time of Enoch to the end of days.[3]

Fourth Ezra is an apocalypse that forms chaps. 3–14 of the Christian apocryphon 2 Esdras. (The Christian Greek additions of 2 Esd. 1–2 and 15–16 are known as *5 Ezra* and *6 Ezra*, respectively.) Set thirty years after the destruction of the Solomonic temple (557 BC), the book is allegedly written by Shealtiel, father of Zerubbabel, who built the second temple (cf. Ezra 3; 5; Hag. 1–2). Yet *4 Ezra* identifies Shealtiel with Ezra the scribe and was written after the (Roman) destruction of the (Herodian) temple in AD 70. The apocalypse is set in a narrative structure in which Ezra changes from one who mourns over Jerusalem and questions the justice of God to one who perceives God's purposes and comforts

3. This complicated unit is itself divided into five distinct literary segments: the *Apocalypse of Weeks* (*1 En.* 93.1–10; 91.11–17); the *Epistle of Enoch* proper (*1 En.* 92.1–5; 93.11–105.2); an *Exhortation* (*1 En.* 91.1–10, 18–19), the *Birth of Noah* (*1 En.* 106.1–107.3), and an *Eschatological Admonition* (*1 En.* 108.1–15).

his people. Ezra receives his revelations by God and the angel Uriel, one in each of the seven divisions of the book. Throughout, Ezra challenges the justice of God and is again and again corrected through visions and their explanations. The book as a whole is noted for the ambiguity of the answers it provides, which are often scant or none at all. The questions Ezra raises pertaining to God's justice are not brought to satisfactory resolution, but Ezra nonetheless resolves himself to God's promise of eschatological bliss. In the final section (chap. 14) Ezra is seen as a new Moses who exhorts Israel to obey the Torah and is taken to heaven. The purpose of the book seems to be to lament over the destruction of Jerusalem and to denounce Rome for doing it.

The Apocrypha and Pseudepigrapha in Jewish and Christian Tradition

The Apocrypha and Pseudepigrapha in Jewish Antiquity

Jewish tradition attributes to Rabbi Akiba the claim that those who read "the outside books" (sĕpārîm ha-ḥiṣônîm) have no place in the world to come (m. Sanh. 10.1; cf. b. Sanh. 100b; y. Sanh. 28a). Though these references provide no list of what books are in view, Rabbi Joseph is said to have forbidden the reading of Ben Sira (b. Sanh. 100b). Yet even here sources are confused, for later in b. Sanh. 100b Rabbi Joseph is claimed to expound "excellent statements" in Ben Sira, which is quoted positively a number of times (similarly y. Ber. 11b; y. Naz. 54b; Rab. Eccles. 7.12) in this section, alongside Proverbs, Jeremiah, and even Deuteronomy. The distinction between sacred books and others is expressed in a surprising way. Some rabbinic traditions indicate that the holiness of sacred Scriptures "make[s] the hands unclean" (t. Yad. 2.14; m. 'Ed. 5.3; b. Meg. 7a; y. Soṭah 18a). Even containers holding Scripture, materials used to sew scriptural manuscripts, and the scrolls themselves are thought to do the same (m. Kelim 15.6; t. Yad. 2.12). Other sources, such as Ben Sira (t. Yad. 2.13), and even Homer (m. Yad. 4.6; y. Sanh. 28a), have no such effect (b. Meg. 7a). Why it is sacred texts and not other sources that render the hands unclean is not immediately evident. The description may suggest a kind of sanctity, a "sacred contagion," similar to the lethal power of the ark of the covenant (cf. 2 Sam. 6:6; Lim, "Defilement"). Regardless, it is a description employed by some rabbinic texts to differentiate sacred texts from others.

Perhaps some saw the need to distinguish sacred texts from others because of the view that the prophets, and presumably their prophecies with them, have fallen asleep (2 Bar. 85.3; Josephus, Ag. Ap. 1.41; b. Soṭah 48b; cf. Zech. 13:2). Josephus affirms twenty-two authoritative books while acknowledging the existence of a multitude of contradictory and conflicting books of which he is aware (Ag. Ap. 1.38). It may be that such books were marginalized because of a perception of the appropriate number of authoritative books (cf. Josephus, Ag. Ap. 1.38; Rab. Eccles. on Eccles. 12:12; both 2 Esd. 14:45–46 and b. B. Bat. 14b–15a suggest the number is twenty-four).

The Apocrypha and Pseudepigrapha in the New Testament

There are no clear quotations of OT Apocrypha in the NT, but there is at least one clear quotation from the Pseudepigrapha. Moreover, there is a degree to which NT authors are familiar with and assume readers to be familiar with some traditions contained in both apocryphal and pseudepigraphic traditions. For example, Jude (v. 9) makes cryptic reference to a battle between the archangel Michael and Satan for the body of Moses which, according to Clement of Alexandria (*Adumbrationes in Epistolam Judae*) and Origen (*Princ.* 3.2.1), is found in the *Assumption of Moses*. This cannot be confirmed, however, because the sole extant copy of that work is a Latin palimpsest discovered in the Ambrosian Library in Milan in 1861. The manuscript dates from, perhaps, the sixth century AD and is thought to contain less than half of the original. So any account there may have been of this legend is as yet undiscovered or has not survived. Later in Jude (v. 14), however, the author makes a clear quotation from *1 Enoch* (*1 En.* 9)—though he does not explicitly cite it as "Scripture."

Another point of familiarity may be found in Heb. 11:37, where the statement "they were sawn in two" is often taken as an allusion to the fate of Isaiah found in the *Lives of the Prophets* (1.1; also in *Mart. Isa.* 5.1–4, 11–14; cf. Justin Martyr, *Dial.* 120.5; Origen, *Ep. Afr.* 9; Tertullian, *Pat.* 14). Some have suggested an apocryphal source for the quotation in 1 Cor. 2:9: "But, as it is written, 'What no eye has seen, nor ear heard, nor the human heart conceived, what God has prepared for those who love him.'" Though this citation is nowhere found in the OT, it is cited elsewhere in early Christianity (*1 Clem.* 34.8; *Mart. Pol.* 2.3; *2 Clem.* 11.7). Some have taken this to mean the apostle cites from a source known to the ancients, such as the *Apocalypse of Elijah* (Origen, *Comm. Matt.* 10.18), which is a Christian document of obscure provenance. At least since Jerome (*Comm. Isa.* [on 64:4]) scholars have recognized here a loose reference to or paraphrase of Isa. 64:3–4. Whatever Paul's source in this text, citation of an apocryphal work is doubtful.

It has been suggested that Paul's "new creation" (Gal. 6:15) draws from an otherwise unknown "Moses apocryphon" (Photius, *Quaestiones ad Amphilochium* 151). Paul's exhortation "Sleeper, awake!" (Eph. 5:14) has been attributed to Elijah (presumably the *Apocalypse of Elijah*), to Isaiah (26:19; 60:1), or to a Jeremiah apocryphon. But it is more likely an early Christian hymn (similarly 1 Tim. 3:16). The Egyptian magicians Jannes and Jambres are mentioned by name in 2 Tim. 3:8, yet the OT source (Exod. 7:11) does not give their names. Their names were known in rabbinic writings (*Tg. Ps.-J. Exod.* 1.15; 7.11), the DSS (CD 5.17–18), and pagan literature (Pliny the Elder, *Nat. Hist.* 30.1.11). Though some contend it likely that there existed a single book that contained details of their exploits, the diverse and fragmentary nature of extant traditions preclude citation of a singular literary source. But agreement on the names does point to a common familiarity regarding their identity. Other suggested citations or allusions have been posited in Matt. 11:25–30 (Sir. 51:1–30); Matt. 27:43 (Wis. 2:13, 18); Rom. 1:18–32 (Wis. 13–15); and Heb. 1:3 (Wis. 7:25–26), but these are debated. Although examples could be multiplied, these examples suffice to demonstrate that traditions found within apocryphal and pseudepigraphic sources were, at times, familiar to NT authors. However, there is no strong evidence for citation of the Apocrypha in the NT, and only one clear citation from the Pseudepigrapha.

The Apocrypha and Pseudepigrapha in Early Christianity

Important citations of the Apocrypha and the Pseudepigrapha are found in early Christian sources outside the NT. Perhaps the earliest is that of the *Didache*, a Christian work from the end of the first century, which exhibits familiarity with Tobit (Tob. 4:15 in *Did.* 1.2) and Sirach (Sir. 4:31 in *Did.* 4.5). In the *Epistle of Barnabas* the author of *4 Ezra* is cited as "another of the prophets" (citing *4 Ezra* 4.33 and 5.5 in *Barn.* 12.1). The same letter cites *1 En.* 89.56–66 as "Scripture" (*graphē*; *Barn.* 16.5) and makes a number of possible allusions to *1 Enoch* (*1 En.* 99.1–2 and 100.1–2 in *Barn.* 4.3; *1 En.* 91.13 [and Dan. 9:24] in *Barn.* 16.16) and perhaps *4 Ezra* (*4 Ezra* 6.6 in *Barn.* 6.13). Also late in the first century, the author of *1 Clement* (3.4) quotes the Wisdom of Solomon (Wis. 2:24) to make an important point about the entrance of death into the world. Later that same author (*1 Clem.* 27.5) quotes the Wisdom of Solomon again (Wis. 12:12) alongside a psalm (Ps. 19:1–3 in *1 Clem.* 27.7). Polycarp's letter *To the Philippians* (10.2) quotes Tobit (4:10; 12:9) adjacent to a string of exhortations (10.1–3) influenced by and alluding to various biblical texts (Prov. 3:28; Isa. 52:5; Rom. 12:10; 1 Cor. 15:58; 2 Cor. 10:1; Eph. 5:21; 1 Pet. 2:12, 17; 5:5).

There is evidence that Clement of Alexandria (ca. AD 150–215) is familiar with traditions like the *Assumption of Moses* (cf. *Strom.* 1.23; 6.15). Melito of Sardis (d. ca. AD 190; preserved in Eusebius, *Eccl. Hist.* 4.26.14) provides a list of OT books that includes the Wisdom of Solomon. Irenaeus (d. ca. AD 202) likewise acknowledges familiarity in referencing "an unspeakable number of apocryphal and spurious writings" (*Adv. haer.* 1.20.1), which he condemns and advocates avoidance among Christians. Yet he regards the Additions to Daniel as authentic (*Adv. haer.* 4.26.3) and accepts the veracity of accounts from *1 Enoch* (*1 En.* 12–16 in *Adv. haer.* 4.16.2) and the *Letter of Aristeas* (*Adv. haer.* 3.21.2), while exhibiting familiarity with *4 Ezra* (*4 Ezra* 14.37–48 in *Adv. haer.* 3.21.2) and calling none into question. Tertullian (ca. AD 160–220) advocated for the scriptural status of *1 Enoch* (*Apparel* 1.3).

Origen's (ca. AD 185–254) dialogue with Julius Africanus occasions a discussion regarding the acceptance or rejection of texts based at least in part on use or disuse (*Ep. Afr.* 4–5). Africanus questions the authenticity of some of the Additions to Daniel. For his part, Origen appeals to the preservation of these texts by God's providence and their use in the churches thus far to justify his own acceptance of them. Origen uses a similar line of argument for his approval of Tobit and Judith (*Ep. Afr.* 13; see also *Comm. Matt.* 10.18). Yet Origen does acknowledge that some "apocryphal" books contain things that are "corrupt and contrary to the true faith" (*Comm. Cant.* prologue §3). In his thirty-ninth *Festal Letter* (AD 367), Athanasius (ca. AD 296–373) identifies books as canonical based on their presence in the Hebrew canon. He includes Baruch and the Letter of Jeremiah alongside Jeremiah.

In Jerome's introduction to the books of Kings (1–2 Samuel and 1–2 Kings; see Jerome, *Prologus Galeatus*), he indicates that he will, in his labors, render the Scriptures from Hebrew into Latin. He also shows his familiarity with books not attested in Hebrew and therefore set aside among the "Apocrypha." These he lists as Wisdom of Solomon, Sirach, Judith, Tobias (Tobit), *Shepherd of Hermas*, and also 1–2 Maccabees, though the former is in Hebrew and the latter in Greek. Elsewhere, Jerome (*Epist.* 107.12, ca. AD 403) instructs a certain Laeta to have her daughter treasure—both read and memorize—the Holy Scriptures. Yet she is to avoid all apocryphal writings. If she does read them, however, she is not to do so for the truth of their doctrine and is to be instructed that they are not really written by those to whom they are ascribed. Moreover, "many faulty elements have been introduced into them, and . . . it requires infinite discretion to look for gold in the midst of dirt." Such works, as with others, she is to read "rather to judge them than to follow them" (W. H. Fremantle, *NPNF²* 6:194).

Catechetical Lectures 4.33 by Cyril of Jerusalem (ca. AD 315–386) exhorts the audience to "read none of the apocryphal writings," for such is to trouble oneself in vain about books that are disputed (presumably in origin; E. H. Gifford, *NPNF²* 7:26–28). His view is often compared with that of Rufinus (ca. AD 345–410; *Commentarius in symbolum apostolorum* 37–38), who distinguishes three classes of books: canonical books, which are the only ones used in proof of doctrine; ecclesiastical, which may be read in churches (such as Wisdom, Ecclesiasticus [Sirach], Tobit, Judith, and the books of Maccabees, among some others); and finally ones called "apocryphal," which are not to be read in churches—though Rufinus in no way defines his terms or distinguishes between the latter two. Yet like Jerome, Rufinus affirms the reading of such works in ecclesiastical contexts for the purpose of edification but not doctrine (Rufinus, *Commentarius in symbolum apostolorum* 37–38). The convention seems to conflate what we consider apocrypha with our category of pseudepigrapha. Augustine (AD 354–430) sought to include in the OT canon the books of Tobit, Judith, 1–2 Maccabees, Wisdom of Solomon, and Sirach (*Doctr. chr.* 2.8.12–13). He recognized that not all would embrace their inclusion but nonetheless made use of some of these texts (Wisdom of Solomon and Sirach) on doctrinal matters.

The Apocrypha and Pseudepigrapha in Later Christian Traditions

The Reformer Martin Luther included the Apocrypha (except 1–2 Esdras) in his translation of the Bible (1534), indicating that while they are not sacred Scripture, they are nonetheless profitable to read. Similar inclusions were made in the Dutch Bible (1526) and the Swiss-German Bible (1527–29). In 1520 Andreas Bodenstein of Karlstadt (*De canonicis scripturis libellus* 114, 118) reckoned some works as sacred (Wisdom of Solomon, Sirach, Tobit, Judith, 1–2 Maccabees), while others were to be censored (1–2 Esdras, Baruch, Prayer of Manasseh, Prayer of Azariah, Song of the Three Young Men, Susanna, Bel and the Dragon). Similar sentiments were affirmed in other statements (Belgic Confession [1561], the Synod of Dort [1618–19], and the Westminster Confession [1647]). In response to such criticisms, the Roman Catholic Church's delegates to session VI of the first Council of Trent (1546) pronounced a curse on any who refuse to recognize all books contained in the Latin Vulgate (1–2 Esdras and the Prayer of Manasseh were thereby rejected from the canon, only to be reinstated in the Clementine Bible of 1592). Another term used by Roman Catholic scholars for the Apocrypha is the "Deuterocanonical" books, a term first posed by Sixtus of Sienna (1566) in recognition of the comparatively late acceptance of their canonical status rather than to indicate that they are secondary in authority.

Outside of Protestant and Roman Catholic traditions, Orthodox confessions have adopted various components of apocryphal and pseudepigraphic texts, perhaps even allowing for some fluidity (Trullan Synod [692]). Five of these are additions to other canonical books, such as Psalm 151, the Letter of Jeremiah, Additions to Esther, and Additions to Daniel (which includes the Prayer of Azariah, the Song of the Three Young Men, Susanna, and Bel and the Dragon).

Other works often included in Orthodox canons are Tobit, Judith, Wisdom of Solomon, 1–2 Maccabees, Sirach, and Baruch. At the Synod of Jerusalem (1672), the Greek Orthodox Church adopted the term "deuterocanonical" for these writings. This designation was likewise used for the Prayer of Manasseh, 1 Esdras, and 3 Maccabees (with 4 Maccabees in an appendix). Since the publication of the Old Church Slavonic Bible (1581), the Russian Orthodox Church includes the writings of the Prayer of Manasseh, 2 Esdras (commonly known elsewhere as 1 Esdras), *3 Esdras* (commonly known elsewhere as 2 Esdras), and 3 Maccabees. Fourth Maccabees is omitted, and the Esdras writings are designated differently. More fluid is the Ethiopian Orthodox canon, which contains the Prayer of Manasseh, 2 Esdras, 2 Esdras 3–14 (known also as *4 Ezra*), *1 Enoch*, and *Jubilees*. The Syriac language–based Orthodox traditions (Syriac Orthodox and Monophysite Orthodox) include such works as *2 Baruch*, *4 Ezra*, and 4 Maccabees (from Peshitta manuscript 7a1), five additional Psalms (Pss. 151–55), and a work known as the *Canons of the Apostles* (which includes Judith, Tobit, and Sirach).

Modern translations, such as the NRSV, often divide the Apocrypha into four units. The first unit contains books found in Roman Catholic, Greek, and Slavonic Bibles (Tobit, Judith, Additions to Esther, Wisdom of Solomon, Sirach, Baruch, Letter of Jeremiah, Additions to Daniel, 1 and 2 Maccabees). The second division contains books found in the Greek and Slavonic Bibles but not in the Roman Catholic corpus (including 1 Esdras, Prayer of Manasseh, Psalm 151, and 3 Maccabees). Third is a work found in the Slavonic Bible and in the Vulgate appendix (2 Esdras), and fourth is a single work in an appendix to the Greek Bible (4 Maccabees).

Apocrypha, Pseudepigrapha, and New Testament Interpretation

The development of scholarly inquiry into these sources has significantly enhanced the ability of the NT student to handle such sources with care. The publication of collections of primary sources has exposed documents to a wide readership. Yet their publication in single volumes, or collections of volumes, should not be taken to indicate they are in any sense a uniform collection. Among NT students unfamiliar with this field, it is common to unwittingly presume that the publication of a collection of ancient sources within an accessible set of volumes with a title like Charlesworth's OTP means that the documents contained therein are both of sufficient antiquity for NT background (say, prior to the Bar Kokhba revolt) and of such an origin that it can unquestioningly be consulted for Jewish "background" to the NT. In reality, in the Charlesworth volumes alone there are Jewish and Christian documents, some early and others late, and some of unknown provenance.

Such diversity serves to illustrate that the "OT Pseudepigrapha" is a loose collection of documents that defies uniformity. Each document must be examined on its own prior to being assessed for its place in the study of the NT, both with respect to provenance and dating. One is on more sure footing with regard to the Apocrypha, all of which are Jewish and date prior to Bar Kokhba. The late Martin Hengel purportedly told his students with some regularity that those who know only the Bible do not really know the Bible. His point was simply that familiarity with primary sources roughly contemporaneous with, say, the NT exposes the student to the context in which the NT was written. The attentive student of the NT has unprecedented access to these sources that, with sufficient caution and respect for these texts first as texts in their own right, can provide fruitful illumination to biblical texts.

See also "The Scriptures and Scriptural Interpretation"; "Pseudonymous Writings and the New Testament."

Bibliography

Bauckham, Richard J. "The Continuing Quest for the Provenance of the Old Testament Pseudepigrapha." Pages 9–20 in *The Pseudepigrapha and Christian Origins: Essays from the Studiorum Novi Testamenti Societas*. Edited by Gerbern S. Oegema and James H. Charlesworth. London: T&T Clark, 2008. Challenges Davila and Kraft on Christian manuscript traditions as the starting place for the provenance of the OT Pseudepigrapha.

Bauckham, Richard J., James R. Davila, and Alexander Panayotov, eds. *Old Testament Pseudepigrapha: More Noncanonical Scriptures*. 2 vols. Grand Rapids: Eerdmans, 2013. Collection of Pseudepigrapha supplementing that of Charlesworth.

Charlesworth, James H., ed. *The Old Testament Pseudepigrapha* [OTP]. 2 vols. Garden City, NY: Doubleday, 1983–85. The standard English translations and collections, with critical introductions and notes, for a wide variety of pseudepigraphic documents.

————. *The Old Testament Pseudepigrapha and the New Testament: Prolegomena for the Study of Christian Origins*. Rev. ed. Harrisburg, PA: Trinity Press International, 1998. Helpful companion to the OTP volumes. Some survey of the thought world of the Pseudepigrapha and its overlap with NT.

Collins, John J., and Daniel C. Harlow, eds. *The Eerdmans Dictionary of Early Judaism*. Grand Rapids: Eerdmans, 2010. Essential reference tool for anything related to Second Temple Judaism, by expert contributors. Prior to dictionary entries are important articles on select topics in the field, including "Apocrypha and Pseudepigrapha," by Loren T. Stuckenbruck.

Davila, James R. *The Provenance of the Pseudepigrapha: Jewish, Christian, or Other?* JSJSup 105. Leiden: Brill, 2005. Recent attempt to develop criteria for discerning the religious origin and orientation to various books.

deSilva, David A. *Introducing the Apocrypha: Message, Context, and Significance*. Grand Rapids: Baker Academic, 2002. Accessible and thorough introduction to the subject. Offers a detailed description of the structure, historical context, and contents of each book. Best single volume available on the subject; ideal starting place.

————. *The Jewish Teachers of Jesus, James, and Jude: What Earliest Christianity Learned from the Apocrypha and Pseudepigrapha*. New York: Oxford University Press, 2012. Examines the formative influence of select books of the Apocrypha and Pseudepigrapha on the Synoptic Jesus traditions and the Letters of James and Jude.

DiTommaso, Lorenzo. "Pseudepigrapha Research and Christian Origins after the OTP." Pages 30–47 in *The Pseudepigrapha and Christian Origins: Essays from the Studiorum Novi Testamenti Societas*. Edited by Gerben S. Oegema and James H. Charlesworth. London: T&T Clark, 2008. Summary of development of scholarly publications in the field since Charlesworth's OTP.

Evans, Craig A. *Ancient Texts for New Testament Studies*. Peabody, MA: Hendrickson, 2005. Comprehensive introduction to all NT backgrounds. Provides brief synopsis of content and scholarly issues of each work, accompanied by bibliography of primary and most important secondary literature. Essential reference tool.

Kraft, Robert A. "The Pseudepigrapha and Christianity Revisited: Setting the Stage and Framing Some Central Questions." *JSJ* 32 (2001): 371–95. Advocates discerning provenance of a pseudepigraphon initially from its Christian setting in the manuscript tradition in which it is preserved.

————. "The Pseudepigrapha in Christianity." Pages 55–86 in *Tracing the Threads: Studies in the Vitality of Jewish Pseudepigrapha*. Edited by John C. Reeves. Atlanta: Scholars Press, 1994. As above, and calls for greater methodological controls than have been used.

Lim, Timothy H. "The Defilement of the Hands as a Principle Determining the Holiness of Scriptures." *JTS* 61, no. 2 (2010): 501–15. Explains the rabbinic notion of hand defilement regarding sacred Scripture in terms likened to the lethal effects of touching the ark of the covenant.

Metzger, Bruce M., and Roland E. Murphy. *The New Oxford Annotated Apocrypha: The Apocryphal/Deuterocanonical Books of the Old Testament*. New York: Oxford University Press, 1991. Standard translation with brief introduction and notes for each text.

Najman, Hindy. *Seconding Sinai: The Development of Mosaic Discourse in Second Temple Judaism*. Leiden: Brill, 2003. Advocates pseudopigraphy as a re-creation of the discourse of the esteemed figures of the past.

Nickelsburg, George W. E. *Jewish Literature between the Bible and the Mishnah*. 2nd ed. Philadelphia: Fortress, 2005. Survey of the literature within respective historical contexts. Excellent source for both history and literature of Second Temple Judaism.

Reed, Annette Yoshiko. "The Modern Invention of 'Old Testament Pseudepigrapha.'" *JTS* 60, no. 2 (2009): 403–36. Traces historical development of modern research in the field, including the categorization of texts, terminology, and publication set in respective historical and cultural contexts of European ecclesiastical and scholarly settings from which the field developed.

Stuckenbruck, Loren T., et al., eds. *Commentaries on Early Jewish Literature*. Berlin: de Gruyter, 2003–. Developing commentary series devoted to Jewish documents and traditions from ca. 300 BC to AD 150.

Wyrick, J. *The Ascension of Authorship: Attribution and Canon Formation in Jewish, Hellenistic, and Christian Traditions*. Cambridge: Cambridge University Press, 2004. Wyrick claims that pseudonymity is an accepted mode of composition for a tradition that discouraged individual authorial glory.

25

Jewish Identity, Beliefs, and Practices

ARCHIE T. WRIGHT

The four issues addressed here—circumcision, Sabbath, food, and purification rites—are inherently linked to the theological debates that took place in the Second Temple period and the early Jewish Christian community. At the heart of these debates is the issue of "sectarianism" in Palestine prior to and during the emergence of Christianity in the first century AD. Disputes between the "sects" were due in part to the Jerusalem temple, the mainstream institution of the society. From the heart of the city, those in control of the temple established policies for the function of the cult and the daily ritual practices of Jews. As a result, the various sects who left behind literature—Qumran, the church, and the rabbis—sought to establish their own rules to govern the practices by either reinterpreting or rejecting the temple rules.

Each of the issues discussed here played an important role in maintaining Jewish identity (Neusner, "Purity," 17). Laws governing the Sabbath, circumcision, food, and purity were interpreted by the sects as boundary markers that normally served to separate Jew and gentile but now differentiated between those considered insiders and the outsiders of each sect. Jewish sectarianism began to emerge in the Maccabean period (second century BC), when changes in Jewish life were rapidly taking place. (Some argue that sectarianism began earlier, during the Persian period, 539–334 BC; see Grabbe, *Judaic Religion*, 207–9.) Several factors contributed to these changes to Jewish life in Palestine, including (1) the introduction of Hellenism, beginning with the conquest of Palestine by Alexander the Great in 334 BC; (2) the persecution by Antiochus IV Epiphanes, who sought to abolish the temple cult and outlaw Jewish laws (cf. 1 Macc. 1:44–50); (3) the successful revolt by the Maccabeans against these decrees in 168–164 BC (cf. 1 Macc. 1–4); and (4) the establishment of a semiautonomous state under the Hasmonean dynasty.

The resulting authority of the Hasmonean dynasty displayed inconsistency in its attitude toward surrounding cultures; despite leading the rebellion against the Seleucid rulers, they showed a particular affinity to the Greek culture. In their ensuing disappointment, the sectarians recognized that a life of purity was needed to protect their way of life from the gentiles and also from Jews who demonstrated unfaithfulness to God.

Christianity emerged in this period with a similar sectarian mind-set (Nickelsburg, *Ancient Judaism*, 182–84), though Jesus and the leaders of this Jewish sect took a different approach to interpreting the laws of the Sabbath, circumcision, food, and purity—an approach that could be described as less rigid or even liberal in relation to other groups, such as the Pharisees or the Essenes. In addition, contrary to other Jewish sects, the early Christian community offered an open door to gentiles, while claiming exclusivism by defining itself around the messianic identity of Jesus of Nazareth rather than Torah. Similarly, each of these somewhat pious Jewish sects claimed that it was the true Israel and that its interpretation of the laws in question was the divinely inspired interpretation (Talmon, "Internal Diversification," 31).

The commandments governing these issues are established in the biblical tradition. The Sabbath is first mentioned in the creation account in Gen. 2:2–3. The covenant marker of circumcision is called for in God's covenant with Abraham in Gen. 17:10–14. Food laws are introduced in Lev. 11:1–47 and Deut. 14:2–20, although other OT texts speak to the issue. The fourth issue, purity laws, is central to the discussion of the other three subjects. Any debate or rulings put forth in the Second Temple period concerning the Sabbath, circumcision, or food hinges on their affect on the purity of an individual or the nation. The implementation of purity rules was necessary to allow continued participation in worship and to prevent pollution of holy places or objects. Leviticus offers the basis for governing the purity issues—for example, unclean animals (Lev. 5), clean animals and how they are to be used in the sacrificial cult (Lev. 11; 17), purification after childbirth (Lev. 12), illness and bodily discharges (Lev. 13; 15), and sexual relations (Lev. 18).

Circumcision

Circumcision in Second Temple Judaism had its origins in Gen. 17. While establishing a covenant with Abraham, God promises him that he will be the father of many nations. The sign of agreement to this covenant is the physical circumcision of every male in Abraham's family, including the household servants. In addition God tells him that every male should be circumcised on the eighth day throughout the generations of Abraham's descendants. Further support for the eighth-day requirement may be suggested from the Qumran scroll 8Q1 Genesis (frg. 4). This fragmentary text contains Gen. 17:12–17, and the suggested reconstruction of the text indicates it may have contained the phrase "on the eighth day" from Gen. 17:14 (Thiessen, "Genesis 17:14").

The practice of circumcision was not exclusive to the Israelites. Archaeological evidence suggests that during the Egyptian Sixth Dynasty the practice was carried out among the Egyptians (their reasons for circumcision appear to be quite different from those of the Israelites). Illustrations from the tomb at Saqqara (2350–2000 BC) depict a circumcised carpenter. A relief discovered at the tomb of Ankh-ma-Hor at Saqqara depicts the circumcision of two puberty-aged boys. A second figure depicts a similar action performed by a second priest. In addition, a twenty-third-century BC stele from Naga-ed-Der indicates that circumcision was performed in a mass ritual. The author states, "When I was circumcised, together with one hundred and twenty men, there was none thereof who hit out, there was none thereof who was hit, and there was none thereof who scratched and there was none thereof who was scratched." Notice that Gen. 17:23–27 recounts an event very much like the stele text (Wilson, "Circumcision," 326).

Further evidence of the practice by the Egyptians is provided by Herodotus, who reports that the Egyptians "practice circumcision for cleanliness' sake; for they would rather be clean than more becoming" (*Hist.* 2.37; A. D. Godley, LCL). He also notes:

> The Colchians, the Egyptians, and the Ethiopians are the only nations that have from the first practiced circumcision. The Phoenicians and the Syrians of Palestine [the Jews] acknowledge that they learned the custom of the Egyptians; and the Syrians [Jews] of the valleys of the Thermodon and the Parthenius, as well as their neighbors the Macrones, say that they learned it lately from the Colchians. These are the only nations that circumcise, and it is seen that they do just as the Egyptians. (Herodotus, *Hist.* 2.104; A. D. Godley, LCL)

Additional archaeological evidence was discovered in an eleventh-century BC relief from Megiddo that portrays a procession coming before a ruler. Included in the group are two naked prisoners who are clearly circumcised and appear to be Semites. According to Jer. 9:25–26, other Semitic groups were practicing circumcision in the seventh century BC—including Edomites, Ammonites, and Moabites. Others—such as the Assyrians, Babylonians, and Philistines—were not circumcised; in fact the Philistines are called the "uncircumcised" in a derogatory fashion.

Scholars have suggested that there is a threefold purpose for circumcision in the HB: metaphorical, ethical, and ritual (Williamson, "Circumcision"). As a ritual, circumcision was demanded in order for a male to be a part of the covenant community. By performing this ritual on one's son, an individual was passing on the privileges and ethical responsibilities to the next generation. In addition it was used to assimilate individuals into the nation and covenant who were not ethnically or biologically related to Abraham.

Circumcision is also used metaphorically in the biblical text. Several passages describe an uncircumcised heart as a heart that does not repent as God requires (Lev. 26:41; Deut. 10:16; 30:6; cf. Jer. 4:4; 9:25–26). Exodus 6:12 and 30 describe uncircumcised lips as those unsuitable for speaking divine communication; Jer. 6:10 suggests that uncircumcised ears are unable to hear divine communication. The issue of unsuitability may be the reason behind the physical human ritual among the Israelites. With physical circumcision, one was identified as suitable for entering into covenant with God.[1]

The ethical significance of circumcision is closely tied to its metaphorical usage. An uncircumcised heart means an individual is unfaithful to God (Deut. 10:16 17; 30:6–7). Leviticus 26:40–42 suggests that Israel must repent of its uncircumcised heart in order for God's covenant to be restored. Jeremiah uses the image of an uncircumcised heart (9:24–26) to compare Israel with the unclean/uncircumcised gentiles. Each significant aspect of circumcision in Israel (metaphorical, ethical, and ritual) was tied theologically and spiritually to covenant obligations and privileges.

During the Second Temple period circumcision was a point of dispute among the Jews. With the Hellenization of Palestine, many Jews became enamored by the Greek culture and customs. Many would take part in the Greek gymnasium, in which exercises were performed in the nude; many Jews became aware of the physical "deformity" of their circumcision and chose to undergo a "de-circumcision" procedure. First Maccabees 1:15 states that a Greek-style gymnasium was constructed in Jerusalem and many Jews "hid their circumcision and abandoned the holy covenant" (author's translation). Josephus reports that "they also hid the circumcision of their genitals that even when they were naked they appeared to be Greeks" (*Ant.* 12.241; author's translation). The difficulty with this practice was that during this period faithful Jews thought that covenant and circumcision were synonymous—that is, anyone who tried to hide the sign of the covenant thus denied his place in the community.

In the ensuing years, Antiochus IV Epiphanes outlawed circumcision along with other identifiably "Jewish" customs, resulting in the Maccabean revolt in the mid-second century BC (cf. 1 Macc. 1:44–49, 60–63). As a result, the faithful in Palestine issued a polemic against the Jews who rejected circumcision (cf. 1 Macc. 1:13–15; Josephus, *Ant.* 12.241). One can thus see the importance that circumcision held in Second Temple Judaism. In the revolt, the Maccabeans defeated the Seleucids and established the Hasmonean Kingdom in Palestine, immediately enacting a ruling requiring mandatory circumcision for Jews and those they subjugated, the

1. John Goldingay, "The Significance of Circumcision," *JSOT* 88 (2000): 3–18.

Idumeans and Itureans (1 Macc. 2:46; Josephus, *Ant.* 12.278; 13.257–58, 318–19). Other Jewish texts from the period stress the continued covenant role of circumcision. *Jubilees* 15.11–14 underscores the magnitude of the ritual by claiming that even the angels were circumcised at creation. As a result circumcised Jews are able to stand in the assembly of the angels. *Jubilees* 15.22–34 states that those who fail to circumcise are identified as "sons of Beliar" or "sons of destruction" and no longer members of the community. The importance of the ritual is also clear from the DSS. According to 1QH^a 14.20 the uncircumcised may not walk on God's holy path, and 4Q458 (frg. 2 2.4) declares that the uncircumcised will be destroyed in the last days. Several scrolls continued the biblical tradition of a metaphorical use of "uncircumcised"—for example, 4Q434 (frg. 1 1.4) affirms that God will save his people with a circumcision of the heart (see also 1QS 5.5, 26; 4Q504 3.11; 1QH^a 10.18; 1QpHab 11.13).

However, when one approaches the NT, a clear shift becomes evident as to the relevance of the ritual of circumcision in the early church. While Jewish believers were allowed to continue the practice, according to Acts 15:1–11; 21:25 new gentile believers were not required to be circumcised. Rather, for Paul and other early church leaders, it is the uncircumcised heart that must be circumcised as a sign of the covenant (Rom. 2:25–5:5; 1 Cor. 7:17–20; Gal. 5:1–15; 6:11–18; Eph. 2:11–12; Phil. 3). It may be argued that water baptism replaced physical circumcision, thus allowing for proper recognition of both males and females in the covenant (Gardner, "Circumcised"; Martin, "Circumcision").

Food Laws

From the quantity of biblical texts dedicated to instructions concerning food and its consumption (e.g., Lev. 11:1–47; Deut. 14:2–20), it is clear that the contents of the Israelite diet were extremely important to God's people (Eidelman, "Food"). However, this is an issue not simply of dietary health but also of covenant purity. In these texts a close link is established between what the people should eat and what was required in the sacrificial cult of the temple.

Leviticus 11:1–47 and Deut. 14:2–20 identify what living creatures may and may not be eaten. These laws are expounded in the *Letter of Aristeas* (142–71) and in Philo (*Spec.* 4.95–131). Characteristics are offered for those animals considered clean: they must part the hoof (i.e., have cloven feet) and chew the cud. Both features must be present; otherwise the animal is considered unclean (Lev. 11:4–8). Also, an Israelite is forbidden to touch the dead carcass of any of these creatures. Leviticus 11:9 states that any water creature with fins and scales may be eaten. A list of seafood considered unclean and inedible follows (vv. 10–12). Verses 13–19 identify species of birds that are detestable and should not be eaten or their carcasses touched. Verse 20 begins a list of detestable insects to be avoided. Verses 20–47 identify creatures that will render an individual unclean, along with cooking practices that result in the ritual impurity of a vessel or an individual. Leviticus 11:45 (not found in the listing in Deut. 14) holds the key to all the food laws of the Pentateuch: "For I am the LORD who brought you up from the land of Egypt, to be your God; you shall be holy, for I am holy." The food laws are given in order to establish further purity guidelines for the people.

Some dietary laws may have been discarded by Jews in the Diaspora in an effort to assimilate (Barclay, *Jews*, 434), although some literature suggests the general Jewish population remained diligent in keeping the food laws (see Philo, *Migr.* 89–93). Although eating with gentiles was taboo, it seems to have been tolerated if a Jew hosted the dinner or brought his own food to the gentile's house (see Jdt. 12:1–4, 19; Add. Esth. 14:17; Josephus, *Life* 14; Rom. 14:1–2). During these meals one would dispense with the prayers and libations of the gentiles (*Let. Aris.* 184–85) and would often sit at a separate table with distinct food (*Jos. Asen.* 7.1). Gentiles saw adherence to the food laws as misanthropic, suggesting that this separation was a common practice (e.g., Philostratus, *Vit. Apol.* 33; *Let. Aris.* 139–42, which describe the setting up of walls between the Jews and gentiles due to food laws; 3 Macc. 3:4 describes how Jews are hated by others due to the religious distinctions). But for the Jews, the food laws bound the community together by solidifying their ethnic identity on a daily basis.

Sabbath

The observance of the Sabbath was the clearest marker of ethnic identity of the Jewish community in the Second Temple period. However, there appears to have been no uniform way for Jewish observance of the Sabbath (Doering, "Sabbath and Festivals"). Practices varied concerning many issues, including marital sex, saving human life, conducting warfare, fasting, travel, and work. According to John Barclay, granting these variations in practice, for Jews the Sabbath was the most important of the Jewish feasts; it was "so regular, so noticeable, and so socially problematic, affecting . . . not only personal but also financial, legal, and political relationships." Gentiles despised the Jews for this practice, calling it "stupidity or laziness or both" (Barclay, *Jews*, 440). They found it remarkable that Jews should neglect work for one day during the week. However, Sabbath observance, like circumcision and observance of the food laws, was an issue of purity for Jews.

The origins of the weekly Sabbath observance are debated. Exodus 20:8–11 establishes the commandment for the Israelites to keep the seventh day holy. Verse 11 suggests that the author of Exodus understands the roots of this commandment to originate in Gen. 2:2–3 and the creation narrative. Exodus 31:14–17 stresses the need for Israel to keep the Sabbath as a sign of the covenant, with further mention of its origins in the creation narrative. The author makes it clear that anyone who profanes the Sabbath with work is to be put to death. Further, Exod. 35:2–3 emphasizes observing the Sabbath and the threat of death to those who do not. In addition, the Day of Atonement in Lev. 16:31 is described as Sabbath rest that is an eternal statute. Furthermore, Lev. 23–26 and Num. 28 describe various sacrificial rites to be performed on the Sabbath.

Despite the limited evidence as to its origins, the Sabbath is a well-established feast by the early Second Temple period (cf. Isa. 56:2; Neh. 13:15–22). Herold Weiss argues that the Jews gave the Sabbath significance during the Babylonian exile in the sixth century BC (*Day of Gladness*). It is possible that the feast was firmly established by Ezekiel and the Priestly authors and editors of the Pentateuch (Andreasen, *Sabbath*). The end result established a dominant covenantal identity marker for the Jews. Further evidence of the Sabbath's importance is found in the Elephantine papyri that record concerns for the Sabbath among a Jewish community in Egypt during the fifth century BC. The issues raised reflect the question of work that could be performed on the Sabbath. We discover similar questions in Palestine during the same period. Nehemiah records that there were many violations taking place in Jerusalem concerning conducting business on the Sabbath. Nehemiah 13 presents the actions necessary to reestablish the nation's commitment not to profane the Sabbath.

During the Hasmonean and Roman periods the Sabbath held a central position in the ideology of the Jews in Palestine (and the Diaspora). In very much a negative sense the Sabbath served as an identity marker of the Jews among the gentiles. As a result many Jews felt a great deal of pressure to hide or neglect its observance in order to assimilate to the surrounding cultures. Many argue that this was the first step in the process of the apostatizing of the nation. Philo states:

> Moreover, it is only a very short time ago that I knew a man of very high rank, one who was prefect and governor of Egypt, who, after he had taken it into his head to change our national institutions and customs, and in an extraordinary manner to abrogate that most holy law guarded by such fearful penalties, which relates to the seventh day, . . . was compelling us to obey him, and to do other things contrary to our established custom, thinking that that would be the beginning of our departure from the other laws, and of our violation of all our national customs, if he were once able to destroy our hereditary and customary observance of the seventh day. (*Somn.* 2.123)[2]

During the Greco-Roman period, several Jewish texts note the necessity of a variety of Jewish communities to maintain a stringent observance of the Sabbath. This practice often required a strict separation from their gentile neighbors in order to prevent a violation of the Sabbath, which, as noted above, resulted in a negative view of the observant Jews and the Sabbath practice among the Gentiles. The *Damascus Document* states that, on the Sabbath, Jews were supposed to remain distant from their gentile neighbors (CD 11.14b–15a). *Jubilees* 50.8 calls

---

2. C. D. Yonge, trans., *The Works of Philo of Alexandria* (Peabody, MA: Hendrickson, 2005), 396.

for the death penalty for those who violate the Sabbath (CD 10.14–11.18 does not take such a harsh stance against a violation). The Gospels also suggest that such a prescription was being enforced during the time of Jesus. Mark 3:1–6 and John 5:1–18 mention the desire of the Pharisees to kill Jesus after his violation of the Sabbath. In these texts, the point of contention for Jesus may have been Pharisaic halakah, not a rejection of the Torah or its commandments per se. Several scholars argue that Qumran and related documents offer stricter sectarian rulings concerning Sabbath observance (Weiss, *Day of Gladness*, 15); others maintain that the so-called stricter rules of Qumran are not sectarian but are the normative Jewish tradition at an early stage (see Josephus, *J.W.* 2.145–49).[3] The Essenes appear more particular about Sabbath observances than do other Jewish groups (cf. CD 10.14–11.18).

Several points of contention concerning the Sabbath were apparent among various Jewish groups during the Greco-Roman period. The most prominent issue appears to be the adoption of the Hellenistic calendar by the high priest (cf. Dan. 7:25), which may have established the mainstream Jewish feast dates, including the Sabbath. The Hellenistic calendar was a luni-solar model of 354 days in a year with intercalary months added when necessary. The calendar was first introduced in 167 BC at the Jerusalem temple. In conflict with the Hellenistic calendar, the Jewish solar calendar contained twelve thirty-day months and an additional four intercalary days—one every three months. This solar calendar would fall short of the 365¼ days of the astronomical calendar (see Dan. 7:25; 1 Macc. 1:59; 2 Macc. 6:7 may suggest that the solar calendar was in use during the Second Temple period). The solar calendar had exactly fifty-two weeks, allowing the days of the month to be fixed, and thus the feasts and Sabbaths were fixed days of the year. It was of absolute importance for the feast days and the Sabbath days to fall on the same day as those celebrated in the heavenly court; otherwise the whole nation could be found in violation of the Sabbath.

With the victory by the Maccabeans in 165 (or 164) BC and the cleansing of the Jerusalem temple, many thought the Jewish solar calendar would be reinstated. However, in 150 BC Jonathan the high priest (appointed in 153 BC; see 1 Macc. 10:1–46; Josephus, *Ant.* 13.35–61) reaffirmed the use of the luni-solar calendar, resulting in many faithful Jews abandoning the temple due to the untimely keeping of the festivals. Those who followed the Jewish solar calendar claimed that the Sabbath began at Saturday sunrise and ended at Sunday sunrise, while those who followed the temple's luni-solar calendar claimed that the Sabbath began at sundown on Friday and ended at sundown on Saturday. Scholars have argued that this dispute may have resulted in the establishing of the Qumran community (Talmon, "Internal Diversification," 35–43; VanderKam, *Calendars*). Still others suggest that this was only one of several reasons the covenanters abandoned the temple.[4]

---

3. S. T. Kimbrough, "The Concept of the Sabbath at Qumran," *RB* 5 (1966): 483–502.

4. Philip R. Davies, "Calendrical Change and Qumran Origins: An Assessment of VanderKam's Theory," *CBQ* 45 (1983): 80–89.

Josephus records that the Jews were granted religious rights that included Sabbath observance (see *Ant.* 13.52; 14.226–27, 242, 244–46, 256–58, 262–64; 16.162–63, 167–68). Several of these passages describe the failure of the Jews to defend themselves in war because they refused to take up arms on the Sabbath (cf. 1 Macc. 2:29–38). On several occasions their enemies may have used this as a military tactic, including the invasion by Nebuchadnezzar (Johns, "Military Strategy"). Josephus argues that some thought that keeping the Sabbath was a weakness on the part of the Jews in that it allowed Ptolemy to take Jerusalem on the Sabbath without a fight (*Ant.* 12.4–6; *J.W.* 2.517–18). After the deaths of Jews who refused to defile the Sabbath by fighting, the Maccabees took an oath to fight on the Sabbath to assure the continued existence of the Jewish people (1 Macc. 2:39–41). Josephus, however, argues that the laws against work on the Sabbath must be observed, and that Sabbath observance is both a measure of piety and an identity badge for those who keep it faithfully. He identifies the Essenes as devoted, pious Jews for their Sabbath observance (*Ant.* 1.33; 3.91, 281; 12.4, 274; 13.252; 14.63; 18.318, 359; *J.W.* 2.456; *Ag. Ap.* 1.212; 2.174).

Proper observance of the Sabbath continued to be a central issue in early Jewish communities, including the Jewish Christian communities.

Purity

Within the HB we find the development of distinct strategies for defining, achieving, and maintaining purity. These include the priestly program presented in Leviticus and also those found in Ezekiel and Deuteronomy. Each of the programs has a certain focus on the tabernacle/temple cult, and particularly on the priests. Bruce Chilton contends that "all laws of cleanness are Israel's means of maintaining solidarity of sacrifice with God, apart from which the land may not be retained" ("Purity," 875). Leviticus 18:24–30 makes it clear that the previous inhabitants of the land were expelled because of their failure to keep rules of purity concerning the land.

Hannah Harrington defines "purity" as "the state of cleanness effected by physical purification rituals required for lay participation in the cult" ("Halakah," 79). Jacob Milgrom defines "impurity" as an "active, malevolent force that grows in strength unless checked and reduced through ablutions" ("Ablutions," 570). For the Qumran community the ablutions (based on Gen. 35:2) must accompany repentance (1QS 3.4–6). These characterizations provide working definitions of purity rites in the Greco-Roman period.

Purity laws varied among Jewish groups in the Second Temple period. The group that stands out the most is the Qumran community. The strict degree of purity imposed at Qumran is likely due to the group's connection to the priesthood. The lifestyle they kept was similar to that of the Zadokite temple priesthood (Sanders, *Judaism*, 359; see the *Temple Scroll* for rulings concerning purity in the temple). In fact, the Qumran community considered itself the temple; as such, all forms of impurity, according to the priestly code, prevented an individual from entering the community. The purification rites that were performed allowed one to participate again in the temple cult activity following defilement.

The archaeological evidence at Qumran suggests the ritual bath (Hebrew *mikveh*; pl. *mikva'ot*) was a centerpiece of the purity rituals of the community (thus far, approximately three hundred *mikva'ot* have been discovered from the late Second Temple period). This feature may be due to the priestly nature of the occupants. It was a priestly ritual to bathe after touching anything unclean or anyone less pure. They treated their meals as holy food eaten outside of the temple by the priests. They abstained from wine because wine was not consumed in the temple. They strictly avoided sexual intercourse due to the impurity issues caused by semen.

The issue of purity and sexual relations is raised in several Qumran documents. The *Damascus Document* prohibits any sexual relations within the city of Jerusalem due to the holiness of the temple (CD 12.1). Biblical law requires the priest to immerse following sexual relations prior to entering the temple (Lev. 15:18); CD 10.10–13 expands this ruling to the entire city: the priest must be completely immersed prior to entering Jerusalem.

For the Qumran community, holiness went hand in hand with purity. According to the *Temple Scroll* (11QT^a 45.12–14), the *War Scroll* (1QM 7.3–5), and the *Halakic Letter* (4QMMT B42–57), physically impaired persons (blemished) were not allowed within the entire temple city or the war camp (in 1QM). This restriction goes beyond what is mandated in the HB, which requires physical perfection only for the officiating priest (Lev. 21:23). It may be proposed that the goal of the Qumran legal material was the achievement of maximum holiness (Harrington, "Halakah," 80–81, 86). The desire for this "pure holiness" is due in part to the presence of the holy angels in the community; this divine presence required a community that strictly adhered to the Torah (1QM 12.1). Some may argue that Jesus also goes beyond the Levitical standards of Torah; in Matt. 5:27–28 Jesus states, "You have heard that it was said, 'You shall not commit adultery.' But I say to you that everyone who looks at a woman with lust has already committed adultery with her in his heart."

Jacob Neusner maintains that the idea of purity in ancient Judaism suggests that there is no difference between moral and ritual impurity. He states, "The impurity of the menstrual woman and that of the arrogant person are not distinguished in any way. . . . For the *yahad* [i.e., members of the strict Qumran community], one cannot distinguish between cultic and moral impurity" (*Purity*, 54). Purity and impurity are closely identified with the anthropology of the period in that it was thought that individuals who were considered sinners had a "spirit of impurity" that could only be cleansed by a spirit of holiness (see esp. 1QS 4.20b–22a; also, more broadly, 1QS 3.13–4.26). The *Rule of the Community* at Qumran indicates that sinners participate in the same ritual immersion as one who has a ritual impurity (1QS 3.6–11; 5.13–14). This does not suggest that all who were considered impure were sinners—for example, menstruation was not a sin; burying the dead was not a sin; the burning of the red heifer results in the priest's becoming impure, but not by sin. Leviticus 11:32 and Num. 19:14–15; 31:23 declare that objects that have become impure by contact must be immersed to be cleansed. Impurity that is not related to sin is easily purified by immersion, while two categories of impure individuals first require a physical healing and then a period of impurity from which they must be cleansed. These individuals include the leper (Lev. 14:3) and the *zāb*, that is, one suffering from an abnormal genital discharge (Lev. 15:3; Harrington, "Impurity").

For Jews living in this period, to be unclean meant to belong to the realm of death. Any acknowledged impurity must be kept away from the sacred, because what is holy is distinct from the ordinary, the profane, or the unclean. The concept of impurity in the first century AD affected three primary activities for the individual—eating, procreation, and attendance at the Jerusalem temple. (The rules of impurity did not apply to participation in the activities of the synagogue.) The temple priests were required to eat under the conditions of cultic cleanness. All Israelites were required to abstain from foods deemed unclean in the Torah. All Israelites had to abstain from sexual intercourse when the woman was in her menstrual cycle. Any Jew wishing to participate in the temple cult first had to pass through a ritual bath. This was especially true during the festivals of Passover, Pentecost, and Tabernacles and during the Sabbath. Uncleanness came about through liquids related to the human body—blood, semen, or the viscous gas of a corpse. The impurity was reversed and cleanness restored through immersion in the natural flow of water in the correct volume.

The Qumran community reflects some of the more stringent regulations concerning purity and uncleanness in the Second Temple period. The legal texts contain a multitude of laws centered on purity issues. There are at least twenty-three legal passages in the *Damascus Document*, and other references can be found in 4QMMT, 4Q159, 4Q513, and the *Temple Scroll* (Harrington, "Halakah," 78). Several regulations are specific to the Sabbath and perhaps deserve special note (Doering, "Purity Regulations"). 4Q512 (frgs. 33+35 4.1–5) identifies the "ritual purification on the eve of the Sabbath" as involving water "to sanctify oneself" and is typical of purification rituals in the DSS, which usually include references to "in water" and "to sanctify oneself." Sanctification takes place in ritual immersion (1QS 3.4–5, 9; 4Q512 frgs. 1–6 12.10; 1QH^a 11.10–11). The authors of these Qumran texts may be drawing from the immersion tradition found in Exod. 19:10, 14–15, where Moses is told to sanctify the people in order to prepare them to come before the Lord at Sinai.

Second Maccabees 12:38 offers a similar incident concerning the Maccabean army's ceremonially purifying themselves "according to the custom" in order to prepare for the coming of the Sabbath. The purification rite may be due to the bloodshed from battle (cf. Num. 31:19), but Num. 31 suggests contact with a corpse, which is not in the text of 2 Maccabees. In CD 11.3–4 and 4Q265 6.2–4 it is specified that, in addition to washing the body for the Sabbath observance, the member will also launder his clothes or at least wear fresh clothing (cf. Num. 31:20). It is likely that "soiled garments," found in both texts, signifies a purity issue. The term "soiled" equates to feces, which of course was a matter of impurity among the Essenes (Josephus, *J. W.* 2.149; see Doering, "Purity Regulations," 603).

The issue of purity played an important part in differentiating between two sects during the Second Temple period—the Qumran *yaḥad* and the Pharisaic *ḥavurah* (an association for the promotion of ritual purity). As a result, one must ask what the Israelites understood as pure and impure and how these ideas were developed into a ritualized set of commandments. It appears that those connected to the priesthood focused on things directly relevant to the temple cult. The language of purity comes to prominence beginning in the late second century BC through the first century AD, in particular in the writings of the Qumran sectarians, Josephus, Jesus' polemic against the Pharisees, and Paul. From these texts we can see that the issue of purity arose due to sectarian conflict within the Jewish community at large.

The idea of purity is typically used as a metaphor in the Second Temple period for such issues as sexual intercourse, idolatry, evildoings, and purity in connection with the cult. Philo uses the purity metaphor for moral purity and addresses the biblical commandments concerning impurity. In Christian literature the main sources of uncleanness are food and sexual intercourse. In the Gospel accounts, impurity becomes a source of the demonic, while a ritual of purification can drive off the spirit of impurity or remove the effects it has on the individual. Purity was a major point of contention between Jesus and the various Jewish sects in Palestine.

Conclusion

In this brief discussion of circumcision, Sabbath, food laws, and purity we have seen that during the Greco-Roman period significant influences, both internal and external to Judaism, resulted in a strong sectarian atmosphere in Palestine. As a result, we can identify various levels of observance for each of these issues due to the level of piety within various Jewish groups.

Bibliography

Andreasen, Niels-Eric. *The Old Testament Sabbath: Tradition-Historical Investigation.* Missoula, MT: Society of Biblical Literature, 1972. Examines the origins of the Sabbath in ancient Israel and suggests that the feast was firmly established by Ezekiel and the Priestly authors and editors of the Pentateuch.

Barclay, John M. G. *Jews in the Mediterranean Diaspora from Alexander to Trajan.* Berkeley: University of California Press, 1996. Barclay compiles and analyzes evidence concerning the Jewish communities dispersed throughout the Mediterranean. The results of the work offer a description of the levels of assimilation, acculturation, and accommodation by which the Jews interacted with the non-Jews that surrounded them.

Chilton, Bruce. "Purity." *DNTB* 874–82. Discusses the idea of purity during the Second Temple period and the variations in practice among Jews.

Cohen, Jeffrey M. "*Hatan Damim*: The Bridegroom of Blood." *JBQ* 33 (2005): 120–26. Discusses the concept of the "bridegroom of blood" in relation to Exod. 4:24–26.

Doering, Lutz. "Purity Regulations concerning the Sabbath in the DSS." Pages 600–609 in *The Dead Sea Scrolls Fifty Years after Their Discovery: Proceedings of the Jerusalem Congress, July 20–25, 1997.* Edited by Lawrence H. Schiffman et al. Jerusalem: Israel Exploration Society, 2000.

———. "Sabbath and Festivals." Pages 566–86 in *The Oxford Handbook of Jewish Daily Life in Roman Palestine.* Edited by Catherine Hezser. Oxford: Oxford University Press, 2010. Examines various levels of Sabbath observance among Jews in the Greco-Roman period and the effects this observance had on the individual and on the nation as a whole.

Eidelman, Jay M. "Be Holy for I Am Holy: Food, Politics, and the Teaching of Judaism." *JRitSt* 14 (2000): 45–51. Discusses the phrase "Be holy, for I am holy" (Lev. 11:44) and its central role in the observance of food laws in ancient Israel.

English, Patrick T. "Cushites, Colchians, and Khazars." *JNES* 18 (1959): 49–53. Discusses the practice of circumcision in the various cultures outside Israel, their reasons for the practice, and how their practices differed from that of Israel.

Gardner, Paul D. "Circumcised in Baptism, Raised through Faith: A Note on Col. 2:11–12." *WTJ* 45 (1983): 172–77. Examines the role of baptism as a substitute for circumcision among believers in the early church.

Grabbe, Lester. *Judaic Religion in the Second Temple Period: Belief and Practice from the Exile to Yavneh.* London: Routledge, 2000. Grabbe discusses the various religious practices of the Jewish people during the Second Temple period.

Harrington, Hannah K. "The Halakah and Religion of Qumran." Pages 74–89 in *Religion in the Dead Sea Scrolls.* Edited by John Collins and Robert Kugler. Grand Rapids: Eerdmans, 2000. Examines the Sabbath under the halakah of the Qumran community and how it differed from other Jewish groups of the period.

———. "The Nature of Impurity at Qumran." Pages 610–16 in *The Dead Sea Scrolls Fifty Years after Their Discovery: Proceedings of the Jerusalem Congress, July 20–25, 1997.* Edited by Lawrence H. Schiffman et al. Jerusalem: Israel Exploration Society, 2000. Examines the rules of dealing with the issue of impurity within the Qumran community and how an individual became ritually impure and was restored to purity.

Johns, Alger. "The Military Strategy of Sabbath Attacks on the Jews." *VT* 13 (1963): 482–86. Discusses the problem that Sabbath observance caused for Jews who were observing the Sabbath law of no work and how this created opportunities for their enemies to overcome them in battle.

Larue, Gerald A. "Religious Traditions and Circumcision." Paper presented at the Second International Symposium on Circumcision. San Francisco, April 30–May 3, 1991. http://www.nocirc.org/symposia/second/larue.html. Examines the history of the religious traditions tied to circumcision throughout the ancient world.

Martin, Troy W. "The Covenant of Circumcision and the Situational Antitheses in Galatians 3:28." *JBL* 122 (2003): 111–25. Examines the problems circumcision created in the early church, in particular with the numbers of gentiles entering the church.

McKay, H. A. *Sabbath and Synagogue: The Question of Sabbath Worship in Ancient Judaism*. Leiden: Brill, 1994. Discusses how Jews in the synagogue observed the Sabbath and the particular rituals and traditions that were present in Sabbath worship in the synagogue.

Milgrom, Jacob. "First Day Ablutions in Qumran." Pages 561–70 in *The Madrid Qumran Congress: Proceedings of the International Congress on the Dead Sea Scrolls, Madrid, 18–21 March, 1991*. Edited by Julio Trebolle Barrera and Luis Vegas Montaner. Leiden: Brill, 1992. Examines the practice of ritual bathing in the Qumran community and how it compared to other Jewish practices concerning purity and how to deal with impurity.

Neusner, Jacob. "The Idea of Purity in Ancient Judaism." *JAAR* 43 (1975): 15–26.

———. *The Idea of Purity in Ancient Judaism*. Leiden: Brill, 1973.

———. *Judaism When Christianity Began: A Survey of Belief and Practice*. Louisville: Westminster John Knox, 2002. Examines the various religious beliefs and practices of Jews in the first century AD and their relationship to the beliefs and practices of the emerging Jewish-Christian and Gentile Christian church.

Nickelsburg, George W. E. *Ancient Judaism and Christian Origins*. Minneapolis: Fortress, 2003. Examines the religious practices and traditions and how they were taken up and further developed or transformed in the early church.

Sanders, E. P. *Judaism: Practice and Belief; 63 BCE–66 CE*. London: SCM, 1992. Examines the various religious beliefs and practices of Jews in the first century AD and their relationship to the beliefs and practices of the emerging Jewish-Christian and Gentile Christian church.

Talmon, Shemaryahu. "The Internal Diversification of Judaism in the Early Second Temple Period." Pages 16–43 in *Jewish Civilization in the Hellenistic-Roman Period*. Edited by Shemaryahu Talmon. Sheffield: Sheffield Academic, 1991. Discusses the issue of sectarianism in the Second Temple period and how that brought about various interpretations of the biblical laws.

Thiessen, Matthew. "The Text of Genesis 17:14." *JBL* 128 (2009): 625–42. Discusses the issue of circumcision of Jewish males on the eighth day of life and when exactly this became a normative practice in Judaism.

VanderKam, James. *Calendars in the Dead Sea Scrolls: Measuring Time*. New York: Routledge, 1998. Examines how the Qumran community managed the problem of proper observance of the heavenly feasts ordained by God in the biblical text. Proper observance required the use of the correct calendar that aligned the feast days on earth with those in the heavenly realm.

Weiss, Herold. *A Day of Gladness: The Sabbath among Jews and Christians in Antiquity*. Columbia: University of South Carolina Press, 2003. Examines the practice of Sabbath keeping and its cultic significance to the Jews of the Second Temple period and the early Christians.

Williamson, P. R. "Circumcision." Pages 122–25 in *Dictionary of the Old Testament: Pentateuch*. Edited by T. Desmond Alexander and David W. Baker. Downers Grove, IL:

InterVarsity, 2003. Offers a review of the practice of circumcision in the ancient world of the OT.

Wilson, John. "Circumcision in Egypt." Page 326 in *Ancient Near Eastern Texts Relating to the Old Testament*. Edited by James B. Pritchard. Princeton: Princeton University Press, 1950. Examines the practice of circumcision in ancient Egypt and how the practice was taken up by surrounding peoples, including the Jews.

26

Jewish Education

KENT L. YINGER

The nature of Jewish education in the first century has clear relevance for a number of issues in NT interpretation. How did Jesus learn Torah—at home, at school? Could he even read and write? Were his disciples illiterates? Could Peter or John have written letters? What sort of rabbinic training did Paul have, and did he study Greek rhetoric and use it in his letters?

Methodology

The variety and contradictory nature of depictions of first-century AD Jewish education in standard handbooks is bewildering. Some speak of elementary schools being widespread throughout Israel; subjects studied, hours of attendance, and teacher pay are all clearly defined (Safrai, "Education"). Others find such elementary schools present only in Jerusalem and only for the children of the most elite in society; elsewhere, illiteracy reigned (Hezser, "Education").

The difference lies in the sources used and in the interpretation of these sources. Most are agreed that the OT provides relevant, though scant, background information for Jewish praxis in the first century. Deuteronomy 6:7 ("Recite [these commands] to your children and talk about them when you are at home and when you are away, when you lie down and when you rise") points to the family- and Torah-centered nature of Jewish education. Equally relevant for nearly all writers on the subject are Second Temple writings such as Sirach, Philo, Josephus, and the DSS. Sirach 51:23 ("Draw near to me, you who are uneducated, and lodge in the house of instruction") has been particularly influential, since it seems to speak of early public education ("house of instruction"; Hebrew *bêt midrāš*); however, this evidence must be treated with caution (see below).

Most of the discrepancy between depictions can be traced, however, to the use of rabbinic sources. Since the written form of these texts is usually dated to the third century AD and later, scholars have become increasingly hesitant to use their statements as a reflection of first-century praxis (e.g., Hezser, "Education"; Victor, *Colonial Education*). Thus, when *m. 'Abot* 5.21 speaks of an age-graded curriculum (Scripture at five years of age, Mishnah at ten years, Talmud at fifteen years), some depictions will import this picture into the first century, whereas others will see it as an ideal of a later generation, not a description of first-century reality.

Our sources provide scarce data for reconstructing the nature of Jewish education in the first century. This article adopts a minimalist approach, drawing conclusions only from sources that are generally accepted as illuminating first-century praxis (see Victor, *Colonial Education*, for an example of this trend).

Family-Centered Instruction Rather Than Formal, or Institutional, Instruction

The home provided the primary source of education for children throughout the Greco-Roman world; this was also the case for Jews in the OT period and in the ANE at large. Although elementary schools existed for the upper classes in Roman cities, for the vast majority of the population, education was largely a private affair.

Fathers were the primary educators of sons, in keeping with the Torah (Exod. 13:8, 14; Deut. 6:20–21; cf. Prov 4:1, 10–11), but mothers and extended family were also involved (Prov 1:8; 6:20; 31:1; Tob. 1:8; 2 Tim. 3:15). The education of daughters was largely in the hands of mothers, but, as with sons, both parents could be involved (Sus. 3). In addition, children received some education in public gatherings (synagogues), during pilgrimages to Jerusalem (cf. Luke 2:41–51), and from visiting scribes, priests, and teachers (Deut. 33:10).

Were there "schools" in first-century Palestine? On the one hand, schools limited to scribal training probably existed in Jerusalem and possibly in other urban centers. Some think John the Baptist's father, Zechariah, evidences such schooling when he writes, "His name is John" (Luke 1:63); at best, this text points only to a minimal writing ability, however. Some upper-class Jewish families, especially in Jerusalem, sent their sons to private elementary and secondary schools for Greek education (Philo, *Spec.* 2.228–30). However, such schools were private affairs, not publicly supported, and thus limited to the upper echelons of society.[1] The pres-

---

1. John T. Townsend, "Education (Greco-Roman)," *ABD* 2:312–17.

ence of such Hellenizing educational institutions was a major point of contention in Jewish society (1 Macc. 1:14; 2 Macc. 4:9, 12), and there is no firm evidence of their existence outside of major urban centers. Qumran's attempt to provide a broader education for children and young adults appears to be an exception to the limited educational offerings throughout most of Palestine (Victor, *Colonial Education*, 118–24).

Most of the Jewish populace in first-century Palestine had no access to institutional education. Many scholars have thought that Sirach's "house of instruction" (*bêt midrāš*; Sir. 51:23) suggests that formal schools were present in Israel prior to the first century. However, the text may simply be a proverb-like call to the foolish to learn wisdom's discipline (LXX: *paideia*). The Jerusalem Talmud speaks of "480 synagogues in Jerusalem, and every one of them had a school-house and a house for learning" (*y. Meg.* 3.1).[2] However, the late date of this tradition and the likelihood of an idealized presentation argue against accepting this at face value. Thus, Jesus and most of his followers would have received only an informal education through home, extended family, village, and occasional visitors or pilgrimages.

The apostle Paul appears as a more highly educated person than most of the other followers of Jesus (Acts 26:24). Although he denies rhetorical skill or "eloquent wisdom" (1 Cor. 1:17; 2:4; 2 Cor. 11:6), his letters testify to some degree of learning, and his opponents give a high estimate of his writing skills (2 Cor. 10:10). If born and raised in Diaspora Tarsus (so Acts), and depending on the social status of his family, he may have received some formal Hellenistic schooling there. However, his use of the Koine rather than more polished Attic Greek makes any secondary or higher Greek education unlikely. In addition, he is reported to have received more advanced Jewish religious training in Jerusalem in connection with Gamaliel (Acts 22:3; Gal. 1:14).

Although later rabbinic sources uniformly disparage the education of daughters, matters may not have been quite so restrictive in the first century, especially in areas with greater Hellenistic influence. Nevertheless, the interest shown by Jesus and the early Christian movement in a woman's religious learning would probably have stood out to contemporary observers (Luke 10:39; Acts 18:26).

Torah-Centered Instruction

If the venues for Jewish education are not unlike their Greco-Roman counterparts, the same cannot be said for the content of that education. For Jews, God's Torah was the controlling center of all education, as both Philo and Josephus emphasize.

> For looking upon their laws as oracles directly given to them by God himself, and having been instructed in this doctrine from their very earliest infancy, they bear

2. J. Neusner, trans., *Megillah* (vol. 19 of *The Talmud of the Land of Israel*; Chicago: University of Chicago, 1987), 117.

in their souls the images of the commandments contained in these laws as sacred. (Philo, *Legat.* 210)[3]

Above all we pride ourselves on the education of our children, and regard as the most essential task in life the observance of our laws and of the pious practices, based thereupon, which we have inherited. (Josephus, *Ag. Ap.* 1.60, Thackeray, LCL; see also Deut. 6:7; 2 Tim. 3:15)

The aim of Jewish education also differed from that of education in the surrounding culture: it prized divine wisdom and virtue above knowledge. Thus, learning God's ways in Torah was foremost, and discipline was strict (as in all ancient education). Jewish education also differed through the inclusion of vocational training, whereas manual labor was disdained among the educated more widely in Greco-Roman society. Thus, Jesus learned woodworking, Paul the leather trade, and Peter fishing, and females learned household duties and other skills (e.g., Lydia was skilled in working with dyes; Acts 16:14).

The precise content of such home-centered Jewish education is nowhere made explicit. Much, of course, would have depended on the educational level of the parents and other relatives. At a minimum, children would have learned the Shema ("The LORD is our God, the LORD alone"; Deut. 6:4 NJPS), the Ten Commandments, the basics of Jewish tradition, and common liturgical elements (including some psalms). Oral repetition and memory, versus written lessons, were undoubtedly the primary medium of instruction. The ability to memorize was surely greater in such oral cultures than in modern literate societies, and a number of NT characters appear to have stored significant amounts of Scripture in their heads (e.g., Paul), but unsubstantiated claims that first-century rabbis (or, in some cases, children) memorized the entire HB should be taken as later exaggeration.

The vast majority of the Jewish population was nonliterate and without formal education. Even Josephus, who could read Greek literary works, needed assistance to compose in good Greek and acknowledged his deficiency in Greek diction (*Ag. Ap.* 1.9; *Ant.* 20.263–66). Jesus' early followers appear to others as unlearned (Acts 4:13). John 7:14–15 ("How does this Man know letters?" [NKJV]) is sometimes taken as counterevidence for Jesus' literacy (see also Luke 4, where Jesus "reads" from Isaiah), but the text more likely refers to the crowd's surprise at Jesus' knowledge of Scripture without formal religious education.

Bibliography

Crenshaw, James. "Education in Ancient Israel." *JBL* 104, no. 4 (1985): 601–15. Examines OT, inscriptions, and ANE parallels.

3. C. D. Yonge, trans., *The Works of Philo* (Peabody, MA: Hendrickson, 1993), 776.

Drazin, Nathan. *History of Jewish Education from 515 B.C.E. to 220 C.E. (During the Periods of the Second Commonwealth and the Tannaim)*. Baltimore: Johns Hopkins University Press, 1940. One of the best treatments from a more maximalist perspective.

Hezser, Catherine. "Education." Pages 39–109 in *Jewish Literacy in Roman Palestine*. Tübingen: Mohr Siebeck, 2001. Best recent interaction with primary and secondary sources on Jewish education (from a minimalist perspective).

Morris, Nathan. *The Jewish School: An Introduction to the History of Jewish Education*. London: Eyre & Spottiswoode, 1937. Judicious and thorough treatment of rabbinic and Second Temple evidence.

Riesner, Rainer. *Jesus als Lehrer: Eine Untersuchung zum Ursprung der Evangelien-Überlieferung*. Tübingen: Mohr Siebeck, 1981. A recent examination coming to maximalist conclusions. See especially chapter 2, "Jewish Education"; and pages 206–45, "Education of Jesus."

Safrai, Shmuel. "Education and the Study of the Torah." Pages 945–70 in *The Jewish People in the First Century: Historical Geography, Political History, Social, Cultural and Religious Life and Institutions*. Edited by S. Safrai and M. Stern. CRINT 1.2. Philadelphia: Fortress, 1987. Standard treatment with maximalist conclusions.

Victor, Royce. *Colonial Education and Class Formation in Early Judaism: A Postcolonial Reading*. LSTS 72. London: T&T Clark, 2010. Chapter 5, "Hellenistic Education and Early Judaism," shows the minimalist direction of more recent studies.

Zolty, Shoshana. *And All Your Children Shall Be Learned: Women and the Study of Torah in Jewish Law and History*. Northvale, NJ: J. Aronson, 1993. Best recent treatment of education of Jewish females in the Second Temple period (esp. pp. 101–13).

27

Healing and Healthcare

JOEL B. GREEN

For much of the twentieth century, the study of health and healing in the NT followed the predictable path of attempting to identify in today's medical terms the nature of the reported disease, then discussing the sometimes varied means by which the patient was granted relief. Debate typically ensued regarding the historical veracity of the miracles of healing recounted by the writers of the Gospels, the causal role of sin in relation to sickness, or the role of demons as agents of certain maladies.

Interestingly, such questions as these are not entirely contemporary but arose with vigor in the wake of the "new science" that emerged in the seventeenth century, with its materialist and empiricist focus. At first, religious and scientific explanations rarely competed. Even with the materialistic focus of new science, its practitioners recognized that science *could* marginalize God but that it did not *need* to do so. Robert Boyle's *A Free Enquiry into the Vulgarly Received Notion of Nature* (1686), for example, insisted that the new, mechanistic science was actually religion's invincible ally. Within a century, however, the Anglican priest John Wesley was aware that some educated people had begun to question reports of Jesus' miracles of healing and exorcism. For example, in a note on Jesus' commission to the disciples that they should "cast out devils" (Matt. 10:8 KJV), Wesley observes that someone has said that diseases ascribed to the devil in the Gospels "have the very same symptoms with the natural diseases of lunacy, epilepsy, or convulsions," leading to the conclusion "that the devil had no hand in them." Wesley continues:

> But it were well to stop and consider a little. Suppose God should allow an evil spirit to usurp the same power over a man's body as the man himself has naturally, and suppose him actually to exercise that power; could we conclude the devil had no hand therein, because his body was bent in the very same manner wherein the man himself bent it naturally?
>
> And suppose God gives an evil spirit a greater power to affect immediately the origin of the nerves in the brain, by irritating them to produce violent motions, or so relaxing them that they can produce little or no motion, still the symptoms will be those of over-tense nerves, as in madness, epilepsies, convulsions, or of relaxed nerves, as in paralytic cases. But could we conclude thence, that the devil had no hand in them?[1]

Wesley himself had embraced as an avocation the study of anatomy and physiology, so he represented in the eighteenth century an interest in the new vistas that science had begun to open and a desire to take seriously the importance of science for biblical interpretation. In this case, his solution was openness to the truth of both faith and science; rather than deny the truth of stories of demonized persons in the Gospels or their scientific explanation, he allowed that both could be true.

Why mention the biblical insights of an eighteenth-century cleric? First, this illustration demonstrates immediately the importance of the lens through which one views texts related to healing and health from the first-century Mediterranean world; and second, it demonstrates that the rise of modern science (i.e., the disciplined, systematic examination of the universe by means of physical evidence) changed how many people would understand those accounts. It is one thing to puzzle over Wesley's conundrum: How might we make sense of reports of exorcism in a world where psychological phenomena are tied to neural activity rather than to the work of demons? It is quite another to puzzle over phenomena related to sickness and healing as these are recounted in ancient documents, that is, to think *with the ancients* about how they experienced and described sickness and healing. Were we to do so, we would take seriously that their reports of healing and health occur within an interpretive framework that is in many ways alien to the biomedical paradigms of medical thought and practice that we take for granted in the Western world. What would it mean to replace the *Journal of the American Medical Association* with the pamphlets of ancient healers?

Perceptions of health are heavily networked with a host of values and practices, with the result that it makes sense to talk about healing and health as a "system." A "healthcare system," then, "refers to the network of beliefs, resources, institutions, and strategies concerned with the maintenance of health and the identification and

---

1. John Wesley, *Explanatory Notes upon the New Testament* (1754; repr., London: Epworth, 1976), 53.

treatment of sickness. Integral to a healthcare system are assumptions about the etiology and diagnosis of sickness, judgments concerning acceptable and unacceptable options for therapeutic intervention in cases of sickness, and a person's ability to gain access to [certain] healthcare options" (*DSE* 358).

The NT itself refers to a number of options for restoring health, including prayer and other forms of appeal to God (e.g., 2 Cor. 12:6–9; James 5:13–16) and such curative interventions as the intercession of a divinely endowed healer (Acts 3:1–10), care within one's own or another's household (Acts 16:25–34; cf. Luke 10:33–35), use of traditional medicaments (1 Tim. 5:23), or employment of a professional physician (Luke 8:43). The Bible explicitly rejects recourse to magic and generally, though not universally, views physicians with disdain (e.g., Mark 5:26). This general bias against physicians is congruent with the biblical view that Yahweh alone is the source of life and therefore the source of renewed health. Agents of healing, whether those empowered by the Spirit to heal or trained physicians, then, are healers only in a derivative sense. In the biblical tradition, the role of Yahweh is decisive and nonnegotiable: "I am the LORD who heals you" (Exod. 15:26 CEB; cf. 2 Kings 5:7–15; Isa. 57:19).

Perspectives on Sickness and Healing

Adopting an appropriate lens for reading and studying ancient reports of sickness and healing is the first, critical step in interpreting NT accounts.[2] We simply must refuse the temptation to imagine that all people in all times and all places experience health and its lack in ways familiar to us. Persons who study ethnomedicine or engage in medical anthropology understand that different societies construct in different ways how the society's members think about and respond to sickness and healing. One society identifies a certain condition within the boundaries of its definition of health while another views that same condition as sickness. Moreover, different societies provide different accounts of sickness, constructing a system by which people identify both the etiology (or cause) of the sickness and prescribe the therapeutic interventions necessary for recovery of health. One widely used classification of sickness introduces three categories (Hahn, *Sickness*):

1. *Disease accounts* focus on the body of the individual as the source of sickness. Patients are treated as individuals, with the site of disease sought in the structure and function of bodily organs and functions. Biomedical interventions serve as the primary mode of therapy.
2. *Illness accounts* identify patients as embodied persons in a nest of relationships. The cause and treatment of sicknesses thus require attention to

2. Portions of this and the following section are adapted from my article "Healthcare Systems in Scripture," *DSE* 358–60. Also see Joel B. Green, *Salvation* (Understanding Biblical Themes; St. Louis: Chalice, 2003), 40–43.

persons in their social environments, with recovery of health measured not only in biomedical but also relational terms.

3. *Disorder accounts* focus not only on the patient's body and social networks but also on the cosmic order of things. "When the universe is unbalanced, sickness may be manifested in particular locales and individual patients" (Hahn, *Sickness*, 28).

Of course, this is a catalog of ideal types, with actual accounts of sickness and recovery sometimes blurring the lines between these categories.

The importance of such a classification rests in our recognition that, for most of us and our contemporaries in the modern West, sickness is understood in terms of *disease accounts*. Indeed, our healthcare systems are dominated by biomedical diagnoses and therapies, whereas related legislation or narrated episodes of sickness and healing in the biblical materials are typically *illness* or *disorder accounts*. To give one illustration, in following the thought of René Descartes, Western medicine has until very recently universally distinguished the mind from the body and treated them as disparate things. This dichotomy led the renowned scientist Trinh Xuan Thuan to remark, "To this day, the brain and mind are regarded as two distinct entities in Western medicine. When we have a headache, we consult a neurologist; when we are depressed, we are told to see a psychiatrist."[3] This way of thinking would have seemed foreign to most people in the world of the Gospels.

Consider the case of "leprosy." In the Bible, this is rarely if ever true leprosy (or Hansen's disease: an infectious condition caused by the organism *Mycobacterium leprae*, characterized by sensory loss in the skin and muscle weakness leading to disfigurement) but instead includes any of a number of skin conditions. (See the translation of *lepra* in the CEB as "skin disease," e.g., in Mark 1:42.) Leviticus 13–14 has it that leprosy is a sign of divine curse (cf. 2 Chron. 26:20), with the result that persons diagnosed as lepers by a priest (acting not as a physician but as a kind of healthcare consultant) are quarantined.

> Anyone with an infection of skin disease must wear torn clothes, dishevel their hair, cover their upper lip, and shout out, "Unclean! Unclean!" They will be unclean as long as they are infected. They are unclean. They must live alone outside the camp. (Lev. 13:45–46 CEB)

In this case, "leprosy" is not life threatening from a biomedical point of view, nor is this skin disease contagious. Instead, the contagion is ritual impurity. Leprosy thus exemplifies how religious, social, and physical considerations coalesce in a single diagnosis.

3. Trinh Xuan Thuan, *Chaos and Harmony: Perspectives on Scientific Revolutions of the Twentieth Century* (Oxford: Oxford University Press, 2001), 294.

Cases of exorcism similarly correlate what might appear to moderns as discrete spiritual, social, mental, and physical factors, both in the presentation of the disorder and in its resolution. In Luke's account (Luke 8:26–39), a Gerasene man expresses the following symptoms: he is from the city but lives among the tombs and is ritually impure, as though himself a corpse; he is "naked and homeless" (v. 27 CEB), hardly human at all; he is demonized, engages in self-torture, and is uncontrollable. After Jesus' therapeutic intervention, the man formerly demon possessed "was sitting at Jesus' feet [a sign of submission], fully dressed and completely sane" (v. 35 CEB). The story ends with Jesus returning the man to his home, tasked with telling the story of what God has done for him.

We can further illustrate the importance of thinking systematically about healthcare by referring to the important work of Larry Hogan, whose study of "healing" in Second Temple Judaism appeared twenty years ago (Hogan, *Healing*), that is, before our heightened sensitivity to intercultural perspectives on sickness and healing. Hogan summarizes his study with a list of six "causes of illness" and five "means of healing" (302–10).

Causes of Illness
1. God, who causes illness in the service of his own purpose (e.g., to discipline or punish)
2. Divine intermediaries (e.g., angels or God's Word)
3. Evil spirits (e.g., demons or fallen angels)
4. Astrological phenomena
5. Natural factors
6. Sin

Means of Healing
1. Faith and/or prayer
2. Virtuous living (esp. effective for avoiding illness)
3. Exorcism
4. Physicians (whether professional physicians or practitioners of folk medicine)
5. Magical or quasi-magical means (whether amulets, magic bands, or related means, which might be regarded as expressions of divine mercy)

What is striking about these lists in the present context is the way they demonstrate how bringing a biomedical paradigm to these ancient texts is like trying to force the proverbial round peg into a square hole. We find references to spiritual and psychological factors, in addition to physical and astrological. Throughout, Hogan shows that any line between medicine and religious belief is at best blurred—as befits a shared, pervasive understanding that the ultimate source of healing in all of its manifestations is the one God of Israel (see Exod. 15:26). If a report traces a malady to sin or evil spirits, clearly the problem cannot be diagnosed or treated in terms limited to the physical body. To push further, though, the question arises whether it makes sense to speak in such terms of healing and health in antiquity. When is a "spiritual" or "physical" problem simply a problem of *human* health?

Ancient Physicians, Ancient Medicine

Healing practices in ancient Israel centered in the home, where the sick were kept. Care might have taken the form of maintaining vigil and soliciting the help of Yahweh through prayer and fasting (e.g., 2 Sam. 12:15–23). Persons with leprosy, on the other hand, were segregated (Lev. 13–14). Women in childbirth received the aid of midwives (e.g., Gen. 35:17; 38:28). Only rarely do physicians appear in the OT. When they do, they are typically seen as negative alternatives to Yahweh (e.g., 2 Chron. 16:12; Jer. 8:22–9:6) or as persons offering worthless advice (Job 13:4). This is consistent with the biblical portrait of Yahweh as the only God. It is also consistent with the state of medical knowledge in antiquity, and thus with the mysteriousness of the human body and its processes, which encouraged hope in magic and/ or miracle. Old Testament faith explicitly excluded magic (or sorcery, the manipulation of the spirits) as a remedy, in preference to divine intervention and care (e.g., Lev. 19:26–28; Deut. 18:10–14; Ezek. 13:17–18).

Prejudice against physicians is not unique to the OT world. Due to the association of medicine with the Greeks and an anti-Greek bias characterizing many of the elite of the Roman Republic, traditional healing practices among the Romans could be asserted over against Greek medicine. This, together with Cato's disavowal of fee-based medical practices among physicians, explains his advice to his son to stay

27.1. A statue of Asclepius, the Greek god of healing, with a snake entwining a staff (left side of statue). The figure is now located in the archaeological museum at Iconium (modern-day Konya).

Lee Martin McDonald

clear of doctors. Instead, he had "written a book of prescriptions for treating those who were sick in his household" (Plutarch, *Cato* 23.3–6, author's translation).

The role of physicians takes a different turn among Jews in the Second Temple period (516 BC–AD 70). Writing in the first quarter of the second century BC, Ben Sira carves out a place for them:

> [1]Honor doctors for their services,
>   since indeed the Lord created them.
> [2]Healing comes from the Most High,
>   and the king will reward them.
> [3]The skill of doctors will make them eminent,
>   and they will be admired in the presence of the great.
> [4]The Lord created medicines out of the earth,
>   and a sensible person won't ignore them.
> [5]Wasn't water made sweet by means of wood
>   so that the Lord's strength might be known?
> [6]And he endowed human beings with skill
>   so that he would be glorified through his marvelous deeds.
> [7]With those medicines, the doctor cures and takes away pain.
> [8]Those who prepare ointments will make a compound out of them,
>   and their work will never be finished,
>   and well-being spreads over the whole world from them.
>
> [9]My child, when you are sick,
>   don't look around elsewhere,
>   but pray to the Lord, and he will heal you.
> [10]Stay far from error,
>   direct your hands rightly,
>   and cleanse your heart from all sin.
> [11]Offer a sweet-smelling sacrifice and a memorial of fine flour,
>   and pour an offering of oil, using what you can afford.
> [12]And give doctors a place, because the Lord created them also,
>   and don't let them leave you, because you indeed need them.
> [13]There's a time when success
>   is in their hands as well.
> [14]They will also ask the Lord
>   so that he might grant them rest
>   and healing in order to preserve life.
> [15]May those who sin against their creator
>   fall into the hands of a doctor. (Sir. 38:1–15 CEB)

Two intertwined motifs run through this text. The first is the coordination of divine sovereignty with respect to healing and health, together with an affirmation, even authorization, of practitioners of medicine. This is explicit in verses 1–2, 4, 13, for example, but verse 5 is particularly interesting in this regard. The phrase "Wasn't water made sweet by means of wood . . . ?" recalls Exod. 15, when the

Israelites complained to Moses that they had nothing to drink. In turn, "Moses cried out to the Lord, and the Lord pointed out a tree to him. He threw it into the water, and the water became sweet" (15:25 CEB). In the very next verse, Exod. 15:26, we read the paradigmatic claim of Yahweh: "I am the Lord who heals you" (CEB). Accordingly, just as God's strength as divine healer can be known through a piece of wood thrown into the water, so God's strength as divine healer can be manifest in a physician's ministrations and medicines. The second motif is the almost seamless coordination of different causes of disease. This is suggested by the instruction first to turn to the Lord and only then to "give doctors a place" (v. 12), to "cleanse your heart from all sin" (v. 10) as well as to submit to the physicians, who themselves will offer prayers as well as medicaments. The point is not that one turns to the doctor if prayer fails, nor that one must address both spiritual and physical needs; such dualities belong more to our era than to the text before us. When life is an integrated whole, then healing and health must be approached in an integrated way.

As a barometer of how much the world of healthcare changed during the Second Temple period, consider the case of the Alexandrian Jew Philo of Alexandria. Two centuries earlier, Ben Sira needed to defend the therapeutic role of physicians, and he did so underneath the umbrella of divine provision and care. In the first century AD, though, Philo regards physicians in a positive light; indeed, it has been urged that Philo himself possessed a medical background (see Hogan, *Healing*, 191–206). The body may heal itself, medical interventions may be unsuccessful, but physicians nevertheless think in terms of drugs, surgery, and changes in diet (e.g., *Leg.* 3.226; *Congr.* 53). In terms reminiscent of Ben Sira, though, Philo affirms that all healing is God's doing:

> God bestows health in the simplest sense, preceded by no illness in our bodies, by Himself only, but health that comes by way of escape from illness He bestows both through medical science and through the physician's skill, letting both knowledge and practitioner enjoy the credit of healing, though it is He Himself that heals alike by these means and without them. (*Leg.* 3.178 LCL)

Consistent with his Platonism, Philo distinguishes the healing of the body from that of the soul, with bodily health having secondary significance in the service of soulish health.

The Jewish historian Josephus received the attention of physicians after injuring his wrist in a fall from his horse (*Life* 404). In his interpretation, Exod. 21:18–20 encourages the payment of physicians. This legislation concerning two people fighting has it that the one who injures the other "shouldn't be punished, except to pay for the loss of time from work and to pay for his full recovery" (Exod. 21:19 CEB); Josephus's version replaces that last phrase with this one: "and all that he hath given to the physicians" (*Ant.* 4.277 LCL). He also demonstrates awareness of folk remedies, such as the healing potential of plants (e.g., *J.W.* 7.181–85).

Undoubtedly, the increasing presence of physicians in Jewish literature of the Second Temple period is due to increased cultural interchange—both in the Diaspora and in the lands of the Jews following the military successes of Alexander the Great. Hellenistic rule promoted advances in the sciences, including anatomical studies, the rise of pharmacology, and major developments in surgical techniques and instruments (Nutton, *Ancient Medicine*, 140–66). Another strand of Hellenistic medicine avoided research curiosities related to anatomy and physiology, however. These empiricists, as they were called, regarded controversy over the cause of diseases as beside the point. What mattered was successful treatment. For them, medical practice focused on astute clinical observation and the importance of a considerable memory, written and/or oral, of which therapeutic interventions had been effective in similar situations in the past.

Lest we imagine that in antiquity concerns with healing and health had taken a decisive turn toward the natural world of biomedicine, consider two important caveats. First, such innovations in Hellenistic medicine as I have begun to outline were localized predominately in urban centers, and even there among the urban elite. Medical practitioners at the end of the Roman Republic and onset of the empire enjoyed certain privileges: even if they filled their ranks with slaves and freed slaves, they are reported to have received immunity from taxes and from military conscription, and in some cases citizenship. Rural medicine and peasant health, however, continued to feature its snake charmers, herbalists, and other folk healers. For these remedies, no trained physician needed to be consulted, no exchange of money was required. These forms of medical treatment were available to everyone. Second, in the Greek and Roman worlds people continued to look to the gods, and their intermediaries, for both personal and national health. Religion and science could not be separated simply by the introduction of new surgical instruments.

Although the Greek terms associated with "salvation"—*sōzō* ("to save"), *sōtēr* ("savior"), *sōtērios* ("saving"), and *sōtēria* ("salvation")—related generally to rescue from misfortune of all kinds, by far the most common usage of these terms in the Greco-Roman world was medical (*TLNT* 3:346–47).[4] Even if other terms might be used for "healing" and "healers," quite often "to save" was "to heal." People might refer to their physicians as "saviors."

Among the deities, Hercules, Asclepius, and Isis were particularly known for their healing ministrations. Though exalted from mortal existence to the Greek pantheon, Hercules remained compassionate toward humanity and acted on humans' behalf to heal diseases of all sorts, including raising the dead (Aelius Aristides, *Her.* 40.12; Apollodorus, *Lib.* 1.9.15). The goddess Isis was well known for her healing and was recognized as queen of the universe, dispenser of life, healer, and bringer of salvation.

> In proof of this, as they say, they advance, not legends, as the Greeks do, but manifest facts; for practically the entire inhabited world is their witness, in that it eagerly

---

4. Portions of this discussion are adapted from Green, *Salvation*, 36–38.

Hanina ben Dosa, a Galilean Healer

According to tradition, Hanina ben Dosa was active in the mid-first century AD. These two stories likely date to the period before AD 70, and were related to illustrate the value placed on fluent prayers.

Our Rabbis taught: Once the son of R. Gamaliel fell ill. He sent two scholars to R. Hanina b. Dosa to ask him to pray for him. When he saw them he went up to an upper chamber and prayed for him. When he came down he said to them: Go, the fever has left him. They said to him: Are you a prophet? He replied: I am neither a prophet nor the son of a prophet, but I learnt this from experience. If my prayer is fluent in my mouth, I know that he is accepted: but if not, I know that he is rejected. They sat down and made a note of the exact moment. When they came to R. Gamaliel, he said to them: By the temple service! You have not been a moment too soon or too late, but so it happened: at that very moment the fever left him and he asked for water to drink.

On another occasion it happened that R. Hanina b. Dosa went to study Torah with R. Johanan ben Zakkai. The son of R. Johanan ben Zakkai fell ill. He said to him: Hanina my son, pray for him that he may live. He put his head between his knees and prayed for him and he lived. Said R. Johanan ben Zakkai: If Ben Zakkai had stuck his head between his knees for the whole day, no notice would have been taken of him. Said his wife to him: Is Hanina greater than you are? He replied to her: No; but he is like a servant before the king, and I am like a nobleman before a king. (*b. Ber.* 34b)[a]

[a] ET in David Instone-Brewer, *Prayer and Agriculture* (vol. 1 of *Traditions of the Rabbis from the Era of the New Testament*; Grand Rapids: Eerdmans, 2004), 70.

contributes to the honours of Isis because she manifests herself in healings. *For standing above the sick in their sleep she gives them aid for their diseases and works remarkable cures upon such as submit themselves to her*; and many who have been despaired of by their physicians because of the difficult nature of their malady are restored to health by her, while numbers who have altogether lost the use of their eyes or of some other part of their body, wherever they turn for help to this goddess, are restored to their previous condition. (Diodorus Siculus, *Lib. Hist.* 1.25.4–5; ET in Cotter, *Miracles*, 33 [1.35.2], italics original)

Devotees of Asclepius labeled their god "Savior." He was the god of healing, who, it was presumed, guided the hands of the physicians. Hygeia, personified Health, was said to be his daughter (see Cotter, *Miracles*, 15–30).

Acts of healing were not limited to the gods. Indeed, worship of Jesus as Lord was challenged in the Roman world by the ever-expanding worship of the emperor. Rome's emperors could be recognized as bringing salvation (health, prosperity, peace, security) to the known world, and their saving work was regarded as proof of their enjoying the blessings and support of the gods. The Latin historian Tacitus (ca. AD 56–118) credits Vespasian (AD 9–79) with acts of healing; these were interpreted by the emperor—and perhaps more important, by the masses—as demonstrations of the lofty esteem in which Vespasian was held by the gods (Tacitus, *Hist.* 4.81).

Miracles of healing in the Roman Mediterranean were claimed by and for "holy men," such as the Jewish charismatic Hanina ben Dosa (first century AD) and the gentile philosopher and mystic Apollonius of Tyana (first century AD, though the historicity of Apollonius is debated), as well as for kings, emperors, and military leaders. For example, expanding on the description of Solomon in 1 Kings 4:29–34, Josephus says that God enabled Solomon to heal and expel demons (*Ant.* 8.44–49). Concerning the emperor Augustus, Philo writes:

> And again the great regions which divide the inhabited world, Europe and Asia, were contending with each other for sovereign power . . . so that the whole human race exhausted by mutual slaughter was on the verge of utter destruction, had it not been for one man and leader, Augustus, whom men fitly call the averter of evil. This is the Caesar who calmed the torrential storms on every side, who healed pestilences common to Greeks and barbarians, pestilences which descending from the south and east coursed to the west and north sowing seeds of calamity over the places and waters which lay between them. (*Legat.* 144–45 LCL)

Philosophers, too, could be spoken of as though they were "physicians," whose teaching was to heal the vices of their auditors and to promote the good health of virtue. In fact, Galen, the second-century AD physician whose medical theories and practices were studied and followed from his day into the seventeenth century, titled one of his books *That the Best Physician Is Also a Philosopher*. Continuing the metaphor, a philosopher might call for a change of diet and medicine, or even the surgical knife or hot iron to cauterize a wound. The Roman philosopher Seneca (first century AD) says of himself, "I am to be cauterized, operated upon, or put on a diet" (*Epist. mor.* 75.6–7; R. M. Gummere, LCL). Healing was also claimed to be available by means of magical paraphernalia. Acts records the burning of magical books at Ephesus by former magicians who had become believers (19:18–19), thus disclosing what must have been a characteristic Christian response to such practices.

As their parables rooted in life on the family farm make clear, the NT Gospels represent a world generally far removed from the household of physicians of the Roman elite or the anatomy lessons of Alexandria. Nevertheless, physicians were sufficiently common that Jesus can allude to their activity metaphorically (e.g., Mark 2:17 par.). At the outset of his ministry according to the Lukan narrative, Jesus predicts that some will say, "Doctor, heal yourself" (4:23 CEB). This proverb reflects a widespread viewpoint that medical attention should be reserved to one's family and friends; in effect, Jesus was anticipating the demands on him of his townspeople: "Attend to people of your own community and not to outsiders!" (cf. Luke 4:42). Only the wealthy could afford the care of a trained physician, however, and village people were especially vulnerable to the abuse of charlatans who took what little money they had but provided little by way of a cure. Mark 5:26 is illustrative: "She had suffered a lot under the care of many doctors, and had spent everything she had without getting any better. In fact, she had gotten worse" (CEB).

Village and rural folk depended less on persons who publicly professed the physician's oath, and they found the prospect of divine healing especially attractive (e.g., Acts 5:16). Hospitality might take the form of healthcare (e.g., Luke 10:30–35; Acts 16:33–34), and the author of 1 Timothy, while recognizing the potential of intoxication, nonetheless reflects medical tradition when he advises "a little wine because of your stomach problems and your frequent illnesses" (5:23 CEB; for an extensive registry of practical medicaments, see Pliny the Elder, *Nat. Hist.* 23–32). Even relative wealth could not certify medical competence, however. Medical treatises might sneer at root cutters, drug sellers, and purveyors of amulets and incantations, but even the best of ancient physicians understood little of the ways of the body.

Bibliography

Avalos, Hector. *Health Care and the Rise of Christianity*. Peabody, MA: Hendrickson, 1999. A good introduction to exploring healthcare as a "system" in the context of the early church.

Cotter, Wendy. *Miracles in Greco-Roman Antiquity: A Sourcebook*. London: Routledge, 1999. A key collection of, and introduction to, primary resources of ancient Greco-Roman texts concerned with miracles, healing, exorcisms, and so forth.

Good, Byron J. *Medicine, Rationality, and Experience: An Anthropological Perspective*. Lewis Henry Morgan Lectures 1990. Cambridge: Cambridge University Press, 1994. An exercise in medical anthropology that undermines the capacity of Western biomedicine to provide a universal account of health and healing.

Hahn, Robert A. *Sickness and Healing: An Anthropological Perspective*. New Haven: Yale University Press, 1995. An important work demonstrating that how people understand and respond to sickness differs greatly across social contexts.

Hogan, Larry O. *Healing in the Second Tempel [sic] Period*. NTOA 21. Göttingen: Vandenhoeck & Ruprecht, 1992. A survey and analysis of the etiology of illness and the means of healing in the literature of Second Temple Judaism.

Kee, Howard Clark. *Medicine, Miracle and Magic in New Testament Times*. SNTSMS 55. Cambridge: Cambridge University Press, 1986. An exploration of the three approaches to healing—medicine, miracle, and magic—in the NT and its world.

Nutton, Vivian. *Ancient Medicine*. SA. London: Routledge, 2004. A comprehensive history of the development of medical ideas from ancient Greece to late antiquity.

Pilch, John J. *Healing in the New Testament: Insights from Medical and Mediterranean Anthropology*. Minneapolis: Fortress, 2000. Develops and applies the concept of a healthcare system to relevant material in the NT Gospels.

PART 4

THE LITERARY CONTEXT OF EARLY CHRISTIANITY

Because the majority of the surviving ancient artifacts of early Christianity are literary documents, it is important to ask questions about the nature and transmission of those artifacts and to acknowledge parallels with other literature of the same period.

Early Christianity emerged within a social and literary context that was influential on the writings that would eventually be recognized as the NT. Consequently, we ought to inquire into the usual writing practices, genres, and materials in antiquity, and to explore how they might have influenced the NT writers. What did writing materials cost? How were manuscripts carried from place to place?

Christianity emerged on Palestinian soil in the first-century Greco-Roman world. We rightly anticipate Jewish, Roman, and Greek influence in the NT writings, including dependence here and there in terms of literary forms, turns of phrase, a common "dictionary," and so on. And, of course, literature from antiquity helps to fill in social, political, economic, and religious background—much of which is simply taken for granted in the NT materials. For example, did the works of Homer influence the writers of the NT, whether consciously or otherwise? Since Homer was at the core of the educational system in antiquity, with schoolchildren regularly taught to read and recite the *Iliad* and the *Odyssey*, one might expect that those who were converted to the Christian faith on Hellenistic soil would also be well acquainted with these works and even show occasional familiarity with them.

Likewise, contemporary Jewish writings offer much to the NT interpreter. What can we learn from Philo, the Alexandrian Jewish philosopher? What of Josephus, the noted Jewish historian who writes about the history of the Jewish people and even names persons known to us from the NT (John the Baptist, James the brother of Jesus, and even Jesus himself)? Without Josephus we would know very little about the Herodians, Essenes, Pharisees, Sadducees, and Zealots, not to mention the various social and political circumstances before, during, and after the time of Jesus. In the rabbinic tradition, much of which postdates the NT period, readers will also find valuable information on the context of early Christianity and some passages in the NT, and they may wonder about the relationship of the NT materials to other early Christian writings.

Finally, an interesting and often-challenging subject for NT students is the ancient practice of writing documents in someone else's name. We call this "pseudonymous" writing and refer to such texts as "pseudepigraphic." In our period, the names associated with such writings are generally those of famous prophets and apostles. For NT study, the pressing question is often whether pseudonymous writings have been included in the Bible. Scholars have debated this matter at length without any consensus, except to agree that this kind of writing was well known in early Judaism and early Christianity, most of it from the second century BC to the third century AD. Some writings in the NT were anonymously written (e.g., the Gospels, Hebrews), and other NT writings have had serious questions raised about their authorship, especially the Pastoral Epistles, 2 Thessalonians, 2 Peter, Ephesians, and Colossians.

28

Reading, Writing, and Manuscripts

E. RANDOLPH RICHARDS

R eading someone else's mail" is a phrase commonly used by NT professors to remind students of the challenges of exegeting NT letters. Ours is a faith firmly grounded in written texts; thus, it is appropriate to examine how documents were made in the first-century AD Mediterranean world. Most ancient documents were written on perishable materials. Papyrus needed to stay constantly dry, while wooden tablets needed to be constantly waterlogged. Thus, most everyday documents survived only in a few (and usually less hospitable) places in the ancient world where the climate has remained optimal for the last two thousand years, such as the deserts of Egypt and the bogs of England. In such places we have found many documents from the NT world. For example, a traveler wrote home: "Artemis to Socrates, greeting. Before all else I pray for your health. I arrived in the city on the 9th" (P.Mich. 8.507).[1] Although this is only a brief note, the recipient kept the letter.

Reading and Writing

It would seem tautological to say that if you are reading this chapter, then you can read. In antiquity it was trickier. The "readers" of a Gospel would more correctly

1. Herbert Chayyim Youtie and John Garrett Winter, eds., *Papyri and Ostraca from Karanis* (2nd series; Michigan Papyri 8; London: Oxford University Press, 1951).

be called the "hearers." In antiquity, reading was done aloud. James cautions his church to be doers and not merely *hearers* (James 1:22–25). The parenthetical remark "Let the reader understand" (Matt. 24:15) was a word of caution to the one reading aloud the passage. The material was politically sensitive: be careful who might overhear. For a church to hear a Gospel or letter, only one reader was needed. In some situations, the person who delivered it was expected to read it aloud, as was likely the case with Tychicus (Col. 4:7).

Reading as Oral Performance

If you have ever been asked to read a passage aloud in church, you know that a good reading requires a bit of practice. In antiquity, since words and sentences were written without spaces between them (*scriptio continua*) and split at the end of a line of text often without regard to syllables, reading was more difficult. Ancients also valued oral rhetoric. Saying something well included cadence in speech, good pronunciation, and intonation. Pliny the Elder, himself a skilled orator, had a slave (*lector*) whose task was to read to him (Pliny the Younger, *Ep.* 3.5; B. Radice, LCL). Pliny the Younger (*Ep.* 8.1) laments at length the temporary loss of his reader. Most people did not have a trained *lector*, but performing a document (reading aloud) was important (Col. 4:16). Letters were written from the viewpoint of when it would be read; thus, Paul wrote "I sent him" (*epempsa*), which we translate "I am sending him" (Phil. 2:28). When a worried mother heard the letter from her son "Apollinarius to Taesion, his mother, many greetings" (P.Mich. 8.490), at that moment her son greeted her.

People in the NT world read aloud even when alone. Augustine was surprised by Ambrose's silent reading of the text (*Conf.* 6.3.3; W. Watts and W. H. D. Rouse, LCL). Michael Slusser, building on the landmark work of Paul Achtemeier,[2] has argued that reading a text was aurally, not visually, interacting with the text.[3] Reading privately was still reading aloud. Thus, "Philip ran up to the chariot and heard the man reading Isaiah the prophet" (Acts 8:30 NIV).

Writing as Calligraphy

From *Webster's* to Wikipedia, literacy has been defined as "the ability to read and write." In fact, in our modern society, these terms are so connected that we often see the expression "reading/writing" as if they are merely two sides of the same coin. In the NT world, literacy was the ability to *read*. Writing was a practiced skill, much like the modern art of calligraphy. Since we were taught to write at the same time we were taught to read, this often surprises us. Let me illustrate. My professor wrote out his books by hand, and a secretary typed them. He was

---

2. Paul Achtemeier, "*Omne verbum sonat:* The New Testament and the Oral Environment of Late Western Antiquity," *JBL* 109 (1990): 3–27.

3. Michael Slusser, "Reading Silently in Antiquity," *JBL* 111 (1992): 499.

quite literate, but he did not know how to type (other than pecking out the letters one by one). The ability to read a typed book did not mean one could type. Handwriting is the same issue. It is a matter of practice. Put your pen in your opposite hand. How well do you write? For me, suddenly I write slowly with large, clumsy letters, because I rarely write with my left hand. Likewise, when Paul states, "See what large letters I make" (Gal. 6:11), we should not read anything unusual into this. Like most letter writers of his day, he used a secretary. Someone who could read probably was able to scratch out letters (write), but we are suggesting that even a literate person might handwrite poorly and only with much labor. Thus, by literate, we mean someone who could read.

Literacy Rates

Although the NT world circulated and stored lots of written documents, we are not suggesting even that most people could read. When modern tourists visit ancient Ephesus, they see scratched into the pavement of the main road from the harbor the picture visually indicating the direction to the local brothel. Likewise, tourists are amused if not scandalized by the "menu" of services painted on the walls of brothels in Pompeii. Like a modern fast-food restaurant, a visual menu helps those who cannot read or who read poorly to order what they wish. When sailors arrived in a port, such as Ostia, the mosaic pictures in front of each local trade guild announced the business. Rome also understood that propaganda must be communicated to be effective. Titus's sestertius coin has an image of the goddess Eirene ("peace") with an olive branch in her right hand and holding a cornucopia in her left to remind everyone that Roman peace brought prosperity. The Roman promise was clear even to those who could not read.

In addition to comments in the literature from antiquity, ancient documents also help us to assess literacy rates. "Inscriptions" commonly refers to writings carved into stone. Yet, we cannot assume that the presence of an inscription indicates a literate audience. Putting something in stone (then and now) had other purposes. Manuscripts, though, do seem to expect a subsequent reader. A "manuscript" in the technical sense refers to a document written by hand (*manu*). As suggested above, we cannot judge literacy rates merely by comparing handwriting and assuming that those with poor handwriting were only marginally literate.

It seems best to assume that there was not a widespread public education system in the NT world (so Gamble, *Books*, 7). Yet we should not be too skeptical. Graffiti in Pompeii shows that at least some soldiers, weavers, and barmaids were able to write (marginally) and expected at least some fellow patrons to be able to read.

Alan Millard argues that Jewish men were taught to read at least Scripture for synagogue services (Millard, *Reading*, 157), citing Simon ben Shetah (100 BC), who commanded all (Israelite) children to attend school (*y. Ketub.* 8.32c), as well as the remarks of Philo (*Legat.* 210; F. H. Colson, LCL) and Josephus (*Ag. Ap.* 2.178; H. St. J. Thackeray, LCL). Jesus seemed to be expected to be able to read (Luke

Graffiti in Pompeii

Scratched on the wall of a bar is the plight of two men (Successus and Severus) who both loved a barmaid (Iris):

> [Severus]: "Successus, a weaver, loves the innkeeper's slave girl named Iris. She, however, does not love him. Still, he begs her to have pity on him. His rival wrote this. Goodbye."
>
> [Answer by Successus]: "Envious one, why do you get in the way? Submit to a handsomer man and one who is being treated very wrongly and good looking."
>
> [Answer by Severus]: "I have spoken. I have written all there is to say. You love Iris, but she does not love you." (*CIL* 4:8258; 4:8259)

On the wall of the gladiators' barracks we find graffiti even more lurid than this one: "Floronius, privileged soldier of the 7th legion, was here. The women did not know of his presence. Only six women came to know, too few for such a stallion" (*CIL* 4:8767). Scratched on walls of offices and elsewhere, we likewise read of broken hearts: "Secundus says hello to his Prima, wherever she is. I ask, my mistress, that you love me" (*CIL* 4:8364); "Cruel Lalagus, why do you not love me?" (*CIL* 4:3042). Finally, some messages are heartwarming: "I don't want to sell my husband, not for all the gold in the world" (*CIL* 4:3061).

4:16–17), or it was already known that he could. Also, papyrus letters in Egypt show some marginal literacy by a wide assortment of people. Since handwriting could be used to determine authenticity (2 Thess. 3:17), a letter sender who could write even a little would take up the pen to "sign" any final comments. When the sender wished to point it out, a comment such as Paul's was typical: "I, Paul, write this greeting with my own hand" (1 Cor. 16:21; cf. Gal. 6:11; Philem. 19; see also Cicero, *Q. Fr.* 2.2.1; 2.16; 3.1; W. A. Falconer, LCL). Therefore, many people could probably read their own signature or perhaps a few very basic words, but we must admit that to read a lengthy text fairly quickly and with understanding was probably beyond the skill of most people.

Although determining literacy in antiquity has challenges, some reasonable estimates have been made. The prevailing opinion suggests that 10 percent of the Mediterranean population could read with any proficiency. Literacy was not, though, evenly distributed across the empire. Moreover, in the NT a literate person might read Aramaic fluently, Hebrew slowly, and Greek with difficulty and be unable to read Latin at all.

While Millard may be correct that Jewish men had a higher literacy rate, we would not want to suggest that more than 15 percent could read, and even that percentage is probably too high. Although we may be discouraged by such a low number, it does indicate that the ability to read was not uncommon. Thus, Millard (*Reading*, 158) is likely correct that it is significant that Jesus introduces Scripture with the words "Have you not *read?*" when speaking to Pharisees (Matt. 12:3), to Sadducees (Matt. 22:31), to scribes (Matt. 21:16), or to a lawyer (Luke 10:26), but says to the crowd, "You have *heard* that it was said" (Matt. 5:21).

Literacy and the Use of Both Oral and Written Material

Conventional wisdom suggests that people in Jesus' day preferred oral sources. It seems likely that early Christians enjoyed hearing from an eyewitness (Luke 1:2). Greek historians argued that a firsthand account was preferred. Nonetheless, the difference between oral and written material was less distinct in antiquity. The written material was still read aloud and heard by the audience (even if an audience of one).

Some of our best sources of information are the ultra-elite aristocracy of Rome, particularly Cicero, who wrote about all manner of mundane matters. Obviously, there are challenges in making comparisons to the practices of NT characters. One should not assume the same quality or resources. Pliny had a *lector;* Caesar wrote while riding in a litter or on a ship; Cicero had slaves merely for carrying letters; they all held lavish dinner parties with other aristocracy. None of these excesses are analogous to the NT. Nevertheless, the basic social structures underneath these extravagances are likely the same. For example, someone read the letter to others; documents could be written while away from home; letter carriers were used (Col. 4:7–9); Corinthian Christians also held dinner parties with apparently the same vices as aristocratic dinners, including dinner "escorts" (1 Cor. 6), idol meat (1 Cor. 8–10), immorality (1 Cor. 10), and drunkenness (1 Cor. 11).

> **The Multilingual New Testament World**
>
> A tablet contains an official request (in Latin) for two sons to be registered. The father (a Roman citizen) writes the subscription in his own hand but must write it in Greek since apparently he cannot write Latin (nor probably speak it). He notes that he is actually writing the subscription on behalf of the children's mother "because she did not know letters" (Winter, *Life*, 54–55).

Scholars are now examining more closely these dinner parties. When philosophers traveled from town to town, a patron (or often a widowed patroness) would host them in his or her home. The guest was expected to reciprocate by "entertaining" the others after dinner, usually sharing philosophical thoughts (e.g., Plutarch, *Caes.* 63.4; B. Perrin, LCL). Early apostles probably used this system for propagating the Christian message. Cicero, although gifted in oratory, often read from a current project. A guest who enjoyed it would ask for a copy, a request Cicero was evidently quick to grant (Cicero, *Att.* 8.9; E. O. Winstead, LCL). Harry Gamble suggests this model to explain the spread of Paul's Letters (Gamble, *Canon*, 36–43).

Reading, Writing, and the Study of the New Testament

A comment like Paul's in Col. 4:16—"After this letter has been read to you, see that it is also read in the church of the Laodiceans and that you in turn read the letter from Laodicea" (NIV)—should not surprise us. Writings were valued and shared. For example, Brutus mentions to Cicero, "I have read the short extract from the note you sent to Octavius. Atticus sent it to me" (Cicero, *Br.* 1.16.1; also see P.Zen. 10).

Early Christians received and handed on tradition (e.g., 1 Cor. 11:23; 15:3). Presumably, the illiterate majority did so orally, but scholars have suggested that notes and other written memoirs played a role in the NT world. It is not preposterous to assume that some of Jesus' hearers took notes. Collections of sayings and parables circulated (Luke 1:1 mentions "many").

It is also reasonable that NT writers took care with the appearance of the documents. A Gospel written to a benefactor (Luke 1:3) or a letter to a church intended to be read publicly (Col. 4:16) would not be scratched messily across some sheet. Ancients had a sense of propriety. For an important letter, Cicero had the final copy prepared on fine, large sheets of papyrus (*macrocolla*) in careful script (see Cicero, *Att.* 13.25; 13.21a).

> ### Biblically Literate
>
> The phrase "biblically literate" often refers to how well one knows the biblical stories, whether from an oral or a written source. First Peter (3:6) seems to know the stories of Abraham from the popular *Testament of Abraham* (where Sarah calls him "lord" five times) and not from the Genesis narrative (where she does not). Similarly, most Christians today know the story of Noah's ark, not from reading Gen. 6 but from hearing (or seeing) popular retellings, and thus have never read Gen. 6:1–4. We should not assume that NT writers knew *all* the biblical stories nor necessarily knew them from the Tanak (i.e., the HB), and we should also not be surprised when they refer to later versions (Jude 9; 2 Tim. 3:8).

The Making of Manuscripts

The basic technology for the nib pen has been the same from NT times until today. Reeds were later replaced by quill pens, which were cut from feathers and drew finer lines. In NT times, the preferred pen (*calamus*) was the sea rush (*juncus maritimus*, a small coastal reed), which was cut about eight to ten inches long and had a split tip; it was stiff but easy to cut and cheap. A red ink mixed from ochre, gelatin, gum, and beeswax was sometimes used, but Greeks and Romans commonly used a black ink from mixing lamp black (or ground charcoal) with gum Arabic (or an animal glue). Sometimes cuttlefish ink or wine dregs were used to enhance the color. Ancients liked the basic carbon ink because it was cheap and easy to make and did not fade. Ink did wash off with water, though, which

28.1. Modern reproduction of a writing palette and reed pen.

is how it was erased. Unfortunately, an accidental soaking also caused many an ancient letter to be "lost" (Cicero, *Q. Fr.* 2.12.4).

Greeks and Romans wrote in lines from left to right, writing the letters pendant, hanging from the line. (We write our letters on top of the line.) The typical sheet, *pagina*, for purchase was a bit smaller than the standard American page and slightly less wide, depending on the quality: *augusta* sheets were thirteen digits wide (about ten inches), while *emporetica* sheets were about six digits wide (nearly five inches). In more formal writing, narrow columns were used, so that less of the scroll had to be unrolled for reading. Each line (Greek *stichos*) was about thirty-six letters, or about three inches long. In fact, copyists charged by the number of lines, or *stichoi*. The average sheet held three to four columns of usually thirty to forty lines (rows) of text, with a half-inch space between columns and wider top and bottom margins. In shorter letters or less-polished documents, the scribe often wrote nearly edge to edge, apparently more concerned with maximizing space than following convention.

Categorizing the Materials

While pen and ink remained largely unchanged, the NT world was experiencing a plethora of new writing materials. (The Chinese invented paper about AD 100, but it took over a thousand years to enter the Mediterranean world.) Ancients wrote on just about anything—walls, pavements, bar counters, and in the dirt (John 8:6). Some materials, though, were just better suited for writing. Availability, price, and the characteristics of the material often determined which was chosen.

Ostraca. Clay pots were cheap but fragile. Most kitchen floors were littered with fragments. These broken shards, called "ostraca," provided a great surface for short, quick notes. Although the glazed side would not hold ink, the unglazed surface was smooth enough and neutrally colored and held ink well. Thus, on an ostracon we commonly find a receipt, vote, invitation, prescription, prayer, or student's exercises. By their very nature, ostraca had no standard size.

Tablets. While ostraca were great for jotting a quick note, they were small, clunky, and not really erasable and thus not reusable. For notes, drafts, lessons, and especially temporary documents, tablets (*tabula*) were preferred. Leaf

Blotted from the Book of Life

Ancient writers usually sat cross-legged. Their tunic was stretched taut between their knees, making a desk of sorts. Desks were not used until several centuries after the NT. A short block of wood with a hollowed inkwell (*atramentarium*) and a slot for holding reeds was held in one hand and the reed pen in the other. Scribes commonly tied a wet cloth on a string to their palette for erasing, which they termed "blotting out." This practice is referred to in Rev. 3:5: "I will never blot out the name of that person from the book of life" (NIV).

tablets, very thinly cut sheets of birch or alder sapling, were used (Cassiodorus, *Variae* 11.38).[4] These sheets were lightweight and adequately durable and could even be folded. Since these were highly perishable, it is possible that leaf notebooks were far more popular than the few surviving examples (from Vindolanda, a Roman fort in northern England) might imply. Nonetheless, the common tablet (judging from remains) was a thin wooden tablet, incised to create a recessed middle with a raised outer border. Tablets were generally made the size of a sheet, or *pagina*. Sometimes ancients wrote directly on the wood, such as found on tablets recovered at Vindolanda. More commonly, the middle was covered in a thin layer of colored wax. The raised rim protected the wax when tablets were stacked.

For wax tablets, the stylus was often bronze or iron with a point. Since one was scratching lightly into the surface of the wax, the verb *exarare* ("to plough") was used for writing and often is translated "jotting" to reflect that tablets were commonly used for notes. The opposite end of the stylus was often rounded or flat to erase by smoothing out the wax.

Parchment. For more permanent writing, two major materials were used: parchment and papyrus. Parchment sheets were leather from the hide of a sheep, goat, or calf. The inner side of the sheet, which was smoother and lighter in color, was preferred. This side has traditionally been termed the "recto" (Latin *rectus*), as the "proper" side of the sheet. The flipside of the sheet has appropriately been called the "verso" (Latin *versus*), although "hair side" and "flesh side" are becoming common terms. Sheets were sewn together with animal or vegetable fibers to make a longer strip that was rolled up to make a scroll. The seams of a scroll were strong but were not smooth. One could not write across them. Properly, one wrote only on the inside (recto) of a scroll, but many took the savings and wrote on the back as well, an opisthograph (cf. Rev. 5:1). Along with many other rolls that Pliny the Elder left to his nephew, he bequeathed 160 rolls that were written on both sides (Pliny the Younger, *Ep.* 3.5.17).

Papyrus. By the time of the NT, papyrus had been popular for millennia. The reed grew along the Nile and was considered unequaled for writing (Cassiodorus,

---

4. S. J. B. Barnish, ed. and trans., *The Letters of Cassiodorus [Variae epistolae]* (Liverpool: Liverpool University Press, 1992).

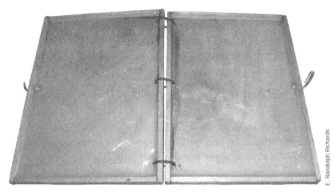

28.2. Wax writing tablet.

Variae 11.38.3). Growing five to fifteen feet in height, the reeds were cut into lengths of about a man's forearm (twelve inches or so). The roughly triangular stalk was about as thick as a man's wrist. The inner pith was sliced into tape-like strips about two to three inches wide. These strips were placed side by side on a pattern board. A second layer was placed on top at a right angle. Pounding or pressing the layers squeezed out most of the juice. The remaining cellulose glued the strips together. (Pliny the Elder mistakenly claims the Nile water was the glue [*Nat. Hist.* 13.23; H. Rackham, LCL].) The dried sheet was trimmed and then polished smooth with pumice. The result was a surprisingly strong, flexible, smooth, white surface.

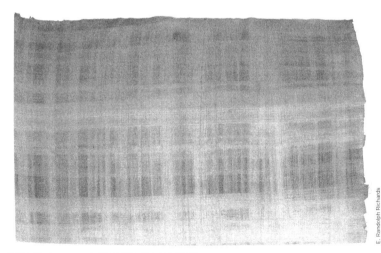

28.3. Modern reproduction of a papyrus sheet.

Pliny the Elder considered papyrus quite durable and (incorrectly) blamed an Alexandrian embargo of papyrus for forcing Pergamum to develop parchment (Turner, *Papyri*, 9). It remains debated why one was preferred over the other. It is commonly asserted that parchment was stronger and more durable than papyrus but that parchment was more expensive. Roger Bagnall has recently argued that (in Egypt, several centuries later) parchment was twice the price of papyrus (*Books*, 55). It does appear the NT world preferred papyrus, perhaps because parchment was more expensive in NT times.

Roll (Scroll). Rolls were typically made from either parchment (see above) or papyrus. With papyrus, the side with the horizontal fibers was considered the recto, for it was easier to write on. Sheets were then glued so that the right edge overlapped the left edge of the next sheet, allowing seams to be easily written across. According to Pliny the Elder (*Nat. Hist.* 13.23), papyrus manufacturers glued twenty sheets together to make a standard *volumen* ("book roll," from the Latin *volvere*, "to roll") of about fifteen feet. This standard roll, a *charta*, cost about four denarii (Millard, *Reading*, 165) and held fifteen hundred to two thousand lines. The roll, or scroll, was the standard book of antiquity. (Purists like to point out that the noun is "roll" and the verb is "to scroll"; thus, one would scroll a roll. The resulting roll, though, is commonly today called a "scroll.")

Although papyrus rolls were sold in a set length, sheets could be either cut off or pasted on to adjust the length. Galen (ca. AD 200) insists that his books are "well proportioned" and "useful" for the reader, although he concedes that some volumes are more than four thousand *stichoi* and may need to be divided in half (*On Consolation from Grief*, 28–29). This matches other comments of long scrolls reaching about thirty-five feet. This practical limit effectively established the length for a volume. Rolls were transported in a cylindrical container called a *capsa*. "Bring . . . the books" (2 Tim. 4:13) certainly refers to a collection of scrolls and likely in a

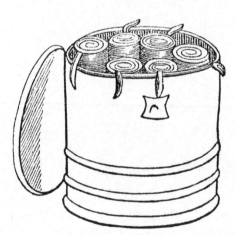

capsa (see photo). Scrolls were read by unrolling with the right hand while gradually rerolling with the left hand so that only a column or two of text was exposed for reading.

Codex (Book or Notebook). While the official form of an

28.4. Scrolls were transported in a cylindrical carrying case called a *capsa*. This sketch is from William Smith, *A School Dictionary of Greek and Roman Antiquities* (New York: Harper & Brothers, 1873), 65.

ancient book was the roll, ancients did use also the codex format. (A codex is the format of modern books, where the pages are attached on one side.) Probably the origin of the term "codex" (meaning "a block of wood") came either from slicing a block into tablets or from the fact that a stack of tablets resembled a block of wood. Holes were bored in the wood, and tablets were tied together to make a tablet book (*codicilli*). Two leaves (a diptych) were most popular, but up to five are common. The well-known painting of the couple from Pompeii shows her holding a four-leaf tablet (see photo). No examples of tablets with more than ten leaves have been found.

Tablets were used for quick notes. Acidinus informs Servius Sulpicius by *codicilli* that Marcellus is dead (Cicero, *Fam.* 4.12.2; W. G. Williams, LCL). Cicero (*Fam.* 6.18.2) sent Balbus *codicilli* when he needed some quick information about a law or when Atticus wanted a swift reply (*Att.* 12.7). Such notes were easy and inexpensive, since tablets were reusable: one washed ink off the wood or smoothed out the wax. Tablets were also used "for first drafts" of writings (Turner, *Papyri*, 6). Thus tablets were viewed as informal or unofficial writing.

> **Having a Bible**
>
> Scriptures were not gathered into a single volume or discrete collection until after the NT period. A complete "Bible" would require seventy-eight papyrus rolls (Bagnall, *Books*, 55). Also, writings were very expensive. Most synagogues in Jesus' day could afford only a few scrolls. This may explain why Jesus quotes from Deuteronomy, Isaiah, and Psalms. Perhaps Nazareth could afford only one from each section of Scripture. Certainly a complete OT (an anachronistic term for several reasons) would have been found in few places, perhaps only in the Judean temple. Likely there were entire books of the Jewish Scriptures that Peter or John had never even heard. Having a complete set of Scripture is a modern experience.

By the time of the NT, parchment notebooks (similar to our modern books) were becoming popular. Sheets were stacked, sewn down the middle, and folded over. The sheet was called a *quaternion* (Latin) or *tetradia* (Greek) because, once folded, it made four pages. Unlike papyrus, which did not tolerate water well, parchment, when prepared appropriately, was easily washed off and reused. These parchment notebooks (*membranae*) were used for the same purposes as the tablets (Roberts and Skeat, *Codex*, 15–23) but were lighter and more durable. Yet such notebooks still carried the stigma of not being official books (Roberts and Skeat, *Codex*, 29). Thus, Paul requests both his books (rolls) *and* his notebooks (*membranae*) that were left in Troas (2 Tim. 4:13).

The Making of Manuscripts and the Study of the New Testament

Christians appear to be the first widespread adopters of the new codex book form. In Egypt the "codex scarcely counted" among documentary remains (Roberts and Skeat, *Codex*, 37); yet, all surviving copies of Christian Scriptures were in the

28.5. A wall fresco found at Pompeii. In this portrait of a Roman couple, the woman is holding a writing tablet and stylus, and the man is holding a scroll.

codex form (except those copied on the back on a used roll; Bagnall, *Books*, 58–59). This wholesale switch from roll to codex cannot be explained merely by preference. The three common explanations all argue that something *Christian* precipitated adopting the codex. C. H. Roberts and T. C. Skeat suggest the publication of the four Gospels as one book. Gamble suggests the publication of a collection of Paul's letters as a single book. I have argued that Paul retained copies of his letters and kept them in *membranae* (Richards, *Letter Writing*, 210–15). This was a common practice. I then suggest that the original set fell into the hands of disciples after his death. Copies were made keeping (somewhat arbitrarily) the original format. No matter the theory, we can say that Christians were avid users of the codex.

The Author in the New Testament World

When you imagine Luke penning his Gospel, you might superimpose a picture of how we used to write college papers before computers. I slipped into a quiet room and sat at a desk with pen and paper. After some thought, I composed as I wrote. If I had sources, I was careful not to plagiarize. When I finished, I turned it in. Ancient writing differed in just about every way.

Sources and Preformed Material

Pliny the Elder had a slave to write down excerpts from books he was reading (Pliny the Younger, *Ep.* 3.5). Ancients commonly pulled material from other writings, sometimes indicating the source and sometimes not. Usually the writer was expecting the hearers to recognize the material and therefore did not call attention to it. Ancients did not use quotation marks. Modern readers sometimes struggle to recognize a piece of quoted material, as in 1 Cor. 6:12. New Testament writers often quoted hymnic fragments, standardized arguments (*topoi*), and early kerygma, often without identifying it. When we modern readers have the source, such as the OT, then we recognize it as quoted.

Collaborative Ancient Authorship

We should not superimpose modern values on the dyadic culture of the NT. They valued teamwork. Paul included others in the letter opening of at least six of his letters. There is no evidence that this was merely a sign of courtesy or humility. The role of Paul's cosenders (coauthors?) is still disputed (so Adams in Porter and Adams, *Ancient Letter Form*, 40–44). The community of a Gospel writer likely heard the material many times (John 21:24). Likewise, team members probably made comments during the editing process as they heard the draft read. Westerners value individualism, but Paul asserted that the hand could not devalue the foot (1 Cor. 12:15).

Authors and the Study of the New Testament

No matter the original source of some material (e.g., the use of a tradition from the *Testament of Moses* in Jude 9) or the contributions of colleagues, the author assumed complete responsibility for the content (see Richards, *Letter Writing*, 109–21, for a fuller discussion).

Secretaries and the Art of Composition

If a friend could write, why hire a secretary? Actually, a friend was likely sufficient for quick notes, receipts, and short letters. Asclepiades wrote to Portis about receiving a shipment of fruit. The letter ends: "Written for him hath Eumelus the son of Herma . . . , being desired to do so for that he writeth somewhat slowly" (Deissmann, *Light*, 166–67, notes this is probably a euphemism for illiteracy). From other ancient letters where we recovered the original, we can clearly see a change in handwriting at the end of the letter, where (likely) the sender wrote—commonly a summary of sorts and a greeting or well-wish—in his or her own hand. In P.Mich. 8.496, the subscription in the sender's (?) original hand is as long as the main letter.[5]

Secretarial Skills

There were other reasons a secretary was a better choice than a friend: if the project was longer or needed to impress, or if the writer was away from home.

---

5. Youtie and Winter, *Papyri from Karanis*, 109.

In fact, we should assume that a secretary was used for a document unless the writer indicates otherwise. Secretaries had the writing materials and the rolls of *charta*. They knew how to cut off the needed length, prick and score the lines on the sheets, and mix the ink. Since the papyrus probably cost at least twice as much as the secretary's labor, why pay so much for the materials and risk an ineffective or embarrassing document?

Table 1. Common Letter Formulas

	Format	Papyri	Paul
Disclosure Formula	"I want you to know that . . .	P.Oxy. 1155, 1481, 1493, 1670	Gal. 1:11
Thanksgiving Formula	"I give thanks to [usually a god or goddess] for [usually good news] . . ."	P.Oxy. 1299, 1070, 1481	Eph. 1:15–16; Col. 1:3; 1 Thess. 1:2; 2 Thess. 1:3; 2 Tim. 1:3; Philem. 4
Astonishment Formula	"I am amazed that [usually a failure to write] . . ."	P.Mich. 8.479	Gal. 1:6
Petition Formula	A verb of request [usually *parakaleō*], vocative, and the request	P.Oxy. 292, 1480, 1666	Rom. 12:1; 15:30; 16:17; 1 Cor. 1:10; 16:15; 2 Cor. 2:8; 10:1

Letters used certain conventions, in which secretaries were well versed. For example, letters had stereotyped phrases (see table 1). Then as now, messing up a set phrase (like an idiom) implies a certain ignorance or incompetence in the language. Officials had titles. There were polite ways to ask something or to inform someone. Secretaries protected a writer from social as well as linguistic blunders.

More important, a secretary knew the appropriate style for the letter or document, including the proper rhetoric. In which type of letter does one appeal to *exempli*? Ancient documents had a very set method of presentation (rhetoric). An argument was to be arranged in a certain order (*dispositio*). How embarrassing (and ineffective) it would be to fail to appeal to *ethos* in one's *exordium*! The average person (then and now) was not trained in this; secretaries were. Even a very highly skilled orator like Cicero noted (privately) that his secretary Tiro provided "assistance" (Cicero, *Fam.* 16.4.3, 11.1).

Secretarial Roles

The role a secretary played in the writing of a particular document depended on the wishes of the author and the skills of the secretary. A secretary could transcribe dictation. Usually this meant syllable by syllable (*syllabatim*). Seneca (*Epist. mor.* 40.10) ridicules someone who stammered badly by saying he spoke as if he were dictating. Cicero mentions fretting over the wording of a document and dictating it *syllabatim* (*Att.* 13.25). In the case of standardized receipts, appeals, and official letters, a secretary could be given the general guidelines, being expected to choose the appropriate format and diction—that is what the secretary was paid for!

These two examples, though, are the extremes. Probably the most common method was for the secretary to take detailed notes on tablets as the author spoke slowly. Later, the secretary would return with a draft, almost certainly on a notebook (wooden or parchment). This process of hearing the draft read, editing, and expanding, was done not in a private room—only a sleeping room (*cubiculum*) was really private—but likely in one of the common rooms, such as the open-air colonnaded garden (*peristylium*), where we have pictures of philosophers gathering, or in the dining area (*triclinium*), perhaps as part of a meal. Depending on its importance, a document might go through many drafts over a period of weeks or months.

Arguments that note the influence of a secretary are sometimes critiqued, as Bart Ehrman does for 1 Peter, by suggesting that this makes the secretary the "real author."[6] This argument, however, suggests there were only two options: the author either dictated the material or capitulated and allowed a secretary free rein. Actually, neither was the common method. Moreover, ancients were not confused as to who was in charge. The author assumed full responsibility for everything in the document. For this reason, authors carefully checked the final draft (see Richards, *Letter Writing*, 81–84).

Secretaries and the Study of the New Testament

We should assume that all the NT epistles were written with the assistance of a secretary. Paul specifically notes it five times (1 Cor. 16:21; Gal. 6:11; Col. 4:18; 2 Thess. 3:17; Philem. 19). Also, long subscriptions were not unknown. If 2 Cor. 10–13 is a subscription in Paul's own hand, it is just another way Paul deviated from pattern. He had long paraenetic (moral exhortation) sections. Paul also wrote more (and longer) thanksgivings than any known writer in antiquity.

The author's unique writing style was often muddied since so many others provided input during the composing and editing and because of the influence of a secretary. Robert Tyrrell and Louis Purser, the undisputed authorities on Cicero's letters, note that the writing style of some of Cicero's letters was so influenced by the secretary that Cicero's unique writing style was lost (*Cicero*, 2:lxix–lxx). Likewise, Trajan's letters display similar variation in style (Sherwin-White, *Letters of Pliny*, 541). Josephus mentions having "assistants" (*Ag. Ap.* 1.50). Henry Thackeray, a leading scholar on Josephus, notes that the "immense debt" Josephus

6. Bart D. Ehrman, *Forged: Writing in the Name of God—Why the Bible's Authors Are Not Who We Think They Are* (New York: Harper Collins, 2011), 139.

owes them "is apparent on almost every page of the work" (*Life*, 1:xv). For this reason, stylistic analyses of ancient letters are rarely helpful for ascertaining authenticity (see Kenny, *Stylometric*, esp. 99–100).

Dispatching/Publishing

When the author was satisfied with the draft, the secretary prepared a nice copy on good papyrus for distribution (or dispatch if a letter). Appearances (Cicero, *Q. Fr.* 1.15b.1) as well as word choice (Cicero, *Att.* 7.3) mattered. In modern editions of ancient papyri, editors often note that a papyrus was written in a neat and careful script. For example, the secretary's handwriting for P.Mich. 8.496 was "large and elegant," and the hand of letter 468 "creates an impression of skill and long practice."[7] Of course, skill levels varied. A copy was retained by the author, probably in a notebook. If multiple copies were needed, the secretary was tasked with the job.

The Cost of Writing

A soldier from Egypt wrote home to his mother that he had reached his assignment safely (P.Mich. 8.490). After the secretary prepared the final copy for dispatch, someone else (probably the soldier) added, "Know that I have been assigned to Misenum, for I learned it later." This letter likely cost about a half denarius for the materials and a secretary. Since the typical papyrus letter, like this one, was brief, all but the poorest could afford to send a letter when needed. We must caution, however, that NT documents were not typical. What we consider brief, 3 John, was a typical letter of that time. Paul's Letters were long by comparison (see table 2). Paul's opponents ridiculed his letters with a pun that worked in Greek as well as English: his letters were "weighty" (2 Cor. 10:10). The biggest surprise to the Roman church was likely the size of Paul's letter. Although letter writing was "affordable" to most, NT documents were more expensive just because of their length.

Table 2. Length of Paul's Letters Compared

Length by Number of Words	Paul	Seneca	Cicero	All Extant Papyrus Letters (~14,000)
Shortest	335	149	22	18
Longest	7,114	4,134	2,530	209
Average	2,495	995	295	87

Note: The estimates are derived from Alfred Wikenhauser and Josef Schmid, *Einleitung in das Neue Testament* (Freiburg: Herder, 1973), 245. The numbers for Paul have been adjusted to reflect NA[27].

7. Youtie and Winter, *Papyri from Karanis*, 16, 24.

Also, it is difficult to convert ancient expenses into today's equivalent. Technically, a denarius had a set amount of silver (1/10 of a troy ounce); yet the cost of silver today is a fraction of the Roman price. If we use silver as a measure, a denarius is worth a few dollars. Historians will commonly use the price of wheat to determine the value of a denarius (see Bagnall, *Books*, 52); yet Americans pay far less for food than did ancients. If we use bread as a measure, a denarius is worth twenty to thirty US dollars. It is commonly stated that a denarius equaled a day's wage. The evidence for such an assertion is usually Jesus' parable of the generous employer (Matt. 20:1–15). Millard (*Reading*, 165) and I (Richards, *Letter Writing*, 168) agree that an unskilled worker probably earned closer to half a denarius per day. This would set a denarius at roughly 110 US dollars. Papyrus cost four denarii per roll. Scribes charged twenty-five denarii per ten thousand lines (P.Lond. Inv. 2110), probably writing about four hundred *stichoi* (lines) per day, earning roughly a denarius a day as a skilled laborer.

Table 3. Approximate Cost of Writing New Testament Letters

	Number of Lines	Percentage of a Standard *Charta*	Cost in Denarii for Materials and Labor	Estimated Equivalent in Today's US Dollars
Romans	979	136%	20.68	$2,275
1 Corinthians	908	126%	19.16	$2,108
2 Corinthians	607	84%	12.80	$1,408
Galatians	311	43%	6.56	$722
Philippians	221	31%	4.68	$515
2 Thessalonians	111	15%	2.32	$255
Philemon	44	6%	0.92	$101

Taking these numbers into consideration, table 3 shows the estimated cost involved in the composition of various NT letters.[8] With regard to a copy of Isaiah, Millard concludes it would cost six to ten denarii to reproduce, and he notes, "While that is not cheap, it would not put books out of the reach of the reasonably well-to-do" (Millard, *Reading*, 165). Although we may quibble over exchange rates, the main point remains: the length of most NT documents made them quite expensive.

8. For a fuller explanation, see Richards, *Letter Writing*, 165–69. These estimates consider the cost of preparing one dispatched copy and one retained copy. I used the lower rate of twenty-five denarii per ten thousand lines, but P.Mich. 8.855 suggests a higher rate. Bagnall (*Books*, 52–57) notes also the challenges of using the Edict of Diocletian (AD 301) to calculate the cost. Even if quite a bit inaccurate, these estimates (which were consistently rounded downward) still serve to show that preparing NT documents was no trivial expense.

The Challenges of "Original Autographs"

An autograph is literally a document in one's own handwriting. When referring to NT writings, however, scholars typically mean the original document. For Romans they mean the original letter that Paul sent to Rome. There are several challenges with this concept. First, no original of any NT document has been found. It is universally thought that all have perished. Second, to call a text an "autograph" is somewhat ill fitting. Paul's original Letter to the Romans was largely in the handwriting of Tertius, the secretary (Rom. 16:22). Last and most important, the term is a bit anachronistic. Collaborative aspects of authorship aside, which copy of Paul's Letter to the Romans was the original, the copy he dispatched or the copy he retained? This is not merely a Pauline problem. In a work for publication, sometimes the work needed redacting to fit onto a standard roll. Clearly, Luke-Acts was written to be a two-volume work (roll). The longer, so-called Western version of Acts is perhaps too long. Was it the rough or retained draft while a shorter, tighter version was sent to Theophilus, or was it just a later expansion, as is commonly suggested? To take an example from the OT: How do we discuss the original autograph of Jeremiah? Baruch wrote it down (Jer. 36:4), but the original was cut up and burned (36:23) and had to be rewritten (36:27–28, 32). At the time of the NT, was the shorter version of Jeremiah (represented by the LXX and two DSS fragments) the original, or was the longer version (represented by the MT and several DSS fragments) the original? While I personally hold a high view of Scripture, I must admit that there are challenges to the concept of original autographs.

> ### Happenstance Letter Carriers
>
> "From Cyrene, where I found a man who was journeying to you, I deemed it necessary to write to you about my welfare." (P.Mich. 8.490)
>
> "As an opportunity was afforded me by someone going up to you I could not miss this chance of addressing you. I am amazed, my son, that to date I received from you no news of your welfare." (P.Oxy. 123)
>
> "I found the boat sailing down, and I thought that I ought to let you know about what I have said." (P.Oxy. 1153)

Letter Carriers

The (highly efficient) Roman postal system was only for official business, and so individuals had to find other means to send letters. Typically, a letter was entrusted into the hands of someone already going that way, a happenstance carrier (see sidebar). Often the sender wrote not because of some pressing need but because someone happened to be going there. Otherwise, a private carrier, usually a slave, had to be sent. The aristocracy maintained private carriers: Cicero complained that Cassius's private carrier had rushed Cicero to finish the letter so that he could get on his way (Cicero, *Fam.* 15.17.1–2). We should not rule out private carriers for most NT letters (1 Cor. 4:17; 1 Pet. 5:12).

Private Letter Carriers

A private letter carrier was someone, often a slave, who was sent to a specific place for the task of delivering a letter. If able, a private carrier might transport supplies as well. Often this was mentioned in the letter, perhaps to encourage the honesty of the carrier. For example, Apollinarius writes to his "father" Sabinus:

> A number of times I asked Longinus, who brings you the letter, to take something for you, and he refused, saying that he was unable; but I want you to know that Domitius the [. . . took along a basket in which] there was a [. . .] for you. . . . If then you love me, you will straightway take pains to write to me concerning your health and, if you are anxious about me, to send me linen garments through Sempronius, for merchants come to us from Pelusium every day. (P.Mich. 8.466)

Another letter reads:

> Having learned that you are in Bacchias, I salute you, brother, and urge you to write to us immediately concerning your health. For I have already used up a papyrus roll [charta] in writing to you, and I received barely one letter from you, in which you informed me that I should receive the cloaks and the pig. The pig I did not receive, but the cloaks I did get. Farewell. (P.Mich. 8.496)

Similarly, Paul assures the church that Epaphroditus has faithfully delivered their gift (Phil. 4:18).

A private carrier could assure the recipient that the letter was authentic, since forgeries occurred (2 Thess. 2:2). Brutus writes to Cicero: "Please write me a reply to this letter at once and send one of your own men with it, if there is anything somewhat confidential which you think it necessary for me to know" (Cicero, *Fam.* 11.20.4). Private carriers were commonly expected to elaborate. Often a letter would commend the carrier as "trustworthy" to validate any additional information (1 Pet. 5:12; Col. 4:7; Cicero, *Fam.* 11.20.4; 11.26.5). Paul states he has told Tychicus to inform them about his imprisonment (Eph. 6:20–22). Paul is not ashamed of his chains, and he does not want the Ephesians to think Tychicus is revealing secrets (as sometimes happened; 1 Cor. 1:11). Paul may initially have used happenstance carriers. Surely even a modestly informed carrier could have sorted out the confusion in the "previous letter" (1 Cor. 5:9–10).

Scriptoria

In a third-century AD copy of the *Iliad*, a scribe once noted in a colophon (a scribal comment) that writing was the result of the hand, pen, *and knee*.[9] This copy of the *Iliad* was prepared in a scriptorium (a book-copying workshop). Before the printing press, copies of books were made by hand and on demand. It has long

---

9. Theodore Cressy Skeat, "The Use of Dictation in Ancient Book-Production," *Proceedings of the British Academy* 42 (1956): 179–208, esp. 183.

been argued that books were made by one person reading from the original, while several or perhaps a room full of people wrote it down. Two reasons are usually given. First, it just seems a more practical way to make multiple copies. Recently, D. C. Parker has called this assumption into question (*Sinaiticus*, 54–55). The practice has no evidence, and it presumes booksellers stocked books rather than making individual copies to order. Also, Parker questions if it was more efficient. I would also add that ancients did not particularly prize efficiency. The cost was by the line, not the time involved. The second argument for copying by lector is that scholars have noted a common error (called an "itacism") in copies: two words that sound alike (e.g., homophones such as "their" and "there" in English) are confused with each other so that the wrong word is written. The usual explanation is that the reader said the correct word, and the hearer wrote the wrong one. Yet, even today, itacisms are common errors.

Dispatching/Publishing and the Study of the New Testament

We should not assume that NT documents were dashed off one evening amid a flurry of mission activities. They were not carelessly written—rhetorical criticism is showing us just how carefully composed they were. Paul's comment about baptizing the household of Stephanas (1 Cor. 1:16) is usually considered a spontaneous or parenthetical remark, but it may well be careful rhetoric to imply that the Corinthians were boasting about matters that were trivial and hard even to remember. Cicero writes what looks like a spontaneous correction: "Well, then, his arrival—I mean Caesar's—is being eagerly awaited"; but the editors caution us that "it is a serious error to ascribe carelessness" to Cicero (Tyrrell and Purser, *Cicero*, 1:76). Seneca calls his letters "carelessly written" (Seneca, *Epist. mor.* 75.1; R. M. Gummere, LCL), but Richard Gummere warns us that this remark should not be taken literally.[10]

We should not imagine that when Luke finished his Gospel, he sent it to a scriptorium that prepared a dozen copies to sell to various churches. Publishing a document was more than merely disseminating copies of an "original autograph." A community could fund the expense for the text's composition but could also validate the document's authenticity and even the reason(s) for its publication. John 21 perhaps should be read in this light. To produce the Gospel and Acts, Luke needed the equivalent in today's currency of perhaps as much as four thousand US dollars for each text. It is no surprise he needed a benefactor.

Earle Ellis has suggested that Christianity had four centers in the first century; each had an apostolic founder, a Gospel, and some letters (*Making*, 32–45). Certainly, we should not assume that most local churches had a copy of even one Gospel. Initially, because it was too expensive to have a copy of everything, churches tended to copy what was "useful."

10. Richard M. Gummere, ed. and trans., *Seneca: Epistles [Ad Lucilium epistulae morales]* (3 vols.; LCL; Cambridge, MA: Harvard University Press, 1917–25), 1:x.

See also "Education in the Greco-Roman World"; "Jewish Education"; "Pseud-onymous Writings and the New Testament."

Bibliography

Bagnall, Roger S. *Early Christian Books in Egypt.* Princeton: Princeton University Press, 2009. A thorough study estimating the cost of parchment and writing for the fourth Christian century.

Deissmann, Adolf. *Light from the Ancient East: The New Testament Illustrated by Recently Discovered Texts of the Graeco-Roman World.* London: Hodder & Stoughton, 1912. Repr., Grand Rapids: Baker, 1978. Deissmann introduced NT readers to the then recently discovered Egyptian papyri, opening up a new age in biblical interpretation.

Ellis, E. Earle. *The Making of the New Testament Documents.* Leiden: Brill, 1999. A summary work by a world-class scholar. His comprehensive reconstruction of early Christianity (four centers and all NT documents pre–AD 70) has not found widespread acceptance.

Exler, Francis X. J. *The Form of the Ancient Greek Letter: A Study in Greek Epistolography.* Washington: Catholic University Press of America, 1922. The classic study of the stereotyped formulas, especially the illiteracy formula. This work began a series of studies in epistolographic formulas.

Gamble, Harry. *Books and Readers in the Early Church: A History of Early Christian Texts.* New Haven: Yale University Press, 1995. Excellent source. Gamble argues that the publication of a Pauline corpus precipitated the Christian adoption of the codex.

———. *New Testament Canon: Its Making and Meaning.* GBS. Philadelphia: Fortress, 1985. Although becoming dated, the series in which this volume appears provides students a simple but solid introduction to a broad range of topics.

Head, Peter M. "Named Letter-Carriers among the Oxyrhynchus Papyri." *JSNT* 31 (2009): 279–99. Using Richards's framework of letter carriers, he does a comprehensive study for this selection of papyri.

Kelber, W. H. *The Oral and Written Gospel.* Philadelphia: Fortress, 1983. The seminal study of orality. Aspects of his thesis (i.e., that written Gospels were intended to supersede oral sources and that Mark's paucity of sayings indicates an early suspicion of sayings sources) are disputed.

Kenny, Anthony. *A Stylometric Study of the New Testament.* Oxford: Clarendon, 1986. The best analysis of this kind. He uses a better text and method than Andrew Morton. Kenny's conclusion is that there is no data to support any group of letters (including the *Hauptbriefe* [i.e., Romans, 1–2 Corinthians, and Galatians]) as being any more similar with one another (stylistically). Kenny concludes that the thirteen Pauline letters were written either by thirteen different individuals or by one very diverse author. He does not factor in secretarial influence, which I think explains the diversity.

Klauck, Hans-Josef. *Ancient Letters and the New Testament.* Waco: Baylor University Press, 2006. This English edition of his German workbook is unquestionably the finest resource on NT letters. It is designed for students and is suitable for doctoral or advanced seminary use.

Millard, Alan. *Reading and Writing in the Time of Jesus.* BibSem 69. Sheffield: Sheffield Academic Press, 2000. An excellent resource, although many think that he overstates the case for Jewish literacy in the first century.

Murphy-O'Connor, Jerome. *Paul the Letter-Writer.* GNS 41. Collegeville, MN: Liturgical Press, 1995. A delightful, brief introduction to the subject.

Parker, David C. *Codex Sinaiticus: The Story of the World's Oldest Bible.* London: British Library, 2010. The executive editor of the International Greek New Testament Project re-creates how the manuscript was made.

Porter, Stanley, and Sean Adams, eds. *Paul and the Ancient Letter Form.* PAST 6. Leiden: Brill, 2010. This collection of essays includes Adams's contribution on letter openings and Jeffrey Weima's on letter closings. Both are good summaries.

Richards, E. Randolph. *Paul and First-Century Letter Writing: Secretaries, Composition and Collection.* Downers Grove, IL: InterVarsity, 2004. Designed for advanced undergraduate and early graduate student use.

————. *The Secretary in the Letters of Paul.* WUNT 2.42. Tübingen: Mohr Siebeck, 1991. The only comprehensive study of the role or function of the ancient amanuensis (secretary).

Roberts, Colin Henderson, and Theodore Cressy Skeat. *The Birth of the Codex.* 2nd ed. London: Oxford University Press, 1983. Considered the authoritative history of the codex. (The lasting influence of Bagnall, *Books*, is not yet clear.) This work argues that the publication of a fourfold Gospel precipitated the Christian adoption of the codex.

Sherwin-White, A. N. *Letters of Pliny: A Historical and Social Commentary.* Oxford: Oxford University Press, 1966. Repr., with corrections, 1985. The authoritative work on the letters of Pliny the Younger.

Stirewalt, M. Luther. *Paul the Letter Writer.* Grand Rapids: Eerdmans, 2003. A study that compares Paul's Letters to official correspondence.

Turner, Eric G. *Greek Papyri: An Introduction.* Oxford: Clarendon, 1968. Repr., 1980. The classic introduction to papyri.

Tyrrell, Robert Yelverton, and Louis Claude Purser. *The Correspondence of M. Tullius Cicero.* 7 vols. 3rd ed. London: Longmans, Green, 1901–33. This remains the authoritative resource on the letters of Cicero.

Weima, Jeffrey. *Neglected Endings: The Significance of the Pauline Letter Closings.* JSNT-Sup 101. Sheffield: Sheffield Academic Press, 1994. The best current study of Pauline "subscriptions."

Winter, John Garrett. *Life and Letters in the Papyri.* Jerome Lectures. Ann Arbor: University of Michigan, 1933.

29

Pseudonymous Writings and the New Testament

LEE MARTIN MCDONALD

Because we live in an age when plagiarism, forgery, stolen identities, and writing in another person's name are not only unethical but also illegal, it is easy to conclude that ancient authors of pseudonymous religious writings also had unethical intentions, that those writers intended to deceive their readers. Indeed, some claim that ancient pseudonymous writings cannot be divinely inspired and further that no such writings exist in the Bible. How could a book that was written to deceive be in the Bible? These concerns are understandable, given modern attitudes toward pseudonymous writings, but are such writings in the Bible? Further, if we find pseudonymous writings in the Bible, what about traditional views of authorship of the biblical books? Is it possible that some authors wrote in the name of a well-known apostolic or biblical figure in order to enhance the writing's acceptability, or perhaps to carry on that person's legacy or purposes? Scholars debate such issues today.

There is considerable evidence in antiquity for the widespread presence of pseudonymous writings. By pseudonymous writings, we refer to writings put forward or published in someone else's name. This is not the same as when a writer uses a pen name, as in the case of the well-known Mark Twain; rather, we refer to cases in which the writer produces a document under a false name, often, but not always, with the intent to deceive readers. Of course, the motivation *may* have been to deceive readers in order to have a wider distribution of the author's views, but some pseudonymous writings may have stemmed from a desire to honor a renowned leader, for example, when an author attempted to express a celebrated figure's views or to indicate that the author's views are in keeping with the views of a well-known person. There are many examples of this practice in the ancient world before, during, and after the NT era. Three examples that are especially relevant for this discussion are Iamblichus (ca. 250–330; *Life of Pythagoras* 31), Olympiodorus (*Prolegomenon* 13.4–14.4), and Elias (500–550; *In Porphyrii Isagogen et Aristotelis Categorias Commentaria* 128.1–22; see Ehrman, *Forged*, 131–33, 282).

A pseudonym is a fictitious name or an assumed name normally used by authors who for various reasons chose to conceal their own identity. The practice of writing under an assumed name was fairly common from the late fourth or early third century BC and extending well into the early Christian era. The collection of Jewish religious literature usually identified as the OT Pseudepigrapha ("pseudepigrapha" refers to writings produced under a false name) contains more than sixty-five documents. Given the precedent of such writings among their Jewish siblings, it should not be surprising that some Christians also produced writings pseudonymously. There are more than eighty *known* Christian pseudonymous writings, often referred to as New Testament Apocrypha [or Pseudepigrapha], generally written in the name of celebrated NT figures (Peter, Paul, James, Andrew, and others) and in literary genres similar to those found in the NT: gospels, epistles, acts, and apocalyptic writings. Below is a list of known Christian apocryphal writings.[1]

1. Gospels[2]

> *Protevangelium of James*
> *Infancy Gospel of Thomas*
> *Gospel of Peter*
> *Gospel of Nicodemus*
> *Gospel of the Nazoreans*

---

1. This list is from D. R. MacDonald, *HBD* 38–39. For a discussion of this literature, see J. K. Elliott, ed., *The Apocryphal New Testament: A Collection of Apocryphal Christian Literature in an English Translation based on M. R. James* (Oxford: Clarendon, 1993); Wilhelm Schneemelcher, ed., *New Testament Apocrypha* (2 vols.; rev. ed.; Louisville: Westminster John Knox, 1991–92); W. Barnstone, ed., *The Other Bible* (New York: Harper & Row, 1984); Rod Cameron, *The Other Gospels: Non-canonical Gospel Texts* (Philadelphia: Westminster, 1982). For a discussion of Jewish pseudonymous literature, likely the catalyst for this practice among Christians, see chapter 24 above. A number of pseudonymous writings also appear in the gnostic Christian writings that circulated in the second and later centuries. A helpful edition of these writings is Marvin Meyer, ed., *The Nag Hammadi Scriptures* (San Francisco: Harper SanFrancisco, 2007).

2. For a careful discussion of the apocryphal Gospels, see Charlesworth and Evans, "Jesus in the Agrapha"; see also Koester, *Ancient Christian Gospels*, 20–31, 173–240.

Gospel of the Ebionites

Gospel of the Hebrews

Gospel of the Egyptians

Gospel of Thomas

Gospel of Philip

Gospel of Mary

2. Acts (the first five of these are called the "Leucian Acts" and were sometimes circulated together)

Acts of John

Acts of Peter

Acts of Paul

Acts of Andrew

Acts of Thomas

Acts of Andrew and Matthias

Acts of Philip

Acts of Thaddaeus

Acts of Peter and Paul

Acts of Peter and Andrew

Martyrdom of Matthew

Slavonic Acts of Peter

Acts of Peter and the Twelve Apostles

3. Epistles[3]

3 Corinthians

Epistle to the Laodiceans

Letters of Paul and Seneca

Letters of Jesus and Abgar

Letter of Lentulus

Epistle of Titus

4. Apocalypses[4]

Apocalypse of Peter

---

3. Some would add here the canonical Pastoral Epistles and Epistles of Peter.

4. "Apocalypse" is a transliteration of the Greek *apokalypsis* ("revelation, disclosure"). Aune (*Prophecy*, 108) defines this literary genre as "a form of revelatory literature in which the author narrates both the visions he has purportedly experienced and their meaning, usually elicited through a dialogue between the seer and an interpreting angel. The substance of these revelatory visions is the imminent intervention of God into human affairs to bring the present evil world system to an end and to replace it with an ideal one. This transformation is accompanied by the punishment of the wicked and the reward of the righteous."

Coptic Apocalypse of Paul
First Apocalypse of James
Second Apocalypse of James
Apocryphon of John
Sophia of Jesus Christ
Letter of Peter to Philip
Apocalypse of Mary[5]

Klaus Koch has noted that the most popular names attached to pseudonymous literature attracted entire genres. For example, divine law came from Moses, wisdom from Solomon, and church regulations were produced in apostolic names—or groups, as in the case of the *Didache* (or *Teaching of the Twelve Apostles*) and the *Apostolic Constitutions* (Koch, "Pseudonymous Writing"). A common justification for pseudonymous literature is that many of these writings imply on the part of their authors a consciousness that "association with a tradition confers legitimacy." Koch explains:

> In many cases the authors to whom the writings are ascribed are considered as alive in heaven and therefore still effective in the present. To this extent attribution of authorship to men of God is similar to ascribing it to God, Christ, or angels. Since what is involved is not the conscious use of an inaccurate name, the designation "pseudonymous" should be used only with reservations. (Koch, "Pseudonymous Writing," 713)

Charlesworth agrees, and he warns against calling all such literature "forgeries" (Charlesworth, "Pseudepigraphy"). All pseudonymous literature may not necessarily be painted with the same brush; although some of it was undoubtedly intended to deceive readers, it may be that some ancient writers considered it acceptable to attribute their writings to one who had inspired them.

The Debate over Canonical Pseudonymous Literature

Biblical scholars continue to debate whether the NT contains pseudonymous writings, but generally those who think this was the case question whether the authors of such writings intended to deceive their readers. Those who argue that the NT contains pseudonymous writings generally point to the Pastoral Epistles, Ephesians, Colossians, 2 Thessalonians, James, 2 Peter, and possibly Jude and

5. There are many other examples of pseudepigrapha in antiquity beyond those produced within Judaism and early Christianity. Many classical writers also were honored by pseudonymous writings published in their names, among them Lysias, Galen, Apollonius, Plato, Pythagoras, Socrates, and Xenophon.

1 Peter as well. In the case of 1 Peter, the question has to do with the letter's remarkably good Greek and style—uncommon among working-class persons from Galilee; others respond that 1 Peter was written through a skilled secretary, Silvanus (5:12). Likewise, scholars question whether the book of Revelation was written by John the apostle. This is an interesting case because Revelation makes no claim to have been written by the apostle, though the author does name himself as "John" (1:9); yet, it is likely that Revelation was included in the biblical canon because people believed that this John who wrote it was indeed the apostle John. Today, though, we recognize that the style, content, and vocabulary of Revelation are considerably different from other writings attributed to John the apostle—the Gospel of John and 1–3 John. We should add that the Gospels, Acts, Hebrews, and 1–3 John were all written *anonymously*, not under a pseudonym, and that the names we now use for them were attached to them later in the second century.

Lewis Donelson (*Pseudepigraphy*, 11) may be right when he claims that no acknowledged pseudonymous writing was accepted in any collection of approved writings in the ancient Greco-Roman world—Jewish, Christian, or secular. Is it therefore possible that, despite good intentions, some deceptive mechanisms were put in place in order to secure the acceptance of some NT writings into the biblical canon? In antiquity it was not illegal to write in a pseudonymous name, but the practice was generally despised.

David Aune (*Prophecy*, 109) lists four common explanations for the existence of pseudonymous literature in antiquity (Aune is referring specifically to apocalyptic literature, but the points are also relevant to other types of literature): (1) it arose at a time when the biblical canon was virtually closed and well-known names were used to secure acceptance; (2) it was used to protect the identity of the writer, who might be in danger if his or her true identity were known; (3) apocalyptic visionaries may have had visions from those figures to whom they attributed their work; and (4) the writer may have identified with a person of the past and written as his representative. Aune suggests that the first of these options is the most likely, but not without qualifications. As a device to legitimate a piece of literature, he posits that pseudonymous authorship was intended to accord the writing in question the esteem and prestige given to the earlier well-known figure. However, he concludes that "pseudonymity is functional only if readers accept the false attribution" (*Prophecy*, 110).

No one denies that pseudonymous literature circulated throughout the Greco-Roman world, including in Jewish and Christian communities, and scholars agree that church leaders in the third and fourth centuries regularly rejected writings that they deemed to have been written pseudonymously.

If we conclude that deception *may* have played a role in the construction of some or many of the pseudepigraphic or pseudonymous writings, can we conclude with assurance that all pseudonymous writers wrote with deception in mind? Here nuance is important. For example, James Charlesworth identifies seven possible categories of Christian pseudonymous literature:

(1) works not by the named author, but probably containing some of his own thoughts (Ephesians and Colossians); (2) documents by someone who was influenced by another person to whom the work is ascribed (1 Peter and maybe James); (3) compositions influenced by earlier works of an author to whom they are assigned (1 Timothy, 2 Timothy, Titus); (4) Gospels (eventually) attributed to an apostle but deriving from later circles or schools of learned individuals (Matthew and John); (5) Christian writings attributed by their authors to an Old Testament personality (*Testament of Adam*, *Odes of Solomon*, *Apocalypse of Elijah*, *Ascension of Isaiah*); (6) once-anonymous works now correctly (perhaps Mark, Luke, and Acts) or incorrectly credited to someone (some manuscripts attribute Hebrews to Paul); (7) compositions that intentionally try to deceive the reader into thinking the author is someone famous (2 Peter). ("Pseudepigraphy," 2:961)

For several centuries some Jews and Christians accepted as Scripture many writings that are now identified as pseudonymous writings. Eventually that changed (McDonald, *Biblical Canon*, 190–214, 230–32). Much of this literature was shaped and inspired by the language, metaphors, and symbols of the OT or pivotal early Christian leaders (apostles). Authorship was often attributed to OT figures such as Enoch, Abraham, Shem, Moses, Solomon, Levi, and other Hebrew patriarchs, but also to early Christian leaders such as Peter, Paul, and James and others in the apostolic community. Although the designation "pseudepigrapha" is commonly used to identify a specific collection called Pseudepigrapha, some pseudonymous literature is found in the Apocrypha, that is, in the collection of Jewish religious writings included in Roman Catholic and Eastern Orthodox Bibles (e.g., Wisdom of Solomon).

Some ancient pseudonymous writings were clearly treated as sacred Scripture by many of the early church fathers, but also in the NT. For example, *1 Enoch*, a pseudonymous collection of five books written from the late fourth century BC to the latter part of the first century BC, is cited in the NT in a scriptural fashion (Jude 14 cites *1 En.* 1.9), and some NT writers are aware of its teachings. In Matt. 19:28 Jesus refers to the "Son of Man . . . seated on the throne of his glory" (cf. Matt. 25:31), which has its only parallel in *1 En.* 61.8; 62.2–5; 69.27–29. Many early church writers, from Justin Martyr to Origen in the middle of the third century, cite *1 Enoch* as Scripture. Indeed, Tertullian specifically calls *1 Enoch* "Scripture"—that is, citing the book he speaks of "the Scripture of Enoch" (*Apparel* 4.15–16). (James VanderKam ["1 Enoch," 47–54] has a helpful discussion of the role of *1 Enoch* in early Christianity.) We can add that the Wisdom of Solomon appears to have been cited as Scripture in Heb. 1:3 (cf. Wis. 7:25), and the many other verbal parallels to apocryphal and pseudonymous literature in the NT suggest that the biblical writers had some familiarity with this literature (McDonald, *Biblical Canon*, 452–64). These parallels indicate that the NT and early church writers knew and welcomed many of these writings.

Again, were *all* pseudonymous writings from antiquity intended to deceive readers? Bart Ehrman (*Forged*, 115–42) says "yes" and contends that those who suggest other, more honorable motives in its production can show no evidence for their position. On the other hand, some scholars argue that the production of pseudonymous writings, while unacceptable to our generation, was common and a widely accepted practice in antiquity, including in the early churches. Consequently, they ask whether it is inappropriate to judge ancient writings by modern standards. Do instances exist where ethical motivations were present in the production of pseudonymous writings? Some scholars contend that there was a time when it was acceptable to write in the name of some recognized biblical figures to honor their memory and earlier achievements—as in the cases of Enoch, Solomon, Peter, Paul, or others. Yet, by the fourth century many church leaders decided that such literature could not be welcomed as the church's sacred Scripture. Nevertheless, for several centuries there was a dispute in churches over whether some NT and other widely used Jewish and Christian writings that were earlier welcomed as sacred Scripture (e.g., *1 Enoch*, *Epistle of Barnabas*, *Didache*) were pseudonymous. That, of course, raises the question of whether some writings could have been rightly accepted into the biblical canon (based on content) yet for the wrong reason (authorship).

The debate about pseudonymous writings in the Old and New Testaments continues among biblical scholars, and some important contributions have emerged as a result (cf., e.g., Beale and Carson, *Commentary*). There are many references to some of this literature in early Christian writings, with many verbal parallels even in the NT writings. Settling this matter is not simple. Although many biblical scholars agree that some of the biblical books are pseudonymous, they do not all agree on which, or on what the author's motivation was, or even whether to continue to recognize them as Scripture. For example, is the book of Daniel in its present form pseudonymous? Some would argue that the earliest form of the book did in fact derive from the Hebrew prophet Daniel and that only its latest or final revised form stems from the mid-second century BC. Does it qualify, then, as a pseudonymous writing? Similarly, if there is a "Second Isaiah" (i.e., Isa. 40–55), should that writing be considered pseudonymous?

Some scholars question whether Matthew and John wrote the Gospels that bear their names, but since all four Gospels were written anonymously, they cannot properly be called "pseudonymous" literature. Many biblical scholars deny that Mark and Luke wrote the Gospels of Mark and Luke, but it is unlikely that their nonapostolic authorship would have been accepted by the ancient churches without some justification. Pseudonymous names from the NT are generally apostolic names, and those names only *began* to be placed on Christian writings after the middle of the second century, though interestingly not on Mark and Luke.

What might have motivated someone to write in another's name? Those who agree that there are pseudonymous writings in the NT generally hold one of four views: such writings were (1) written to deceive; (2) written in honor of a renowned personality (apostle or patriarch)—in humility and not to deceive; (3) written in the name of an apostle to continue the teaching that the renowned figure likely would have said was relevant for a subsequent generation; or (4) written by a secretary who was able to correct the style and sometimes the content of the writing itself, as perhaps in the case of Tertius who wrote Romans for Paul (Rom. 16:22). (For other possibilities, see Ehrman, *Forged*, 115–41.)

Ehrman contends that the biblical authors falsely claimed to be someone they were not, namely, celebrated apostolic or other biblical figures. He rejects the notion that pseudonymity was widely acceptable in antiquity and even asks how such writings could be the Word of God if they are deceitful. He concludes that those who wrote in another's name were liars and deceitful, and he recognizes that this conclusion has serious implications for those who look on the Bible as an infallible and authoritative guide to the truth of God (*Forged*, 1–32). Not everyone agrees with his assessment. I. Howard Marshall, for example, rejects Pauline authorship of the Pastorals in their current condition—especially 1 Timothy and Titus—and thinks there is sufficient authentic Pauline material in 2 Timothy to allow him to speak of Timothy or Titus as the final author/editor of the corpus. Instead of using the term "pseudonymity" to describe authorship, Marshall prefers "allonymity" and "allepigraphy," by which he urges that the anonymous writer continued (lengthened or completed) what Paul had intended to say.[6] Interestingly, Ehrman himself acknowledges that some pseudonymous writings could have been written by authors with good intentions, but he concludes that they nevertheless lied and that in such matters they should have been more honest (*Forged*, 262–65). Perhaps the ethically loaded terms he uses—"liars" and "forgeries"—should be softened, given his own conclusions.

Some biblical scholars reject Pauline authorship of the Pastoral Epistles but defend the practice of pseudonymous writing in the first century.[7] Since there are likely authentic Pauline traditions in the Pastorals—such as the rejection of Paul in Asia Minor (2 Tim. 1:15–18), the manner of the apostle's death (2 Tim. 4:6–8), and many of the closing comments to colleagues in 2 Tim. 4:14–22—should 2 Timothy be separated from 1 Timothy and Titus? If the author of the Pastoral Epistles simply wanted apostolic sanction for his views on organization and discipline in the church, and therefore attached Paul's name to his own writings, what conclusion(s) should we draw about the Pastorals? Since most of the important theological issues in the universally acknowledged letters of Paul (Romans, 1–2 Corinthians, Galatians, Philippians, 1 Thessalonians, and Philemon) are absent in the Pastoral Epistles (reconciliation, eschatology, "in Christ," justification by faith, the prominent role of the Holy Spirit, and a simple church organizational structure), a strong case can be made that the Pastoral Epistles were written not by Paul but

6. I. Howard Marshall, in collaboration with Philip H. Towner, *The Pastoral Epistles* [ICC; Edinburgh: T&T Clark, 1999], 79–89.

7. Among these are Meade, *Pseudonymity*; J. D. G. Dunn, "The Problem of Pseudonymity," in *The Living Word* (Philadelphia: Fortress, 1987), 65–85; idem, *DLNTD* 977–84; Donelson, *Pseudepigraphy*; and the earlier, important article by Kurt Aland, "The Problem of Anonymity and Pseudepigraphy in Christian Literature of the First Two Centuries," *JTS* 12 (1961): 39–49.

rather by someone who followed him. Many conservative scholars continue to argue, however, that the Pastoral Epistles were written by the apostle Paul at the end of his life, and they welcome as Paul's all of the NT writings attributed to him, including Ephesians, Colossians, and 2 Thessalonians.

Many popular ancient Christian writings outside the NT are generally acknowledged as pseudonymous works, including the *Didache*, *2 Clement*, the *Apostolic Constitutions*, the *Epistle of Barnabas*, the *Gospel of Thomas*, and many others. By the fourth century, as we see in the works of Eusebius, writings that were believed to be pseudonymous were regularly rejected (*Eccl. Hist.* 3.25.4–7). Such discussions, however, are rare before the fourth century, and several eminent, early church fathers accepted pseudepigraphic books as sacred Scripture. As we saw above, Tertullian cited *1 Enoch* as Scripture when dealing with women's attire (*Apparel* 1.3). It is remarkable, then, that the pseudonymous *Apostolic Constitutions* (ca. mid-fourth century)—itself written in the name of the apostles—warns Christians against reading pseudepigraphic literature. Notice first how its author claims to be reflecting words of the apostles:

> On whose account also *we*, who are now assembled in one place,—Peter and Andrew; James and John, sons of Zebedee; Philip and Bartholomew; Thomas and Matthew; James the son of Alphaeus; Simon the Canaanite, and Matthias, who instead of Judas was numbered with us; and James the brother of the Lord and bishop of Jerusalem, and Paul the teacher of the Gentiles, the chosen vessel, *having all met together, have written to you this Catholic doctrine* for the confirmation of you, to whom the oversight of the universal Church is committed. (6.14; *ANF* 7:456, emphasis added)

Two chapters later the author writes:

> We have sent all things to you, that you may know our opinion, what it is; and that you may not receive those books which obtain in our name, but are written by the ungodly. For you are not to attend to the names of the apostles, but to the nature of the things, and their settled opinions. For we know that Simon and Cleobius, and their followers, have compiled poisonous books under the name of Christ and of His disciples, and do carry them about in order to deceive you who love Christ, and us his servants. And among the ancients also some have written apocryphal books of Moses, and Enoch, and Adam, and Isaiah, and David, and Elijah, and of the three patriarchs, pernicious and repugnant to the truth. The same things even now have the wicked heretics done, reproaching the creation, marriage, providence, the begetting of children, the law, and the prophets; inscribing certain barbarous names, and as they think, of angels, but to speak the truth, of demons, which suggest things to them. (6.16; *ANF* 7:457)

Apparently, by the middle of the fourth century, *known* pseudonymous writings were no longer held in high esteem in the churches, even if they were still being produced.

The Contribution of Pseudonymous Writings

The value of all so-called apocryphal and pseudepigraphic literature for the study of the NT and early Christianity cannot be overestimated. Along with the canonical literature, this literature provides us with a portrait of the life and thought of the early church. Without it we have only a vague understanding of the emergence and growth of early Christianity and are left with less understanding of important terms such as "Son of Man," angels, the notion of apocalyptic eschatology, kingdom, messianic expectations, and many more topics of special interest. Most NT interpreters today, across the theological spectrum, see the immense value of this literature for informing our understanding of the context of the NT literature. This is true not only of the OT Apocrypha and Pseudepigrapha but also of the NT Apocrypha writings.

Conclusion

What can be made of the ancient practice of producing pseudonymous writings and their circulation among early Christians? One standard that made pseudonymous writings more acceptable, no doubt, was orthodoxy. If a particular writing cohered theologically with the kerygma of the larger Christian community, and if it was useful in the life of churches, that writing was more likely to find acceptance. By the third and fourth centuries, pseudonymous writings were generally more easily recognized and rejected by Christians, though some of the second-century church fathers identified and rejected some pseudonymous writings (Justin, Irenaeus, and others). Some of the cherished writings may well have been attributed to an apostle, as in the case of Hebrews, in order to secure their place in the Christian Scriptures. In the final analysis, *the* deciding factors in the acceptance of ancient writings likely had more to do with their orthodoxy and use among the churches, even if beliefs about the authorship of documents was not unimportant.

When most of the pseudonymous writings were produced, there was little or no discussion of the parameters of the biblical canon (contrary to Aune's point 1 above). The acceptance of much of this literature should imply not necessarily naïveté on the part of its first readers but rather that different concerns and a different understanding of that genre of literature existed at the time it was produced. It is more likely that the teaching in each of the presumed pseudonymous writings commended themselves to some Christians. Also, if those writings were in widespread use in the early churches, this ensured their continuing inclusion in the NT. In time, some writings were likely attributed to apostles in order to secure their acceptance in the Christian Scriptures, as in the cases of Hebrews, Revelation, and probably others.

Since pseudonymous writings were well known both in ancient Judaism and early Christianity, as well as in the wider Greco-Roman world before, during, and after the time of Jesus, it may be better to be more cautious about discussing notions of forgery and unethical intentions in all authors who wrote such literature. How the church decided what literature to include in its biblical canon is a matter of debate, but the issue of pseudonymity should probably not be a major criterion in settling the matter.

Bibliography

Aune, David. *Prophecy in Early Christianity and the Ancient Mediterranean World.* Grand Rapids: Eerdmans, 1983. Includes a useful and informed discussion of pseudonymous writings of antiquity and how they are interpreted.

Beale, G. K., and D. A. Carson, eds. *Commentary on the New Testament Use of the Old Testament.* Grand Rapids: Baker Academic, 2007. Generally, the authors deal carefully with examples of the NT's use of some of the apocryphal and pseudepigraphic writings, along with its use of the OT writings. Comments about Jude's use of *1 Enoch* are inaccurate, though, since this book was cited as Scripture in various texts in early Christianity, especially by Tertullian, but by others also.

Charlesworth, James H. *Old Testament Pseudepigrapha and the New Testament.* Cambridge: Cambridge University Press, 1985. Good discussion of the value of this literature for understanding early Christianity and the NT.

———. "Pseudepigrapha." *HBD* 836–40. A helpful discussion of this genre of ancient literature.

———. "Pseudepigraphy." *EEC* 2:961–64. Useful summary of the kinds and functions of pseudonymous writings in antiquity.

Charlesworth, James H., and Craig A. Evans. "Jesus in the Agrapha and Apocryphal Gospels." Pages 479–533 in *Studying the Historical Jesus: Evaluations of the State of Current Research.* NTTS 19. Leiden: Brill, 1994. Helpful discussion of the identity and function of noncanonical writings in early Christianity.

Donelson, Lewis R. *Pseudepigraphy and Ethical Argument in the Pastoral Epistles.* HUT 22. Tübingen: Mohr Siebeck, 1986. An informed discussion of whether pseudonymous literature exists in the Bible and how it can be evaluated in its historical context.

Ehrman, Bart D. *Forged: Writing in the Name of God—Why the Bible's Authors Are Not Who We Think They Are.* New York: Harper Collins, 2011. A popularly written work that promises a later, full-length, and scholarly discussion of this subject in a subsequent volume. Critically assesses denials of pseudonymous writings in the NT and claims that pseudonymous writings were not acceptable in antiquity and were intended to deceive readers. Includes helpful references to important sources.

Koch, Klaus. "Pseudonymous Writing." *IDBSup* 712–13. A brief but helpful discussion of pseudonymous writings.

Koester, Helmut. *Ancient Christian Gospels: Their History and Development.* Philadelphia: Trinity Press International, 1990. One of the best discussions of the function of the canonical and noncanonical Gospels in early Christianity and also their influence in the ancient churches.

McDonald, Lee Martin. *The Biblical Canon: Its Origin, Transmission, and Authority.* Peabody, MA: Hendrickson, 2006. Shows that the faith of the early Christians was informed by more than the Old or New Testament literature, including some writings that are now identified as pseudonymous.

Meade, David G. *Pseudonymity and Canon: An Investigation into the Relationship of Authorship and Authority in Jewish and Earliest Christian Tradition.* Grand Rapids: Eerdmans, 1986. Provides helpful information on the role of pseudonymous writings in antiquity, claiming that this practice began in OT times. Contains a dated but still useful bibliography.

Metzger, Bruce M. "Literary Forgeries and Canonical Pseudepigrapha." *JBL* 91 (1972): 3–24. A dated but still excellent discussion of the presence and function of pseudonymous writings in the ancient world. Not to be missed!

VanderKam, James C. "1 Enoch, Enoch Motifs, and Enoch in Early Christian Literature." Pages 33–101 in *The Jewish Apocalyptic Heritage in Early Christianity*. Edited by J. C. VanderKam and W. Adler. CRINT. Minneapolis: Fortress, 1996. Includes a helpful discussion of the history of the use of *1 Enoch* in early Christianity and cites many ancient sources.

30

Literary Forms in the New Testament

THOMAS E. PHILLIPS

At the most basic level, the NT is a piece—or several pieces—of literature. Too often people forget—or ignore—this most basic and undeniable fact. All of the literary forms in the NT would have been familiar to the Greek-speaking people of the first and second centuries. Of course, some varieties of NT literature would have been more easily recognizable by particular subgroups within the Greco-Roman world than other varieties. For example, the genre of apocalyptic literature (like the book of Revelation) would have been well known to many Jews and virtually unknown to many non-Jews. Overall, however, most of the NT writings were written in literary forms that were commonplace within the Greco-Roman world.

The investigation of the literary forms in the NT can proceed on two levels—at the level of individual literary units within the NT "books" and at the level of the NT books themselves. Our focus here is on the level of the literary forms (genres) of the NT books themselves.

Literary Forms (Genres) of the New Testament Documents

The twenty-seven books of the NT can be divided broadly into five literary forms: biographies (the Gospels), history (Acts), letters proper (Paul's Letters, James,

1–2 Peter, 2–3 John, and Jude), sermons and tracts (Hebrews and 1 John), and apocalypse (Revelation).

Biographies

New Testament scholars once commonly asserted that the Gospels belonged to a unique genre of literature that was unparalleled in the Greco-Roman world, a sui generis. However, subsequent research has demonstrated that this assertion is not supported by careful comparison between the Gospels and other ancient literature. Biographies, comparable to Gospels, were widely known in the first century. Writers like Plutarch, Suetonius, and Cornelius Nepos produced biographies of Alexander the Great, the emperors, and various other political leaders and philosophers.

In the Greco-Roman world, biographies were recognized by their focus on one primary character, by their emphasis on that person's (almost always commendable) character, by their relative lack of interest in formal political and military processes, and by their tendency to conclude quickly after the main character's death. These four traits of biography are all evident in the Gospels, and it is likely that ancient readers would have quickly associated the Gospels with this widely known ancient genre.

In the case of the Gospels, Matthew and Luke begin their biographies with the birth of Jesus (Matt. 1:18–2:23; Luke 1:5–2:40). These two Gospels also contain a genealogy of Jesus' family of origin (Matt. 1:1–17; Luke 3:23–38). Besides these brief birth narratives (and one very brief reference to one of Jesus' childhood experiences in the temple; Luke 2:41–52), the Gospels focus entirely on Jesus' adult life and ministry from the time of his baptism by John, a event that Luke reports occurred when Jesus was about thirty years old (Luke 3:23). Mark and John limited their narratives entirely to the events in Jesus' adult life and the events that immediately followed his death and resurrection. The Gospels all climax with their telling of the crucifixion and the resurrection. All these characteristics of the Gospels—their occasional inclusion of genealogies and birth narratives, their relative disinterest in their primary character's childhood, their strong emphasis on the adult life of a single person, their rapid conclusions after Jesus' death and resurrection, and even the brief preface to Luke's Gospel—are entirely consistent with the genre of biographies in the first century. While genre categories—both in antiquity and today—are fluid and not without exceptions and variation, the Gospels fit quite well within the ancient genre of biography.

History

The book of Acts, the sequel to the Gospel of Luke, is the NT's only historical monograph. Greek and Roman writers had a rich legacy of history writing that stretched back to the fifth century BC, when Herodotus and Thucydides wrote their great military and political histories. By the late first and early second centuries

AD, when the Gospels and Acts were written, history writing had developed into a widespread and quite diversified set of subgenres. By the beginning of the Christian era, history no longer focused exclusively on military and political events and characters. Writers who were roughly contemporary with the author of Acts often produced histories of various people groups. Such "ethnic histories" were marked by their focus on some people group that was distinguished from the dominant culture. The groups chronicled in these histories were typically united by their shared geographical, cultural, or religious traits. These histories often showed a strong interest in the group's internal political processes (like the "apostolic conference" in Acts 15) and in the group's interactions with political authorities external to the group (like the church's frequent interaction with the Roman Empire in Acts). Such histories could be expected to pay particular attention to the group's internal customs and practices. Josephus's late first-century history of the Jewish people is one of the best known of the extant ethnic histories. Acts was probably written in a historical genre similar to Josephus's *Antiquities of the Jews*.

The question of the relationship between Luke and Acts attracted considerable scholarly attention during the second half of the twentieth century. Acts opens with the author's claim to have written an earlier book about Jesus' words and deeds (Acts 1:1–8). Interpreters have long recognized that this preface to Acts is alluding to Luke's Gospel, and few Lukan scholars have seriously challenged the likelihood that Luke and Acts were composed by the same author. Together these two books, the two longest books in the NT, contain a two-part story. Luke's Gospel relates the story of Jesus, and Acts relates the story of Jesus' followers in the early church. The key question has been, not the common authorship of Luke and Acts or the function of Acts as a sequel to Luke, but whether the two books share a common genre. The Gospels are typically regarded as biographies, but only the Gospel of Luke has a sequel, the book of Acts. Should Luke and Acts (or Luke-Acts, as many scholars prefer to designate the books) be read as one continuous narrative that belongs to a single genre, or should the Gospel and Acts be read separately—that is, as a biography with a follow-up history of the church?

The question of the genre(s) of Luke and Acts may seem like a mere scholarly trifle, but one's answer to this question does have interpretive implications. On the one hand, if the two books belong to the same genre, the determination of their shared genre is largely dependent on Acts. Acts (with its focus on multiple characters and multiple overlapping story lines) hardly fits within the genre of biography, but the Gospel of Luke fits loosely within the genre of history (Jesus, being the founder and key personality within the history of the Christian people). On the other hand, if the two books belong to different genres, then their genres are viewed as the biography of the unique founder (Luke's Gospel) and as the subsequent history of his followers (Acts). The issue at stake is the unique authority of Jesus. Were Peter and Paul (in Acts) Jesus' successors who possessed the authority to lead the Christian movement in new directions; or were Peter and Paul Jesus' followers who worked to preserve Jesus' original words and deeds?

Reading Luke-Acts as one history favors the successor model; reading Luke and Acts as a biography and a history favors the follower model. (Of course, many factors bear on such theological questions, and the designation of genre is only one of these factors.)

Letters

Letters, typically brief notes exchanged between friends or family members, are the most commonly preserved type of literature from the Greco-Roman world (many of these letters were preserved in the detritus of landfills and garbage dumps, but preserved nonetheless). Letters are also the most common type of literature in the NT. Depending on what one determines to be the defining characteristic of a letter, the NT contains between nineteen and twenty-one letters. Using the more restrictive definition (see below), the NT contains thirteen letters attributed to Paul, two letters attributed to Peter, two letters attributed to John, one letter attributed to James, and one letter attributed to Jude.

These nineteen books can be confidently regarded as letters because each contains the three typical features of an ancient letter: a letter opening, a letter body, and a letter closing. The most consistent feature, and therefore the most important feature for recognizing the literary form of letters, is the letter opening. Letters in Greco-Roman antiquity typically opened with three standardized formulas: a sender formula, a recipient formula, and a salutation (often in the form of a prayer or health wish). As documents of the Greco-Roman world, the letters in the NT follow these standard conventions quite closely. As examples, consider the openings of 2 Peter and James:

> From Simon Peter, a slave and apostle of Jesus Christ [sender formula].
>   To those who received a faith equal to ours through the justice of our God and savior Jesus Christ [recipient formula].
>   May you have more and more grace and peace through the knowledge of God and Jesus our Lord [salutation]. (2 Pet. 1:1–2 CEB)

> From James, a slave of God and of the Lord Jesus Christ [sender formula].
>   To the twelve tribes who are scattered outside the land of Israel [recipient formula].
>   Greetings! [salutation]. (James 1:1 CEB)

These two letter openings were chosen in part to illustrate two issues—first, the relative consistency of letter openings, and second, some of the complexities of interpreting sender and recipient formulas. All nineteen of the NT letters listed above contain a letter opening with a sender formula, a recipient formula, and a salutation, even though few NT scholars accept that all of the NT letters were actually written by the person (or persons) listed in their sender formulas, and NT scholars commonly doubt the wisdom of reading every letter's recipient formula as a reliable guide to the letter's original readers. For example, most NT scholars doubt that the apostle Peter wrote 2 Peter (pseudonymity will be discussed below), and NT scholars commonly interpret the "twelve tribes" in James's recipient formula metaphorically. In spite of the prevalence of nonliteral readings of these two letters' openings, few scholars doubt that each of these documents was written in the literary form of a letter.

The body of ancient letters varied widely in antiquity. Still, most ancient letters were relatively brief—closer in size to the body of Jude (vv. 3–23) than to the size of 1 Corinthians (1:10–16:12). The diverse content and forms of the NT's letter bodies are consistent with the diverse content and forms contained in the other ancient letters.

Ancient writers commonly, but not consistently, employed letter closings. In keeping with this cultural practice, most of the NT letters also end with some sort of letter closing (e.g., 2 John 13; Jude 24–25; 1 Pet. 5:12–14), even though these closings vary more widely than do the NT's letter openings (James has no clearly discernible letter closing).

Within the broad literary form of letters, scholars have developed several different classifications of the subgenres of letters. First, the letters can be divided into subgenres on the basis of their implied readership: pastoral letters to churches and personal letters to individuals. If the traditional designations of authorship (the author identified in the letter opening) are accepted, the vast majority of NT letters are what could be broadly defined as pastoral letters, letters from a senior Christian leader to a community. Nine of the thirteen letters of Paul and the letters of 1–2 Peter, 2 John, James, and Jude all fall within this category of pastoral letter. The remaining NT letters (1–2 Timothy, Titus, Philemon, and 3 John) are personal letters, ostensibly written to a single person. Even these may presume a wider audience, however; note, for example, the designation of the recipients of Paul's letter to Philemon: "To Philemon our dearly loved coworker, Apphia our sister, Archippus our fellow soldier, and the church that meets in your house" (vv. 1b–2 CEB).

Second, the letters could be divided into subgenres on basis of their implied (or traditional) authorship. Using this approach, the letters would be grouped into the thirteen letters of Paul, the two letters of Peter, two letters of John (2–3 John), and the single letters from James and Jude. This approach is problematic, however, because few contemporary scholars accept the traditional authorship designations of all the NT letters.

A third and equally problematic approach to locating the letters within subgenres is based on the letters' content and purposes. Although some of the letters can be placed within known literary traditions from the Greco-Roman world with relative ease (e.g., 1 Peter and James are letters of moral exhortation, Romans is probably Paul's ambassadorial letter introducing Paul to the Roman church, and Philemon is Paul's letter of personal appeal in behalf of Philemon's returning slave Onesimus), other letters, like Philippians and Jude, are very difficult to place within a subgenre strictly on the basis of content or purpose.

The complexities involved in placing the NT letters into clearly defined sub-genres has resulted in a series of overlapping, often imprecise, and sometimes competing scholarly taxonomies for discussing the subgenres of the letters. Most scholars speak of the "authentic," "genuine," or "undisputed" letters, by which they mean the letters that an overwhelming majority of NT scholars regard as having been written by the authors whose names appear in their letter openings.

Scholarship, therefore, has yet to provide any consistent or well-established definitions of the appropriate subgenres under the general category of "letters." Scholars seldom deny the relevance of distinguishing between subgenres within the genre of letters—and most agree that such subgenres will eventually coalesce around some combination of the criteria of authorship, readership, and content. At this point, however, most scholars employ a series of loose describers—such as "authentic," "pseudonymous," "pastoral," "personal," "ambassadorial," and "paraenetic"—when speaking about the characteristics of individual letters. No clearly defined subgenres have been established within the broad genre of letters.

What of the question of pseudonymity as a NT literary form? Simply defined, "pseudonymity" is the phenomenon of a person writing in the name of some other figure, typically a deceased person of greater renown. Pseudonymity was common in antiquity. Persons composed letters in the names of Plato and other intellectual figures either to promote their interpretations of such figures or else to seek to update the master's teachings for a new situation. There can be no doubt that some early Christians wrote pseudonymous letters in the names of various apostles. We possess several noncanonical letters attributed to Paul, Peter, and James, all of which are universally recognized as pseudonymous. The question is whether any of the writings in the NT are pseudonymous. Of course, it is possible that none of the NT letters are pseudonymous, but it is also possible that many are. Indeed, it is probable that at least some of the NT letters are pseudonymous. Given the NT's Greco-Roman context, this is not surprising.

In his monumental volume on the literature of the Roman Empire, Albrecht Dihle places the issue of NT pseudonymity within the context of pseudonymity in the larger Greco-Roman world:

> Many contemporary and later Christian authors . . . emulated the example set by Paul's letters. Some of their works were ascribed to him, and some to other apostles. . . . That they should have laid claim to apostolic authority cannot simply be condemned as literary forgery, just as this term can not be applied to the letters which were published under Plato's name. Choosing the name of an apostle signified no more than the author's public declaration that he was advocating the pure, true faith; and it was this very criterion which later caused church authorities to canonise some of the non-genuine letters. (*Greek Literature*, 207)

In some cases, the actual authorship—whether pseudonymous or apostolic—is largely insignificant to the interpretation of the letters. For example, 1 Peter and James are letters of moral exhortation (paraenesis), regardless of their authorship (though James offers this paraenesis in profound dialogue with the OT wisdom tradition and 1 Peter offers advice that is more acculturated to Greco-Roman categories). In other cases, however, the "pseudonymous" designation profoundly influences both one's interpretation of the document in question and one's construction of early Christianity. For example, consider the implications of deciding that 2 Peter and 1 Timothy are pseudonymous. If Peter wrote 2 Peter, it offers an original apostle's vigorous defense of the authentic faith against those who have fallen away from that faith. However, if 2 Peter is pseudonymous (as many scholars believe), it can be read as part of a second-century debate over competing interpretations of the shared Christian faith. Similarly, if 1 Timothy is authentically Pauline, then Paul was content to work within a hierarchical and office-structured church that endorsed the social values of the Greco-Roman world. However, if 1 Timothy is pseudonymous, 1 Timothy (as well as the other disputed and doubted Pauline letters) can be read as a movement away from Paul's original impulse toward a countercultural and gift-structured church that tended in the direction of egalitarianism.

Letters are the most common literary form in the NT. The NT contains many letters—pastoral letters, personal letters, paraenetic letters, ambassadorial letters, and quite likely, pseudonymous letters.

Sermons and Tracts

One book of the NT, Hebrews, is a sermon, and it identifies itself as a "word of exhortation" (13:22). In negative terms, even though Hebrews has a letter-like closing (13:17–25), few ancient readers would have seen any connection between the opening lines of Hebrews and the standard literary features of the letter form. The opening of Hebrews contains none of the traditional features of a letter opening (i.e., sender, recipient, peace or health wish, and thanksgiving). The absence of a sender formula particularly distances Hebrews from the letter form, because an anonymous letter would have been without parallel in antiquity. In positive terms, the tightly reasoned structure and sustained engagement with Scripture in Hebrews has many parallels to the sermons that Peter and Stephen reportedly preached to Jewish groups in Acts (2:14–41; 7:2–53).

A recognition of the sermonic character of Hebrews is significant for three reasons. First, setting aside the "sermons" in Acts, each of which might be read as a sermon précis, Hebrews is probably the earliest surviving example of early Christian preaching. Second, Hebrews illustrates both how deeply reliant early Christianity was on the OT for its own self-understanding and how important symbolic (allegorical) interpretation of the OT was for Christian discourse. Third, the preservation of Hebrews establishes the probability that early Christian groups shared sermons with one another.

The NT also contains one tract, the anonymous book of 1 John, which looks even less like a traditional Greco-Roman letter than Hebrews. With neither a letter opening nor a letter closing (cf. 1 John 5:21), 1 John offers theological and ethical advice to a divided Christian community. First John contains extensive allusions to the Gospel of John (which was probably produced by the same community at some earlier time), but 1 John contains none of the direct appeals to the OT so common in the sermonic Hebrews. The exhortations in 1 John are rooted in the authority of the anonymous author and in that author's appeal to generalized Christian traditions about the centrality of love and the character of God (e.g., 2:7; 3:16; 4:11). This tract stems from a respected member of the Johannine community (a member identified as "the elder" in 2 John 1:1 and 3 John 1:1).

Apocalypse

Of all the literary forms in the NT, none is less familiar to modern readers than apocalyptic literature. Apocalyptic literature, the genre of the book of Revelation, flourished in ancient Judaism and early Christianity from the third century BC until the third century AD. Two documents in the contemporary Christian canon, the books of Daniel and of Revelation, stand toward each end of the apocalyptic movement. Daniel was probably written in the 160s BC, and Revelation was probably written in the mid- to late AD 90s. However, these two books represent only a small sample of the vast array of apocalyptic documents produced by ancient Jews and Christians.

The apocalyptic movement, and the literature created by that movement, arose as a religious response to ancient Jewish perceptions of social, political, and religious oppression by the gentile powers that ruled over them. The identity of the perceived oppressors changed as time passed. In Daniel's time, the oppressors were Greek; by the time of Revelation, the Romans had replaced the Greeks as the intractable foes of righteousness. The specific point of apocalypticism's entry into early Christianity is widely debated. Some scholars argue that Jesus and John the Baptist were apocalyptic figures; other scholars argue for a later (possibly Pauline) introduction of apocalypticism into Christian circles. Regardless of the exact timing of apocalyptic thought's emergence within Christian circles, two facts are clear. First, early Christianity and the NT were deeply influenced by apocalyptic thought, and second, apocalyptic literature was a Jewish rather than a gentile literary genre.

Apocalyptic thought is marked by profound convictions about good, evil, judgment, and divine action. Apocalyptic writers always believed themselves to be a good and righteous minority that suffered at the hands of an evil and unrighteous dominant power. Apocalyptic thought presumed that the present age was evil and would soon be judged by God in a decisive moment of divine action—an *apocalypse*, a revealing of divine justice. Although this ideology originated among Jewish groups that regarded themselves as God's true people and the Greeks as their evil oppressors who would be judged in the apocalypse, many Christian thinkers adopted this same ideology and simply placed themselves in the role of the oppressed righteous and the Romans in the role of their evil oppressors. Both Christian and Jewish apocalyptic writers often identified themselves with the past leaders of God's people (e.g., Moses, Elijah, and Enoch) and their persecutors with the traditional enemies of God's people (particularly the Babylonians, who destroyed Judah's temple in 586 BC).

Apocalyptic literature follows a predictable arc, an arc that parallels the apocalyptic vision of history. The story begins with the persecution of the righteous and the seeming invincibility and prosperity of their persecutors. Then the narrative experiences a sweeping intervention of divine justice that fully vindicates the righteous, decisively defeating God's enemies and establishing God's righteous rule over all creation. This arc is well illustrated by the manner in which the ubiquitous images of kings, thrones, and court authorities function in apocalyptic literature. Apocalyptic literature often contains images of kings and rulers who assert their authority in the place of the one true God. At first their arrogance appears to proceed unchecked; they typically are initially depicted as triumphing over the people of God (nearly always acquiring their dominance through ruthless militarism and violence). Eventually, however, God intervenes, asserting God's rightful place on the throne as Lord of all creation. In apocalyptic literature this arc of justice may be temporarily invisible to those who currently suffer, but God—often through an angel or other divine guide—has revealed these truths to the document's author, who has been charged with delivering the message of impending judgment to God's elect.

Apocalyptic literature is inherently subversive to the dominant powers. Therefore apocalyptic writers often employed various literary techniques to conceal their message from outsiders. Thus apocalyptic literature is renowned for its use of symbolism, numerology, and other insider language. In keeping with these stern dichotomies between God's righteous people and God's evil enemies, apocalyptic literature tends to employ stylized images of good and evil. The enemies of God are frequently identified as beasts of various kinds (e.g., lions, leopards, whales, and various mythological creatures, like fire-breathing dragons). The people of God are typically identified as human sufferers, as martyrs, and as the devout. Violence—both realistic military violence (swords, spears, war horses, and chariots) and symbolic cosmic violence (floods, famines, earthquakes, and severe storms)—is commonplace. This violence is often sexualized. The righteous often portray themselves in terms of virgins and brides, while the wicked are characterized as sexually indulgent or exploitive. Wealth and political power are consistently viewed as the earthly but temporary possession of the wicked. The saints see themselves as impoverished and disempowered; their oppressors are wealthy and powerful. In apocalyptic thought, divine judgment brings a cataclysmic end to the present order. The rich and powerful are judged; the present sources of military, economic, and political oppression are decisively defeated, often through acts of cosmic violence. The righteous are rewarded and vindicated.

The book of Revelation stands squarely within this apocalyptic tradition in terms of symbolism (the beast, the dragon, the whore of Babylon, the four horsemen), numerology (7 bowls, 7 trumpets, 24 elders, 144,000 righteous, and the evil of 666), and contrast between the righteous and the unrighteous. However, Revelation also challenges this literary tradition. In Revelation the central image of God's righteous judgment is a slaughtered lamb (5:6–14), and the moment of God's decisive victory over evil is imaged in terms of divine self-sacrifice rather than divine violence and conquest.

Conclusion

The NT contains five common genres from antiquity—biography, history, letters, sermons and tracts, and apocalypse. Early Christian writers adapted these common literary forms to suit their individual needs, but the genres within the NT are all recognizable literary forms in the first-century Mediterranean world.

See also "Reading, Writing, and Manuscripts"; "Pseudonymous Writings and the New Testament."

Bibliography

Attridge, Harold. "Paraenesis in a Homily." *Semeia* 50 (1990): 210–26. Examines the implications of reading the book of Hebrews as an early Christian homily.

Aune, David. *The New Testament in Its Literary Environment*. LEC. Louisville: Westminster John Knox, 1987. The best monograph-length discussion of the literary forms of the NT books.

Burridge, Richard A. *What Are the Gospels? A Comparison with Graeco-Roman Biography*. Grand Rapids: Eerdmans, 2004. A sustained argument for understanding the Gospels as ancient biographies.

Dihle, Albrecht. *History of Greek Literature: From Homer to the Hellenistic Period*. New York: Routledge, 1994. Although Dihle mentions the NT only briefly, his work provides the most complete survey of the literature and literary genres that were common at the time of the NT's composition.

Graves, David. *The Seven Messages of Revelation and Vassal Treaties: Literary Genre, Structure, and Function*. Piscataway, NJ: Gorgias, 2009. Examines the genre of Revelation in the context of political treaties in the ANE in which a sovereign power entered into treaty with a subordinate power.

Klauck, Hans Josef. *Ancient Letters and the New Testament: A Guide to Context and Exegesis*. Waco: Baylor University Press, 2006. This work discusses the genre of NT letters in the context of Greco-Roman letters.

Malina, Bruce. *On the Genre and Message of Revelation: Star Visions and Sky Journeys*. Peabody, MA: Hendrickson, 1995. Explains how visions and heavenly imagery in Revelation functioned in ancient apocalyptical literature. The author draws heavily from both historical and social-science tools in his analysis.

Phillips, Thomas E. "The Genre of Acts: Moving toward a Census?" Pages 46–77 in *Acts in Diverse Frames of Reference*. Edited by Thomas E. Phillips. Macon, GA: Mercer University Press, 2009. Surveys recent scholarly discussions regarding the genre of Acts, particularly Acts as a subgenre of ancient historiography.

Sterling, Gregory E. *Historiography and Self-Definition: Josephos, Luke-Acts, and Apologetic Historiography*. NovTSup 64. Boston: Brill, 1997. Argues that Acts is written in the same genre as Josephus's history of the Jewish people and that it serves as an introduction to and self-definition of early Christianity.

31

Homer and the New Testament

If you lived in the Roman Empire in the mid- to late first century, when most of the NT was written, you may or may not have heard of Jesus and the early Christians, you may or may not have had any awareness of the content of the writings that Christians now call the OT, and you may or may not even have been able to read, but you would have possessed a fairly detailed knowledge of Homer's two great epics, the *Odyssey* and the *Iliad*. For contemporary interpreters of the NT, the key question is this: In what way(s) should the NT world's undeniable immersion in the Homeric traditions inform our contemporary reading of the NT?

Homer's *Iliad* and *Odyssey*

No one doubts the presence and influence of the Homeric tradition within the first-century AD Greek-speaking world. The two Homeric Greek epic poems, the *Iliad* and the *Odyssey*, were the most read and studied books in antiquity. The basic plot of the *Iliad* relates the battle between the Greeks and the Trojans at Troy's city walls. The story particularly emphasizes the struggle between two ill-fated warrior heroes, the Greek Achilles and the Trojan Hector. The *Odyssey* relates the struggle of a Greek man, a veteran of the Trojan War named Odysseus, and his multiyear journey back to his home and his wife, Penelope.

390

Little is known of Homer's life and biography. The fifth-century BC historian Herodotus dates Homer's life four centuries prior to his own life, or in the ninth century BC. Other ancient sources date Homer as far back as the thirteenth century BC. Based on the orthography of his name, some traditions regard Homer as a hostage, as a blind man, or both (the Greek word *homēros* can signify someone who is a "hostage" or even "blind"). Several locations around the eastern Mediterranean Sea have been associated with Homer's birth, life, and death. However, none of these claims about Homer's origins are particularly useful or even—some would say—significant. In fact, most scholars doubt the appropriateness of thinking in terms of a single ancient author behind these texts.

In all probability, the *Iliad* and the *Odyssey* were produced and modified by an assortment of largely anonymous authors and editors over an extended period of time. Most scholars today agree that these epics probably took their established form in the eighth century BC or shortly thereafter. However, the larger tradition of Homeric literature extends to several other documents and spans several more centuries. This larger literary tradition includes several hymns to the gods and a host of books about Homer's life and works, which have been universally recognized as derivative from the *Iliad* and the *Odyssey* and are clearly inferior to these texts in literary quality and significance. Therefore, I will limit my comments to the Homeric *Iliad* and *Odyssey*.

Homer's Influence within the Greco-Roman World

No texts within the Greco-Roman world were more widely read, studied, and imitated than were Homer's *Iliad* and *Odyssey*. Homer's influence was impressed on Greco-Roman culture through education, art, theater, and literature.

The *Iliad* and the *Odyssey* were the primary texts in Greek education. These Homeric epics were the first Greek texts that most students read. Children's exposure to these texts began with simple reading exercises, then progressed to memorization of key portions of the texts, and eventually culminated in the imitation of the epics' scenes and discourses. This repeated and in-depth exposure to Homer's writing undoubtedly explains why no author is more quoted in ancient literature than Homer and why brief quotations from Homer's epics so commonly appear in both Greek and Latin writers. Those writers include two first-century Jews whose importance for understanding the NT world is pivotal: Philo, who refers to Homer as "the greatest and most reputed of poets" (*Conf.* 4); and Josephus, who calls on Homer as a witness to the antiquity of Israel's Torah (*Ag. Ap.* 2.152).

Although literacy rates in the Greco-Roman world are notoriously difficult to establish, it is safe to assume that nearly every literate person in the Greek-speaking eastern empire had read from Homer. The literate elite had probably also read the pseudo-Homeric hymns, an assortment of commentaries on Homer, and various secondhand accounts of his life. Most of the highly educated persons in antiquity had also likely spent time composing their own imitations of Homer's poetry—such imitation was a standard practice for advanced students of Greek.

Exposure to Homer was not the exclusive privilege of the literate classes. Even the illiterate masses would have known many of the stories and scenes within Homer's epics. Public and semipublic readings of Homer's works were common; mosaics and paintings throughout the Roman Empire routinely incorporated images from Homer's epics; Greek and Roman theaters echoed with productions based on Homer's writings; and coins were even sometimes minted with images drawn from the Homeric stories. This ubiquitous onslaught of theatrical productions, public readings, and artistic representations of Homer's stories ensured that no one in the Greco-Roman world was unaware of the characters, the plots, and many of the key lines from Homer's epics.

Homer and the New Testament

The first-century's cultural immersion in Homer and the Homeric tradition provides important background for interpreters of the NT. No other cultural icon more fully embodies the values and ideals of Greco-Roman society than do the Homeric epics. To be clear, most—if not all—of the NT writers had probably read Homer's *Iliad* and *Odyssey*; most—if not all—of the NT writers had probably memorized at least portions of these epics; and all of the NT writers were certainly familiar with the stories contained in the epics (just as contemporary North Americans are familiar with images like "the yellow brick road" and with quotations like "I don't think we're in Kansas anymore, Toto" from *The Wizard of Oz*). Still, the NT's literary character is significantly different from Homer's literary character. At the most basic linguistic level, in terms of the evolution of the Greek language, the NT was written in the first century's Koine Greek, and the Homeric epics were written in the much more complex Homeric or Ionic Greek of the classical period. Similar differences exist on the level of literary style. Homer wrote hexameter poetry with highly stylized patterns of rhythm and rhyme, but not even the most sophisticated NT writers (e.g., the author of Hebrews) offer any clear parallels to this Homeric style. Perhaps, most important of all, the NT never clearly and directly quotes Homer. (A few recent scholars have suggested that some of the New Testament writers imitated Homer's narrative structures; see below.)

In spite of the NT's lack of overt and obvious reliance on the Homeric tradition, a sustained engagement with the Homeric tradition provides valuable background for understanding the cultural terrain of the NT world. Let me briefly explain how an understanding of two of the key cultural ideals presumed and promoted within Homer's epics can help inform one's appreciation for the work of the NT writers. These two ideals are the forces that guide human affairs in Homer and the NT and the presumed and proper order for society and households in Homer and the NT.

First, in the *Iliad* and the *Odyssey*, human affairs are guided and controlled by fate, the interaction of competing gods, the love of honor, and the quest for (male) glory. On the human level, the central characters are all motivated by the desire for glory and honor. A few brief examples: in the *Iliad*, Achilles goes to battle against Troy in order to attain eternal glory for his name. He does so even though he knows beforehand that this glory will come at the cost of his own life (Achilles prefers a short life followed by eternal glory rather than a long life followed by eternal obscurity). Also in the *Iliad*, Priam, the honorable king of Troy, risks his own life to retrieve—and properly honor—the dishonored body of his defeated son Hector. In keeping with this emphasis on honor, Hector refuses to flee Troy even when he has learned both that the battle against the Greeks was fated to failure and that he would die in the course of the ill-fated battle. Similarly, in the *Odyssey*, Odysseus's decadal journey is completed only when he returns to his home and regains his personal honor by defeating the young usurpers who would take over his property, marriage bed, and family honor.

Even though Homer's major characters are consistently motivated by the desire to possess personal honor and to acquire glory in the eyes of their peers and of subsequent generations, their lives are not solely—or even primarily—controlled by these desires. Instead, in the Homeric tradition, human lives are ultimately controlled by fate and by the will of competing gods. Throughout the *Iliad*'s days and weeks of battle around the walls of Troy, the true fate of the battle lies outside human control. The battle's outcome is determined more by the attention or inattention of Zeus and by the competition between Poseidon and Apollo than by the feats and struggles of the human participants. Seventeen different gods, with at least seventeen different goals, directly intervene in the battles in the *Iliad*! Both of the two most distinguished combatants, Hector and Achilles, are fated to die in this epic battle. Their fates lie in the hands of the gods and beyond their personal control. Neither can avoid his fate without dishonor—and the central characters in Homer's *Iliad* and *Odyssey* always make honorable decisions. They are, above all else, honorable men.

Of course, these cultural ideals of honor, glory, fate, and competing deities were appropriated in diverse ways by those who read Homer. Nonetheless, some form of these ideals was widely presumed by the inhabitants of the Greco-Roman world. The NT writers were aware of these cultural ideals and broke with them at nearly every point. For example, John's Gospel repeatedly denounces any attempt to seek glory for one's own name and person (John 5:41–44; 7:18; 8:50–54). The parables and teachings of Jesus chasten those who seek their own honor (Matt. 6:2; 23:6; Mark 12:39; Luke 14:7–10; 20:46). The apostle Paul even sarcastically glories in his own dishonor and weakness (1 Cor. 4:10; 2 Cor. 11:30). The NT writers praise the Christ who suffered the most dishonorable of all deaths, death on a cross (Phil. 2:8; Acts 2:23; 5:30; 10:39; 1 Cor. 1:17–18), and they seek to imitate Christ's example of self-humiliation and cross bearing (Matt. 10:38; 16:24; Mark 8:34; Luke 14:27). The central Christian message of the cross and the crucified

Messiah was completely antithetical to Homeric celebration of personal glory and honor. In the face of the culturally formative traditions embedded in the pervasive Homeric epics, Paul could only make a radically countercultural plea: "May I never boast except in the cross of our Lord Jesus Christ" (Gal. 6:14).

The NT writers were equally dismissive of the Homeric tradition of polytheistic fatalism. The NT writers, of course, stood within the Jewish tradition of monotheism in their rejection of polytheism. In keeping with the Jewish roots of Christianity, the apostle Paul regards polytheism as a catalyst to evil of all manner (Rom. 1:18–32), and the book of Acts attributes polytheism to human ignorance (Acts 17:30).

Second, as a complementary pair, the *Iliad* and the *Odyssey* each presume a clearly defined order for society and family. In the *Iliad*, men distinguish their place in society through battles that they perceive either to advance the interests of their homeland (the Greeks) or to defend the safety of their homeland (the Trojans). From either perspective, the well-ordered society is characterized by men who gain glory for themselves and their homeland by protecting their personal and corporate honor against any perceived threat. (Remember that the Greeks decided to wage their war of aggression against the Trojans because of the insult inflicted on their honor by Helen's stealthy departure from Agamemnon's marriage bed.) The central societal norm in the *Iliad* is an ethos of the violent suppression of any perceived threat to the honor of one's person or homeland. The *Odyssey*'s central theme is homecoming, the warrior Odysseus's return to his home and his faithful wife, Penelope. This homecoming story presumes a clearly established ideal of what proper family life looks like—the norms of the Greek world's paterfamilias, a code of male authority and honor and of female submission and fidelity. Both Odysseus and Penelope embody this ethic. Penelope remains faithful to her departed husband year after year in spite of his extended absence and likely death. On his eventual return, however, Odysseus restores himself to a place of honor by slaying the coterie of young men who have impinged on his honor by pursuing his wife's affections. Helen, the most prominent female in the *Iliad*, stands as a counterexample of this pattern. Her infidelity to Agamemnon brings a disastrous fate on her former husband, on her lover, on his family, and on the entire city of Troy. The same disdain for uncontrolled female sexuality is displayed in the *Odyssey* as the muses seek to seduce and destroy any man who sails within the sound of their seductive voices. Female sexuality in Homer is dangerous unless kept faithfully subordinated to a man's control.

Although the NT consistently endorses an ethic of marital fidelity (Matt. 5:27–32; 1 Thess. 4:1–11), and sometimes appears to endorse an ethic of female subordination (Eph. 5:22; Titus 2:1–8), the NT breaks with the prevailing Homeric tradition by imposing demands for sexual fidelity on men and women equally. The NT shares none of Homer's presumption that female sexuality is more dangerous or destructive than male sexuality. In fact, the NT even commands husbands to fulfill their wives' sexual needs and places the husband's body under his wife's

31.1. Lion Gate at Mycenae. This gate is the most famous landmark of the ancient site of Mycenae, home of the Agamemnon of Homer's *Iliad*. The gate is on the northwest corner of the Cyclopean wall of the citadel and depicts two heraldic lions, each of which is three meters tall.

authority (1 Cor. 7:3–4). The NT sometimes even dismisses the significance attached to gender (Gal. 3:28). The leadership roles played by women like the deacon Phoebe (Rom. 16:1–2), the apostle Junia (Rom. 16:7), the preacher and doctrinal corrector Priscilla (Acts 18:1–26; Rom. 16:3; 1 Cor. 16:19; 2 Tim. 4:19), and the congregational leader Chloe (1 Cor. 1:11) are unparalleled in Homer. Just as important, the NT decisively breaks with the Homeric tradition regarding the violence that men are expected to employ as the appropriate instrument for establishing, protecting, and restoring their personal honor. The NT writers almost unanimously reject violence (Matt. 5:39; 26:52; Luke 6:29; Rom. 12:19; Rev. 13:10).

Dennis MacDonald and *Mimēsis* Criticism

Recently the NT scholar Dennis MacDonald, many of his students, and some sympathetic readers of his work have argued that Mark, the oldest Christian Gospel, and many other narratives within the NT were modeled on Homer's *Iliad* and *Odyssey*. Early in his career, MacDonald became convinced that the *Acts of Andrew* and several other postbiblical Christian texts deliberately imitated Homer's epics and engaged in what MacDonald came to call *mythomachia* and transvaluation. By *mythomachia*, MacDonald meant that these Christian authors deliberatively imitated the Homeric myths—a skill they had mastered during the course of their Greek education—and sought to replace Homeric fictions with competing Christian fictions. By *transvaluation*, MacDonald meant that these Christian authors were intentionally replacing Homeric values with their own Christian values.

Before long, MacDonald extended his thesis and argued that Mark used Homer's *Odyssey* as a model for the first fourteen chapters of his Gospel and the *Iliad* (esp. the story of Hector's death and his father's ransom of his corpse) as a model for the last two chapters. Eventually MacDonald extended his research into Acts and came to insist that much of Mark's Gospel and large portions of Acts were exercises in *mythomachia*, that is, Christian fiction writing for the sake of establishing a new and alternative fiction for Christians to orient their social, political, and religious lives around (that is, transvaluation). Although NT scholars universally recognize that educational practices in the ancient world included imitation (*mimēsis*) of Homer, few scholars have been convinced by MacDonald's arguments. The two central criticisms of his work are that (1) no ancient reader—neither Christian nor pagan—noticed the subtle Christian *mimēsis* in the NT that MacDonald found nearly two millennia later; and (2) neither Acts nor Mark ever quotes or even mentions Homer. If Mark and Acts were imitating anything, MacDonald's critics maintain, they were probably imitating the LXX, which they repeatedly cited.

Conclusion

An acquaintance with Homer's epics provides important insights into the cultural presuppositions of the Greco-Roman world regarding the forces that guide and control human actions and regarding the properly ordered society and home. Although a few scholars would disagree, I argue that the NT never directly interacts with Homer. Still, knowledge of Homer's epics can inform one's appreciation for the accomplishment of the NT writers.

Bibliography

Andersen, Øivind, and Vernon K. Robbins. "Paradigms in Homer, Pindar, the Tragedians, and the New Testament." *Semeia* 64 (1993): 3–31. A brief overview of rhetorical features that overlap between ancient Greek poetry and the NT.

MacDonald, Dennis R. *Does the New Testament Imitate Homer? Four Cases from the Acts of the Apostles*. New Haven: Yale University Press, 2003. A careful treatment of selected texts in Acts that may reflect awareness of or use of Homeric writings.

———. *The Homeric Epics and the Gospel of Mark*. New Haven: Yale University Press, 2000. MacDonald's work argues, with limited success, for the NT's dependence on Homer for narrative plot lines.

Mitchell, Margaret M. "Homer in the New Testament." *JR* 83, no. 2 (2003): 244–60. This classic work explores the manner in which the NT engages common motifs from Homer's epics.

Sandnes, Karl Olav. *Challenge of Homer: School, Pagan Poets and Early Christianity.* LNTS 400. New York: T&T Clark, 2009. The author shows the widespread familiarity of Homer in the ancient world and its near universal influence, not only in the Greco-Roman world at large but also in early Hellensitic Christianity.

———. *The Gospel "according to Homer and Virgil": Cento and Canon.* NovTSup 138. Boston: Brill, 2011. Sandnes examines both the similarities and dissimilarities between Homer's epics and the NT, offering a strong criticism of MacDonald's theses.

Stanley, Christopher D. "Paul and Homer: Greco-Roman Citation Practice in the First Century CE." *NovT* 32, no. 1 (1990): 48–78. This classic article offers a model for discerning literary dependence and allusions between the NT and other ancient texts.

32

Josephus and the New Testament

MICHAEL F. BIRD

Who Was Josephus?

Flavius Titus Josephus was appointed as the Judean general charged with the defense of Galilee during the First Jewish Revolt against Rome (AD 66–70). He subsequently was captured, changed sides in the conflict, and later wrote significant historical, autobiographical, and apologetic works under imperial patronage in Rome. His significance lies in the fact that he is arguably the single most important witness to the history and religion of the Jewish people in the Greco-Roman world of the first century. The works for which he is known are *Jewish War* (*Bellum judaicum*), *Antiquities of the Jews* (*Antiquitates judaicae*), *Life of Josephus* (*Vita*), and *Against Apion* (*Contra Apionem*).

Josephus was born Yoseph ben Mattiyahu in Jerusalem to a wealthy priestly family in AD 37. His elevated social status is implied by his Greek education, his dispatch to Rome on a diplomatic mission at age twenty-six, his landholdings in Jerusalem, and his appointment as regional commander of Galilee during the war against Rome. In his teenage years Josephus allegedly tried all three major Jewish sects (Essenes, Sadducees, Pharisees) and for a time followed a Judean ascetic named Bannus, who lived in the wilderness. Josephus then purportedly returned to Jerusalem and joined the Pharisees. He was selected by a revolutionary council to prepare Galilee for the Roman invasion, during which time he was opposed by John of Gischala. He eventually surrendered to Vespasian's forces at Jotapata (Josephus, *J.W* 3.340–92). Josephus was kept alive only because he prophesied Vespasian's accession to the Roman throne (*J.W* 3.400–408). For two years (ca. AD 68–69) he was kept in Roman custody, but he won favor by acting as a translator, adviser, and negotiator in the siege of Jerusalem. For his cooperation, Josephus was rewarded with Roman citizenship and patronage in the Flavian house, which had acceded to power, with Vespasian, Titus, and Domitian each taking the throne in turn.

While living in Rome, Josephus published *Jewish War*—initially in Aramaic (ca. AD 73), later in Greek (ca. AD 75–81). Its principal purposes were, first, to be an apology for the Romans to the Jews that God had in effect gone over to the side of the Romans because of Judean impiety and, second, to defend Judean character from vitriolic criticism following the disaster of AD 70. Later, around AD 93–94, Josephus composed *Jewish Antiquities*, with his *Life* attached as an appendix. The *Antiquities* fits the genre of "rewritten Bible"; that is, it summarizes and redacts sacred accounts of Israel's history, combined with extensive information about the events leading up to the Jewish war. The *Life* was written to exonerate Josephus from charges of falsehood raised by Justus of Tiberias concerning Josephus's account of the Jewish war and to extol Josephus's character and credentials. Soon afterward, Josephus composed *Against Apion*, a defense of Judaism and the Jewish people against objections posed by the Alexandrian scholar and politician Apion. Josephus probably died sometime around AD 100.

The relevance of Josephus's writings for understanding the NT is manifold. First, he provides a great deal of background information about Judaism and Jewish history. Indeed, we may regret that he never got around to writing his work *Customs and Reasons* about the Jewish people (Josephus, *Ant.* 4.198; 20.268). Second, he writes about events, institutions, groups, customs, places, and people known in the NT, such as Pilate, Herod Agrippa, the census of Quirinius, the Jerusalem temple, and more. Third, independent of the NT accounts, he provides attestation to the careers of John the Baptist, Jesus, and James the brother of Jesus.

Josephus on the Jewish Background to Christianity

The significance of Josephus as a background source and contemporary of the first Christians can be demonstrated with several examples.

First, Josephus provides information about the Pharisees, Sadducees, and Essenes, which he describes as the "three forms of philosophy" (*J.W.* 2.119; *Ant.* 13.171; 18.11; *Life* 10). Josephus's account is somewhat jaundiced. He is favorably disposed to the Pharisees (and even claims to be one), probably because they were the Jewish sect that emerged as leaders of the Palestinian Jews after the destruction of Jerusalem. So Josephus disparages the Sadducees as "barbarous" and presents the Pharisees as "friendly" (*J.W.* 2.166). Josephus also describes the sects in largely Hellenistic terms, likening them to a "philosophy," with the Essenes believing in the immortality of the soul and Pharisees in reincarnation (*J.W.* 2.154–57, 163). Nonetheless, Josephus remains our best source outside the NT for information about these Jewish sects, including their practices, politics, and beliefs.

Second, Josephus refers to the body of "traditions" that the Pharisees preserved and transmitted to others (*Ant.* 13.297–98, 408; 18.15). Evidence for a Pharisaic oral tradition of halakah (i.e., legal interpretation) is attested in the Gospels (Matt. 15:2–6; Mark 7:3–13) and Paul's Letters (Gal. 1:14). The traditions of the elders may not have been a technical "oral Torah" distinct from the "written Torah" (see *m. 'Abot* 1.1), but Josephus and the NT confirm the existence of such a body of Pharisaic traditions before the codification of the Mishnah (ca. AD 200).

Third, Josephus is also an excellent source of information about banditry, royal pretenders, prophetic movements, and revolutionary leaders in Judea. He writes about how Judea was filled with "imposters and demagogues, [who] under the guise of divine inspiration, provoked revolutionary actions and compelled the masses to act like madmen. They led them out into the wilderness in order that there God would reveal to them signs of imminent liberation" (*J.W.* 2.259 LCL [amended]; cf. *Ant.* 20.160). This is an important factor for considering popular and Roman responses to Jesus' messianism.

Fourth, Josephus shows that the dilemma of whether converts to Judaism should be circumcised was not limited to the early Christian movement (e.g., Galatians; Acts 15). Josephus recounts how King Izates and Queen Mother Helena of Adiabene (modern-day Armenia) converted to Judaism (*Ant.* 20.17–96). Yet Izates received conflicting advice as to whether he should be circumcised. A Jewish merchant named Ananias told him that he could worship God without circumcision, whereas a Pharisee named Eleazar chastised him for spurning the commandment to be circumcised (*Ant.* 20.41, 44–45).

Fifth, Josephus's works have a particular parity with Luke-Acts. The prologues to Luke (1:1–4) and Acts (1:1–2) parallel the prologues to both books of *Against Apion* (1.1–5; 2.1–3), and both have patrons in, respectively, "Theophilus" and "Epaphroditus." Luke and Josephus refer to similar people, places, and events, including the watershed census under Quirinius and political leaders like Pontius Pilate and Herod Antipas, as well as such revolutionary leaders as Judas the Galilean, Theudas, and the Egyptian. Both also have written broadly historical works with the purpose of defending a group against calumnious accusations and to demonstrate the inherent virtue of the group's way of life. Josephus writes about Jews and Romans from the top down in his position as a Flavian client representing Judean interests; Luke writes about Christians and Romans from the bottom up as a gentile Christian in a group regarded as a foreign sect by Roman elites.

Josephus on John the Baptist

In the canonical Gospels, John the Baptist is regarded as the forerunner of Jesus. According to the synoptic evangelists (Mark 6:17–28; Matt. 14:3–11; Luke 3:19–20) the reason for the Baptist's arrest and execution was that he criticized Herod Antipas for marrying Herodias, his brother Philip's wife, contrary to Levitical law (Lev. 18:16; 20:21). Josephus mentions John the Baptist in a parenthetical remark in *Ant.* 18 concerning the defeat of Herod Antipas's army by the Nabatean King Aretas IV. There Josephus recounts:

> But to some of the Jews the destruction of Herod's army seemed to be divine vengeance, and certainly a just vengeance, for his treatment of John, surnamed the Baptist. For Herod had put him to death, though he was a good man and had exhorted the Jews to lead righteous lives, to practice justice toward their fellows and piety toward God, and so doing to join in baptism. In his view this was a necessary preliminary if baptism was to be acceptable to God. They must not employ it to gain pardon for whatever sins they had committed, but as a consecration of the body implying that the soul was already cleansed by right behavior. When others too joined the crowds about him, because they were aroused to the highest degree by his sermons, Herod became alarmed. Eloquence that had so great an effect on mankind might lead to some form of sedition, for it looked as if they would be guided by John in everything that they did. Herod decided therefore that it would be much better to strike first and be rid of him before his work led to an uprising, than to wait for an upheaval, get involved in a difficult situation and see his mistake. Though John, because of Herod's suspicions, was brought in chains to Machaerus, the stronghold that we have previously mentioned, and there put to death, yet the verdict of the Jews was that the destruction visited upon Herod's army was a vindication of John, since God saw fit to inflict such a blow on Herod. (*Ant.* 18.116–19 LCL)

From Josephus we can deduce the following: (1) John was regarded as a Judean holy man, popular with the masses, who attracted large crowds; (2) he was known for and named after his activity as a "baptizer" (*baptistēs*); (3) John exhorted his audience to return to appropriate covenantal behavior, marked by righteous conduct, justice, and reverence for God; (4) a commitment to a righteous life was a prerequisite for baptism and not a license for lawlessness, implying that baptism was for the remission of sins; (5) Josephus links baptism to purification, though he adds a gloss couching this activity in Hellenistic philosophical terms by regarding it as a symbol of the soul that has been cleansed by noble conduct; (6) Herod Antipas imprisoned John because he feared the influence of John over the masses, who might be led to revolt; and (7) it was a commonly held view that the defeat of Antipas's army by King Aretas of Arabia was a sign of God's anger with Antipas for executing John the Baptist.[1]

1. Michael F. Bird, "John the Baptist," in *Jesus among Friends and Enemies* (ed. C. Keith and L. Hurtado; Grand Rapids: Baker Academic, 2011), 63.

Josephus on Jesus

The most famous passage from Josephus is the *Testimonium Flavianum*, which contains the first of two mentions of Jesus in *Antiquities of the Jews*. The received form of the text reads:

> About this time there lived Jesus, a wise man, *if indeed one ought to call him a man.* For he was one who performed surprising deeds and was a teacher of such people as accept the truth gladly. He won over many Jews and many of the Greeks. *He was the Messiah.* And when, upon the accusation of the principal men among us, Pilate had condemned him to a cross, those who had first come to love him did not cease. *He appeared to them spending a third day restored to life, for the prophets of God had foretold these things and a thousand other marvels about him.* And the tribe of the Christians, so called after him, has still to this day not disappeared. (*Ant.* 18.63–64 LCL, italics added)

The authenticity of the passage is disputed because it sounds far too positively disposed toward Jesus to have been penned by someone who was not a follower of Christ. (See the italicized portions of the quotation, above.) Origen, writing in the third century, states that Josephus "did not believe in Jesus as the Messiah" (*Comm. Matt.* 1.15; *Cels.* 1.47), perhaps indicating that no "Jesus passage" was in the version of Josephus available to Origen. Others argue that the *Testimonium* interrupts the context that deals with upheavals and the folly of Roman governors, while no such upheaval occurs here. We could say regarding context, however, that Josephus is prone to rather obtrusive digressions in his works. In any case, the *Testimonium* is not really a digression, since it continues to recount the events occurring under Pilate's procuratorship. Origen's remark about Jesus only indicates that Josephus did not believe in Jesus as the Messiah, not that Josephus did not mention Jesus at all. Finally, the glowing account of Jesus is explainable by the fact that the text has been touched up by a Christian scribe (i.e., the italicized portions above).[2]

In summary, the evidence favors the authenticity of the *Testimonium*, though not in its present form. (1) The language in the *Testimonium* is consistent with

---

2. For example, on the phrase "He was the Messiah," Alice Whealey ("The Testimonium Flavianum in Syriac and Arabic," *NTS* 54 [2008]: 573–90) draws attention to the *Testimonia* preserved by Michael the Syrian (twelfth century) and Jerome (fourth century), which independently attest to the reading "he was thought to be the Messiah." This corresponds to Origen's claim that Josephus did not believe in Jesus as the Messiah. A variant is also found in the Arabic chronicles of Agapius of Hierapolis (tenth century): "he was perhaps the Messiah." In light of this, there probably was a reference to Jesus as Messiah in the *Testimonium* but probably in a way that held that the messianic status of Jesus was dubious. Christian scribes who transmitted the text of Josephus removed this dubiety from the *Testimonium* and instead inserted "He was the Messiah." Alternatively, Jerome's version may be an assimilation from *Ant.* 20.200. Overall, I think there was a reference to the Messiah in *Ant.* 20.200 and probably in *Ant.* 18.63, but it was expanded (rather than interpolated) by a Christian scribe.

Josephus's style elsewhere.[3] (2) There is no emphasis on the role of the Judean leadership in Jesus' death. (3) The brief mention of Jesus again in *Ant*. 20.200 presupposes the mention of Jesus in *Ant*. 18.63–64. If a Christian scribe interpolated the Jesus passages in Josephus, it is likely that he would have put them into one location rather than spread them over books 18 and 20. (4) Arabic and Syriac versions of the *Testimonium* differ slightly from the received Greek textual form and either omit or alter the seemingly positive descriptions of Jesus.[4]

Stripped of the obviously Christian glosses and embellishments, the original form of the text probably was something like this:

> At this time there appeared Jesus, a wise man. For he was a doer of startling deeds, a teacher of people who receive the truth with pleasure. And he gained a following both among many Jews and among many of Greek origin. And when Pilate, because of an accusation made by the leading men among us, condemned him to the cross, those who had loved him previously did not cease to do so. And up until this very day the tribe of Christians (named after him) has not died out.[5]

Josephus on the Martyrdom of James

Josephus narrates how, during an interregnum between Roman governors in Judea, the high priest Ananus had a man "named James the brother of Jesus called the Messiah" and his companions summarily executed about AD 62.

> Festus was now dead, and Albinus was set upon the road. He [Ananus] convened the council of judges and brought before it the brother of Jesus—who was called "Christ"—whose name was James, and certain others. Accusing them of transgressing the law he delivered them up for stoning. But those of the city considered to be fair-minded and strict concerning the laws were offended at this and sent to the king secretly urging him to order Ananus to take such actions no longer. (*Ant*. 20.200 LCL)

James was venerated as a martyr in Christian tradition and was even called "James the Just" (see *Gos. Thom*. 12). The precise reason for James's death is not given in any of the sources, including Josephus. The charge of being "breakers of the law" is a form of sociological deviant labeling where the beliefs and praxis of someone are regarded as a threat to a shared identity and common way of life. Most likely, James was a victim of intra-Jewish sectarianism, where Christians

3. H. St. J. Thackeray, *Josephus, the Man and the Historian* (New York: Jewish Institute of Religion, 1929), 137; see, however, Ken Olson, "Eusebius and the *Testimonium Flavianum*," *CBQ* 61 (1999): 305–22.

4. For discussion, see John P. Meier, *A Marginal Jew* (4 vols.; ABRL; New York: Doubleday, 1991), 1:56–69; Alice Whealey, *Josephus on Jesus: The Testimonium Flavianum Controversy from Late Antiquity to Modern Times* (New York: Peter Lang, 2003).

5. Meier, *Marginal Jew*, 1:61.

in general and James in particular were regarded as a dangerous threat to the integrity of the Judean laws on account of their messianic faith and so warranted violent censure.

Conclusion

Josephus is the single most important source for understanding first-century Judaism. He provides crucial background information about the politics, sects, culture, laws, and religion of Judea. Josephus also provides independent historical attestation for many events recounted in the NT, not the least of which is the existence of the man Jesus of Nazareth in the *Testimonium Flavianum*.

Bibliography

Major translations of Josephus's works include Henry St. John Thackeray et al., trans. and eds., *Josephus* (9 vols.; LCL; Cambridge, MA: Harvard University Press, 1929–53); and Steve Mason, ed., *Brill Josephus Project*. The translation by William Whiston (*The Complete Works of Josephus* [1737; repr., Peabody, MA: Hendrickson, 1997]) is dated and unreliable.

Barclay, John M. G. *Jews in the Mediterranean Diaspora: From Alexander to Trajan (323 BCE–117 CE)*. Edinburgh: T&T Clark, 1996. Though not written exclusively on Josephus, this is a useful overview of Jews in the Mediterranean Diaspora that makes constant use of Josephus (and others, like Philo) for mapping the life, religion, politics, and society of Jews outside Palestine.

Böttrich, Christfried, et al., eds. *Josephus und das Neue Testament*. WUNT 1/209. Tübingen: Mohr Siebeck, 2006. A collection of essays that presents the current scholarly views of Josephus and NT studies; several essays are in English.

Mason, Steve, ed. *Brill Josephus Project*. 9 vols. Leiden: Brill, 2000–. The gold standard for Josephus studies. It includes new translations and commentary on Josephus's works. Not all the volumes are available yet, but the early ones on *Against Apion* and *Life of Josephus*, and the early chapters of *Judean Wars* and *Antiquities of the Judeans*, are well worth consulting.

———. *Josephus, Judea, and Christian Origins: Methods and Categories*. Peabody, MA: Hendrickson, 2009. A helpful collection of essays on the significance of Josephus for study of the NT and early Christianity. Although some of Mason's positions are debated, overall this is a good introduction to the importance of Josephus.

Meier, John P. "Jesus in Josephus: A Modest Proposal." *CBQ* 52 (1990): 76–103. A sober and lucid approach to the *Testimonium Flavianum* and a slightly more expanded account than found in Meier, *A Marginal Jew* (4 vols.; ABRL; New York: Doubleday, 1991), 1:56–88.

33

Philo and the New Testament

TORREY SELAND

Life and Accomplishments

Philo of Alexandria (ca. 20 BC–AD 50) was a Jewish scholar, philosopher, author, and politician who lived in Alexandria all his life and who has had significant influence through his many books. He wrote about seventy treatises, of which about fifty are still extant in whole or in part. His works are of tremendous value for students of the Judaism of his time, of the NT, and of the early churches in the Diaspora.

Until the seventeenth century, many scholars believed that Philo had had some relation to Christianity; some thought he referred to early Egyptian Christian groups in his writings, or that he had met Christians during a stay in Rome. Some ancient sources even consider him to have been a Christian. As far as we know, however, Philo never met any Christians, nor does he tell anything about any Christians, nor did any of the NT writers know him. Nevertheless, it is remarkable that during the many centuries after his death, Jews did not preserve his works, but Christians did, and they came to cherish them and to adopt many of the ideas inherent in his works. Today we can see that his literary remains contain evidence of various relevant traditions about Jewish life and theology and various ways of interpreting the Jewish Scriptures, as well as information about the life of the Jews as a minority group in the Greco-Roman world of the first century AD.

Philo's Works

Most of Philo's writings are expositions of the five books of Moses, the Pentateuch. These expositions are grouped in two main parts: the exposition of the law and his exegetical commentaries. The first group comprises ten volumes that are still preserved: *On the Creation of the World*; *On the Life of Abraham*; *On the Life of Joseph*; *On the Decalogue*; *On the Special Laws 1–4*; *On the Virtues*; *On Rewards and Punishments*; and probably *On the Life of Moses 1–2*.

The exegetical commentaries are of two kinds: two volumes on *Questions and Answers on Genesis and Exodus* and the allegorical commentaries, consisting of twenty-one books dealing with Gen. 2–41: *Allegorical Interpretation 1–3*; *On the Cherubim*; *On the Sacrifices of Abel and Cain*; *That the Worse Attacks the Better*; *On the Posterity and Exile of Cain*; *On the Giants*; *On the Unchangeableness of God*; *On Agriculture*; *On Noah's Work as a Planter*; *On Drunkenness*; *On Sobriety*; *On the Confusion of Tongues*; *On the Migration of Abraham*; *Who Is the Heir of Divine Things*; *On the Preliminary Studies*; *On Flight and Finding*; *On the Change of Names*; and *On Dreams 1–2*.

In addition, Philo wrote some philosophical works (*That Every Good Person Is Free*; *On the Eternity of the World*; *On Providence 1–2*; and *On Animals*) and some historical and apologetic works (*Against Flaccus*; *On the Embassy to Gaius*; *On the Contemplative Life*; and the *Hypothetica*). (For more information on the various volumes, see Kamesar, *Philo*; and Schenk, *Philo*.)

Not much is known about Philo's private life. He most probably belonged to a rich and influential family in Alexandria. He had both a brother and a nephew who were involved in politics, the latter ending up as the prefect of Egypt (AD 66–70)—the highest Roman official in Egypt. Philo himself became engaged in some political duties, even serving as the leader of a delegation to the emperor in Rome in AD 38–40. The work of most interest to us in the present context is his exposition of the Holy Scriptures of the Jews, the Scriptures we call the OT. Philo himself does not explicitly reveal to us the social context of his writings, but Gregory Sterling has strongly argued that Philo "had a private school in his home or personally owned structure for advanced students which was similar to schools of higher education run by individuals throughout the Greco-Roman world" (Sterling, "School," 150). At the time of Philo, Alexandria was one of the three largest cities in the Roman Empire, probably containing a half million people. The city was famous for its great library—though Philo never mentions it—and as being a learning center for its region. Later it was to become a great Christian center, and Philo's works and thoughts had a great impact on the theology of the church fathers living there.

As a philosopher and expositor of the Scriptures, Philo was heavily influenced by Platonism but also by Stoicism and Pythagoreanism. His philosophy, especially his Platonism, is the ideological background of many of his interpretations of the

Scriptures, and he can hardly be understood without taking that conceptual and ideological background into consideration.

Philo and Social Life in the Diaspora

Due to his family context, Philo belonged to the elite segment of the Jewish communities, but he was also an embedded member of the Jewish community in Alexandria. The Jewish community at that time was large. Philo says that they lived primarily in two of the five sections of the city (*Flacc.* 55). They probably had their own institutions of a social, judicial, and religious nature; these were often housed in one and the same building (i.e., the synagogue), and the Jewish Torah was the fundamental and comprehensive law. The Jews were nevertheless living in a minority situation, competing with other minority groups in the same city, all subject to and ruled by the Roman authorities.

According to the Acts of the Apostles, the apostle Paul took the Jewish synagogues as his point of departure for his evangelistic work in the various cities, starting with his fellow Jews (see Acts 13:5, 14; 14:1; 17:1–2; 18:4; etc.). It took ten Jewish men to establish a synagogue; hence, there were synagogues in most major cities. However, as the Christians were soon separated from local Jewish synagogal communities, they had to establish their own social settings and congregations. And thus they were a minority group, subject to conditions comparable to those of the Jews. Reading Philo can help us to see the social processes at work and thus to understand the social conditions of such minority groups in the Roman world.

Let us focus on one important issue. One particular aspect singled the Christians out from the Jews: they were a missionary movement, trying to recruit others as members of their Jesus Messiah–believing congregations. It has been hotly debated whether the Jews were engaged in missionary activities to gain proselytes; probably they were not, but they welcomed those who wanted to be accepted as proselytes. Michael Bird summarizes the present research situation: "Although proselytes to Judaism were made in significant numbers, there is no evidence for concerted, organized, or regular efforts to recruit Gentiles to Judaism via the process of proselytizing. Conversion to Judaism was a difficult affair, and was usually done at the initiative of the Gentile" (Bird, *Crossing*, 13). Philo can illuminate some of the social costs of becoming a Jewish proselyte, or per analogy, of becoming a Christian. He describes, for example, the disruptive functions such conversions might have and the converts' need for being included in their new settings: The proselyte is a person who has "turned his kinsfolk . . . into mortal enemies, by coming as a pilgrim to truth and the honouring of the One who alone is worthy of honour" (*Spec.* 4.178); they have "joined the new and godly commonwealth . . . ; they have left their country, their kinsfolk and their friends for the sake of virtue and religion. Let them not be denied another citizenship or other ties of family and friendship, and let them find places of shelter ready for refugees to the camp of piety" (*Spec.* 1.51–52; see also *Virt.* 102, 181, 219–22).[1] We have similar sayings in Paul: "You turned to God from idols, to serve a living and true God" (1 Thess. 1:9); and exhortations in several of his letters prove the various problems Christians might have in family relations (see 1 Thess. 2:13–17; Eph. 4:17–6:9). Moreover, the author of 1 Peter admonishes his readers to take care not to invite harassment in their neighborhoods, but "always be ready to make your defense to anyone who demands from you an accounting for the hope that is in you" (3:15; cf. 2:11–17; 4:1–4). They are to consider themselves as "aliens and exiles" (2:11). Philo has also several statements about apostasy (*Spec.* 1.54–56, 313–18); these too illustrate possible problems created by conversions. Thus, in reading Philo, we can illuminate the social context and even some of the experiences of the early Christians from a contemporary source.

Philo and the Study of the New Testament

An important starting point for evaluating the significance of Philo for understanding the NT is the fact that both are representing and presenting expositions of the so-called OT. Philo, on his part, probably did not know much Hebrew. His "Bible" consisted of the Greek translations of the Hebrew Scriptures, what later came to be called the Septuagint (LXX). Philo, in fact, provides us with his version of how the Greek translation came into being (see *Mos.* 2.25–44; cf. *Letter of Aristeas*). The "Bible" of the Christians who wrote the NT books was also the LXX. Although some of these authors probably did know Hebrew, they all wrote in Greek, and their quotations from the Scriptures reveal a deep knowledge of the Greek translations in vogue at that time. Sometimes their quotations conform to the Hebrew text, sometimes to the LXX, and sometimes they may come from versions no longer available to us.

The Acts of the Apostles provides two important cases of possible influence from Alexandria. In Acts 6:9 we read that people from Alexandria were among the persons from the synagogue of the Freedmen opposing Stephen, and in 18:24 we find that Apollos, the young man whom Priscilla and Aquila met in Ephesus, was born in Alexandria. Some scholars consider the influence of this Apollos, as reflected in 1 Corinthians, as due partly to his ideological background in Alexandria. Hence, it is at least possible that some early Christians would have met people who had heard Philo, or might have been influenced by him in other ways.

Philo knew about various interpreters and various ways of interpreting the Scriptures. It is clear that he had predecessors, and he points to contemporary exegetes with whom he both agrees and disagrees. It is particularly interesting that he points to expositors who interpret the Scriptures in a more literal way,

---

1. All quotations from Philo in this chapter are taken from the LCL translation.

nowadays often labeled the "literal-
ists," and to some who allegorize, the
"allegorists." Philo himself uses both
methods according to his audiences
or topics, or both, and he criticizes
those who reject the one in preference
for the other.

In addition to the scriptural texts,
Philo also knows traditions that were
carried on from "the fathers," and he
utilizes both in his own works. For
example: "For I will . . . tell the story
of Moses as I have learned it, both
from the sacred books, the wonder-
ful monuments of his wisdom he has
left behind him, and from some of
the leaders of the nation; for I always
interwove what I was told with what I
read, and thus believed myself to have
a closer knowledge than others of his
life's history" (*Mos.* 1.4). Thus Philo
knows many Jewish interpreters and

> ## Philo on the "Literalists" and the "Allegorists"
>
> "There are some who, regarding the laws in their literal sense in the light of symbols of matters belonging to the intellect, are overpunctilious about the latter, while treating the former with easy-going neglect. . . . They ought to have given careful attention to both aims. . . . Why, we shall be ignoring the sanctity of the Temple and a thousand other things, if we are going to pay heed to nothing except what is shewn us by the inner meaning of things. Nay, we should look on all these outward observances as resembling the body, and their inner meaning as resembling the soul. It follows that exactly as we have to take thought for the body, because it is the abode of the soul, so we must pay heed to the letter of the laws." (*Migr.* 89–93)

traditions, but most regrettable for us, he never names any such persons or provides further characterizations of his traditions. Yet, in his love for the Scriptures
as well of oral and written traditions, he sides with his contemporary Jews and
with the early Christians.

In the NT we find that when Paul describes his pre-Christian past, he characterizes himself as one who "advanced in Judaism beyond many among my people
of the same age, for I was far more zealous for *the traditions of my ancestors*"
(Gal. 1:14); later, as a Christian, he emphasizes the role of tradition-awareness
among early Christians (1 Cor. 11:23; 15:1–3). In a society where only two out
of ten could read and write, the role of oral tradition was pivotal. And the NT
confirms the importance of promoting the oral traditions about Jesus and his
gospel. Furthermore, we see various interpretations in use. For example, Paul
had to deal with other interpreters and preachers of the gospel; among the more
obvious are those to whom he refers as other interpreters from Jerusalem (Gal.
2:11–15; cf. Acts 15; 21:21–25), but several of his other letters reflect additional
theological debates and interpretations with which he had to cope (cf. Gal. 3–4;
Rom. 4; Col. 2:16–23; Titus 3:9).

The NT authors do not, however, share the delight of Philo in allegorical
interpretations, and the most prominent NT hermeneutical procedure, involving
typological interpretation, is not found in Philo. In fact, there is only one clearly
allegorical interpretation comparable to those of Philo in the NT. That is the

Paul's Allegory in Galatians 4:21–31

"Tell me, you who desire to be subject to the law, will you not listen to the law? For it is written that Abraham had two sons, one by a slave woman and the other by a free woman. One, the child of the slave, was born according to the flesh; the other, the child of the free woman, was born through the promise. Now this is an allegory: these women are two covenants. One woman, in fact, is Hagar, from Mount Sinai, bearing children for slavery. Now Hagar is Mount Sinai in Arabia and corresponds to the present Jerusalem, for she is in slavery with her children. But the other woman corresponds to the Jerusalem above; she is free, and she is our mother. For it is written,

'Rejoice, you childless one, you who bear no children,
    burst into song and shout, you who endure no birth pangs;
for the children of the desolate woman are more numerous
    than the children of the one who is married.'

Now you, my friends, are children of the promise, like Isaac. But just as at that time the child who was born according to the flesh persecuted the child who was born according to the Spirit, so it is now also. But what does the scripture say? 'Drive out the slave and her child; for the child of the slave will not share the inheritance with the child of the free woman.' So then, friends, we are children, not of the slave but of the free woman."

famous statement of Paul in Gal. 4:21–31. Another comparable saying of Paul is 1 Cor. 10:1–12, concerning the Israelites in the desert and the accompanying rock, which is interpreted as Christ. In this case, though, the role of the event was to provide examples, or "types," for coming generations. Hence this is hardly to be read as an allegory, but rather as a typology. In typology, the OT contains issues, characters, and events that function as models, or rather types, finding their fulfillment in the time of the new covenant. Hebrews abounds in such typologies; see also Rom. 5:12–21; 1 Pet. 3:20–21. This heuristic way of using issues, characters, and events from the OT is not found in the same manner in Philo. The reason for this absence in Philo is to be found in the Christian conception of fulfillment in the messianic times that have been inaugurated with the coming of Jesus, the Messiah.

Several studies have also demonstrated that exegetical debates reflected in Philo might be useful when trying to understand discussions and arguments present in the NT. When Paul, for instance, discusses the role of circumcision (Col. 2:8–13), comparable issues in Philo have proved illuminating (e.g., *Spec.* 1.1–11), and Paul's discussion of Deut. 30:12–14 in Rom. 10:4–17 should be read in light of Philo's *Virt.* 183–84 and *Praem.* 79–84. The use of the manna traditions in John 6 has also been illuminated by a comparison with Philo and rabbinic traditions.

For a long time Hebrews has been considered the letter most influenced by the works of Philo and his Platonism (see esp. Heb. 7–9). In the middle of the twentieth century several scholars suggested that the otherwise unknown author of this letter might even have been a former student of Philo who had converted to Christianity. Nowadays this view is held by only a few; most scholars suggest that we should rather reckon with a kind of influence from comparable traditions and interpretive milieus. But Hebrews is still most often considered to be the NT book closest to many views known from Alexandria.

Furthermore, the roles of the Word (the Logos) in the prologue of the Gospel of John have been investigated for a possible Philonic background. There is in fact a lot about the Logos in the works of Philo, a concept he uses more than fourteen hundred times. Several aspects are also comparable to issues inherent in John 1; we might mention only the role of the Logos as an intermediary between God and the world, as well as its presence at and participation in creation. But again, direct influence from Philo is not necessary. Such OT traditions as Jewish Wisdom theology might be a possible background for both John and Philo.

In a similar way we might consider various issues in the Letters of Paul. Several aspects of the problems of the communities in Corinth have been suggested as due to influences from Alexandrian ideologies, and the terminology of the hymn in Col. 1 has been studied against the background of Philo's works. The list could be considerably prolonged.

Summary

In the study of the NT, the works of Philo should surely be included when investigating exegetical techniques, specific concepts and ideas, their social and ideological background, and theological debates. However, some important precautions should also be taken into consideration.

1. It is improbable that there was any direct contact between Philo and any NT writers.
2. It is possible, however, that there might have been some contact between some persons mentioned in the NT and Philo, or students of Philo.
3. Furthermore, one must not forget that both the NT writers and Philo of Alexandria had the same Scriptures—what we call the OT—as their theological background.
4. Hence, as interpreters of the same Scriptures, they might have drawn on various common techniques, or they might both have been influenced by comparable theological traditions and interpretive milieus.
5. In some cases, it seems that the similarities between Philo and Paul, for example, relate more to what Paul was arguing against; that is, the similarity is less between Philo and Paul and more between Philo and those whom Paul sought to counter. Such cases nevertheless demonstrate the relevance of including Philo in one's reading.

6. When looking for similarities between the NT and Philo, one should not forget the differences that still remain. The Platonist Philo did not know Jesus of Nazareth, the Messiah. Hence, he did not share the developed Christology of the early Christians or the eschatology found in the NT.

Even with these caveats, Philo's works remain extremely important for students of the NT, of the Judaism of his time, and of the early churches of the Diaspora.

Bibliography

The most used translation and text edition of Philo's works is F. H. Colson et al. *Philo with an English Translation*. 10 vols. LCL. Cambridge, MA: Harvard University Press, 1929–62.

Bird, Michael F. *Crossing over Sea and Land: Jewish Missionary Activity in the Second Temple Period*. Peabody, MA: Hendrickson, 2010. The most recent study of the question of possible Jewish missionary activity in the first century AD.

Deines, Roland, and Karl-Wilhelm Niebuhr, eds. *Philo und das Neue Testament*. WUNT 172. Tübingen: Mohr Siebeck, 2004. A collection of scholarly articles on Philo and the NT, in English and German.

Kamesar, Adam, ed. *The Cambridge Companion to Philo*. Cambridge: Cambridge University Press, 2009. A collection of informative introductory articles concerning Philo and his life, works, thoughts, and influence.

Runia, David T. *Philo in Early Christian Literature: A Survey*. CRINT 3.3. Minneapolis: Fortress, 1993. A comprehensive presentation of the influence of Philo in the NT and in the church fathers.

Schenck, Kenneth. *A Brief Guide to Philo*. Louisville: Westminster John Knox, 2005. A general introduction to Philo, also containing an informative section on Philo and the NT.

Seland, Torrey. *Strangers in the Light: Philonic Perspectives on Christian Identity in 1 Peter*. BIS 76. Leiden: Brill, 2005. Five studies reading issues in 1 Peter in light of perspectives from Philo.

Sterling, Gregory E. "The School of Sacred Laws: The Social Setting of Philo's Treatises." *VC* 53 (1999): 148–64. An important study discussing the social setting of Philo's teaching.

34

Rabbinic Literature
and the New Testament

BRUCE CHILTON

Rabbinic literature arose with the emergence of Rabbinic Judaism as the dominant form of Israelite religion after the destruction of the temple in AD 70. Until that time, teachers belonging to the group that framed the oral traditions behind rabbinic literature vied with other groups—priests, apocalyptic teachers, philosophical writers, and separatists—over the definition of Israel's faith and practice. Some of those who are called Pharisees in the NT probably featured among those who developed the rabbinic movement, but they considered themselves as sages and used the common address of "rabbi," which reflected their status as teachers. This has caused them to be known as the rabbis in a preeminent sense, although many teachers—like Jesus of Nazareth—were called "rabbi" who were not Pharisees or exponents of the characteristic rabbinic theology.

Introduction to Rabbinic Writings

Rabbinic writings of the first six centuries AD, together with Scripture, constituted the Torah in the minds of the sages.[1] The Torah is written, yet also formulated

---

1. For further analysis, see Chilton et al., *Comparative Handbook*. The present description draws on that fuller work, with the encouragement of the principal editor concerned, Jacob Neusner.

and transmitted orally. The literature of the sages represents this oral tradition. By AD 200 the rabbis had developed a sophisticated understanding of the Torah as evolved through a tradition of oral law they said also went back to Moses on Sinai. Their authoritative interpretation enabled their form of Judaism to survive after the destruction of the temple, where worship had been an axiom in the HB, and to adjust to the often dislocating changes that came after AD 70. The rabbis taught the Torah on the understanding that they spoke and exemplified the Torah. Throughout, they frequently interacted with the Scripture, the Tanak (an acronym of Torah, Nebi'im, Ketubim—i.e., "Law," "Prophets," and "Writings"), although their activities were by no means limited to formal commentary.

Judah the Patriarch, appointed as the Jewish authority in Palestine by the Romans, brought together the *mišnāyôt* ("the repeated teachings" of the Tannaim [Hebrew *tannā'îm*, "repeaters"]) of key rabbis into the Mishnah, the first document of rabbinic literature. He organized these legal materials into sixty-three tractates, grouped within six major divisions: tithes on agricultural produce (*Zera'im*), feasts (*Mo'ed*), women and marriage (*Našim*), violations of the rights of others (*Neziqin*), sacrifice at the temple (*Qodašim*), and ritual purity (*Ṭoharot*). This written distillation of oral Torah included regulations concerning the temple, for which any practical hope of rebuilding perished with the collapse of the Bar Kokhba revolt in AD 135. But since so much of the Mosaic law dealt with the temple cultus, it had to be treated in any comprehensive discussion of the legal tradition. In effect, meditation on and discussion of the laws of sacrifice took the place of sacrifice itself.

This adjustment to the circumstances after AD 70 fed the growing rabbinic conviction that, whatever conditions on the ground might look like, the Torah of Moses remained eternal and inviolate in heaven. The principal concern of the Mishnah is halakah, or the way in which Israel should "walk" (*hālak*) in the matters covered. An additional tractate, *'Abot* ("the fathers," or founders), conveys additional sayings, and another, *'Abot de Rabbi Nathan* ("the fathers according to Rabbi Nathan"), contains narrative concerning those authorities.

The Tosefta is a compilation of supplementary sayings; the word *tôseptā'* in Aramaic means "addition." Organized around nearly the whole of the Mishnah as citation and gloss, secondary paraphrase, and freestanding complement, the entire Tosefta appears to have emerged around AD 300.

Instead of taking the route of supplementing the Mishnah, the two Talmuds (one called Palestinian, the other Babylonian) offer sustained and systematic commentaries on the Mishnah. Because the Talmuds focus on the Mishnah as their base text, the status of the Mishnah within the dual Torah (i.e., the biblical text and its oral counterpart as promulgated by the rabbis) is at every turn reinforced.

That Talmudic move represents the signal concern of Rabbinic Judaism with the oral Torah as embodied in the Mishnah, although it is frequently misunderstood. Readers often suppose that commentary on the written HB is the principal issue. Although Scripture features frequently in the Talmud, as throughout rabbinic literature as a whole, the Talmudic aim is the elucidation of the Mishnah, the oral Torah given on Sinai.

The Talmud of the land of Israel, usually known as the Palestinian Talmud, reached closure around AD 400 and offers commentary on most of the tractates of the Mishnah's first four divisions. The Babylonian Talmud, concluded around AD 600, provides a sustained exegesis of most of the tractates of the Mishnah's second through fifth divisions. The Palestinian Talmud consists of discussion of the first four themes of the Mishnah, and the Babylonian Talmud offers interpretations concerning feasts, women, rights violations, and sacrifices. These collections present detailed discussions of the same and related materials presented in the Mishnah, together with comparisons between the differing points of view and disparate perspectives. Although most of the Talmud was written in Aramaic, parts of it are in Hebrew, and some elements in both languages may claim great antiquity. Since the Mishnah and Talmud emerged centuries later than the NT, and since they picture a Judaism with structures and concepts for which there is no evidence in the first century, only a small segment of the material from the Mishnah and Talmud is appropriate as a basis for comparison between Jewish and early Christian interpretation of the law of Moses. By the Middle Ages the Babylonian Talmud had attained the status of the paradigmatic document of Rabbinic Judaism.

Although the two Talmuds are no more designed as commentaries on the written Torah than the Tosefta is, Scripture did attract sustained commentary in another genre of literature. This is midrash (pl. midrashim); the term "midrash" means the "searching out" (from the verb *dāraš*) of meaning. One prominent collection is called the Tannaitic midrashim, after the Tannaim who contributed to the Mishnah. In fact, however, these writings often come from a later period; the third and fourth centuries are the likely period of composition. They include two commentaries on Exodus—the *Mekilta de Rabbi Ishmael* and the *Mekilta*—one on Leviticus, *Sipra*; and one on Numbers and Deuteronomy, *Sipre*. These midrashim are also known as halakic because they deal with issues of practice, although they are not systematic in the way that the Mishnah is. But they are not as discursive as the *Midrash Rabbah*, the famous collection developed between the third and the seventh centuries that covers the Pentateuch and other Scriptures key to liturgy in synagogues: Ruth, Esther, Lamentations, and Song of Songs. Taken together, they provide a rich source of narrative, homily, commentary, and theological teaching. In view of that variety and the concern of the material for belief, appropriate attitude, and virtue, *Midrash Rabbah* is known as haggadic, or concerned with rabbinic lore (haggadah).

The relationship between written and oral Torah also proves key to understanding the genre of targum within rabbinic literature.[2] The term "targum" simply

---

2. The development of the targumim is dealt with more fully in Flesher and Chilton, *Targums*. The present discussion draws on that collaborative work with Professor Flesher's permission.

means "translation" in Aramaic, but the type and purpose of the renderings from Hebrew into Aramaic varied widely.

Aramaic survived the demise of the Persian Empire as a lingua franca in the Near East. It had been adopted by Jews (as by other peoples, such as Nabateans and Palmyrenes), and the Aramaic portions of the HB (in Ezra and Daniel) testify to a significant change in the linguistic constitution of Judaism by the second century BC. Abraham himself, of course, had been an Aramaean, although the variants of the Aramaic language during its history are dramatic. Conceivably, one reason for Jewish enthusiasm in embracing Aramaic was a distant memory of its affiliation with Hebrew, but it should always be borne in mind that Hebrew is quite a different language. By the first century AD, Aramaic appears to have been the common language of Judea, Samaria, and Galilee (although distinctive dialects were spoken); Hebrew was understood by an educated (and/or, perhaps, a nationalistic) stratum of the population, and some familiarity with Greek was a cultural necessity, especially in commercial and bureaucratic circles.

The linguistic situation in Judea and Galilee demanded that translation be effected for the purposes of popular study and worship. Although fragments of Leviticus and Job in Aramaic, which have been discovered at Qumran, are technically targumim (that is, "translations"), they are actually unrepresentative of the genre of targum in literary terms. They are reasonably "literal" renderings; some attempt at formal correspondence between the Hebrew rendered and the Aramaic is present. The other extant targumim, documents deliberately guarded within Rabbinic Judaism, are of quite a different character.

In that the aim of targumic production was to give the sense of the Hebrew Scriptures, paraphrase is characteristic of the rabbinic targumim. Theoretically, a passage of Scripture was to be rendered orally by an interpreter (*mĕtûrgĕmān*) after the reading in Hebrew; the *mĕtûrgĕmān* was not to be confused with the reader, lest the congregation mistake the interpretation for the original text (cf. *m. Meg.* 4.4–10; *b. Meg.* 23b–25b). (Regulations specifying the number of verses that may be read prior to the delivery of a targum probably date from well after the period of the NT.) Although the renderings so delivered were oral in principle, over the course of time, traditions in important centers of learning became fixed, and coalescence became possible. Moreover, the emergence of the rabbis as the dominant leaders within Judaism after AD 70 provided a centralizing tendency, without which literary targumim could never have been produced.

The targumim that were developed and handed on over centuries are paraphrases, but the theological programs conveyed in them are not always consistent, even within a given targum. Although the rabbis attempted to control targumic activity, the extant targumim themselves sometimes contradict rabbinic proscriptions. For example, *m. Meg.* 4.9 insists that Lev. 18:21 ("You must not give of your seed, to deliver it to Moloch") should not be interpreted with respect to sexual intercourse with gentiles; the *Targum Pseudo-Jonathan*—a late work, produced long after rabbinic authority had been established—takes just that line. The targumim evince such oddities because they are the products of a dialectical interaction between folk practice and rabbinic influence. That tension is sometimes mediated through a love of dramatic and inventive speculation, the interplay of conflicts over interpretations, and delight in the interpretive process, all enriched during the extensive period of transmission. Each of the extant targumim crystallizes that complex process at a given moment.

The targumim divide up among those of the Torah (the Pentateuch), those of the Prophets (both "Former Prophets," or the so-called historical works, and the "Latter Prophets," or the Prophets as commonly designated in English), and those of the Writings (or Hagiographa), following the conventional designations of the HB in Judaism. Although the HB is almost entirely rendered by the targumim in aggregate, there was no single moment, and no particular movement, that produced a comprehensive Bible in Aramaic. The targumim are irreducibly complex in provenances, purposes, and dialects of Aramaic.

Among the targumim to the Pentateuch, *Targum Onqelos* appears to correspond best of all the targumim to rabbinic ideals of translation. Although paraphrase is evident, especially in order to describe God and his revelation in suitably reverential terms, the high degree of correspondence with the Hebrew of the MT (and, presumably, with the Hebrew text current in antiquity) is striking. The dialect of *Onqelos* is commonly called "Middle Aramaic," which would place the targum between the first century BC and AD 200. A better designation, however, would be "Transitional Aramaic" (200 BC–AD 200), embracing the various dialects (Hasmonean, Nabatean, Palmyrene, Arsacid, Essene, as well as targumic) that came to be used during the period after the Imperial Aramaic of the Persians ceased to be an agreed standard. What followed was a strong regionalization in dialects of Aramaic, which we can logically refer to as Regional Aramaic (AD 200–700).

Various targumim were produced in Transitional Aramaic even after its demise as a common language, because it remained understandable even after the time during which it was spoken as the current language. For that reason, the year AD 200 is not a firm date, after which a targum in Transitional Aramaic cannot have been composed. *Onqelos* should probably be dated during the third century, in the wake of similar efforts to produce a literal Greek rendering during the second century, and well after any strict construal of the principle that targumim were to be oral. By contrast with the rabbinic ethos that permitted the creation and preservation of *Onqelos*, one might recall the story of Rabbi Gamaliel, who is said during the first century to have immured a Targum of Job in a wall of the temple (*t. Šabb.* 115a).

The *Targum Neofiti I* was discovered in 1949 by Alejandro Díez Macho in the Library of the Neophytes in Rome. The paraphrases of *Neofiti* are substantially different from those of *Onqelos*. Entire paragraphs are added, as when Cain and Abel argue in the field prior to the first case of murder (Gen. 4:8); such "renderings" are substantial additions, and it is impossible to predict when remarkable freedom of this kind is to be indulged. The dialect of *Neofiti* was called "Palestinian Aramaic" in older scholarship (and was produced during the period of

Regional Aramaic AD 200–700), to distinguish it from the Babylonian Aramaic of *Onqelos*. The distinction between "Palestinian" and "Babylonian" manifests the regionalization in the Aramaic language to which we have referred. But *Neofiti* is produced in a frankly Regional Aramaic, while *Onqelos* appears in a Transitional Aramaic that is on the way to becoming Regional. The chronology of the two targumim is about the same, although *Neofiti* appears somewhat later; the differences between them are a function more of program than of dating. The rabbis of Babylonia, who called *Onqelos* "our targum," exerted greater influence over Aramaic renderings there than did their colleagues to the west.

The latest representative of the type of expansive rendering found in *Neofiti* is *Targum Pseudo-Jonathan*. Its reference to the names of Mohammed's wife and daughter in Gen. 21:21 put its final composition sometime after the seventh century AD. This oddly designated targum is so called in that the name "Jonathan" was attributed to it during the Middle Ages because its name was abbreviated with a *yod*. But the letter probably stood for "Jerusalem," although that designation is also not established critically. The title *Pseudo-Jonathan* is therefore a tacit admission of uncertainty.

Neofiti and *Pseudo-Jonathan* have together been known as Palestinian targumim, to distinguish their dialects and their style of interpretation from those of *Onqelos*. In fact, however, *Pseudo-Jonathan* was produced at the dawn of the period of Academic Aramaic (AD 700–1500), during which rabbinic usage continued to develop the language in a literary idiom after Arabic as a lingua franca had supplanted Aramaic in the Near East.

Neofiti and *Pseudo-Jonathan* are to be associated with two other targumim, or, to be more precise, groups of targumim. The first group, in chronological order, consists of the fragments from the Cairo Geniza. They were originally part of more complete works, dating between the seventh and the eleventh centuries, that were deposited in the geniza of the Old Synagogue in Cairo. In the type and substance of their interpretation, these fragments are comparable to the other targumim of the Palestinian type. The same may be said of the *Fragmentary Targum*, which was collected as a miscellany of targumic readings during the Middle Ages. An interesting feature of the targumim of the Palestinian type is that their relationship might be described as synoptic, in some ways comparable to the relationship among the Gospels. All four of the Palestinian targumim, for example, convey a debate between Cain and Abel, and they do so with those variations of order and wording that are well known to students of the Synoptic Gospels.

Both the Former and the Latter Prophets are extant in Aramaic in a single collection, although the date and character of each targum within the collection needs to be studied individually. The entire corpus, however, is ascribed by rabbinic tradition (*t. Meg.* 3a) to Jonathan ben Uzziel, a disciple of Hillel, the famous contemporary of Jesus. On the other hand, there are passages of the Prophets' targumim that accord precisely with renderings given in the name of Joseph bar Hiyya, a rabbi of the fourth century (see *Isaiah Targum* 5.17b; *t. Pesaḥ.* 68a). As it happens, the *Isaiah Targum* (which has been subjected to more study than any of the other Prophets' targumim) shows signs of a nationalistic eschatology that was current just after the destruction of the temple in AD 70, and of the more settled perspective of the rabbis in Babylon some three hundred years later. It appears that *Targum Jonathan* as a whole is the result of two major periods of collecting and editing interpretations by the rabbis, the first period being Tannaitic, and the second, Amoraic (a term that refers to the Amoraim, "interpreters," who succeeded the Tannaim).

After *Targum Jonathan* was composed, probably around the same time the *Fragmentary Targum* (to the Pentateuch) was assembled, targumic addenda were appended in certain of its manuscripts; they are represented in the Codex Reuchlinianus and in a manuscript in the French Bibliothèque Nationale that is mislabeled as Hébreu 75.

Of the three categories of targumim, that of the Writings is without question the most diverse. Although the *Targum of Psalms* is formally a translation, at certain points its character seems better described as midrashic. The *Targum of Proverbs* appears to be a fairly straightforward rendition of the Peshitta (the Syriac version), and the *Targum(im) of Esther* seems designed for use within a celebration of the liturgy of Purim. The targumim of the Writings are the most problematic within modern study but also of the least interest of the three general categories of targumim from the point of view of understanding the NT, in view of their late (in certain cases, medieval) date.

The New Testament and Rabbinic Writings

New Testament scholarship has long been aware that rabbinic literature can illuminate the context and meaning of events within the NT. Telling examples include Jesus' action in the temple and Paul's teaching in regard to idols.

Money changers for the payment of the half-shekel tax each year prior to Passover played an integral role in the atonement rite on behalf of the entire community of Israel throughout the world.[3] They took the coins brought by pilgrims and changed them into the half shekel that every Israelite male owed for the maintenance of the daily whole offerings that were presented for the forgiveness of sin. There was no evident reason to drive them out of the temple court; so understood, the action of Jesus is difficult to understand.

In throwing out those buying and selling, Jesus would have disrupted the holy offerings and treated the rites as null, contradicting the esteem for them reflected in the first-century writers Philo and Josephus, quite apart from rabbinic literature. Disputes concerning how the offerings were to be made were well known (*m. Šeqal.* 3.3), and this makes Mark's presentation of Jesus' action appear surreal.

---

3. This example and discussion is drawn from Chilton, *Galilean Rabbi*, supplemented by the anthropological analysis in idem, *The Temple of Jesus: His Sacrificial Program within a Cultural History of Sacrifice* (University Park: Pennsylvania State University Press, 1992) and the commentary in Chilton et al., *Comparative Handbook*.

Moreover, because the operation of changing money began in the provinces before Jerusalem was involved (*m. Šeqal.* 1.3), intervening in the temple would not have prevented the collection of the half shekel. Cicero devoted himself to the defense of a client in 59 BC (*Pro Flacco*) who had plundered a synagogue where the tax was collected in the Diaspora. The account in Mark in its received form may have such an attack on Judaism in mind, and its initial hearers and readers would clearly have understood this to refer to the collection of the half-shekel tax, but to that extent the Gospel does not represent conditions in Jerusalem accurately or plausibly.

Yet if Jesus' action did not target the collection of the half shekel in particular, what was its purpose? Alongside the collection of the tax, the temple also accommodated a system for exchanging seals or tokens (*m. Šeqal.* 5.3–4). To that extent, the setting of the action in Mark seems plausible after all.

The location of the vendors of animals themselves was usually on the Mount of Olives (Josephus, *J.W.* 5.504–5; *y. Ta'an.* 7.4), and the assumption of Mishnah tractate *Šeqalim* itself is that offerings were not directly available in the Great Court of the temple (*m. Šeq.* 5.3–4). An arrangement in which they were actually sited in the Great Court would have been controversial. According to the Babylonian Talmud (*b. 'Abod. Zar.* 8b), around AD 30 Caiaphas indeed imposed drastic changes: "Forty years prior to the destruction of the temple the Sanhedrin went out into exile from the temple and held its sessions in a stall."[4] The counterpart of exiling the Sanhedrin from the temple to Hanuth, the word for "market stall" in Aramaic, is what Mark focuses on: the introduction of trade into the temple. Jesus is depicted as protesting the new setting of the animals, rather than the exile of the Sanhedrin, which is the concern of the Talmud.

His protest is portrayed in prophetic terms (Isa. 56:7; Jer. 7:11) and incorporates the symbolism of the fig (Prov 27:18; *b. 'Erub.* 54a–b). The use of force, not an overt attack on the temple, has a precedent in *t. Ḥag.* 2.11 (see Neusner, *Tosefta*), where a rabbi named Baba ben Buta drove animals *into* the temple to protest high prices in Jerusalem—by offering them for free. The last chapter of the *Targum of Zechariah* predicts that God's kingdom will be manifested over the entire earth when the offerings of Sukkoth are presented by both Israelites and non-Jews at the temple. It further predicts that these worshipers will prepare and offer their sacrifices themselves without the intervention of middlemen (*Targum Zech.* 14.21). The thrust of the targumic prophecy brought on the dramatic confrontation that Jesus provoked in the temple, and Mark preserves the recollection of the circumstances beneath the surface of the text. Jesus' act raises the issue of authority, which becomes a point of focus in Mark.

Unlike in the case of Jesus, Acts 22:3 directly claims on Paul's behalf that he studied "at the feet of Gamaliel," that is, with the patriarch of the Pharisaic party

4. For the most influential renderings in English, see Epstein, *Babylonian Talmud*; and Jacob Neusner, *The Talmud of Babylonia: An American Translation* (Brown Judaic Studies; Chico, CA: Scholars Press, 1984–94). Unless otherwise noted, all translations in this chapter are my own.

of the land of Israel in the succession from Hillel.[5] Paul identifies himself as a
Pharisee (Phil. 3:5), but what can he have learned from Gamaliel? Whether or not
he personally studied with the sage, they were contemporaries, and a comparison
of their teachings is in order.

The issue of idolatry brings us to an analogy between the positions of Gamaliel and Paul, rather than a contrast. Paul's principle is simple: "We know that
there is no idol in the world and that there is no God but one" (1 Cor. 8:4). So
the notional sacrifice of food to idols (contrary to the position of James as cited
in Acts 15:19–21) must be beside the point. Yet if the freedom of action that this
principle implies were to lead a fellow believer to falter, Paul says he would prefer
not to eat meat at all (1 Cor. 8:13; cf. Rom. 14:13, 20).

Paul's statement of the principle is emphatic, and one might expect to see it
at odds with a conventionally Pharisaic opinion. But Gamaliel's proves to offer a
contrast, not of substance, but of the degree of vehemence (in *m. 'Abod. Zar.* 3.4):

> Peroqlos b. Pelosepos asked Rabban Gamaliel in Akko, when he was washing in
> Aphrodite's bathhouse, saying to him, "It is written in your Torah, And there shall
> cleave nothing of a devoted thing to your hand [Deut. 13:17]. How is it that you're
> taking a bath in Aphrodite's bathhouse?" He said to him, "They do not give answers
> in a bathhouse." When he went out, he said to him, "I never came into her domain.
> She came into mine. They don't say, 'Let's make a bathhouse as an ornament for
> Aphrodite.' But they say, 'Let's make Aphrodite as an ornament for the bathhouse.'
> Another explanation: Even if someone gave you a lot of money, you would never
> walk into your temple of idolatry naked or suffering a flux, nor would you urinate in
> its presence. Yet this thing is standing there at the head of the gutter and everybody
> urinates right in front of her. It is said only, '. . . their gods' [Deut. 12:3]—that which
> one treats as a god is prohibited, but that which one treats not as a god is permitted."

Although Gamaliel is no less dismissive of Aphrodite than Paul is of idols as a
whole, Paul is more cautious in expressing and applying the principle. After all,
he is dealing with some people who have actively served idols. For all that, it is
striking that Paul simply asserts the view that idols are nonentities, as if a position
along the lines of Gamaliel's has been widely accepted.

There is still a persistent tendency to assume that, if the NT and another Judaic
source speak about more or less the same thing, they must be referring directly to
the same issues. Then they are contrasted without further reflection, as if they were
having an argument. For example, until the last quarter of the twentieth century,
scholarship widely supposed that the phrase "kingdom of the heavens" in Judaic
sources must mean something very different from "kingdom of God" in Jesus' teaching. The former is a matter of law, the latter is a matter of grace; this much we were
to know before any source was permitted to speak. But because *Targum Jonathan*

---

5. This example and discussion is drawn with permission from Chilton and Neusner, "Paul
and Gamaliel."

persistently uses the phrases "kingdom of God" and "kingdom of the LORD" with an eschatological meaning comparable to Jesus' usage, scholarly opinion has been revised. The many rabbinic parables of God as king demonstrate that the easy characterization of Jesus as a subversive teacher is facile. He never told a parable as surreal as that of the king who left his property with servants and returned to discover that they had so defrauded one another that they were left poor and naked outside the walls of the city (see Rabbi Nathan in the *Semaḥot de Rabbi Ḥiyya* 3).

Jesus' action of expelling merchants from the temple is certainly illuminated by the common context of Baba ben Buta's action of driving sheep into the temple and offering them freely to whoever would sacrifice as he saw fit (so *b. Beṣah* 20a–b). But that common context should not lead us to assume either identical or diametrically opposed understandings of purity. Then again, the vow of *qorbān* in Matt. 15:3–9 and Mark 7:6–13 is helpfully illustrated with the common reference in the Mishnah (tractate *Nedarim*, esp. 9.1) to that same vow, and it is interesting that the Mishnah is concerned to control abuses of the practice in respect of parents, much as in the Gospels. Even Paul's teaching in regard to idols appears to offer an analogy with rabbinic literature.

Inferences for New Testament Studies

The wider question we confront in the comparative reading of the NT and rabbinic literature is the manner in which the sources unfolded. That development may be illuminated by greater clarity in the first instance concerning the type of analogy that appears to be at issue (and why). Beyond that, there must be sensitivity to the literary contexts of rabbinic sources, and far greater accuracy and specificity in regard to questions of dating. On that basis, we may proceed to inferences in regard to the generative moment of texts and sources, be they Jesus or Paul or even other tradents and writers from whom the NT unfolded. Rabbinic literature is only one resource for understanding the context of that process, yet it also offers analogies for the nature of the process itself.

Bibliography

Blackman, Philip. *Mishnayoth: Pointed Hebrew Text, English Translation, Introductions, Notes, Supplement, Appendix, Indexes, Addenda, Corrigenda.* Gateshead: Judaica, 1990. A commonly used translation of this classic rabbinic text, with English and Hebrew in parallel columns.

Bowker, John. *The Targums and Rabbinic Literature: An Introduction to Jewish Interpretations of Scripture.* Cambridge: Cambridge University Press, 1969. An early introduction to the corpus, which remains useful for its accessibility and critical rigor.

Chilton, Bruce. *A Galilean Rabbi and His Bible: Jesus' Own Interpretation of Isaiah.* London: SPCK, 1984. Analyzes how materials in the *Targum of Isaiah* shaped Jesus' understanding of the kingdom of God and other key themes in his teaching, and develops a perspective on Jesus' hermeneutics on that basis.

Chilton, Bruce, Darrell Bock, and Daniel M. Gurtner, eds. *A Comparative Handbook to the Gospel of Mark: Comparisons with Pseudepigrapha, the Qumran Scrolls, and Rabbinic Literature.* The New Testament Gospels in Their Judaic Contexts 1. Leiden: Brill, 2010. Instead of assuming any causative relationship between Mark's Gospel and Judaic literature, this compendium sets out the analogies that help to illuminate the sense of Mark and of its development and sources.

Chilton, Bruce, and Jacob Neusner. "Paul and Gamaliel." *BBR* 14, no. 1 (2004): 1–43. Identifies in detail how Paul and traditions associated with Gamaliel developed distinct but related views and manifest analogous theological principles.

Epstein, Israel, ed. *The Babylonian Talmud.* London: Soncino, 1948. The most commonly used translation of this classic rabbinic text, formatted to facilitate reference to the original language.

Evans, Craig A. *To See and Not Perceive: Isaiah 6.9–10 in Early Jewish and Christian Interpretation.* JSOTSup 64. Sheffield: Sheffield Academic Press, 1989. Focusing on a particular but crucial passage within the Jesus tradition, this monograph demonstrates the formative influence of rabbinic and especially targumic traditions on Jesus' theology.

Flesher, Paul V. M., and Bruce Chilton. *The Targums: A Critical Introduction.* Waco: Baylor University Press, 2011. Although critical work on the targumim has been a feature of scholarship for centuries, this general treatment of targumic literature, its formation and principles, individual documents, and relationship to other literature, including the NT, is the first of its kind.

Freedman, H., and Maurice Simon, eds. *Midrash Rabbah.* London: Soncino, 1983. The most commonly used translation of this classic rabbinic text, formatted to facilitate reference to the original language.

Maccoby, Hyam. *Early Rabbinic Writings.* Cambridge Commentaries on Writings of the Jewish and Christian World, 200 BC to AD 200. Cambridge: Cambridge University Press, 1988. A good, solid introduction to this aspect of Judaic literature.

McNamara, M., ed. The Aramaic Bible. Collegeville, MN: Liturgical Press, 1987–. A series providing the most commonly used translation of these classic rabbinic texts, formatted to facilitate reference to the original language.

Neusner, Jacob. *Introduction to Rabbinic Literature.* ABRL. New York: Doubleday, 1994. An analytic treatment of the literature for those preparing to move beyond general introduction and into the critical use of the corpus.

———. *Talmud of the Land of Israel: A Preliminary Translation and Explanation.* Chicago: University of Chicago Press, 1982–94. The most commonly used translation of this classic rabbinic text, formatted to facilitate reference to the original language.

———. *The Tosefta: Translated from the Hebrew.* Peabody, MA: Hendrickson, 2002. The most commonly used translation of this classic rabbinic text, formatted to facilitate reference to the original language.

Safrai, Shemuel, et al., eds. Compendia rerum Iudaicarum ad Novum Testamentum. Assen: Van Gorcum; Philadelphia: Fortress, 1974–. A series of detailed treatments of how Judaic institutions and texts relate to the study of the NT.

35

Early Noncanonical Christian Writings

NICHOLAS PERRIN

Although the very oldest extant Christian literature is preserved in the NT canon, there are other texts, not included in the canon, written not too long before or not too long after the composition of the later NT writings. Leaving aside some of the second-century church fathers (e.g., Justin Martyr [AD 103–165]; Irenaeus of Lyons [ca. AD 130–202]), we might classify the most important writings as falling under one of two categories: the Apostolic Fathers and the apocryphal Gospels. This article will provide a brief overview of both categories as well as more-detailed discussion of three representative texts from each.

Apostolic Fathers

In 1672, the French scholar J. B. Cotelier published a two-volume work that included the *Epistle of Barnabas*, seven epistles by Ignatius of Antioch (ca. AD 50–ca. 117), an epistle by Polycarp of Smyrna (ca. AD 69–156), an account of the martyrdom of the same, *1* and *2 Clement* (the first of which can be reasonably ascribed to Clement and dated AD 96), and the *Shepherd of Hermas*. Assuming that these texts were written by those who knew the apostles personally, Cotelier designated the corresponding authors as "Fathers of the Apostolic Period." It is Cotelier, and not any ancient author or community, who is to be credited for originating the phrase now used as an umbrella term for some of the earliest Christian writings outside the NT. Although the category has remained slightly fluid in the intervening centuries (with certain texts being added, only later to be removed), today it is generally accepted that the term "Apostolic Fathers" refers to Cotelier's original list along with the more recently (re)discovered *Didache* and the *Epistle to Diognetus*.

Considerable guesswork goes into the dating of many of these documents, but it is safe to say that all of them were written within a century-long window (ca. AD 70–ca. 170). Like the NT writings, these texts were written in response to particular needs arising within the early church. As such, they represent a breadth of viewpoint and witness to some of the more pressing issues facing late first- and second-century Christianity. There is also considerable diversity among the kinds of texts represented in the Fathers. For example, in addition to the epistles of Ignatius and *1 Clement*, we in effect have two homilies preserved in *2 Clement* and the *Epistle of Barnabas*, an apology (defense of the faith) in the *Epistle to Diognetus*, a church manual in the *Didache*, and an apocalypse (comparable to Revelation in the NT) in the *Shepherd of Hermas*. The collection is also character- ized by a geographical diversity, with authors hailing from such places as Rome (Clement), Antioch (Ignatius), and Alexandria (*Epistle of Barnabas*). As such, the Apostolic Fathers offer a broad crosscut of subapostolic Christianity, a period that otherwise would have remained largely shrouded in obscurity.

The collection not only affords a fascinating mirror of its own period but has also proved influential on the thinking of later church writers. Those who drew on the Apostolic Fathers include such early theological heavyweights as Irenaeus, Clement of Alexandria (ca. 150–215), Tertullian (160–225), Hippolytus of Rome (ca. 170–236), Origen (ca. 185–254), Eusebius (ca. 260–ca. 340), Athanasius (ca. 296–373), and Jerome (ca. 342–420). Even if the collection fell into disuse in the Middle Ages, these texts commanded respect in their own day and in the imme- diately subsequent centuries. For this reason, the theology contained here must have been at least generally within keeping of the Great Church tradition.

Because space forbids treating all the Apostolic Fathers (for this see Jefford et al., *Apostolic Fathers*), this article will be limited to three representative voices: the *Epistle of Barnabas*, the *Didache*, and Polycarp's letter *To the Philippians*. Not only do these texts give a sense of the wide variety of styles contained in the collection, but they are also among the most important in the study of the NT era.

Epistle of Barnabas

The *Epistle of Barnabas* (ca. 96–100) is an adapted homily of Alexandrian origin. Whereas manuscripts containing a partial text have been handed down through antiquity, the complete Greek text came to light only in the 1844 discov- ery of Codex Sinaiticus. The final form of *Barnabas* was clearly an early editor's attempt to combine the sermon proper (*Barn.* 2.1–17) with material reflecting the so-called Two Ways tradition that has parallels in both Christian (e.g., *Did.* 1–6) and pre-Christian (e.g., 1QS 3.13–4.26) writings.

Even though the text is formally ascribed to Barnabas and a handful of church fathers agree that the author is none other than Paul's partner in ministry (cf. Gal. 2; Acts 11–15), the author's connection with the apostolate is dubious. First, it is unlikely that the Jewish Barnabas of the NT would take the kind of virulent stance against Judaism that we find in this text. Second, if, as most scholars suspect, our text hails from the end of the first century, this would make for a very old author indeed—at least by first-century standards. More than likely, either the text was penned as a pseudepigraphic work (whereby a relatively anonymous author ascribed the work to a well-known, authoritative figure) or was originally anonymous and then later credited to *the* Barnabas by the early church. In any event, the author seems to have been writing to Christian believers who knew him and willingly submitted to his spiritual authority.

For the modern reader, the most striking feature of *Barnabas* is its harsh rhetoric directed against the Jews. In a theological move similar to that of the NT book of Hebrews, the author writes that God has abolished the temple cultus in order to make way for "the new law of our Lord Jesus Christ" (*Barn.* 2.6).[1] Yet no NT book comes even close to *Barnabas* (2.6; 4.6–8; 5.11; 14.5; etc.) in its radical supersessionism (i.e., the view that Christianity completely displaced Judaism in the divine economy). The author's invective against Judaism was likely in response to a situation similar to that which helped spark the writing of Hebrews: Christian believers (re)converting to Judaism. The stated concern, lest "we break ourselves through being converts to that law" (3.6b), seems to show that the gradual "parting of the ways" between church and synagogue was still in process; after all, a text so intent on sharpening socioreligious self-definition would be explicable only in a situation in which, so far as the author is concerned, existing boundaries were uncomfortably fluid (see also, e.g., Evans and Hagner, *Anti-Semitism*). Perhaps, as James Carleton Paget (*Barnabas*) argues, *Barnabas* was written in response to heightened Jewish eschatological fervor following Domitian's demise, which prompted hopes for restoration and a rebuilt temple in Jerusalem.

There are other elements of interest. The Two Ways tradition of chaps. 18–20 belongs in the same Jewish-style genre as the exhortations to righteousness found in Matt. 7:15–20 and parallels; Gal. 5:19–23a; James 3:13–18; Rev. 21:6–8; and so on. Also, like Rev. 17:3–14, the epistle interprets the ten-horned beast of Dan. 7 as imminently being fulfilled in the present eschatological moment (*Barn.* 4.1). Here we have anything but a settled, nonapocalyptic Christianity.

Finally, since most scholars take the wording and arrangement of the numerous OT quotations in *Barnabas* as evidence of preexisting *testimonia* (standardized collections of proof texts), this bolsters the long-standing scholarly argument,

---

1. Translations of ancient texts here and throughout the chapter are my own.

which has enjoyed varying degrees of popularity over the years, that similar such *testimonia* were also put to use by NT writers.

Didache

Ever since the discovery of its complete text in 1873, the *Didache* has piqued the curiosity of NT scholars. Its influence in antiquity is demonstrated not only by the breadth of its transmission (with fragments in Greek, Coptic, and Georgian) but also by its reception history. The *Didache* has exerted its influence on such geographically diverse texts as the fourth-century Greek *Apostolic Constitutions*, the Ethiopic *Church Order*, the Latin *Doctrina apostolorum*, and the Arabic *Life of Shenoute*.

Issues of authorship, dating, and provenance are problematized by the common perception that the *Didache* is the product of an editorial evolution occurring over an undetermined period. Scholars believe that the text took its final form no later than AD 150, with some portions being reduced to writing as early as AD 70 and some of those traditions stemming from an even earlier period (see here esp. Milavec, *Didache*). The whole work seems to be a composite of at least two discrete works: one focusing on individual piety as expressed in the Two Ways (*Did.* 1–6), and the second focusing on such matters as baptism, prayers, the Eucharist, and appropriate treatment of itinerant apostles and prophets (*Did.* 7–15). Most scholars prefer to assign *Did.* 1–6 (closely paralleling *Barn.* 18–20) to the late first century; *Did.* 7–15 was likely written not much later. Evidence of reliance on a written copy of the Gospel of Matthew—together with the instructions regarding itinerant prophets in *Did.* 12–13, which seem to reflect a transitional period between the death of the apostles and the hierarchical ecclesiology of the early second century—points us to the turn of the first century. Whether the text is of specifically Syrian or Egyptian provenance (both positions seem plausible on the evidence) cannot be determined with any certainty.

The *Didache* is relevant to NT studies in at least three respects. First, the Didachist not only makes rather minimal use of the titular "Christ" (occurring only at 9.4) but also renders the Second Person of the Trinity (despite *Did.* 7.1) conspicuous only by his near absence. A strongly Jewish community exhibiting a low Christology, the original audience of the *Didache* may have been very similar to the recipients of the Epistle to the Hebrews, which was written in large part to persuade a Jewish Christian audience of the superiority of Jesus Christ. Second, we find both continuity and discontinuity with the sacramental language of the NT. The Didachist passes along the baptism formulary just as we have it in Matt. 28:19 (interestingly, too, the Lord's Prayer [Matt. 6:9–13 par.] is to be said three times a day). But the instructions regarding the table depart from Paul's language (1 Cor. 11:17–34): there are no words of institution, the fellowship meal has been dropped, and new vocabulary ("holy vine of David" [9.4]) has entered in. Finally, issues of ecclesial authority are of special concern. The Didachist warns against hosting false prophets (cf. 1 John 4:1–6; 2 John 7–11; 3 John 5–8) and seems to assume a two-tier structure of bishops and deacons (*Did.* 15.1). All this is consistent with the instructions in the Pastoral Epistles (1 Tim. 3; Titus 1:5–7) and Clement of Rome (*1 Clem.* 42.4–5), but different from the Ignatian scheme that would later introduce the presbyter as a separate office (Ign. *Magn.* 3.1–2).

Polycarp, To the Philippians

Polycarp (ca. 70–155/56), bishop of Smyrna, wrote a number of letters to various communities over the course of his bishopric, but the only one to survive is *To the Philippians*. The text is fully preserved in a rather loose Latin translation based on the original Greek. Fortunately, nine Greek manuscripts have also come down to us; these uniformly preserve Pol. *Phil.* 1–9, with *Barn.* 5 appended. Eusebius of Caesarea also preserves Pol. *Phil.* 9 and 13 (*Eccl. Hist.* 3.36.13–15).

Although a few scholars deem the text to be essentially unified, most are convinced that *To the Philippians* is not really one letter but two (or pieces of two) fused into one, consisting of Pol. *Phil.* 1–12, 14 as one block, and Pol. *Phil.* 13 as the other. Two reasons stand behind this judgment. First, Pol. *Phil.* 13.1 seems to introduce a radical break in thought. Second, and more persuasive, is the observation that while Polycarp includes Ignatius among the martyrs in 9.1, in 13.2 he is inquiring into Ignatius's welfare and is unaware of his death. Our best guess is that both texts hail from Polycarp's hometown of Smyrna.

Eusebius (*Eccl. Hist.* 5.20.5–8) informs us that Polycarp was a disciple of the apostle John; John in fact appointed Polycarp to the bishopric at Smyrna. We also know that Polycarp had an encounter with the heretic Marcion (ca. 85–160) and clashed with the Roman bishop Anicetus (died ca. 167) over the proper dating of Easter. The *Martyrdom of Polycarp* (ca. 160), written not too long after the bishop's death, affords insight into not only the venerated church leader's demise but also his reputation as a Christian leader. The memory of Polycarp would take on larger-than-life proportions in the fifth-century *Life of Polycarp*.

Noteworthy in the text are the NT roots of Polycarp's theology of persecution. First, his allusion to Christ as "the everlasting high priest" (Pol. *Phil.* 12.2; cf. Heb. 6:20) comes alongside a charge to pray for secular leaders during a season of opposition, all with a view to being rendered "perfect [Latin *perfecti*] in him" (Pol. *Phil.* 12.3). Assuming that "perfect" invokes a cultic context, we discover that Polycarp appreciated the NT's characterization of persecution and martyrdom in cultic terms (1 Pet. 2:4–12; 3:17–22; Rev. 1:5–6; 6:9–11), with Christ himself as the attendant high priest. Second, Polycarp's statement "if we should live worthily as citizens [Greek *politeusōmetha axiōs*] before him, then we will also reign with him" (5.2), was undoubtedly an allusion to one of two occurrences of the same verb in the NT, where Paul in *his* letter to the Philippians writes, "Only, live your life in a manner worthy [*axiōs . . . politeuesthe*] of the gospel of Christ" (Phil. 1:27; cf. Acts 23:1), also in the context of persecution (Phil. 1:27–30). Based in a major center of emperor worship (with its attendant pressures on the Christian community), Polycarp must have been conscious of the conflicting demands placed on those who must serve the imperial rules of Rome and Christ. He also seems to have been well aware of the anti-imperial undertones of Paul's writing, with which Pauline scholars are just now coming to terms. Polycarp's use of letters ascribed to Paul has proved to be an interesting study in its own right (as instanced in Hartog, *Polycarp*).

Apocryphal Gospels

Although many associate the term "Gospel" with any one of the first four books of the NT (i.e., the canonical Gospels: Matthew, Mark, Luke, and John), the term applied much more broadly in antiquity. By the early third century, there were a great number of different Gospels, exhibiting different characteristics and often representing theological trajectories vastly different from that of the canonical Gospels (for overviews and texts, see Klauck, *Apocryphal Gospels*; Cameron, *Other Gospels*). Some of these noncanonical Gospels exhibit heightened interest in Jesus' childhood (*Protevangelium of James*, *Infancy Gospel of Thomas*, *Gospel of Pseudo-Matthew*). Others focus on conversations allegedly taking place between the risen Jesus and his disciples (*Sophia Jesu Christi*, *Epistula Apostolorum*, *Gospel of Mary*, and *Apocryphon of John*). Still others push the lens back to his death and resurrection (*Gospel of Peter*, *Acts of Pilate*, *Gospel of Bartholomew*). Motivated at least in part by a theological agenda, early Christians took to composing texts like these in hopes of filling in the gaps left by prior oral and written traditions.

Interestingly enough, not all the apocryphal Gospels are narrative in character: the *Gospel of Truth* appears to be a homily; the *Gospel of Thomas* and the *Gospel of Philip* are sayings of Jesus with little or no setting or narrative framework. The absence of such narrative elements has made some of these texts difficult to date. It has also led some scholars to posit connections with one of the earliest strands of Christianity, represented by Q (see discussion below), which itself, according to some scholars, may have been the very first Gospel. If the Synoptic Gospels share a close resemblance, and the Gospel of John is different from these, the apocryphal Gospels constitute a clear departure from all four in form as well as content.

Scholars freely grant the possibility that at least some, if not all, of the four canonical Gospels were written by the apostolic authors to which tradition has ascribed them, but the same cannot be said for the apocryphal Gospels. They are clearly pseudepigraphic works, passed off (against our better historic judgment) as having been written by an apostolic figure. Whether the original hearers of these texts took these ascriptions at face value is difficult to say. In any event, it is clear that at least in some cases claims of apostolic authorship were meant to compete directly with the apostolic authority attached to the now-canonical Gospels.

By the end of the second century, some were objecting to the existence of any Gospels beyond the now-canonical four. Irenaeus insists that "it is not of the nature of the gospels that they be either more or less than the number than they are": there must be four—no less, no more (*Adv. haer.* 3.11.8). According to the same church father, the proliferation of Gospels was a function of heresy (*Adv. haer.* 3.11.7). Although we must be cautious in reading the words of the bishop of Lyons uncritically, there is certainly some substance to his concerns. Scholars can draw clear lines between certain of these apocryphal Gospels and gnostic movements of the day. The *Gospel of Truth* and the *Gospel of Philip*, for example, derive from a Christian sect originating with Valentinus (ca. 100–ca. 160). In this respect, the apocryphal Gospels shed light on the diversity of early Christian belief as well as the convictions and practices of those who would eventually be deemed to lie beyond the pale of right belief.

Three texts, selected for their significance in contemporary discussion, are treated below: the *Gospel of Thomas*, the *Gospel of Peter*, and the *Gospel of Judas*. Their relevance to the reconstruction of earliest Christianity remains under discussion. Some claim that the existence of such texts demands a complete re-evaluation of Christian origins and the theological landscape of Christianity as we have known it. Others remain skeptical. At the very least, we learn from these Gospels something about how Jesus Christ was understood by some of his later interpreters.

Gospel of Thomas

Discovered in the winter of 1945 in the village of Nag Hammadi, Egypt, the thirteen codices (books) making up the so-called Nag Hammadi library proved to be a rich treasure trove of both familiar and unfamiliar texts. The most important of these is no doubt the *Gospel of Thomas*, a collection of some 114 sayings, most of which are attributed to Jesus, and about half of which have parallels in the Synoptic Gospels (Matthew, Mark, and Luke). Although the Nag Hammadi version of *Thomas* (our only complete text) was written in Coptic (a scribal language of late Egypt), scholars quickly connected this find with certain Greek fragments (P.Oxy. 1, 654, 655) discovered a half century earlier outside Oxyrhynchus, Egypt. Influenced by the judgment of the discoverers of the Oxyrhynchus fragments, the first commentators on Coptic *Thomas* dated the collection to AD 140. In recent decades, the window of possibility has widened considerably: April DeConick (*Gospel of Thomas*) envisages a compositional evolution with a core of material going back very close to the time of Jesus (AD 30s); Nicholas Perrin (*Thomas*) positions the text after a Syriac Gospel harmony called the *Diatessaron* (making it the late 170s); and Elaine Pagels (*Belief*) splits the difference (ca. 100) by putting *Thomas* in conversation with the canonical Gospel of John. (No scholar believes the text to have actually been written by the apostle Thomas himself.)

The current lack of consensus on the issue of dating has not helped to resolve debates on other fronts. For example, if *Thomas* is the written residue of a long-running and evolving oral performance, free from the influence of the Synoptic tradition, then it is more appropriate to talk about settings (plural) rather than setting (singular). On the other hand, if *Thomas* is directly or indirectly dependent on the Synoptic Gospels, then we are virtually forced to imagine an editor or oral performer consciously reworking the text that has come down to us in the first three Gospels.

One point on which there is broad agreement is that of provenance. Since *Thomas* bears certain Syriacisms, including reference to the apostle as "Didymus Judas Thomas" (unique to the Syriac tradition), most scholars are content to ascribe the (final) text to a Syrian setting, most likely the city of Edessa. Over time, *Thomas* attracted the notice of certain church fathers, including Hippolytus of Rome (ca. 220), who warns against using the Gospel, and Eusebius, who lists the sayings collection among the *antilegomena* (those texts that ought to remain outside the canon). Whether the Great Church's ultimate rejection of *Thomas* marks a narrowing tolerance cannot be determined with great certainty. Arguments that the Coptic Gospel bears some affinities with the gnostic doctrines of Valentinianism (a second-century heresy stemming from the Alexandrian exegete Valentinus) were once rendered unfashionable but have in the past several years been resuscitated.

The relevance of *Thomas* to NT studies depends in large measure on prior judgments of its independence or dependence vis-à-vis the Synoptic Gospels. Some scholars, impressed by the formal similarities between the Coptic sayings collection and the sayings collection Q (an alleged source standing behind Matthew and Luke), have advanced the theory that earliest Christianity—as evidenced in reconstructed Q and *Thomas*—knew neither cross nor resurrection. Others remain unconvinced by the analogy between Q and *Thomas*, or even of the collection's status as an independent witness. For all practical purposes, the text has made little palpable difference to the results of Jesus research, even in the accounts of those who lay great store by it.

Gospel of Peter

The *Gospel of Peter* was discovered in Akhmîm, Egypt, in 1886–87. It is contained in a fifth- or sixth-century Greek manuscript, now identified as Cairo 10759, along with the *Apocalypse of Peter*. Nearly a century later, in 1972, P.Oxy. 2949 and 4009 (late second- or early third-century papyri) were published. Dieter Lührmann has identified these papyri (along with P.Vindob. G 2325, P.Egerton 2, and an ostracon) as fragments of the Petrine Gospel. The connection he posits between P.Oxy. 2949 and *Gos. Pet.* 2.3–5 seems reasonably secure, despite the objections of a few (e.g., Foster, *Gospel of Peter*). It is also almost certainly the same Gospel that Serapion of Antioch (d. 211) first accepted for general use only to reject it later due to concerns about its orthodoxy (cf. Eusebius, *Eccl. Hist.* 6.12.2).

Like the *Gospel of Thomas*, the *Gospel of Peter* has provoked considerable debate regarding its putative relationship to the Synoptic Gospels. Whereas most twentieth-century scholarship has judged the Petrine Gospel to be of secondary character and dependent on the canonical Gospels, John Dominic Crossan (*Historical Jesus*) has dated the Gospel to about AD 50. While Crossan admits that the Gospel in its final form shows marks of dependence, he attributes this mid-first-century date to a narrative core, a "Cross Gospel," embedded within the present text, a view that has met with both support and disapproval. Various factors—not least among them anti-Semitic sentiments, the repeated use of the christological title "Lord," and the bizarre quality of the miracle material—has induced most scholars to assign the Gospel as a whole to the second century.

The narrative of the *Gospel of Peter* breaks down into three basic scenes: a passion account (1–6), an epiphany of judgment (7), and a resurrection account (7–15). Unlike many dialogues between the disciples and the risen Lord, this text conjoins the crucified and resurrected Lord—in a way not entirely different from the so-called Longer Ending of Mark (16:9–20). The narrative departs most glaringly from the canonical accounts in its recounting of a walking and talking cross reaching up to the heavens. Frustratingly, the text both begins and ends abruptly: the copyist behind the Akhmîmic fragment seems to have been restricted to a fragmentary copy.

The *Gospel of Peter* provides interesting background to the NT at a number of points, especially so far as early Christian interpretation is concerned. For example, by providing the first extracanonical reference to Christ's descent to hell (cf. 1 Pet. 3:18–22; Eph. 4:7–10), *Gos. Pet.* 10.31–42 contributes to the history of interpretation of the *descensus Christi* ("descent of Christ"). Elsewhere, the Jesus of *Peter* makes an unusual last declaration: "My power, the power, why have you forsaken me?" (*Gos. Pet.* 5.19). Although some interpret "power" merely as a circumlocution for God, the wording of the Greek seems hauntingly reminiscent of the early second-century heresy of Cerinthianism, which radically separated the two natures of Christ. Finally, whereas Gospel commentators down through the ages have differed as to the intention of the one who offered Jesus wine vinegar on a sponge (Mark 15:36 par.), in *Peter* it seems clear enough that the intention was to poison Jesus (*Gos. Pet.* 5.16).

It is uncertain whether the *Gospel of Peter* was composed by an author who subscribed to docetism (the heretical belief that Jesus only appeared to take on human form). The most crucial passage reads: "He was silent as one who experienced no pain" (*Gos. Pet.* 4.10). The phrase need not have been docetic in intent, especially since the orthodox *Martyrdom of Polycarp* contains a similar line in reference to its hero (8.3). At the same time, if Serapion thought that *Peter* left too many open doors to an unbalanced Christology, one might suspect that it became a favorite of docetically inclined Christians.

Gospel of Judas

In the 1970s a certain ancient codex, now called Codex Tchacos and dateable to 220–340, was discovered outside of El Minya, Egypt. Following numerous changes of hands, including a stint in a safe deposit box in Long Island, New York, the same book, containing the Coptic *Gospel of Judas*, was acquired in 2004 by the National Geographic Society, who in turn announced the acquisition two years later. Scholars had already been aware of such a Gospel on account of Irenaeus, the second-century bishop of Lyons (*Adv. haer.* 1.31.1), who seems to be familiar with the community that composed the *Gospel of Judas* as well as the text itself. As for the original (probably Greek) autograph manuscript standing behind the extant Coptic text, a window of AD 130–150 may be inferred. This is sustained by its marks of a full-blown version of Gnosticism, in this case, Sethian Gnosticism.

The plot of *Judas* revolves around a conversation between Jesus and his disciples. In the initial scene, Jesus laughs at his disciples as they offer a prayer of thanksgiving over bread (clearly a jab at Eucharist-observing Christians [*Gos. Jud.* 34]). Next Jesus holds private conversations with Judas regarding the mysteries of the kingdom, while the rest of the Twelve are characterized as foolish for worshiping the God of Israel, who is variously termed Nebro (rebel) and Saklas (fool). The narrative draws to a close with Jesus informing Judas that he will "sacrifice the man that clothes me" (*Gos. Jud.* 56.17–18). As DeConick (*Thirteenth Apostle*) rightly argues, Judas is no hero; after all, he is "a demon" (*Gos. Jud.* 44.18–21). Nevertheless, despite his negative characterization, which is consistent with his profile in early Christianity, he is superior to the apostolate and has insight that the rest of the disciples lack (e.g., *Gos. Jud.* 35.17–18). The Gospel closes with Judas making arrangements for Jesus' betrayal.

Like the *Gospel of Peter*, the *Gospel of Judas* exhibits a thoroughgoing docetism. This is inherent in the way Jesus is described. Moreover, like the *Gospel of Thomas*, this Gospel exhibits an anti-Jewish character; for the author, early Christianity's claim to be an extension of Judaism is abhorrent. Behind both of these polemical positions may stand a metaphysical dualism that rejects the coidentification of the creator god with the highest God.

Finally, we find in *Judas*, as in a good many gnostic Gospels, a posture of radical individualism. This follows simply from the mode of Jesus' revelation: even if the Jesus of the *Gospel of Judas* makes no special claim for himself, the mysteries he discloses are revealed to Judas alone, apart from the community. In the end, Judas is referred back to his star, that is, his spirit, which Hellenistic philosophy saw as providing guidance. Thus there are obvious differences between the canonical Gospels and the *Gospel of Judas*. As a background to the NT, the gnostic Gospel is witness to the fact that many of the doctrinal battles engaged during the first century (e.g., 1 Tim. 1:3–10; 1 John 4:1–5; Rev. 2:15–16) were still underway well into the second century. Unfortunately, as far as research into the historical Jesus or historical Judas is concerned, we have no reason to suspect that this Gospel affords us anything of historical value.

Conclusion

Together the Apostolic Fathers and the apocryphal Gospels shed light on early Christianity and by extension the NT as well. In both collections we find the rumblings of battle over the controversy of docetism, a battle first instanced in texts like 1 John (4:2–3). Already by the turn of the first century, theological trajectories initiated by the first NT texts were splitting off into various directions: some leading to what is—or would later be—recognizable as a brand of Gnosticism, others to what would culminate in Nicene orthodoxy. Both collections appeal to either the NT writings or oral traditions that find parallel in our now-canonical texts. In this regard, the Apostolic Fathers and the apocryphal Gospels constitute an important source in discussions of NT canon. Finally, these texts testify to the parting of ways taking place between the local church and the local synagogue. Such divisions are already discernible in some of the earliest NT writings (e.g., 1 Thess. 2), but also and more conspicuously in some later texts as well (e.g., Gospel of Matthew, Gospel of John, Revelation). Just when and how early Christianity began to identify itself over and against the Judaism that gave it birth is a complex question, but one for which, thankfully, we have certain textual bearings outside the canon.

Bibliography

Cameron, Ron, ed. *The Other Gospels: Non-canonical Gospel Texts*. Philadelphia: Westminster, 1982. Repr., Cambridge: Lutterworth, 2006. A collection of primary sources, this text helpfully provides the noncanonical Gospels in readable translation.

Crossan, John Dominic. *The Historical Jesus: The Life of a Mediterranean Jewish Peasant*. San Francisco: HarperSanFrancisco, 1991. Although this book concerns the historical Jesus, it is noted for its interesting and provocative understanding of the *Gospel of Peter*.

DeConick, April D. *Recovering the Original Gospel of Thomas: A History of the Gospel and Its Growth*. LNTS 286. London: T&T Clark, 2005. In this technical study, the author offers her own reconstruction of the compositional history of the *Gospel of Thomas*.

———. *The Thirteenth Apostle: What the Gospel of Judas Really Says*. London: Continuum, 2007. One of the leading books on the *Gospel of Judas*, correcting errors contained within earlier responses to the unveiling of the Gospel.

Evans, Craig A., and Donald Alfred Hagner, eds. *Anti-Semitism and Early Christianity: Issues of Polemic and Faith*. Minneapolis: Fortress, 1993. Although now somewhat dated, this book still constitutes an array of useful essays.

Foster, Paul. *The Gospel of Peter: Introduction, Critical Edition and Commentary*. TENTS 4. Leiden: Brill, 2010. A technical work, this book will likely prove to be a standard.

Hartog, Paul. *Polycarp and the New Testament: The Occasion, Rhetoric, Theme, and Unity of the Epistle to the Philippians and Its Allusions to New Testament Literature*. WUNT 2/134. Tübingen: Mohr Siebeck, 2002. The author provides an interesting study of Polycarp's use of the NT material, particularly relevant for its focus on the church father's appropriation of writings ascribed to Paul.

Jefford, Clayton N., et al. *Reading the Apostolic Fathers: An Introduction.* Peabody, MA: Hendrickson, 1996. A handy and well-designed introduction to the Apostolic Fathers—eminently readable.

Klauck, Hans-Josef. *Apocryphal Gospels: An Introduction.* London: T&T Clark, 2003. One of the best and most succinct overviews of the apocryphal Gospels.

Milavec, Aaron. *The Didache: Text, Translation, Analysis, and Commentary.* Collegeville, MN: Liturgical Press, 2004. Although overly sanguine in some of his claims regarding the *Didache*, Milavec nevertheless combines top-notch scholarship with clarity.

Pagels, Elaine H. *Beyond Belief: The Secret Gospel of Thomas.* New York: Random House, 2003. A *New York Times* bestseller, this book is written at a semipopular level and brings history to bear on an agenda applicable to modern Western religion.

Paget, James Carleton. *The Epistle of Barnabas: Outlook and Background.* WUNT 2.64. Tübingen: Mohr Siebeck, 1994. One of the few major writings on the *Epistle of Barnabas*.

Perrin, Nicholas. *Thomas, the Other Gospel.* Louisville: Westminster John Knox, 2007. Identifies the *Gospel of Thomas* within the setting of early Syriac Christianity and assigns the text a late second-century dating.

PART 5

THE GEOGRAPHICAL CONTEXT OF THE NEW TESTAMENT

Having a broad sense of the location, history, and social context of the world of the NT, including several leading cities where early Christianity made significant inroads, helps students to understand what early Christians encountered and largely took for granted in their writings. In addition, archaeological work has sometimes clarified biblical texts.

In this final section, readers will find valuable information on the archaeological and geographical context of the NT, especially during the time of Jesus and the emergence of the early church's mission. Archaeology has until recently been one of the most neglected subjects in NT study; consequently, it is not unusual

for biblical interpreters to miss some of the highly significant features of the locations where the early Christians lived and ministered—features that undoubtedly
influenced the NT writings.

We begin with an important focus on archaeology, particularly on its benefits
for understanding Jesus and the times in which he ministered. Unfortunately, biblical scholars have often known little about archaeology, and archaeologists have
known little about the Bible. As these chapters suggest, this is beginning to change.

Having a basic introduction to the background and history of the locales
mentioned in the NT writings is critical to our understanding of the message
of the NT writers. In what follows, readers will find discussion of many of the
important places mentioned in the NT, often by scholars who have repeatedly
visited the regions and cities they describe and who have investigated them carefully for many years.

36

Jesus Research and Archaeology

JAMES H. CHARLESWORTH

Jesus research is in full bloom.[1] Recent years have witnessed impressive contributions from the academy, the synagogue, and the church, but no major works significantly include archaeological work in lower Galilee and Judea, especially in and near Jerusalem and Qumran. This deficiency seems odd since it is widely recognized that many methodologies are now essential in Jesus research, including philology, exegesis, rhetoric, eyewitness studies, memory, oral tradition, sociology, anthropology, carbon dating, numismatics, geology, ground-penetrating radar, topography (including soil analyses), and—of course—archaeology.

Since Jesus lived and worked in Palestine, Galilee, and Judea during the Herodian dynasty, it is helpful to know what factors and hopes defined life then, how terms were defined, and what concepts were regnant. Since the NT authors were mostly Jews who lived before the Bar Kokhba rebellion and focused their attention, informatively and paradigmatically, on the Holy Land, what we learn about that time and place helps us better comprehend their mind, traditions, and memory, and especially their Christologies. J. L. Reed aptly summarizes the new scene: "There can be no doubt that Galilee, once mere background to historical Jesus research, has moved to the foreground."[2]

1. In memory of Hanan Eshel, Yizar Hirschfeld, Ehud Netzer, and Shemaryahu Talmon.
2. J. L. Reed, "Instability in Jesus' Galilee: A Demographic Perspective," *JBL* 129 (2010): 343–65 (343).

Why have students of Jesus been slow to learn from archaeology? First, NT experts often shy away from archaeology because they are usually not trained or experienced in excavations and the distinct, advanced science of archaeology. For their part, archaeologists are often uninterested in NT study, and some view it with disdain because it can be confessional and theological. Second, NT scholars are understandably offended by the archaeologists' penchant for employing guild language and technical terminology, such as "balk," "stratum," "*in situ*," "*locus*," "pottery chronology," "curvilinear walls," "lithics," "AMS C^{14}," "thermolumines-cence," and "*guffah*."[3] Third, NT scholars have cause to be leery of archaeology because of the continuing tendency of some authors to use archaeology apologeti-cally (see Freyne, *Galilee*, 160–82).

Fourth, it is also true that repetitive and false claims can cause embarrassment. Over the past decade the global community has been bombarded by archaeological claims—some true, others false. An ossuary (burial bone box usually of stone) purporting to belong to Jesus' brother has been recovered. Authenticating this claim has been controversial; it is likely that the ossuary and the beginning of the inscription are authentic, but there are doubts about the phrase "and the brother of Jesus." A tomb in southern Jerusalem was initially hailed as "the Jesus Tomb" because an ossuary was found *in situ* bearing the inscription "Jesus, son of Joseph." Some scholars concluded that it was the bone box of Jesus from Nazareth, but it probably belonged to an unknown Joseph and Jesus (these were popular names in the first century). Yet it is possible that some remains found in the tomb belonged to Jesus' clan or to members of the Palestinian Jesus movement.

Other claims mar the advance and importance of archaeological research. Lead scrolls have been announced, and some scholars claim that they are as important as the DSS, but they turned out to be fakes. The "Jesus Scroll" announced in 2000 had far more to do with the date of the millennium than with antiquity. The *Gospel of Judas* was not composed by Judas, and the *Secret Gospel of Mark* should be viewed with caution.

No one today suggests that archaeology is unimportant for Jesus research, but NT experts have often missed the importance of archaeology for Jesus research and the NT. In 1941, Millar Burrows succinctly summarized the significance of archaeology for biblical studies:

> What has been presented here, even though given only in broadest outlines, may suffice to show the service archeology has rendered biblical history by tying it into its framework in world history, connecting it with the rise and fall of nations and their relationships one with another, and orienting it to the outstanding movements and developments in the cultural and social history of mankind. By the aid of archeology the study of the Bible ceases to be, as it were, suspended in the air, and gets its feet upon the ground.[4]

3. For reading reports, many NT experts find helpful Dever and Lance, *Field Excavation*.
4. Millar Burrows, *What Mean These Stones? The Significance of Archeology for Biblical Studies* (New Haven: American Schools of Oriental Research, 1941), 115.

Burrows wrote when many scholars used the Bible as a key in archaeology and most shared a dream that someday scholars would achieve a grand synthesis of the Bible and archaeology.

When he wrote in 1941 Burrows could not have known that before the decade closed, he would be involved in one of the greatest archaeological discoveries that would revolutionize virtually all facets of biblical studies and the perception of Jesus within his culture: the discovery of the famous DSS (= Qumran Scrolls). William F. Albright authenticated the Scrolls, and on April 12, 1948, the news of the discovery swept the world with an excitement not seen since the discovery of Tutankhamen's tomb and still not presently matched.

36.1. Ossuaries (bone boxes) discovered on the Mount of Olives, dating from the first century BC/AD. An ossuary constituted a second phase of burial, after the body had decomposed and only the bones remained.

How has archaeology shaped the study of the historical Jesus and NT studies? In the early 1940s, Burrows made few historical references to Jesus, only mentioning that archaeology helps us ascertain the year of Jesus' birth (8–6 BC) because of papyri records and the evangelists' reports. He concluded that archaeological research provided nothing that illuminates the life of John the Baptizer or Jesus' baptism. That has all changed. He knew about the ossuary that Eleazar Sukenik found in a warehouse, but he dismissed the inscription "Jesus son of Joseph" as indicative only of the popularity of these names in the time of Jesus from Nazareth. Burrows opined that scholars will never find confirmation regarding the facts of Jesus' life or even of his existence. After all, "a wandering preacher who writes no books, erects no buildings, sets up no organized institutions, but leaves to Caesar what is Caesar's, seeking only his Father's kingdom, and who commits his cause to a few poor fishermen . . . leaves no coins bearing his images and superscription."[5]

To be sure, archaeologists should not expect to find a document written by Jesus, or a building he built, even if he may have been a *tektōn* (Greek, "builder"; see Mark 6:3)—though he may have helped build the pre–AD 70 stone terraces and towers that have now been excavated in Nazareth. Burrows would undoubtedly be surprised to learn that archaeologists have uncovered and studied streets on which Jesus probably walked, houses which he may have lived in and frequented, gates and monumental stairs leading to the temple, *mikva'ot* (Jewish ritualistic baths) he probably entered (Siloam and Bethesda [or Bethzatha]), and most important, a synagogue in which he most likely taught.

Since 1946, archaeologists have received or discovered scrolls that Jesus' contemporaries held and considered sacred. These scrolls clarify terms that Jesus used but never defined, and they provide descriptions and symbolic language that make some of his difficult sayings meaningful for the first time or provide the historical context for their full meaning.

Perspective Shifts: From Existentialism to Archaeology and Sociology

Rudolf Bultmann and his school in Germany and the United States were deeply influenced by existentialism and showed virtually no interest in archaeology in Israel-Palestine, though some of his students did, most notably Helmut Koester. The major German NT scholar Joachim Jeremias was devoted to archaeology from 1920 to 1960.

Over the past forty years, scholarly interest has shifted to archaeology and its corollary, the social description of Jesus' world. Interest in the world that shaped thinking in Second Temple Judaism now includes sociological studies that are focused on pilgrimages, charisma, purity, liminality, and barriers, among other things. More important for our present focus is evidence of pre–AD 70 life in ancient Palestine. Vast amounts of evidence indicate a continuity of sacred traditions from preexilic Israel to Second Temple Judaism. Although the influence of Persia, Greece, and Egypt is evident and the influence of Aramaic on Hebrew is evident, more important is the exceptional influence of the Pentateuch and the appearance of texts categorized as "rewritten Bible." That is, the biblical text was the catalyst for new expressions. Deuteronomy, for example, was one of the most formative texts for Qumran and the Palestinian Jesus movement, and it also appeared in a new form. The *Temple Scroll* "re-creates" Deuteronomy by shifting God's third-person discourse to direct revelatory speech ("I say to you . . . "). The book of Isaiah flowed from the eighth-century prophet, was expanded by Second and perhaps Third Isaiah, becoming (most likely) the most influential biblical

5. Burrows, *Stones*, 283.

text for the prophetic community at Qumran and for the prophet from Nazareth and his followers. The moral code remains anchored in the Ten Commandments. The living God known in and through history remains the one and only deity, and reverence for Yahweh causes Jews to elevate the name so that it is ineffable (at Qumran in 1QS we see the tetragrammaton [YHWH] represented by four dots—warning one not to pronounce the name).

In 1968, many specialists in archaeology thought that archaeology was important for OT studies, but they did not have the same opinion for NT studies. Old Testament scholars pointed out that they had over a millennium to study, but NT scholarship had only one century. They had cities, armies, and empires to study; the Jesus movement left no *realia* (no concrete evidence) but made claims that left little physical evidence. It was widely believed that excavating would uncover no evidence of Jesus' followers, since all the symbols that distinguished them appeared only much later, in the fourth century, and one could not distinguish between a bone, ring, coin, or fibula that belonged to a member of the Palestinian Jesus movement from those that belonged to Greeks, Romans, or (other) Palestinian Jews. It was argued that archaeology was virtually unimportant for NT research.

Over the past forty years, thanks to the recovery of architecture and artifacts left by Jews and others when the Romans burned cities and villages in AD 67, 68, 70, 74 (when Masada fell), and 136 (when Bar Kokhba was defeated), a revolution has occurred in the study of Christian origins. Thanks to archaeological discoveries and research, since about 1947 (when the DSS were first discovered in Cave I), and especially 1967 (during excavations in Jerusalem), scholars who are devoted to reconstructing life in pre–AD 70 Palestine are now enriched by the following (selected) archaeological discoveries:

- hair, mirrors, necklaces, and perfume bottles
- leather sandals and wool clothing
- weapons, including helmets, shields, swords, spears, knives, ballista stones, catapult arrowheads, and arrowheads
- mirrors, earrings, rings, bracelets, glass ungentaria, wooden combs, tweezers, and gold pendants
- numismatics (esp. "widow's mites" and Tyrian shekels)
- bronze and iron vessels, rings, and phallic images worn by many
- glass and bronze serpents that are clearly Herodian
- ceramic lamps, inkwells, oil fillers, plates, bowls, and jars used in Judea and Galilee during Jesus' time
- glass spoons, inkwells, oil fillers, plates, bowls, and ungentaria
- gold and silver earrings worn by women in Jerusalem and its environs
- metal plates, spoons, bowls, and wine dippers used during Jesus' time

- marble, ceramic, and bronze statuettes of Aphrodite and Hermes
- stone vessels, plates, tables used by Jews contemporaneous with Jesus
- stone gates, walkways, tunnels, and sewers in Jerusalem
- ornamental plaster in Yodafat, Migdal, Jerusalem, Masada, and elsewhere
- liquefied bones (human?) on columns from Herod's royal stoa in the Jerusalem temple
- frescoed walls in many mansions in Jerusalem
- a palace south of the temple, perhaps belonging to the rulers of Adiabene, and the massive stones of the temple's retaining walls built by Herod's builders (Ritmeyer and Ritmeyer, *Secrets*; Ben-Dov, *Shadow*; Mazar, *Complete Guide*)
- a boat, anchors, net sinkers, and fishhooks used in Galilee of Jesus' time (Wachsmann, *Ancient Boat*)

36.2. This first-century AD boat was discovered in the northern Sea of Galilee and is now located at the Ginosar kibbutz.

- anchors and docks in the Dead Sea
- ossuaries dating from Jesus' period
- baths, bathtubs, cisterns, and *mikva'ot*
- scrolls found in many places on the western and eastern sides of the Dead Sea
- a lighthouse on the northwestern edge of the Dead Sea
- many cities built by Herod the Great in Judea and Samaria
- theaters, especially in Jerusalem and Sepphoris
- aqueducts, valleys, rivers, hills, mountains, and a lake familiar to Jesus

- villages, like Yodefat and Gamla, that lie in ruins since the Roman conquest of AD 67
- the amphitheaters, gates, and monumental buildings in pre–AD 70 Tiberias
- Herodium and Herod's tomb
- Herod's desert retreats and palaces
- Caesarea Maritima and architectures seen by Peter and Paul as they went to Rome
- the site of the monumental Augusteum on "the way" to Caesarea Philippi
- a synagogue in which Jesus sat and taught, according to the Gospels
- inscriptions from ordinary people on shards, ossuaries, and monuments
- tombs from Jesus' time in Galilee and Judea (some with rolling stones) (see Hachlili, *Funerary Customs*)

Two final notes to this list must suffice. First, combs were not used primarily, or only, for cosmetic purposes (as today); they were delousing instruments. Today many wooden combs from the first century are known, and they usually contain lice eggs. Second, especially significant are finds in Yodefat and Gamla. The material remains of these two villages are similar. Although Yodefat and Gamla are not mentioned in the Gospels, they lie abandoned since the Romans destroyed them in AD 67 and today provide "an archaeological snapshot of Jewish life at the time of Jesus" (Crossan and Reed, *Excavating Jesus*, 5).

The Stimulus of the Qumran Scrolls

We can summarize only briefly how Qumran research changed our understanding of Second Temple Judaism and early Christianity. Most important, the study of the DSS and the literature we know as the OT Apocrypha and Pseudepigrapha has proved that, during the Second Temple period, there were not simply four Jewish groups (namely, Pharisees, Sadducees, Essenes, and Zealots). Instead, over twenty groups and subgroups defined Second Temple Judaism, including the Baptist groups, the Enoch groups, the Samaritans, the Palestinian Jesus movement, and others.

36.3. Rare glass from the early Roman period.

James H. Charlesworth

Study of the DSS has revealed the following important information:

- manuscripts, architecture, and *realia* that help expose a community living in "the wilderness" and collecting scrolls from many Jewish groups
- the fundamental importance of "pseudepigrapha," and the pre-Christian origins of many works, especially *Jubilees*, the *Books of Enoch* (all of them), and most likely the earliest strata of the *Testaments of the Twelve Patriarchs*
- the earliest evidence of what becomes Mishnaic Hebrew (esp. 4QMMT) and of halakot (4QMMT and esp. 11QT[a])
- proof that pre–AD 70 Jews were fascinated by and believed in angels, God the King, kingdom, the Messiah, the Son of God, resurrection, and technical terms used by Jesus but never defined by him
- evidence that clarifies some of Jesus' most difficult sayings, especially in the *Damascus Document*
- evidence that John the Baptizer may have been connected in some ways to Qumran and may have left that community (e.g., Charlesworth, *Bible and DSS*, vol. 3)
- a better comprehension of Jesus' deeds, especially the exorcisms
- criteria for discerning the Messiah (4Q521)
- background for Paul's thought, especially "the works of the Law" (see Charlesworth, *Bible and DSS*, vol. 3)
- the source of some of the dualism in the Gospel of John (see Charlesworth, *John and DSS*, 76–106)

Archaeological explorations and excavations near Qumran have continued. Some scholars imagine they have found the *mĕqôm yād* ("latrine") in the higher areas to the west of Khirbet Qumran. Others have discovered subterranean caves and carved areas in the marlstone terrace to the north of Khirbet Qumran; there some Qumranites dwelt in the wilderness but within man-made caves in which the space was cooled as water evaporated. Excavations on the plateau have disclosed further evidence of an earthquake (probably from 31 BC) and jars. The area just south of locus 77 was unearthed; it is a cobbled area in which figs were found. One team has recovered near the eastern wall an ostracon that clearly refers to the region of Jericho and may contain the word *yaḥad* (perhaps referring to the covenant Community at Qumran). Another has excavated areas of Ein Feshka and discovered extensive ruins that seem to be related to the production of balsam and not scrolls.

Since the discovery of the DSS and excavations in the surrounding region, most scholars readily admit that archaeology is now on center stage in virtually every aspect of biblical research. However, biblical scholars should take into consideration two caveats. (1) For those devoted to Jesus research and NT studies, the first century is trifurcated: 4 BC to AD 30 (the approximate time of Jesus' death), 30 to

36.4. Authentic jar in which the first Dead Sea Scrolls were discovered in 1947, now housed in a shop in Bethlehem.

70 (the time of the destruction of the temple), and 70 to 132. These are important distinctions; for example, if we discover a synagogue at Khirbet Qana with plaster that dates from AD 50 to 150, Jesus could not have been within the building if it dates, at the earliest, to twenty years after he left Galilee. (2) Focus should be directed to the question: Was the object found by an archaeologist *in situ* (its undisturbed setting), or did it fall into this place? What is found *in situ* sometimes is misleading for historical reconstructions, due to disturbances caused by earthquakes, ancient building projects, the unevenness of the land, and the slow process of gravity.

Regionalism and the Historical Jesus

The most important insight unknown to most NT specialists is the vast amount of archaeological evidence that many Judeans (= Jews) migrated northward to Galilee after the Hasmonean conquests of Galilee by John Hyrcanus (135/34–104 BC), Aristobulus I (104–103 BC), and Alexander Jannaeus (103–76 BC). In many ways, Josephus's reports are reliable, especially for Yodefat and Gamla and the conquests of Galilee by Judean armies (= Hasmoneans). This new perspective is illustrated and documented by the excavations in Migdal (see also Leibner, *Settlement and History*).

The pre–AD 70 buildings on Mount Gerizim have been excavated and studied, but the four hundred Aramaic, Hebrew, and Samaritan inscriptions and thirteen thousand coins are not yet published. The place along the Jordan where John the Baptist probably worked (at least on some occasions) and which was venerated by early Christians has been located and exposed.[6] The Jordan Rift Valley served as a regional barrier, but culture and life flowed across it. The Samaritans defined a special culture that was protected by the sheer mountain ranges separating it from Judea and lower Galilee.

Jerusalem: A Special Treasure

Archaeological excavations in Jerusalem, especially in 1967, have revealed some surprising and challenging evidence of life before AD 70. First, Jerusalem was a

6. See Michele Piccirillo, "The Sanctuaries of the Baptism on the East Bank of the Jordan River," in Charlesworth, *Jesus and Archaeology*, 433–43.

36.5. The trumpeting stone. This is a replica of a stone discovered next to the southwest corner of the temple mount. The Hebrew reads "to the place of trumpeting to," likely a reference to the place where a trumpeter stood to announce the beginning and close of the Sabbath.

major metropolitan city before 70. Second, foreign influences are evident, notably by the rulers of Adiabene who converted to Judaism, moved to Jerusalem, and built palaces within Jerusalem, as well as a monumental series of tombs north of the city walls. Third, the city boasted some of the most impressive houses in the Roman world, rivaling those of the emperors in Pompeii and Herculaneum. Fourth, the whole area was sealed for us to explore when Jerusalem and its environs were buried beneath ashes and collapsed structures.

Archaeologists have uncovered the foundation of the ancient walls of Jerusalem and have been able to date many of them. Some foundations are Hellenistic or Hasmonean; others were built by Herod Agrippa I (AD 37–44). Jerusalem's walls today date from the sixteenth century, encompass a city much smaller than the one Hillel and Jesus knew, and in places have much earlier foundations. Recent finds include the Hellenistic or Hasmonean wall, found recently in the northern sides of the Hinnom Valley; the conflagration of seventy buried houses and palaces of the procurator and high priests; the "Burnt House" belonging to the Kathros family of priests; and the bones of a woman recovered near a door along with stone vessels. Jewish purity laws are brought to mind by the numerous *mikva'ot* and stone vessels.

Central in debates about the reasons for Jesus' arrest are his actions in the temple, which also included parables uttered in the temple, perhaps before a high priest, and polemics against the Sadducees (e.g., Luke 20:9–19). Archaeology supplies data for a more informative assessment of that event and its interpretation by the evangelists. First, Jesus' explosive actions would be in the area of the temple mount that was extended southward by Herod the Great. Thus, some Jews did not consider the area in the southern section of the temple mount to be "sacred area."

Lee Martin McDonald

36.6. Ruins of a first-century AD street that ran alongside the Western Wall of the Jerusalem temple.

Second, during Jesus' last year, the *ḥanut* ("meat market," or place for the large animals for sacrificing; cf. Josephus, *Ant*. 15.393, 411–17) may have been moved from Gethsemane to the lower southeast sections of the temple mount. In the late first century BC, Rabbi Baba ben Buta is reported to have brought three thousand large animals for sacrifice and placed them on "the temple hill" (*t. Ḥag.* 2.11; *y. Beṣah* 2.4). Perhaps the *ḥanut* was moved within the temple precincts just before AD 30. That is the year Jesus exploded with rage within the temple area because he thought the temple was being polluted. Did Jesus observe large animals, perhaps oxen, which he had never seen before within the sacred space? Had the priests tethered these large beasts previously outside the temple (cf. *m. Pesaḥ.* 7.11)? Large animals would have polluted the temple area. Jesus would have been offended by this desecration, even if it were within Herod's extension to the temple. Only the Fourth Evangelist's report attests to this alteration, recounting a narrative that presupposes the presence of large animals and ropes for tying them within the temple area:

> In the temple he [Jesus] found those who were selling oxen, sheep, and pigeons, as well as the money changers at their business. And making a whip of cords, he drove them all, with the sheep and oxen, out of the temple. And he poured out the coins of the money changers and overturned their tables. (John 2:14–15)[7]

7. All translations in this chapter are my own, unless otherwise noted.

When he attempted to "cleanse" the temple, Jesus would have been outraged if he had known that the *ḥanut* had been moved within what he judged to be holy space. Recently a passageway leading from the so-called Solomon's Stables to the southeastern Huldah Gates, and suitable for such large animals, seems to have been located.

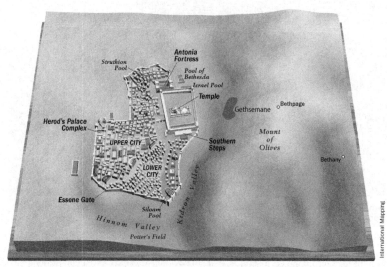

36.7. Jerusalem at the time of Jesus.

Third, a weight for a scale belonging to "Bar Kathros" was recovered (January 1970) in the upper city of Jerusalem, in an elegant house named the "Burnt House." The inscription on the weight was in the square Aramaic script (with brackets indicating doubtful letters): "of Bar Kathros" (*[d]b[r] [q]trs*). One is reminded of the oligarchic oppression of this priestly family, mentioned in the Talmud:

> Woe is me because of the House of Kathros,
>   woe is me because of their pens.
> Woe is me because of the House of Ishmael, son of Phiabi,
>   woe is me because of their fists.
> For they are the High Priests, and their sons are treasurers,
>   and their sons-in-law are trustees, and their servants beat the people
>   with staves.
>
> <div align="right">(<i>b. Pesaḥ.</i> 57.1; cf. <i>t. Menaḥ.</i> 13.21–22)</div>

We also should contemplate a growing gap between priests and laity before AD 70. A. M. Berlin states that the material culture indicates "a marked fissure between

Jerusalem elites, including some priests, and the majority of Jews living in the Judean countryside, Galilee, and Gaulanitis."[8]

Fourth, we now have thousands of coins used in the temple, including the so-called widow's mite and the silver coin for paying the temple tax. Since the latter has the image of a heathen god (Melkart of Tyre), it breaks the first commandment. Maybe Jesus was disturbed by more than one offense within the temple. Reasons (perhaps the most important) for Jesus' arrest are now less imaginative and more reinforced; and the significance of the temple for the life of Jews receives pre–AD 70 palpable data known to those who considered the temple to be the "House of God," or just "the House."

Thanks to vast archaeological research to the west and south, the temple mount rises before us today. The Herodian ashlars are stunningly well cut. Among the many discoveries related to or contiguous to the temple are the following (all antedate AD 70): remains of the balustrade to warn non-Jews not to continue further than the Court of the Gentiles; massive stones far heavier than those in the pyramids (one weighs about 470 tons); shops, streets, sewers, numerous *mikva'ot*, monumental steps, and gates leading up and into the temple.

The Pool of Bethesda (variant: Bethzatha) and the Pool of Siloam have been recovered. The author of John's Gospel knows a vast amount about pre–AD 70 Jerusalem, including the place of houses and these pools. Each antedates AD 70 and is a *mikveh* that receives "living water," that is, water that has not been drawn by humans (*m. Miqwa'ot*; *Sipra*, Shemini, parasah 9). The remains of Herod's palace and perhaps Caiaphas's house have been excavated or recovered. Although the present-day Via Dolorosa is sacred because of almost a thousand years of reverence, Jesus most likely took another route to Golgotha. The elevated stone within the Church of the Holy Sepulchre (or nearby) may well be the place where Jesus was crucified, though J. E. Taylor argues that the site of Golgotha (Mark 15:22; Matt. 27:33; Luke 23:33; John 19:17) may be south of the present traditional site; it would be on the junction of two roads.[9] The traditional site, however, is the only traditional site, and it was clearly visible for the public to see, on a road, and outside Jerusalem walls in AD 30 but not in AD 44. Quintilian (*Declamationes* 274) notes that crucifixions were organized on busy highways so the maximum number of people would see and fear Roman power (the road to Jaffa and elsewhere, especially Caesarea Maritima, ran south and beneath Golgotha). Shimon Gibson reports on executions just outside the Jaffa Gate in Jerusalem and notes that according to Tacitus (*Ann.* 2.32.2) all crucifixions must be outside a city.[10] Interestingly, the author of Hebrews claims that Jesus was crucified (suffered) outside the city (13:12).

Numerous Jewish tombs are evident within the Church of the Holy Sepulchre, and an ancient quarry is exposed in the lower levels of the church. The remains

8. A. M. Berlin, "Jewish Life before the Revolt: The Archaeological Evidence," *JSJ* 36 (2005): 417–70.

9. J. E. Taylor, *Christians and Holy Places* (Oxford: Clarendon, 1993).

10. Shimon Gibson, *The Final Days of Jesus: The Archaeological Evidence* (Oxford: Lion, 2009), 116–17.

of a temple to Aphrodite have been found east of the church, along with a boat and inscription meaning "We have come, O Lord" inscribed below Constantine's church and some of the fourth-century pillars that are visible behind others (see Charlesworth, "Passion of Jesus").

36.8. View of the top of the Church of the Holy Sepulchre in Jerusalem, built over the hill where many believe that Jesus was crucified. Construction was begun in the fourth century AD by the mother of Constantine.

One person who was crucified about the time of Jesus' death has been identified. His bones were found with the bones of a child in an ossuary unearthed at Giv'at HaMivtar, now within northern Jerusalem. His name was Jehohanan, and he was between twenty-four and twenty-eight years old. An iron nail and parts of the cross (Latin *stipes*) are still attached to his right heel bone (*calcaneum*). Outside the present sixteenth-century walls are numerous tombs. Some are monumental (probably robbed by Romans to build the circumvallation wall), and some have rolling stones before the door precisely as reported by the evangelists regarding Jesus' tomb (or the tomb of Joseph of Arimathea). Hundreds of ossuaries (boxes for bones that were disarticulated) have been recovered; in almost all cases they date from Herod to the destruction of the temple, when the industry necessary for their creation ceased. Names on them—like "Jesus the son of Joseph," "Mary," and "Jude"—and incised images that look like crosses do not indicate, let alone prove, that the remains are related to the Palestinian Jesus movement.[11] Most likely

11. The "cross" is one of the oldest symbols. It can denote the dot, the circle, and the square—and also the cross. Images that look like crosses antedate Christianity by at least one thousand years. See J. F. Strange's sane advice in "Archaeological Evidence of Jewish Believers?," in *Jewish Believers in Jesus* (ed. O. Skarsaune and R. Hvalvik; Peabody, MA: Hendrickson, 2007), 710–41.

the tombs or ossuaries of Herod, Caiaphas, Annas, and (conceivably) Simon of Cyrene have been recovered. Debates rage regarding the Talpiot Tomb and its connection, if any, with Jesus from Nazareth.

Major Archaeological Discoveries for Jesus Research

The following are the most sensational of many amazing archaeological discoveries for Jesus research and NT study.

Migdal

What was previously claimed to be a synagogue in Migdal is a monumental fountain in the Hellenistic style built about 100 BC. Water still flows into it from the north. In 2011, Stefano De Luca unearthed a latrine to the east of the Hellenistic fountain with toilet seats and a mosaic floor. It postdates 63 BC, when Pompey brought Roman control to the region. The tower, or *migdāl*, is early; the pottery in the drain is Hasmonean.

One finds there the remains of elegant glass and a harbor. The latter is plastered in color and reminds one of Caesarea Maritima's harbor. The area for docking the large ships has been found. It has stones with circular holes for tying small flat-bottom boats. Migdal was an ideal site for ships and boats. The current went counterclockwise from Migdal to Capernaum, Hippus, and Tiberias, then finally back to Migdal.

A massive road was uncovered in the western part of Migdal; could this be the famous *via maris*, the main artery from Egypt to the East? If Mary Magdalene's home was near the spring, as early pilgrims reported, and if a church was built above it, perhaps someday we will find what they claimed was Mary's house. This optimism may be diminished by the discovery of many springs at Migdal and the massive building projects there; they destroy all ancient evidence.

The Israel Antiquities Authority sponsored an excavation north of the Franciscan property there, in order to prepare for the building of a hotel on Migdal beach. In the mud, archaeologists have recovered remains of an elegant synagogue with mosaics (never finished), plastered and frescoed walls and pillars, and stone benches for the worshipers. Coins *in situ* date from about 100 BC to AD 66, the time of the First Jewish Revolt. Migdal was burned by Titus's troops. There is reason to imagine that the synagogue was destroyed during that famous battle at Migdal. Most likely, the burning of the Migdal synagogue was in Josephus's mind when he referred to "sanctuaries [Greek *hiera*] set on fire" by the Roman soldiers (*J.W.* 7.144).

A stone was discovered in the main hall of the synagogue. Carved in the stone is a unique menorah; it has a square pedestal with a triangular base and is flanked by two amphora and columns. On the top of the stone one can see carvings; perhaps they are trees and a rosetta. We now have abundant proof that the Jews in lower Galilee were fond of the Jerusalem temple. Galilean Jews shared a culture with Judeans. The menorah probably mirrors the famous one in the temple, and the columns may represent the temple (as in the Bar Kokhba coins).[12]

Now, archaeologists have found a synagogue in which, according to the Gospels, Jesus could have worshiped and taught. Each of them reports that Jesus taught in the synagogues in Galilee. Migdal is only one hour by boat from Capernaum, Jesus' headquarters for his itineraries. We may ask: Where did Jesus meet Mary of Migdal, and why was she named after that city (Mary Magdalene)?

Bethlehem

It is no longer wise to jettison all references to Jesus' connection with Bethlehem as editorial additions created by the desire to prove Jesus' Davidic connection. First, it is likely that we now have archaeological evidence that descendants of David were known in Second Temple Judaism; an inscription on an ossuary found in 1971 in Jerusalem denotes that the bones inside belong to "the House of David." If there were descendants of David active in Jerusalem, then the Mishnaic report that they periodically brought "the wood offering" in the temple can preserve reliable history (*m. Taʿan.* 4.5). Second, if many Jews living in lower Galilee in the first half of the first century AD were descendants of Jews who migrated from Judea, then maybe Jesus had relatives (such as Elizabeth and John) in Judea. Some noncanonical traditions give Joseph's birthplace as Bethlehem; he allegedly fled to Galilee due to poverty. Unearthed only recently are at least two pre–AD 70 houses in Nazareth. Jesus, who spent over twenty years there, most likely had been in these houses. We need to reconsider all the historical data that may be preserved in the traditions regarding Jesus' birth.

Capernaum

This small Jewish fishing village is of undetermined size and population; perhaps one thousand to two thousand people lived there in Jesus' time. The excavators have found no *mikvaʾot* at Capernaum; perhaps immersing in the "living waters" of the Kinneret (Sea of Galilee) would suffice. It was filled with "living water" pouring from the northern mountains. The size of homes and bedrooms are now clarified. It is now easier to imagine all sleeping in the same bed, and sometimes awakening to find a loved one dead at one's side. The white marble synagogue is late fifth century, at the earliest, since a coin from the late fifth century was found *in situ* under the basalt foundation. In the center of the foundation are remains

12. A correct perspective on Galilee is now provided by five main publications: Aviam, *Jews, Pagans and Christians*; Chancey, *Myth*; M. H. Jensen, *Herod Antipas in Galilee* (2nd ed.; WUNT 2/215; Tübingen: Mohr Siebeck, 2010); Leibner, *Settlement and History*; Zangenberg, Attridge, and Martin, *Ancient Galilee*.

36.9. Ruins of first-century AD residences next to a synagogue at Capernaum.

of another building. Could it be a foundation from the synagogue in which Jesus is reported to have taught?

Tiberias

Water was always a problem at Tiberias, even though the Kinneret was nearby. The first-century massive gates at Tiberias are probably to be associated with Antipas's building of Tiberias, which began between AD 18 and 20. Tiberias had no walls; to add them would be to threaten Rome. The walls appeared in the fifth century. Antipas knew not to upset Rome; massive gates without walls also make a pro-Roman political statement. Jesus may well have walked through these gates as he went southward to Jerusalem for the annual festivals.

Bethsaida

Bethsaida is mentioned by Pliny the Elder (*Nat. His.* 5.71), Josephus (*Ant.* 18.4–6, 28, 106–8; *J.W.* 2.168; 3.57, 515; *Life* 398–406), Ptolemy (*Geogr.* 5.16.4), and the NT Gospels. Digging at et-Tell, archaeologists have discovered evidence from which they claim the site is Bethsaida. Is this the home of Philip, Andrew, and Peter, and perhaps James and John, the sons of Zebedee? Perhaps Jesus stayed sometimes at Bethsaida. The evangelists report that Jesus visited Bethsaida, and this site (Bethsaida-Julias) existed before and after the First Jewish War (AD 66–74). No evidence of destruction is mentioned by Josephus or found *in situ*.

36.10. Ruins of a church dating from the fourth to the sixth centuries at Bethsaida, home of the apostles Peter, Philip, and Andrew (John 1:44; 12:21–22).

Coins of Philip, the ruler of this area from 4 BC to AD 34, have been recovered. In one locus a lance, a dagger, and a gold coin of Antoninus Pius were found dating from AD 138.

The Likely Site of Peter's Confession

From earliest times until now, most commentators have located Peter's confession at Caesarea Philippi (Banias). Mark reports that Jesus asked his disciples the question about his identity while "on the way" to Caesarea Philippi (Mark 8:27). Some NT exegetes have ignored the prepositional phrase and placed Peter's famous confession near the altars of Pan, where water cascades from the mountains to the north. They incorrectly assumed the Augusteum was there by the waters flowing out of the large cave.

If we take Mark's text seriously, though, we note that there must be a road heading from the Kinneret to Caesarea Philippi and some monument "on the way" there. In fact, an ancient road, a colonnaded way (which is Byzantine but seems to presuppose an earlier passage), and temples—one from Jesus' time—have been found at Horbat Omrit. There are three temples, which may be hypothesized as follows:

1. The Shrine (50–40 BC). It is conceivable that something antedated the Shrine.
2. Herod's Augusteum (ca. 20 BC)
3. Hadrian's temple (early second century AD)

36.11. Niches in the hillside at Caesarea Philippi that honored the Greek god Pan, the son of Hermes and native to Arcadia. Pan's recognition as a god spread to Athens, and eventually he was celebrated by the Greeks who lived in this region from the third century BC. The modern name of this place is Banias, a variation of the ancient name of Pan(ias), before it became Caesarea Philippi.

Each subsequent temple is larger than the previous one. The early structures have colored frescoes. The marble is of exceedingly fine quality. An altar area is constructed separately and to the east. Many small bird bones found *in situ* prove that this was a place for sacrificing.

Most likely, Horbat Omrit is the site of the Augusteum built by Herod the Great. Augustus was hailed as the son of Julius Caesar, and hence "the [by then deceased] son of god"; although Augustus forbade his cult within Rome, he permitted it in the provinces. Thanks to archaeology, we know that governors built temples to emperors when they were alive; recall the temple at Caesarea Maritima built by Pontius Pilate and dedicated to Tiberius with the inscription "[Dis Augusti]s Tiberieum / [Po]ntius Pilatus / [Praef]ectus Iuda[ea]e / [fecit d]e[dicavit]" ("To the honorable gods [this] Tiberium Pontius Pilate, Prefect of Judea, had dedicated"). The Augusteum is an indication of how Herod poured a heavy dose of Roman influence on Israel-Palestine. Herod met Augustus (Octavian) at Rhodes shortly after he defeated Antony (Herod's former Roman leader). Again, in 20 BC, Herod met Augustus in Syria (not far from Horbat Omrit) and was rewarded with more territory; most likely about that time Herod built the Augusteum to honor the emperor (and Herod may have imagined it possible to claim that Augustus was "the son of god"). When he toured the Holy Land in 14 BC, did Marcus

36.12. Ruins of a portion of Herod Philip's and Herod Agrippa II's palace at Caesarea Philippi, first century AD.

Vipsanius Agrippa—who was close to Augustus (and sometimes second only to the emperor)—hear about or even see the Augusteum and report it to Augustus?

"The Son of God" may well be Mark's favorite title for Jesus; would it not make more historical sense for Jesus to ask about his identity as he neared a tall marble temple, blazing in the bright sun, dedicated to "the son of god"? Either Mark preserved reliable historical tradition, or his rhetoric is informed with precise details from the upper Galilee. Reflections turn to Paul's report of his "conversion" experience; where did he have his christophany? Horbat Omrit is on the way to Damascus. Did Paul experience something life changing where he knew Jesus had asked his question?

Other Sites

Samaria. The cities in Judea were Jerusalem and Jericho (Caesarea Maritima was on the coast); Jesus visited both of them. The city in Samaria is Sebaste; Jesus visited it. The major city on the Sharon was Caesarea Maritima; there is no evidence Jesus visited that area or city. It is precarious, then, to seek reasons why Jesus never visited the cities in Galilee, namely, Ptolemais, Scythopolis, Hippos, Sepphoris, and Tiberias. The evangelists never report that Jesus was in the wealthy estate Ramat Ha-Nadiv (which includes Horvat Eleq, Ein Tzur, and Horvat Aqav), a most appealing place to relax and enjoy life. It is conceivable that Antipas lived there before he moved to Galilee.

Ancient Samaritan inscriptions and mosaics prove that the Samaritans—who have for millennia claimed to be "Israelites" (Greek *Israēlitai*)—have for millennia called God "Abba," frequently referred to "One God," and revered images of the menorah (a seven-branched candelabra), jugs, chalices, the pomegranate, sheaves of wheat or barley, a grapevine, trees or branches (palm fronds), the showbread table, and two trumpets (Num. 10:1–10). These symbols derive from the Pentateuch and the tabernacle images. Archaeological research on pre–AD 70 copies of the Pentateuch and the Samaritan versions of it (as well as readings suggesting that the Samaritan Pentateuch sometimes preserves superior readings) proves not only how much the Samaritans consider it God's Word but also how close the Samaritan Pentateuch is to the Pentateuch used by Jews and Christians today. Both the latter (the MT) and the Samaritan Pentateuch are clearly edited traditions.

Archaeological studies indicate that Samaritans rejected many Jewish or Judean symbols, believing that only Mount Gerizim was the traditional and official place to sacrifice. The most important of the rejected symbols were connected to the Jerusalem temple, such as the lulav, the ethrog, the shofar, and the *hanukeia* (the nine-branched candelabra used to celebrate the Hanukkah of the Hasmoneans, who attacked the Samaritans).

Finally, Samaritans and Jews were believed to be against icons, yet bird images appear on the stucco from the "House of Caiaphas." All Jews, especially the priests on Mount Gerizim and on Mount Zion, sought to obey the purity laws specified in the Torah; but in Judea and elsewhere (e.g., the groups behind the *Temple Scroll*) purity became an obsession and could be dangerous anthropologically and theologically.

Synagogues. Archaeological advancements often make major studies obsolete; for example, how and in what ways does archaeology help in assessing the evangelists' report that Jesus taught in the synagogues throughout Galilee, as in Mark 1:39? What evidence exists that there were synagogues—not buildings but, as the term "synagogue" implies (Greek *synagōgē* means "a gathering together"), public gathering places for Jews?

In conclusion, I will mention only three more sites. First, Khirbet Beza is located on the western ridge of Galilee. From this site one can see Ptolemais (Acco). The village appeared in the first century AD and disappeared in the second. The large olive installations were probably used until the third century, since third-century pottery was found *in situ*. The early inhabitants were Jews, since broken stone vessels were found on the surface. Second, Tel Rekesh is far to the east in lower Galilee, and southeast of Mount Tabor. It appeared in the first century AD and ceased to exist in the second. Was it a village or a wealthy estate that was perhaps given to a Roman centurion after the First Jewish Revolt? Third, a cave has been found west of Jerusalem's walls. It seems to have some connection with devotees of John the Baptist, and Gibson is convinced that John the Baptizer immersed Jews in the cave.[13]

---

13. Shimon Gibson, *The Cave of John the Baptist* (London: Century, 2004).

36.13. Ruins of the Herodium fortress/palace, east of Bethlehem, which was built by Herod the Great. The remains of a synagogue can be seen in the center of the photo.

Hard evidence of first-century buildings that are most likely synagogues includes the following: (beginning in the south) Masada, Herodium, Jerusalem [Theodotus inscription], Qiryat Sefer, Modiin, Jericho, Capernaum [?], Khirbet Qana, Gamla, and Migdal.[14] Jesus most likely knew only one of these synagogues. The synagogues at Masada and Herodium date thirty-six years after Jesus' death and should not be conceptualized as typical synagogues of the early first century (they were probably built by Zealots). The synagogue mentioned by Theodotus has not been located, and the inscription was not found *in situ*. There is no text that reports Jesus was at Qiryat Sefer or Modiin; and he passed through Jericho, so one can only assume that he visited the Jericho synagogue. The Capernaum synagogue of Jesus' time has not been recovered; it may have been demolished when a later one was constructed. The synagogue at Kefar Qana may date from AD 50–150, if the dating of the plaster is reliable. Gamla is in the Golan, contiguous to and east of Galilee. Only the synagogue at Migdal meets all the criteria for Jesus to have taught there: it is within his main area of work, and it was operative during the 20s, when he preached to crowds and in synagogues.

It is likely that synagogues were buildings in first-century Galilee for four main reasons: (1) The pre–AD 70 Theodotus inscription proves a synagogue (a building with rooms for "guests") existed in Jerusalem long before AD 70; the inscription refers to building a synagogue. (2) Inscriptions refer to building a "prayer hall" in Alexandria (37 BC) and repairing or refurbishing a synagogue at Acmonia

14. See, e.g., D. D. Binder, *Into the Temple Courts: The Place of the Synagogue in the Second Temple Period* (SBLDS 169; Atlanta: Society of Biblical Literature, 1999); L. I. Levine, *NEAEHL* 4:1421–24.

in Phyrgia (first century AD), Berenice (AD 55), and Olbia (late second century AD); these inscriptions demand a building and not simply a public place for gathering. (3) If a small village like Qiryat Sefer (northwest of Jerusalem) had a synagogue before Jesus' time, so did other villages. (4) The numerous pre–AD 70 references to a Jewish prayer hall (*proseuchē*)[15] indicate a building for praying, that is, a synagogue. This is also supported by the discovery of a synagogue in lower Galilee at Migdal.

There is certainty now that the building in Migdal is a synagogue, and it clearly antedates not only 67 but also the first century AD. It is an elaborate edifice, if rather small, and it may have had a scriptorium or place for depositing sacred scrolls to its west. The newly uncovered synagogue at Migdal ceased to exist after AD 67, when Titus burned Migdal. Archaeologists now wisely suggest that Jesus most likely taught in that synagogue.

Although there is certain evidence of buildings that are synagogues in Israel-Palestine during Jesus' time, it is unlikely that all were oriented toward Jerusalem, and it is not yet clear what functions they served. Were synagogues buildings used for social and legal functions, as well as for reading and learning, but not for liturgy and worship? It is certain that rich diversity is obvious before AD 70 (Levine, *Ancient Synagogue*, 297); it is best not to distinguish between reading Torah and liturgy or to force one answer on all issues. If worship means sacrifice, festivals, and priestly services, then worship for Jews in Judea and Galilee was only in Jerusalem (except for Samaritans and Qumranites). Before AD 70, the synagogue apparently was a house for reading the Pentateuch and Prophets and for learning. The reading served a didactic function, rather than a liturgical one.

Summary and Conclusion

We have summarized some of the most important advances in the field of archaeology, with a focus on pre–AD 70 Judea, Samaria, and Galilee. Virtually all aspects of NT research are impacted by archaeological advancements and insights, including exegesis, rhetorical criticism, and hermeneutics, and new perceptions and paradigms are beginning to appear. Archaeological research has produced amazing and fundamental data. For the first time in biblical research, we have abundant, tangible evidence of life two thousand years ago in Israel-Palestine.

It is imperative to use "cognitive archaeology," that is, to be informed by the branch of archaeology that seeks to discern the ancient mind and the development of human cognition. As is clear, the ancient human mind comes slowly to our perceptions with each turn of the trowel. In Capernaum, for example, all in a family slept in the same bed. Such experiences (and the loss of intimacy during

---

15. A *sabbateion* may also refer to a synagogue; see Josephus, *Ant.* 16.164, and the inscription found on Thyatira.

marital sex) shaped the cognitive mind of those who lived (and slept in the same bed) during the time of Hillel and Jesus.

Let me reiterate three important and recent archaeological advances for Jesus research and NT studies. First, excavations of towns and cities in Galilee indicate that most lay abandoned since the Assyrian conquest or were founded sometime around 100 BC following the Hasmonean conquests. Second, it is conceivable that Peter's confession should be located at Horbat Omrit. Third, a synagogue in which Jesus could have, and probably did, preach has been unearthed in northern Migdal; hence, the evangelists correctly refer to synagogues as buildings.

Six observations indicate that archaeology is fundamental to Jesus research and NT studies. First, archaeological research provides scrolls and papyri that constitute the primary texts from which all biblical translations and interpretations derive and are improved. That is, the printed texts that all biblical scholars use today throughout the world are improved by the discovery of early biblical manuscripts dating from the earliest manuscripts in the Qumran library to early Christian papyri and uncials. The earliest "biblical" texts would be inscriptions found on preexilic silver scrolls from Ketef Hinnom, which preserve the Aaronic Prayer. The earliest manuscript of a book in the NT is Papyrus 52 (Rylands Gr. P. 457), dating from 100–125, though this has been challenged.

Second, the primary data for research into Second Temple Judaism and Christian origins—and especially the NT—is no longer limited to texts. All interested in biblical research know that texts must have contexts to be meaningful. The contexts for understanding documents are sometimes surprisingly clarified by archaeological discoveries and research. Although some of NT papyri date from four hundred years or more after Jesus' death, some archaeological evidence and images are contemporaneous with Jesus.

Third, Jewish and Christian beliefs are grounded not in ideas but in real events in human history; archaeology supplies an avenue to many of those events. For instance, archaeological discoveries shed light on Jesus' passion (e.g., Pilate's name; Caiaphas's house; Antipas's palace; remains of a crucified man from Jesus' time; the ossuaries of Caiaphas, Annas, and Simon from Cyrene; the location of Golgotha; and the vast evidence of Jewish tombs like Jesus' tomb according to the evangelists' description). Jesus chose to center his ministry within a small triangle of villages on the northwest of the Kinneret (the Sea of Galilee); these villages have been located, and ancient ruins can be seen in Chorazin, Bethsaida, and Capernaum, although the ruins at Chorazin postdate the Bar Kokhba rebellion. Material culture (here and elsewhere in Galilee and rural Judea) seems to be a code for religious unity and identity.

Fourth, Jewish thought, especially in Jesus' parables, tends to be pictorial. A study of topography (including fauna and flora) and archaeology often supplies what was imagined by ancient listeners. Today one can see, as in the first century, an agrarian industry of grain, olives, and grapes. Neither in the first century nor now is Galilee exclusively agricultural. Pottery was made at Kefar Hananya and

Shikhin, Yodefat had an advanced weaving industry, and Migdal was a center for exporting pickled fish.

Fifth, a scientific discipline can be judged valuable, even fundamental, by the new questions it fosters; thus archaeology is enriching NT research and the study of Second Temple Judaism. Creative reconstructions of Hillel's and Jesus' time are now shaped by such fresh questions as these: Why did Jesus choose to center his ministry in Capernaum, Bethsaida, and Chorazin? These villages may be economically similar to the cities, but are they culturally and ideologically distinct from Sepphoris and Tiberias? Jesus cursed his three chosen villages:

> Woe to you, Chorazin! Woe to you, Bethsaida! If the mighty works that happened in you had happened in Tyre and Sidon, long ago in sackcloth and ashes they would have repented. . . . And you, Capernaum: Will you be heavenly exalted? Unto Hades you will be cast down. For if the mighty words that happened in you had happened in Sodom, it would have remained until today. (Matt. 11:21–23; cf. Luke 10:12–15)

The Semitic flavor and the pre-Matthean and pre-Lukan (Q?) date of these curses are obvious; can archaeology help us obtain better answers for Jesus' curses?

Other questions are even more recent: Where did Jesus meet Mary of Migdal? Did Jesus shun some cities because they were aligned with the Herodian dynasty and perhaps too compromising with Greek culture? How and in what ways are stone vessels, *mikva'ot*, and the Jewish purity laws (found, for example, in the *Temple Scroll*) determinative for discerning the opposition to Jesus and his eventual crucifixion?

Sixth, for nearly two thousand years ecclesiastical leaders have attempted to establish that Christian faith is not focused on a far-off celestial Christ. It is grounded in an incarnational theology and the world in which all humans live from womb to tomb (see, e.g., Charlesworth and Weaver, *Faith*). Christian faith presupposes a real human that was crucified. Archaeology helps reveal life in ancient Israel-Palestine, discloses contexts for texts that contain Jesus' biography, and provides palpable data for comprehending symbolic language that represented fears and hopes.

Bibliography

The major works that should be consulted in an exploration of archaeology and the NT in ancient Israel-Palestine include Stern, Lewinson-Gilboa, and Aviram, *The New Encyclopedia of Archaeological Excavations in the Holy Land* (NEAEHL); Meyers, *The Oxford Encyclopedia of Archaeology in the Near East* (OEANE); Negev and Gibson, *Archaeological Encyclopedia of the Holy Land*; and Charlesworth, *Jesus and Archaeology*. Biographical summaries of active archaeologists appear in H. Shanks, *Who's Who in Biblical Studies and Archaeology* (2nd ed.; Washington, DC: Biblical Archaeology Society, 1993).

Works on archaeological excavations and summaries of archaeological work are considerable. The following works are first-rate (now up to date) and will guide the reader to other publications: Geva, *Jewish Quarter Excavations in the Old City of Jerusalem*; and Reich, *Excavating the City of David*. The best books on archaeology and Jesus include Reed, *Archaeology and the Galilean Jesus*; Crossan and Reed, *Excavating Jesus*; and Charlesworth, *Jesus and Archaeology*. Resources that are erudite and full of important archaeological data include Leibner, *Settlement and History in Hellenistic, Roman, and Byzantine Galilee*; and Hezser, *The Oxford Handbook of Jewish Daily Life in Roman Palestine*. A marvelously illustrated and attractive overview of topography and archaeology is provided by D. Tal et al., *Flights into Biblical Archaeology* (3rd ed.; Israel: Albatross and Israel Antiquities Authority, 2010). Promising to be a landmark publication is Magness, *Stone and Dung, Oil and Spit*.

These reference notes are selective but representative of the best works available. One should note the rule, however, that when a book or article on archaeology is published, it is already out of date. Biblical studies may move like a glacier, but archaeological insights, when published, move like a tsunami.[16]

Aviam, Mordechai. *Jews, Pagans and Christians in the Galilee*. Land of Galilee 1. Rochester: University of Rochester Press, 2004. An enlightening discussion by one of the leading archaeologists in Galilee.

Ben-Dov, Meir. *In the Shadow of the Temple: The Discovery of Ancient Jerusalem*. New York: Harper & Row, 1985. Though dated, this publication contains superb information.

Chancey, Mark A. *The Myth of a Gentile Galilee*. SNTSMS 118. Cambridge: Cambridge University Press, 2002. Exposes the myth that Galilee was defined by gentiles.

Charlesworth, James H. "Archaeology and the Passion of Jesus." *SI* 4, no. 1 (2010): 45–68. An attempt to clarify the many archaeological discoveries that relate directly to the story of Jesus' passion.

———, ed. *The Bible and the Dead Sea Scrolls*. 3 vols. Waco: Baylor University Press, 2006. Leading authorities address the major ways the DSS have impacted biblical studies.

———. "Does Archaeology Help Christian Belief?" Pages 125–47 in *Origins Matter*. Manila: Catholic Biblical Association of the Philippines, 2009. An argument that archaeology can provide some understanding for Christian belief.

———, ed. *Jesus and Archaeology*. Grand Rapids: Eerdmans, 2006. A major collection of studies on archaeology and Jesus; many of the contributors are archaeologists.

———, ed. *John and the Dead Sea Scrolls*. New York: Crossroad, 1991. A team of experts explain how and in what ways the Dead Sea Scrolls have enriched our understanding of John.

Charlesworth, James H., and Walter P. Weaver, eds. *What Has Archaeology to Do with Faith?* Philadelphia: Trinity Press International, 1992. Urges that archaeology does not form but can inform faith.

16. Unfortunately, the publication of excavations often is not timely.

Claussen, Carsten, and Jörg Frey, eds. *Jesus und die Archäologie Galiläas*. BThS 87. Neukirchen-Vluyn: Neukirchener Verlag, 2008. A good indication of the importance of archaeology for Jesus research.

Crossan, John Dominic, and Jonathan L. Reed. *Excavating Jesus: Beneath the Stones, Behind the Texts*. New York: HarperCollins, 2001. Rich and detailed with reliable insights.

Dever, William G., and H. Darrell Lance. *A Manual of Field Excavation: Handbook for Field Archaeologists*. Cincinnati: Hebrew Union College; New York: Jewish Institute of Religion, 1982. Explains archeological methodologies.

Freyne, Sean. *Galilee and Gospel*. WUNT 125. Tübingen: Mohr Siebeck, 2000. Groundbreaking but now dated.

Geva, Hillel. *Jewish Quarter Excavations in the Old City of Jerusalem Conducted by Nahman Avigad, 1969–1982*. 4 vols. Jerusalem: Israel Exploration Society and Institute of Archaeology, Hebrew University of Jerusalem, 2000–2010. A window into the material culture that defined life in Jerusalem (esp. among the elite and rich) in pre–AD 70 upper Jerusalem.

Hachlili, Rachel. *Jewish Funerary Customs: Practices and Rites in the Second Temple Period*. JSJSup 94. Leiden: Brill, 2005. Contains unique and valuable data.

Hezser, Catherine, ed. *The Oxford Handbook of Jewish Daily Life in Roman Palestine*. Oxford: Oxford University Press, 2010. Definitive and helpful.

Leibner, Uzi. *Settlement and History in Hellenistic, Roman, and Byzantine Galilee*. TSAJ 127. Tübingen: Mohr Siebeck, 2009. The major monograph on Jewish life in lower Galilee.

Levine, Lee I. *The Ancient Synagogue: The First Thousand Years*. New Haven: Yale University Press, 2000. The standard text on the origin and development of the ancient synagogues. It is dated but still contains a wealth of useful information.

Magness, Jodi. *Stone and Dung, Oil and Spit: Jewish Daily Life in the Time of Jesus*. Grand Rapids: Eerdmans, 2011. Informative and highly recommended.

Mazar, Eilat. *The Complete Guide to the Temple Mount Excavations*. Jerusalem: Shoham Academic Research and Publication, 2002. Authoritative.

Meyers, Eric M., ed. *The Oxford Encyclopedia of Archaeology in the Near East*. 5 vols. New York: Oxford University Press, 1997. Dated but full of data for reflection.

Moreland, Milton C. *Between Text and Artifact: Integrating Archaeology in Biblical Studies Teaching*. SBLABS 8. Atlanta: Society of Biblical Literature, 2003. Reflections by some leading professors on how to use archaeology in teaching.

Negev, Avraham, and Shimon Gibson, eds. *Archaeological Encyclopedia of the Holy Land*. New York: Continuum, 2001. The best small encyclopedia.

Reed, Jonathan L. *Archaeology and the Galilean Jesus*. Harrisburg, PA: Trinity Press International, 2000. Focused and erudite.

————. *The HarperCollins Visual Guide to the New Testament: What Archaeology Reveals about the First Christians*. New York: HarperCollins, 2007. An attractive guidebook on how archaeology reveals aspects of the NT.

Reich, Ronny. *Excavating the City of David: Where Jerusalem's History Began*. Jerusalem: Israel Exploration Society, 2011. Authoritative and full of fresh data.

Ritmeyer, Leen, and Kathleen Ritmeyer. *Secrets of Jerusalem's Temple Mount*. Washington: Biblical Archaeology Society, 1998. Superb drawings.

Stern, Ephraim, Ayelet Lewinson-Gilboa, and Joseph Aviram, eds. *The New Encyclopedia of Archaeological Excavations in the Holy Land.* 5 vols. New York: Simon & Schuster; Jerusalem: Israel Exploration Society and Carta, 1993–. The best encyclopedia on archaeology; it is updated with supplements.

Vamosh, Miriam Feinberg. *Food at the Time of the Bible.* Nashville: Abingdon, 2004. A simple introduction to the use of food in biblical times.

Wachsmann, Shelley. *The Excavations of an Ancient Boat in the Sea of Galilee.* Jerusalem: Israel Antiquities Authority, 1990. Professional discussion of a wooden boat from Jesus' time.

Zangenberg, Jürgen, Harold W. Attridge, and Dale B. Martin, eds. *Religion, Ethnicity and Identity in Ancient Galilee.* WUNT 210. Tübingen: Mohr Siebeck, 2007. Essays (including those by S. Freyne, D. R. Schwartz, D. R. Edwards, and R. Deines) discuss evidence that Galilee represents many different cultures.

37

Egypt

JOHN D. WINELAND

Christian Origins in Egypt

Much of the information about the origins of Christianity in Egypt is uncertain, mingled with long-held traditions and speculation. Clearly Egypt played an important role in the development of Christian thought and practice, and many written sources relating to the early development of Christianity have been found in Egypt, but none of them gives an account of the beginnings of Christianity in this ancient land.

The first record of any connection between Jesus of Nazareth and Egypt comes in the birth narrative found in the Gospel of Matthew. Matthew 2 reports that Mary, Joseph, and Jesus fled to Egypt to avoid the wrath of Herod the Great. The duration of their stay in Egypt is described only as "until the death of Herod [the Great]" (v. 15). The route of their journey is also not described. A tradition within the Coptic Orthodox Church of Egypt posits a detailed itinerary of a four-year sojourn; each year many tourists visit the fourth-century church of Saints Sergius and Bacchus in Coptic Cairo, said to have been built over the site where the holy family rested after their initial journey to Egypt. However, the historical value of such traditions is doubtful.

Acts 2, which records the events of the day of Pentecost, describes the apostles praising God in foreign languages among those assembled in Jerusalem—a crowd that includes Jews from all over the Roman Empire, including Egypt. If some of those Jews from Egypt heard Peter's sermon, accepted his challenge to repent, and were added to the number of three thousand converts that day, they could have returned to spread the message in Egypt. It is clear that many Jews lived in Egypt in the first century. Josephus reports a first-century Jewish population of some 7.5 million, excluding the large Jewish population of Alexandria (*J. W.* 2.385). Since Josephus would have had access to the Roman census information in Rome, his population estimates seem credible. This means that there would be ample opportunity for the message of Christianity to spread in Egypt through the Jewish population (see Goehring and Timbie, *Early Egyptian Christianity*). But we have no written accounts of such activity.

Greek was the predominant language of the Jewish population in Egypt during the first century. The Septuagint—the Greek translation of the Hebrew Scriptures written in Alexandria—attests to the widespread use of Greek in the Jewish population in Egypt by the second century BC. The Jewish leaders in Alexandria realized the necessity of translating the Hebrew Scriptures into Greek to ensure that the Jewish population could access the Scriptures. The widespread use of Greek in Egypt later facilitated the communication of the gospel there.

An indication of the early spread of Christianity to Egypt can be found in the references to Apollos in 1 Cor. 1:12; 3:5–6; and Acts 18:24–19:1. In Acts 18, Apollos is described as a native of Alexandria, Egypt. He is also described as a leader within the first-century church. Since Apollos arrived in Ephesus with a thorough knowledge of the Scriptures and of Christ, this would presumably mean that he was educated about Christianity in Alexandria. Thus we have some evidence for Christianity in Egypt by the mid-first century AD, at least in the city of Alexandria. However, we lack details about how Christianity arrived and spread in Egypt.

Another text sometimes connected with Christianity in Egypt is 1 Pet. 5:13. The author of the epistle sends greetings from the church at Babylon and from Mark. Most commentators think that Babylon signifies Rome, and some that it refers to Babylon in Mesopotamia. A few, however, argue that Babylon here actually refers to a fortress in Egypt near Cairo (often called Coptic Cairo today). A fortress there had the name "Babylon," and it is home to some of the oldest structures in Coptic Cairo. There is little evidence, however, to support the conclusion that 1 Peter was written from Egypt. The mention of Mark in that passage might have led some to this idea, since he is listed as the founder of the church in Egypt by Eusebius. It seems unlikely that this small military fortress would have been the base of operations for the church in Egypt.

Eusebius of Caesarea (ca. AD 260–339) was the first major historian of the church. In the early fourth century Eusebius produced his *Ecclesiastical History*, an attempt to detail the history of the church from its beginnings. He revised his work to include recent events in his lifetime, including the persecution of Decius (303) and Constantine's edict of toleration (313). Eusebius states that Mark was the first sent to preach in Egypt (*Eccl. Hist.* 2.16; Pearson, "Egypt," 137–45), but he cites no sources, and his language is vague, so scholars doubt the veracity of his account. The lack of references to leaders of congregations in Egypt in early Christian literature also complicates the situation. As his authority, Eusebius uses the writings of Philo of Alexandria (ca. 20 BC–ca. AD 50). Philo mentions the Therapeutae, a Jewish group related to the Essenes, whose name derives from a Greek term meaning "healers" or "worshipers." They lived in a monastic style near Lake Mareotis, south of Alexandria. Eusebius argues that their lifestyle of fasting, having all things in common, and celibacy proves they were a Christian group (*Eccl. Hist.* 2.17). Since Eusebius's argument on this point is unconvincing, his reference to Mark's beginning the church in Egypt is also called into question. So we know very little indeed about the origins of Christianity in Egypt.

Early Christianity in Egypt

Papyri and Manuscripts

While there is little reliable evidence about Christianity in Egypt in the apostolic era, for postapostolic times there are abundant literary remains. One of the most important collections of documents was found at Oxyrhynchus, located about 125 miles south of Cairo. It served as a provincial capital and became a large and important city during the Hellenistic period. It is best known for the thousands of Greek papyrus documents found at the site, which was excavated by Bernard P. Grenfell and Arthur S. Hunt (1897–1907), William F. Petrie (1922), and A. Evarist Breccia (1927–28; see Luijendijk, *Oxyrhynchus Papyri*, 6–8). These documents are both pagan and Christian in origin. They include fragments of classical literature, Gospels, OT materials, apocryphal works, patristic texts, and inventories of churches. The documents date from the first to the sixth centuries AD, including the earliest fragment of any NT manuscript—the Rylands Greek Papyrus 457 ($\mathfrak{P}^{52}$), which dates to no later than about AD 125–150 and contains a fragment of John 18. This indicates that Christianity must have arrived in Egypt at least in the latter part of the first century AD and that Christian documents were being circulated and copied by the early second century AD (Luijendijk, *Oxyrhynchus Papyri*, 227–34).

Other examples of Christian documents from Egypt are the Bodmer papyri, found in 1952 and named for Martin Bodmer, who purchased them. This collection has some documents in Greek and others in Coptic. One part of the Bodmer collection, Papyrus 66 ($\mathfrak{P}^{66}$) is dated to around AD 200 and preserves about two-thirds of the Gospel of John on full pages. The Chester Beatty papyri collection also contains thirty leaves of Acts in Greek dated to around AD 250 ($\mathfrak{P}^{45}$), most of Paul's Epistles in Greek dated to around AD 175–225 ($\mathfrak{P}^{46}$), and sections of the book of Revelation in Greek dated to the third century AD ($\mathfrak{P}^{47}$). These collections attest to the availability of Christian writings in the second century AD, and they are some of the most important collections of NT documents available.

Additionally, several important texts were found in 1945 at the village of Nag Hammadi. They are written in Coptic and bound in a book format (codex) rather than as scrolls. Twelve complete codices, with eight pages of a thirteenth text, preserve fifty-two tractates of ancient texts (Robinson, *Nag Hammadi Library*). The texts, written in the fourth century AD, mostly reflect gnostic theology. Most experts agree that they were translated from early Greek texts dating most likely to the second century AD. The codices were found in jars in the caves near the village of Nag Hammadi, about 250 miles south of Cairo. The most important of these texts is the *Gospel of Thomas*, a collection of 114 sayings of Jesus. This collection highlights the influence of gnostic thought on Christianity especially in the second century AD.

Christian Scholars and Leaders

In addition to the vast collection of important Christian texts found in Egypt, a wide range of Christian scholars and leaders from the region have greatly influenced Christianity. One of the earliest is Clement of Alexandria (ca. AD 160–215), a Christian thinker heavily influenced by Greek philosophy. (He should not be confused with the Apostolic Father Clement of Rome, the bishop of Rome [AD 88–97].) Clement of Alexandria, according to Eusebius, established a school of philosophy at Alexandria and eventually trained the great Christian scholar Origen. Clement taught a mystical form of Christianity that focused on Christ as the Logos—a type of teaching that has sometimes been described as docetic in its Christology (i.e., Christ only "seemed" [from the Greek verb *dokeō*, "to seem"] to be human). Others have labeled Clement as a proto-gnostic thinker. Scholars think Clement was born in Athens and spent most of his adult life in Alexandria. He later moved to Caesarea in Cappadocia (modern Turkey) after the persecution of Christians in Alexandria in AD 202.

Origen (ca. AD 185–254), one of the greatest scholars of early Christianity, was born in Alexandria and, according to Eusebius, was trained by Clement of Alexandria. Eusebius tells us much about Origen; for example, when Origen was a teenager his father was arrested and eventually executed during a persecution of Christians in Alexandria in AD 202. Origen would have joined his father on the day of his arrest and eventual martyrdom, if not for the intervention of his mother. She hid his clothing and knew that his modesty would prevent him from leaving the house. Origen ran a school to train Christians in Alexandria and stayed in the city until AD 232. He left for Caesarea Maritima in Palestine after a dispute with the bishop of Alexandria. Origen lived in Caesarea until his death in AD 254. Eusebius, who served as bishop in Caesarea, developed a great interest in Origen, no doubt kindled by his access to Origen's library, which was available in Caesarea.

Origen was a prolific writer of sermons, commentaries, and tracts—which Epiphanius of Salamis estimated at over six thousand works. He was systematic in his approach to writing and theology. One of his most important works is *De principiis* (*On First Principles*), a description of his theology and of his approach to hermeneutics with its threefold meaning of the Scriptures. Origen wrote an excellent commentary on the Gospel of John. His *Hexapla* is a monument to his dedication to textual studies of the Scripture. This work sets the text of the OT side by side in six columns—one containing the Hebrew text, another Origen's own Greek translation, and the other four columns with four additional Greek translations available at the time. This work, bound in codex format, allowed for a side-by-side comparison of all six versions simultaneously. Origen is also famous for his defense of Christianity in his work *Contra Celsum*. Celsus was a Platonist philosopher who attacked Christianity in his work titled *True Doctrine*. The content of this work is known only from Origen's references to it in his refutation.

37.1. Important cities and early Christian monasteries established in Egypt.

Monasticism

Christian monasticism can be traced back to its beginnings in the deserts of Egypt. The pivotal figure in the origin of monastic life is Anthony (ca. AD 251–356), known to us through the *Life of Anthony*, written by Athanasius (ca. 296–373), bishop of Alexandria. According to Athanasius, Anthony was born to a wealthy family and inherited all of their money as a young man. He gave away his wealth after hearing a sermon about the rich ruler, in which Jesus commended the ruler to sell all that he owned and give it to the poor. Anthony began to live in the tombs near his hometown and to practice an ascetic life of denial. After fifteen years he decided to withdraw from society and live in isolation in the desert. He seems to have been the first to attempt to live in isolation in order to concentrate on holy living. His attempt to live in solitude led to fame and to others following him into the desert for instruction and inspiration. Anthony would train them for a while and then retreat further into the desert to continue his hermit existence. He died at the age of 105, and his life inspired others to seek a monastic life. This monastic movement came to be known as the Anchorites, desert fathers, or hermit monks.

Monasticism developed further in Egypt under the influence of Pachomius (ca. 292–346). Pachomius was born in Egypt and converted to Christianity at the age of twenty. As a soldier in the Egyptian army, he was influenced by the practice of Christian kindness to convert (Veilleux, *Saint Pachomius*, 36). After he ended his service in the army, he returned to his home and submitted to baptism. Pachomius is credited with developing cenobitic ("common life") monasticism. He also developed the first monastic rules to oversee the life of monks—their shared meals, prayer, and work within a walled monastery. His first monastery at Tabennisi grew quickly and was expanded several times. After six years it was clear that a second monastery was needed, and one was built at Pabau (Faou). A third was later added at Chenoboskion (Schenisit). Before his death, Pachomius started a total of nine monasteries and two nunneries. He eventually had a total of three thousand monks under his rule. His life and work became well known through a *Life of Pachomius* that circulated widely in various dialects and revisions. Eventually Pachomian monasteries died out in Egypt in the fifth century AD on account of christological controversies in church. The idea of cenobitic monasteries was transferred to the West through the influence of Jerome and Benedict.

Summary

The influence of Christianity in Egypt as it developed is varied, and the impact is tremendous. The discovery of various Christian writings, including several early and important copies of NT manuscripts, bears witness to the spread of this literature as Christianity developed. Great thinkers and scholars, like Origen, shaped the theological discussions of the early church. The rise of monasticism in Egypt served as model for Christians in the West. Although we may never know how the seeds of Christianity were planted in Egypt, it is clear that the fertile soil gave rise to important early thinkers, writers, and leaders. They influenced the rest of Christendom through their writings, teachings, and monastic living.

Bibliography

Bell, H. I. "Evidences of Christianity in Egypt during the Roman Period." *HTR* 37, no. 3 (1944): 185–208. Provides a detailed overview of the evidence for Christianity in Egypt under Roman rule; makes use of many papyri available on the subject, with a useful appendix on the use of papyri.

Goehring, James E., and Janet Timbie, eds. *The World of Early Egyptian Christianity: Language, Literature, and Social Context*. Washington, DC: Catholic University of America Press, 2007. Offers important essays about Coptic language, literature, and social history; advances Coptic studies, including the emergence of Christianity in Egypt and its later development in the Coptic Church.

Griggs, C. Wilfred. *Early Egyptian Christianity: From Its Origins to 451 C.E.* New York: Brill, 1993. An excellent overview of the development of Christianity in Egypt. Griggs argues that Christianity was present in the first century AD.

Luijendijk, AnneMarie. *Greetings in the Lord: Early Christians and the Oxyrhynchus Papyri*. HTS 60. Cambridge, MA: Harvard University Press, 2008. A recent and well-structured presentation of the papyrological material relating to early Christianity at Oxyrhynchus—divided into three parts ("Meeting Christians at the Marketplace," "Papa Sotas, Bishop of Oxyrhynchus," and "Legal Matters and Government Dealings"), preceded by a general introduction ("Destination Oxyrhynchus: Historical Detective Work in the Footsteps of Monks and Papyrologists"), and concluded by a chapter on "Early Christians in the Oxyrhynchus Papyri: New Voices in Ancient History."

Pearson, Birger A. "Earliest Christianity in Egypt: Some Observations." Pages 132–57 in *Roots of Egyptian Christianity*. Edited by Birger A. Pearson and James E. Goehring. SAC 1. Philadelphia: Fortress, 1986. An excellent overview of the available evidence by a scholar in the field. It focuses on the evidence for the presence of Christianity in Egypt in the first and second centuries AD.

Robinson, James M., ed. *The Nag Hammadi Library*. 3rd ed. San Francisco: Harper & Row, 1988. An overview of the discovery of the Nag Hammadi library together with excellent translations of each of the documents discovered.

Veilleux, Armand. *The Life of Saint Pachomius and His Disciples*. Kalamazoo, MI: Cistercian Publications, 1980. A translation of all existing documents from the cenobitic monasteries of Pachomius (AD 292–346); an excellent look at patristic scholarship covering the early history of cenobitism and religious life.

38

Palestine

THOMAS R. HATINA

From approximately 450 BC to 1948, "Palestine" was the name given to the geographical region between the eastern part of the Mediterranean Sea and the Jordan River. The term's origins are difficult to trace, but many conjecture that it probably derives from the ancient word for "Philistines" and perhaps comes from the Hebrew *pělešet*. Its diverse topography can be divided into four major regions: the Jordan valley, the coastal and inland plains, the rugged mountainous terrain, and desert. The climate fluctuates with the seasons but on average remains mainly dry and moderate in temperature. The highest fluctuation occurs in the winter, which can last two to three months, and the height of summer, which can be very hot.

The land of Palestine is the center of Judaism and the cradle of Christianity. It is where Jesus was born and raised, where he ministered and died; for this reason, students of the historical Jesus over the last century have contributed immensely to the study of ancient Palestine. It is where Jesus' earliest followers (the disciples) resided and ministered after his death; it was also the residence of the apostle Paul, often regarded as the father of Christianity. The earliest stories about Jesus are set primarily in three of the major regions of Palestine: Galilee (where he was raised in Nazareth), Samaria, and Judea (where Jerusalem and Bethlehem are located). An informed understanding of the ministries of Jesus, his earliest followers, the Gospels, and select parts of the NT are contingent on a familiarity with the context out of which they emerged. It was a world that differed significantly from modern Western society on almost every level.

History

The history of Palestine is riddled with the conquest, exile, strife, revolution, and perseverance of the Jewish people. Palestine of the first century AD was no different. It was occupied by the Romans, who annexed Palestine to its empire, first as a territory under the provincial rule of Syria, and then as the province of Judaea, or *Iudaea*, which is not to be confused with the small region of Judea located between Samaria and Idumea. The province of Judaea consisted of Samaria, Judea, and Idumea.

The history of occupation is extensive, but a good place to begin is the Babylonian exile. In 587/86 BC, the small independent kingdom of Judah was invaded by the Babylonians. At that time, "Judah" was a political term referring to the central area of Palestine, with Jerusalem as its capital. Over time the term "Jew" came to be applied to those who adhered to the customs and practices of the Judeans. The Babylonian invasion was devastating. Many of Judah's inhabitants were massacred, several thousand of its elite were deported, and the temple was destroyed. Approximately fifty years later, when the Babylonians were conquered by the Persians (539 BC), the Persians permitted the Judeans to return to Palestine to rebuild a modest temple (see Ezra; Nehemiah). The dedication of this temple, usually dated to 516 or 515 BC, marks the beginning of what is commonly called Second Temple Judaism. Dramatic changes to Judaism occurred during this period, from the completion of the temple under the Persians to its eventual destruction by the Romans in AD 70. The Persian era (539–333 BC) set the stage for further religious developments inaugurated by the conquest of Alexander the Great (who died in 323 BC), traditionally called the Hellenistic period. The end of this period is debated—some point to 146 BC, when Rome conquered Greece, others to the battle of Actium in 31 BC, which marked the end of the Ptolemaic dynasty—but its impact on Judaism, the culture of the region, and later the formation of Christianity is immeasurable.

When Alexander the Great died, his vast empire was divided among his generals. For over a century, Palestine was first controlled by Ptolemy I Soter, who declared himself pharaoh of Egypt. After repeated conflicts, Palestine was eventually controlled by the Seleucid dynasty, which was established by another one of Alexander's generals, Seleucus I Nicator, who ruled over a vast territory to the north and east of Palestine. The Seleucid control of Palestine under Antiochus III and later Antiochus IV was one of the most brutal periods in Jewish history, especially for devout Jews who refused to embrace Hellenism. Shortly after Antiochus IV (Epiphanes) took the throne (175–164 BC), Jason, the high priest in Jerusalem, attempted to reform Judaism by making "a covenant with the Gentiles" (1 Macc. 1:11), and in essence he made Jerusalem a Greek city. Although this period is difficult to reconstruct, it appears that Jason's Hellenistic reforms (2 Macc. 4) somehow instigated an inner-Jewish power struggle that was (mis)understood by Antiochus as insurrection. This instability led Antiochus and his forces to take Jerusalem in 167 BC. Those who resisted were killed. Jewish religious practice

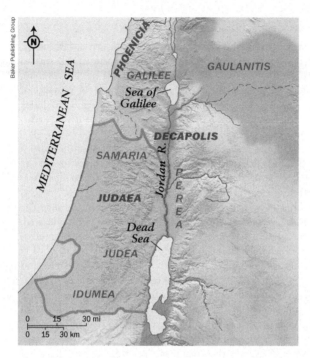

38.1. The Roman province of Judaea, which consisted of Samaria, Judea, and Idumea.

was prohibited (1 Macc. 1:54–64), and Jewish temple worship was replaced with the cult of Zeus Olympios (this is referred to as the "desolating sacrifice" or "the abomination of desolation" in Dan. 9:27; 11:31; 12:11; see also 2 Macc. 6:1–2). As more gentiles began to inhabit a number of the cities in Palestine, those cities took on a Hellenistic appearance.

In reaction to the oppressive policies of Antiochus IV, a small band of Jews under the leadership of a priest named Mattathias, of the Hasmon family (nicknamed the Maccabees), initiated a revolt that gained considerable momentum. After several decades of fighting, the Hasmonean vision of a new independent state was realized in 142 BC. Independence, unfortunately, soon led to a civil strife over power among the Hasmoneans. Some were content with the victory over the Seleucids because it established the freedom to practice their Jewish faith (1 Macc. 14:4–15), whereas others were eager to continue with their expansionist and antigentile policies. The latter group eventually seized power. Under the leadership of John Hyrcanus (135–104 BC), a vast amount of land was taken. The (Samaritan) temple on Mount Gerizim was destroyed, and a program of religious and ethnic intolerance against non-Jews was inaugurated. The Greek cities in Palestine were forcibly altered to Jewish cities. Gentiles were forced to convert. The animosity between the Samaritans and the Jews, reflected in the NT, goes back to the harsh policies of John Hyrcanus.

The Hasmonean dynasty came to an end in 63 BC when the Roman general Pompey entered Palestine with his forces and abolished the constitution initiated by the Hasmoneans. The reaction of the Jews was split. Some welcomed the Romans, whereas others resisted them with force, but to no avail (Josephus, *Ant.* 14.69–75, 77–79). Due to an increased military threat posed by the Parthians in the east, Rome installed a strong client king in Judea, Herod the Great (37–4 BC), who secured Palestine as Rome's territory. Herod managed to keep much of Palestine united, though his rule was not without rebellion. Galilee was especially a hotbed for revolutionary activity incited by frustrated peasants (Josephus, *J.W.* 1.303, 328–30). His reign was a blend of ruthless attacks against alleged (or real) threats to his throne and of maintaining relative peace and social order, without interfering with the temple and its practices. To his credit, Herod defended Jewish worship outside Palestine, remitted taxes during a famine, and engaged in extensive building projects, the greatest of which was the reconstruction of the temple in Jerusalem (Josephus, *J.W.* 5.238; 7.172–77; *Ant.* 15.331–41, 380–425; 16.142–45). Peace reigned during his rule, the economy was generally strong, and his "rule was probably the high point of Judea's prestige in the world" (Grabbe, *Judaic Religion*, 84).

After Herod's death, the kingdom was divided among his three sons. Judea, Samaria, and Idumea fell to Archelaus; Herod Antipas received Galilee and Perea; and the areas north and east of the Sea of Galilee were given to Philip. After a short reign, Archelaus was deposed (Josephus, *J.W.* 2.111–17; *Ant.* 17.342–44), and Judea began to be governed by prefects, or procurators. During Jesus' ministry, Judea was governed by Pontius Pilate (AD 26–36), who had his headquarters in the port city of Caesarea but traveled to Jerusalem with troops when the need arose. The day-to-day governance of Jerusalem was the responsibility of the high priest and his council.

Herod's grandson Agrippa was made king of Judea from AD 41 to 44 by the emperor Claudius, but the region returned to Roman control after Agrippa's early death. The next two decades gave rise to tensions between the Jews and the Romans, which escalated to an all-out war in AD 66. The destruction of the temple in AD 70 marked the end of the war and the close of the Second Temple period. A second revolt was launched against the Romans by Bar Kokhba in AD 132–135, with a disastrous outcome: Jerusalem was turned into a Roman city, renamed Aelia Capitolina, and the remaining Jews were deported and prohibited from entering their sacred site.

Politics, Infrastructure, and Institutions

When Augustus came to power, the Roman provinces were categorized as either imperial or senatorial. The difference lay in who appointed the governor (though no such general term was used). Rulers of imperial provinces were appointed by the emperor; those over senatorial provinces were appointed by the Senate. The province of Syria, annexed by Pompey in 64 BC, initially included most of Palestine but was later subdivided into smaller provinces. Judaea (called *Iudaea*), for

38.2. A recently excavated palace on top of Machaerus, Herod the Great's easternmost palace and fortress. The story of John the Baptist's death is situated here (see Mark 6:17–29).

example, became a province in AD 6, after Herod's son Archelaus was deposed. The province of Judaea consisted of Samaria, Judea, and Idumea.

Herod the Great followed the Hellenistic tradition of kings having the monarchic authority of Alexander the Great and the Hasmoneans, which meant that he was not only a warlord but also the supreme judge and legal authority. As king he commanded the army and had control over socioeconomic affairs, but his authority was not extended to religious matters. Only high priests had ultimate control of Jewish religious life.

Herod's most important legacy was his building projects in urban centers. Two of his grandest projects were the city of Caesarea and the Jerusalem temple. When Herod began the reconstruction of Caesarea Maritima (named in honor of Caesar Augustus) in about 22 BC, it was largely a pagan city. The project was extensive, employing thousands of workers. In addition to the famous harbor that rivaled the one in Athens, the construction included temples, public buildings in grand Roman style, warehouses, baths, wide roads, and markets. When the harbor was complete (ca. 13 BC), Caesarea became the capital of the province of Judaea and the official residence of its prefects (including Pontius Pilate). Next to Jerusalem, which had a population of about 200,000, it was the largest city in Judaea, with a population of approximately 125,000.

Herod's expansion of the Jerusalem temple (ca. 19 BC) was a massive undertaking (Josephus, *Ant.* 15.380–90; *J.W.* 1.401). The old temple, originally constructed under the leadership of Zerubbabel almost five hundred years earlier and renovated under the Hasmoneans, served as the platform. It was situated on top

Lee Martin McDonald

38.3. The southern steps into the temple mount, from the first century BC/AD. Jesus may well have entered the temple this way.

of the temple mount, also known as Mount Moriah. According to Josephus, the project employed ten thousand skilled laborers and another thousand priests as masons and carpenters in order to conform to ritual requirements of working on a sacred site (*Ant.* 15.389–90). When it was finally completed in AD 63, it measured 280 meters (south wall) by 485 meters (west wall) by 315 meters (north wall) by 460 meters (east wall), for a total of 144,000 square meters; that is, it had doubled in size and was enormous compared to other temples in the empire (Ben-Dov, *Temple*, 77).

Although Herod boasted that the temple was his gift to the Jews and for the glory of God, there was no mistaking that the temple and "the whole world" was under Roman rule (Josephus, *Ant.* 15.382–87). To show Rome's supremacy, a Roman golden eagle was hung over the eastern ("great") gate. Just prior to Herod's death, Josephus reports, a few youths pulled it down (*Ant.* 17.151–63; *J.W.* 1.649–55). This would not be the last time that Roman supremacy was symbolized in the temple. In AD 40, the emperor Caligula attempted to install a statue of himself in the temple (Josephus, *Ant.* 18.257–62).

The temple was the focal point of religious activity, not only for Judea and Galilee, but also for the Diaspora Jews. It was also an ethnic, political, and economic center that wielded justice and power. It required an annual half-shekel contribution and in essence served as the national treasury. The high priest and his family, under the oversight of the Roman prefect, controlled the operations of the temple. Josephus calls the chief of everyday operations a *stratēgos* (*J.W.* 2.409), a military term meaning "captain," who may have also been in charge of the Jerusalem markets. Part of the duties of the Levitical families included security, as temple "police." They were responsible not only for maintaining temple purity, peace, and order, however. Since certain areas of the temple complex were restricted to Jews and priests, the police force guarded the gates of the temple and had the authority to deal severely with transgressors (Hengel, "Geography").

The temple attracted Jewish pilgrims from around the empire, especially for the celebration of Passover. Most would arrive on Palestine's shores, usually at the port of Jaffa (today's Tel Aviv) by boat, and then travel south for three days to Jerusalem. The glistening white marble structures would have been an impressive sight as pilgrims neared the city. Since the temple was the focal point of Jerusalem, the city's economy was closely tied to temple worship. Pilgrims needed food, lodging, sacrificial animals, and other supplies. Josephus writes that at Passover in AD 65, there were 2,700,000 people, with only 200 priests (*J.W.* 6.425). It is hard to know how exaggerated this number might be.

38.4. This portion of the ruins of Herodium shows the recently discovered burial site of Herod the Great. The platform in the foreground is where the sarcophagus was found, and the town of Bethlehem appears in the background.

After Herod's death, the political and economic landscape became more precarious. Since Palestine was divided among Herod's sons, and eventually prefects, there was less money in the central coffers for grand projects. Building projects in Judea were minimal, but some parts of Galilee flourished. After having been under the rule and authority of Jerusalem, Galilee was now under a separate political administration. Herod Antipas ruled as a tetrarch—a lesser title than king—having powers similar to those of his father. As a result of his position, he was not directly under the administration of the Romans and could decide the fate of individuals, such as John the Baptist, without reference to anyone else (see Matt. 14:10; Luke 3:20; 9:9; Mark 6:17; Josephus, *Ant.* 18.116–19). Although Antipas paid tribute to Rome, taxes went directly to him. It is difficult to know how supportive the Galileans were of the temple. Scholars have argued in contrary directions, for both a strong allegiance (Chancey, *Galilee*, 54–55; Freyne, *Jesus*, 200–203) and disfavor due to a corrupt establishment (Horsley, *Galilee*, 33). The saturation of Greco-Roman culture and the number of gentile residents is hotly debated. Some argue that Galilee was primarily Jewish (e.g., Chancey, *Galilee*); others argue that it boasted a large contingent of Roman officials and a substantial gentile population (e.g., Batey, *Jesus*; Kee, "Galilee").

Perhaps Antipas's most notable project was the rebuilding of the fortress city of Sepphoris, which was earlier destroyed by the Romans after a revolt led by a certain Judah ben Hezekiah. It was located in the center of Galilee, about four miles northeast of Nazareth. Having been built on a hill, it was also visible for miles around. Antipas made Sepphoris his capital in 4 BC (Josephus, *Ant.* 18.27). During Jesus' day, it was the largest city in Galilee and regarded by Josephus as its jewel. The rebuilding project included lavishly decorated residences for the elite, as well as Antipas's palace, roads paved with limestone, a 4,500-seat theater cut into the hillside, and two markets.

Sepphoris housed a number of elite families, who would have been estate owners and wealthy merchants. Many of the peasant residents worked within the city walls as merchants or as government officials; the rest were farmers supplying the city. According to James Strange, who resumed excavation of the city after a fifty-year hiatus, Sepphoris would have had a well-represented middle stratum, including

> the professional scribe, the teacher, the lawyer, the hand worker, mason, carpenter, or cooper, the small shop keeper, the family farmer, the banker or money-changer, fisherman (on Lake Tiberias), tax collectors, foremen, the money lender, the master of a household, the manager of a household or steward, the ironsmith, coppersmith, silversmith, or goldsmith. To these one may add from other sources, whose status we do not know, the caravaneer, peddler, charcoal maker, lime maker, tanner, leather-worker, soldier, healer, exorcist, physician, herbalist, and actors and entertainers. ("Sepphoris")

In AD 19, Antipas replaced Sepphoris as his capital in favor of Tiberias (named in honor of the emperor), situated on the western shore of the Sea of Galilee, also called Lake Tiberias and Lake Kinneret (Josephus, *Ant.* 18.37–38). The surrounding area was famous for grapes, barley, figs, and wheat. In addition to the construction of impressive residences, a market, and a theater, it contained a number of natural hot springs that fed baths. Unlike Sepphoris, its importance grew. Antipas had coins minted there with the city's name on them. When Claudius became emperor, he added his own name to the city, calling it Tiberias Claudiupolis. In the second century, it was known as one of the four holy cities of Judaism (along with Jerusalem, Hebron, and Safed). Our best primary record of Tiberias under the rule of Antipas comes from Josephus, who writes,

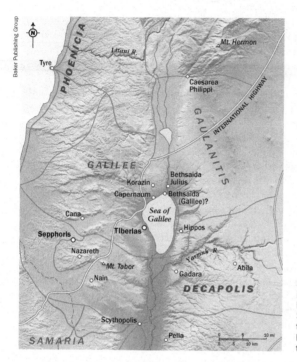

38.5. The Galilee region in the first century AD. Herod Antipas rebuilt Sepphoris and made it the capital of the region but later made Tiberias the capital city.

And now Herod the tetrarch, who was in great favor with Tiberius, built a city of the same name with him, and called it Tiberias. He built it in the best part of Galilee, at the lake of Gennesareth. There are warm baths at a little distance from it, in a village named Emmaus. Strangers came and inhabited this city; a great number of the inhabitants were Galileans also; and many were necessitated by Herod to come thither out of the country belonging to him, and were by force compelled to be its inhabitants; some of them were persons of condition. He also admitted poor people, such as those that were collected from all parts, to dwell in it. Nay, some of them were not quite free-men, and these he was benefactor to, and made them free in great numbers; but obliged them not to forsake the city, by building them very good houses at his own expense, and by giving them land also; for he was sensible, that to make this place a habitation was to transgress the Jewish ancient laws, because many sepulchers [that] were to be here [were] taken away, in order to make room for the city Tiberias whereas our laws pronounce that such inhabitants are unclean for seven days. (*Ant.* 18.36)[1]

These building projects affected village peasants in several ways. The social impact was considerable, for they required huge resources to be extracted from

1. William Whiston, *The Works of Flavius Josephus: Complete and Unabridged* (updated ed.; Peabody, MA: Hendrickson, 2005), 478.

the peasants. In addition, a political shift was felt when power was transferred away from distant Jerusalem to two centers within a half-day's walk (Horsley, *Galilee*, 34). Scholars have recently tried to ascertain what impact the rebuilding of both Sepphoris and Tiberias would have had on urban-rural relations. The dialogue seems to be at a standstill, with some arguing that Antipas's urbanization of Galilee would have drawn a deeper wedge between village farmers and the urbanites, and others arguing that villagers would have prospered and thus welcomed the change (Reed, "Jesus' Galilee").

After Antipas was deposed in AD 39, Caligula gave Galilee to Herod the Great's grandson Agrippa I, and in 41 he was made ruler over the whole territory formerly controlled by his grandfather. Agrippa was raised "within the circle of Claudius" in Rome, and he was more interested in the political affairs of the Jewish Diaspora than in the mundane activities of the remote district of Galilee (Horsley, *Galilee*, 35). He sponsored games in honor of the emperor and took an active role in the politics of the temple and high priesthood. After three years Agrippa died, and Galilee was given to his son, Agrippa II. Judea was again governed by Romans of the equestrian class. However, just prior to the war with Rome in AD 66, Agrippa II found it increasingly more difficult to control the growing protests throughout Galilee. The region eventually fell into political disarray, with some villages supporting government forces and others supporting the rebels (Josephus, *Life* 228–89). After the war, Palestine was governed by a succession of legates who had legionary armies under their command. Toward the end of the first century, Palestine became a Roman colony, with its seat of government remaining in Caesarea.

The central government was not the only governing body. Local councils functioned as the community's local government, which kept census records of all persons within their territory, collected taxes, and allocated resources for local needs. One of the major organizations was the local market (cf. Matt. 20:3; Luke 20:46), which enabled residents to exchange goods and services. It appears that the council's responsibilities included maintaining the infrastructure by providing water for its residents (cf. John 4:6) and by keeping streets, roads, gates, and walls serviceable. It is important to realize that local communities in the Mediterranean world were not administered by central governments, such as the Herods. Rulers interfered little in the affairs of the villages, except to collect taxes and keep the peace. Villages and towns were semiautonomous local communities that held assemblies twice a week, Mondays and Thursdays, the same days on which courts were held and the market was opened for selling and bartering (Horsley, "Synagogues," 56–57).

Although politics and religion were blended, civil and religious authorities frequently had an uneasy relationship. The religious establishment was challenged by Herod the Great and Roman governors, who were concerned that the temple not become a flashpoint for civil unrest. It is no accident that the Jewish rebellion began in AD 66 in the temple and that it remained the center of unrest until its destruction in AD 70. The destruction of the temple was an appalling tragedy, both for the Jews in Judea and for those in the Diaspora.

Another important political/religious institution was the synagogue. It has a long and complicated history. It seems to have been an amalgamation of a prayer house, which most likely originated in the Diaspora in the Hellenistic era; a study hall or school, possibly originating in Israel in the Hellenistic times; and a meeting house, which served different needs in both the Diaspora and Israel (Cohen, *Maccabees*, 109). It functioned as an effective means of constructing meaning in the lives of the common people by using liturgy in a broad sense, reading and teaching the Torah, and reciting prayers and hymns. But it also was a place where community affairs were handled, such as fund-raising, public projects, funerals, education, and social conflicts.

Legal System

The legal system in first-century Palestine was not founded on equality. A person's status as freedman or slave, citizen or foreigner, child or adult, and male or female determined their legal rights.

Civil justice in Palestine during the reign of Herod and his sons was under the jurisprudence of the client rulers, who administered the province to meet the objectives set by Rome. Herod used three ruling bodies: the *boulē*, the *ekklēsia*, and the *synedrion* (Rocca, *Herod's Judaea*, 263–72). It appears that the *boulē*, which was the city council (mentioned by Josephus in *Ant.* 20.11; *J.W.* 2.331, 405; cf. Dio Cassius, *Hist.* 66.6.2; Luke 23:50) in Jerusalem, was a well-established political entity and should not be viewed as an ad hoc committee. On one occasion, Herod supposedly summoned the "most eminent men" of the city to convince them that the theater and the hippodrome were not contrary to Jewish beliefs and sensibilities (Josephus, *Ant.* 15.277–79). This governing organization consisted of several hundred members, who met to discuss matters dealing with the economy, such as setting market prices, certifying and providing weights and measures, and ensuring the purchase of wheat and supplies, which was always a concern in overpopulated areas. In Jerusalem, the *boulē* included magistrates, who were responsible for the theater and the water system (which Herod had installed) and for public health, including urban disposal and hygiene. It seems that the *boulē* was called to decide or ratify decisions concerning civic legislation. Joseph of Arimathea (Mark 15:43; Luke 23:50) was most likely a member of this council.

The popular assembly, the *ekklēsia*, had no real decision-making power, but it enabled Herod to sense the mood of the people concerning his policies and in turn allowed the population to be perceived as partners in important decisions. For example, Josephus reports that Herod called together an assembly of the masses for their input on the building of the temple (*Ant.* 15.381). Josephus also refers to a popular assembly that acted as an informal judge, jury, and executioner (*Ant.* 16.393–94; *J.W.* 1.648–50). This public body consisted of priests and lay, free men of military age and convened whenever a need arose. It is probable that after Herod's death, when Judea was ruled by Roman magistrates, the *ekklēsia* was replaced by the Sadducees and the Herodian upper classes.

The *synedrion* (Sanhedrin) appears to have been created during the Herodian era, probably as a reconstruction of the council of elders in the Hasmonean court. It is unclear who served on this body, what its structure was, or who convened its assembly. Its function, however, is clearer. It was the supreme legislative body that ruled on all legal matters that affected Jewish law, including criminal cases. The Sanhedrin could punish convicted offenders, but it is unclear whether it had the authority to enact capital punishment without Roman oversight. It appears that at times Roman governors intervened in local Jewish affairs and at other times they did not. In any case, the Roman authorities could take initiative themselves, without the approval of the Jewish court, and bring to trial anyone suspected of a political offense.

There were other Jewish courts in addition to the Sanhedrin. The communal judicial system was operated by local officials, who appointed magistrates throughout Galilean and Judean villages (cf. Matt. 5:22, 25; John 7:51). This informal system of local governments was independent of central authority, such as the Sanhedrin, and functioned much as it had done for centuries. The judiciary depended on seven elders, who had experience, wealth, or power in a community and whose main task was to settle legal cases. Josephus states that two Levites had to be appointed by the local village courts and serve together with the seven judges (*Ant.* 4.214; cf. Matt. 5:25). If expertise was needed, it is conceivable that other Levites, priests, and scribes were available for consultation (Mark 3:22; Matt. 9:3; Luke 11:45), with difficult cases being referred to a regional council (cf. Acts 4:5; Josephus, *Life* 79). Decisions and punishments could be meted out according to Jewish law by local officials, which could include flogging (cf. Matt. 10:16–18), excommunication (cf. Luke 6:22), or restitution (cf. Matt. 18:23).

Economy

Much of the information about the first-century economy in Palestine is sporadic. What can be said with certainty is that the society was primarily agrarian (see Josephus, *Ag. Ap.* 1.60). The traditional crops were grain (wheat, barley), olives, figs, and grapes. Of these, grain was the primary staple in the diet of the populace. It was grown wherever possible, but apparently the optimal crops were grown in the northern part of Samaria. Many of the crops grown around small villages served the needs of the local populations, the regional military, and the elite who wanted to be viewed as devoting themselves to "higher" interests of philosophy, leisure, and tranquility (see Cicero, *Sest.* 98). Only a few crops were exported. The hill country was well suited for growing olives and grapes. From pre-Roman times, Palestine made much of its excellent wine production, which was cultivated and exported in great quantities. But olive oil was Palestine's main surplus crop, with about half of the production being exported.

Jesus was associated with fishermen, some of whom were his disciples. Commercial fishing was not a free enterprise but was controlled by the wealthy, who sold fishing rights to brokers who in turn sold leases to fishermen (Oakman, *Jesus*, 106). At the bottom of this industry were hired laborers, who engaged in tasks like cleaning and mending nets and managing oars and sails (see Mark 1:19–20).

In addition to farming and fishing, peasants in villages had a variety of specializations that were handed down in families, such as making clothing; processing grain; manufacturing pottery, leather goods, metal, and wooden goods; weaving; and pressing olive oil and grapes. This allowed for self-sustaining village life.

The taxation system weighed heavily on peasants. Josephus writes that when Antipas was appointed ruler of Galilee, he enforced a special levy, collecting the vast sum of one hundred talents (*J.W.* 1.220; *Ant.* 14.274). Other taxes and tributes included a head tax of one denarius yearly (Appian, *Syr.* 50.8), a tribute of one-quarter of the crops every second year, an imperial tribute amounting to 12.5 percent per year, and tithes and offerings expected by the temple priests amounting to 20 percent of the crops. It is not known if all these taxes were collected or whether there was a fluctuation in tax rates. It is also unknown if the rates varied among regions. It should be noted that, although Tacitus (*Ann.* 2.42) records that the Jews pressed the Roman government for tax reduction in AD 17, there is no record of an organized tax revolt in first-century Palestine. This could be attributed to controls placed on the people, which made the organization of a revolt difficult. It can also be attributed to the possibility that the tax burden, although great, was common throughout the empire. Nonetheless, an inability to pay taxes or tributes would have indebted farmers to their creditors and reduced the landowners to tenant farmers.

A smoothly run port infrastructure was crucial to profitable trade. The port city of Tyre (today in southern Lebanon), for example, was an important economic center of Palestine. Its geographical layout allowed for two harbors and a fortified military port. In ancient times, the main part of Tyre was on an island situated in close proximity to the mainland, which eventually became an extension of the city. Distribution centers like Tyre had storage facilities and roads that connected the port to major inland arteries. The ports provided employment for large numbers of people and attracted numerous ancillary businesses of all types. Port cities were also cosmopolitan in the sense that they became natural points of philosophical and religious convergence.

The road system in Palestine consisted of four north–south arteries and a series of east–west secondary routes. Since towns and cities were destinations, they served as the intersections. In Galilee, the Romans built three major east–west roads from the Jordan valley to the sea, usually to port towns and cities. A major north–south route extended from Caesarea Philippi south to the east side of the Jordan Rift, then to Bethsaida, and branched off to encircle both sides of the Sea of Galilee. A well-traveled route that linked communities along the Mediterranean Sea was the Via Maris, which went the full length of Galilee and Judea and continued to Egypt (Isaac, "Infrastructure," 148–49).

See also "Economics, Taxes, and Tithes"; "Temple and Priesthood"; "Synagogue and Sanhedrin."

Bibliography

Alon, Gedaliah. *The Jews in their Land in the Talmudic Age (70–640 CE)*. Cambridge, MA: Harvard University Press, 1989. Highly recommended for its masterful use of rabbinic sources. Examines numerous social, legal, economic, and political issues concerning Jewish life under Roman rule.

Batey, Richard A. *Jesus and the Forgotten City: New Light on Sepphoris and the Urban World of Jesus*. Grand Rapids: Baker, 1991. A good introduction to the cosmopolitan culture of Sepphoris and urban Galilee, with a fine selection of illustrations and photos. Argues that Jesus was well acquainted with Galilean urban life.

Ben-Dov, Meir. *In the Shadow of the Temple: The Discovery of Ancient Jerusalem*. New York: HarperCollins, 1985. This report on the excavations at the temple mount contains valuable sections on Herod's reconstruction. Highly accessible.

Chancey, Mark A. *The Myth of a Gentile Galilee*. SNTSMS 118. Cambridge: Cambridge University Press, 2002. An important contribution to the ongoing question of whether first-century Galilee was primarily Jewish or pagan. The author argues for the former.

Cohen, Shaye J. D. *From the Maccabees to the Mishnah*. 2nd ed. Louisville: Westminster John Knox, 2006. Excellent introduction to the history, politics, texts, and beliefs of early Judaism. Accessible to all students.

———. "Were Pharisees and Rabbis the Leaders of Communal Prayer and Torah Study in Antiquity? The Evidence of the New Testament, Josephus and the Early Church Fathers." Pages 89–105 in *Evolution of the Synagogue: Problems and Progress*. Edited by H. C. Kee and L. H. Cohick. Harrisburg, PA: Trinity Press International, 1999. Important essay on the role of Pharisees during the time of Jesus. Very good contribution to the study of the social background of rural and urban peasant life.

Crossan, John Dominic, and Jonathan L. Reed. *Excavating Jesus: Beneath the Stones, Behind the Texts*. New York: HarperCollins, 2001. A historical Jesus scholar and an archaeologist examine the most significant archaeological discoveries that shed light on Jesus and his teachings. Well illustrated and accessible.

Fiensy, David A. *The Social History of Palestine in the Herodian Period: The Land Is Mine*. SBEC 20. Lewiston, NY: Mellen, 1991. A valuable contribution to the long-standing discussion on the impact of urbanization in Palestine. Good evaluation of how the archaeological and textual records have been (mis)interpreted. Provides a good example of how sociological and anthropological models can be applied.

Freyne, Sean. *Jesus a Jewish Galilean: A New Reading of the Jesus Story.* London: T&T Clark, 2004. An excellent resource for understanding the social, religious, and political context of the historical Jesus' ministry in Galilee in the late 20s.

Grabbe, Lester L. *Judaic Religion in the Second Temple Period: Belief and Practice from the Exile to Yavneh.* London: Routledge, 2000. The focus is the development of early Jewish beliefs, structures, and their connections with political movements and ideals. It is clearly written, accessible, and filled with primary data.

Hanson, K. C., and Douglas E. Oakman. *Palestine in the Time of Jesus: Social Structures and Social Conflicts.* Minneapolis: Fortress, 1998. An accessible treatment of peasant life in rural and urban Palestine. Includes valuable discussions of family life, institutions, politics, economy, and religion. A fine textbook.

Hengel, Martin. "The Geography of Palestine in Acts." Pages 27–79 in *The Book of Acts in Its Palestinian Setting.* Edited by Richard Bauckham. A1CS 4. Grand Rapids: Eerdmans, 1995. A thorough treatment of the social and physical geography of Palestine as it relates to the book of Acts. Includes a rich array of textual data.

Horsley, Richard A. *Galilee: History, Politics, People.* Valley Forge, PA: Trinity Press International, 1995. A valuable analysis of the political and social dimensions of both rural and urban Galilee. His interpretations of the data raise provocative questions. Excellent summary of prior works on Galilee.

———. "Synagogues in Galilee and the Gospels." Pages 46–69 in *Evolution of the Synagogue: Problems and Progress.* Edited by H. C. Kee and L. H. Cohick. Harrisburg, PA: Trinity Press International, 1999. Valuable summary of the institution and function of synagogues in Galilee and their later impact on nascent Christianity.

Isaac, Benjamin. "Infrastructure." Pages 145–64 in *The Oxford Handbook of Jewish Daily Life in Roman Palestine.* Edited by C. Hezser. Oxford: Oxford University Press, 2010. Recommended summary of studies on rural and urban infrastructure, such as the layout of cities, their relationship to the countryside, roads, and markets.

Kee, Howard Clark. "Early Christianity in the Galilee: Reassessing the Evidence from the Gospels." Pages 3–22 in *The Galilee in Late Antiquity.* Edited by L. Levine. New York: Jewish Theological Seminary of America, 1992. Well-written and well-documented essay on urban and rural life and interaction in first-century Galilee. Argues for a strong Roman presence in the Galilean urban centers.

Oakman, Douglas E. *Jesus and the Economic Questions of His Day.* SBEC 8. Lewiston, NY: Mellen, 1986. Situates Jesus' life within the economics of peasant societies. Valuable discussion of how the urban redistribution system of the elites (Rome and temple) exploited peasants.

Reed, Jonathan L. "Instability in Jesus' Galilee: A Demographic Perspective." *JBL* 129 (2010): 343–65. Provides a helpful summary of the long-standing debate on the urban-rural divide in Galilee. Argues that Galilee was not a demographically stable region under Antipas's reign.

Rocca, Samuel. *Herod's Judaea: A Mediterranean State in the Classical World.* Tübingen: Mohr Siebeck, 2008. A valuable study into the relationship between King Herod, who modeled his reign after Alexander the Great and Augustus, and his Jewish subjects in Judea.

Sanders, E. P. "Jesus' Galilee." Pages 3–41 in *Fair Play: Diversity and Conflicts in Early Christianity: Essays in Honour of Heikki Räisänen.* Edited by I. Dunderberg et al. NovTSup

103. Boston: Brill, 2002. Offers a helpful summary of recent research on first-century Galilee. Includes valuable contributions to the interrelationship between the residents of Galilee and Roman power.

Strange, James F. "Sepphoris." http://www.bibleinterp.com/articles/sepphoris.htm. Brief, but informative, summary of the archaeological findings at Sepphoris by a leading scholar. The home page includes links to several primary texts.

————. "Tiberias." *ABD* 6:547–49. One of the best introductory articles on first-century Tiberias, with numerous references to primary sources.

39

Syria, Cilicia, and Cyprus

MARK WILSON

Syria

Ancient Syria was the geographic region that encompassed the mountains and fertile plains between the Mediterranean coast and the desert of northern Arabia in the northeastern Levant. During the Persian period (ca. 539 BC), Syria became a satrapy known as "Beyond the River," that is, beyond the Euphrates, Syria's eastern boundary. This distinguished it from "Syria between the Rivers," which was Mesopotamia. Alexander the Great incorporated Syria into his kingdom after defeating the Persians at Issus in 333 BC. Following the battle of Ipsus in 301 BC, the Macedonian general Seleucus I Nicator assumed control of northern Syria while his counterpart Ptolemy I Soter ruled southern Syria. Seleucus is noted for founding four great cities in Syria—Seleucia, Antioch, Laodicea, and Apamea. He made Seleucia the first capital of Syria, but his son Antiochus I moved the capital to Antioch in 281 BC. After the Romans gained control of Syria in 64 BC, Antioch continued as the capital. The Roman province of Syria was an important administrative district on the empire's eastern border. Its territory stretched as far south as Petra. Three to four legions were usually stationed in Syria. This large force protected Rome from the feared Parthians, who threatened from across the Euphrates, and from the volatile Jews in Judea.

Around 27 BC Augustus changed Syria's status from a senatorial province to an imperial province. The post of legate of Syria was one of the most important appointments in the empire. Around 44 BC Cilicia Pedias (see below) was incorporated into the province of Syria and remained a part of it until AD 72. Luke 2:2 mentions that Quirinius was the province's governor at the time Jesus was born. This reference presents a historical difficulty because Josephus (*Ant*. 18.1–10, 26–28) states that Quirinius served as governor in AD 6–7 and that the census for Judea occurred in AD 6, a decade after Jesus' birth. One proposed solution for this quandary suggests that Quirinius held an extraordinary command in the East when the first census was made and that the second census was held during his governorship.[1]

Damascus

Three Syrian cities—Damascus, Antioch, and Seleucia Pieria—have importance for NT students. Damascus is located on a plateau between the Anti-Lebanon mountain range and the Syrian Desert, 2,230 feet above sea level. Two rivers flow through the city, the ancient Abana and Pharpar (2 Kings 5:12). It is one of the oldest continuously occupied cities in the world. Damascus is mentioned numerous times in the OT. From the tenth century to the eighth century BC it was the capital of Aram, acting as both a rival (cf. 2 Sam. 8:5–6) and an ally of Israel (cf. 1 Kings 15:18–20). The Assyrians captured Damascus in 732 BC and made it a provincial capital, a status that continued through the Babylonian (572–532 BC) and Persian (532–325 BC) periods.[2] After the Seleucids made Antioch their capital, Damascus lost its preeminent place in Syria.

The city was situated at the crossroads of an important north–south caravan route, and travel southward to Jerusalem was relatively easy, a distance of approximately 175 miles. In the first century AD, Damascus had a substantial Jewish population, with a number of synagogues (see Acts 9:2, 20). At the beginning of the Jewish rebellion in AD 66, Josephus records, its residents killed 10,500 Jews (*J.W.* 2.561; the number is 18,550 in *J.W.* 7.368). Acts never describes how the church was founded there, only that disciples like Ananias lived in the city (Acts 9:10).

Damascus was an important nexus for Paul's early life as a disciple of Christ (see Acts 9; Gal. 1:13–17). The "many days" of Acts 9:23 (NIV) is apparently the period mentioned by Paul in Gal. 1:17 when he spent time in Arabia and later returned to Damascus. Paul was forced to flee the city because of a plot against his life. Acts 9:23 states that he was fleeing a conspiracy of the Jews, while Paul himself writes that the Nabatean king Aretas IV was seeking to arrest him (2 Cor. 11:32). He escaped when his disciples lowered him in a basket over the city wall, traditionally at the gate Bab Kisan (Acts 9:25; 2 Cor. 11:33). Today there are few archaeological remains from Paul's day. The Straight Street (Via Recta; Acts 9:11), the Roman *decumanus maximus* (the central east–west street) where Paul stayed

1. I. H. Marshall, *The Gospel of Luke* (NIGTC; Grand Rapids: Eerdmans, 1978), 102–4.
2. Ross Burns, *Damascus: A History* (London: Routledge, 2005), 23–26.

with Judas, is still lined with shops. An underground chapel marks the traditional site of the house of Ananias.

Antioch

History. Antioch (modern Antakya, Turkey) was located on the east bank of the Orontes River in northwestern Syria. It was founded in May 300 BC by Seleucus I Nicator, who moved settlers from nearby Antigonia and named the new city after his father. (Although there were sixteen Antiochs in the ancient world, this and Pisidian Antioch are the only two mentioned in the Bible.) An inland city, Antioch was a half-day journey upriver from its port, Seleucia Pieria. Antioch was strategically situated at the crossroads of several major routes that connected Asia Minor, Mesopotamia, and Judea. At an elevation of 220 feet, the city was situated at the foot of Mount Silpius. The fortifications on this citadel were never adequate to defend the city; hence it was vulnerable to attack. Four gates led into the city, and its grid plan was unusual because it followed a northeast to southwest orientation. This design accommodated the cooling Mediterranean breezes that flowed up the Orontes valley.

After Seleucus's assassination in 281 BC, his son Antiochus I Soter made Antioch the capital of the Seleucid Empire. After the defeat of Antiochus III by the Romans in 190 BC, the Seleucids lost control of Asia Minor north of the Taurus Mountains. Antioch's power and status was therefore greatly reduced. Antiochus IV (175–163 BC) restored the city's magnificence through an extensive building program. A series of weak rulers followed, and from 83 to 69 BC Tigranes II of Armenia occupied the city. The last ruler of the Seleucid dynasty was Antiochus XIII (69–64 BC).

In 64 BC Pompey the Great ended Seleucid rule and made Syria a Roman province with Antioch as its capital. When Julius Caesar visited the city in 47 BC, he introduced a new timekeeping system, replacing the Seleucid dating with a Julian calendar. In 40–39 BC the Parthians again occupied Antioch, but Antony soon reestablished control. Augustus twice visited the city, in 31–30 BC and 20 BC, and through his benefaction more building projects resulted. Herod the Great was responsible for paving the city's main colonnaded street with polished stones, and Tiberius built its impressive colonnades. In AD 37 Caligula sent funds to rebuild the city after a damaging earthquake.

Antioch's population in the first century AD is estimated conservatively at two hundred thousand people,[3] making it the third-largest city in the Roman Empire (Josephus, *J.W.* 3.29), behind Rome and Alexandria. Tyche (Fortune) was the principal goddess of the city and regarded as its protector. A Roman imperial cult existed in the late first century BC, and Augustus appears on coins depicted as the high priest of his own cult.

Jews in Antioch. Seleucus I settled Jews in Antioch and granted them special civic rights (Josephus, *J.W.* 7.44; *Ag. Ap.* 2.39). During the reign of Antiochus IV

---

3. F. W. Norris, *ABD* 1:265.

the Jewish community was forbidden to circumcise, Torah scrolls were confiscated, and Hellenization was imposed. The most famous example of Jewish resistance was the Maccabean martyrdom. According to one tradition, the scribe Eleazar, seven brothers, and their mother died in Antioch (2 Macc. 6:18–7:41; 4 Macc. 17:7–10). In 169 BC Antiochus IV attacked the Jerusalem temple, rededicated it to Zeus, and carried its sacred treasures to Antioch. After the death of Antiochus IV in 164 BC, his successors restored the property of the Jews of Antioch, whose population soon became the largest in Syria (Josephus, *J.W.* 7.33).

After the Jewish revolt began in AD 66, the Jewish community was again persecuted when a fire in the city was falsely blamed on them (Josephus, *J.W.* 7.54–62). Following the destruction of Jerusalem in AD 70, Titus visited Antioch to celebrate the victory. Despite the petitions of Antioch's citizens, he sustained the traditional rights of the Jewish community and refused to expel them from the city. Titus, however, did erect on the Daphne Gate the bronze cherubim taken from the temple to remind the Jews of his triumph.

39.1. Important cities of Syria, Cilicia, and Cyprus.

Christians in Antioch. In the first century AD Antioch developed into an important center of Christianity. According to Acts, Barnabas and Paul taught great numbers in an early type of discipleship training (11:23–26), and members of the nascent community were first called "Christians" here (v. 26). The aid brought to Judean believers as a result of Agabus's prophecy was an early example of Christian relief work (Acts 11:27–30; cf. Gal. 2:1–10). This famine struck Antioch as well as Judea around AD 46. After returning from Jerusalem, in Antioch Paul and Barnabas were commissioned for their first missionary journey (Acts 12:25–13:3). They, along with John Mark, were sent out around AD 46. Scholars who hold to the early dating of Galatians typically see this letter as having been written from Antioch after the apostles returned there around AD 48. It is Paul's only letter that has a church, probably Antioch, named as a cosender (Gal. 1:2). Acts never mentions the presence of Peter in Antioch. However, Paul describes Peter's visit wherein the latter vacillated over eating with gentiles, prompting a confrontation by Paul (Gal. 2:11–14). A disagreement in Antioch over the necessity of circumcision for salvation prompted the apostolic council in Jerusalem (Acts 15:1–21). Paul once again made the four-hundred-mile journey there and back with Barnabas (Acts 15:2, 30). Paul also started his second and third journeys from Antioch (Acts 15:40; 18:22–23).

Peter appears to have ministered in and around Antioch until AD 54. Eusebius (*Eccl. Hist.* 3.32) names Evodius as the first bishop of Antioch. His assumption of leadership at that time might relate to Peter's departure, although Paul continued to have ties to Antioch until the mid-50s too. Peter was the first of Jesus' twelve apostles to visit Antioch, and in later centuries the Antiochian church, eager to associate itself with the Twelve, claimed Peter as a main figure in its history. Catholic and Orthodox tradition holds that Peter was the first bishop of Antioch. Some scholars have suggested that Matthew wrote an early draft of his Gospel for an Antiochian audience. Around AD 114 Ignatius, the bishop of Antioch, was dispatched to Rome for execution. As he traveled through the province of Asia, he wrote seven letters to Christians there that are now collected in the Apostolic Fathers. The *Didache* ("Teaching"), also found in the Apostolic Fathers, is sometimes connected with Antioch. The pseudepigraphic *Odes of Solomon*, a collection of early Jewish Christian hymns and known to Ignatius, probably originated from Antioch around AD 100.

Seleucia Pieria

Seleucia Pieria (modern Çevlik) is located sixteen miles southwest of Antioch on the Mediterranean Sea. In 300 BC Seleucus I Nicator founded Seleucia as Syria's first capital. Following his assassination in 281 BC by Ptolemy Ceraunus, Seleucus I was buried in Seleucia. His son Antiochus I then moved the capital to Antioch. Seleucia's strategic coastal location caused the Ptolemies and Seleucids to vie continually for its control. In 241 BC Ptolemy III Euergetes secured Ptolemaic control for the next twenty-two years. Finally, in 219 BC Antiochus III the Great recaptured the city. Ptolemy VI later captured Seleucia again for Egypt in 146 BC (1 Macc. 11:8). Records from 186 BC show that Seleucia was self-governing, a status confirmed by the Seleucids in 109/8 BC and by Pompey the Great in 66 BC. During the imperial period, Seleucia served as a base for the imperial fleet, and its harbor had to be continually maintained because of silting. Paul and Barnabas set sail with John Mark from Seleucia to Cyprus on their first journey (Acts 13:4). However, Seleucia is unmentioned as the apostles' disembarkation point when they sailed back to Antioch (Acts 14:26). Cut stones from the mole that lined the channel to the inner harbor are still visible in Seleucia.

Cilicia

Cilicia was a region of Asia Minor located on the northeastern coast of the Mediterranean Sea. It was divided into two sections—Tracheia (Greek, "Rough"; Latin *Aspera*) and Pedias (Greek, "Smooth"; Latin *Campestris*). The boundary stood at the Lamus River, west of Soli-Pompeiopolis. Because only Cilicia Pedias relates to the biblical text, our discussion will focus on it. Pedias consisted of three areas—the western Aleian Plain, a northeastern plain, and a coastal strip along the Amanus Mountains. The Aleian Plain was drained by three important rivers—the Cydnus, the Sarus, and the Pyramus. A limestone ridge running south from the Taurus to the Amanus Mountains separated the northeastern plain from the Aleian Plain. A narrow gorge at Mopsuestia provided the only means of transit between them. The Cilician Gates (elevation 3,445 feet) provided entrance to Cilicia from the north through the Taurus Mountains. At Tarsus the Pilgrim's Road joined the coastal road, which ran westward to Soloi and Cilicia Tracheia and eastward to Adana and Mopsuestia. East of Mopsuestia travelers encountered another junction. Those going to Zeugma on the Euphrates took the northern branch. Abraham is depicted in the *Genesis Apocryphon* (1QGenAp 21.16–17) as following this route in his circular journey of the Near East. Travelers bound for Syria took the southern branch through the Amanian Gates, reaching the coast above Issus. This coastal road continued southward past Baiae, where it passed through the Cilician-Syrian Gates (*Pylae*). Here stood Jonah's Pillar, where, according to tradition, the prophet Jonah was washed ashore. This ridge of the Amanus Mountains that ran down to the sea formed a natural boundary between Cilicia and Syria (Strabo, *Geogr.* 14.5.19 [676]). Alexandria ad Issum was located further south along the coast, before the road climbed southeast over the Syrian Gates (elevation 2,428 feet) to Antioch.

A critical question for interpreting Acts 15:23 and 41 is whether Luke is talking about geographical Cilicia or political Cilicia. The sequence of names—Antioch, Syria, Cilicia—suggests a geographical progression following the established route northward. Rhosus and Alexandria were cities in northwestern Syria where churches might have existed. At the Cilician-Syrian Gates Paul would pass into Cilicia. This natural boundary was used by Vespasian in AD 72 to establish the political border separating Cilicia from Syria.

After Alexander defeated Darius III in 333 BC at Issus, Cilicia experienced rapid Hellenization. Seleucus I Nicator (ca. 282 BC) and Antiochus IV (171 BC) urbanized many cities, including Tarsus, Mopsuestia, and Adana. The original province of Cilicia was organized in 102 BC as Rome's second province in Asia Minor. However, the province did not include either Tracheia or Pedias. In the early decades of the first century BC Cilicia declined due to pirates plundering the coast and the invasion of the Armenian king Tigranes. After Pompey defeated the pirates in 67 BC, Cilicia was resettled with some of the pirate captives. At this time Pompey finally attached Pedias to Cilicia and made Tarsus the provincial capital (Dio Chrysostom, *Or.* 34.7–8). He also refounded many cities between 67 and 65 BC and divided Pedias into seventeen cities. However, Cilicia's status was diminishing; Cicero served as its last governor of consular rank in 51–50 BC. Pedias was joined to the province of Syria around 44 BC, an affiliation that continued until AD 72, when Vespasian finally joined Pedias and Tracheia into their own province.

In Gal. 1:21 Paul states that he returned to Syria and Cilicia after his conversion on the road to Damascus. How long he remained there is unknown, but various chronologies of Paul's life suggest a period of five to ten years. Acts 15 suggests that these "silent years" may not have been so quiet after all. The Jerusalem church sent a letter summarizing the results of the apostolic council to gentile believers in Cilicia (Acts 15:23, 41). This is the first mention in Acts of churches in Cilicia. No other person is known to have been in Cilicia except Paul. Following his return to Cilicia, it appears that Paul was active in church planting there. Although Paul may have attempted to evangelize many of Cilicia's seventeen cities, three are likely candidates for Pauline churches: Tarsus, Adana, and Mopsuestia.

Tarsus is one of the few cities in Turkey to retain its ancient name. It is located about ten miles from the Mediterranean coast. The Cydnus River flowed through Tarsus and, before reaching the sea, entered the Rhegma, a lagoon that served as an arsenal and harbor for Tarsus. Tarsus was first inhabited around 3000 BC, and it became the capital of a small kingdom around 2500 BC. In the second millennium BC it was an important Hittite city because of its strategic location near the Cilician Gates. Around 1200 BC it was destroyed by the Sea Peoples, but it was refounded soon afterward by Greeks from Argos in the Peloponnesus. Tarsus is among the towns mentioned on the Black Obelisk that Shalmaneser captured in the middle of the ninth century BC. During both the Assyrian and Persian periods, Tarsus served as an administrative center. In 333 BC Alexander the Great pronounced Tarsus a free city, and it functioned as such during most of the Seleucid period. After Tarsus revolted against Antiochus IV in 171 BC (2 Macc. 4:30–31), the city was reorganized and renamed Antiocheia on the Cydnus. Julius Caesar visited Tarsus in 47 BC, and in 41 BC Mark Antony met Cleopatra on a barge that sailed up the Cydnus (Plutarch, *Ant.* 26).

With Cilicia's incorporation into Syria around 44 BC, Tarsus lost its status as a provincial capital. Augustus restored it as a free city in 19 BC before he visited

Tarsus. The emperor's teacher, the Stoic philosopher Athenodorus, came from Tarsus, and in 15 BC Augustus appointed him to expel the tyrant Boethus and reform the city. Tarsus was a provincial administrative center (*conventus*) during Paul's day. Strabo (*Geogr.* 14.5.13) stated that the city "not only has a flourishing population but also is most powerful, thus keeping up the reputation of the mother-city." Dio Chrysostom (*Or.* 33.17, 28; 34.7–8, 37 LCL) later called it "the greatest of the cities of Cilicia." Among the ruins still in Tarsus is a well-preserved section of a colonnaded and guttered street lined with shops that dates to the time of Paul.

Lee Martin McDonald

39.2. Ruins of an ancient Roman forum in Tarsus, from the time of the apostle Paul.

Adana, like Tarsus, retains its ancient name to the present. Located on the main highway, it was also a likely site for one of the Cilician churches. Dio Cassius (*Hist.* 47.31.2) records that Adana had a long-standing rivalry with Tarsus. The city was founded during the Hittite period, although it appears in literary sources only from the Hellenistic period onward. It was an important river crossing, situated on the west bank of the Sarus. Little remains of ancient Adana, although the acropolis area is still visible. A bridge built by Hadrian in the second century AD and restored by Justinian continues to span the Sarus River.

Mopsuestia (modern Misis) was named after its eponymous founder, the legendary Mopsos, who migrated to Cilicia after the fall of Troy. Like Adana, the city was on the main highway. A stone bridge, dating from the Roman period and recently renovated, is still used to cross the Pyramus River. A small mosaic museum contains the remains of Turkey's earliest biblical mosaic, with scenes depicting the accounts of Noah's ark and Samson. Scholars differ as to the building's function, whether it was a synagogue or a basilican church. Mopsuestia's Christian heritage is recalled through its famous bishop and church father Theodore (AD 342–408).

The founding of the Cilician churches during Paul's "silent years" has several important implications for early Christian history. First, these churches antedate even the establishment of the church in Antioch, which Luke emphasizes in Acts. A corollary is that they precede the establishment of the churches in south Galatia during Paul's first journey. The churches in Cilicia would thus have been the first Christian churches in Asia Minor. Second, the presence of these churches influenced the itinerary of Paul's first journey. The Mediterranean coast southward was already evangelized (Acts 11:19). Because the boundary of the Roman Empire was just east of Antioch, evangelization in that direction was difficult. Because of the existence of the Cilician churches, Paul had no incentive to travel northward. West was the only direction open, and Cyprus was an inviting first stop since it was the home of Barnabas (Acts 4:36). Finally, the experience Paul gained in Cilicia would later prove valuable as he planted churches during his later journeys. He generally evangelized key cities along major roads where there was a significant Jewish population. In these cities he first went to the synagogues, where he would usually be rejected and persecuted (2 Cor. 11:24). Then he would preach to the gentiles. Taking a core of Jewish and gentile believers, Paul would establish a church and appoint local leadership, while maintaining contact through personal visits and letters. Paul visited the Cilician churches again at the beginning of his second journey in order to share the letter from the apostolic council (Acts 15:23, 41). Paul also passed through Cilicia and on to Ephesus at the beginning of his third journey (Acts 18:23).

Twice in Jerusalem, Paul specifically associated himself with Tarsus and Cilicia (Acts 21:39; 22:3). Later the governor Felix asked Paul from which *eparcheia* he came, and he responded, "from Cilicia" (Acts 23:34). As mentioned earlier, Cilicia was not a province at this time but rather a part of Syria. Inscriptional evidence suggests that *eparcheia* might be better translated "district" rather than "province" in this verse.

Literary and archaeological evidence validates the presence of Jews in Cilicia. Acts 6:9 mentions Cilician Jews who, with other Diaspora Jews, formed a synagogue of the Freedmen in Jerusalem. Agrippa I confirms the presence of Jews in Cilicia in his letter to Caligula (Philo, *Legat.* 281). Although archaeological objects such as the menorahs on lead coffins found at Aegeai date later than the biblical period, the accumulated evidence points to a long-established Jewish community. This population must have been large and is estimated around seventy thousand.

Cyprus

Cyprus is the third-largest island in the Mediterranean, after Sicily and Sardinia. It is 138 miles long and 60 miles wide, with an area of 3,571 square miles. It lies

39.3. According to local legend, Paul was beaten on the rounded stone pillar in the foreground when he and Barnabas ministered here in Paphos, Cyprus (Acts 13:6–13).

only 47 miles off the southern coast of Asia Minor. The distance from Salamis to Seleucia Pieria was about 130 miles. The island's Greek name is *Kypros*, while its Hebrew name, *Kittim*, is probably derived from the southeastern coastal city of Kition (Num. 24:24; Dan. 11:30). In the OT, Kition might also have been known as Elishah (cf. Ezek. 27:7). Two mountain ranges dominate the island's topography, the Kyrenia along the northern coast and the Troodos in the southwest. Between these ranges lies the central plain, called the Mesaoria. Cyprus was located along important sea trading routes; hence, throughout its history it became subject to Rhodes, Phoenicia, Persia, Egypt, Greece, and Rome. In 58 BC it was annexed by Rome, and in 30 BC it became a Roman province. In the imperial period, Cyprus was divided into four districts: Paphos, Salamis, Amathus, and Lapethos. After an earthquake destroyed Salamis in 15 BC, the capital was shifted from there to Nea (New) Paphos. Salamis, however, remained the island's most important city. Agrippa, in his letter to the emperor Gaius Caligula, stated that Cyprus was an island with a significant Jewish community (Philo, *Legat.* 282). Barnabas was a Levite from Cyprus (Acts 4:36), and a Cypriot disciple named Mnason hosted Paul in Jerusalem (Acts 21:16). Salamis was the port city at the northeastern end of the island, where Paul, Barnabas, and John Mark landed on their first journey (Acts 13:5). Here they began to preach in the Jewish synagogues. The apocryphal *Acts of Barnabas* (22–23) claims that Barnabas was later martyred here by a mob. The nearby Church of St. Barnabas stands over his supposed burial site. After leaving Salamis, the apostolic party traveled along the Roman road that ran across the southern coast to Paphos. According to Acts, there Paul encountered the sorcerer Elymas, who was subsequently blinded. This event amazed the Roman governor

Sergius Paulus, who became his first important gentile convert (Acts 13:6–12). Through Sergius's influence the apostolic party was apparently redirected to his home colony of Pisidian Antioch (Acts 13:13–14). After Paul and Barnabas split at the beginning of the second journey, Barnabas and John again sailed to Cyprus from Seleucia (Acts 15:39). The most important ruins at Paphos are the remains of the palace of the Roman governor and the mosaics of the house of Dionysus. Outside a Byzantine church is a pillar on which Paul was scourged, according to local tradition.

Bibliography

Butcher, Kevin. *Roman Syria and the Near East*. Los Angeles: Getty, 2003. A comprehensive survey of the history and archaeology of Syria under Roman rule.

Downey, Glanville. *A History of Antioch in Syria from Seleucus to the Arab Conquest*. Princeton: Princeton University Press, 1950. An in-depth history of Antioch on the Orontes.

Jones, A. H. M. *The Cities of the Eastern Roman Provinces*. 2nd ed. Oxford: Clarendon, 1971. An enlightening look at the urbanization of the Greek East by a leading scholar of antiquity.

Karageorghis, Vassos. *Salamis: Recent Discoveries in Cyprus*. New York: McGraw Hill, 1969. A dated but still useful overview of the history and archaeology of Salamis.

Kondoleon, Christine, ed. *Antioch: The Lost Ancient City*. Princeton: Princeton University Press, 2000. A beautifully illustrated volume on the current state of research regarding various aspects of life in Antioch.

Maier, F. G., and V. Karageorghis. *Paphos: History and Archaeology*. Nicosia: A. G. Leventis Foundation, 1984. An illustrated guide to the Roman capital of Cyprus.

Nobbs, Alanna. "Cyprus." Pages 279–89 in *The Book of Acts in Its Graeco-Roman Setting*. Edited by David W. J. Gill and Conrad Gempf. A1CS 2. Grand Rapids: Eerdmans, 1994. An insightful article on Cyprus's role in the NT.

Tracey, Robyn. "Syria." Pages 223–78 in *The Book of Acts in Its Graeco-Roman Setting*. Edited by David W. J. Gill and Conrad Gempf. A1CS 2. Grand Rapids: Eerdmans, 1994. A comprehensive article on Syria during the biblical period.

Wilson, Mark. "Cilicia: The First Christian Churches in Anatolia." *TynBul* 54, no. 1 (2003): 15–30. An article discussing Cilicia and its role in early Christianity.

———. "Was Paul a Cilician, a Native of Tarsus?: A Historical Reassessment." *Olba* 8 (2003): 93–107. An article evaluating how the book of Acts presents Paul's relationship to Cilicia and Tarsus.

Zoroğlu, Levent. *A Guide to Tarsus*. Ankara: Dönmez, n.d. A basic guide to the history and archaeology of Tarsus.

40

The Province and Cities of Asia

PAUL TREBILCO

The early church grew rapidly in the province of Asia, and a significant part of the NT relates to cities in this province. Asia was also one of the regions to which 1 Peter was addressed (1 Pet. 1:1).

The Province of Asia

The Roman province of Asia extended along the western coast of the Anatolian Peninsula, now modern Turkey, from the Propontis in the north to the Mediterranean in the South. In the time of Paul the province of Asia incorporated the areas of Mysia, the Troad, Aeolis, Ionia, the coastal islands, Lydia, Caria, western Phrygia, and Cibyra.

In 334 BC Alexander the Great ended Persian control of what later became the province of Asia. The Seleucids ruled most of Asia Minor during the third century, with the Romans being drawn into the affairs of the area during the rule of Antiochus III. Under the Treaty of Apamea of 188 BC, most of Anatolia was taken from the Seleucids and granted to Eumenes II, king of Pergamum, and other monarchs friendly to Rome. The kings of Pergamum ruled western Asia Minor until 133 BC, when Attalus III of Pergamum bequeathed supremacy over the area to the Roman people.

40.1. The Library of Celsus in Ephesus was built between AD 105 and 120 and restored between 1970 and 1978. It was named after the Roman governor of Asia, who lived in Ephesus. His tomb lies below the west wall of the library.

Manius Aquillius created the province between 129 and 126 BC. After Mithridates VI of Pontus unsuccessfully revolted against Rome between 89 and 85 BC, there were no further attempts to oust Roman power. The reconstruction of the province by Sulla in 85 BC and the associated levies he required led to considerable economic hardship in Asia. After his defeat of Pompey in 48 BC, Julius Caesar's general policy in Asia was considerate; both he and some of those he appointed to office granted favors and privileges to the cities, which evoked widespread gratitude. After Caesar's assassination, Brutus and Cassius regarded the eastern provinces primarily as a source of wealth and power and used Asia as a source of money and troops. Mark Antony entered Ephesus in triumph and, in order to pay his soldiers, demanded that the taxes due from Asia for the next nine years should be paid within two years. The effect of the civil wars was to leave Asia totally depleted of capital.

Octavian, known as Augustus from 27 BC, defeated Antony at the battle of Actium in 31 BC. As Robert Broughton notes, "The first aim of Augustus was to rebuild a vigorous city life out of the wreckage of the civil wars; that of most of his successors was to maintain and extend it" ("Roman Asia Minor," 711). The importance of Octavian in the eyes of the people of Asia was shown by the development of the imperial cult in Asia from 29 BC. He also stimulated urban development in the province, and throughout his long reign, which ended in AD 14, he generally adopted policies that were beneficial for the province.

Tiberius, who was emperor until AD 37, continued the policy of his predecessor with respect to Asia; his government was generally beneficial, and he attempted to prevent extortion and cruelty and to maintain law and order (see Magie, *Roman Rule*, 1:491–510). The province was little affected by Caligula's grandiose ideas and desire to play the part of an Oriental ruler (AD 37–41). Claudius's policies generally promoted the welfare of the province (AD 41–54), while Nero (AD 54–68) continued the bureaucratic methods of Claudius, including allowing imperial procurators to have increased power; he also adopted measures for the benefit of the province, which overall was not impacted by his cruelty and folly.

Vespasian's reign (AD 69–79) was marked by a continuation of the trend toward centralization, and his efforts to ensure the allegiance and contentment of the cities of Asia seem to have met with success. The Flavian period (AD 69–96) was a time of great urban growth and architectural development in the cities of Asia.

David Spender/Wikimedia Commons

40.2. Ruins of the temple of Athena in Assos (ca. 530 BC). Assos was the home of Aristotle before he became the teacher of Alexander the Great. The apostle Paul came to the city overland from Troas and set sail from here with his missionary colleagues (Acts 20:13–15).

Overall, Augustus's rule began a long period of peace and development in Asia that lasted throughout the first and second centuries AD and brought recovery first to the great coastal cities and then to smaller cities and the inland regions. The Pax Romana, and the confidence engendered by peace, along with improvements throughout the empire, made it possible for Asia's great natural resources to be developed, introducing an era of unprecedented prosperity. This becomes most apparent in the commencement of building work undertaken in the cities. In the first century AD the increase in building work, financed primarily by municipal funds and private gifts, leaves the impression that a gradual and sound recovery had taken place. This recovery laid the foundation for the wide expansion of urban life and culture and the widespread prosperity of the second and early third centuries in Asia. As Stephen Mitchell (*Anatolia*, 1:198) notes, "The great age of urban building in Asia Minor, running from the beginning of the principate to the Severan period, with the most intense activity in the second century, marks the climax of Roman civic life in the provinces."

There were some significant and well-established Jewish communities in Asia, dating back at least to the third century BC. We have evidence that some of these communities were involved in the life of their cities, and they clearly had an impact on the development of early Christianity in the province.

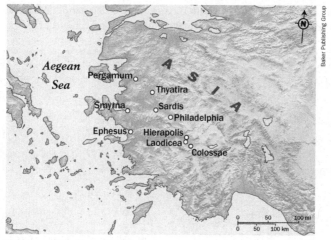

40.3. Important cities of Asia.

Main Cities

Cities in the province of Asia feature as recipients of Paul's Letters, in the book of Acts, and as the "seven churches" of Revelation. The main cities will be discussed below. Other cities in Asia mentioned in the NT include Adramyttium (Acts 27:2), Cnidus (Acts 27:7), and Cos (Acts 21:1).

Assos

According to Acts 20:13–14, Paul traveled from Troas to Assos by foot, while his companions traveled by ship. Assos was opposite the northern end of the island of Lesbos, on the southern coast of the Troad, and was situated on the coast road from Adramyttium to Troas.

By the sixth century BC, Assos had become the most important city in the Troad. The city was of military significance to the Attalids, since it commanded

40.4. The theater at Assos.

the easiest passage from Pergamum to the Troad. An artificial harbor gave the city considerable importance in coastal trade (see Strabo, *Geogr.* 13.1.57, 66), but with the growth of Alexandria Troas to the north into a great commercial center, Assos declined in significance. However, it continued to be a port where coastal traders called, and we know of some construction work in the city in the first century AD (Broughton, "Roman Asia Minor," 716–17). Buildings at Assos include the city walls, the temple of Athena, an agora, gymnasium, baths, bouleuterion, and theater.

Colossae

Paul wrote a letter to the Christians in Colossae, and Philemon and his wife, Apphia, hosted a house church in the city (Philem. 1–2). Along with the other churches of the Lycus valley, the church of Colossae was founded by Epaphras, Paul's colleague (Col. 1:7; 4:12). Colossae was located about 120 miles east of Ephesus and was on the southern bank of the Lycus River; it was 11 miles south-east of Laodicea and 15 miles south-southeast of Hierapolis.

Colossae was by far the oldest of the cities in the Lycus valley, with Herodotus (*Hist.* 7.30) describing it as "a great city of Phrygia" in 480 BC. In the first century AD it was still an important city. Like the other cities in the Lycus valley, its economic success was connected to textile industries, with Colossae being famous for its distinctive black wool (Pliny the Elder, *Nat. Hist.* 21.51). It was also on major trade routes from Ephesus and Sardis to the hinterland.

Colossae was probably hit by the earthquake in AD 61/62 (Tacitus, *Ann.* 14.27.1; Magie, *Roman Rule*, 564, 1421n73), but we do not know how quickly it recovered.

Lee Martin McDonald

40.5. The unexcavated mound of ancient Colossae. Colossae was destroyed by an earthquake in AD 61/62. It was never fully restored and was abandoned in the ninth century. The stones in the foreground are remnants of the ancient burial site, or necropolis, of Colossae.

Angela Standhartinger writes, "The claim that it [Colossae] was abandoned in AD 61/62 in the wake of an earthquake, though often made, is improbable as far as we can know from the archaeological remains like coins and known inscriptions."[1]

The city has not yet been systematically excavated; there is evidence on the site for a theater, a necropolis, and other ancient buildings. Coins indicate that a range of deities were worshiped there, including Ephesian Artemis, Men, and Zeus.

Ephesus

Ephesus is a significant city in the NT. Paul had an extensive mission there (Acts 18:19–20:38) and mentions the city in 1 Cor. 15:32; 16:8. Although the phrase "in Ephesus" in Eph. 1:1 was probably not part of the original text of the letter, this letter has traditionally been associated with the city. Both 1 and 2 Timothy are written to Ephesus (1 Tim. 1:3; 2 Tim. 1:18; 4:12), and there is a strong tradition that John's Gospel and 1–3 John are connected with the city. In Revelation, John writes to the Christians in the city in the first of his seven letters (Rev. 2:1–7).

Ephesus was located at the mouth of the Cayster River on a number of important land and sea routes, with the result that it was a major center of international trade. In addition to good land routes to the north and the south, two great highways led from Ephesus to the east—one that went from Ephesus up the Maeander

1. Angela Standhartinger, "Colossians and the Pauline School," *NTS* 50 (2004): 572–93, here 586.

Lee Martin McDonald

40.6. The first-century AD theater in Ephesus (see Acts 19:28–41).

valley to Tralles, Laodicea, and further eastward and a second that went to Sardis and then on the ancient Persian Royal Road, which went to Susa.

From around 1000 to 550 BC the city was located at the northern base of Mount Pion, and from 550 BC it was situated near the Artemisium. Because of land subsidence, Lysimachus founded a new city around 290 BC on higher ground, in the general area where the city was located in the imperial period, and also established a new harbor (Strabo, *Geogr.* 14.1.21). In the third century BC Ephesus was in turn under the Seleucids and then the Ptolemies of Egypt. After the defeat of Antiochus III, the city was made subject to the rule of Eumenes II in 188 and then came under the control of Rome after Attalos III bequeathed his kingdom to the Romans in 133 BC, although Ephesus was granted its freedom by Rome. Ephesus supported Mithridates in his first war against Rome and was deprived of its freedom in 85 BC by Sulla after he had defeated Mithridates; the city did not regain its freedom until around 47 BC. After Octavian's victory at Actium in 31 BC, Ephesus seems to have remained at least nominally free.

Ephesus prospered and grew during Augustus's reign and was elevated by him to the status of the capital of the province of Asia in place of Pergamum. As the whole province recovered, and as communications with the interior of Asia Minor improved and new cities were founded there, the importance of cities at the head of the great roads to the interior increased. Ephesus, along with Pergamum and Smyrna, benefited greatly.

In 29 BC Augustus granted Ephesus and Nicea the right to dedicate sacred precincts to *Dea Roma* and *Divus Iulius* because, according to Dio Cassius (*Hist.* 51.20.6 LCL), "these cities had at that time attained the chief place in Asia and in Bithynia respectively." Ephesus also received the much prized title "the first and greatest metropolis of Asia," which it used in inscriptions of this period. Around AD 20 Strabo wrote of Ephesus that "the city, because of its advantageous situation, . . . grows daily, and is the largest emporium in Asia this side of the Taurus" (*Geogr.*

Lee Martin McDonald

40.7. The Harbor Street of Ephesus led both to the ancient harbor, now silted over, and to the Hellenistic tower known as St. Paul's prison (see the hill just to the left of the Harbor Street).

14.1.24 LCL). Pliny the Elder, writing in AD 77, after having spoken of Smyrna, wrote of Ephesus as "the other great luminary of Asia" (*Nat. Hist.* 5.120 LCL). These are indications of the prominence of the city of Ephesus from the time of Augustus.

Another indication of the wealth and growth of Ephesus in the first and second centuries AD was the number of donations made and public buildings constructed during this period. In the first century the population of Ephesus was around 200,000–250,000, which would probably make Ephesus the third-largest city in the empire, after Rome and Alexandria.

The right to establish the third provincial imperial cult in Asia in Ephesus was granted by Domitian in the early to mid-80s, and the temple was dedicated in AD 89/90. A very large bath-gymnasium complex was also built in Domitian's honor. Ephesus used the term *neōkoros*, or "temple warden," to describe its bond with Artemis (see Acts 19:35) but also as an official title for the city in relation to the imperial cult.

Ephesus was the home of many cults, but the most significant and powerful deity was Artemis of Ephesus. The temple of Artemis, or the Artemision, was outside the city wall and about two kilometers from the center of Roman Ephesus. The temple, which stood during the first century AD, had been built in the fourth century BC and measured 130 meters by 70 meters; it was thus about four times the size of the Parthenon in Athens. It contained 127 columns, each of them 2 meters in diameter and 20 meters high. It was richly adorned with the works of the greatest painters and sculptors of the age and featured in many lists of the seven wonders of the ancient world.

Numerous buildings and over four thousand inscriptions have been discovered in Ephesus. In the time of Paul the notable buildings of the city would have included the temple of Artemis; the Magnesian Gate; the Upper or State Agora, including an

Augustan basilica and chalcidicum; the bouleuterion; the temple of Dea Roma and Divus Iulius; the Prytaneion; the Memmius monument; the temple of Isis or Augustus; the monument of Pollio; the Heroon of Androklos; the Gate of Mazaeus and Mithridates; the Tetragonos Agora; the Fountain House; the theater; the Harbor Gate; the temple of Apollo; the stadium; and the Koressos Gate. Many of these buildings had been constructed or significantly renovated during or since the reign of Augustus.

Hierapolis

Colossians 4:13 shows that a Christian group existed in Hierapolis at the time of its writing; the group was probably formed during the work of Paul and his missionary team in AD 52–55 (Acts 19:10). Hierapolis was situated on a road that left the main Ephesus-Iconium road at Laodicea and led to Philadelphia, Sardis, and the Hermus valley. Hierapolis was on a three-hundred-foot-high terrace and looked across to Laodicea. The Lycus flowed into the Maeander in the plain beneath this terrace.

Hierapolis was probably founded in the third century BC by Antiochus I, and it became part of Eumenes II's kingdom after the Treaty of Apamea (188 BC). The city was built on a Hippodamian grid plan; the main colonnaded street ran northwest and southeast and had a monumental gate at either end. It was a commercial center, and like the other cities in the Lycus valley, it was known for its textile industry. It was also the birthplace of the Stoic philosopher Epictetus (ca. AD 55–135). A hot mineral spring wells up behind the site of the city, overflows pools, and has formed amazing calcified cliffs. In antiquity the spring was thought to have medicinal value and so attracted visitors.

The city was badly affected by the earthquake of AD 61/62. A range of buildings has been excavated, including the temple of Apollo, an

Lee Martin McDonald

40.8. This figure of the goddess Artemis Ephesia (second century AD) is now located nearby at the Ephesus museum in modern-day Selçuk. The breast-like objects on her chest may reflect the ancient belief that she was the mother of everything and therefore ruled everything (see Acts 19:23–20:1).

40.9. The recently discovered burial site of the apostle Philip, who died some time in the AD 80s, likely at the order of Emperor Domitian. This site in Hierapolis is near the martyrium built to honor Philip and his daughter (see Eusebius, *Eccl. Hist.* 3.39.9; 5.24.2).

agora, a nymphaeum, a bath-gymnasium complex, and a theater. An extensive necropolis with over twelve hundred tombs has also been preserved. A cave to the south of the temple of Apollo was known as the Plutonium and was believed to be an entrance to the underworld. A significant Jewish community also lived in the city.

Laodicea

Paul mentions the church in Laodicea in Col. 2:1; 4:13, 15–16, and John writes to the church in the city in Rev. 3:14–22. The city was probably first evangelized by Epaphras (Col. 4:13). Laodicea was located on the south bank of the Lycus, eleven miles downstream from Colossae and six miles south of Hierapolis. It was refounded on the site of an earlier settlement by Antiochus II sometime between 261 and 253 BC and named after his sister-wife, Laodice. The city grew quickly and surpassed its older neighbor Colossae in importance.

The prosperity of the cities of the Lycus valley was greatly indebted to their location. Laodicea in particular was at the junction of two important roads—first, the road that went from Ephesus up the Maeander valley to Laodicea and then on to the Euphrates; and second, the north–south route from Pergamum to Sardis, Philadelphia, Laodicea, and Cibyra and on to the Mediterranean.

By the first century BC, Laodicea had become a center of financial operations (Cicero, *Att.* 5.15; *Fam.* 3.5), and the Cibyratic conventus met in the city. In 62 BC

40.10. The Syria Street (the *decumanus maximus*) in Laodicea measures some nine hundred meters and stretches from the city center to the Syrian Gate on the east side of the city.

Flaccus seized a large amount of Jewish temple tax from Laodicea and elsewhere (Cicero, *Flac.* 28.66–69), which indicates that a fairly large number of Jews lived in the cities of the Lycus valley. Strabo (*Geogr.* 12.8.16) testifies to Laodicea's economic prosperity at the beginning of the first century AD. The city suffered from a severe earthquake in AD 17, when it received Roman help, and Tacitus (*Ann.* 14.27.1) tells us that, although Laodicea was destroyed in the earthquake of AD 61/62, it was rebuilt using only its own resources.

The city was known for its textiles, particularly the local black wool, and it seems to have been the chief medical center of Phrygia (Strabo, *Geogr.* 12.8.20). Buildings on the site include two theaters, two agoras, a bath-gymnasium complex, a stadium, a bouleuterion, a nymphaeum, an odeion, and two gates, one of which has three arches.

Miletus

Paul addresses the Ephesian elders in Miletus (Acts 20:15, 17), and 2 Tim. 4:20 tells us that Trophimus was ill in the city. Miletus was situated on the west coast of Asia Minor, near the mouth of the Maeander River, thirty miles south of Ephesus.

Miletus was one of the oldest and most important cities in Ionia and was the site of an important Mycenean colony from the middle of the second millennium onward. By the sixth century BC it was the most prosperous Greek city in Asia Minor. Beginning in 479 BC, the city was reconstructed on a grid system by Hippodamos, a native of Miletus, who gave his name to this system of city planning. Its four separate harbors made it an important center for transshipment, but the

40.11. This second-century AD temple near the Syria Street in Laodicea is now called simply Temple A. It is one of the more impressive reconstructions of ancient Laodicea.

city's trade by land was hampered by the lack of good road access. Although Miletus waned in prominence in the Hellenistic period, it remained an important center of commerce and art in Ionia. Its population in the second century BC is estimated at one hundred thousand, and it is doubtful if the size of the city increased greatly under the Roman Empire (Broughton, "Roman Asia Minor," 813). In the late second century BC the commercial life of Miletus suffered as a result of the increased importance of its rival Ephesus, but it continued to be prosperous.

During the Roman period, Miletus continued to be a significant city, although the silting up of its harbors was an ongoing problem. Strabo can still describe Miletus as "one of the principal places" (*Geogr.* 14.1.4 LCL).

In Paul's time, the city had three impressive agoras, indicative of the abundance of trade stimulated by its harbors. Other buildings included a theater, a gymnasium, a stadium, a nymphaeum, a bouleuterion, and a *hērōon* (shrine to a hero). Apollo Delphinios was the principal deity of the city and was worshiped in the Delphinion. The temple of Athena was an Ionic temple, dating to 499–450 BC. The territory of Miletus included the famous temple of Apollo at Didyma, ten miles to the south and connected to Miletus by a "Sacred Way."

Patmos

We learn from Rev. 1:9 that John wrote the book of Revelation on Patmos, one of the Sporades Islands, probably after being exiled there. It was a small island of

40.12. The probable route of Paul's third missionary journey.

twenty-four square miles shaped like a horseshoe, thirty-seven miles southwest of Miletus and sixty-five miles from Ephesus. The earliest inhabitants were Dorians, with Ionians settling there later. A Greek settlement has been excavated on the isthmus at the center of the island. Roman prisoners were often exiled to islands, and Pliny the Elder (*Nat. Hist.* 4.69–70) and Tacitus (*Ann.* 4.30) tell us that three islands in the Sporades were used for exiles.

Pergamum

The church in Pergamum is addressed by John in Rev. 2:12–17. Pergamum was located fifteen miles from the Aegean and was built on an acropolis thirteen hundred feet above the valley below, and on two plateaus below the acropolis.

Pergamum was settled as early as the eighth century BC, and it emerged as a major military and political center in the third century BC, with the acropolis becoming one of the key fortresses in Asia Minor. Philetaerus began to build the Pergamene Kingdom from 283 to 263 BC, and his successor Eumenes I (263–241 BC) continued to expand Pergamum's power. Eumenes's son Attalus I (241–197 BC) was even more important in this regard. Attalus also forged an alliance between Pergamum and Rome in 212, an alliance that led to the end of Seleucid power in Asia Minor after the Treaty of Apamea in 188 BC, when Attalus's son Eumenes II (197–159 BC) was ruler. This treaty led to Pergamum's gaining massive amounts

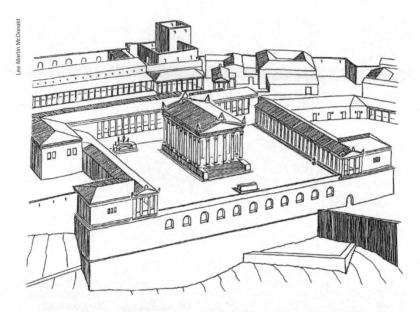

40.13a and b. Artist's reconstruction of the second-century AD Trajan temple at Pergamum and the current temple remains (see Rev. 2:12–17).

of former Seleucid territory. When Attalus III died without an heir in 133, he bequeathed his kingdom to Rome. The Romans then created the province of Asia from the Attalid Kingdom, with Pergamum as the first capital.

In the second century BC, Pergamum became one of the key artistic and intellectual centers of the Greek world, which was reflected in many of the buildings constructed on the acropolis by Eumenes II. In the Upper City buildings included a theater with an associated temple of Dionysus; a palace; the altar of Zeus, which included a frieze constructed of 118 panels; the upper agora; the temple of Athena; and a new library, which became one of the ancient world's great centers of learning and which Plutarch says contained two hundred thousand volumes (*Ant.* 58.5). Later, a Trajaneum was built here. The Middle City featured a bath complex; a podium hall; temples of Demeter, Hera Basileia, and Asclepius; and a large gymnasium. The Lower City featured an agora and the gate of Eumenes.

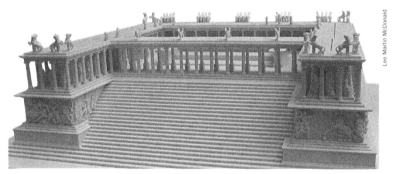

40.14. Replica of the altar of Zeus from Pergamum, located at the Pergamum Museum in Berlin. The primary remains of that temple were taken to Berlin and can be seen in their reconstructed condition there.

Since the Attalids had built on most of the available space in the acropolis, during the Roman period the city expanded in the plain around its base. Buildings here included an amphitheater, a theater, and a huge Serapion. By the first century AD, the Asclepion, founded around 400 BC, was a major medical and intellectual center.

The position of Pergamum slowly declined in relation to other Asian cities after the beginning of direct Roman rule, due in part to the revolt of Mithridates and the subsequent heavy exaction from Pergamum levied by Sulla. Only in the reign of Augustus did the city begin to recover. The first provincial imperial cult, dedicated to Rome and Augustus, was built in Pergamum in 29 BC. Eventually Ephesus replaced Pergamum as the leading city in the province. In the first century AD, Pergamum's population was between 180,000 and 200,000 (Mitchell, *Anatolia*, 1:243–44).

Philadelphia

The church in Philadelphia is addressed by John in Rev. 3:7–13. The city was located in a fertile plateau in the valley of the Cogamus River, which was a tributary of the Hermus River. Philadelphia was probably founded by Seleucus I between 321 and 280 BC (see Mitchell, *Anatolia*, 1:180), as is suggested by a recently discovered inscription. The city was renamed after Attalus II Philadelphus, the king of Pergamum from 159 to 138 BC; his loyalty to his brother Eumenes II (197–159 BC), who ruled before him, earned Attalus II the nickname "Philadelphus" ("brotherly love").

The Persian Royal Road that went from Sardis to Susa passed through Philadelphia. A severe earthquake in AD 17 destroyed the city (Strabo, *Geogr.* 12.8.18; 13.4.10); Pliny the Elder (*Nat. Hist.* 2.86.200) describes it as the greatest earthquake in human memory. The tribute from Philadelphia was remitted for five years to enable it to recover; the city was very grateful to Tiberius for this assistance. Of the seven cities to which Revelation was written, only Philadelphia is not to be thought of as one of the major cities of Asia.

The few remains of the ancient city that have been discovered include part of the city wall, a theater, a Roman temple, a late basilica-style building, and a monumental entrance.

40.15. A second- or third-century gymnasium at Sardis. Gymnasiums in antiquity were a place of both exercise and learning.

Sardis

Sardis, whose church is addressed by John in Rev. 3:1–6, dominated the fertile Hermus valley and was located on the Royal Road that went to Susa. The acropolis of the city was on a spur of Mount Tmolus, with the city lying to the west.

Sardis was in turn the capital of the Lydian Empire (ca. 680–547 BC), the seat of a Persian satrap, an administrative center of the Seleucids, part of the Attalid Kingdom, and then a leading city in the Roman province of Asia. Although Sardis lost its power as a key administrative center to Ephesus, it was an important center throughout the Roman period.

The earthquake of AD 17 devastated the city, and Tiberius remitted taxes for five years to enable it to recover (Strabo, *Geogr.* 12.8.18). The new city was laid out on a grid, with a fifty-foot-wide, marble-paved, colonnaded main avenue, begun under Tiberius and finished under Claudius.

Buildings included the temple of Artemis (who was seen as protector of the city), a large bath-gymnasium complex that included a marble court, a stadium, a theater, and a hippodrome. A major synagogue, which was part of the bath-gymnasium complex and was located on a major thoroughfare, has been discovered in Sardis. It probably dates to the third century AD; Josephus (*Ant.* 14.259–61) preserves a decree from the first century BC that probably concerns an earlier synagogue in Sardis.

Smyrna

The church in Smyrna is addressed by John in Rev. 2:8–11. Smyrna, modern Izmir, was situated at the foot of Mount Pagros and the mouth of the Melas River, on the southern shore of the Gulf of Izmir. It was the terminus for a major road that went to Sardis and then on to Susa in the east. The first Greeks in the region were

the Aeolians, who arrived probably in the eleventh century BC and dominated the indigenous peoples. In the seventh century, the city was captured by the Lydian Kingdom, which was centered in Sardis.

Lysimachus refounded the city, probably in 288/87 BC; it grew rapidly in importance because of its strategic location, becoming a major seaport. In 195 BC it became the first city in Asia Minor to erect a

40.16. The synagogue entrance at Sardis, the largest known synagogue in the ancient world.

Lee Martin McDonald

Lee Martin McDonald

40.17. The mosaic floor inside the synagogue ruins at Sardis.

temple to the goddess Roma. After the Roman army defeated Antiochus III in 189 BC, Smyrna was a free city for a century, a status it lost after the defeat of Mithridates VI of Pontus (whom Smyrna aided) in 85 BC.

In the Roman period, Smyrna was famous for its fine buildings and wealth. Writing early in the first century AD, Strabo (*Geogr.* 14.1.37 LCL) called Smyrna the "most beautiful city of all." It was also one of the four centers of the provincial assembly, alongside Ephesus, Sardis, and Pergamum, which indicates that the Romans thought of Smyrna as one of the most important cities in the province. The second provincial imperial cult in Asia was permitted by Rome in AD 26 and built in Smyrna, after intense competition between the cities of the province with regard to where it would be located; it was dedicated to Tiberius, Livia (his mother, and Augustus's widow), and the Senate. The remains of the city include aqueducts, a theater, and a state agora.

Thyatira

The church in Thyatira is addressed by John in Rev. 2:18–29, and Lydia, a purple dealer Paul met in Philippi (Acts 16:14–15, 40), was originally from this city. Thyatira was located on the plain of the river Lycus (a different Lycus River from the one near Colossae, Laodicea, and Hierapolis), on the road from Sardis to Pergamum. It was founded as a Lydian town and served as the central junction in northern Lydia. Seleucus I Nicator refounded the city in 281 BC; under the Treaty of Apamea the city was given to the Attalids. By the first century AD, it was a major inland commercial center; its textile industry was particularly important.

We know of shrines in the city to Apollo Tyrimnaeus and Artemis Boreitene, to Helius and to Hadrian; we also have evidence for three gymnasia, stoas and shops, and a place where the gerousia met.

40.18. Ruins of the Roman forum of ancient Smyrna (modern-day Izmir).

Troas

After being forbidden by the Holy Spirit from preaching the gospel in Asia or Bithynia, Paul and Timothy go through the region of Mysia and arrive at the coast at Troas, where Paul has a vision, which results in his going on to Macedonia (Acts 16:6–11). In Acts 20:5–12 Paul and his companions revisit Troas and stay there for seven days. Paul finds an open door for preaching the gospel in the city (2 Cor. 2:12–13), and from 2 Tim. 4:13 we learn of the cloak, books, and "above all the parchments" Paul has left with Carpus at Troas.

The city was founded by Antigonus, one of Alexander's successors, in 310 BC and named Antigoneia (Strabo, *Geogr.* 13.1.26). After his death, his rival Lysimachus improved the city and renamed it Alexandria in honor of Alexander; it came to be known as Alexandria Troas to distinguish it from other cities called Alexandria. The city grew quickly due to the construction of an artificial harbor that enabled it to become the main seaport of northwestern Asia Minor and a city of great commercial importance.

Augustus created a Roman colony at Alexandria Troas. The city continued to flourish as a commercial and maritime center, so that around AD 20 Strabo could describe it as "one of the notable cities of the world" (*Geogr.* 13.1.26 LCL). It was the largest city in the Troad and one of the great ports of the Roman Empire. Among the few ruins that remain of the city are a stoa, the Roman forum and agora, an odeion, a Doric temple, a theater, and a bath-gymnasium complex.

Bibliography

Akurgal, Ekrem. *Ancient Civilizations and Ruins of Turkey.* 5th ed. London: Kegan Paul, 2002. The most recent edition of a widely used guide to archaeological sites in Turkey.

Broughton, T. Robert S. "Roman Asia Minor." Pages 499–918 in vol. 4 of *An Economic Survey of Ancient Rome*. Edited by T. Frank. Baltimore: John Hopkins University Press, 1938. A mine of historical and economic information on the province of Asia.

Cadwallader, Alan H., and Michael Trainor, eds. *Colossae in Space and Time: Linking with an Ancient City*. Göttingen: Vandenhoeck & Ruprecht, 2011. The latest work on the site of Colossae.

Fant, Clyde E., and Mitchell G. Reddish. *A Guide to Biblical Sites in Greece and Turkey*. Oxford: Oxford University Press, 2003. A detailed guide to the history and archaeology of the key biblical cities of Asia, along with site maps.

Friesen, Steven J. *Imperial Cults and the Apocalypse of John*. New York: Oxford University Press, 2001. A detailed analysis of the imperial cult in the province of Asia, and a reading of Revelation against this background.

———. *Twice Neokoros: Ephesus, Asia and the Cult of the Flavian Imperial Family*. Leiden: Brill, 1993. A study of the imperial cult that was established in Ephesus in the late first century AD.

Hemer, Colin J. *The Letters to the Seven Churches of Asia in Their Local Setting*. JSNTSup 11. Sheffield: Sheffield Academic Press, 1986. An exegetical study of the seven letters of the book of Revelation in the context of the local situations to which they were addressed, drawing on literary, epigraphical, archaeological, and numismatic evidence.

Koester, Helmut, ed. *Ephesos, Metropolis of Asia: An Interdisciplinary Approach to Its Archaeology, Religion, and Culture*. Valley Forge, PA: Trinity Press International, 1995. Studies of Ephesus from a range of disciplines, including classics, history of religions, NT studies, and archaeology.

———, ed. *Pergamon, Citadel of the Gods: Archaeological Record, Literary Description, and Religious Development*. Harrisburg, PA: Trinity Press International, 1998. Studies of Pergamum from a range of disciplines, including classics, history of religions, NT studies, and archaeology.

Macro, Anthony D. "The Cities of Asia Minor under the Roman Imperium." *ANRW* II 7.2:658–97. A sociopolitical analysis of the cities of Asia Minor under the Roman Empire.

Magie, David. *Roman Rule in Asia Minor to the End of the Third Century after Christ*. 2 vols. Princeton: Princeton University Press, 1950. The classic and indispensable work on the topic.

Mitchell, Stephen. *Anatolia: Land, Men and Gods in Asia Minor*. 2 vols. Oxford: Clarendon, 1993. The most recent comprehensive study of the history of Asia Minor in antiquity.

Murphy-O'Connor, Jerome. *St. Paul's Ephesus: Texts and Archaeology*. Collegeville, MN: Liturgical Press, 2008. A helpful collection of ancient texts relating to Ephesus.

Price, S. R. F. *Rituals and Power: The Roman Imperial Cult in Asia Minor*. Cambridge: Cambridge University Press, 1984. The standard work on the imperial cult in Asia Minor.

Schnabel, Eckhard J. *Early Christian Mission*. 2 vols. Downers Grove, IL: InterVarsity, 2004. A comprehensive discussion of the topic, with detailed information about ancient sites.

Trebilco, Paul R. "Asia." Pages 291–362 in *The Book of Acts in Its Graeco-Roman Setting*. Edited by David W. J. Gill and Conrad Gempf. A1CS 2. Grand Rapids: Eerdmans, 1994.

———. *The Early Christians in Ephesus from Paul to Ignatius*. WUNT 166. Tübingen: Mohr Siebeck 2004. A study of the evidence for early Christians in Ephesus.

————. *Jewish Communities in Asia Minor.* SNTSMS 69. Cambridge: Cambridge University Press, 1991.

Wilson, Mark. *Biblical Turkey: A Guide to the Jewish and Christian Sites of Asia Minor.* Istanbul: Yayinlari, 2010. The most recent guide to the history and archaeology of the cities of Asia.

41

Galatia

MARK WILSON

Ancient Galatia was a region of central Asia Minor characterized generally by a flat, open landscape. It was situated at the headwaters of the Sangarius (Sakarya) River and the middle course of the Halys (Kızıl Irmak) River. Its name comes from the mercenary Celts who emigrated from Thrace in 278–277 BC to serve the Bithynian king Nicomedes I. For decades the Galatians pillaged western Asia Minor. However, in 232 BC the three Galatian tribes settled in three cities—the Tolistobogii at Pessinus, the Tectosages at Ancyra, and the Trocmi at Tavium. Within ethnic Galatia they practiced their traditional culture, language, and religion. They also adopted the worship of the indigenous mother goddess Cybele, whose main temple was at Pessinus. The Galatians were governed by a council and tetrarchs. However, in 63 BC Deiotarus killed the other two tribal kings and assumed the sole monarchy. In 25 BC the final Galatian king, Amyntas, willed his kingdom to Rome. At this time Augustus made Galatia a Roman province and established Ancyra as its capital. The new province of Galatia included not just the area of the Celtic tribes but also Pisidia, eastern Phrygia, Lycaonia, Isauria, and for a time, Pamphylia. Thirteen colonies, most in the southern part of the province, were founded by Augustus. Galatia's size is estimated at 15,625 square miles. The province's boundaries were changed again by Vespasian in AD 72 for military reasons, as Galatia was joined to Cappadocia to form a new double province.

41.1. Galatia and surrounding regions.

The name "Galatia" was used in two ways during the first century AD—as the geographic name of the northern Celtic region and as the political designation for the large Roman province. Which Galatia, ethnic or political, Paul visited on his journeys, or to which audience Paul addressed the book of Galatians, has been a source of ongoing debate among NT scholars. Luke, in describing the routes of Paul's first and second journeys, shows Paul traveling and planting churches only in southern Galatia (Acts 13:14–14:23; 16:1–6). Therefore Stephen Mitchell (*Anatolia*, 2:3) argues, "There is virtually nothing to be said for the north Galatian theory. There is no evidence in Acts or in any non-testamentary source that Paul ever evangelized the region of Ancyra and Pessinus, in person, by letter, or by any other means." Nevertheless, some scholars, such as Jerome Murphy-O'Connor (*Paul*, 159–62), still see Paul as visiting north Galatia and identify the audience of Galatians as the ethnic Celts. Galatia is mentioned as the second province in the address of 1 Peter (1 Pet. 1:1). Although it has been suggested that the Galatian cities to which the messenger delivered the letter included Iconium and Pisidian Antioch, it seems preferable to view the audience residing in the north Galatian cities of Tavium, Ancyra, and Pessinus (Wilson, "Cities," 2). If we accept that 2 Timothy is Pauline and written from Rome, Paul's companion Crescens is said to have left the apostle and traveled back to Galatia (2 Tim. 4:10).

Pisidian Antioch

Pisidian Antioch (modern Yalvaç) was one of the sixteen eponymous cities founded by the Seleucid ruler Antiochus I before 261 BC. He invited colonists from Magnesia on the Maeander to settle the site. Antioch was located in Phrygia Paroreius, not in Pisidia; hence, to speak of Antioch "in" or "of" Pisidia, as many Bible translations do, is geographically and politically inaccurate for the first century AD. "Antioch toward [*pros*] Pisidia" (Strabo, *Geogr.* 12.8.14) is most correct, but "Pisidian Antioch" is often used to distinguish it from the other nearby Antiochs—Carian Antioch and Antioch on the Meander. The city is set in the southern foothills of the Sultan Dağ ("Mountain") at an elevation of 4,055 feet.

Below the eastern face of its acropolis flows the Anthius River. Antioch sat on the *koinē hodos*, or "common road," that linked Ephesus to the Cilician Gates and Syria. It was also at the apex of a triangle that reached southward through Pisidia to the Mediterranean region of Pamphylia. Because of its strategic location, Augustus established a Roman colony called Colonia Caesarea Antiochia here in 25 BC. Veterans of legions V Gallica and VII and their families settled Pisidian Antioch. These three thousand men with families constituted an initial colony of an estimated ten thousand persons. In addition, Greek and Phrygian residents continued to inhabit the city. The colonists had an assembly (*ekklēsia*), while its wealthier members formed the *ordo*, the Roman equivalent of the Greek *boulē*.

In 6 BC Augustus authorized the praetor Cornutus Aquila to construct the Via Sebaste, a road that ran from Perga to Pisidian Antioch. Its initial purpose was to secure the region from the hostile tribe of Homanadensians, but it also advanced the political and economic success of the other colonies along the route. The road was later extended eastward from Pisidian Antioch to Iconium and Lystra. At the Climax Pass northwest of Antalya a gate complex still contains a milestone *in situ* marking 139 Roman miles (1 Roman mile = 4,856 feet) to Climax from Pisidian Antioch, the *caput viae* ("head of the road"). Along this road Paul and Barnabas arrived in the colony around AD 46 (Acts 13:14). Pisidian Antioch had a typical Roman street plan with a north–south *cardo maximus* intersecting an east–west *decumanus maximus*. A Greco-Roman theater rested in a hillside in the city's center; a bouleuterion (council hall) stood to the east. The *cardo maximus* led to the Tiberia Platea, a colonnaded street thirty-six feet wide. A triple-arched propylon (portico) with twelve steps stood at the east end of the street. Nearly sixty pieces of the Latin text of the *Res gestae divi Augusti* ("the deeds of divine Augustus") were found in the Platea area during archaeological excavations in 1924. These are now on display at the local museum in Yalvaç. The propylon served as the entrance to the imperial cult sanctuary. The temple of Augustus was the most important building in the city. Situated on the city's highest level and visible from all points, this Roman temple was built in AD 25 by the emperor Tiberius to honor Augustus. Its foundations suggest a size of 85 by 49 feet. The surrounding sanctuary area was approximately 328 by 279 feet. Its raised style on a podium with its two-story curved portico is typically Roman. The semicircular portico was mostly cut from the natural rock; the rock wall was 21 feet at its highest point. Approximately 150 columns were used in the portico and stoas that formed the backdrop of the sanctuary. The design of the temple resembled that of the temple of Mars Ultor built in Rome in 2 BC.

Paul's first and longest sermon in Acts was delivered at the synagogue to Jews and God-fearers (Acts 13:16–41). Although Acts mentions the presence of synagogues in Pisidian Antioch and Iconium, no archaeological evidence exists to document them. The city's main religion revolved around the Anatolian moon-god Men, whose worship occurred at a sanctuary on a peak southeast of the city. A sacred way linked the city with the sanctuary. The southwestern wall of the temple

Lee Martin McDonald

41.2. Remains of the imperial temple of Augustus at Pisidian Antioch (modern-day Yalvaç in Turkey).

still contains inscriptions as well as numerous votive aediculae (a small room or a niche used as a shrine) decorated with a crescent moon sign, the symbol of Men.

The apostolic visit to Pisidian Antioch was a seeming consequence, unstated in the book of Acts, of the conversion of the Roman proconsul Sergius Paulus at Paphos (Acts 13:7–12). Paul apparently saw the meeting as providential and changed their itinerary toward Pisidian Antioch. This deviation is probably why John Mark left the apostles in Perga (Acts 13:13). The proconsul apparently gave Paul and Barnabas an introduction to the leading officials in Pisidian Antioch because his senatorial family, the Sergii Paulli (the Latin spelling has a double *l*), held large estates northwest of the city (Witherington, *Acts*, 403–4). William Ramsay, on the other hand, thinks it was an illness contracted in Pamphylia that drove Paul to the higher elevation of Pisidian Antioch (*Paul the Traveler*, 88). Latin inscriptions mentioning L. Sergius Paullus *filio* and Sergia Paulla, the son and daughter respectively of the proconsul mentioned in Acts, have been found at Pisidian Antioch. Acts implies that Paul visited the city again on his two later journeys while traveling to points farther west (Acts 16:6a; 19:1). Epigraphic evidence suggests that the city's territory extended about 540 square miles from villages southwest as far as modern Gelendost and northwest to Sağır. This is the "whole region" reached by Paul and Barnabas during their stay (Acts 13:49 NIV). Under Diocletian, Pisidian Antioch became the capital of the newly formed province of Pisidia in AD 292; in this new political configuration it could then be called Antioch of Pisidia.

41.3. A four-arch gateway into the large ancient city of Perga. Paul and Barnabas stayed here briefly on their first missionary journey (Acts 13:13–14; 14:25).

Iconium

Iconium (Konya) is situated on the northwest edge of a high and fertile plateau 3,770 feet above sea level, 92 miles southeast of Pisidian Antioch. It is one of the oldest occupied cities in the world, dating to the third millennium BC. Iconium's foundation myth combines a disastrous flood tradition with two legends about its name: (1) an image (Greek *eikōn*) of Medusa was brought there by Perseus or (2) clay images, or icons, of people were produced by Prometheus after the flood to replace those who had drowned. Originally founded as a Phrygian settlement, it was geographically connected with the Lycaonian cities of Lystra and Derbe (cf. Acts 14:6; 16:2). After 25 BC, Augustus granted Iconium its status as a full Roman colony. The native Greek *polis* ("city") was allowed to exist alongside the Roman colony. Iconium functioned as a double community until the time of Hadrian (ca. AD 135), when the Roman colony absorbed the *polis* (cf. Mitchell, *Anatolia*, 1:77, 89, 90). After AD 41, the emperor Claudius honored the city with a new name, Claudiconium. At Iconium the Via Sebaste intersected roads leading to Ancyra, Caesarea Mazaca, and Tarsus, making the city an important transportation hub. Paul and Barnabas began their ministry in Iconium at a synagogue, with a church resulting from their evangelistic efforts in the city (Acts 14:1). Paul visited Iconium on his second journey, delivering the results of the apostolic council with Silas (Acts 16:1–4). Another visit on his third journey is likewise implied in Acts 18:23. If Paul's letter to the Galatians was directed to southern Galitia, then Iconium was one of the churches addressed in the letter. One of Justin Martyr's companions at his trial in Rome in AD 165 was Hierax, who testified that he had been dragged away from Iconium in Phrygia" (*Martyrdom of Justin* 3). A church council was held in Iconium in AD 232. Few archaeological remains of ancient Iconium are extant, because the modern city of Konya is built over them.

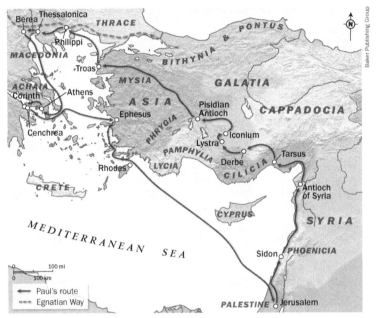

41.4. The probable route of Paul's second missionary journey.

The apocryphal *Acts of Paul and Thecla* (second–third century AD) recounts the story of a woman named Thecla, who is described as a convert and associate of Paul. She was from Iconium, where her family was part of the Roman nobility. When Thecla heard Paul preach about virginity, she broke off her engagement to a young noble and followed Paul. She then miraculously survived various persecutions, including attempted execution by fire. After being sentenced to death by the Roman governor at Pisidian Antioch, she was miraculously delivered from wild beasts at a *venatio* ("hunt"). The Pontic queen Tryphena, who happened to be in Pisidian Antioch, then took her into protective custody. The queen's household was subsequently converted by Thecla (*Acts Paul Thec.* 26–39). To escape further persecution, Thecla disguised herself as a man and renewed her search for Paul in Myra. Surprised to find Thecla still alive, Paul commissioned her to teach God's word. Thecla returned home to Iconium and later moved to Seleucia ad Calycadnum

(Silifke). There a martyrium in her honor was built in the fourth century AD. The only extant physical description of Paul is found in the *Acts of Paul and Thecla*. Onesiphorus, Paul's host in Iconium, was waiting along the road to Lystra and looking for a man who had been described by Titus. "And he saw Paul coming, a man small in size, bald-headed, bandy-legged, well built, with eyebrows meeting, rather long-nosed, full of grace. For sometimes he seemed like a man, and sometimes he had the countenance of an angel" (*Acts Paul Thec.* 3; *ANF* 8:487).

Lystra

Lystra was located in the region of Lycaonia (Acts 14:6) approximately twenty-one miles southwest of Iconium. Situated in the northern foothills of the Taurus Mountains, Lycaonia was successively under the rule of the Persian, Seleucid, and Attalid Kingdoms. Starting in 129 BC, the Romans placed the area under a series of client kings. After the death of the final king, Amyntas, in 25 BC, Augustus incorporated western Lycaonia into the new province of Galatia. It was subsumed into Vespasian's new province of Galatia-Cappadocia after AD 72. Before the introduction of Roman rule, Lycaonia had no urban centers. When Paul healed a crippled man at the city gate, the Lystrans declared in their native Lycaonian language that the gods had visited them. This declaration of amazement is translated into Greek in Acts 14:11. Thus Lycaonian, along with Phrygian, Lycian, Lydian, Carian, and Pamphylian, was among the native Anatolian languages still spoken in the first century AD. This suggests that many residents of Asia Minor were bilingual and spoke both a native language and Greek (cf. Acts 2:8).

Lystra was situated on a small rise along a fertile river valley. In 25 BC, Lystra became the final military colony that Augustus formed as a protective ring around the hostile Pisidians. Lystra's full Roman name was *Colonia Iulia Gemina Felix Lustra*. Its Latin spelling, *Lustra*, provided a seeming connection with *lustrum*, indicating the ritual cleansing of the state by the Romans.

Approximately a thousand retirees from two Roman legions constituted the initial settlement, suggesting an estimated population of approximately three thousand, including women and children. Intermarriage with the local population undoubtedly did occur; nevertheless, Lystra continued to have a Roman identity, as evidenced by numerous Latin inscriptions and a typical Roman civic organization. Lystra lost its strategic importance after Pisidia was completely pacified in the third century AD. Nevertheless, in the Byzantine period Lystra was second in status only to Iconium in the region.

Timothy, Paul's closest associate and disciple (1 Tim. 1:2; 2 Tim. 1:2), was raised in Lystra by his Jewish grandmother, Lois, and his mother, Eunice (2 Tim. 1:5). Timothy's father, however, was not Jewish. Since Lystra was never Hellenized, it is better to consider Timothy's father to be a "gentile" rather than a "Greek," contrary to most English translations of *Hellēn* in Acts 16:3. Lystra had a significant native Lycaonian population; however, a Jewish woman would typically not marry a local pagan. It is more likely that Timothy's mother married a Roman resident of the colony, and Timothy was the product of that mixed marriage. As a result, Timothy was never circumcised (Acts 16:3). The Jewish population of Lystra was probably too small to support a synagogue. So the two women would have undoubtedly attended the nearby synagogue in Iconium whenever possible (Acts 14:1) and taught Timothy the Greek Scriptures from his infancy (2 Tim. 3:15). Timothy perhaps met Paul on his first visit to Lystra and at some point became a believer, like his mother and grandmother (Acts 14:21–22?). Timothy joined Paul and Silas on their second journey at Lystra because the believers in Iconium and Lystra spoke well of him (Acts 16:2).

Derbe

Derbe (modern Ekinözü) was situated in eastern Lycaonia (Acts 14:6) in the shadow of Mount Boratinon (Karadağ). It was located eighty-one miles southeast of Lystra and eighteen miles south of the main highway running from the Cilician Gates to Iconium. The city's early history is largely unknown. Some Hellenization occurred

Lee Martin McDonald

during the Seleucid period; after 129 BC Derbe came under Roman rule. It was added to Cappadocia as the eleventh *stratēgia* ("administrative unit") around 65 BC but was soon seized by a local dynast, Antipater. In 36 BC Amyntas defeated Antipater and added Derbe and nearby Laranda to his kingdom. Upon Amyntas's death in 25 BC, Derbe was incorporated into the newly formed province of Galatia. Early in the reign of Claudius (ca. AD 41/42) Derbe received the honorific title Claudioderbe. The site of Derbe was unknown to archaeologists until the twentieth century. J. R. R. Sterrett and W. M. Ramsay had

41.5. A Greek inscription discovered at Derbe. This artifact, which helped archaeologists determine the location of the ancient city of Derbe, is now in the archaeological museum at Iconium (Konya).

suggested a site near Gudelisin, northwest of Laranda (Karaman). In 1956 Michael Ballance found an inscription dated to AD 157, now in the Konya Archaeological Museum, establishing that the site was near Ekinözü. This is twelve miles northeast of Karaman, at a place almost thirty miles from the Gudelisin site. In 1962 Bastiaan van Elderen found a second inscription in the same area mentioning a bishop of Derbe named Michael ("Archaeological Observations," 156–60). After Paul's stoning in Lystra, the apostles went to Derbe, the easternmost point of their first journey (Acts 14:19–20). Why they bypassed Laranda, the major city of the region, is an interesting question. Probably a personal contact was made in Lystra that prompted an invitation to Derbe. Instead of returning directly to Tarsus and Antioch via the Cilician Gates, Paul and Barnabas instead revisited the newly planted churches in Lystra, Iconium, and Pisidian Antioch. Despite the great suffering and persecution experienced in these cities (2 Tim. 3:11), the apostles thought it important to appoint elders in each church to provide leadership in their absence. Paul passed through Derbe on his second journey, delivering the apostolic decree to the believers there as well as in Lystra and Iconium (Acts 16:1–4). On his third journey to Ephesus, Paul probably again visited Derbe to strengthen the disciples (Acts 18:23). Gaius, one of Paul's traveling companions to Jerusalem, was from Derbe (Acts 20:4).

Bibliography

Elderen, Bastiaan van. "Some Archaeological Observations on Paul's First Missionary Journey." Pages 150–61 in *Apostolic History and the Gospel: Biblical and Historical Essays Presented to F. F. Bruce*. Edited by W. Ward Gasque and Ralph P. Martin. Exeter: Paternoster, 1970. Discusses the inscriptions that helped to determine the location of Derbe.

Gazda, Elaine K., and Diana Y. Ng, eds., in collaboration with Ünal Demirer. *Building a New Rome: The Imperial Colony of Pisidian Antioch (25 BC–AD 700)*. Ann Arbor, MI: Kelsey Museum Publications, 2011. Using state-of-the-art computer re-creations, this volume provides a look at the city in the time of Paul.

Levick, Barbara. *Roman Colonies in Southern Asia Minor*. Oxford: Oxford University Press, 1967. The standard work on Augustus's colonization efforts in Pisidia and Galatia in the first century BC.

Magie, David. *Roman Rule in Asia Minor*. 2 vols. Princeton: Princeton University Press, 1950. The classic treatment of the history of Roman hegemony in Asia Minor.

Mitchell, Stephen. *Anatolia: Land, Men and Gods in Asia Minor*. 2 vols. Oxford: Oxford University Press, 1993. The current magnum opus on the history and archaeology of Galatia.

Mitchell, Stephen, and Marc Waelkens. *Pisidian Antioch: The Site and Its Monuments*. London: Duckworth with the Classical Press of Wales, 1998. An outstanding summary of research on the site of Pisidian Antioch.

Murphy-O'Connor, Jerome. *Paul: A Critical Life*. Oxford: Oxford University Press, 1997. One of many volumes on the apostle Paul written by a highly regarded NT scholar.

Ramsay, William M. *St. Paul the Traveler and Roman Citizen*. Edited by Mark Wilson. Rev. ed. Grand Rapids: Kregel, 2001. Ramsay's classic biography of Paul updated and expanded.

Wilson, Mark. *Biblical Turkey: A Guide to the Jewish and Christian Sites of Asia Minor*. Istanbul: Ege Yayınları, 2010. A guidebook to the history and archaeology of all the biblical sites in Turkey.

———. "Cities of God in Northern Asia Minor: Using Stark's Social Theories to Reconstruct Peter's Communities." *VEcc* 32, no. 1 (2011): 1–9. http://www.ve.org.za/index.php/VE/article/view/422/540. Uses social-science methodology to locate the cities probably addressed in 1 Peter.

———. "The Route of Paul's First Journey to Pisidian Antioch." *NTS* 55 (2009): 1–13. Seeks to identify which route Paul and Barnabas might have traveled to and from Pisidian Antioch.

Witherington, Ben, III. *The Acts of the Apostles: A Socio-Rhetorical Commentary*. Grand Rapids: Eerdmans, 1998. A highly recommended commentary on the book of Acts written by an outstanding NT scholar.

42

Macedonia

GENE L. GREEN

During the second of Paul's missionary journeys recorded in Acts, the apostle arrives at the great port city and Roman colony called Colonia Alexandria Augusta Troas, located on the western coast of the Roman province of Asia (16:8), near the ancient city of Troy. Although Troas was named to honor the emperor Augustus, King Lysimachus (ca. 355–281 BC) had previously called Troas "Alexandria" in a show of devotion to the memory of the great Macedonian king Alexander III ("the Great"), under whom he had served as an officer (Strabo, *Geogr.* 13.1.26). From this large principal seaport in northwest Asia Minor, travelers could easily secure passage across the Aegean Sea to the Roman province of Macedonia. A "man of Macedonia," whom Paul sees in a vision during the night, summons him and his companions to sail over and provide the divine aid the Macedonian people need: "Come over to Macedonia and help us" (Acts 16:9). The person in the vision is an ethnic Macedonian, not simply a man residing in Macedonia. Paul may have identified him by the traditional Macedonian garb he wore, possibly the "broad-brimmed hat" (*kausia*) made of felt, which Antipater of Thessalonica said in one of his epigrams was the Macedonians' "comfortable gear" (Gow and Page, *Greek Anthology*, 1:37).

Although Macedonia was no more than a Roman province during Paul's time, it was once a kingdom ruled by Philip II, which his son Alexander III expanded to become the largest empire the world had ever seen. During their era, the Macedonians spoke standard Greek (*koinē*) but also communicated in *Makedonisti* ("in Macedonian"; Plutarch, *Alex.* 51.6; Hammond, *History*, 1:39–54). Although Philip and

Alexander claimed Greek descent (Hammond, *Alexander*, 257–58), the history and culture of Macedonia was distinct from that of the Greeks to the south (P. Green, *Alexander to Actium*, 3–5), a point often lost in discussions about ancient Macedonia. Now, in Acts 16, the descendants of the great Macedonian Kingdom of Philip and Alexander need the help that Paul can bring through the gospel of Jesus Christ.

The History of Macedonia

King Philip II (ruled 359–336 BC) brought the Greek city-states under Macedonian rule, a state of affairs that endured until the intervention of Rome in the second century BC. Philip was an intelligent, strategic ruler whose diplomatic prowess and military strategy had turned Macedonia into the principal power on the Aegean Sea. The Macedonian army had become the greatest in the world through Philip's reorganization and the development of a phalanx formation using the *sarissa* (an iron-tipped pike of twelve to fifteen feet) in addition to small shields and swords. Philip also had designs on conquering the Persian Empire, whose rule extended through Asia Minor at that time. However, early in the time of the campaign against the Persians, Philip was knifed and assassinated by his bodyguard Pausanius at the lavish wedding of his daughter Cleopatra in the theater of the Macedonian capital of Aigai (or Aegae). Though believed to be descended from Zeus, King Philip lay dead. The very same day, his twenty-year-old son, Alexander III, was elected successor to the Macedonian throne.

Although young in years, Alexander III (ruled 336–323 BC) had been groomed to assume rule over Macedonia. Philip had assured that he was well educated by placing him under the tutelage of the great Macedonian philosopher Aristotle (though educated in Plato's Academy in Athens, he was Macedonian by birth). Alexander learned the Greek way of life from Aristotle. Demosthenes, the Athenian orator, had railed against Alexander as a base coward who was "content to saunter around in Pella," referring to his studies under Aristotle (Aeschines, *Ctes.* 160 LCL; P. Green, *Alexander of*

42.1. A small ivory portrait head, possibly of Philip II.

Building for the Protection of the Royal Tombs of Vergina

Macedon, 118). Philip had also trained Alexander in the art of war when he was a youth by naming him a general in the army and sending him to lead numerous military campaigns. After Philip's death, Alexander, by adding cavalry as protection along the flanks and rear, perfected the phalanx formation that his father had developed. The young king surrounded himself with experienced and wise men as well.

Alexander reasserted Macedonian control over Greece and also led campaigns through the Balkans. His eye, however, was on Asia, as had been that of his father. Alexander led his army to victory as he crossed the Hellespont and went for Troy; upon landing, "he flung his spear from the ship and fixed it in the ground, and then leapt ashore himself, the first of the Macedonians, signifying that he received Asia from the gods as a spear-won prize" (Diodorus Siculus, *Lib. Hist.* 17.17.2 LCL). He crisscrossed and took control of Asia Minor, sacrificing to the gods as he went, in his quest to become the king of Asia and to "liberate" the peoples of Anatolia from Persian oppression. Moving eastward, he traversed the Cilician Gates, passed through the city of Tarsus, and then confronted and defeated the Persian king Darius III in 333 BC at Issus, on the northeastern Mediterranean. According to the sources, 110,000 Persians died in the melee, although Darius escaped, leaving his wife, mother, and children behind. Alexander, however, honored Darius's family members. He was proclaimed "King of Asia" (Plutarch, *Alex.* 34.1), a title subsequently inscribed in a dedication to Athena: "King Alexander, having mastered Darius in battle and having become Lord of Asia, made sacrifice to Athena of Lindus in accordance with an oracle" (cited in Hammond, *Macedonian State*, 207).

Alexander and his army continued southward to capture the lands along the Mediterranean coast, sacking Tyre, sweeping down through Palestine, passing through Dor (where in 2009 archaeologists found a gemstone with Alexander's image), capturing

42.2. A marble bust of Alexander the Great (second–first century BC) from Alexandria, now in the British Museum.

42.3. Mosaic of the battle of Issus from Pompeii, laid during the Roman period. Alexander (left) faces the retreating Darius and his Persian troops.

Gaza, and arriving in Egypt. There in 331 BC he founded a new city and named it after himself: Alexandria. The Egyptians gave him the title "King of Upper Egypt and King of Lower Egypt, beloved of Ammon and selected of Ra" (Ra was the supreme deity; Hammond, *Genius*, 99). When Alexander visited the sanctuary of Zeus Ammon at the oasis in Siwah, the priest greeted him as "Son of Ra," identifying Alexander as pharaoh and the Son of Zeus. Alexander became convinced that he had been "born of Zeus" and was celebrated as Zeus the King.

Alexander did not remain in Egypt but turned eastward to expand further the kingdom of the Macedonians. In 331 BC he campaigned in northern Mesopotamia, where he again faced and defeated Darius, at the battle of Gaugamela. Alexander swept southward through Babylon and Persia. He pursued Darius up through Media. Darius was assassinated before Alexander could reach him, yet Alexander was regarded as Darius's successor. Alexander continued his campaigns eastward all the way to "Indike," the land of the Indus River valley, in order to extend his reign over all Asia. Alexander's army, however, was exhausted and longed for their homeland. So the king turned south along the Indus and then, at last, headed westward, toward Babylon. But there, on June 10, 323 BC, Alexander died at the age of 33 of causes still disputed. In just over a decade he and his Macedonian troops altered the course of history; through him the "Hellenistic world" extended as far as India.

References to Alexander of Macedon appear within the biblical text (Dan. 2:39; 7:6; 8:5–8, 21; 11:2–4; and possibly Zech. 9:1–8; see also 1 Macc. 1:1–9; 6:1–2).

Down into the first century AD and beyond, people universally remembered his Macedonian legacy well. Pliny the Elder, for example, wrote in AD 77: "After comes Macedonia, with 150 nations, and famous because of its two kings [Philip II and Alexander III] and their former world empire" (*Nat. Hist.* 4.10 LCL). Many Roman emperors sought to imitate Alexander. Augustus traveled to Alexandria in Egypt to see the sarcophagus of Alexander, and when asked whether he wanted to see the tombs of Alexander's successors the Ptolemies, Augustus remarked, "My wish was to see a king, not corpses" (Suetonius, *Aug.* 18.1–2 LCL). Caligula donned the breastplate of Alexander that he had taken from Alexander's sarcophagus (Suetonius, *Cal.* 52). Later, Nero planned to use a legion of Roman troops he called "the phalanx of Alexander the Great" in a military campaign to the Caspian Gate, where Alexander had pursued Darius (Suetonius, *Nero* 19.2 LCL). At the beginning of the second century AD, the Roman emperor Trajan expressed an unfulfilled desire to conquer as far as the Indus, as had Alexander (Dio Cassius, *Hist.* 68.29.1). Even lesser Roman rulers, such as the proconsul of Macedonia Lucias Calpunius Piso, were inspired by the image of Alexander. Alexander's image remained on the coinage in certain areas, such as the issue minted by the Macedonian *koinon* (federation of Macedonian cities) centered in Beroea during the mid-third century AD.

Various rulers, such as the Macedonian king Ptolemy I, established and promoted the cult of Alexander, which became a prototype for the later development of the Roman imperial cult. The exploitation of Alexander's name and image for political purposes was commonplace, as witnessed by the silver tetradrachms minted by Lysimachus (see figure 42.4) and by Aesillas, a Roman quaestor (supervisor of financial affairs) in Thessalonica, both of which bore the image of the divinized Alexander. After the assassination of Julius Caesar, Brutus and Cassius fled to Macedonia, where, before being defeated by Octavian (Augustus) and Mark Antony, Brutus minted a Lysimachus-style gold stater to pay his mercenaries.

As a result of Alexander's conquests, there emerged a new consciousness of the world (the *oikoumenē*, "inhabited world"), as well as the idea of a universal kingdom. In Alexander's wake the Greek language spread throughout the East, giving the world Koine Greek as the lingua franca and facilitating cultural exchange and governance, including the later spread of the gospel. The tetradrachm became universal coinage, minted from Amphipolis in Macedonia all the way to Babylon in Asia, and set down new economic patterns by facilitating commerce across vast regions. Greek ideas, such as the nature and design of the *polis* ("city") and Greek philosophy, as taught to Alexander by Aristotle, became normative across Alexander's former empire. Indeed, Alexander founded some seventy cities (Plutarch, *Mor.* 328E) and celebrated the virtues of "excellence" (*aretē*), courage, and loyalty among his commanders (Hammond, *Alexander*, 264). Although Alexander freely adopted the religious customs of conquered peoples—even honoring and worshiping God in the Jerusalem temple, according to Josephus (*Ant.* 11.329)—the Macedonian troops brought with them the worship of the deities associated with Mount Olympus in Macedonia. He also integrated conquered peoples into his army and administration,

42.4. The Macedonian king Lysimachus, one of Alexander's successors, minted tetradrachms (3 cm.) bearing the image of the deified Alexander with the horn of Ammon.

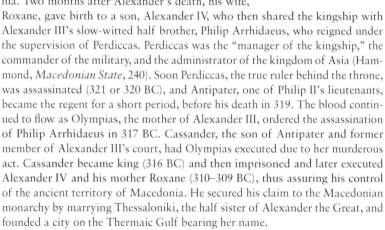

allowing considerable diversity within his kingdom. The idea of a universal king, one who would be granted divine honors, finds its expression in Alexander as well. The world was forever changed, both politically and culturally, by the conquests of Alexander of Macedon.

After the death of Alexander, there was no clear line of succession to his rule as the king of Asia and the king of Macedonia. Two months after Alexander's death, his wife, Roxane, gave birth to a son, Alexander IV, who then shared the kingship with Alexander III's slow-witted half brother, Philip Arrhidaeus, who reigned under the supervision of Perdiccas. Perdiccas was the "manager of the kingship," the commander of the military, and the administrator of the kingdom of Asia (Hammond, *Macedonian State*, 240). Soon Perdiccas, the true ruler behind the throne, was assassinated (321 or 320 BC), and Antipater, one of Philip II's lieutenants, became the regent for a short period, before his death in 319. The blood continued to flow as Olympias, the mother of Alexander III, ordered the assassination of Philip Arrhidaeus in 317 BC. Cassander, the son of Antipater and former member of Alexander III's court, had Olympias executed due to her murderous act. Cassander became king (316 BC) and then imprisoned and later executed Alexander IV and his mother Roxane (310–309 BC), thus assuring his control of the ancient territory of Macedonia. He secured his claim to the Macedonian monarchy by marrying Thessaloniki, the half sister of Alexander the Great, and founded a city on the Thermaic Gulf bearing her name.

Cassander was just one of the *diadochoi* ("successors") to Alexander III's kingdom. While he became the king of Macedonia and exercised sovereignty over the territories of the ancient Macedonian Kingdom and Greece, Lysimachus ruled Thrace to the north and then Asia Minor also, after Antigonos fell in battle in 301 BC. Ptolemy ruled as sovereign over Egypt and Cyrene, and Seleucus held the eastern portion of Alexander III's empire all the way to the Indus River. The conflicts between the Seleucids and Ptolomies over Palestine were, in the end, conflicts between Macedonian rulers. Queen Cleopatra VII in Egypt, the last pharaoh and one who with Mark Antony attempted to wrest control of the Roman Empire, bore a traditional Macedonian name and became

42.5. The Seleucid and Ptolemaic kingdoms following the death of Alexander the Great.

the last of the Macedonian monarchs. The world had been under the control of Macedonians and their successors until the triumphal eastward expansion of the Romans.

Macedonia experienced considerable upheaval from the time of Cassander until the reign of Philip V (238–179 BC). Philip managed to bring great economic prosperity to the kingdom. But in 215 he made a treaty with Hannibal of Carthage, the rising power in the West and the enemy of Rome. The Macedonians plunged into two wars with the Romans (214–205 BC and 200–196 BC), the second of which ended in a resounding defeat of the Macedonians at the battle of Cynoscephalae. The Roman general Titus Flamininus liberated the Greeks to the south and declared their freedom in the stadium at Isthmia, just outside Corinth. The enduring domination of Greece by the Macedonians had come to an end.

The Third Macedonian War brought the Macedonian Kingdom to its knees as the Romans defeated Philip V's successor, King Perseus, at the battle of Pydna (168 BC) by the Thermaic Gulf. In its eastward expansion, Rome considered Macedonia to be a real and present danger. Perseus had assembled an army so great that it could only be compared to that of Alexander the Great (Livy, *Hist*. 42.51.11). But the Roman general Aemilius Paulus broke through the Macedonian ranks, even though the general confessed "that he had never seen anything more terrible and dreadful than a Macedonian phalanx" (Polybius, *Hist*. 29.17.1 LCL). As Roman soldiers plundered Macedonia, King Perseus fled to the island of Samothrace, the ancient Macedonian cult site of the deities called the Cabeiri, where Philip II had met his wife, Olympias. The booty from war was so great that Rome exempted its citizens from taxation for the next century. Rome proclaimed itself the "liberator" of the kingdom of Macedonia, but freedom only meant submission to Rome. The world took note. Even 1 Macc. 8:5 refers to Roman victory in the Second and Third Macedonian Wars: "They had crushed in battle and conquered Philip [V], the King Perseus of the Macedonians, and the others who rose up against them."

Rome broke the back of Macedonia by dividing the kingdom into four districts (cf. Acts 16:12; Philippi was in the first district) so that it could not be reunified. The Romans prohibited trade across the districts as well as marriages between those of different districts. They ordered the gold and silver mines shut and curtailed shipbuilding by forbidding the Macedonians to cut timber. Macedonia was mangled and disjointed as the Romans sought to ensure that it would never again rise to power (Livy, *Hist.* 45.18, 29–30).

Andriscus, who claimed to be the son of King Perseus, led some Macedonian cities in an uprising against Rome. The Romans, under the military leadership of the praetor Quintus Caecilius Metellus Macedonicus, handily quelled the rebellion that began in 149 BC. The kingdom finally ended when Rome incorporated Macedonia as a province in 148 BC. Rome joined the territory of Macedonia with the southern portion of Illyria, thus extending the newly formed province from the Aegean on the east to the Adriatic Sea on the west. Late in the second century BC (146–120), Rome built the Via Egnatia, which stretched from Apollonia and Dyrrachium on the Adriatic all the way eastward through Edessa, Pella, Thessalonica, and Philippi and up to Byzantium. Cicero called it "our great military road through Macedonia as far as the Hellespont" (*Prov. cons.* 2.4). This all-weather road

Lee Martin McDonald

42.6. Ruins of the Via Egnatia (Egnatian Way) near Philippi. This Roman road extended from Byzantium to Neapolis (Kavala), on to Philippi and Thessalonica, and then westward through western Greece to the coast of the Adriatic Sea.

helped assure Rome's control of the province but also provided one of the main east–west arteries of the rising empire. Along with military troops, government officials, merchants, pilgrims, and other travelers, the apostle Paul and his companions traveled this road during their mission through Macedonia (Acts 16:11–17:10; 19:21–22; 20:1–6). At some time Paul reached its western terminus in the region of Illyricum (Rom. 15:19). When in exile in Thessalonica during the mid-first century BC, Cicero complained that he did not like to travel the road, since it was so crowded (*Att.* 3.14). Macedonia became fully integrated into the life and politics of the Roman Empire, so much so that when Cicero was in Thessalonica he noted the loyalty of Macedonia to Rome as one of its allies (*Pis.* 84; *Font.* 44).

42.7. Important cities in Macedonia and environs.

The Cities and Government of Macedonia

In 27 BC the emperor Augustus recognized that the province of Macedonia was at peace and loyal to Rome, so he placed it under the jurisdiction of the Roman Senate. During a period of unrest it was joined with the province of Achaia to the south, and the two became an imperial province under the emperor's supervision (AD 15–44). Under Claudius's administration the provinces were divided again, and Macedonia reverted to a senatorial province. The capital of the Roman province of Macedonia was not the ancient Pella of Philip II and Alexander III but Thessalonica, located at the head of the Thermaic Gulf. Thessalonica had become the capital of the second district of Macedonia after the battle of Pydna, but when

Rome converted the former kingdom into a province, it made Thessalonica the capital of the whole due to its loyalty to Rome at the time of the rebellion of Andriscus. Later, Mark Antony granted Thessalonica free-city status (*Thessalonice liberae condicionis*, according to Pliny the Elder, *Nat. Hist.* 4.10.36), since it sided with him and Octavian against Cassius and Brutus after their assassination of Julius Caesar. This meant that the city was honored with exemption from taxation to Rome and was not required to have Roman troops garrisoned within its walls. Thessalonica became, according to Strabo the geographer, "the metropolis ["mother city"] of what is now Macedonia" (frg. 7.21 LCL). The city showed great loyalty and honored the Romans, so much so that it built a temple in honor of Julius Caesar and his adopted son, Augustus, who was called "the son of god," and established a priesthood in honor of "Dea Roma and the Roman benefactors" (Hendrix, "Romans"). Roman and traditional Macedonian names appear together in inscriptions enumerating the politarchs (see Acts 17:6, 8), the governing officials of the city. In addition, the city had a governing assembly, there called the *dēmos* (see Acts 17:5), as well as a council (*boulē*). As the provincial capital, the city was also the home of the Roman proconsul, the highest governing official in a senatorial province, as well as the quaestor, the Roman official responsible for the financial affairs of the city.

Philippi, though a leading city within the province's first district (see Acts 16:12), was not its capital, since that honor fell to another city along the Via Egnatia, the ancient city of Amphipolis (Acts 17:1; see the tetradrachm in fig. 42.8). Philippi became a Roman colony (named Colonia Augusta Iulia Philippensis) after the battle of Philippi (42 BC), when Octavian and Mark Antony defeated the assassins Brutus and Cassius. Since it had the status of a Roman city, its free citizens enjoyed Roman citizenship. Latin was the language of the majority of inscriptions in the city, and its law and governance were Roman. The colonial officials in Philippi were the two principle magistrates, or *duoviri* (Greek *stratēgoi*; see Acts 16:20, 22, 35–36, 38); the *aediles*, who were supervisors of buildings and public works; the *quaestores*, who were in charge of financial affairs; and the *lictores*, who maintained order (Greek *rhabdouchoi*; see Acts 16:35, 38). Philippi was

42.8. Silver tetradrachm (31 mm.) minted in Amphipolis, capital of the first district of Macedonia. Inscribed: *Makedonōn prōtēs*, "Of the first of the Macedonians."

Harlan J. Berk, Ltd.

served by a well-sheltered port, Neapolis (Acts 16:11), which lay just ten miles (sixteen kilometers) eastward.

Beroea, another Macedonian city visited by Paul and his associates (Acts 17:10), was the seat of the Macedonian *koinon*, a council composed of upper-class members of the Macedonian cities. The *koinon* represented the interests of the province before the emperor, promoted the imperial cult, had authority to mint coins, and sponsored games during its yearly assembly. After Paul escaped from the city, he likely traveled to the ancient religious center of Macedonia, Dion, located near the base of Mount Olympus. Like Philippi, Dion had become a Roman colony. Since Dion lay by the Aegean Sea, Paul could easily find passage from there aboard a freighter bound for Athens (Acts 17:14–15). The NT contains no record of other principal Macedonian cities that lay along the Via Egnatia, such as Pella (the ancient Macedonian capital) and Edessa, although churches were at some time established within them.

42.9. The theater at Philippi was built by Philip of Macedon about 350 BC but was enlarged by the Romans in the first and second centuries AD.

Bibliography

Errington, R. Malcolm. *A History of Macedonia*. Berkeley: University of California Press, 1990. Provides a clear picture of the centrality of Macedonia in the development of Hellenistic history.

Gow, A. S. F., and D. L. Page. *The Greek Anthology: The Garland of Philip and Some Contemporary Epigrams*. 2 vols. Cambridge: Cambridge University Press, 1968. A collection of epigrams from Philip and Antipater of Thessalonica.

Green, Gene L. *The Letters to the Thessalonians*. PNTC. Grand Rapids: Eerdmans, 2002. Includes an extensive introductory section on the history and social world of Macedonia, with a focus on Thessalonica.

Green, Peter. *Alexander of Macedon 356–323 B.C.: A Historical Biography*. Berkeley: University of California Press, 1991. One of the best histories on Alexander the Great.

———. *Alexander to Actium: The Historical Evolution of the Hellenistic Age*. Berkeley: University of California Press, 1990. An overview of Hellenistic history that frames Macedonia within developments occurring in the wider Hellenistic world.

Hammond, N. G. L. *Alexander the Great: King, Commander and Statesman*. London: Bristol Classical Press, 1980. An accessible and insightful history of Alexander the Great.

———. *The Genius of Alexander the Great*. Chapel Hill: University of North Carolina Press, 1997. A more popular version of Hammond's 1980 publication.

———. *The Macedonian State: The Origins, Institutions and History*. Oxford: Clarendon, 1989. A shorter version of Hammond's three-volume *History of Macedonia*.

———. *The Miracle That Was Macedonia*. London: Sidgwick, 1991. A popular survey of Macedonian history and its historical significance. A good first text to read on the history.

Hammond, N. G. L., G. T. Griffith, and F. W. Walbank. *A History of Macedonia*. 3 vols. Oxford: Clarendon, 1972–88. No scholar is more versed in the history of Macedonia than Nicholas Hammond. His three-volume work runs up only to the beginning of the Roman period but is detailed and comprehensive up to the battle of Pydna.

Hendrix, Holland Lee. "Thessalonicans Honor Romans." ThD diss., Harvard Divinity School, 1984. A key text for understanding the relationship between the Macedonian capital Thessalonica and the Romans. Hendrix emphasizes the economic dimension of the imperial cult.

Roisman, Joseph, and Ian Worthington, eds. *A Companion to Ancient Macedonia*. Malden, MA: Wiley-Blackwell, 2010. An excellent contemporary introduction to the history, politics, and social world of Macedonia up through the Roman period.

Sakellariou, M. B., ed. *Macedonia: 4000 Years of Greek History and Civilization*. Athens: Ekdotike Athenon, 1983. A basic illustrated guide to the history of Macedonia.

43

Achaia

GENE L. GREEN

During his second missionary journey recorded in Acts, the apostle Paul sets sail from Macedonia and arrives in the Roman province of Achaia for the first time when he lands in Athens (17:13–15). After preaching the gospel in Athens, he continues on to Corinth, the provincial capital of Achaia (18:1–17). Paul then sets sail for Ephesus in the province of Asia (18:18–19), embarking from Cenchreae, Corinth's port on the Saronic Gulf that empties into the Aegean Sea. On the so-called third missionary journey, he decides to return to the churches in the provinces of Macedonia and Achaia (19:21–22; 20:1–3). Unsurprisingly, the apostle occasionally mentions the churches of these provinces together in his letters (Rom. 15:26; 2 Cor. 9:2; 11:9–10; 1 Thess. 1:7–8), although at times he speaks solely of the converts in the province of Achaia (1 Cor. 16:15; 2 Cor. 1:1). The province covered the ancient lands of the Greeks, and so in some texts "Greece" becomes the alternate name for Achaia (e.g., Acts 20:1–3). Not all who are called "Greeks" in the NT, however, were from Achaia. The NT writers often employ the term to speak about all non-Jews whose language is Greek (John 7:35; 12:20; Acts 14:1; 18:4; 19:10; Rom. 1:14; 3:9; 1 Cor. 1:22, 24).

The History of Achaia

The name "Achaia" (also spelled "Achaea"; Greek *Achaia*) was originally the name of the peoples who settled along the northern part of the Peloponnese, the southern peninsula of Greece, bounded on the north by the Gulf of Corinth (Herodotus, *Hist.* 7.94; Strabo, *Geogr.* 8.7.1; Pausanias, *Descr.* 2.5.6, who also notes in 7.1.1 that Achaia was formerly called Aegialus). Herodotus records that there were twelve districts, or divisions, in Achaia (*Hist.* 1.145). The historian Polybius recalls that twelve cities of Achaia banded together to form a league with their own constitution (*Hist.* 2.41–42) in which they rejected monarchic government in favor of democracy (*Hist.* 2.41). This first Achaian League was followed by a second, which held to the original's democratic values (*Hist.* 2.42). The Achaians stood against any rule by a king and so were vigorously opposed to control by the kingdom of Macedonia to the north, which was represented by the Macedonian fortress located at Corinth. The Achaian League embraced the values of "equality and freedom" and sought liberty for all the states of the Peloponnese with a view to uniting them together. They assured that no advantage accrued to any particular state of the federation over the others. In a mass gathering of the Achaians, they annually elected their chief magistrate, the *stratēgos* ("general") who commanded the league's federated army. The first of these was Margos of Caryneia. Unsurprisingly, the Achaian League sought to oust the Macedonians from their states. Polybius says their goal was "the explusion of the Macedonians from the Peloponnese, the suppression of the tyrants, and the re-establishment on a sure basis of the ancient freedom of every state" (*Hist.* 2.43 LCL; Errington, *History*, 91).

Lee Martin McDonald

43.1. The temple of Hephaestus, the crippled Greek god of artisans, is half the size of the Parthenon, with six columns on the short side and thirteen on the long. This is the best-preserved ancient temple in Greece and is located above the main part of the Athenian agora (completed in the late fifth century BC). Paul visited the agora on his second missionary journey (Acts 17:16–18:1).

While the Achaian League was developing in the Peloponnese, the Aitolian League began to form in central Greece, the region north of the Gulf of Corinth and south of Macedonia. This too was a federation of Greek states that served as the protector of the great oracle at Delphi. The Aitolian League, as the Achaian, eventually spread beyond the traditional land of the Aitolians and embraced other regions, such as Akarnania to the west. These leagues, along with Athens, were in constant interplay and tension with Macedonia down until the time of the Roman expulsion of Macedonian power from Greek soil and the final overthrow of Macedonia. These alliances and conflicts defined their history.

Originally the Achaian League found support from the Macedonians through the period of the First Macedonian War against Rome (214–205 BC). But under the leadership of a new *stratēgos* Aristainos, and by vote of the people, the Achaian League then turned to ally itself by treaty with Rome at the time of the Second Macedonian War (200–196 BC; Livy, *Hist.* 32.19–25). During this period, the Romans liberated the Achaian League and all of Greece from Macedonian control. The Romans dealt the Macedonians a brutal defeat at the battle of Cynoscephalae, after which the Roman general Titus Flamininus declared freedom for the Greeks through an announcement in the stadium at Isthmia near Corinth. This freedom for the Achaians and all the Greeks did not, however, mean freedom from Rome, which imposed taxation on them. And whatever freedom had been assured was also short lived.

Rome invaded the Greek states after conquering Macedonia in 168 BC and quelling the subsequent Macedonian uprising under Andriscus in 149 BC. Unrest erupted in the Peloponnese as Sparta, a member of the Achaian League, challenged the league and was answered with military action. After war broke out in the Peloponnese, the Roman Senate sent Lucius Mummius, who had defeated Andriscus in Macedonia, southward to begin a campaign known as the Achaian War (146–145 BC; Pausanias, *Descr.* 7.12–16). The Roman proconsul Mummius defeated the Achaian League and destroyed the city of Corinth, torching it and tearing down its walls. The devastation of Corinth was the beginning of the destruction of the whole of Achaia. As Pausanias says, "It was at this time that Greece was struck with universal and utter prostration, although parts of it from the beginning had suffered ruin and devastation at the hand of heaven" (*Descr.* 7.17.1 LCL). Pausanias also recounts the earlier ruin of other cities at the hands of the Macedonians, through plagues and by other wars before the one with Rome. Indeed, even after Rome conquered the Achaian League, civil war broke out, which led to closer control by Roman power (*Descr.* 7.17.4). The Achaian War meant that Greek independence, which had been won after the Second Macedonian War (200–196 BC), had come to an end. From the time of the Achaian War onward, the whole of Achaia came under the control of Rome and was supervised by the Roman proconsul in Macedonia. As a subject of Rome, Achaia was obliged to pay taxes to the power in the West (Errington, *History*, 252–53).

Achaia became a province of the Roman Empire in 46 BC (although some date the grant of provincial status earlier). According to the geographer Strabo, "the

Provinces have been divided in different ways at different times" (*Geogr.* 17.3.25 LCL), and this holds true for the province of Achaia as well. Strabo notes that at the time of Augustus Caesar, Achaia stretched "as far as [Greek *mechri*; this may imply inclusion] Thessaly and Aetolia and Acarnania and certain Epeirotic tribes which border on Macedonia" (*Geogr.* 17.3.25 LCL). This area embraces the lands that lay south of the provinces of Macedonia and Epirus, including the traditional lands of the Achaians in the Peloponnese. According to Strabo, at that time Achaia was a senatorial province, or "Province of the People," that is, one under supervision of the Senate, or "assigned . . . to the Roman people" and governed under "praetors and proconsuls." Such provinces "were peaceful and free from war" (Dio Cassius, *Hist.* 53.12.1–4 LCL). For a period, however, the emperor Tiberius joined the provinces of Achaia and Macedonia together and placed them under the jurisdiction of Moesia due to complaints over their tax burden (AD 15; Tacitus, *Ann.* 1.76.4; 1.80.1; Dio Cassius, *Hist.* 58.25.4–5). The two became one of the Roman imperial provinces that, as Strabo noted, were under the direct control of the emperor rather than the Senate. The emperor sent legates and procurators as the principal governing officials of these "provinces of Caesar." Some years later, however, the emperor Claudius reversed Tiberius's policy by separating the provinces and returning Achaia to senatorial supervision (AD 44; Suetonius, *Claud.* 25.3; Dio Cassius, *Hist.* 60.24.1).

In AD 67 the emperor Nero freed Achaia from Roman control entirely (Pliny the Elder, *Nat. Hist.* 4.6.22; Suetonius, *Nero* 24.2), a state of affairs that lasted for only a short period. In AD 69 Vespasian took away their freedom and made Achaia a senatorial province once again, "since," he said, "the Greek people had forgotten how to be free" (Pausanias, *Descr.* 7.17.3–4 LCL; cf. Suetonius, *Vesp.* 8.4). The former glory of the Achaian League was just a memory, at least from the Roman point of view.

The Cities of Roman Achaia in the New Testament

Athens

Athens once was ruled by kings but, Strabo notes, "they changed to a democracy" (*Geogr.* 9.1.20 LCL). Before the coming of Rome during the time of the Achaian War, Athens had been subject to Macedonia but fostered good relations with the rising power in the West (Polybius, *Hist.* 2.12.8). During the Third Macedonian War (171–168 BC), Athens sided with the Romans against the last king of Macedonia, Perseus, and was rewarded by being given Delos in 166 BC. This was the mythical birthplace of Apollo and Artemis and the center of the archipelago in the Aegean Sea called the Cyclades. The island and its prosperity increased even after the Achaian War and the sacking of Corinth (see Strabo, *Geogr.* 10.5.4). Athens and Athenian Delos prospered together. The pro-Roman stance of Athens meant that many from Italy came to settle there and had their

43.2. The ancient prison in Athens where Socrates was jailed and given poison (fourth century BC).

sons educated in the city. Strabo notes, "The Romans, seeing that the Athenians had a democratic government when they took them over, preserved their autonomy and liberty" (*Geogr.* 9.1.20 LCL).

The city, however, unwisely decided to turn its loyalty from Rome to the king Mithradates IV Eupator Dionysus (120–63 BC), who ruled over Pontus in Asia Minor and was a declared enemy of Rome. Delos did not follow this folly and remained loyal to Rome, leaving Athens to face the Roman proconsul L. Cornelius Sulla, who put Athens under siege in 87–86 BC. Athens fell, as had Corinth before it (Plutarch, *Sull.* 12–14; Errington, *History*, 254–55), but Athens managed to remain a free city, since Sulla "pardoned the city itself" (Strabo, *Geogr.* 9.1.20 LCL). Athens was drawn into the Roman province of Achaia and continued to prosper under Roman rule since it received a considerable amount of benefaction from the Romans.

Although during the Roman period Athens did not enjoy the intellectual glory of the days of Socrates, Plato, and Aristotle, the city continued to be a center for philosophical discourse and became one of the seats of the Second Sophistic movement (Philostratus, *Lives of the Sophists*; Anderson, *Second Sophistic*; Winter, *Philo and Paul*). The author of Acts focuses on Paul's daily discourses in the Athenian agora, the traditional place of philosophical discussion. Paul "dialogued" with those who gathered (Acts 17:17), an echo of the Socratic style of teaching (see Xenophon, *Mem.* 1.2.2–3; 4.4.15). Socrates could be found engaging people in all quarters, from the agora to the gymnasium to the workshops. Paul engaged both the Epicureans and the Stoics while speaking in Athens, challenging their

43.3. The Parthenon sits on top of the acropolis in Athens and is currently being reconstructed.

philosophical assumptions as he argued from the Jewish Scriptures and the gospel of Jesus Christ (Acts 17:22–34).

The agora in Athens was under the shadow of the acropolis and was filled with idols and temples (Acts 17:16). This holds true for the classic Greek agora of the city as well as the newer Roman forum, the central commercial center to the north of the city's central acropolis, built with funds from Julius Caesar and Augustus in the first century BC. The quantity of idols and temples in the city was even noted by ancient authors (see Pausanias, *Descr.* 1.14.1–15.4; Livy, *Hist.* 45.27). Though ancient cities publically honored the gods, Athens could hardly be outdone and even honored unknown gods (Acts 17:23; Philostratus, *Vit. Apol.* 6.3).

Corinth

One of the most graphic moments of the Achaian War was the destruction of the city of Corinth. In his *Description of Greece*, Pausanias tells the story of Mummius's invasion, the downfall of Corinth (7.16), and the subsequent subjugation of Achaia (7.17). Mummius brought 3,500 cavalrymen as well as 23,000 foot soldiers down from Macedonia to the isthmus where Corinth lay. The Achaians came out to attack Mummius's troops and scored a small early victory but did not manage to assess fully the strength of the proconsul's forces. Mummius moved his troops forward, the cavalry leading the way, and easily routed the Achaians (see

Pausanias, *Descr.* 7.16.3–4). The Achaians made their escape, some to Corinth, but then left the city along with many of Corinth's inhabitants. Mummius arrived to find the city gates open and, suspecting an ambush, waited three days before storming the city and setting it ablaze. Those left in Corinth were killed by the sword, while women and children were taken captive to be sold as slaves. Mummius plundered the riches and art in the city and then proceeded to tear down the walls (*Descr.* 7.16.7–10). The wasting of Corinth assured that the city would not rise again. Corinth had been widely known for its wealth, and so the city's destruction meant riches for Rome. As Cicero said in the mid-first century BC, "After that [the defeat of Macedonia], that most excellent and fruitful land of Corinth . . . which by the successful campaign of L. Mummius was added to the revenues of the Roman people" (*Agr.* 1.2.5 LCL). The city of Corinth lay fallow for a hundred years, with just a few native inhabitants remaining.

Lee Martin McDonald

43.4. The temple of Apollo, one of the few structures in Corinth that survived the Roman destruction.

Shortly before his untimely death, Julius Caesar ordered the refounding and colonization of Corinth, in 44 BC. The city became the capital of the province of Achaia. Caesar drew most of the colonists from among the freedmen, *plebs* ("commoners"), and veterans of the Roman legions. The first two were among the more disenfranchised and discontent in Rome, so moving them out relieved some of the overpopulation and took some of the more problematic elements of society out of the city. Rome assured the loyalty of these colonists by relocating them to a place that had lost none of its strategic advantage and giving them land allotments besides.

Strategically the refounding of Corinth was a great boon to Rome, since it gave the Romans a point from which to expand their influence toward the east and to facilitate trade. Such was the importance of Achaia. By the time Paul arrived, Corinth had become the largest city of Roman Achaia, with approximately eighty thousand urban inhabitants along with twenty thousand in the surrounding countryside (Engels, *Roman Corinth*, 84). However, not everyone gloried in the new foundation of Roman Corinth; the epigramist Crinagoras referred to it as a "great calamity to Greece" and described the new inhabitants as "a crowd of scoundrelly slaves" (Patton, *Greek Anthology*, 9.284).

During both the classical and the Roman periods, Corinth was an extremely rich city, since it was located on the isthmus between mainland Greece and the Peloponnese and controlled all north–south trade. It also lay along the principal east–west trade route of the northern Mediterranean and controlled a six-mile-long dry canal, a road named the Diolkos, which allowed passage of goods and even small ships between the Gulf of Corinth and the Saronic Gulf. This portage was built around 600 BC and was the preferred means of passing to the east or west, since sailing around the Peloponnese was dangerous. As the ancient saying went, "But when you double Maleae [that is, sail around Maleae on the southern tip of the Peloponnese, where the sea was dangerous] forget your home" (cited in Murphy-O'Connor, *St. Paul's Corinth*, 53). Julius Caesar had planned to build a canal through the isthmus. Nero attempted to cut one through by using prisoners captured during the First Jewish Revolt (begun in AD 66) but failed. But even without a canal, Corinth grew rich due to its service economy. Roman Corinth helped generate prosperity for many of the new colonists, and this, in turn, meant the revival of the Achaian economy, which had been greatly depressed. One of the most well-known and prosperous early colonists was Gnaeus Babbius Philinus, who erected a monument on the west side of the agora and whose name seems to indicate that he came from servile origins.

But during the Roman period, not everyone enjoyed the wealth of the city. A wide gulf existed between its rich and its poor, a social reality that defined the Corinthian church as well (cf. 1 Cor. 1:26). In the second century the orator Alciphron commented on the stark economic disparity that existed in the town: "for I learned in a short time the foridness of the rich there and the misery of the poor" (*Ep.* 3.24 LCL).

When Paul first came to the city after traveling from Athens (Acts 18:1–28), he went to the Jewish synagogue, where he preached the gospel every Sabbath day (18:4). Archaeologists have found an inscription that reads "Synagogue of the Jews," but they have not discovered where the synagogue was located.

Although there was a Jewish community in the city, Corinth was distinctly Roman. Colonies were established by Rome throughout the empire in order to secure its hold on the territories that had come under its control. These colonies were

43.5. Remains of the ancient Diolkos road that allowed ships and their cargo to be dragged across the Isthmus of Corinth.

"mini-Romes," with Latin being the dominant language, government according to the Roman order, and citizens sometimes exempt from taxation to Rome. The Jews in Acts who ended up in Corinth were known by their Latin names (e.g., Acts 18:2, 8), and some Greek families in the city took on Roman names as well. Though Corinth was located on Greek soil, the coinage from Corinth bore Latin letters, and public inscriptions were written predominantly in Latin, with the exception of inscriptions related to the Isthmian Games, which Corinth administered (from 6 or 2 BC onward) since these were panhellenic. The architecture during the Roman period was Italian and not Greek, and the images of the emperor were portrayed with Roman dress. Corinth hosted gladiatorial contests that the Latins loved but were not part of Greek cultural heritage. Although this was a predominantly Roman city on Greek soil, Paul's Corinthian Letters were written in Greek. There was likely a gradual increase in the presence of Greeks in the city who relocated there due to the economic advantages it offered. Dio Chrysostom's thirty-seventh *Oration* (likely written by Favorinus) to the Corinthians speaks of someone who "has become thoroughly hellenized, even as your own city has" (37.26 LCL).

The Roman proconsul who administered the province of Achaia had his seat in Corinth. He exercised both administrative and judicial functions in criminal cases. The *duoviri* had jurisdiction in civil cases. L. Iunius Gallio was the proconsul during part of Paul's eighteen-month visit to the city. Gallio, the adopted brother of the great philosopher Seneca, assumed the post on July 1, AD 51, and held it for almost a year. Seneca commented that Gallio "began to develop a fever in Achaia and took ship at once, insisting that the disease was not of the body but of the place" (*Epist. mor.* 104.2 LCL). Gallio's arrival in Corinth, which can be dated from an inscription in Delphi, means that Paul likely came to the city in either late AD 49 or early 50. The city itself was under the administration of the chief magistrates, the two *duoviri* who were elected each year by the assembly of the citizens of the city (Latin *comitia tributa*; Greek *ekklēsia*). Not everyone who lived in the city was a *cives* (Latin, "citizen"), as there were also resident aliens in their midst (Latin *incolae*). The city also had a senate called the *decuria* (Latin) or *boulē* (Greek).

We do not meet with these officials in the Epistles or Acts, but in 1 Cor. 9:24–27 Paul does make reference to the games, which were under the administration of the city's *agōnothetēs*. These officials were elected every two years, and the custom seems to have been that they would take part in funding the games, which in Corinth's case were held in Isthmia. Corinth held the games every two years, and they were likely going on when Paul was in the city.

Cenchreae

Although the city does not figure prominently in NT history, Cenchreae is mentioned twice, as the port city of Corinth along the Saronic Gulf and a place where a church was established (Acts 18:18; Rom. 16:1). The church was under the leadership of Phoebe, who also served as a benefactor to Paul and the church in Cenchreae as well. Archaeologists have excavated the harbor area and dock facilities that date from the time when Corinth was a thriving colony. In his novel *Metamorphoses* (also known as *The Golden Ass*), Apuleius describes a procession honoring the Egyptian goddess Isis (*Metam.* 11), which testifies of the way that not only commercial goods but also religions traversed the Mediterranean Sea and arrived in Corinth and the cities of its hinterland.

Other Cities of Roman Achaia

Although not mentioned in the NT, other cities of Achaia are important for understanding the place of the gospel in the setting of Roman history. The city of Epidaurus, south of Corinth on the Saronic Gulf,

Rokaszil/Wikimedia Commons

43.6. The famous Corinthian canal, begun by Nero but completed in the early twentieth century, is near ancient Isthmia and the ancient city of Corinth. The second-most-familiar athletic contests in antiquity were held in Isthmia.

43.7. Ruins of the harbor and dock at Cenchreae.

was the center of the cult of Asclepius, the god of healing. Sanctuaries dedicated to the god were also located in Athens and Corinth and elsewhere. Worshipers would come to the sanctuary of Asclepius and sleep in the *abaton*, awaiting a dream from the god, who would give instruction or effect their cure. Votive offerings were part of the ritual at these sanctuaries. The expectation of physical healing by the Holy Spirit found in the NT (e.g., 1 Cor. 12:9, 30) should be read against the backdrop of this ancient healing cult.

Delphi was well known from antiquity as the central oracular site in Greece. Located north of the Gulf of Corinth, it came under the protection of the Aitolian League before the Roman invasion. The oracle at Delphi was the center for seeking divine revelation and guidance but went into decline during the first century, as had other oracles throughout Greece. Plutarch, the priest of Apollo at Delphi at the end of the first century AD, wrote works defending the oracle's continued efficacy in the face of critiques coming principally from Epicureanism, which denied divine providence and the ability of the gods to predict the future (Plutarch, *De Pythiae oraculis*; *De defectu oraculorum*; see also Cicero, *De divinatione*). The NT argues strongly for the validity of divine speech but points to the church as the true place of divine revelation, through the agency of the Holy Spirit (1 Cor. 14).

By the time of the NT, the legendary games of the great city of Olympia experienced a resurgence after a period of decline. These games, as the ones held in Isthmia outside of Corinth, were not only athletic but also cultural events that drew musicians and orators alike. Those who came to the city could see the great temple of Zeus there. Sparta, another of the cities of Roman Achaia, once a powerful Greek state that had even challenged the Achaian League, was reduced to a memory of its former glory and power.

The Achaian Mission

The gospel of Jesus Christ came to Achaia first through the ministry of the apostle Paul. The scenes of this ministry preserved in Acts and the Epistles, most notably 1–2 Corinthians and 1 Thess. 3:1–5, demonstrate how the gospel addressed the culture and the social issues of the day as it played off against the history and memory of these communities. Achaia, once a seat of power and intellect, now hears the message of the true philosophy (as Jerome called the gospel), the genuine power of God, and the faithful message of divine revelation and healing.

See also "Greco-Roman Philosophical Schools"; "Macedonia."

Bibliography

Anderson, Graham. *The Second Sophistic: A Cultural Phenomenon in the Roman Empire.* London: Routledge, 1993. Along with Winter (*Philo and Paul*, see below) Anderson presents an overview of a key philosophical movement that was influential in Corinth and other cities of Achaia and beyond.

Engels, Donald. *Roman Corinth: An Alternative Model for the Classical City.* Chicago: University of Chicago Press, 1990. An indispensable guide for understanding the social and economic realities in the important Achaian city of Corinth.

Errington, R. Malcolm. *A History of the Hellenistic World, 323–30 BC.* Malden, MA: Blackwell, 2008. As an expert on Macedonian history, Errington frames the history of Achaia within the larger picture of the rise and fall of the Macedonian Empire as well as the spread of Roman power.

Michael F. Mehnert/Wikimedia Commons

43.8. Asclepius, god of medicine and healing.

Gill, David W. J. "Achaia." Pages 433–53 in *The Book of Acts in Its Graeco-Roman Setting*. Edited by David W. J. Gill and Conrad Gempf. A1CS 2. Grand Rapids: Eerdmans, 1994. The articles in this volume, including the one on Achaia, help orient the reader to the culture and provinces of the Greco-Roman world with reference to Acts and other NT literature.

Halstead, Paul, et al. "Greece (Prehistory and History)." Pages 648–53 in *The Oxford Classical Dictionary*. Edited by Simon Hornblower and Antony Spawforth. Oxford: Oxford University Press, 1996. The *Oxford Classical Dictionary* is a well-researched and continuously revised resource for the student of the ancient world. The article on Greece is especially well written by two of the volume's editors, along with others.

Murphy-O'Connor, Jerome. *St. Paul's Corinth: Text and Archaeology*. Collegeville, MN: Liturgical Press, 2002. Presents the student of Corinth with a collection of primary texts and comments relevant for studying the history and social world of this Achaian capital during the Roman period.

Olshausen, Eckart. "Achaea [Roman Province]." Columns 80–83 in vol. 1 of *Brill's New Pauly: Encyclopaedia of the Ancient World*. Edited by Hubert Cancik and Helmuth Schneider. Leiden: Brill, 2002–11. A brief but helpful introduction to Achaia. The *New Pauly* is a massive resource for anyone seeking an overview of the ancient world.

Patton, W. R., ed. *The Greek Anthology*. 5 vols. Cambridge, MA: Harvard University Press, 1916–18. The sixteen books in these volumes contain a wealth of epigrams from the ancient world, as well as other Greek texts.

Tokhtas'ev, Sergej R. "Achaeans, Achaea." Columns 69–77 in vol. 1 of *Brill's New Pauly: Encyclopaedia of the Ancient World*. Edited by Hubert Cancik and Helmuth Schneider. Leiden and Boston: Brill, 2002–11. See comments at Olshausen, above.

Winter, Bruce W. *Philo and Paul among the Sophists: Alexandrian and Corinthian Responses to a Julio-Claudian Movement*. Grand Rapids: Eerdmans, 2002. Winter is the expert when it comes to interpreting Corinthians and the Letters of Paul within the framework of the Second Sophistic movement.

44

Rome and Its Provinces

THOMAS R. HATINA

Although the cradle of earliest Christianity was Palestinian Judaism, Christianity's development and expansion can be credited to the Roman Empire of the first century. Rome's infrastructure, political and social policies, and military created the ideal conditions for early Christian missions. In turn, the Roman Empire (and the inherited Hellenistic traditions) gave expression to the formation of Christianity. The broad use of Greek in the eastern part of the empire and the use of Latin in the west were the means through which the faith was understood and communicated. The philosophical traditions, rhetorical methods, literary genres, and artistry, as well as the political, legal, and ethical structures, and social relations (such as slaves/masters, husbands/wives/children, classes), among other aspects—all influenced how Christianity took shape.

History

The founding of the city of Rome traditionally has been dated to 753 BC, when it consisted of simply a few settlements. Over the next century or so, it developed into a large group of communities spread throughout the seven hills (the Capitoline, Palatine, Quirinal, Viminal, Esquiline, Caelian, and Aventine hills) and eventually united into a city-state. However, the remarkable ancient city, as most people think of it today, did not begin to take shape until the end of the third century BC (Jones and Sidwell, *World of Rome*, 1–48). It was during the republican period (approximately from the fifth century to 31 BC) that grander temples were erected, usually to foreign deities increasingly being incorporated into the Roman pantheon. The imperial period, which began with the reign of Augustus in 31 BC, is considered the high point of construction and incorporation of foreign deities, art, ideas, and architecture. It was within the context of the empire that Jesus ministered and in which Christianity was born.

During the early centuries of Rome, the primary cultural influence came from its eastern neighbors: the Phoenicians, the Etruscans, and mainly the Greeks. Unlike the Phoenicians, whose influence was primarily economic, the Greeks and the Etruscans (who probably came from Asia Minor) established colonies on the Italian peninsula. The Etruscans filled the political gap by establishing a monarchy, but it was short lived. In the late sixth century BC, Etruscan power in the Mediterranean was weakening, and the monarchy gave way to the establishment of the Roman Republic. Due to political instability in the region and ongoing Gallic raids on Rome, Roman political power in the western Mediterranean was not a major force until the second half of the third century BC. The success of Roman expansion can be credited to Rome's policy of incorporating conquered peoples into its empire. Instead of annihilating native populations, the Romans often allowed local political structures to remain in place, encouraged traditional cultural practices, and offered grants of citizenship to compliant groups and especially to wealthy/elite individuals in the provinces. Roman citizens could participate in elections of magistrates, had the right to be tried in Roman courts, had the right to appeal convictions, were exempt from personal tax, and usually could not be crucified, tortured, flogged, thrown to beasts, or sentenced to hard labor (Lintott, *Imperium Romanum*, 161–67).

Roman expansion into the eastern regions of the Mediterranean, such as Palestine and Asia Minor, began to take shape in the first half of the second century BC. Taking advantage of the long-standing strife between the Ptolemaic and Seleucid dynasties, and the threat of the Parthians, the Romans made their way into the region and gained control of Egypt and much of Asia Minor. When the Seleucids (under the rule of Antiochus IV) were defeated by the Romans in Egypt, the Seleucids returned via Jerusalem and enacted policies aimed at eradicating Judaism. Antiochus's oppressive agenda led to the Maccabean revolt, beginning in 168/67 BC, under the leadership of the Hasmonean family. With the help of the Romans, the revolt eventually led to the defeat of the Seleucids and the establishment of an independent Jewish state in 142 BC.

The eastern Mediterranean, which included Palestine, did not fall under Roman supremacy for another eighty years. In 63 BC, Pompey seized control of Palestine and put an end to Jewish independence. The Romans (and later the Byzantine Empire) would remain in control of that region for approximately the next six hundred years. The response by the Jews to Pompey's arrival in Jerusalem was split, with one faction welcoming his arrival and the other opposing it, even militarily.

Barricading themselves in the temple, the opposing Jews could resist for only three months. Palestine was soon annexed to the province of Syria.

Although the Roman conquest of Palestine was successful, the republic was quickly declining. Civil war ensued and was eventually decided at the famous battle of Actium, on the west coast of Greece, between the forces of Antony (and Cleopatra VII) and Octavian (born Gaius Octavius Thurinus; sworn as Gaius Julius Caesar Augustus). By 27 BC, the republic had been replaced by the empire, with Augustus at the helm. This new era was marked by relative political peace, economic prosperity, and cultural expansion (Rostovtzeff, *Roman Empire*, 1:38–74). The success of Roman expansion and unification can be credited to the Pax Romana (Roman peace), achieved by a combination of strong military and political policies that focused on the unification of the provinces through cultural acceptance, incorporation, promise of security, reciprocity, and rewards (Ando, *Imperial Ideology*, 19–48). At the beginning of the first century AD, the empire spanned from Britain to Syria, and from central Europe to North Africa, completely encompassing the Mediterranean Sea and much of the Black Sea. Never before or since has the Mediterranean world been so politically unified (Garnsey and Saller, *Roman Empire*, 12–19).

Roman Emperors

Augustus/Octavian (30 BC–AD 14)
Tiberius (AD 14–37)
Gaius Caligula (AD 37–41)
Claudius (AD 41–54)
Nero (AD 54–68)
Galba (AD 68–69)
Otho (AD 69)
Vitellius (AD 69)
Vespasian (AD 69–79)
Titus (AD 79–81)
Domitian (AD 81–96)
Nerva (AD 96–98)
Trajan (AD 98–117)
Hadrian (AD 117–138)
Antonius Pius (AD 138–161)
Marcus Aurelius (AD 161–180)
Commodus (AD 180–192)
Four emperors (AD 193–194)
Septimius Severus (AD 193–211)

Politics

Augustus's official investiture was not self-initiated but was granted to him by the Roman Senate, the most powerful body in the empire. By 23 BC he was the supreme authority over all the Roman provinces. Although he sought to give the appearance that he cooperated with the Senate, which had six hundred wealthy members, his power transcended it (Talbert, *Senate*; Adcock, *Ideas and Practice*, 26–53, 71–88). Augustus was the monarch and commander in chief of the entire military. The Senate declared him *divi filius*, son of (a) god, since he was the one who brought peace, unity, and prosperity to the empire (Ando, *Imperial Ideology*, 206–70).

By the beginning of the first century AD, Rome's political system was highly effective. Since the empire was vast and culturally diverse, the imperial government

Roman Prefects and Procurators of Judea and Samaria

Coponius (AD 6–9)
Marcus Ambibulus (AD 9–12)
Annius Rufus (AD 12–15)
Valerius Gratus (AD 15–26)
Pontius Pilate (AD 26–36)
Marcellus (AD 36–37)
Marullus (of all of Israel; AD 37–41)
Herod Agrippa I (not a Roman prefect, but takes the title "king"; AD 41–44)
Cuspius Fadus (AD 44–46)
Tiberius Alexander (AD 46–48)
Ventidius Cumanus (AD 48–52)
M. Antonius Felix (AD 52–60)
Porcius Festus (AD 60–62)
Albinus (AD 62–64)
Gessius Florus (AD 64–66)

was constantly challenged with the complexities of controlling conquered peoples. As new lands and peoples were conquered, they were often made into provinces, which were the largest territorial units (Starr, *Roman Empire*). During the republic, provinces were under the authority of magistrates for limited terms. When Augustus came to power, the provinces were categorized either as imperial or senatorial, depending on who held the authority to appoint the governor. Many of the senatorial provinces that were already established during the republic retained their governance policies (Jones and Sidwell, *World of Rome*, 84–110). The governing authority, called a "proconsul" (the highest class of governor), was chosen from the senatorial class, who had governing experience (e.g., former consuls or praetors). Major imperial provinces were governed by procurators, who were also appointed from the senatorial class. Less important imperial provinces, like Judea, were governed by procurators (or prefects) from the equestrian class (second after the senatorial class) and by legates, who were high-ranking officers in command of legions, appointed from the senatorial class (Lintott, *Imperium Romanum*, 22–69; Ando, *Imperial Ideology*, 336–405).

The province of Syria, annexed by Pompey in 64 BC, initially included most of Palestine but was later subdivided into smaller provinces. Judea, for example, became a province in 6 BC after Herod's son Archelaus was deposed by Rome for harsh leadership. In AD 26, Pontius Pilate was appointed as prefect and was subordinate to the legate of Syria. In some provinces, the governing authorities functioned more like regional commanders or ambassadors, working closely with local authorities, whereas in other provinces they took on imperial authority, as was the case with Pontius Pilate.

Clear boundaries were very important to the Roman administration, whether they were between the provinces or at the empire's frontiers. Rome was scrupulous in administering the various forms of taxation and thus needed to have a clear idea of who belonged to which region.

Rome extended its influence and power outside of its official boundaries to "client kingdoms," which usually had more autonomy than provinces. They were regarded as friends of Rome. Some kingdoms were allied with Rome through treaty and retained their own monarch. Other kingdoms had a monarch imposed upon them by Rome. King Herod was a client king who ruled at the pleasure of Rome and in turn promoted and protected Rome's interests, particularly against the Parthians (Braund, *Rome*, 75–85).

Military

Rome's rise to power and the unification of the empire can be directly credited to its military might. After Augustus's victory at Actium, he had an enormous army at his disposal. Augustus initiated reforms that were primarily responsible for turning the army into a professional institution. Shifts in the fiscal system, political structure, taxation, and organizational infrastructure led to successful recruitment, attractive remuneration, and benefits after discharge. The army was divided into legions, composed of regular recruits (who were primarily citizens) and auxiliary units, whose soldiers were not from Italy but from various provinces, often retaining their distinct ethnicity. By the end of Augustus's reign, there were twenty-five legions (each about five thousand men) totaling 125,000 and almost as many soldiers in the auxiliary army, for a total of approximately 250,000 men at his disposal. Later, under Tiberius, the auxiliary forces numbered that of the legions. After the First Jewish War (AD 66–70), which overlapped with a civil conflict in Rome, auxiliaries began to be rewarded with citizenship at retirement (Luttwak, *Grand Strategy*, 13–50; Alston, *Roman History*, 145–65). This was the dawn of the so-called standing army. Two-thirds of the army was located in the western provinces. The other third was primarily in the east: Asia Minor, Syria, Palestine, and Egypt. About a century later, 10 percent of the army was committed to Britain.

Apart from engaging in expansionist campaigns and securing the frontiers, in the provinces most soldiers would have spent their time performing duties within a peaceful context. Their duties would have included such activities as policing (e.g., Palestine and Egypt are well attested); guarding key installations, transportation routes (against opportunistic pirates and bandits), and state assets, like mines and grain supplies; maintaining peace and order; building roads, bridges, and forts; and collecting taxes. At the root of the military's function was the preservation of the empire's economic viability and sustainability (Campbell, *Roman Army*, 28–45; Goldsworthy, *Roman Army*, 68–107, 119–41).

The army in the first century AD was loyal to the reigning emperor. Utmost allegiance was required. Upon enlistment, soldiers pledged to the emperor an oath of obedience with their lives. Oaths were regularly reinforced through ceremonies of honor (Starr, *Roman Empire*, 111–16). In order to maintain strong allegiances, officers were drawn from the aristocracy and commissioned by the highest imperial authorities, including the emperor. A commanding officer of a legion, a legate, was of a senatorial rank and appointed directly by the emperor. Immediately subordinate

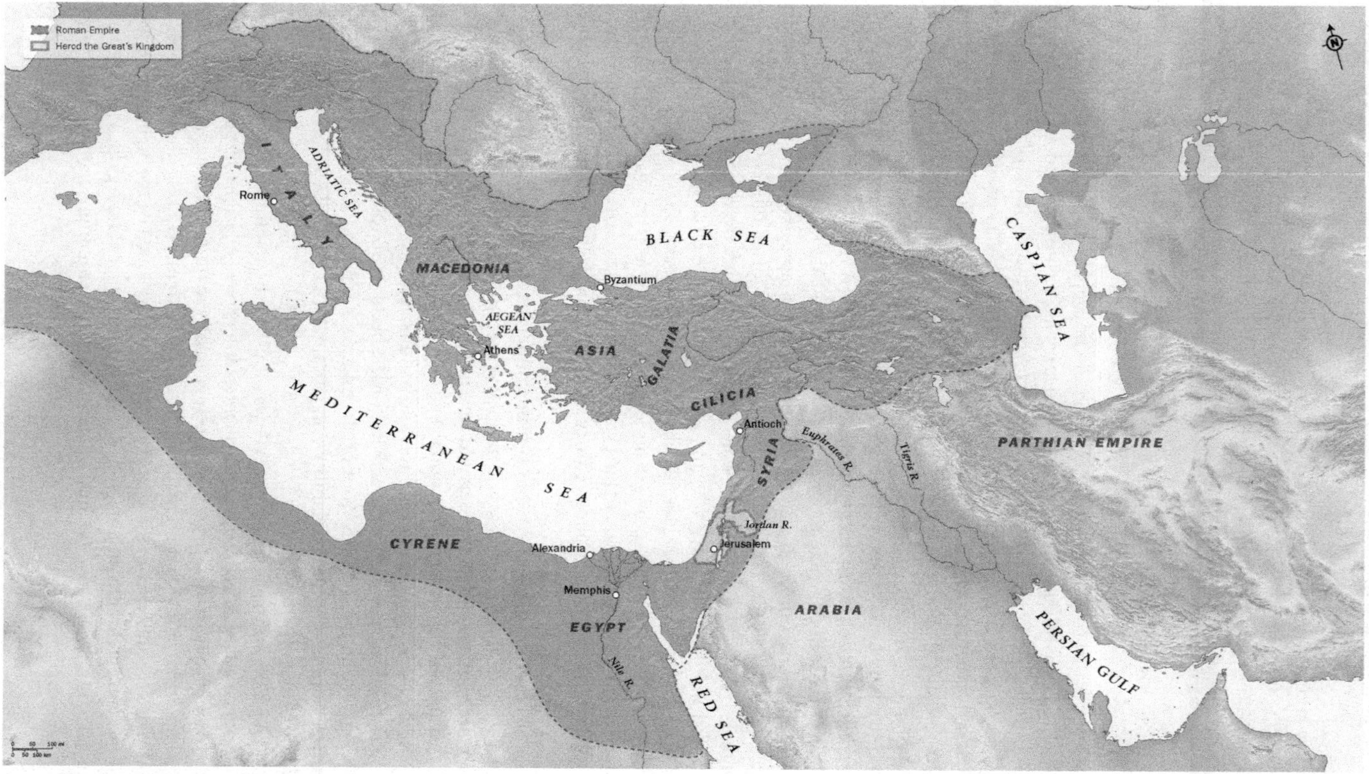

Roman Empire
Herod the Great's Kingdom
ITALY
Rome
ADRIATIC SEA
MACEDONIA
AEGEAN SEA
Athens
BLACK SEA
Byzantium
ASIA
GALATIA
CILICIA
Antioch
SYRIA
Euphrates R.
Tigris R.
CASPIAN SEA
PARTHIAN EMPIRE
MEDITERRANEAN SEA
CYRENE
Alexandria
Memphis
EGYPT
Nile R.
Jordan R.
Jerusalem
ARABIA
RED SEA
PERSIAN GULF
Baker Publishing Group

44.1. The Roman Empire at the time of the birth of Christ.

to each legate were six tribunes, and below them was a centurion. Provincial governing authorities were not permitted to commission officers or raise their own forces. Under normal (usually peaceful) conditions, provincial authorities along with their forces were not permitted to associate with their peers in neighboring provinces, for fear of a consolidation of power. Regular soldiers as well as officers were rotated so as to prevent any ties that might lead to dissidence. Despite the safeguards, occasional rebellions took place, instigated usually by high officials.

In battle, Roman soldiers were trained to be merciless. Retreating enemy forces were pursued and killed. Residents of captured cities were at times slaughtered. After Augustus, Rome was particularly brutal in its campaigns against the barbarians on the frontiers and against revolutionaries within the provinces (Millar, *Roman Empire*; Burns, *Rome*, 140–93). Palestine (esp. Galilee) was a hotbed of revolutionary activity from 4 BC to AD 66. Various kingly aspirants and messianic pretenders arose in opposition to Roman control. Captured insurrectionists were punished publically and painfully (Goodman, *Rome*, 379–423). For the Romans and the Jewish establishment, Jesus fell into the same category. His arrest, trial, and execution, as recorded in the Synoptic Gospels, correspond with the reaction to someone who was a perceived political threat.

Commerce and Travel

During Augustus's reign the population of the city of Rome was about one million, which was a powerful consumer body. An estimated 30 percent were slaves. No other city in the Western world would reach this size until London in the eighteenth century. Rome's growth to such an enormous size can be credited to its dependence on the resources of the provinces (Garnsey and Saller, *Roman Empire*, 83–85). Chief among these was its vast supply and trade of food. Rome alone consumed about 60 percent of the empire's resources. As an agrarian society, Rome's wealth and power was tied to its land. Much of the land in Italy and adjacent provinces that was economically viable was owned by the Roman elite and aristocracy and often managed by tenant farmers. Provincial labor was cheap and often exploited through the use of slaves (D'Arms, *Commerce*; Alston, *Roman History*, 227–45). The owners profited not only from agriculture itself but also from rents and taxes (for consumption, production, and distribution) imposed on tenant farmers. Trade with distant imperial lands, such as Spain and Egypt, was encouraged through tax breaks, subsidies for transportation, and offers of citizenship. Among the provinces, the elite also imported vast amounts of food, textiles, and building supplies in order to raise the profile and economy of their own beloved cities. Provincial elites in port cites—namely, in Spain, Greece, Asia Minor, Palestine, and Egypt—had amassed great wealth, some through shipping. Often these cities were gateways to broader markets. In short, with an estimated population of sixty to seventy million within Roman territory, commerce was extensive (Garnsey and Saller, *Roman Empire*, 43–62).

Taxation was a continuous and constant source of revenue. It extended to all the provinces and provided a continued source of wealth for Rome. Payment of taxes was not limited to cash but also included goods. A farmer would have paid his elite overlord up to 40 percent of his crop. The bounty would then be redistributed to nearby areas and sometimes shipped directly to Rome. Withholding tax was regarded as a violation against the supremacy of Rome and was punished severely.

Rome's economic prosperity was dependent on its transportation system. Most of the traded goods were shipped by sea on freighters due to cost, efficiency, and volume. Rome contracted enough privately owned freighters to transport 135,000 tons of wheat from Egypt annually. The size of the Roman merchant marine would not be rivaled in Europe until the eighteenth century. The ships, some of which measured 180 feet, were also designed to carry passengers. Travel by sea would have been much more comfortable and safer than by land caravans, providing convenience like shelter and water. The major risk to maritime transport was shipwrecks due to inclement weather (Garnsey et al., *Trade*, 36–50; Casson, *Everyday Life*, 109–15).

The Romans were skillful engineers, well known for building extensive aqueducts to pipe water into cities, arched stone bridges over rivers, and especially paved roads. The famous road system made land travel, communication, and distribution relatively easy and secure with the help of the military, but it was not the preferred means of travel. Roads were at times cumbersome and slow, animals and carriages had to be maintained on the journey, and the volume that could be transported was much smaller. Land travelers also had to contend with the climate, which could be unforgiving. Carrying enough water for long journeys would have created an added inconvenience, though in many areas along major routes, towns or hostels were about thirty miles apart, about a day's trip. Also helpful to travelers were distance markers. The road system may have been extensive for its day, including both public and private roads, but they were not all paved. Those that were paved consisted of hewn polygonal stones (granite or basalt) measuring about a foot and a half across and about eight inches thick. They were carefully fitted on tightly packed sand or gravel. Ravines and rivers were crossed with bridges, depressions were filled, and hills were dug in an attempt to keep the roads as straight and as level as possible. Primary roads were eight to ten feet wide.

Alongside exposure to local cultures, travelers would have encountered symbols of Rome's supremacy throughout the provinces. Roman coins with an emperor's head on one side were in broad circulation. Provincial coins also included Roman images to symbolize identity.[1] Cities and temples were adorned with statues of emperors and gods. Many buildings were inscribed with honors given to Roman benefactors, emperors, and gods. Roman architecture often overpowered local structures. And art in various forms (e.g., frescos and reliefs) portrayed the might, wealth, and sophistication of Rome.

1. Christopher Howgego, Volker Heuchert, and Andrew Burnett, eds., *Coinage and Identity in the Roman Provinces* (Oxford: Oxford University Press, 2005), 1–18.

Social Conditions

Roman society across the empire can be divided into the elites and non-elites. The social distance between the two was enormous, and there was no middle class to speak of. Social migration from elite to non-elite was at best extremely rare, since one's birth determined status, and there was little opportunity for financial development.

The elites were in the top 3–5 percent of the population in wealth, power, education, authority, and honor. Their value system was guided by personal gain and security as opposed to the enhancement of the common good. Preservation of the political and economic status quo with its inherent social inequalities factored prominently in public policy. Although the elites showed disdain for manual labor, they depended on it, be it for food, construction, or the trade of other goods and services. The elite were voracious consumers, living lavish lifestyles, exhibiting their status and wealth through clothing, jewelry, estates, exotic artifacts, entertainment, and meals. Although they provided employment at an extensive level, exploitation of laborers was rampant. Not only did the elite profit from the productivity of the laborers, but the taxes and rents they imposed on the non-elites ensured a constant cash flow. The elite coerced and exploited their workforce, but at the same time they needed to maintain productivity and compliance. So on occasion they appeased the masses by sponsoring events, feasts, festivals, games, and the building of public facilities. During times of shortage, the elite ensured that there was enough food to go around (Carter, *Roman Empire*, 8–10; Potter and Mattingly, *Roman Empire*, 75–145).

The inhabitants of the empire can also be categorized into citizens, free people of the provinces, and slaves. It has been said that Rome was built on the backs of its slaves. Though this saying is simplistic, slavery certainly contributed to Rome's growth. Slaves were valuable assets for the elite. Since they were property, they could be bought, sold, traded, and inherited. Slave markets were commonplace in port cities. The quantity of slaves corresponded with one's status.[2] Pliny the Elder (AD 23–79) provides a summary of assets recorded in the will of a Gaius Caecilius Claudius Isidorus, who was probably at the upper end of the elite. Pliny writes that despite his losses in the civil war, Gaius left behind 4,116 slaves, 3,600 oxen, 257,000 head of other cattle, and 60,000,000 sesterces (*Nat. Hist.* 33.47; Casson, *Everyday Life*, 57–64).

Religion

In the ancient world, religion pervaded every aspect of daily life at every social level and every ethnic group. Fundamentally it was believed that the success, peace, and prosperity of the empire depended on the *pax deorum*, the goodwill

---

2. Keith R. Bradley, *Slaves and Masters in the Roman Empire: A Study in Social Control* (New York: Oxford University Press, 1984), 13–46.

Primary Sources for the Study of Rome

Major primary sources for the study of Rome, all available in the Loeb Classical Library, include the following:

Appian (Greek historian, ca. AD 90–160), *Roman History* and *Civil War*

Cicero, Marcus Tullius (politician, orator, 106–43 BC), *Actio prima*, *Philippics*, *Pro Milone* (*In Defense of Milo*), *Pro Roscio Amerino* (*In Defense of Sextus Roscius*), *Pro Flacco* (*In Defense of Flaccus*), *De Officiis* (*On Duties*)

Dio Cassius, or Cassius Dio (senator, historian, AD 164–229), *Roman History*

Josephus (late first century AD), *Jewish War*, *Jewish Antiquities*, *The Life*, *Against Apion*

Livy, or Titus Livius (historian, 59 BC–AD 12), *Roman History*

Lucan, or Marcus Annaeus Lucanus (philosopher, AD 39–65), *On the Civil War*

Ovid (poet, 43 BC–AD 17), *Heroides*, *Amores*, *Remedies for Love*, *Metamorphoses*, and others

Philostratus, or L. Flavius Philostratus (writer, third century), *Life of Apollonius of Tyana*, *Lives of the Sophists*

Pliny the Elder, or Gaius Plinius Secundus (military commander, AD 23–79), *Natural History*

Pliny the Younger, or Gaius Plinius Caecilius Secundus (senator, consul, ca. AD 61–112), *Panegyricus* and many letters

Plutarch, or Mestrius Plutarchus (procurator, before AD 50–120), *Alexander and Caesar*, *Pericles and Favius*, *Tiberius and Gaius Gracchus*, and others

Polybius (historian, ca. 200–118 BC), *Histories*

Seneca, Lucius Annaeus (politician, philosopher, ca. 4 BC–AD 65), *On Anger*, *On Providence*, *On Benefits*, *On the Happy Life*, and others

Strabo (historian, geographer, 64 BC–AD 21), *Geography*

Suetonius, or Gaius Suetonius Tranquillus (historian, ca. AD 70–130), *On Illustrious Men*, *Lives of the Caesars*

Tacitus, or Cornelius Tacitus (historian, politician, ca. AD 56–118), *Agricola*, *Germania*, *Dialogues*, *Histories*, *Annals*

Virgil, or Publius Vergilius Maro (poet, 70–19 BC), *Eclogues*, *Georgics*, *Aeneid*

of the gods. In Rome, while senators occupied the highest political and military positions, they also played important roles in religious matters and held the highest offices, including priesthood. The Roman religious system was organized and led by priests (in conjunction with magistrates), who represented the gods. Organized into colleges, they oversaw the practice of public rituals, such as sacrifices, feasts, and festivals. The overall authority was the emperor, who came to be known as Pontifex Maximus, the chief priest of the empire, a title that would later be applied to the pope. The perception that the emperor had the favor of the gods was perpetuated through ancient literature about the lives of the emperors, which included some kind of divine experience as support, be it omens, a sign, a human mother and a divine father, dreams, or extraordinary works (Casson, *Everyday Life*, 84–97; Potter and Mattingly, *Roman Empire*, 23–50).

Honor of an emperor's divine sanction and role, known as the imperial cult, was celebrated throughout the empire through various rituals (e.g., offerings, sacrifices, prayers), images, inscriptions, and the building of temples. Ascription of divinity to emperors was inconsistent. Some, like Augustus, were made divine posthumously, whereas others were not. Although the meaning of the cult is disputed, it is agreed that it conveyed loyalty. Participation in the cult was not compulsory, but it was encouraged by the elite and the Roman provincial authorities. Broad participation not only elevated the prestige of the elite but also added significantly to the local economy, such as the purchase of sacrificial animals. By the time of the Flavian emperors, the cult was widespread throughout the empire.

Most people throughout the empire practiced religion in much the same way as the Romans. They were polytheistic and inclusive. New gods could be imported, and existing ones could be exported throughout the provinces. Some gods were linked with different places and functions, and other gods had powers that were divided among the temples. The gods were interested and involved in the lives of people, but not always with good intentions. The gods were fickle, and so were their devotees. Changing allegiance from one god to another was common practice. The choice was often pragmatic. When one god seemed to be absent, another was petitioned.

Roman policy toward religion in the provinces was tolerant. As long as there were no political threats, risks to public safety, or abhorrent practices, Rome was neutral on indigenous religious practice. Persecution of Christians was sporadic and regional. Its onset varied but was usually linked with a perceived social threat and violation of the will of the gods (e.g., failure to honor the gods and Caesar), or the denial of them altogether. In the provinces, a number of cities were associated with certain deities. To reject these deities was in effect to reject the traditional power structures and an affiliation with the community's identity. Unlike Judaism, Christianity was new and actively proselytized. The Romans tended to respect and incorporate religions that had a long tradition. Longevity and ancestral customs were respected (Alston, *Aspects*, 315–17).

The transportation routes that linked provinces contributed significantly to both the spread of religions and their syncretism. It also allowed for the blending of cultures, which in turn affected religious language, the retelling of stories, and the development of ideas. In the second century AD, we begin to see a proliferation of syncretism. Judaism still remained prominent as the primary influence on Christianity, but Platonism, Gnosticism, and the Roman pantheon began to play a role in attempts to interpret Jesus. As the church began to institutionalize, its governance was also influenced by the dominant culture. The birth of Christianity as a new religion, distinct from being a sect of Judaism, testifies to culture's transformative effect on religion (Bryan, *Render to Caesar*, 77–112).

See also "The Imperial Cult"; "Economics, Taxes, and Tithes"; "Slaves and Slavery in the Roman World."

Bibliography

Adcock, F. E. *Roman Political Ideas and Practice*. Ann Arbor: University of Michigan Press, 1959. Still a valuable resource for understanding Roman political thought; written in a clear and interesting manner by a superb classicist. Useful for generalists and specialists.

Alston, Richard. *Aspects of Roman History, AD 14–117*. London: Routledge, 1998. An introduction to the early imperial period. The first half provides a good introduction to the emperors from Tiberius to Trajan. The second half is a well-rounded introduction to Roman society.

Ando, Clifford. *Imperial Ideology and Provincial Loyalty in the Roman Empire*. Berkeley: University of California Press, 2000. Examines the function of Roman political ideology in the unification of Rome and its provinces. This is a more advanced volume, written from the perspective of social theorists.

Braund, David C. *Rome and the Friendly King: The Character of the Client Kingship*. New York: St. Martin's Press, 1984. One of the best treatments of the political relationships between client kings, such as Herod the Great, and the Roman administration.

Bryan, Christopher. *Render to Caesar: Jesus, the Early Church, and the Roman Superpower*. Oxford: Oxford University Press, 2005. An illuminating and detailed study of the Roman background to Jesus, Christian origins, and the NT. Tackles Rome's perception of Jesus and his early followers, and the attitude of the early Christians toward Rome as a superpower.

Burns, Thomas S. *Rome and the Barbarians, 100 B.C.–A.D. 400*. Baltimore: Johns Hopkins University Press, 2003. Very helpful for appreciating the military and political complexities on the frontiers. Over the five centuries covered, the author clearly conveys the development of Roman international relations. Filled with a vast amount of literary and archaeological data, but not out of reach for new students.

Campbell, Brian. *The Roman Army, 31 BC–AD 337: A Sourcebook*. London: Routledge, 1994. A rich and indispensable collection of primary sources (including coins, inscriptions, papyri, and literary works) on the organization, function, and impact of the Roman military during the imperial period.

Carter, Warren. *The Roman Empire and the New Testament: An Essential Guide*. Nashville: Abingdon, 2006. A valuable introduction to first-century Roman politics, society, economics, and religion, with an aim to better understanding the NT and early Christianity. Argues that the Roman Empire is the central context in which the NT should be interpreted. Highly recommended as a textbook.

Casson, Lionel. *Everyday Life in Ancient Rome*. Baltimore: Johns Hopkins University Press, 1998. Important series of studies of how different social groups grappled with daily life in cities, villages, and the countryside during the first two centuries of the imperial period, which was an extended time of peace and prosperity. Clearly written and includes numerous quotes and illustrations. Highly recommended.

D'Arms, John H. *Commerce and Social Standing in Ancient Rome.* Cambridge, MA: Harvard University Press, 1981. Series of essays on the economic life of different social groups in the late republican and early imperial periods.

Garnsey, Peter, Keith Hopkins, and C. R. Whittaker, eds. *Trade in the Ancient Economy.* Berkeley: University of California Press, 1983. Scholarly papers on economic topics that span from ancient Greece to the late Roman period. The essay on grain trade is especially recommended.

Garnsey, Peter, and Richard P. Saller. *The Roman Empire: Economy, Society, and Culture.* Berkeley: University of California Press, 1987. An insightful introduction to the unifying challenges and strategies of the empire under imperial control. Its social and economic angle makes it a valuable complement to more-traditional introductions.

Goldsworthy, Adrian. *The Complete Roman Army.* London: Thames & Hudson, 2011. Useful description of the army at war and in peacetime. Includes an impressive array of illustrations (over a hundred in color) and discussions of key battles, tactics, and their commanders. Accessible for new students.

Goodman, Martin. *Rome and Jerusalem: The Clash of Ancient Civilizations.* New York: Knopf, 2007. Provides an extensive introduction to the historical, political, social, and religious interface between the power of Rome and the self-identity of the Jews under occupation.

Jones, Peter V., and Keith C. Sidwell. *The World of Rome: An Introduction to Roman Culture.* Cambridge: Cambridge University Press, 1997. One of the best introductions today for students. The illustrations alone are worth the cost. It traces Rome's history from about 1000 BC to the late fifth century AD. It is also a valuable resource to students undertaking Latin.

Lintott, Andrew. *Imperium Romanum: Politics and Administration.* London: Routledge, 1993. Imperial Roman political policy is described from a postcolonial perspective. Emphasis is on governmental organization and law. Recommended as an introduction and/or textbook.

Luttwak, Edward. *The Grand Strategy of the Roman Empire: From the First Century A.D. to the Third.* Baltimore: Johns Hopkins University Press, 1976. The first fifty pages constitute an outstanding introduction to the organization and strategies of the military during the first century.

Millar, Fergus. *The Roman Empire and Its Neighbours.* London: Weidenfeld & Nicolson, 1967. Dated, but Millar was a prolific scholar who has provided a valuable read for understanding the political relationship between Rome and its frontiers, including the Germanic tribes.

Potter, D. S., and D. J. Mattingly, eds. *Life, Death, and Entertainment in the Roman Empire.* Ann Arbor: University of Michigan Press, 2010. A good entry into the social world of the imperial period. It is a general discussion on topics like family structures, gender, diet, trade, religion, and entertainment.

Rostovtzeff, Michael I. *Social and Economic History of the Roman Empire.* 2 vols. Oxford: Clarendon, 1957. A valuable and comprehensive source for understanding the transformational policies of the empire and their impact on the provinces. It is rich in plates and illustrations.

Starr, Chester G. *The Roman Empire, 27 B.C.–A.D. 476: A Study in Survival.* Oxford: Oxford University Press, 1982. One of the few books that analyzes how, in the face of economic and political challenges, the Roman Empire managed to keep its vast territory unified over five centuries. Given its detail, richness of data, and minimal interpretation, this work is best used as an encyclopedic resource alongside more general introductions.

Talbert, Richard J. A. *The Senate of Imperial Rome*. Princeton: Princeton University Press, 1984. A standard text on the function of the Senate and its relationship to the emperor in the imperial period.

ADDITIONAL
RESOURCES

Money in the New Testament Era

LEE MARTIN MCDONALD

The use of coins for exchange of products began around the eighth or seventh centuries BC. Prior to that some form of a bartering system was used throughout the ancient world. As people moved into larger towns and cities, away from farming communities, the use of coins or money for daily exchanges to purchase goods (wheat, tools for labor, etc.) and services was more common and would gradually become the standard means of purchasing necessary products.

Money was coined in three primary metals: bronze, silver, and gold. By the NT period, silver coins were by far the most common means of exchange for products, followed by gold and bronze. The Romans often allowed subject nations to mint bronze coins (the cheaper kinds) but used their own silver and gold coins. The *lepton* was the primary bronze Jewish coin minted in the land of Israel; it is mentioned in Mark 12:42, where it is translated "small copper coin" (NRSV, NIV; see also Luke 12:59; 21:2).

The basic Roman currency was the *denarius*, which was roughly equivalent to the Greek drachma (see Mark 6:37; 14:5; Luke 7:41; 10:35; John 12:5; also Matt. 22:19; Mark 12:15; Luke 20:24); it seems to have been equal to a full day's wage for an average worker (Matt. 20:1–16). The smallest Roman coin was the *quadrans*, which was equal to two Jewish leptons.

The Greek *drachma* (mentioned only in Luke 15:8–9), the basic standard Greek coin, was equivalent in value to the Roman denarius. The drachma, like the denarius, was equal to 128 leptons. Two drachmas (i.e., *didrachmon*, a double drachma) were used by Jews to pay the Jewish temple tax (Matt. 17:24); the temple tax was prescribed to be a half shekel (cf. Exod. 30:11–16), but the *shekel* (Hebrew *šeqel*) is not referred to in the Bible after the Maccabean period (1 Macc. 10:40–42).

The Greek *talent*, equal to some 240 Roman aurei, is mentioned in Matt. 18:24; 25:15–28. The talent was equal to about fifteen years of full-time salary.

The four-drachma coin (*stater* or *tetradrachm*) is mentioned only in Matt. 17:27. It is likely that this is the coin in which Judas received his "thirty pieces of silver," or 120 denarii (Matt. 26:15). Twenty-five denarii were equal to a Roman gold coin called an *aureus*.

Because of the presence of many currencies in antiquity, money exchanges were common, as we see in the NT when money changers were present in the temple—especially during festival times, when people would purchase sacrificial animals. Inaccurate exchanges were widespread, and such exchanges allowed for abuse. Jesus' disdain for such persons in the temple is well known and led to his overthrowing the tables of the money changers in the temple precincts (e.g., Matt. 21:12–17).

As a subjugated people, Jews in NT times used the currencies of their former (Greek) and present (Roman) occupiers. The occupiers often allowed the Jews to strike smaller bronze coins of lesser value but circulated their own coins in the land for larger purchases. The only Jewish coin mentioned in the NT, the lepton, was likely minted in Judah. Only during the Jewish rebellions against Rome (AD 66–73, 132–135) were silver coins struck in the land of Israel.

Summary of New Testament Monetary Values

Coin/Amount	Value
Assarion	The smallest Roman coin and equivalent to one-sixteenth of a denarius (see Matt. 10:29; Luke 12:6)
Aureus (pl. aurei)	A Roman gold coin equivalent to twenty-five denarii
Denarion, or denarius (pl. denaria, or denarii)	A Roman silver coin roughly equivalent to one day's wages for a day laborer. (Note: Matt. 20:2 = a full day's pay for a day laborer; see also Tob. 5:15.) The reference to two hundred denarii as a sum adequate to offer a minimal meal for some five thousand persons (Mark 6:37, 44) also suggests the value of the denarius.
Drachma (pl. drachmae	Introduced by Alexander the Great, a Greek silver coin roughly equivalent to the Roman denarius (see Luke 15:8–9); slightly heavier than the denarius, but not valued quite as high
Lepto, or lepton (pl. lepta)	The smallest Jewish bronze coin, equivalent to roughly 1/128th of a denarion (= penny, or "widow's mite")
Mina	One hundred drachmas (later devalued, so that one hundred minas = ten thousand drachmas)
Pieces of silver (Matt. 26:15)	Equals 30 shekels (see Zech. 11:12) or 120 denarii or drachmas
Pound	In Luke 19:11–27, the likely reference is to minas.
Quadrans	A small Roman coin roughly equal to two Jewish lepta

Coin/Amount	Value
Shekel	A Jewish monetary value mentioned in the OT; in NT times, a half shekel—the annual temple tax levied against Jews—is roughly equal to a didrachmon (or two drachmas; see Matt. 17:24). A shekel is equal to one tetradrachm (four drachmas) coin. (See also Exod. 38:24–26 for equivalents and Ezek. 45:12 on the relation to a mina.)
Stater, or tetradrachm	The same as a four-drachma coin
Talent	Also 62.5 pounds, equal to some 240 Roman aurei. Sixty minas; one talent is equal to six thousand drachmas.

Note: It is difficult to render precise values of ancient currencies in terms of modern currencies. Like weights and measures, such values vary considerably in short amounts of time, as we see in modern currencies.

Bibliography

Betlyon, John W. "Coinage." *ABD* 1:1076–89.

Bilkes, Gerald M. "Money, Coins." *NIDB* 4:130–37.

Measurements in the
New Testament Era

LEE MARTIN MCDONALD

Various forms of metrology were used from approximately 2200 BC, but the use of some measurement has been dated to around 3500 to 3000 BC. Measurements of any kind in antiquity are difficult to determine with precision since standards varied. The following are generally acknowledged to have been used in NT times.

Lengths and Distances

Lengths were often governed by various parts of the body; for example, the finger, handbreadth, span (from little finger to thumb), and cubit (forearm, or from the tip of the finger to the elbow) were commonly used to measure lengths in antiquity. Since these body parts vary in length, consistent standards are difficult to establish. Often, but not always, the lengths of the body parts of royal family members, especially kings, were used as a standard. Most ancient measurements are at best only within a 5 or 10 percent level of consistency in modern translations. False measurements were common, and false balances were common (cf. Amos 8:5).

In NT times, the *cubit* is mentioned variously (Matt. 6:27; Luke 12:25; John 21:8; Rev. 21:17), but its exact length is uncertain. Likewise, the *fathom*, a measurement from the tip of the fingers of one outstretched arm to the fingertips of the other outstretched arm and sometimes measured as 4 cubits (or 1.8 meters), is used to measure the depth of the ocean in Acts 27:28. The larger distance horizontally is the *stadion*, used variously in the NT (Matt. 14:24; Luke 24:13; John 6:19; 11:18;

Rev. 14:20; 21:16). The Roman *milion* is mentioned in Matt. 5:41 and comes from the Roman *mille passus* (a "thousand paces"), measured by the Romans as 5 feet, or around .296 meters per pace. The Roman mile was approximately 1,480 meters. There were approximately 8.5 stadia (of some 600 Roman feet per stadion) to a Roman mile. There were approximately 360 cubits to the stadion. In Acts 1:12, a Sabbath day's journey, namely, the distance allowed under the law to be traveled on the Sabbath, was approximately 2,000 cubits, or 1 kilometer.

Table 1. Summary of Distances

Term	Distance
Finger	The width of the finger, or about .75 inches
Handbreadth	About three inches or four finger widths, side by side
Span	About nine inches, from the tip of the little finger to the tip of the thumb of an outstretched hand
Cubit	About eighteen to twenty-five inches, the length of the tip of the longest finger to the tip of the elbow, depending on the size of the person whose cubit was the standard measure
Fathom	Approximately six feet, the distance between the fingertips of both out-stretched arms
Stadion (pl. stadia)	Four hundred cubits = about two hundred yards or six hundred feet (see John 21:8: two hundred cubits = about one hundred yards)
Sabbath day's journey (Exod. 16:29; Josh 3:4)	About two thousand cubits (about one thousand yards)
Roman mile (Latin *milion*)	One thousand paces of double steps (or 58 inches), equal to 1,618 yards
Yoke	The distance a yoke of oxen could plow in one day, about .6 of an acre

Weights

Almost all NT weights are monetary measurements. In Matt. 18:24, for example, the silver talents would be approximately 204 metric tons of silver owed to the king—that is, the sum of sixty million denarii (compared to the hundred denarii owed to the unforgiving debtor).

The term "pound" (Greek *litra*) is used to refer to the ointment used by Mary to anoint Jesus' feet in John 12:3 and to refer to the hundred pounds of ointments and perfumes brought by Nicodemus for the burial preparations of Jesus (John 19:39). The Roman pound was equivalent to 326.4 grams (or 96 denarii). The reference in Rev. 16:21 to large hailstones, "each weighing about a hundred pounds," is likely only intended to emphasize their large size and damaging effects.

Table 2. Summary of Weights

Term	Weight
Gerah	8.81 grains (.57 grams)
Beka	Half a shekel, or 10 gerahs, or about 88 grains (5.73 grams)
Shekel	Two bekas, or 176 grains (11.44 grams). The Persians introduced this term for describing amounts of silver, and the Jews later adopted it for their currency. Twenty shekels were deemed equivalent to a daric (named after Darius). See Neh. 5:15.
Pound	A Roman pound of 326.4 grams or about 11.5 ounces (see John 12:3; 19:39; Rev. 16:21, where a hundred weight = a talent). Elsewhere "pound" and "talent" refer to an amount of money (see above).
Mina	About 50–60 shekels, equal to 1.25 pounds (or about 20 ounces, or 1 pound 4 ounces)
Talent (Greek *talanton*)	Also 62.5 pounds, equal to some 240 Roman aurei. Sixty minas; one talent is equal to six thousand drachmas.

Note: It is difficult to render precise values of ancient weights and measures in terms of modern equivalents. As with ancient currencies, such values could vary considerably in short amounts of time.

Bibliography

Kletter, Raz. "Weights and Measures." *NIDB* 5:831–41.

Powell, Marvin A. "Weights and Measures." *ABD* 6:899–908.

Glossary

JOEL B. GREEN AND LEE MARTIN MCDONALD

Abba. Aramaic term for "father."

adoptionism. A form of early Christology that argued that Jesus became God's Son by adoption at his baptism.

agrapha (Greek, "unwritten"). The sayings of Jesus not found in the canonical Gospels. The singular, *agraphon*, is used of individual sayings. Some of these sayings are preserved in the early church fathers, certain biblical manuscripts, and in apocryphal writings, such as the *Gospel of Thomas*.

amanuensis. A scribe or secretary who wrote out documents in the ancient world.

'Am-hā'āres. A Hebrew phrase meaning "the people of the land." The term is often used of low-status persons, possibly with contempt.

Amoraim (Hebrew *amora*, a "teacher" or "reciter"). The rabbinic teachers from AD 220 through the Talmudic period, roughly sixth century AD. The Amoraim composed the Gemara, or commentary, on the Mishnah and the Hebrew Scriptures.

anacoluthon (Greek, "not following"). When one grammatical construction is abandoned for another, in the middle of a sentence.

antinomianism (literally "being against law"). Belief that law, especially the Jewish law, is no longer binding.

Apocalypse, apocalyptic (Greek, "revelation" or "disclosure"). A wide-ranging set of terms, used variously to refer to the last book of the NT (the Apocalypse; i.e., the book of Revelation); a specific genre of visionary literature that focuses on the end times, often using terms with hidden meanings and referring to hidden revelations of the "last days"; the kind of eschatology to which such literature bears witness; or more generally, the disclosure of God's salvific program in Christ.

Some of these terms are adapted from those listed in the longer collections of N. Turner, *Handbook for Biblical Studies* (Philadelphia: Westminster, 1982); and R. N. Soulen, *Handbook of Biblical Criticism* (Atlanta: John Knox, 1976). Other useful terms are found in R. F. Collins, *Introduction to the New Testament* (Garden City, NY: Doubleday, 1983), 409–30; L. M. McDonald and S. E. Porter, *Early Christianity and Its Sacred Literature* (Peabody, MA: Hendrickson, 2000), 653–61; H. Koester, *Introduction to the New Testament* (2nd ed.; 2 vols.; Berlin: de Gruyter, 1995–2000), 2:351–54.

Apocrypha, apocryphal (Greek, "hidden"). Sacred literature that was not accepted into the biblical canon but was highly valued in Jewish and early Christian communities. Often a reference to esoteric writings.

apophthegm/apothegm. A short, pithy saying, often referring to pronouncement stories or paradigms in Gospel studies.

Aramaism. Wording in the Greek of the NT that betrays a Palestinian Aramaic origin—for example, *Abba* (Mark 14:36; Rom. 8:15).

asyndeton. Clauses or phrases that are linked together without connective words, such as "but" or "and."

autograph. The original manuscript of a book. Normally a reference to the original manuscripts of the biblical authors, none of which have survived.

baraita (pl. *baraitot*; Hebrew, "external"). A rabbinic tradition (writing) not included in the Mishnah by Rabbi Judah ha-Nasi (*nasi* = "the prince," "chief," or "president"). It is unclear the extent to which this material was widely known or acknowledged as authoritative in the second century AD or before.

berakah (Hebrew, "blessing"). A Jewish prayer of blessing and thanksgiving.

canon (Greek, "a measuring rod" or "guideline"). Normally used in reference to a collection of literature that was considered by the Christian community to be sacred and authoritative. The term can also be used of any recognized group of authoritative writings.

catechesis. Oral instruction, often in conjunction with teaching given to candidates for baptism.

catena. A collection of biblical quotations found in the church fathers, used to interpret the Scriptures.

chiasmus, chiastic. Terms derived from the Greek letter *chi* (X), which resembles an X. The term "chiasmus" (or "chiasm") refers to a practice in ancient Greek writing of reversing the subject and object of the first line in the second line (see Mark 2:27), though the chiastic structure can also be found in larger portions of text and extend to more than two levels (e.g., passages with an ABC-C′B′A′ structure).

chiliasm, chiliastic (Greek, "thousand"). Literature that focuses on an imminent eschatological kingdom of God. Often referred to as "millenarianism," based on apocalyptic literature in the Bible (esp. Daniel and Revelation).

codex (pl. codexes or codices). Ancient manuscripts put together in the form of a book, unlike the more typical scroll. Christians were the first to use the codex on a large scale to publish their sacred writings.

cognate. Refers to words from the same root or family of words. For example, in the NT, love (*agapē*) has the cognate "beloved" (*agapētos*).

colophon (Greek, "summit" or "finishing touch"). A publisher's identification mark, normally on a title page. In the case of older manuscripts, it is often written by the scribe at the end of a book, giving the time, sometimes authorship, and location of the writing.

covenantal nomism. A category of thought used in recent Pauline studies to describe what many see as ancient Jewish belief regarding covenant and law, namely, the Jewish covenantal relation to God on the basis of grace, not law.

credo (Latin, "I believe"). A creed, or "credo," is a collection of teachings believed by a person or group.

Decalogue. The Ten Commandments.

Demiurge (Greek, "craftsman"). The gnostic term for the creator of the world, to be distinguished from the unknown God of Jesus.

demythologizing. A term made popular in the writings of Rudolf Bultmann, who tried to explain what he called the "myth" of the NT (e.g., the miraculous) in terms of human self-understanding. He intended the term to refer to the need for reinterpreting myth rather than eliminating it.

diachronic (literally "through time"). Historical change over a period of time. When sequence is prominent, the term "diachronic" is used. *See also* synchronic.

Diaspora (Greek, "scattered"). Jews who lived outside Palestine. Sometimes a reference to the Assyrian and Babylonian captivities of the Jews. See James 1:1; 1 Pet. 1:1.

Diatessaron (Greek, "through four"). Term used by Tatian in the late second century AD to refer to his "Gospel made up of four," a harmony of the four canonical Gospels and probably some noncanonical writings.

didache (Greek, "teaching"). Sometimes used of the teaching ministry of the early church as opposed to the proclamation or kerygma of the church. Also a reference to a late first-century writing that summarizes the teaching of the church, called the *Didache* ("The Teaching of the Lord to the Nations by the Twelve Apostles").

docetism (Greek *dokeō*, "I seem" or "I appear"). The belief of a group of Christians of the late first century and throughout the second century who taught that Jesus only *appeared* to have a body. They taught that the Christ descended upon Jesus at his baptism, only appeared to suffer on the cross, and instead ascended just prior to the cross. This is a gnostic belief that emphasized the corruptness of human flesh and sought to preserve the Christ from such corruption.

Ebionites. A Jewish sect of Christians who lived east of the Jordan in the second century and rejected the deity of Jesus.

ecclesiology. A study of the church and its doctrines, practices, and organization.

Eighteen Benedictions. A series of Jewish prayers called the Shemoneh-Esreh, used in the synagogue and in personal prayer. These come mostly from the late first century AD, but also from the second century. Of special note for the Christian community is whether the twelfth benediction is directed against Christians ("Let the Nazarenes [Christians?] and heretics [Hebrew *minim*] perish in a moment").

ekklēsia (Greek, "assembly" or "gathering"). Term used in the NT to identify the group of followers of Christ. It is often modified as the *ekklēsia*, or church, "of God" or "of God in Christ," and so on. The term itself is neutral, but it was quickly adopted by the Christian community. Its meaning is not unlike that of the Greek term *synagōgē* ("synagogue").

encratite (Greek, "self-controlled" or "strengthened"). A term used to identify Christian sects like the Ebionites, docetics, and gnostics, who were known for extreme asceticism barring them from eating meat and from marriage.

epigraphy (Greek, "writing on" or "inscription"). Refers to the study of papyri, inscriptions, and ostraca and writings on these types of surfaces.

epiphany (Greek, "manifestation"). Refers to the manifestation of a deity. Some leaders of the ancient world adopted the term in reference to themselves, for example, Antiochus IV Epiphanes (165 BC).

eschatology, eschaton (Greek, "last" or "end"). Terms used to describe the end times or the end of the ages. As a theological discipline, eschatology focuses on the nature of God's kingdom in the NT, which is also paralleled with a time of judgment. The eschaton is the final reality of the end times.

ethnarch (Greek, "ruler of a nation/people"). A ruler or governor of a province or nation.

euangelion (Greek, "good news"). Term used to describe the "good news" brought by the coming of Jesus Christ. Also translated "gospel," to describe both the first four NT books (Gospels) and the message they and other NT books proclaim.

exegesis (Greek, "explanation," "interpretation"). The interpretation of the biblical text, using a range of skills and disciplines. An exegete is an interpreter of a text.

expiation (Latin *expiare*, "to atone"). In the Bible, normally an offering (sacrifice) made to God as an atonement or covering for one's sins.

florilegium (Latin, "a gathering of flowers"). A collection of proof texts used by the early Christians in their apologies before skeptics and instructions to new converts.

Gattung (German, "kind, type"). A kind, style, or type of literature, art, and so forth. Used in biblical studies to distinguish forms of literature (parable, epigram, apothegm, etc.). *See also* genre.

Gemara (Aramaic, "completion"). The Amoraim's additions to the Mishnah, both in terms of explanations and further teachings or interpretations of the Mishnah. Eventually the Gemara became the Talmuds.

gematria. A method of interpreting ancient terms and/or texts in terms of their numerical value.

geniza/genizah (Hebrew, "hiding place"). A room normally attached to a synagogue for the purpose of discarding worn-out portions of holy writings and Scripture. Even heretical literature, if it contained the divine names, was discarded in a geniza out of respect for the divine names.

genre (French, "kind" or "type"). A kind, style, or type of literature, art, and so forth. Used in biblical studies to distinguish types of literature (Gospel, letter, apocalyptic, etc.).

Geschichte (German, "history"). Although no substantive distinction is made in German usage between *Geschichte* and *Historie* (both can be translated as "history"), the terms have come to refer to the actual event (*Historie*) and its significance (*Geschichte*).

gloss. A brief explanation inserted into a manuscript to explain a point or something unusual in the text.

gnosis, Gnosticism, gnostic (Greek, "knowledge"). Some early Christians claimed to have a special higher knowledge of the divine activity and spiritual mysteries. This dualistic system of thought, widespread in the second century, has earlier, incipient forms in the NT era. Generally the gnostics rejected the God of the OT and Jewish forms of religion; many were ascetic. They saw matter as evil and rejected the notion that the God of Jesus created the world. Docetism is a form of gnostic belief.

Greco-Roman. Descriptive of the period from the first century BC to the fifth century AD, when Greek culture combined with Roman political dominance.

haggadah, haggadic (Hebrew, "narrative" or "telling," as in "telling a story"). Postbiblical narrative writing among the rabbis that is not legal prescription; stories that illustrate the Torah. (The tradition that focused on the legal implications of the law

is called halakah, or halakhah.) Anything not included as halakah.

Hagiographa (Greek, "holy writings"). The collection of sacred Scriptures that makes up the third part of the HB. Also called, in Hebrew, the Ketubim ("Writings").

halakah, halakic (Hebrew, "the way"). Legal regulations of the law, both oral and written, which emerged out of postbiblical Judaism. Viewed by the rabbis as more important than the haggadah or narrative traditions.

hapax legomenon (Greek, "said once"). Term used to identify a word found only once in antiquity or in the Bible, or only once in one person's writing in one of the Testaments.

Haustafel (German, "code of household duties"). Refers to lists of responsibilities of members of a household (see, e.g., Eph. 5:21–6:9).

Heilsgeschichte (German, "salvation history"). The sacred activity of God in human history that is described or foretold in the Scriptures.

Hellenistic period. The period from the third century BC to the fourth century AD, in which the influence of classical Greek spread throughout the Mediterranean world.

henotheism. The belief in and worship of one god, but without excluding the possibility of there being other gods. *See also* monotheism.

hermeneutics (Greek *hermeneuō*, "I interpret"). The theory and process of interpretation. In terms of biblical studies, it refers to all that is involved in interpreting the biblical text. *See also* exegesis.

heterodox. That which is not "orthodox," not in keeping with what is the generally accepted teaching of the church.

higher criticism. A term first widely used in the nineteenth century for interpretation of the text with regard to its literary and historical dimensions, as opposed to the "lower criticism" of textual criticism.

Historie. In theology, an event as it actually happened, or as one can verify that it actually happened. See also *Geschichte*.

hortatory. Language and/or literature that urges a particular course of action or behavior.

hypotaxis. Language that makes use of subordinate grammatical structures, such as participial phrases and subordinate clauses, often linked with words such as "because," "while," and others.

inscription. A text written on stone or a similar surface.

interpolation. When new words are put into a text.

ipsissima verba (Latin, "the very word itself"). Used by scholars to distinguish the words that can be attributed to the historical Jesus in the biblical tradition and in the *agrapha*.

ipsissima vox (Latin, "the very voice"). When the exact words are not discoverable, the actual thought or notion that may still be attributed to the historical Jesus.

Judaizers. Jewish Christians who accepted the law and its traditions and sought to impose circumcision upon the gentiles. See Gal. 2:11–14; Acts 15:1–5.

kerygma (Greek, "preaching"). Early Christian proclamation and evangelistic activity, sometimes distinguished from its teaching (*didachē*) ministry.

Ketubim. The Writings, the third of three divisions of the HB, containing poetry and wisdom literature, as well as some historical books (Ruth, 1–2 Chronicles, Ezra, Nehemiah, Esther) and Daniel. *See also* Nebi'im; Torah.

Koine Greek (Greek, "common"). The common language used in the composition of the NT writings, as contrasted with the more formal classical Greek. Some writings in the NT are of more formal literary quality (Luke-Acts, Hebrews, James, 1 Peter), while others are more informal and common (Paul's Letters, Mark). The Greek of all NT writings can be classified as Koine.

koinōnia (Greek, "fellowship," with idea of sharing). Used in the NT of the gatherings of the early Christian community, which often involved the breaking of bread together in a common meal.

L. Abbreviation for material in Luke's Gospel that is unique to Luke. It may stem from the author of the Gospel or from a written or oral source he used in producing his Gospel.

lacuna. A "gap" or "that which is missing." Often a reference to something absent from a manuscript.

langue. A French term from the early twentieth-century linguist Ferdinand de Saussure, used to indicate a language system, such as English, Greek, or others. See also *parole*.

lectionary. A collection of readings from the Scriptures, used in liturgical services and fixed according to church calendars. The use of lectionaries dates back almost to the beginning of the church.

lingua franca. The common language of a large number of people, such as Koine Greek in the Greco-Roman world of the first century AD.

logion (pl. logia; Greek, "saying"). In scholarly jargon, used of a saying of Jesus.

lower criticism. The name often given to the basic work of establishing the text that one intends to study, as opposed to higher criticism. *See also* textual criticism.

LXX (roman numerals for 70). *See* Septuagint.

M. Abbreviation for material in Matthew's Gospel that is unique to Matthew. It may stem from the author of the Gospel or from a written or oral source that he used in producing his Gospel.

magi (Greek, "wise men"). In Matt. 2:1 "magi" came to honor the newborn king of the Jews. The term was used of masters of the astrological arts (astrologers) but could also have been a reference to persons who were known as wise sages from the East.

Majority Text. The name often given to the collection of Byzantine texts used in establishing the first modern texts and translations of the Bible. The Byzantine texts constitute the majority of manuscripts. The Majority Text is similar to the Received Text.

majuscule. Script that is written in capital letters as opposed to minuscule (lowercase) or cursive letters, or a manuscript written in this script. *See also* uncial.

Maranatha (Aramaic, "Our Lord, come!" or "Our Lord has come"). An early Christian affirmation regarding the desired return of Christ. Paul uses this term in its transliterated Greek form (1 Cor. 16:22).

Masorah (Hebrew, "tradition"). Commonly used of the rules that govern the passing down of the biblical text. The Masoretes were Jewish scholars who stabilized the text of the HB and added vowel points so that it could be properly pronounced.

Megilloth. A reference to the "festival" books of the HB (i.e., Ruth, Song of Songs, Ecclesiastes, Lamentations, Esther), that is, the books read during the celebration of five Jewish festivals.

messianism. Belief in a coming messiah (Judaism) or that the messiah has come in the person of Jesus (Christians). How widespread messianism was among Jews in the first century is debated.

midrash (Hebrew, "investigation," "to inquire," "to search" or "to interpret"). An interpretation of Scripture, or a commentary. The oldest Hebrew commentaries on the Scriptures are the *Mekilta* (on Exodus), the *Sipra* (on Leviticus), and the *Sipre* (on Numbers and Deuteronomy).

minuscule. A Greek manuscript written in lowercase (or minuscule) characters, typically dating from the tenth to the twelfth centuries. *See also* majuscule.

Mishnah (Hebrew, "what is repeated" or "repetition"). Codified oral tradition that dates from before the time of Jesus to the time of Rabbi Judah ha-Nasi (AD 200–219). Citations of the Mishnah consist of the tractate name (preceded by *m.* for Mishnah) followed by chapter and verse numbers.

monotheism. The belief that there is only one God, as opposed to polytheism, the belief that there are many gods. *See also* henotheism.

mystērion (Greek, "mystery"). Used of the mystery of God or of the Christian gospel itself (e.g., Eph. 3:3–6; Col. 1:27).

myth. A term used in a specialized sense indicating the transcendent activity of God spoken of in this-worldly categories. "Myth" is a way of speaking about the otherworldly activity of God in terms of concrete this-worldly activity.

Nebi'im. The Prophets, the second of three divisions of the HB, containing the Former Prophets (Joshua, Judges, 1–2 Samuel, 1–2 Kings) and the Latter Prophets (the major and minor prophets). *See also* Ketubim; Torah.

nomina sacra (Latin, "sacred names"). Term used to designate the use of abbreviated names, such as "God" and "Jesus," in papyrus and parchment manuscripts.

Old Latin. The Latin versions of the Bible that predate or are independent of Jerome's Vulgate.

ossuary. A box or container in which the bones of a dead person were placed.

ostracon (pl. ostraca). An inscribed potsherd or piece of pottery. This was a common writing material for receipts, notes, and so forth. A number of ostraca have been found dating to the Hellenistic period.

paleography (Greek, "old writing"). The study of ancient handwriting, especially as found on papyri, inscriptions, ostraca, and other sources.

palimpsest (Greek, "rubbed again"). A manuscript that has been reused, with the first text removed so as to receive the second text.

papyrus (pl. papyri). Plant used in ancient times, especially in Egypt, to make a writing material. Many documents written on papyrus have been found in Egypt and have helped to illuminate the language and customs of the Hellenistic world. The term is used of the texts themselves, especially in the plural ("papyri").

parablepsis (Greek, "look over"). When a copyist's eyes jump to a similar word or expression, resulting in either omission (haplography) or repetition (dittography) of the intervening section.

paraenesis, paraenetic. Admonitory or exhortative teaching, usually concerning moral behavior in everyday life. The latter chapters of Paul's Letters often contain paraenetic teaching (e.g., Rom. 12:1–15:13; Gal. 5:1–6:10), whereas in 1 Peter and James such exhortations appear throughout the letter.

parataxis (Greek, "placing side by side"). Language typified by clauses and phrases joined by the simple connective "and."

parole. A French term from the early twentieth-century linguist Ferdinand de Saussure, indicating an individual's particular use of a language. See also *langue*.

parousia (Greek, "being present"). The presence of someone; used especially of the returning presence of Christ at the end of this age.

patristics. The study of the church fathers or their writings through the sixth or even seventh century.

Peloponnese. A mountainous peninsula forming southern Greece, connected to the mainland by the isthmus of Corinth.

pericope (Greek, "cut around"). A defined section of biblical material, such as a parable.

pesher (pl. pesharim; Hebrew, "interpretation" or "realization"). A form of biblical interpretation similar to midrash that sees the fulfillment of the passage in the context of the current interpreters. Pesher interpretation was popular at Qumran.

Peshitta. The translation of the Bible of the Syrian Church. The OT was translated around the second century AD, while the NT dates to probably the fifth century.

pleonasm. The use of more words than are necessary to express an idea. Redundancy is implied by a pleonastic construction.

pneumatic (Greek, "spirit, wind"). Concerned with or related to a spirit, often with reference to the Holy Spirit.

praetorium/praetorian. Initially the Latin term *praetorium* referred to a general's tent, but eventually it was used for the official residence of a provincial governor (Mark 15:16; Acts 23:35). See also Phil. 1:13, which refers to a praetorium guard.

Pre-Tannaim. Rabbinic teachers from 200 BC to AD 10.

prolegomenon (pl. prolegomena; Greek, "what is said first"). An introductory section, or introduction.

propitiation. The ancient belief that the wrath or anger of God or the gods must be appeased through sacrifice, and the means of accomplishing this.

proselyte. A person converted from one belief system to another. In the NT, "proselyte" is especially used of gentiles who convert to Judaism.

protreptic (Greek, "to urge forward"). A form of literature that is exhortatory, that attempts to persuade to a course of action.

provenance. The place of origin of a document.

pseudepigrapha, pseudepigraphic. Documents written under another person's name. Ancient pseudepigrapha were typically done under the name of a famous person, such as Enoch or Plato.

Q. Abbreviation for German word *Quelle* ("source"), which refers to an alleged collection of Jesus' sayings, typically understood as a source for Gospel material in Matthew and Luke not found in Mark.

Qumran. Remains of a settlement near the Dead Sea, where in eleven nearby caves numerous biblical and extrabiblical texts, commonly known as the Dead Sea Scrolls (DSS), were discovered.

Received Text. The Received Text, or *Textus Receptus*, designates the Greek edition of the NT by Erasmus that came to be the text received by the church. The 1633 Elzevir edition was the specific edition to which this name was given.

recension. A revision of a text, and the product of that revision.

redaction. The editing of written material.

Second Temple period. A designation for the period in Jewish history before, during, and after the time of Jesus—roughly the late sixth century BC through the destruction of the Jerusalem temple in AD 70.

Seder (pl. Sedarim; Hebrew, "Order"). Name for the six major divisions of the Mishnah, each of which contains seven to twelve subdivisions called "tractates." The word is also used to refer to the order of service for celebrating the Passover.

semeion (pl. *semeia*; Greek, "sign"). One of the words used for the miracles Jesus performed as evidence of his messianic role.

Semitic. Characteristic of the Semites, especially the Jews, as descendants of Noah's son Shem.

Semitism. Expression in NT Greek betraying intervention or influence from Hebrew or Aramaic, either directly or indirectly through the Septuagint (Septuagintalism).

Septuagint. The various translations of the Hebrew Scriptures into Greek that began around 280 BC and were completed sometime around 100 BC. According to legend, the translation was made by seventy or seventy-two Jewish scholars brought to Alexandria, Egypt. The abbreviation "LXX" (for "seventy") is the common siglum for the Septuagint. The scope of the LXX at the time of Jesus is debated. When quoting the OT, the LXX is used more than 80 percent of the time by NT writers. It was the Bible of the early Christian communities as well as of the Jews of the Diaspora.

Shemoneh-Esreh. *See* Eighteen Benedictions.

Sitz im Leben (German, "life situation"). The social context of a given text, event, or person.

soteriology. Study of the doctrine of salvation.

stichometry. In the study of manuscripts, the calculation of the letters or syllables on a line and the number of lines on a page. There are some indications in ancient manuscripts of authors' and scribes' concern for these factors. They can be used in trying to reconstruct the parameters of a text.

synchronic (Greek, "same time"). Looking at language or events altogether as a complete system. When the whole is viewed together, "synchronic" is used. *See also* diachronic.

syncretism (Greek, "mixed together"). The mixing together of various ideas from differing sources; often used to refer to the blending of diverse religious concepts and practices.

Synoptic Gospels. The Gospels of Matthew, Mark, and Luke. A synoptic presentation is in parallel fashion, especially when the Gospels are displayed so as to show their similarities and differences.

synoptic problem. Discussion of the issues surrounding the origins and relationships of Matthew, Mark, and Luke, the Synoptic Gospels.

Talmud (Hebrew, "learning"). The combination of the Mishnah and its Gemara make up the Talmud.

Tanak. An acronym for the HB based on the first letters of its three sections: Torah (Law), Nebi'im (Prophets), Ketubim (Writings).

Tannaim (Hebrew, "teacher" or, more specifically, "reciter" or "repeater"). The rabbinic teachers from AD 10 to AD 220.

targum (Aramaic, "translation"). An ancient paraphrase or interpretive translation of the HB into Aramaic.

textual criticism. The principles and standards employed in the establishment and subsequent editing of any text. Also referred to as "lower criticism."

Torah. The Law, or the first five books of the OT; the first of three divisions of the HB. The term is also used more generally for Jewish law. *See also* Ketubim; Nebi'im.

Tosefta (Hebrew, "supplement"). Material not found in the Mishnah and dating from approximately the same period. Citations of the Tosefta consist of the tractate name (preceded by *t.* for Tosefta) followed by chapter and verse numbers.

uncial. Biblical manuscript written in capital (or uncial) letters. The majority of uncial manuscripts date from the third to the tenth centuries. *See also* majuscule.

vaticinium ex eventu, vaticinium post eventum. Both Latin phrases refer to a prophecy or prediction made *after* the event.

Vorlage (German, "lies before"). A document that is thought to lie behind another source or tradition or material and that explains the context of another document, person, or activity.

Vulgate. Latin version of the Bible translated by Jerome, officially adopted by the Catholic Church in the sixteenth century, though used by the majority of Roman Catholics for centuries before then.

Index of Ancient Sources

Dead Sea Scrolls and Related Texts

Rabbinic Literature

Other Ancient Writings

Index of Biblical Texts

Old Testament Apocrypha

New Testament

Index of Modern Authors

606

Index of Subjects

Made in the USA
Las Vegas, NV
06 October 2021